Masters & Legends of Fantasy Art

Techniques for Drawing, Painting & Digital Art from 36 Acclaimed Artists

Contributing Artists:
H. R. Giger
Frank Frazetta
Chris Achilléos
Boris Vallejo & Julie Bell
James Gurney
Rodney Matthews
Chris Foss
Syd Mead
Dave Gibbons
Charles Vess
Brian Froud
Brothers Hildebrandt

The Editors of
FANTASY & SCI-FI DIGITAL ART
ImagineFX
Magazine

FOX CHAPEL
PUBLISHING

FEATURED ARTISTS

Boris Vallejo & Julie Bell
Jean 'Mobius' Giraud
H.R. Giger
Craig Mullins
Mike Mignola
William Stout
Chris Achilléos
Brothers Hildebrandt
Ken Kelly
Nicolas 'Sparth' Bouvier
Luis Royo
Aaron Sims

Frank Frazetta
Jean-Sébastien Rossbach
Brian Froud
Marc Potts
James Gurney
Rodney Matthews
Chris Foss
Peter Oedekoven
Syd Mead
Francis Tsai
Dave Gibbons
Charles Vess

Mélanie Delon
Dan Scott
Adam Hughes
John Kearney
Raymond Swanland
Svetlin Velinov
Andrew Jones
Christian Alzmann

Marta Dahlig
Wayne Barlowe
Bob Eggleton
Henning Ludvigsen

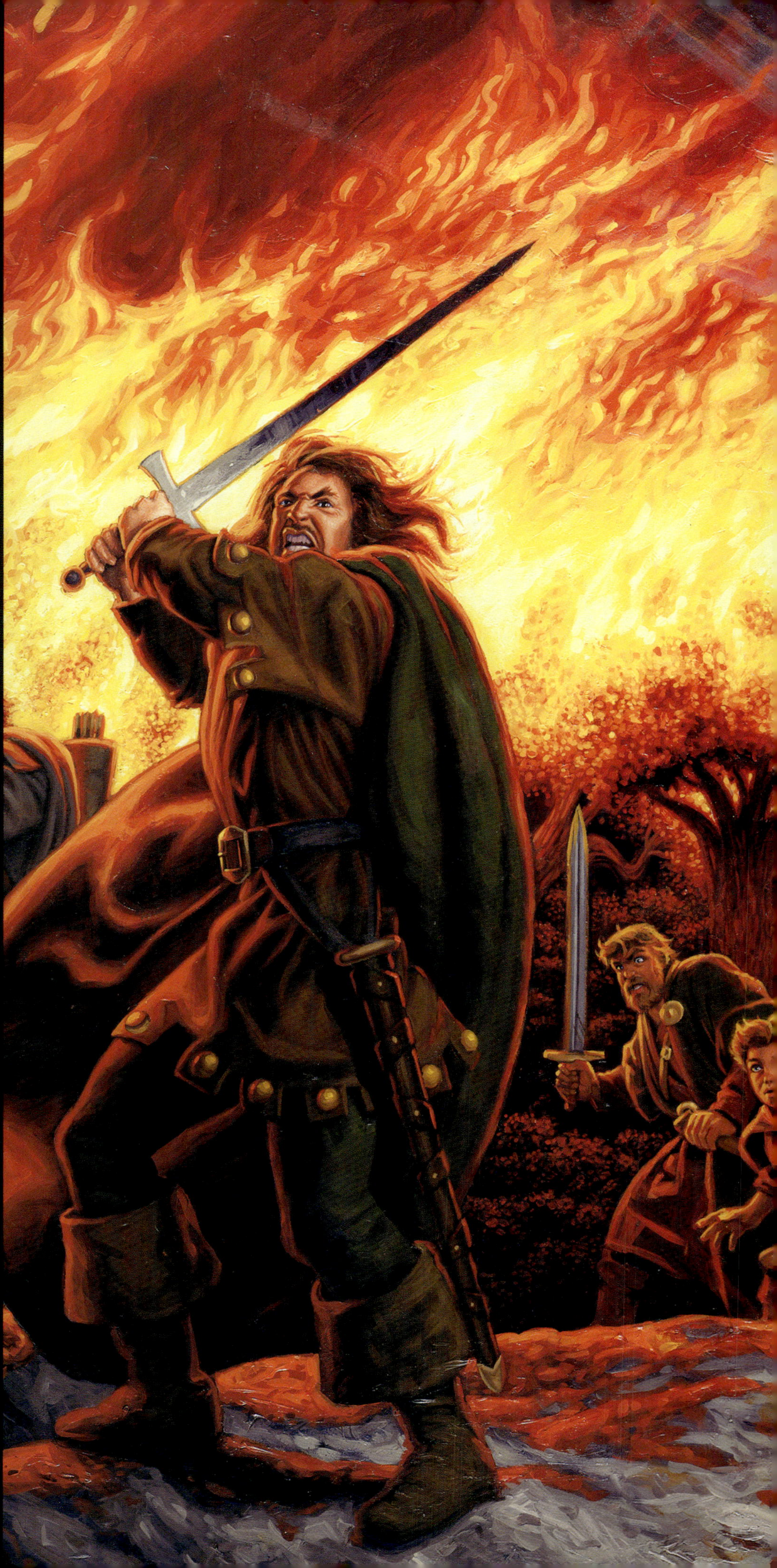

Masters & Legends of Fantasy Art

Techniques for Drawing, Painting & Digital Art from 36 Acclaimed Artists

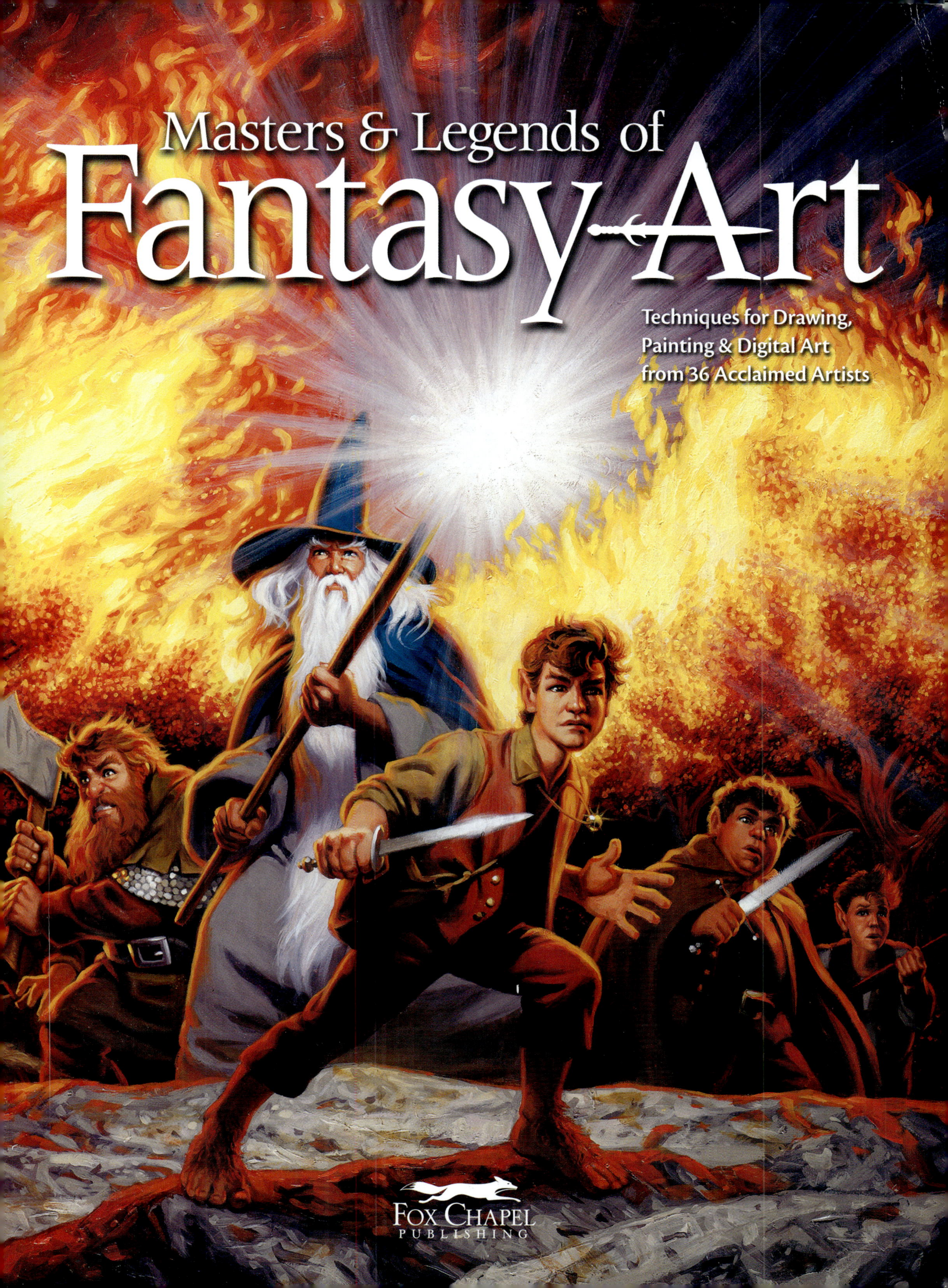

Fox Chapel Publishing

Contents

Learn to paint like the fantasy art masters

Gallery

Cover art by Dan Scott, page 126.

ISBN 978-1-56523-719-3

To learn more about the other great books from Fox Chapel Publishing, or to find a retailer near you, call toll-free 800-457-9112 or visit us at *www.FoxChapelPublishing.com*.

Note to Authors: We are always looking for talented authors to write new books. Please send a brief letter describing your idea to Acquisition Editor, 1970 Broad Street, East Petersburg, PA 17520.

Printed in China

First printing

Art legends

Art masters

Core skills

On your disc

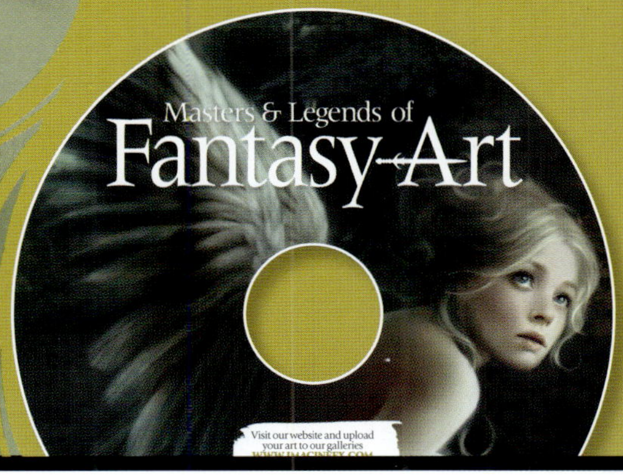

Gallery

Get inspired by the legendary artists behind some of fantasy's most iconic images

Boris Vallejo and Julie Bell

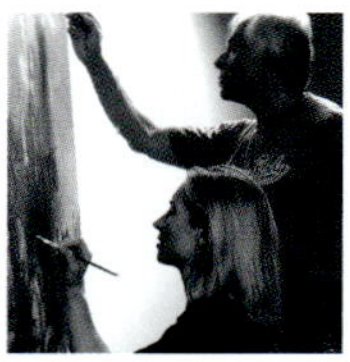

The Peruvian prodigy Boris Vallejo, a professional artist since the age of 16, was amongst the core number of artists that defined the 'classic' fantasy art of the 1960s, making his name with his illustrations of Tarzan, Conan The Barbarian, and Doc Savage.

In the 1990s bodybuilder, model and painter Julie Bell married Boris, and since then they've produced a prolific body of hyperrealist fantasy art, that celebrates the fantastical body beautiful with dynamic heroines and mythical creatures galore.

With a slew of art books and calendars to their names, the couple continue to push each other on, working together for a variety of commissions, from ad campaigns to Meat Loaf's Bat Out of Hell 3 cover. www.imaginistix.com

"We very much inspire each other, our minds work similarly in all kinds of ways. We spend 24 hours a day together and not only do we do it with ease, but we love it that way."

Wise words

PERFECT THE BODY

"By drawing, you're keeping your own little file in your head, of the human body and every time you draw from life you're just adding to it and reinforcing it."

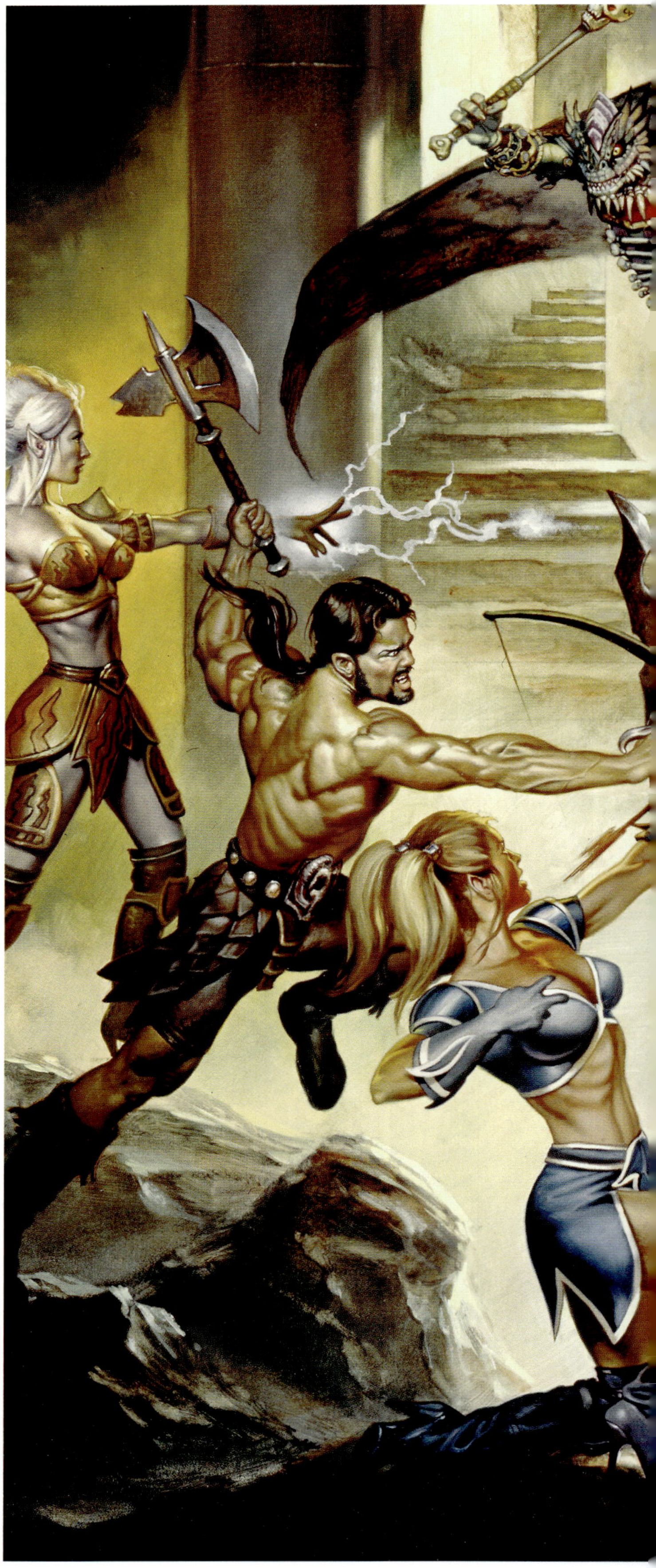

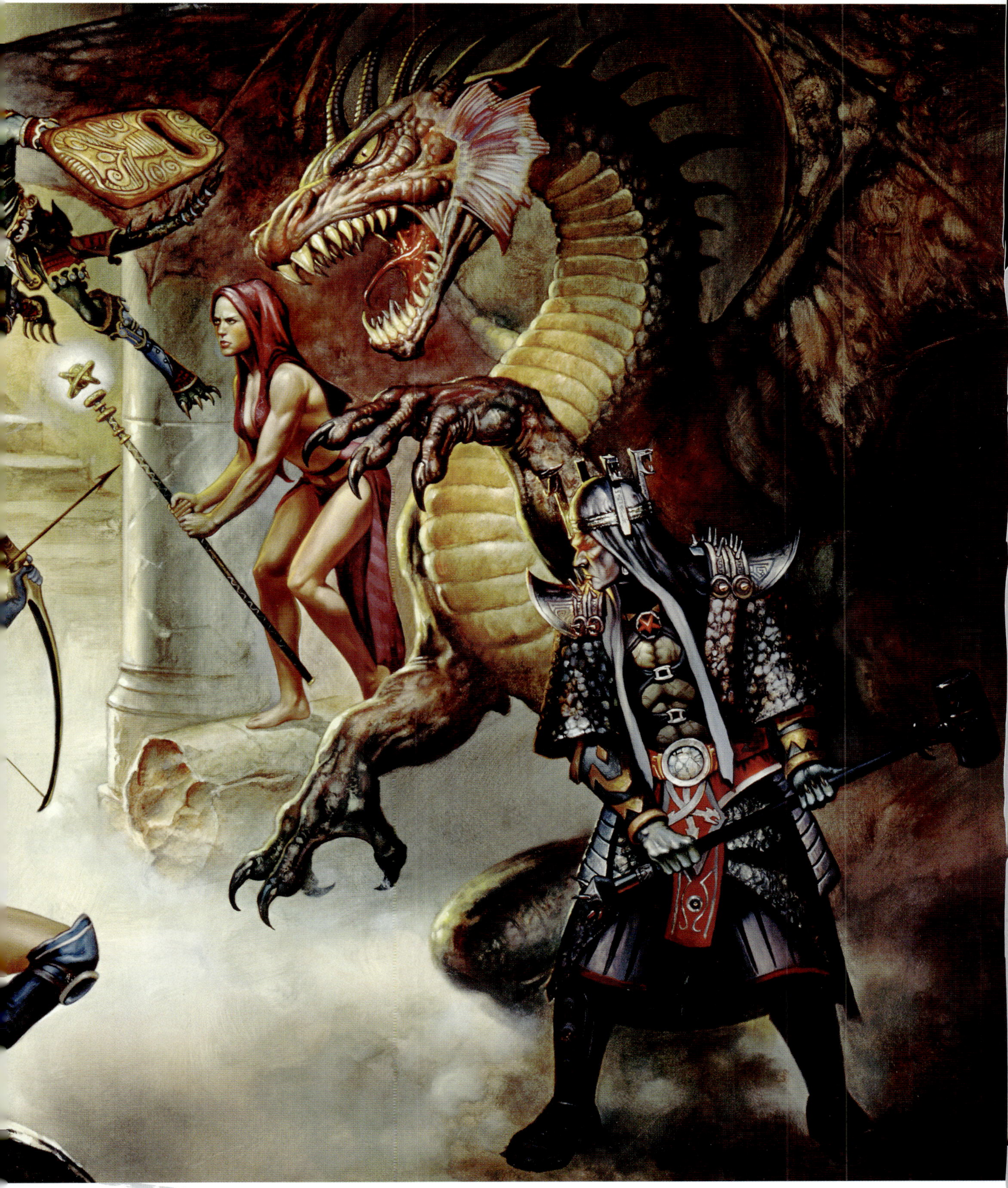

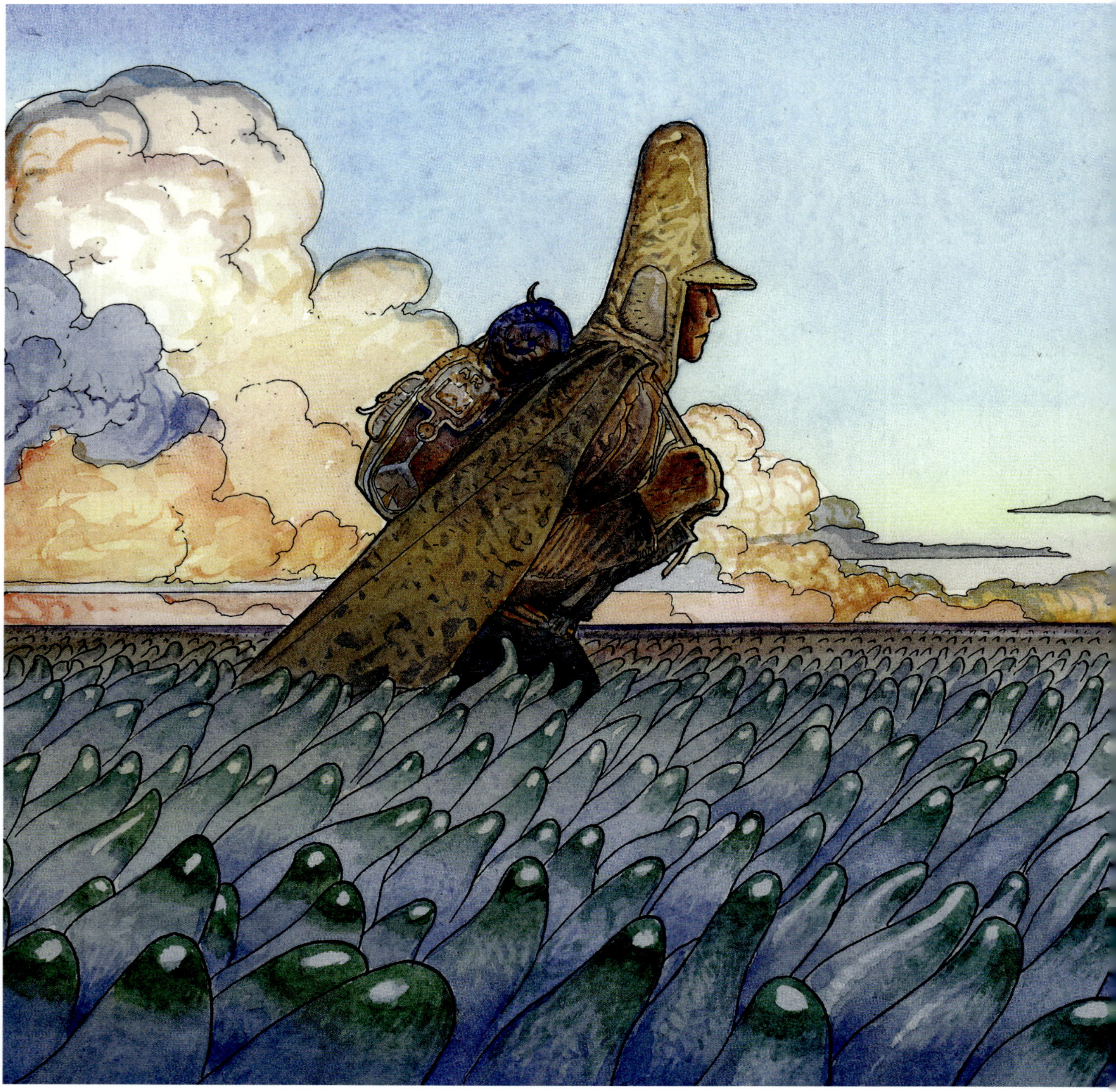

Jean 'Moebius' Giraud

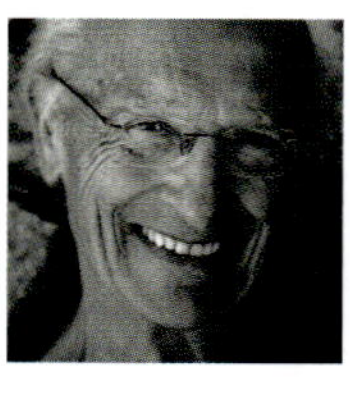

Wise words

FORGET PERFECTION

Learn from the master and shun the idea of achieving a distinct style: "In France, the artist wants to be known and recognised. They're not interested in perfection or examination; they look for style. I search for truth."

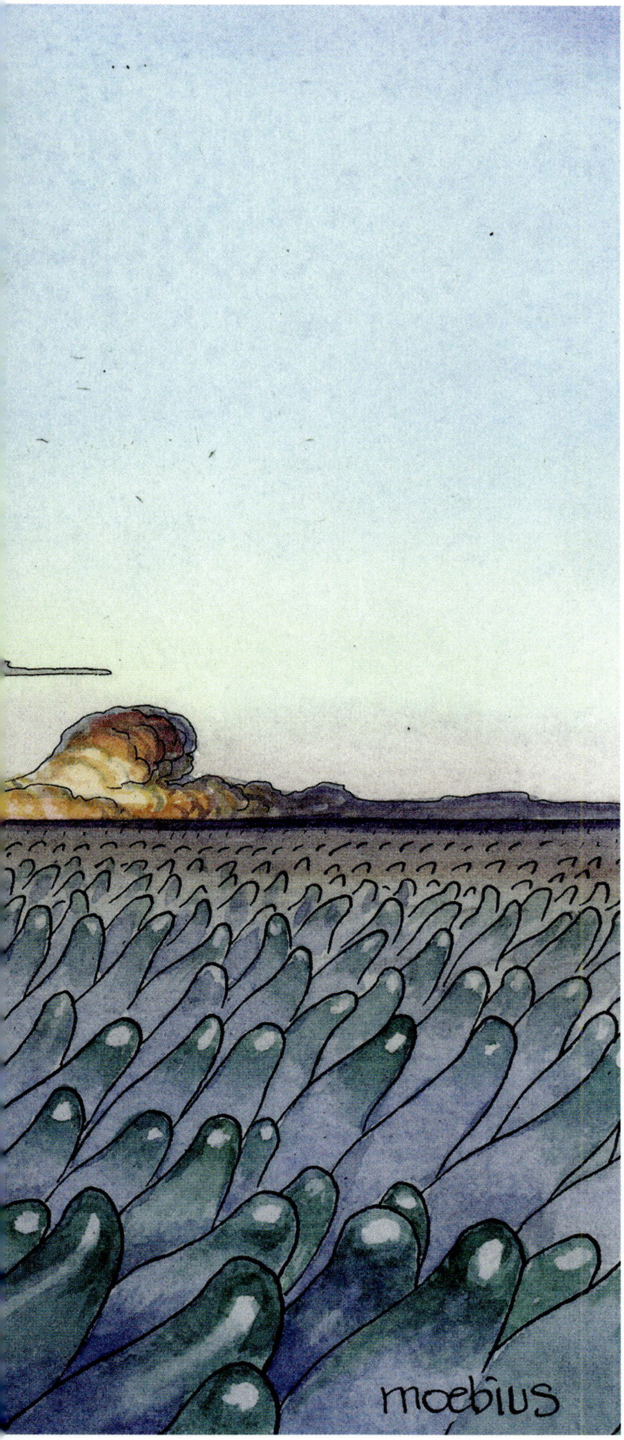

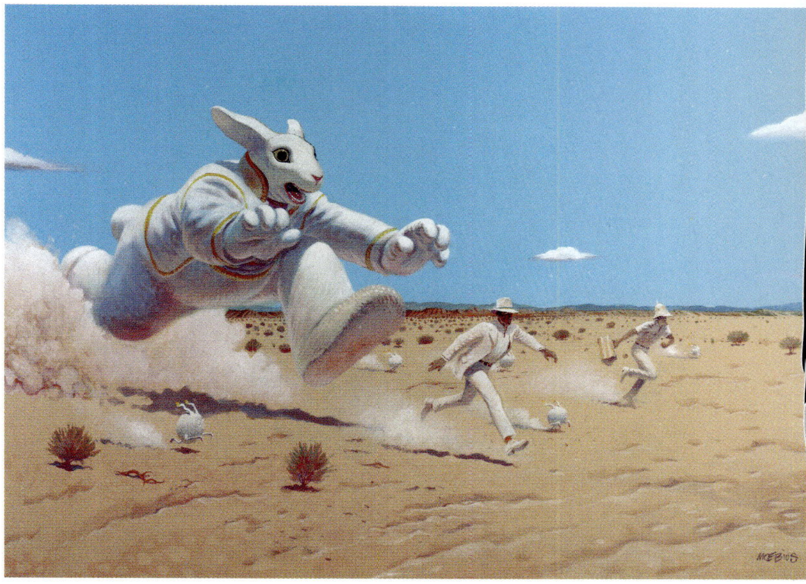

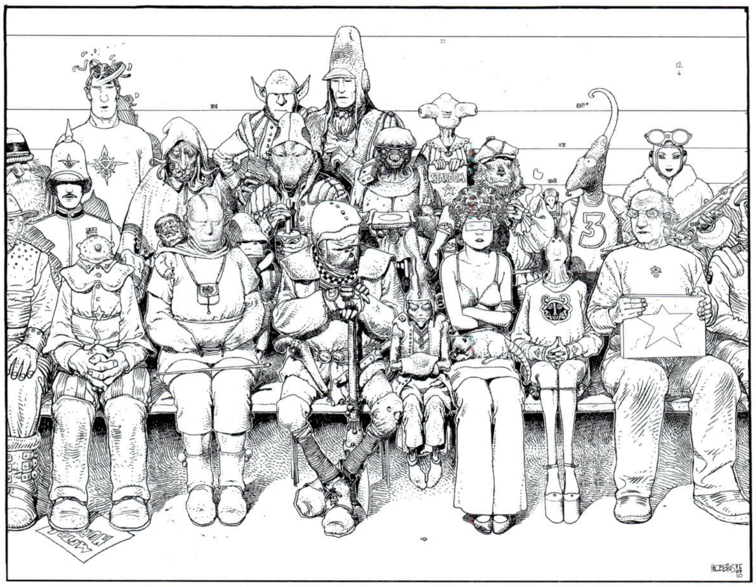

“When I started, I set myself a direction – a trajectory like a rocket in the sky. At the end I will blow up, but I don’t know where.”

It’s easy to forget the influence the man behind fantasy’s most famous alias has had on comics and sci-fi art. Having plucked the name Moebius out of the air at 22, Jean took comics into a new world touched by the surreal and led by the metaphysical. He then went on to help epitomise the face of modern sci-fi.

Making his name with the 1960s comic strip Blueberry (initially using the pseudonym Gri), Jean then formed the United Humanoids in the 1970s, a group responsible for the original Heavy Metal magazine. With Arzach, Moebius popularised a text-free, non-linear comic style. He was then hired as a concept artist for the films Alien and Tron, though he prefers to be remembered for his comic art.
www.moebius.fr

Hans Rudolf Giger

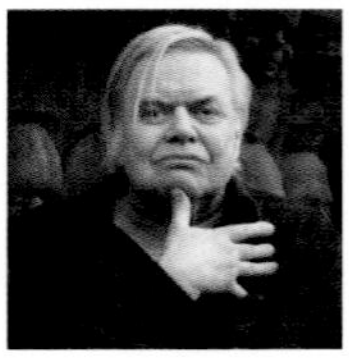

Whether you love or loathe his darkly stylised art, if you've the slightest interest in digital art, the chances are you'll recognise at least some, of HR Giger's work.

Now retired from commercial painting at the age of 71, from the 1970s onwards he transformed himself from an obscure Swiss surrealist to mainstream Academy Award-winning artist for his iconic work on Alien.

Commonly combining themes of elemental eroticism with an aesthetic that involves biomechanical mixtures of machine and alien flesh, his unique style has inspired countless artists.

1998 saw the creation of the Giger museum, at Château St. Germain in the ancient walled city of Gruyères. With this venture Giger signalled a change in his attention towards sculpture and architectural design (which he studied at university), he is now focusing exclusively on this work.

www.hrgiger.com

"In the beginning I had no idea what I was doing. I just did some clouds, then I would add an eye..."

Wise words

MAKING MOVIES

"When I worked on Alien I was in the studio for seven months. If you want to do something really good, you have to travel and work with the film makers."

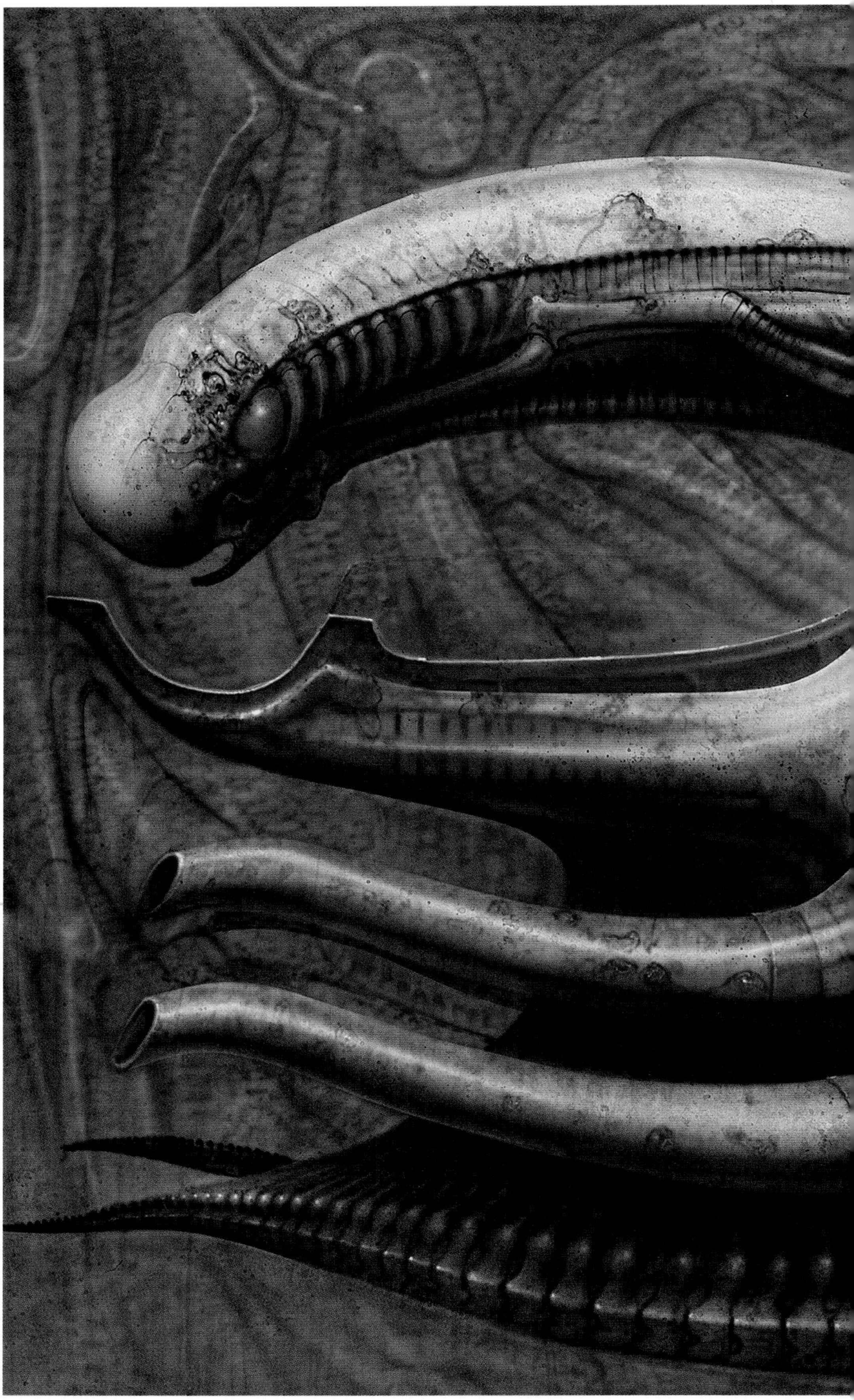

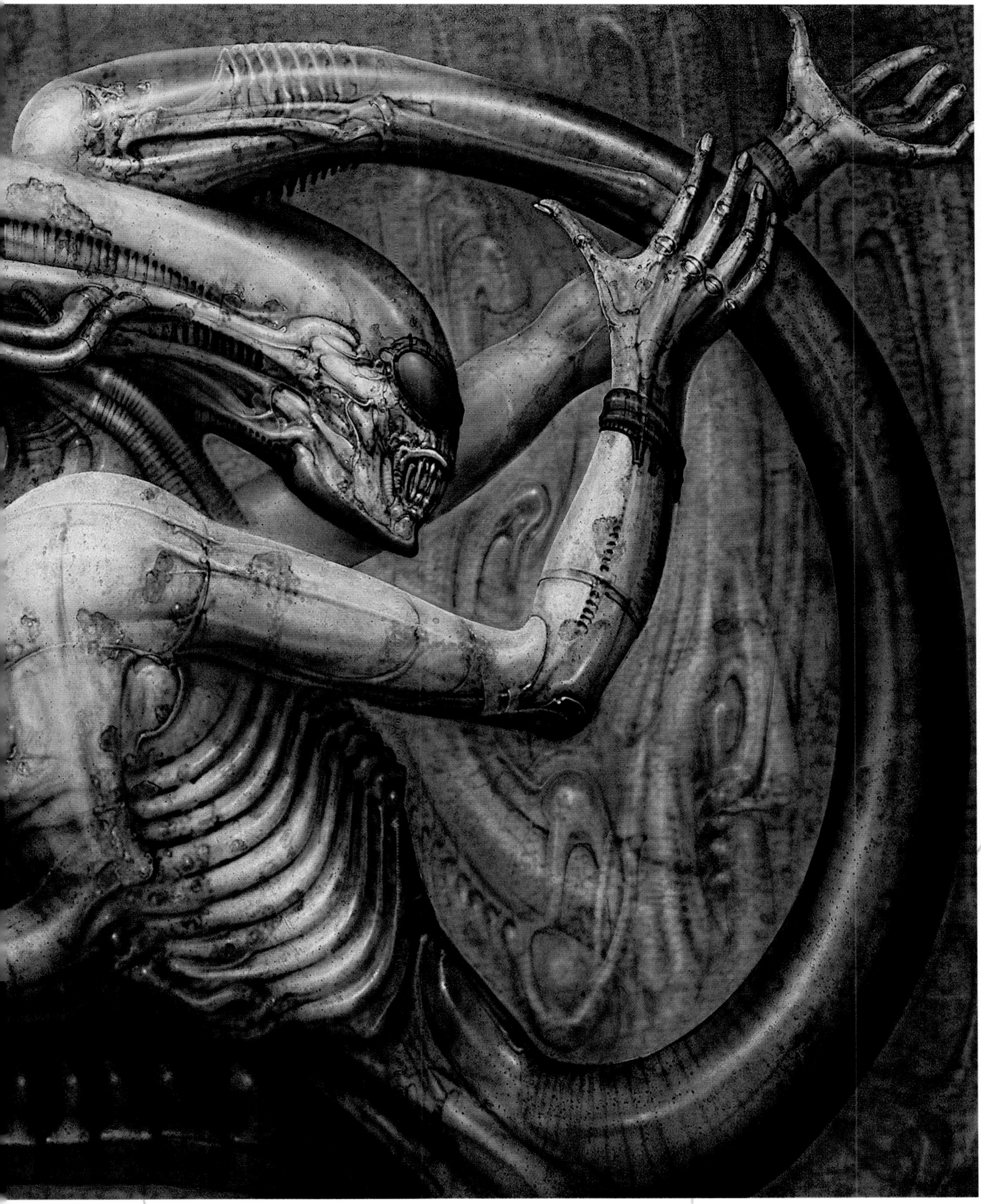

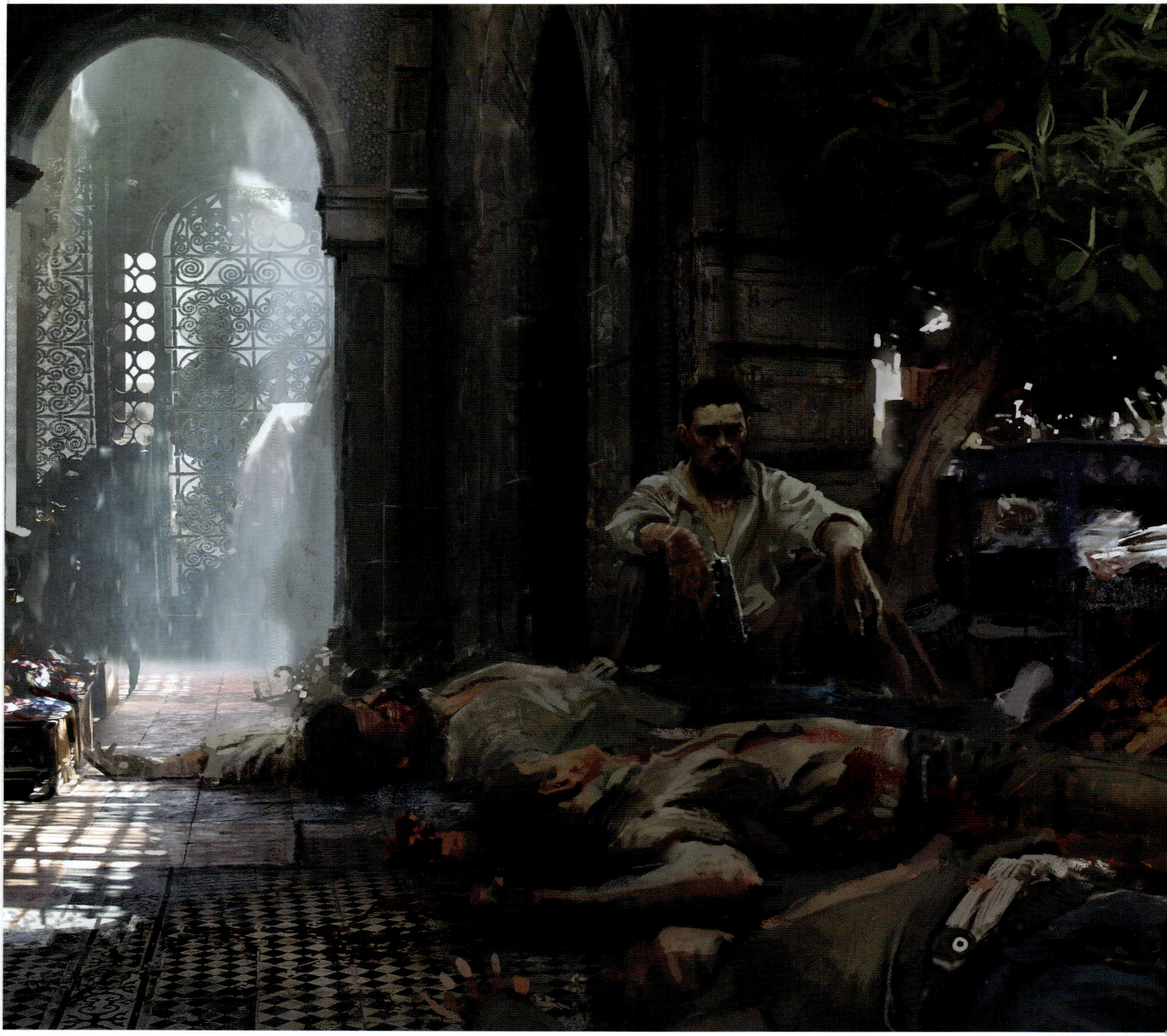

Craig Mullins

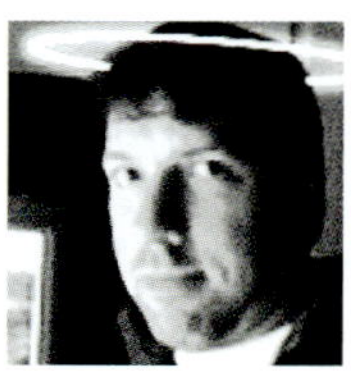

Pioneering digital art in the 1980s, straddling the worlds of industrial design and illustration, and getting his hands on projects like The Matrix Revolutions, Halo, and Fallout 3, Craig Mullins is the consummate digital artist.

Guarded on the specifics of his techniques, Craig is much more open when asked about how he settles on the concept for a painting: Rorschach tests, ink spills, fevered dreams, jokes, mental experiments, the list goes on.

Craig graduated from traditional training in 1990, then turned to digital art because of its speed and flexibility for commercial work. Aware of the medium's shortcomings, he says; "because digital tools are infinitely plastic it's easy for laziness to set in." With a CV that covers and blurs concept art for games and film, industrial design, and illustration with fine art, it's an accusation you'd be hard pressed to level at this artist.
www.goodbrush.com

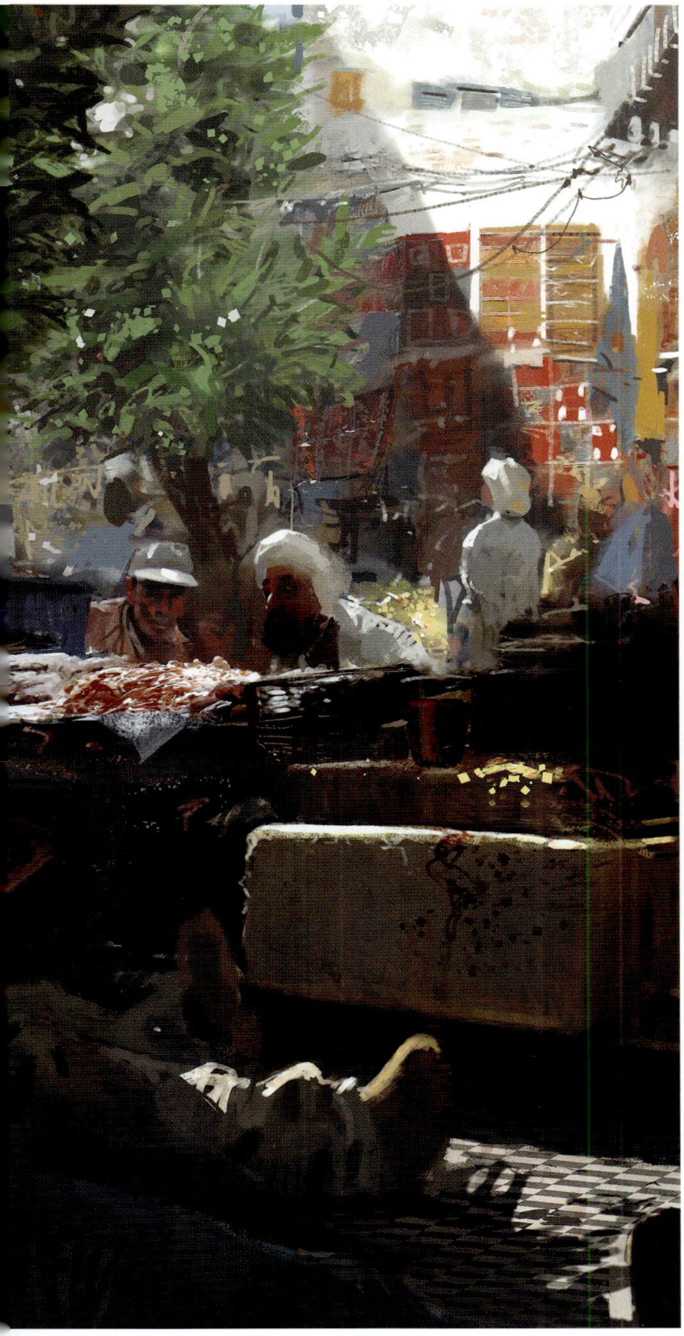

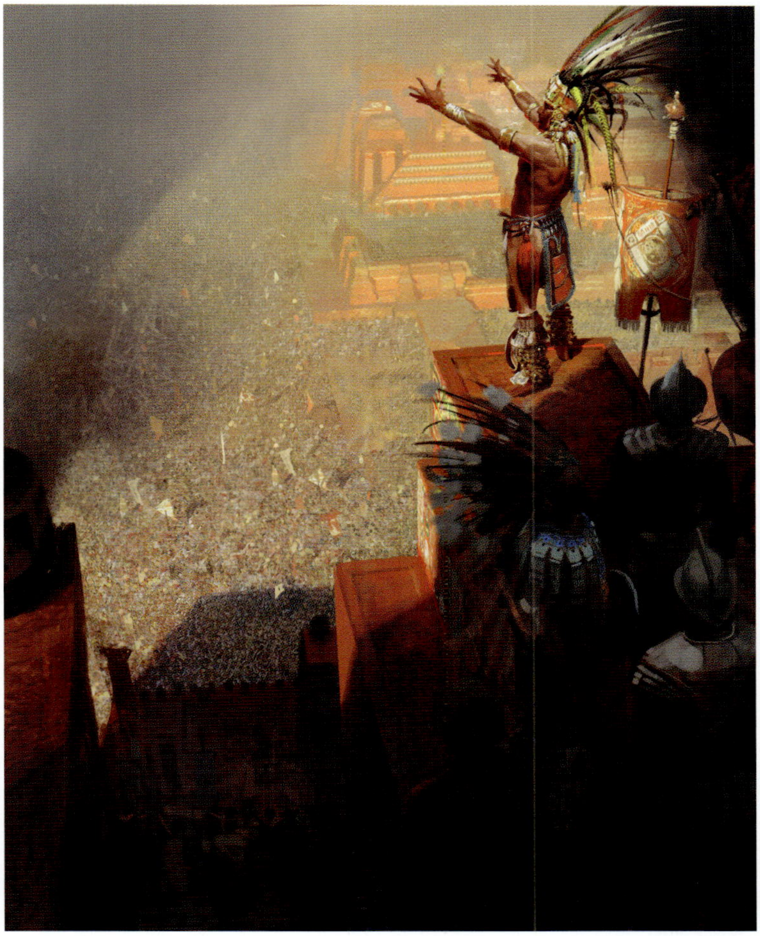

“My style is a combination of a lot of different things. Stuff sticks in your head, like leaves on a wet lollipop.”

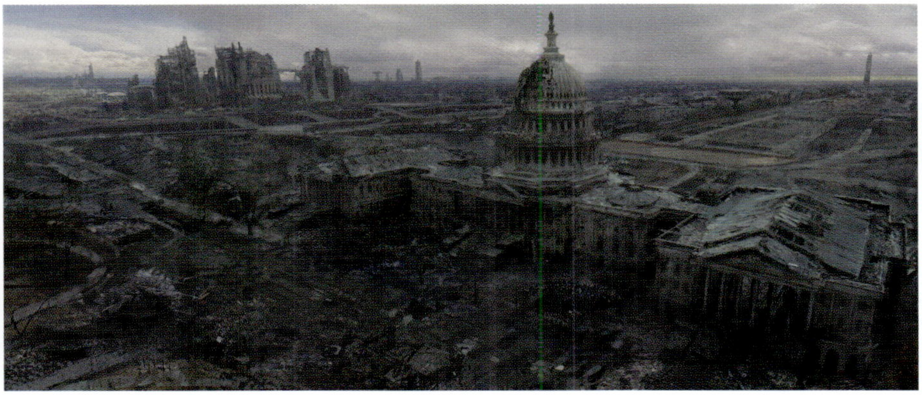

Wise words

STAY OPEN

“Realise that what you like now isn't going to be what you like in five years. Knowing this, it actually allows you to grow. The idea that you know a truth is an illusion...”

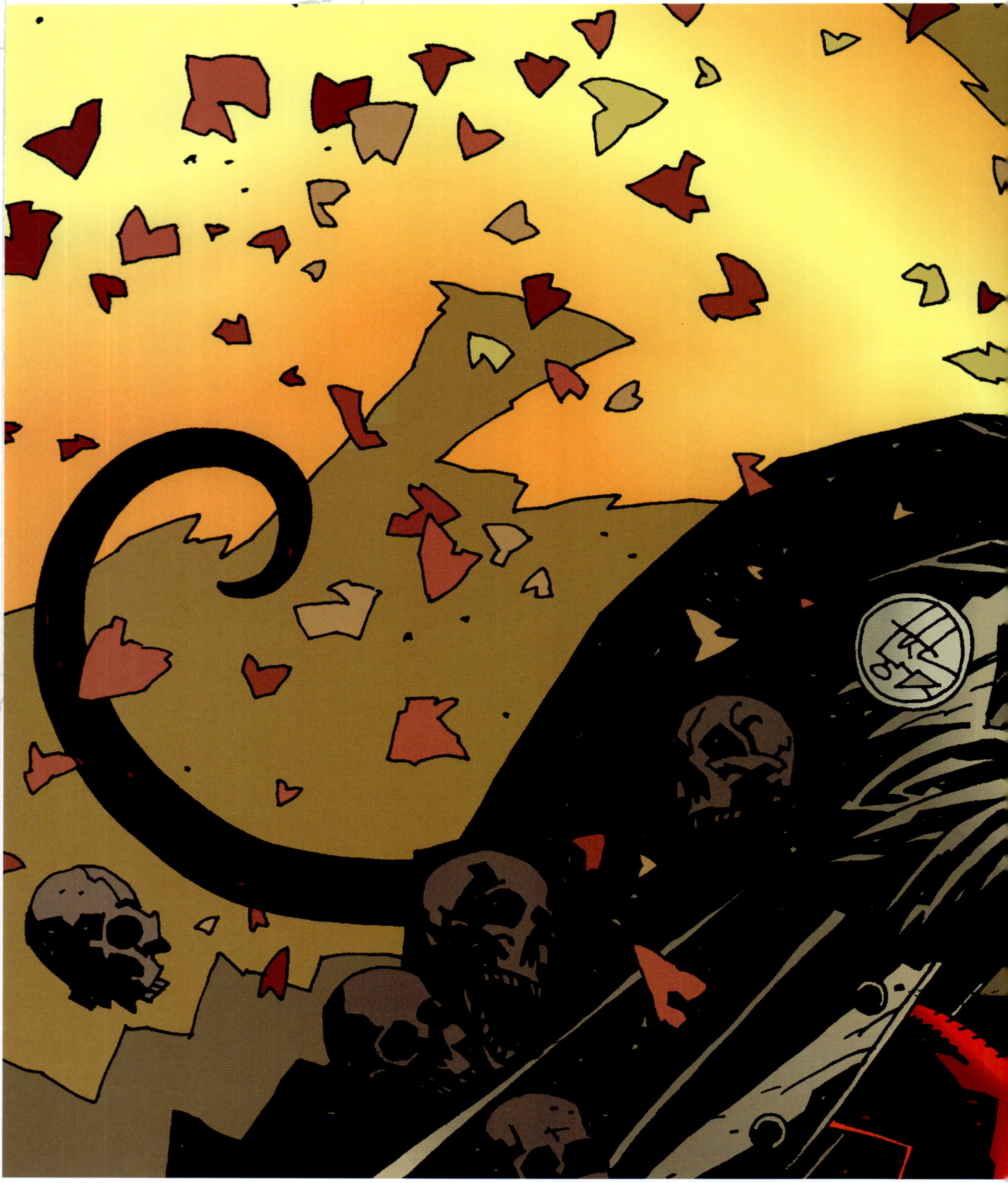

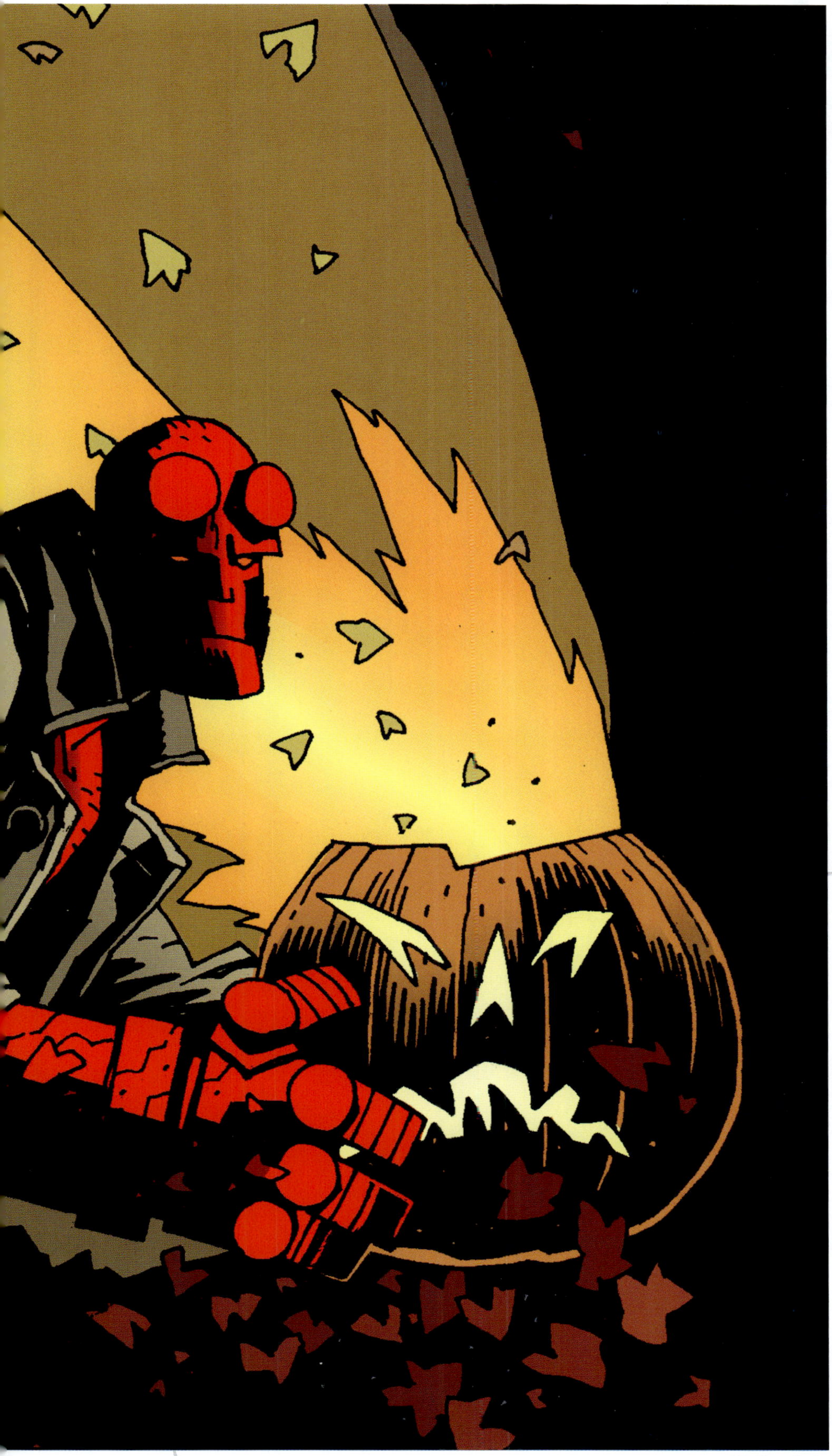

© Darkhorse Comics.

Mike Mignola

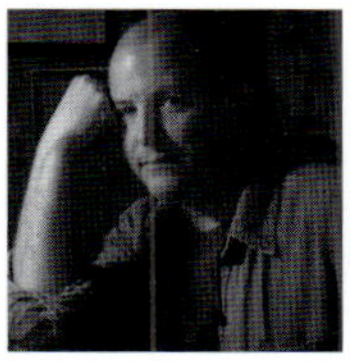

© Photo by Christine Mignola

Having worked as an inker at Marvel in the early 1980s, Mike spent the next decade flitting from Marvel and DC, drawing Batman, Thor and Cosmic Odyssey, before coming up with his most beloved creation.

Drawn on a whim for a 1993 comic convention, Hellboy swiftly developed into the perfect showcase for Mike's unique style and broad genre influences. And with Guillermo del Toro's titular film in, 2004 Mike went from the comic artist's comic artist to a world famous artist.

The first Hellboy storyline was written in 1994 and since then the character has appeared in a range of guises. Two animated Hellboy films, two feature films and several spin-offs have earned Mike and his creation numerous awards. With so much work sprouting from one character, Mike's allowed other artists to contribute to the ongoing Hellboy comics, however, this hellish creation continues to resonate nearly 20 years after its conception.
www.artofmikemignola.com

> "I spent time designing him so he'd be fun to draw, and Hellboy was the only name I came up with."

Wise words

STYLE BY IMITATION

"In high school I wanted to be Frank Frazetta. I learned a lot from copying him. Then I went through phases where I wanted to be a zillion different guys. Now people look at my work and they don't know who I'm influenced by, which I like."

William Stout

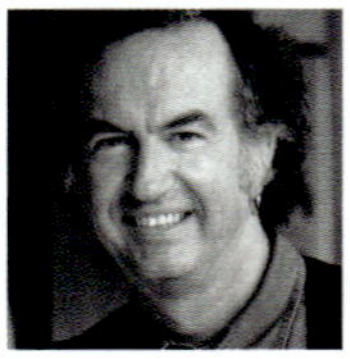

As a profusely creative artist entering the industry in the 1960s, William Stout's career has covered most forms of illustrations and design. Starting in the US underground comic scene, he was in full steam when the world acquired an insatiable appetite for everything sci-fi in the 1970s. William became successfully involved with film design and has worked in many roles from storyboard artist to production design, on more than 30 titles.

An avid fan of natural history, his personal work often involves accurate reconstructions of prehistoric life. Month-long trips to Antarctica and Patagonia inspired him to quit film work and dedicate himself to fine art (with a prolific sideline in illustration). Having never missed a San Diego Comic Con since 1970, he's also a proud champion of comic art, and artists' rights.
www.williamstout.com

"Observing nature and life feeds me with lots of ideas."

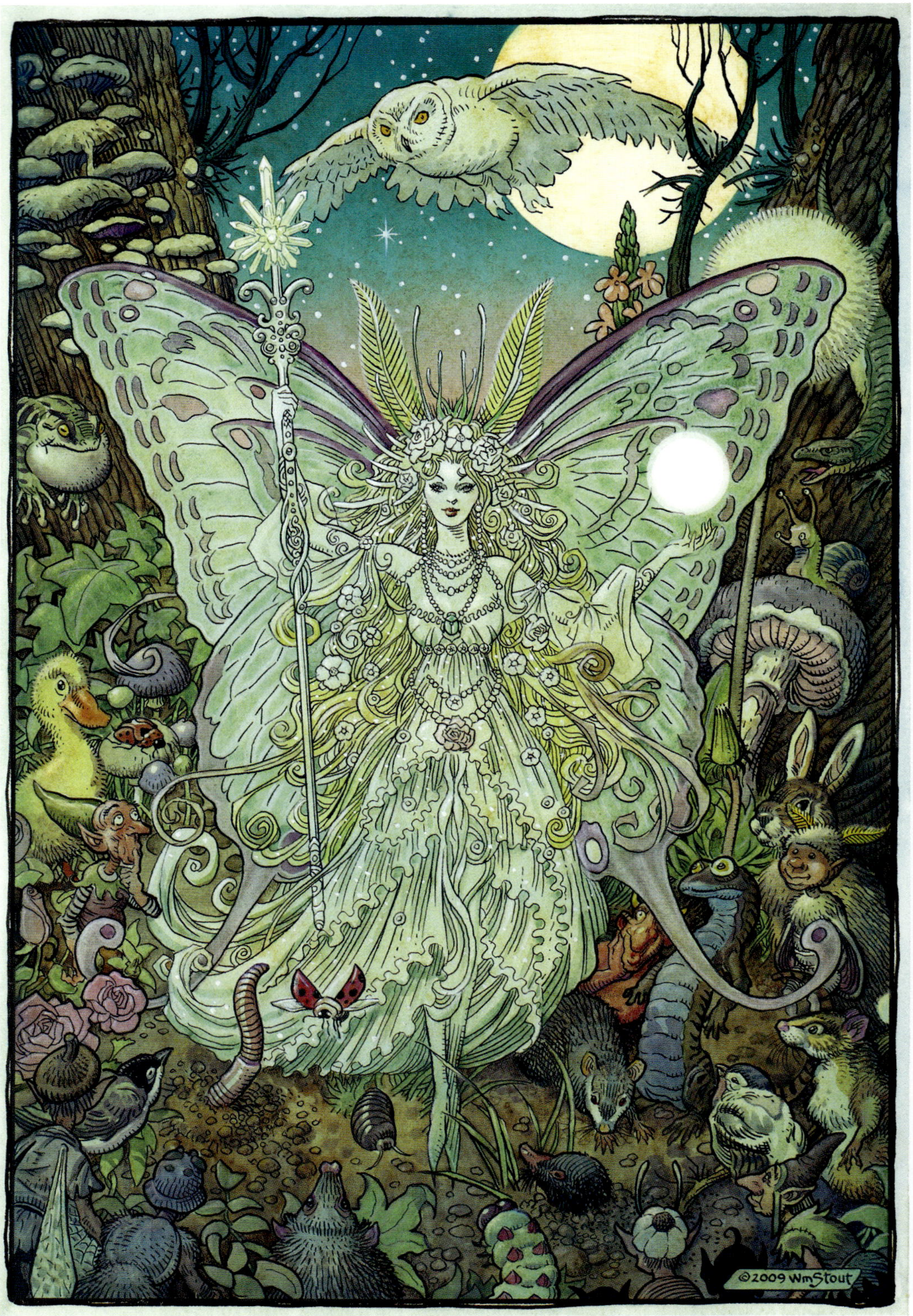

Wise words

MR NICE

"I've seen other pros abuse their fans... My attitude is pretty simple: show up and be nice. It takes just as much energy to be nice as it does to be a jerk, so why not be nice?"

"Get out and see the world; experience different cultures, lands and phenomena. Don't live vicariously through the adventures of others – create your own."

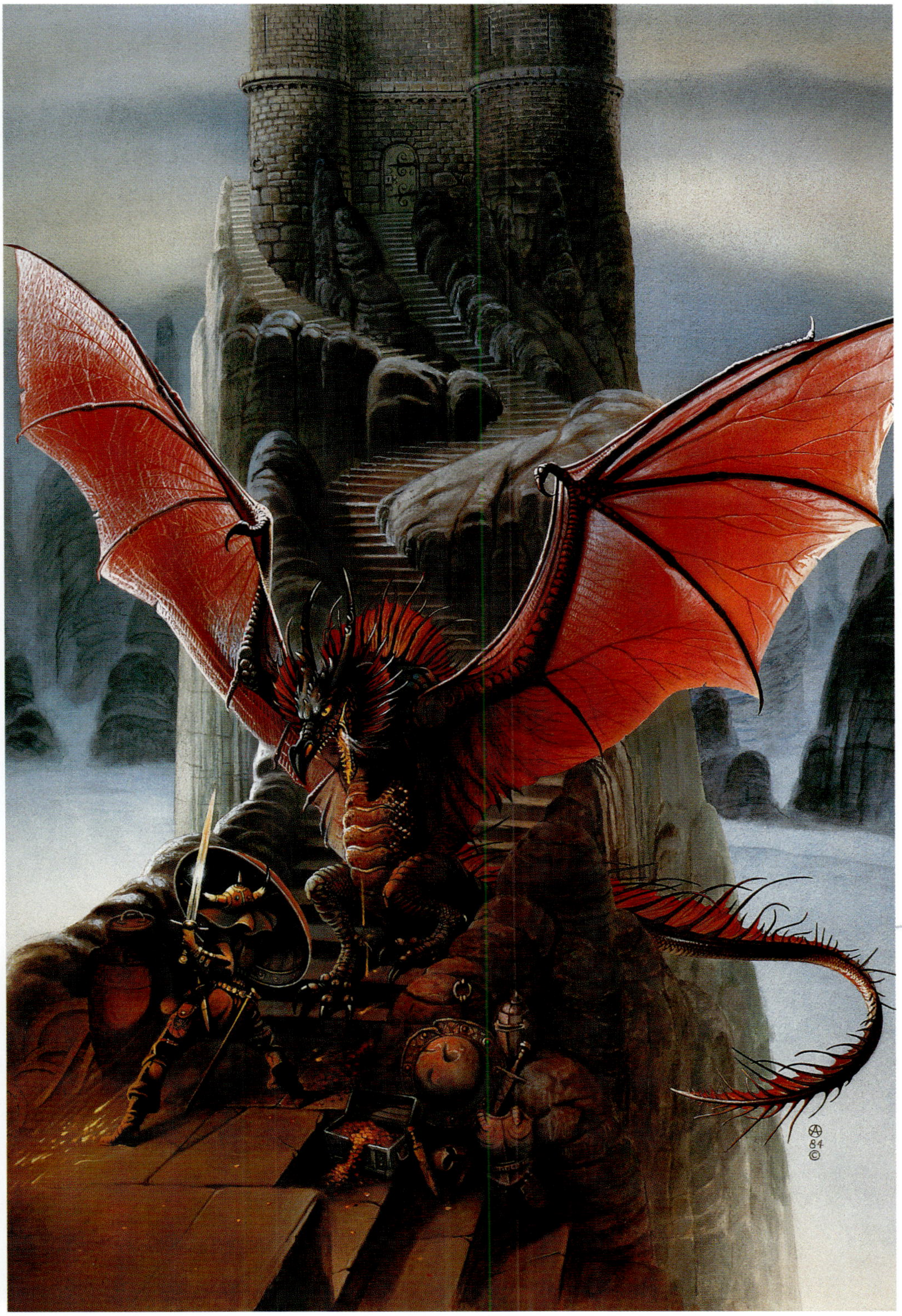

“Most importantly the picture has to be pleasing to the eye. If it also makes one think, then all the better.”

Chris Achilléos

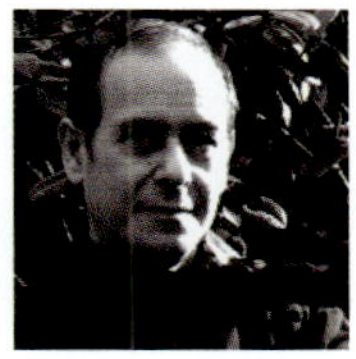

Chris's meticulously detailed art has been at the forefront of British fantasy for more than 30 years, appearing everywhere from hard rock album covers to the BBC TV series Doctor Who.

Graduating from art school in 1969, Chris was equally inspired by Frank Frazetta and airbrush art to dedicate his budding talents to fantasy book jacket designs, then the corporeal world of pin-up art.

After a time of recession-led obscurity, Chris came back as a concept artist on George Lucas's Willow. But he is perhaps best known for his paintings of Amazons. From 1973 to the present he has created a pantheon of female warriors for books, magazines, calendars and posters, finally collecting them for the art book, Amazona, in 2004.

www.chrisachilleos.co.uk

“I have a proud boast of having sold the most trading cards of any artist.”

Wise words

MAGIC INGREDIENTS

"The Alchemy of making Art: Take one person, preferably young, ambitious, and competitive, add visual imagination, hand to eye co-ordination, determination, the ability to concentrate for long periods of time, lots of patience and finally, the ability to work alone!"

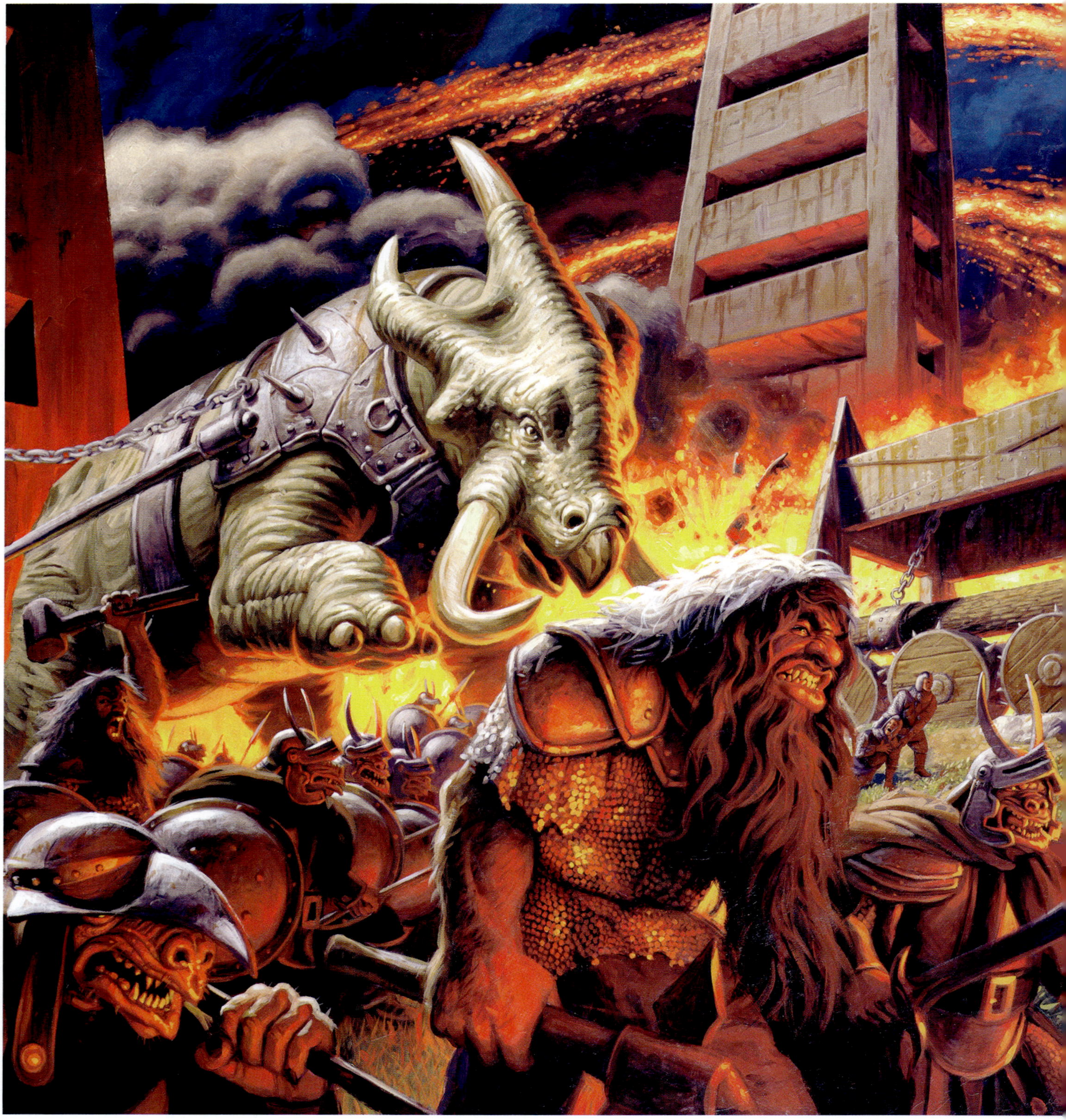

Brothers Hildebrandt

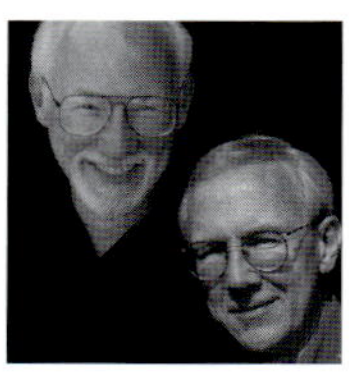

The twin brothers Tim and Greg Hildebrandt may have found fame within the fantasy art world with their classic promotional Star Wars poster, but they had been professional and recognised by the industry artists for 20 years before that.

Bred on golden age comics and Disney, the brothers wanted to be animators. After working in that field on industrial and commercial films, in 1969 they worked as commercial children's book illustrators for six years. Then came the Tolkein calendar.

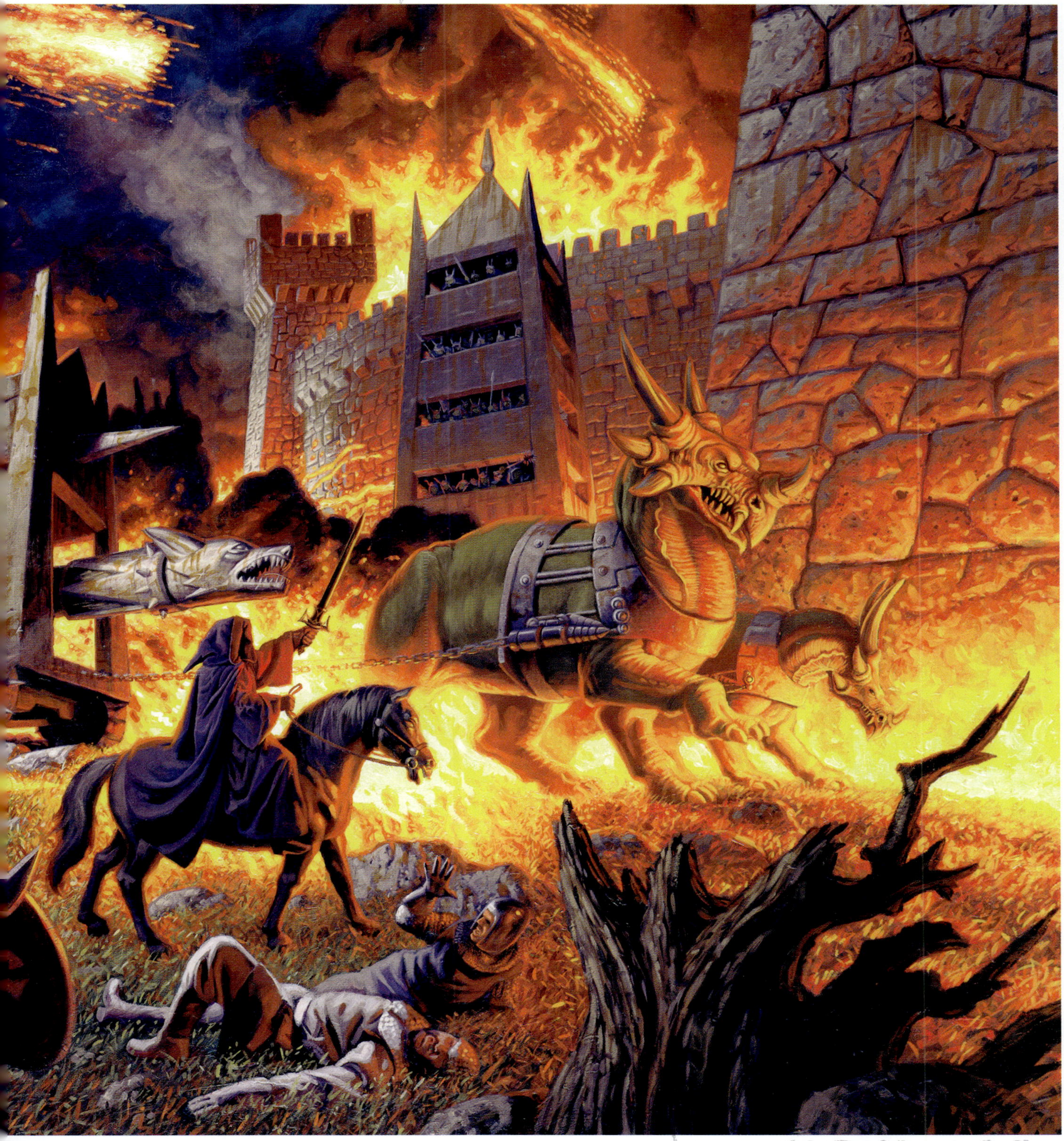

The only professional artists that replied to a call for entries for a Lord of the Rings calendar competition, the brothers' winning paintings immediately made an impression in fantasy art – the third in the calendar series sold more than a million. Later, asked to paint a Star Wars poster eight days before the film's release, their image became an instant classic. A career in comics, ads, D&D and Star Wars books has spread the brothers' self-tutored style, far and wide.
www.brothershildebrandt.com

Wise words

GREG HILDEBRANDT, BE A TWIN

"I'm amazed by any artist as an individual who manages to complete anything. In the early days we'd have these freakouts, throw the art in the corner and say 'I quit'. Then the other one would say, 'well, unless you get back in here, I'm quitting too,' and that would be the end of the freakout."

“To me Conan wasn’t a fictitious cover of a book. He was once a living entity.”

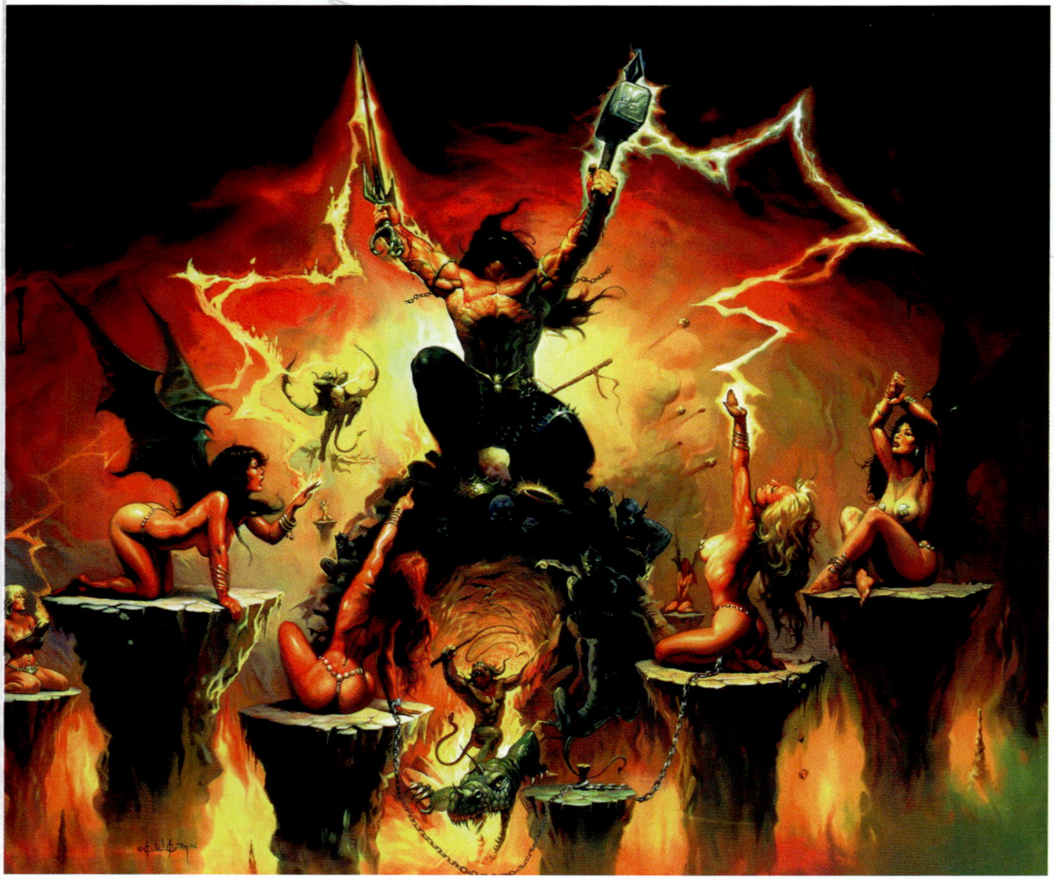

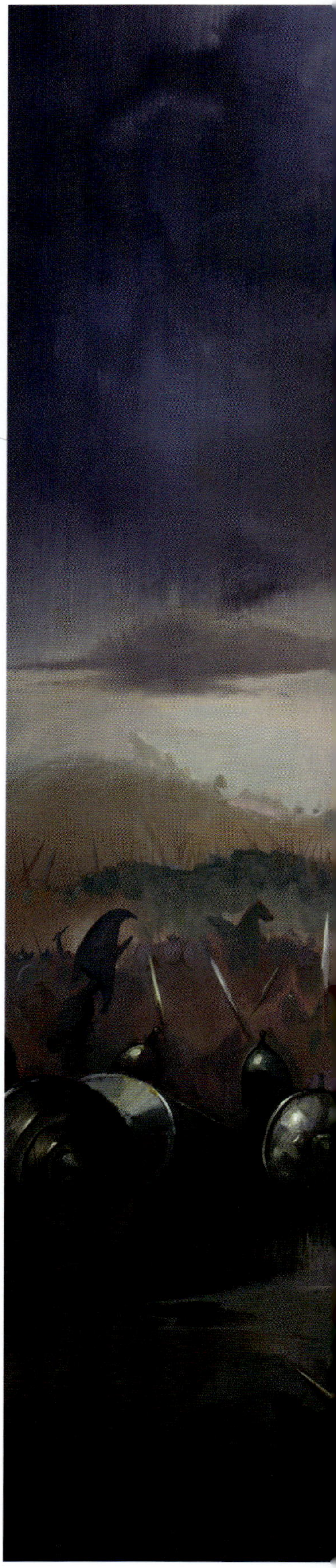

Ken Kelly

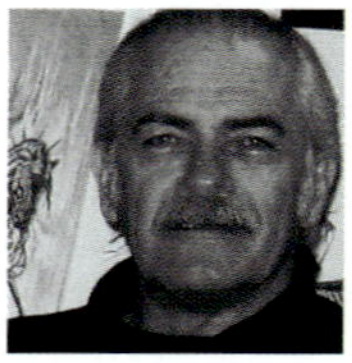

Ken developed his art chops working on horror comics, but it was his work on the cover of rock band KISS’s first platinum album Destroyer that fired him into the big time, introducing him to a whole new world of fans.

Thirty-five years later, Ken’s KISS artwork is still popular on his website. But before the iconic rock images, his work on horror comic titles like Eerie, Creepy and Vampirella was shown alongside art by Frank Frazetta and Neal Adams. Frank was Ken’s tutor in commercial artistry and even reworked Ken’s first commissioned piece.

As KISS became superstars, Ken was making his name as a book artist great, producing a series of timeless Conan the Barbarian images for the likes of Robert E Howard and Robert Adams.

With a spate of dynamic Dark Horse Star Wars comic covers in the 1990s, Ken has continued to produce great art for rock bands, and has even gone full circle painting covers for the revamped Creepy series.

www.kenkellyfantasyart.com

Wise words

BE BASIC

“I’m more Neanderthal than anything. I have a very crude painting style. I go for realistic as far as backgrounds, but I tend to exaggerate main characters and lean towards the dramatic as far as lighting and painting style.”

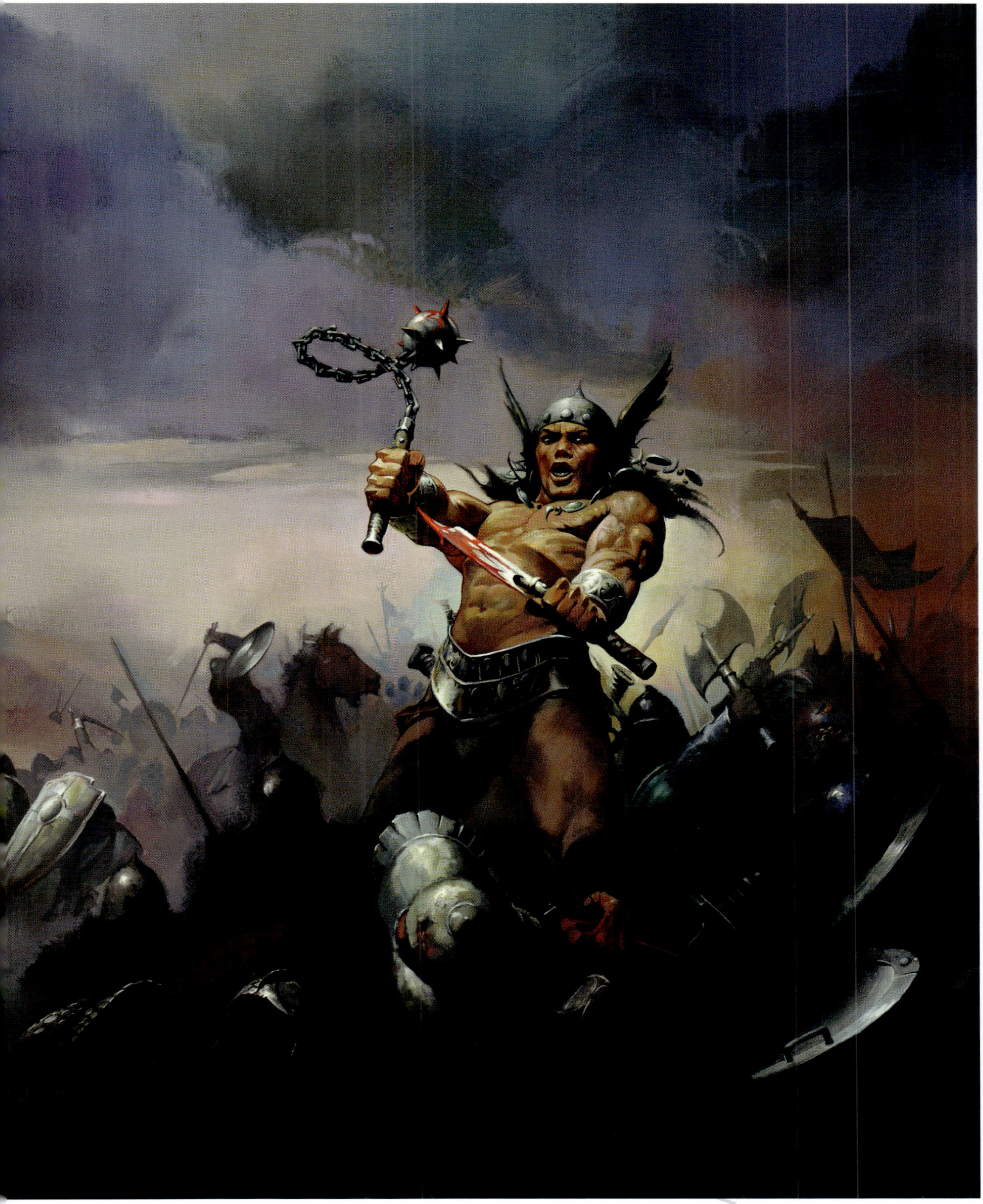

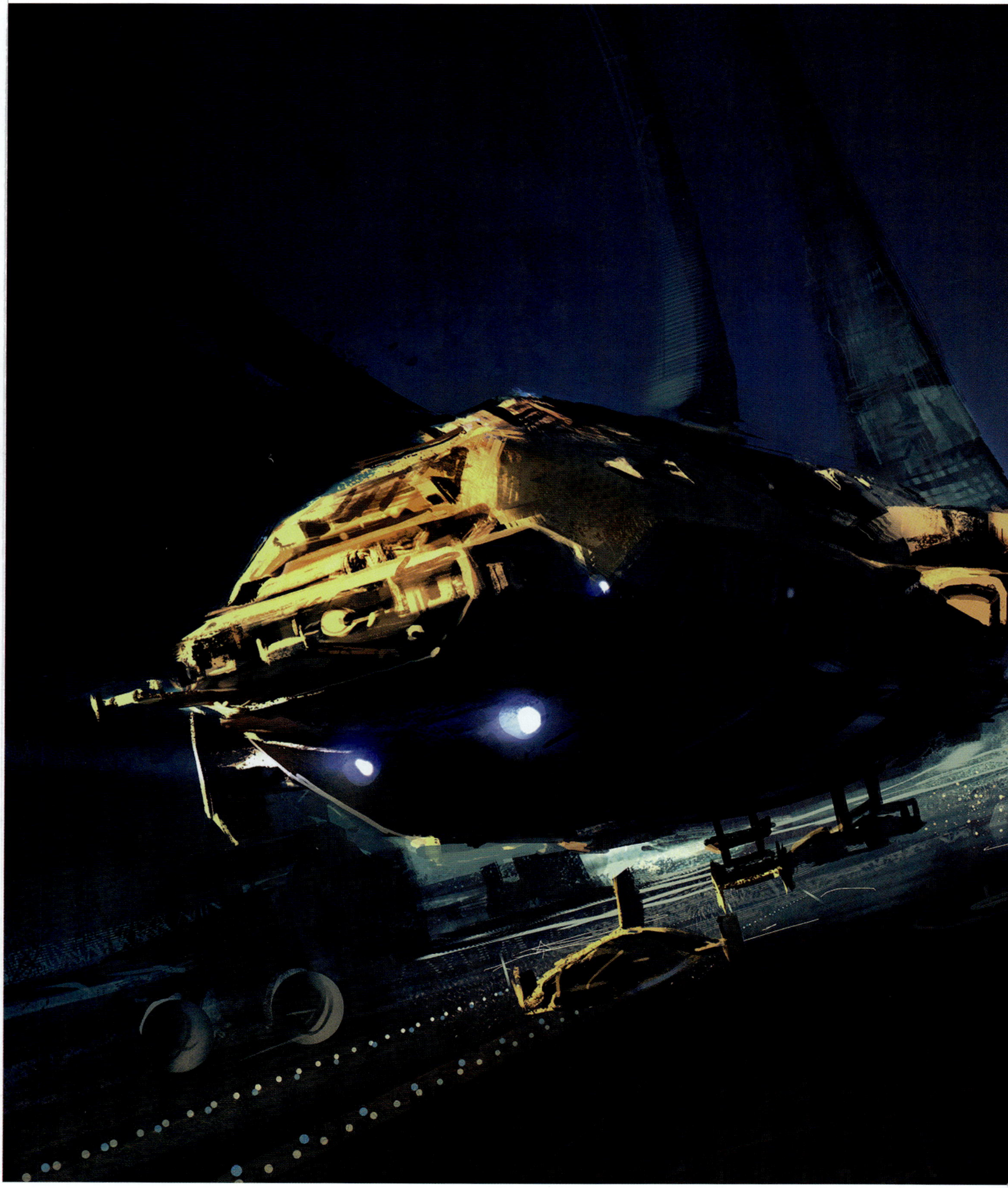

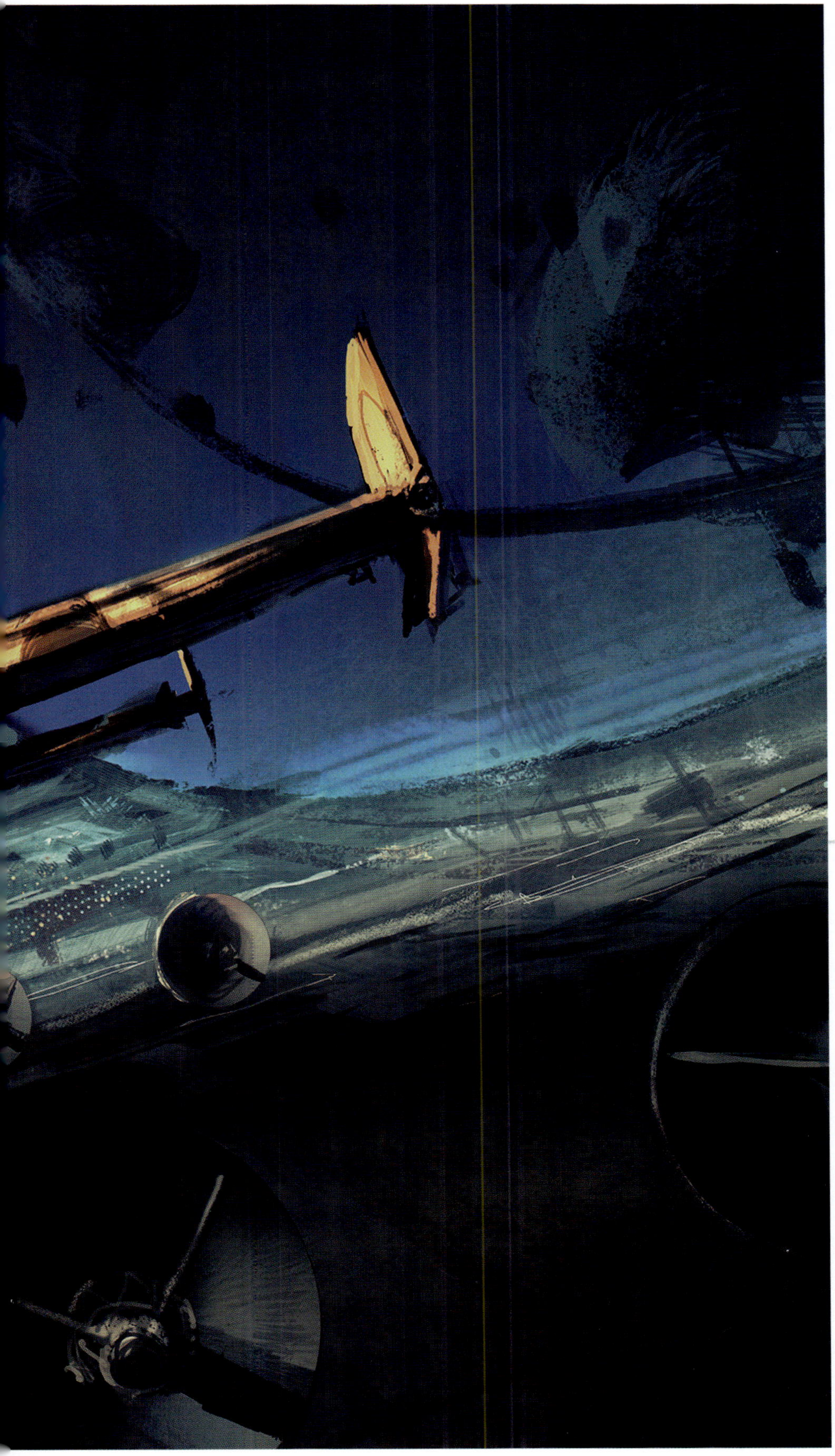

Nicolas 'Sparth' Bouvier

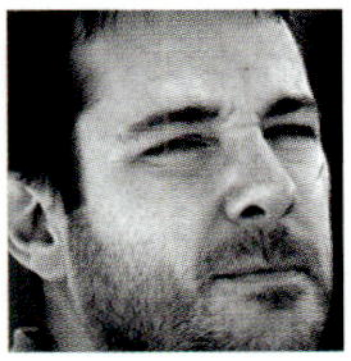

Since 2001 French artist Sparth has exclusively worked in digital. "Going 100 per cent digital greatly helped me to shape my vision," he says, and his army of fans around the world would agree.

Yet Sparth's visions of the future have definite links to the past, and he sees himself as part of the Star Wars generation, with his architect-accurate vistas and sci-fi epics echoing the worlds of Chris Foss and Greg Hildebrandt.

Working for 343 Industries, Sparth helped visualise the computer game franchise Halo, and he's produced more than 50 book cover illustrations since 2004. Inspired by utilitarian styles of architecture, Sparth's images linger in the imagination because as awe-inspiring and vast as they are, they're glimpses of a future that you can imagine inhabiting.

www.sparth.com

"The biggest challenge in sci-fi art is to avoid repeating the same concepts as so much has already been done... But there are still so many doors that haven't been opened yet."

Wise words

ACT NOW, THINK LATER

"I think I'm more effective at getting straight to the point instead of planning an image long term. Most of the time when I do so I end up having an average image."

Luis Royo

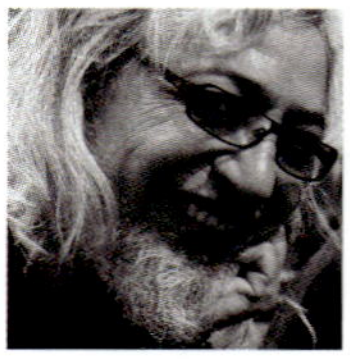

Although brandishing the technical skills of a hyperrealist, Spaniard Luis Royo classes himself squarely as a fantasy artist saying: "I'm not looking for reality… My goal isn't to reflect today's environment or real life."

Luis honed his craft as a draftsman then entered the world of comics in the 1980s, but he is perhaps best known for his 20-odd art books. From the 1990s onwards, he has released 'best of' compilations, as well as erotically charged collections, and also project-specific books, like Dome, which documents his commissioned painting of a huge fresco in a Russian castle.

Seduced by the aesthetics of the female form, nearly all of Luis's art involves the depiction of women. And although his immersive approach to art doesn't involve digital tools, he remains an inspiration to many in the modern medium.
www.luisroyofantasy.com

" It's not only the female form that attracts me. I also feel attracted by everything that revolves around the feminine universe. "

Wise words

EMBRACE YOUR MISTAKES

Once he's set on a final idea, Luis often makes several 'finals' that never see the light of day. "About the mistakes," he says, "there are a lot, but when you've left them behind they're very helpful in strengthening your ideas."

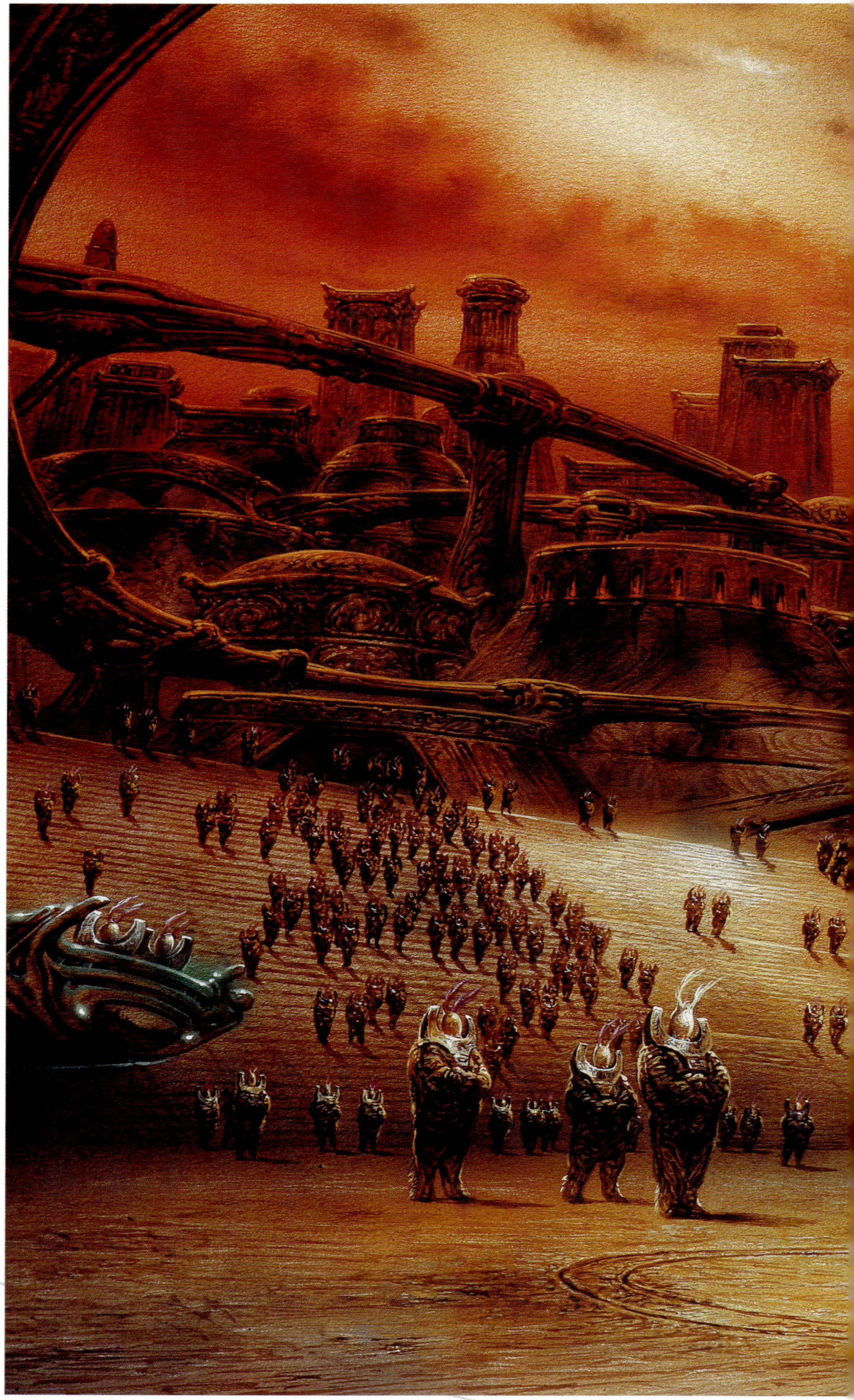

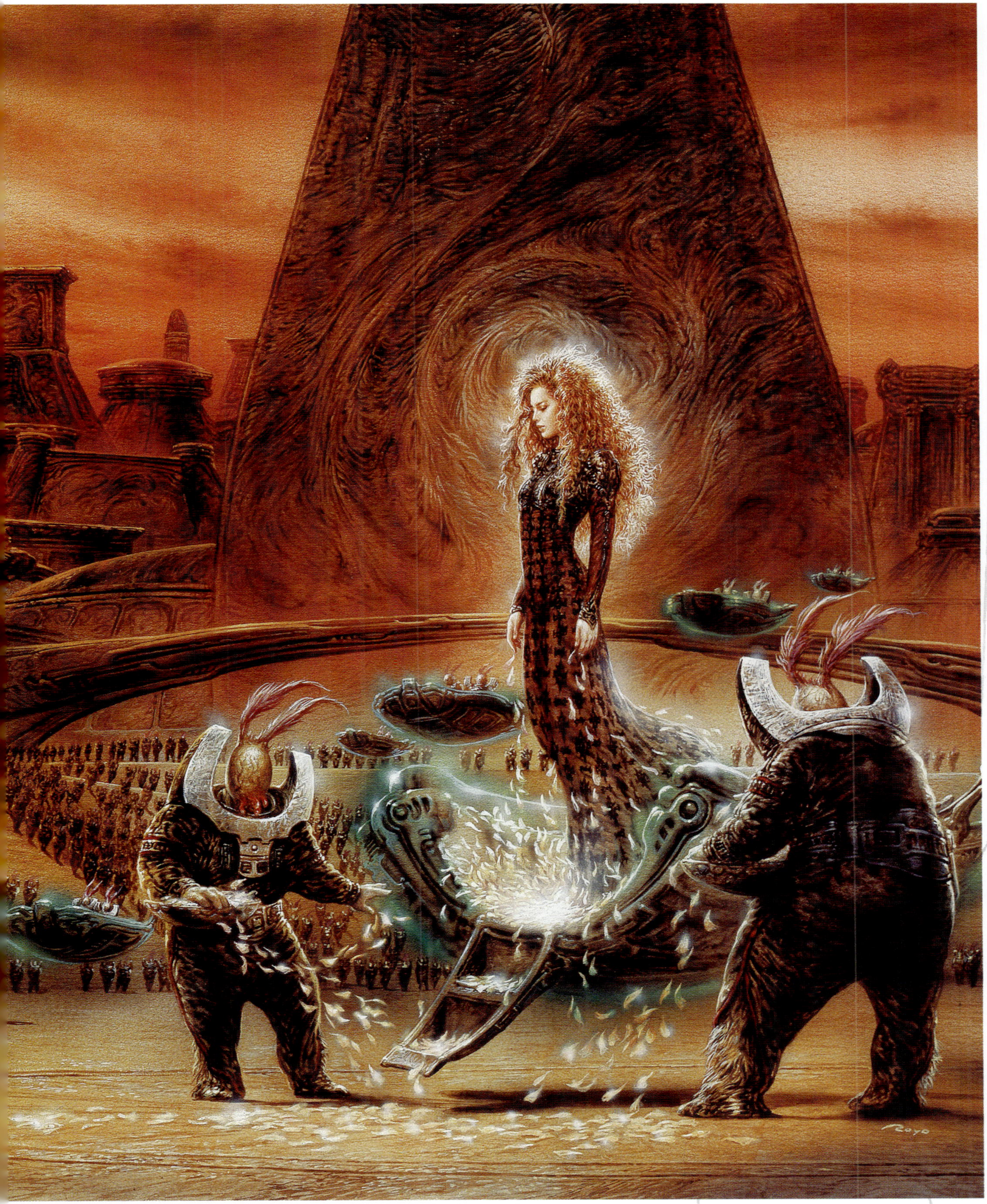

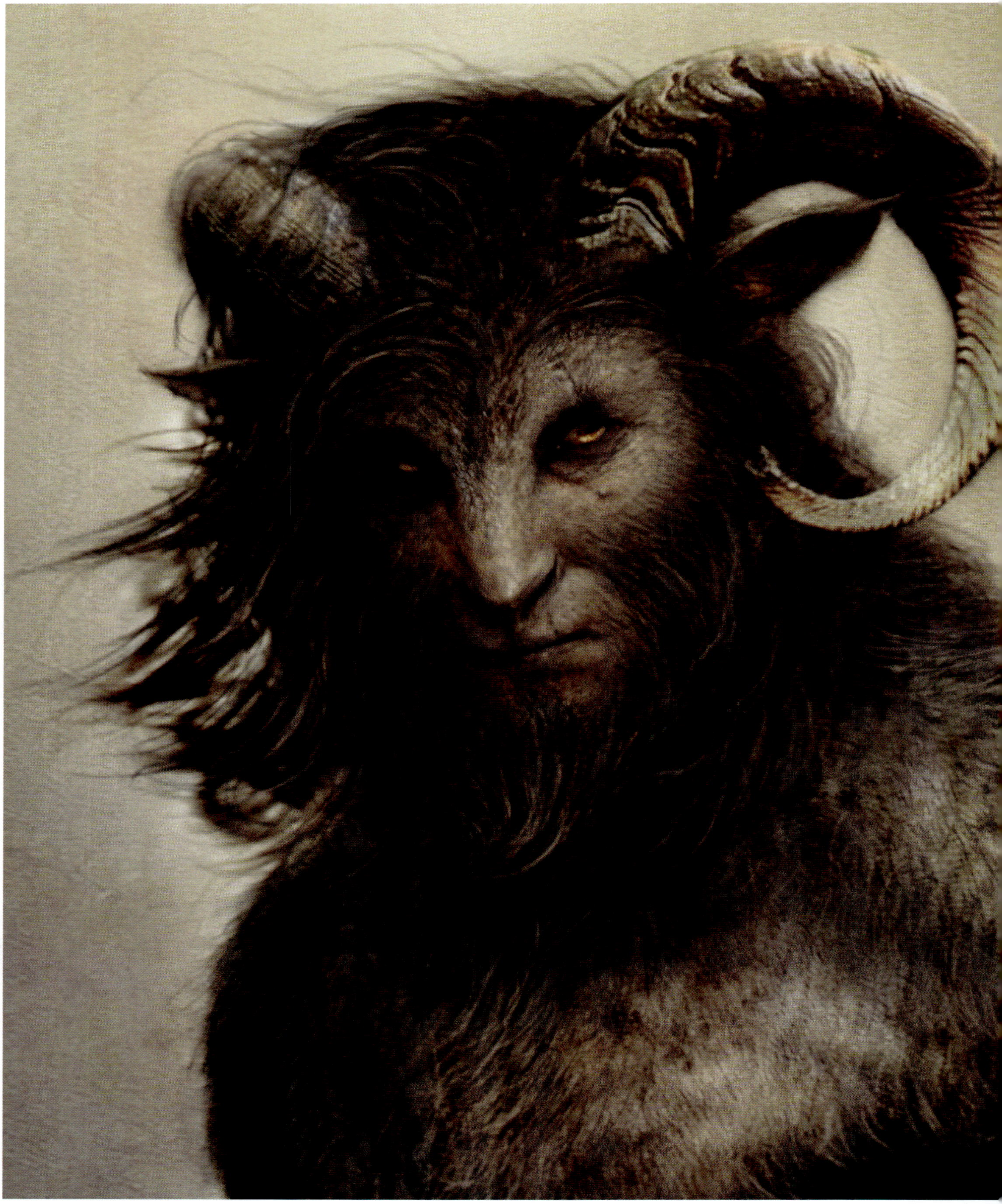

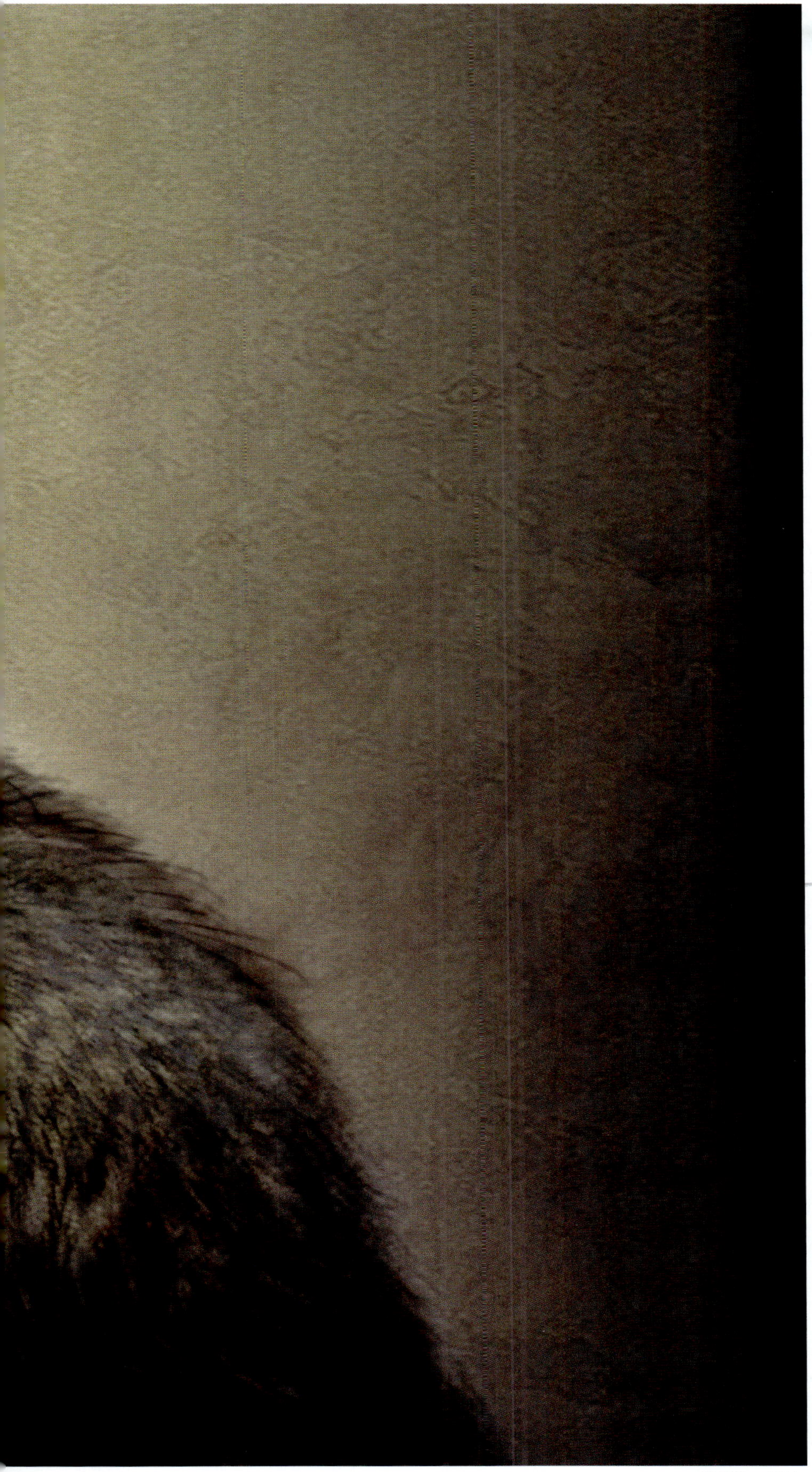

© 2008 Disney/Walden

Aaron Sims

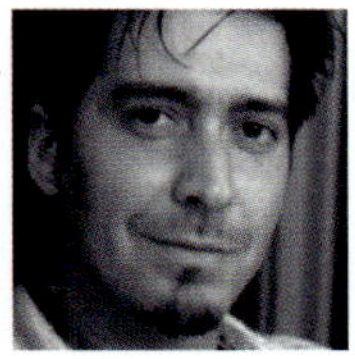

He's worked on some of the biggest Hollywood effects films in recent years, including Ai: Artificial Intelligence, The Chronicles of Narnia: Prince Caspian, The Incredible Hulk, The Mummy: Tomb of the Dragon Emperor, I Am Legend, and Clash of the Titans, he also specialises in creature design beast-fests.

Working as a makeup artist in the 1980s, he switched to special effects, for films like Batman Forever, Gremlins 2 and Men in Black. Riding the digital art wave into the 1990s, Aaron worked with visual effects legend Stan Winston and continued to innovate in the world of digital concept art and creature design. He has made his name by visualising the creatures that directors imagine, in both 2D and 3D, Aaron saves the producers money by creating a concept so accurately that the finished designs are used exactly as they are in the film.

www.aaron-sims.com

“What's changed from when I was doing this in pencil or clay, is that now I render out a final image that the client can sign off and say: 'This is what it'll look like in the movie'.”

Wise words

SELF HELP

"There are so many educational devices that train people what to do. I've done many DVDs through Gnomon, which is a visual effects school. Educating yourself on those, I think, is really good."

ART LEGENDS

Advice and techniques from iconic artists...

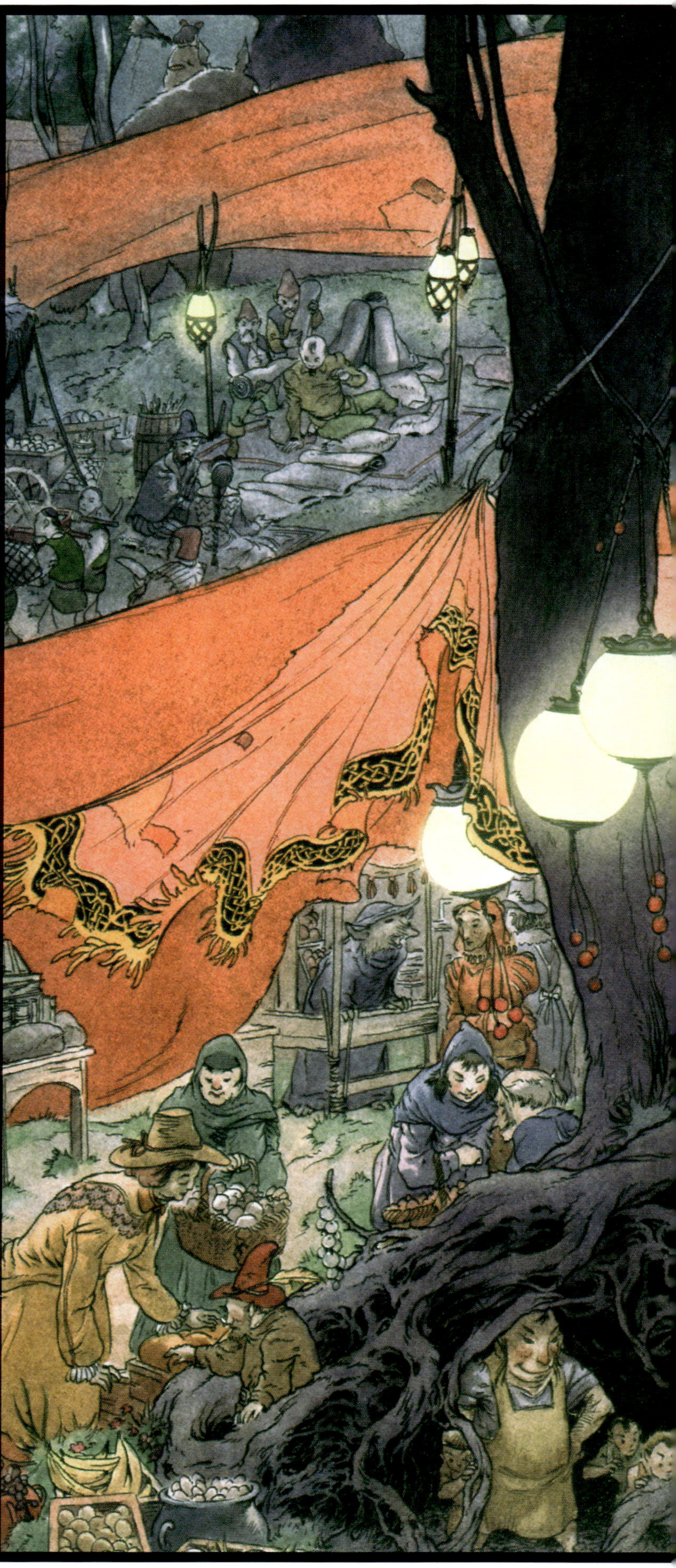

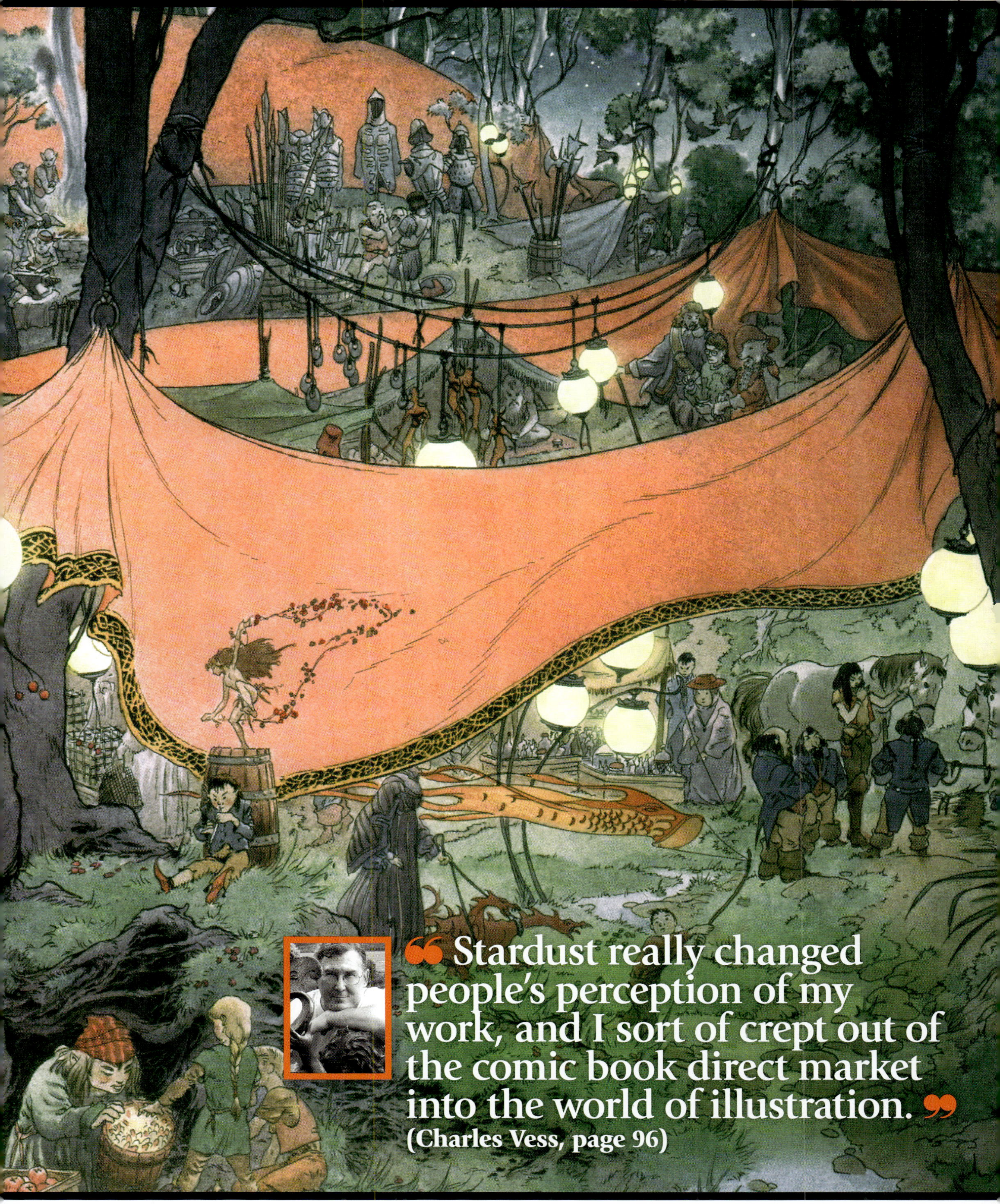

“Stardust really changed people’s perception of my work, and I sort of crept out of the comic book direct market into the world of illustration.”
(Charles Vess, page 96)

Interview

Frank Frazetta

*An icon, a legend and an inspiration – we pay tribute to **Frank Frazetta**, the godfather of fantasy art*

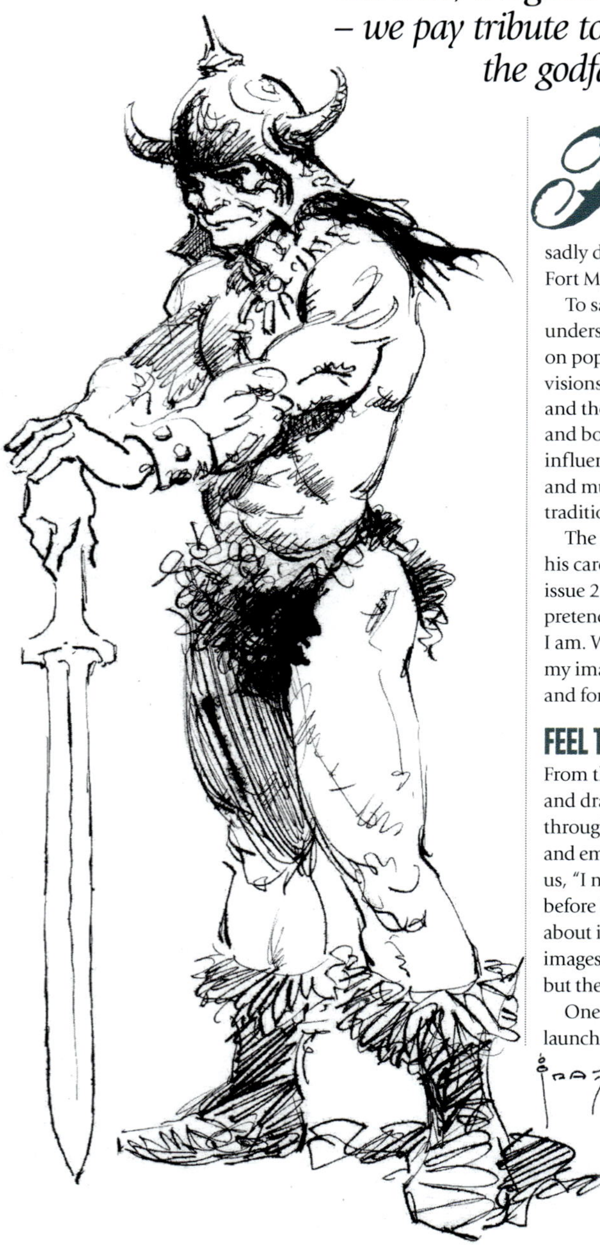

CONAN
In a few short pencil strokes Frank Frazetta captured the essence of Conan the Barbarian for generations of fans.

Frank Frazetta, the artist who defined the Golden Era of fantasy art and brought about new respect for the genre, sadly died of a stroke on 10 May 2010, in Fort Myers, Florida, USA. He was 82.

To say Frank was an inspiration is to understate his impact, not just on art, but on popular culture in its widest sense. His visions of barbarians, fantastical creatures and the female form brought a new realism and boldness to fantasy art that cast an influence as far wide as books, comics, film and music. He mixed art theory and tradition with fantasy and drama.

The man himself was more humble. Of his career and his art he told ImagineFX in issue 28, back in 2008, that, "I'm not pretending I'm a great painter. I don't think I am. What I think I'll be remembered for is my imagination, for my sense of drama, and for not being afraid to take a chance."

FEEL THE SCENE

From the outset, Frank had a loose, yet bold and dramatic style. His images came to life through his use of aggressive brush strokes and empathy for the subject. In 2008 he told us, "I never have a solid image in my head before I start drawing, just a certain feeling about it. On very rare occasions I see the images very clearly once I start sketching, but they're usually just very simple scenes."

One such scene was the image that truly launched Frank's career. In 1965, after

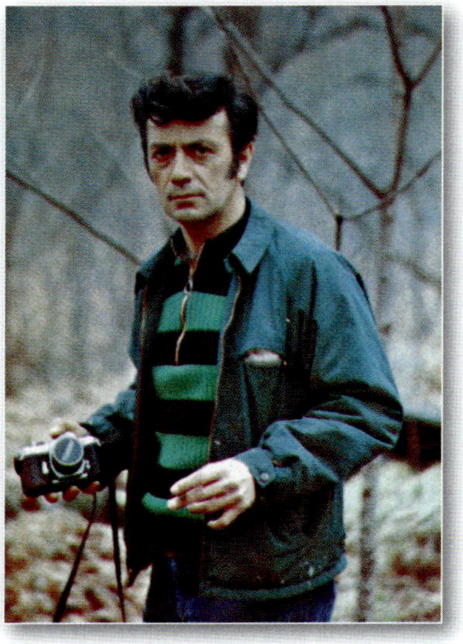

IMAGINATION
Frank never considered himself a great painter, but his art is naturally balanced.

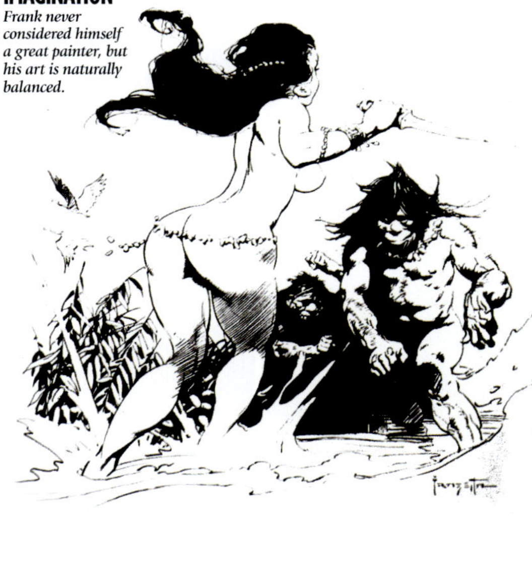

THE DEATH DEALER
Painted in 1973, this is painting inspired its own comic series.

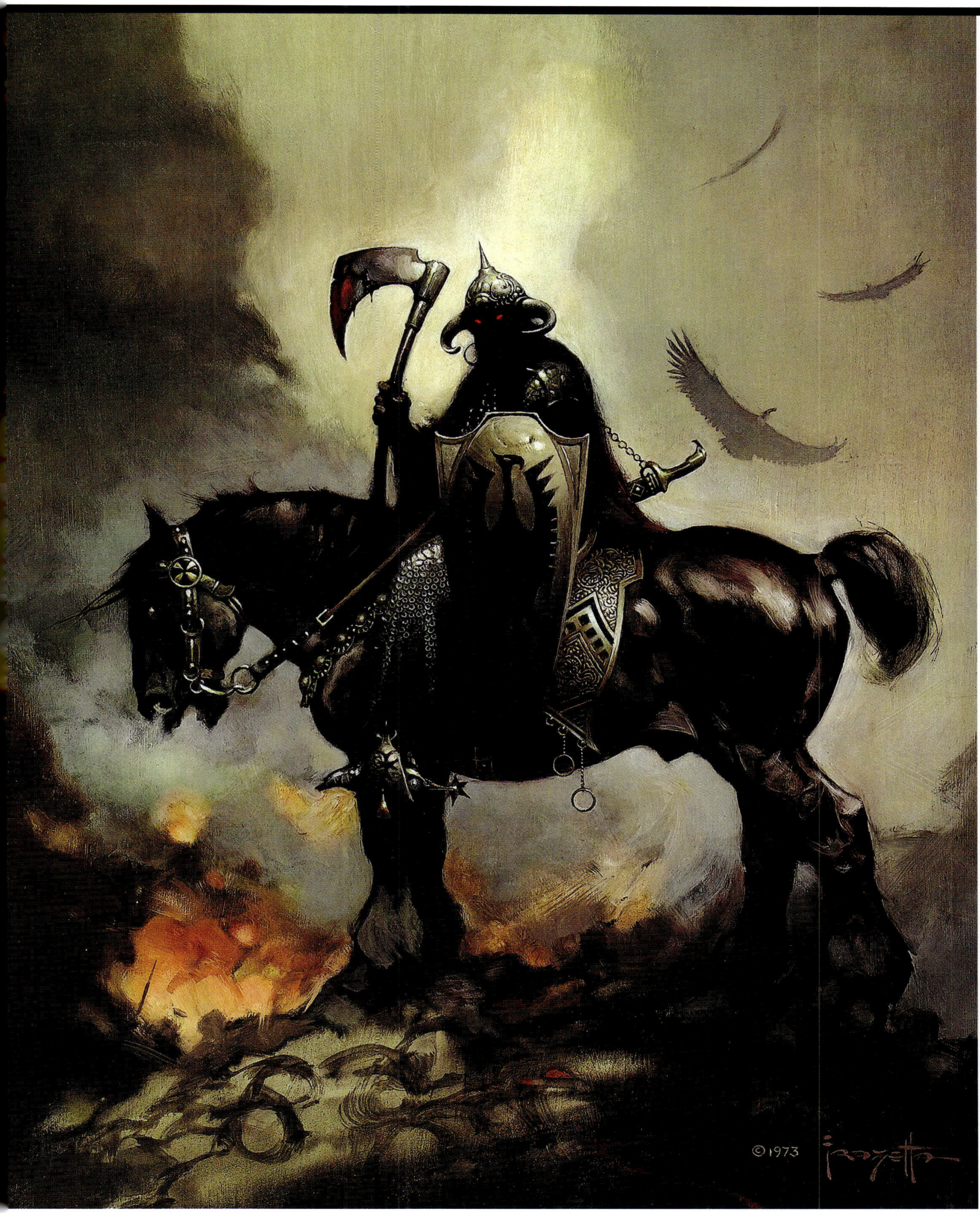
©1973
Frazetta

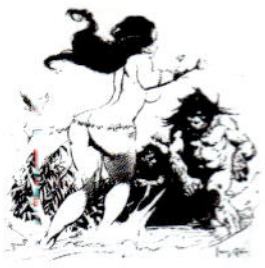

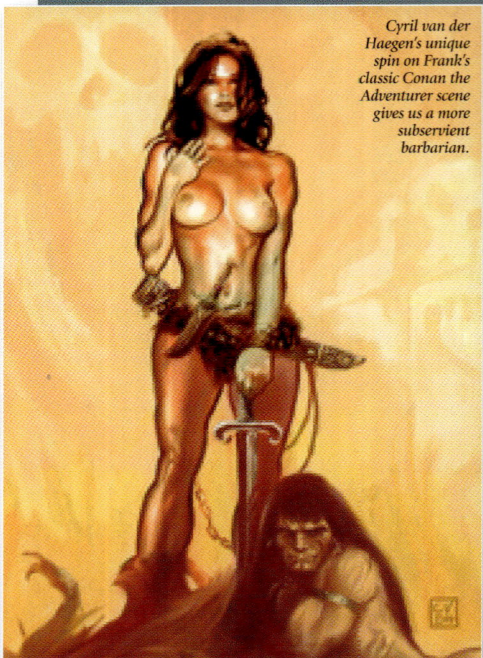

Cyril van der Haegen's unique spin on Frank's classic Conan the Adventurer scene gives us a more subservient barbarian.

FRANK AT 80

In 2008, the leading fantasy art magazine ImagineFX celebrated Frank Frazetta's 80th birthday with the world's art community...

The magazine partnered with 80 artists, including Rodney Matthews, Daniel Dociu and Raymond Swanland, and asked them to create their own take on a Frank Frazetta scene. The end result was a collection of exceptional illustrations, in a variety of styles and media. It proved that Frank's influence spreads to every corner of modern fantasy art, from concept artists to book illustrators and matte painters.

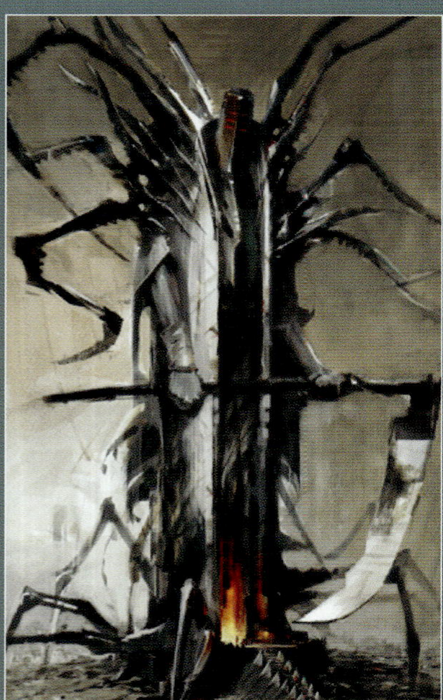

Daniel Dociu puts a digital spin on a classic Frazetta character and re-imagines Death Dealer in his own style.

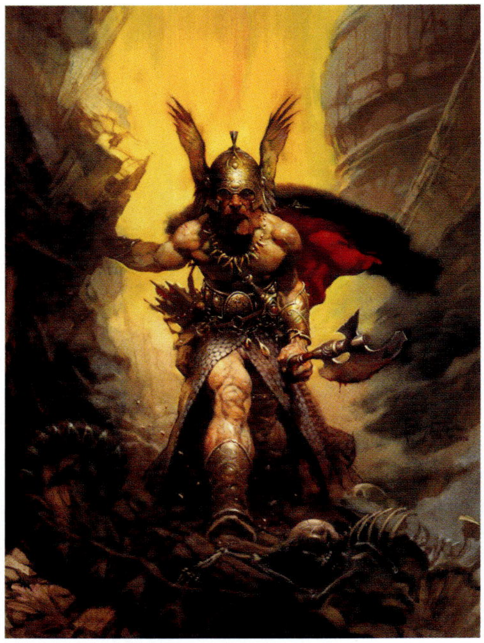

Dark Kingdom, painted in 1976, is typical of Frank's masterful use of composition and contrasting light, that drags you towards his warrior's pose.

years working in comics, painting covers for the jungle adventure Thun'da, Dan Brand and Buck Rogers, Frank was offered a contract to paint the cover of Robert E Howard's Conan The Adventurer. The cover featured a dark, brooding barbarian, standing on a heaped pile of dead bodies, a naked slave girl wrapped around his legs and the glow of a burning village crowning the frame. It was visceral, iconic and exploded the preconception of what fantasy art should be.

"Frank Frazetta was the undisputed daddy of heroic fantasy art, an inspiration to artists across the globe," says Simon Brewer, recalling his love of the artist's work and that famous cover. "His high-impact style is much copied yet rarely replicated, such

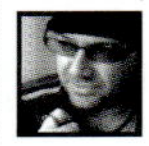

was his skill in communicating energy, dynamism and classic fantasy mood. Frank may have passed on but his legacy will long continue."

It's all the more impressive when you dig deeper into Frank's working process. Paintings such as that first Conan cover, or indeed his later work on Tarzan and John Carter of Mars, began life from an emotional source. "I don't see detail, just a certain atmosphere," he once told us. "That it's warm or cold, that's it's terrible or eerie. I see something, but nothing distinct."

It's that emotional connection, above all, that was Frank's gift. He qualified his

> **"What I think I'll be remembered for is my imagination, for my sense of drama, and for not being afraid to take a chance" FRANK FRAZETTA**

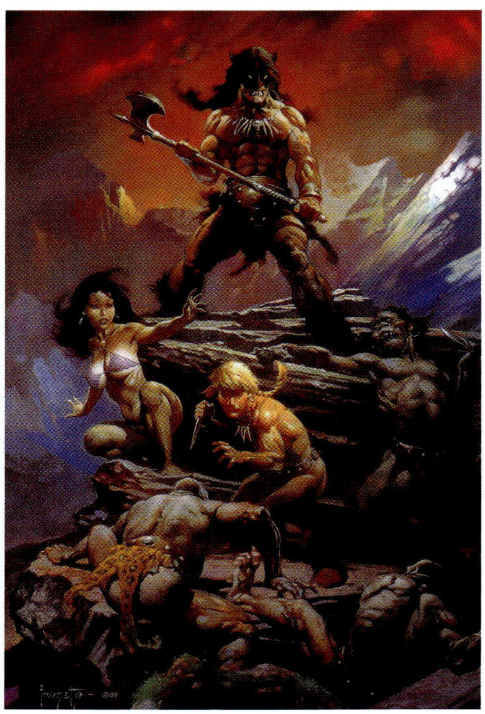

The 1983 movie Fire and Ice was pure Frazetta in motion. Frank created the characters and their world, drafted the script and painted this image, the movie's promotional poster.

feelings for an image through bold strokes, a vibrant colour palette and imaginative character design that seemed to grow from the paint itself. The impact of the first Conan cover was equally emotional. Frank soared to the top of the industry. Publishers craved both him and anything to do with Robert E Howard.

Thanks to Frank's powerful illustrations of warriors and sexualised savagery, long-forgotten pulp characters became contemporary bestsellers. With them, Frank became one of the most influential illustrators of the 20th century.

"When you're struck by the work of an artist, the day remains engraved in your psyche," reflects John Howe. "I may well

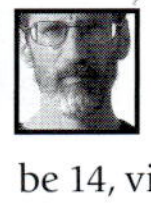

have grown up and now be working in the profession I hoped I might, but somewhere, I'll always be 14, visiting every used paperback shop within cycling distance, searching for book covers by Frank Frazetta. Buried treasure couldn't have lured or enchanted me more." Such was Frank's impact, you have to wonder: did anyone ever read Conan? John recalls the dilemma fondly. "I made horrible copies of them [the illustrations] all in oil pastel. Perhaps I even read some of the books behind those coveted covers. If halcyon days can have a face and a name, it would be Frazetta's."

HARD GRAFT

The Conan cover was the impetus for Frank's most productive period. Between 1965 and 1973, Frank produced most of his more famous illustrations, including Cat Girl, Silver Warrior and the iconic Death Dealer. Frank's success (Conan The Adventurer sold 10 million copies) spawned imitators, and soon barbarians and buxom women were appearing on many book sleeves. Frank stayed ahead of the pack by working at a frenzied pace. He once completed three cover illustrations for Ace Books in two days.

Frank's workrate was again linked to his process. He'd often regarded himself as painting "by instinct" and would "draw almost unconsciously", letting his hand wander the canvas, building shapes and masses. As he told us, "It's like my mind is one place and my hand is another… somehow it all starts to come together."

Taking this at face value would be to deny Frank's gift for composition. Every image is built from an energetic focal point, shapes interact and the pyramid structure holds his paintings together. When working on an image, Frank would look for interesting patterns and work with loose blobs of colour to visualise spaces and shapes, building a hierarchy of importance and positioning. To prevent an image looking too forced, he occasionally introduced a new element, forcing it into the composition to sweep across the hierarchy and set the mind racing.

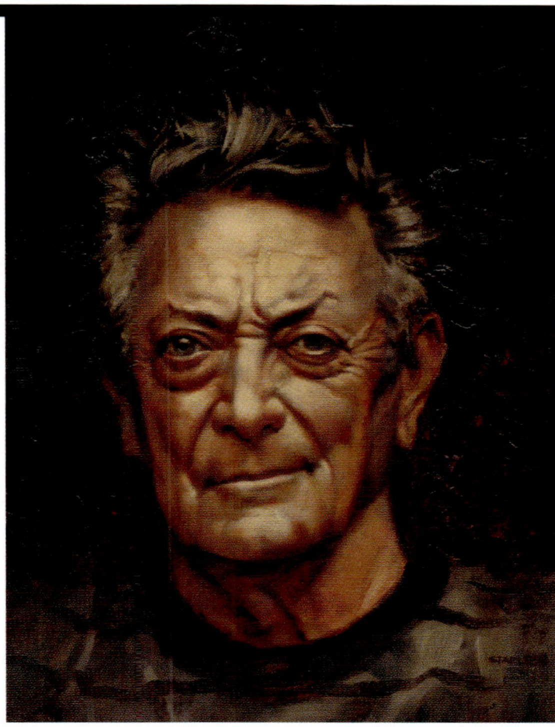

> **"When I finally bought my first Frazetta book when I was 24, I honestly couldn't believe what I was seeing. It wasn't necessarily his painting technique. Frankly I felt there are some who could paint technically just as well, but it was the power and energy that hit me like a lightening bolt! His subjects were alive on the page, his women made of real flesh, his people moved… this was not the fantasy art I was expecting. Everything he touched, worked."**
>
> GREG STAPLES

"Once I'm happy with the composition, I'll work on the forward figures first: they're the most important," said Frank when he spoke to ImagineFX for his 80th birthday celebration. "Above all, there's always an interaction of shapes that provides a feeling of stillness. I think that's why people react to my art, even if they can't figure out why the hell they're reacting to it. It's not posed and fake."

Part of Frank's inspiration to artists was his devotion to learning the craft. While he was a gifted child, having started drawing at the age three and enrolled in the Michele Falanga's Brooklyn Academy of Fine Arts when he was eight, he was instinctive, not technical. Commenting in the 2003 documentary Frazetta: Painting With Fire, he said, "When I was in school with Falanga, the emphasis was on feeling, not on the nuts and bolts." When working in comics in the late 1940s and 1950s, Frank was mentored by Ralph Mayo. "When Ralph took over, he pulled me aside and said, 'Frank, your stuff is great, but you need to learn some anatomy.' I really didn't understand what he meant by anatomy." That night Frank went home and studied an anatomy book Ralph had lent him, and in typically frenzied fashion, he began on page one and redrew the entire human body from the skeleton up.

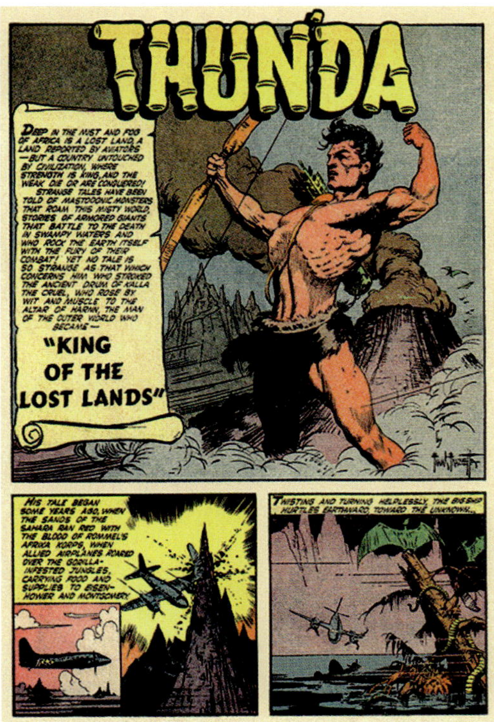

In the 1950s, Frank worked under the guidance of Ralph Mayo on Thun'Da, the only comic he drew cover to cover.

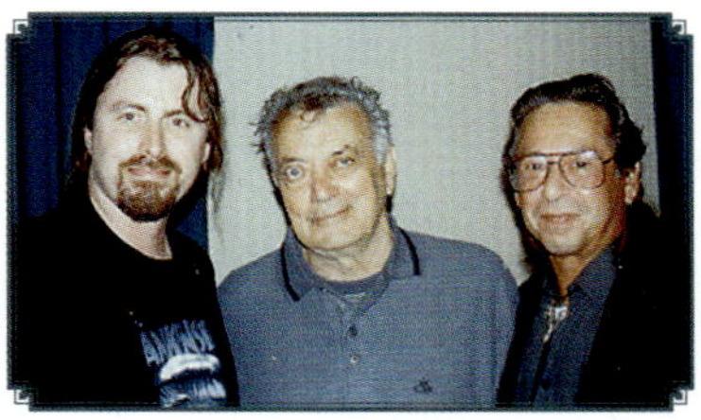

Bob Eggleton and the late Ron Walotsky pictured with Frank in 1997.

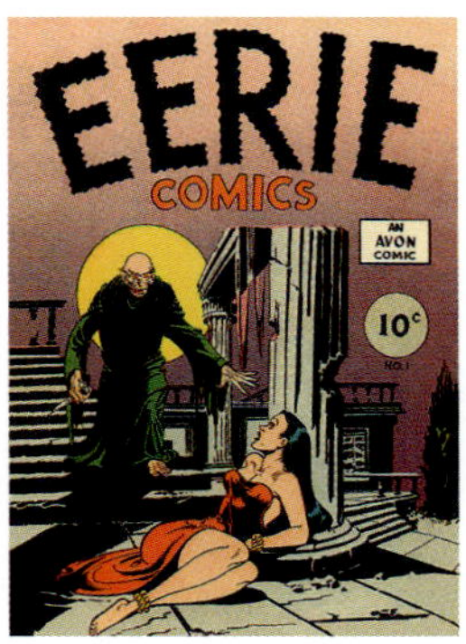

Many young fantasy artists got their first taste for Frank from his work on Eerie and Creepy magazines.

SUPERSTAR SKETCHER

It's these stories that help define Frank as a legendary artists' artist. He worked hard at his craft, and was himself inspired by other artists, such as Howard Pyle and NC Wyeth, picking up on their use of light to punctuate the darker brooding colours of a scene. He turned those influences into his own style, built on instinct, imagination and hard work. Looking back at Frank's early work, his signifying influences, references and details can be seen no matter what the subject. The stylised foliage, the impression of space, the obsession with powerful beasts such as panthers and wolves, and of course, no matter what the scenario, Frank's women were unclothed, buxom and beautiful. Robert E Howard's Conan was funnelled through Frank's vision, not the other way around. In doing so, he stepped over the line that separates a jobbing illustrator from an artist.

"Frazetta revitalised the field of fantasy art with a fresh sense of the iconic image, drawn from his own vivid feeling for drama and conflict," says James Gurney as he ➤

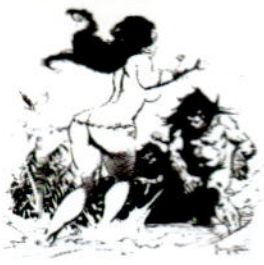

→ recalls what impressed him about Frank's work. "His moon maidens, thundering dragons and sword-wielding barbarians took on a powerful life of their own, which shaped the imagination of many artists working today, me included."

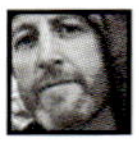

LICENSING BREAKTHROUGH

Frank forged a new kind of relationship between artist and client. His policy of retaining original works and licensing his art, coupled with his wife Ellie setting up a poster business to sell Frank's work, created a business model that has empowered artists to this day. Frank was a 'success'; the professional illustrator admired by his peers, respected by his clients and idolised by his fans. As Liam Sharp says, "Frazetta gave fantasy art credibility – and its first true superstar."

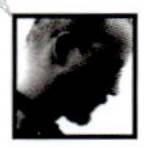

Frank's status in the 1970s and the impact of his art on popular culture exploded in the 1980s, including work on album covers, T-shirts and films, culminating in the movie Fire and Ice. While previous films such as John Milius's Conan The Barbarian drew inspiration from Frank for their art direction, Fire and Ice was more personal. Long-time friend and animator, Ralph Bakshi, fresh from work on Lord of the Rings and Wizards, asked Frank to collaborate on the movie. Working closely with Ralph, Frank designed the characters, their world and even sat in on the casting and live-action filming sessions.

"I had the privilege of working as a background painter on Fire and Ice," says James Gurney as he remembers time spent with Frank at his studio. "We always tried to get Frank to give the studio a class on figure drawing and composition, but he never did, probably because much of what he did was intuitive. That intuition, combined with a fierce confidence in the power of pure imagination, made his images unforgettable and truly immortal."

After a disappointing reception to Fire and Ice, Frank returned to his studio. During the 1980s and 1990s, he continued to paint, creating art for album covers and posters, as well as developing his own themes; he painted new versions of Death Dealer and Cat Woman. Celebrity fans courted him, and included Steven Spielberg, George Lucas and Arnold Schwarzenegger. His value soared and even unfinished sketches would sell for thousands of dollars. Despite this, Frank refused to sell many of his original paintings. Instead, he opened the Frazetta Museum in East Stroudsburg so that they could be enjoyed by the public.

In the 2003 documentary, Frank spoke about the need to create the museum. "It was all Ellie's idea. We were always getting calls from the fans asking if they could come see the originals. The best we had done through the years was to have some exhibits at various conventions, but that got to be a hassle. We did the museum for all the people who have had fun with my art over the years. It wasn't for profit – if I wanted to make money I would've sold the originals. My joy is in showing the work."

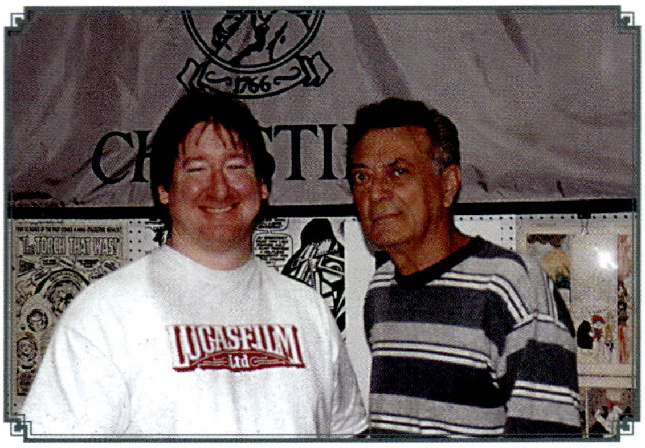

> "I'm constantly asked how I learned to paint. My standard answer is, I taught myself. In reality, I didn't. Frank Frazetta taught me how to paint. I can pinpoint the exact moment when Frank changed my life. It was the day I picked up that copy of Conan the Conqueror from the drugstore paperback rack as a child in Hawaii. It was then that I knew what I wanted to be. I literally copied his paintings to teach myself how to paint. Eventually, he taught me that I couldn't be him – I needed to be my own artist."
>
> Dave Dorman

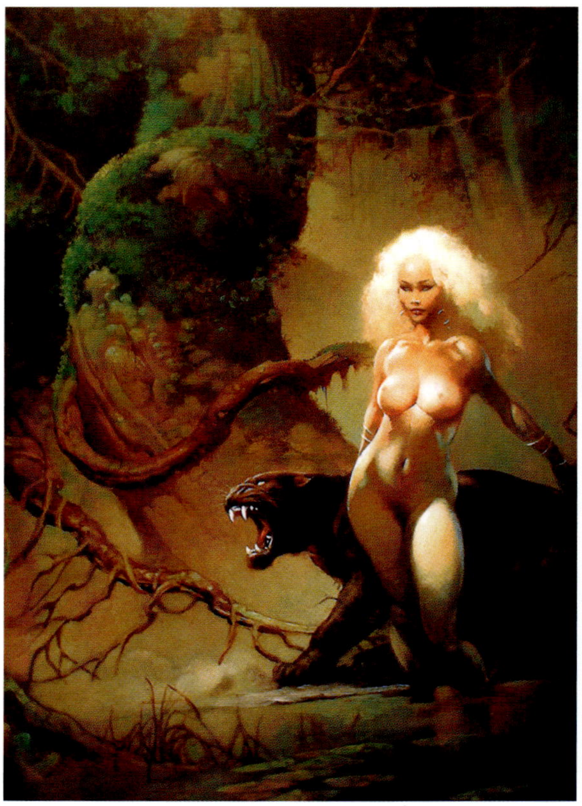

Cat Girl II, painted in 1990, was a reworking of his 1984 original and continued Frank's love affair with the female form and powerful, big cats.

THE SILVER WARRIOR
Painted in 1972.

LATE IN LIFE

Behind the scenes, Frank's health was worsening but, as Bob Eggleton recalls, it didn't prevent him commanding an audience, or painting. "When I met him in 1997, you felt his presence when he entered the room," says Bob. Frank was recovering from a stroke at the time. It had left his drawing hand paralysed, but he had taught himself to draw with his other hand. "He was in great spirits and a very kind man to meet. However, when fellow artist, the late Ron Walotsky and myself met him, and had our picture taken with him, it was such an intimidating experience for us both. Ron aptly titled the photo 'Frank Frazetta and Two Guys'. We'll miss Frank, but his work has left a permanent imprint on not just fantasy art, but the art world as a whole."

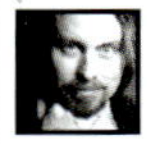

In 2008, the cover illustration for Burroughs' Escape on Venus sold for $251,000. In 2009, the original Conan the Conqueror painting was sold privately for $1 million. Up until that point, Frank had resolutely refused to sell any of his original Conan illustrations, and it became a contentious issue, which for a time divided the Frazetta family. To this day, it's unclear how much Frank knew of the sale.

It's a testament to Frank's legacy that such unseemly squabbles over his collection haven't harmed his reputation. His impact stretches further than a valuation could ever reach. As Brom recalls, "I was six years old when I saw my first Frazetta cover. The impact was so great that I can still recall the adrenaline rush. I've spent my life since then trying to capture an ounce of the life and power of his works. My greatest testament to Frank, is the better I become as an artist, the better his art gets."

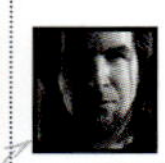

Frank was a unique talent. He bridged the gap between the traditions of the Golden Age masters and artists of the modern era. As artists of all calibre line up to pay tribute, one thing is clear, Frank Frazetta will live on in his paintings and in the brush strokes of myriad fans and artists, all aspiring to follow in his footsteps. ●

Turn the page to learn to paint like Frank Frazetta

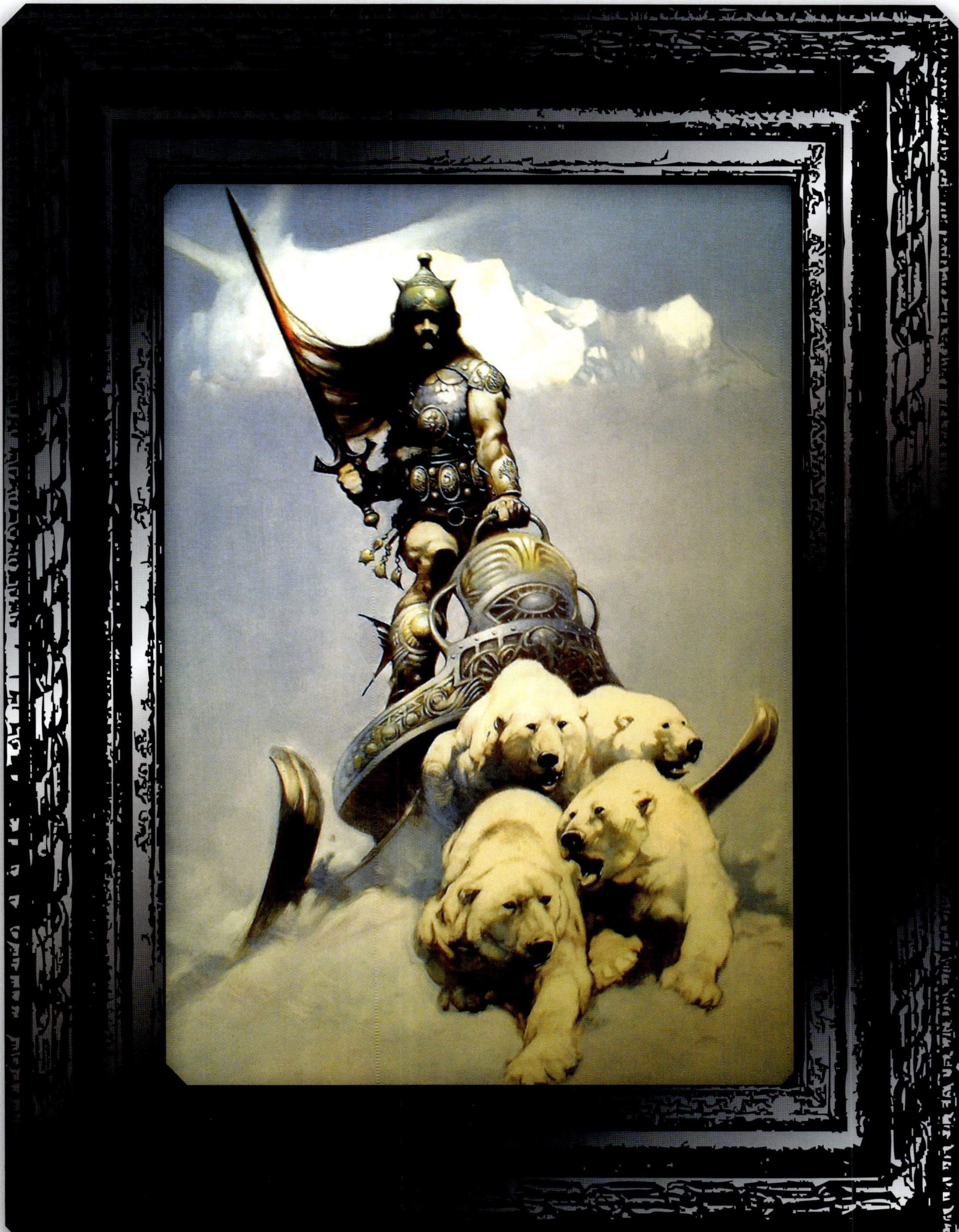

Photoshop

LOOK TO FRAZETTA FOR INSPIRATION

Tap into Frank Frazetta's iconic style of painting without ending up with a poor copy. **Jean-Sébastien Rossbach** tips his hat to the master artist...

I don't know a single fantasy artist who isn't influenced by the art of Frank Frazetta. A combination of his innate sense of movement, the energy, the raw pulse of life he put in his images, and his skills in anatomy and storytelling propelled him to the top of the illustrators' pyramid. I'm going to show you my way of interpreting the legacy this artiste extraordinaire has left us.

Many have tried to steal his magic potion, but no one has been able to give their art even half the power that Frazetta could. So my goal isn't to copy Frazetta. Instead, I ask myself what elements of the great man's production I like, and see if I can incorporate them into my own workflow. And what better subject could there be than a good old Conan piece?

If you look closely at early Frazetta pieces you'll see how he likes to draw human figures like animals. His guys can look like gorillas. I want to draw a Conan thrusting his chest out like a gorilla. You'll also often find him at the top of a triangle composition, with an axe or sword in his hands. I like this a lot because it's a simple type of composition and puts the focus on the main character, giving him potency and strength. I know I'll add a couple of enemies at his feet, but for now I don't know what they'll look like.

Artist **PROFILE**

Jean-Sébastien Rossbach

COUNTRY: France

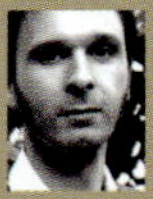

Jean-Sébastien has worked for many major companies including Marvel, Wizards of the Coast and Ubisoft. He's also the author of Merlin, an art book that retells the legendary wizard's story.

livingrope.free.fr

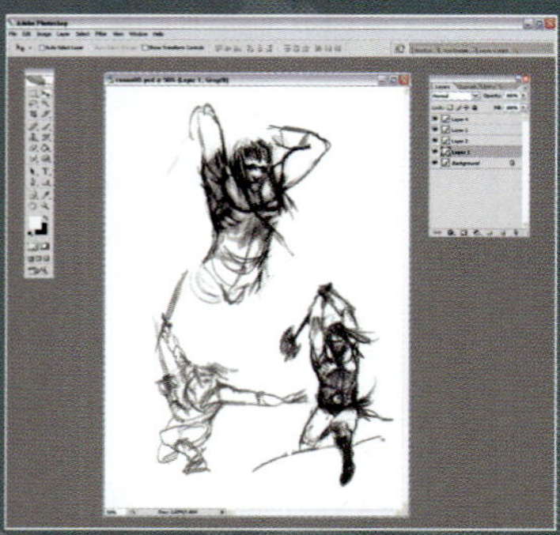

1 The initial sketch

Because the composition is so simple and I'm creating the image in Photoshop (enabling me to correct my composition at any time), I begin drawing Conan directly. I've done a couple of sketches to see what movement would be the most interesting, even though I already have a good idea of what I'm going to end with. I use a bold diamond brush – a personal favourite – for starting to draw the shapes and anatomy. It means I can wander around the canvas without having to be too precise.

2 Focus on movement

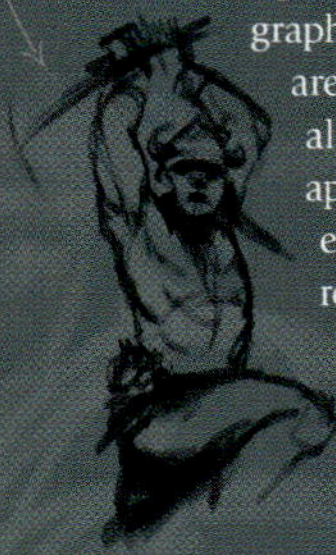

The aim is to first nail the movement of the body, so I don't pay much attention to the muscles and volumes. I'd do the same at a life-drawing session, and begin with a big charcoal or graphite pencil. Big brushes are easy-going – they allow the shapes to appear in front of your eyes. Afterwards I'll rescale anything that's too big or small, and sculpt the shapes more precisely with the eraser.

3 Add a background

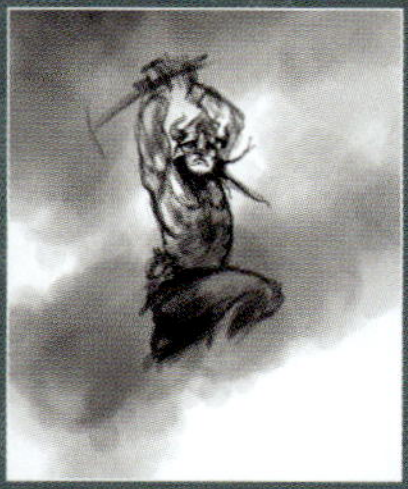

Now that I have an idea of my character's gesture I begin to add some background to the piece. Again, the main character is the focus of the painting, so I'll only use fog and clouds, but the clouds are important and they'll help me build my composition. From the very beginning I knew that I'd put my Conan on top of a small promontory.

WORKSHOP BRUSHES

PHOTOSHOP

DIAMOND BRUSH

The brush I use the most is a big diamond brush. It's very useful for roughing out the first sketches. I also like the marks it makes when you simply paint a subject.

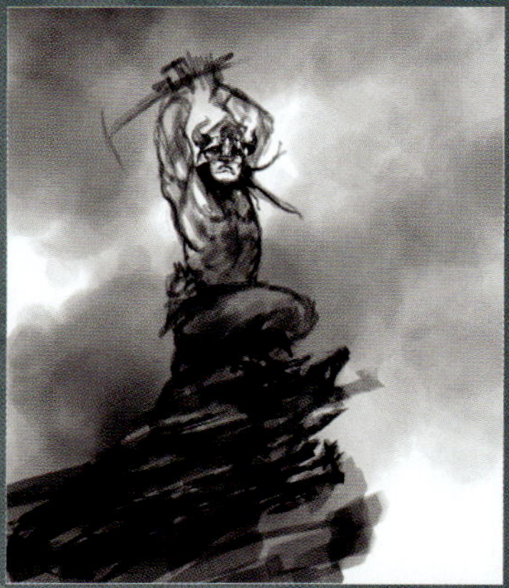

4 Generate energy

My composition now appears clearly. It's a triangle, and inside this triangle I'll use curvy lines that rise and fall from to the bottom left of the plane to the upper right. These wavy lines will bring a sense of energy and movement to my image. I didn't do a proper thumbnail of the composition in the beginning because I knew where I was going, but I strongly recommend that you do so before starting a painting. The composition is the most important step in the construction of an image.

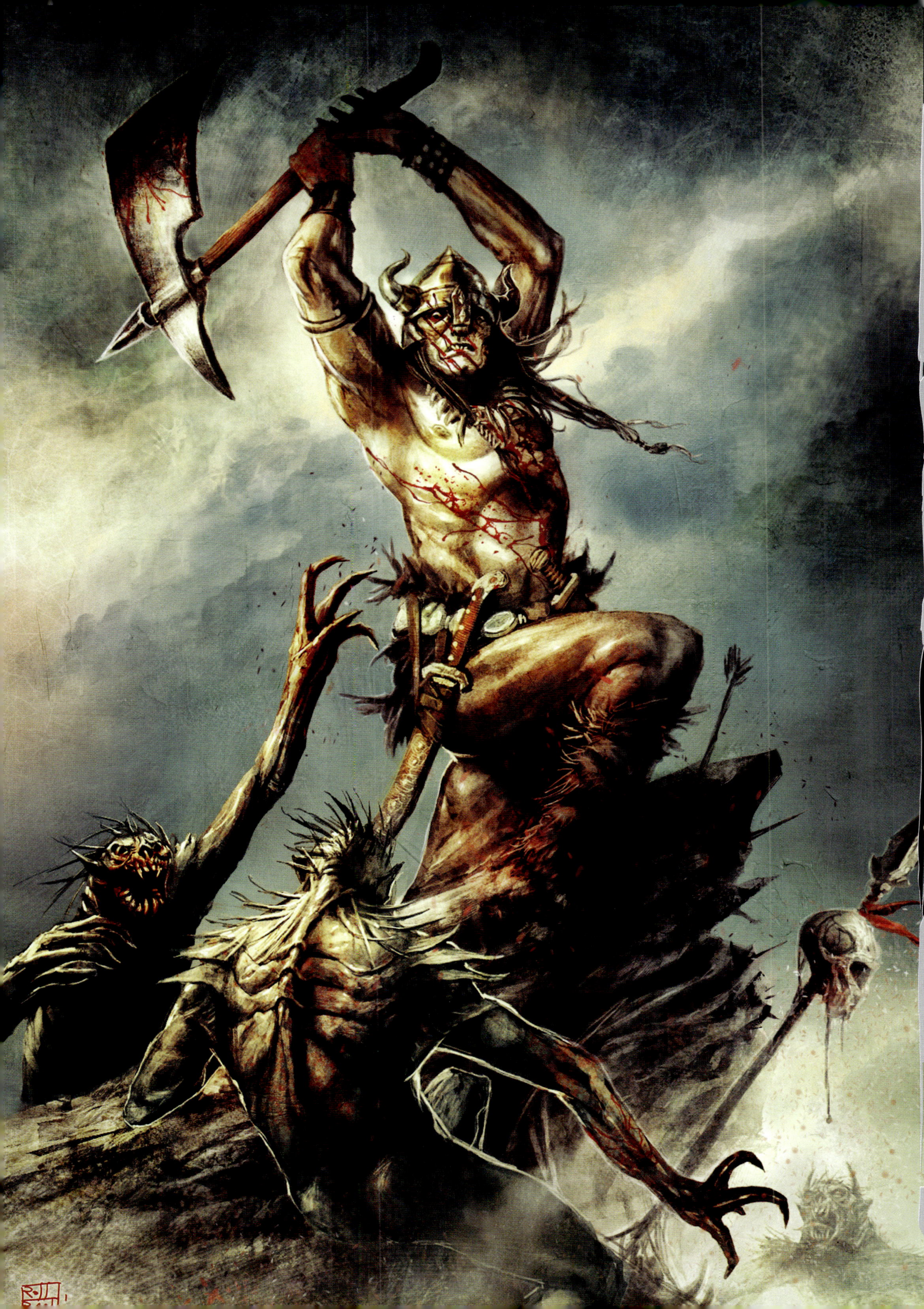

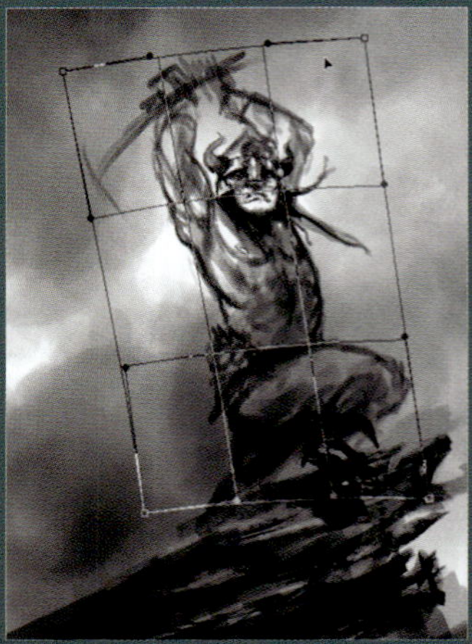

5 Build the anatomy

Now that I've blocked the movement of my character and have a good idea of what my composition will be, I can begin to refine the anatomy. This is the main problem to solve in an image like this. If you're not too comfortable with anatomy I recommend that you use a photo reference. In fact, this is what I do now: because I'm not sure what his arms and hands should look like I take a naked photo of myself, (don't even think about asking me to show it – my woman would kill me!). It helps me to see where the elbow is in relation to the head, for example. I then use Photoshop's Warp tool to adjust his pose.

6 The beast within

Here I'm focusing on Conan's chest because it's what I want to express: the beast inside the man! I don't want to make him look too smart either, so I begin to draw his eyes bulging. He's also biting his lip because of the effort involved (this is a technique you often see in Simon Bisley's art, for example). The man-animal is appearing slowly in front of me.

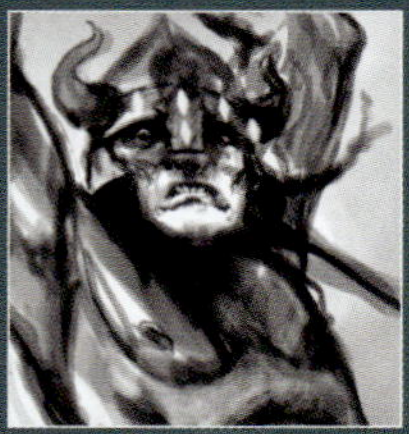

7 Shine a light

Now I need to identify the light sources. Light is a powerful tool that helps create atmosphere, and a character will look different if you throw a light on them from the bottom or from the top. I decide to put a narrow, yet diffuse, spot on Conan's chest; because it's the focal point of the image. I keep part of his face in shadow so that his eyes appear bright and mad-looking. His axe is almost completely treated like a shadow puppet, to emphasise the threat that it represents.

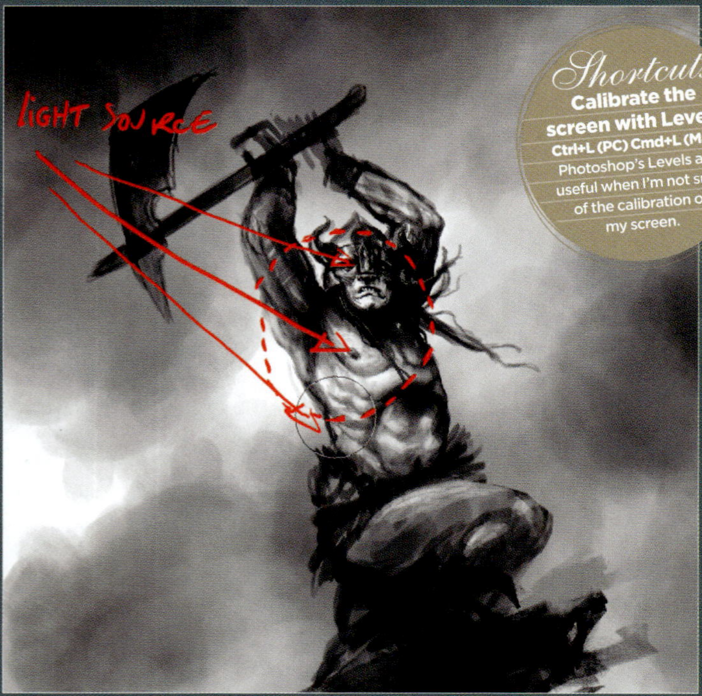

Shortcuts
Calibrate the screen with Levels
Ctrl+L (PC) Cmd+L (Mac)
Photoshop's Levels are useful when I'm not sure of the calibration of my screen.

8 Turn up the volume

Each part of the body, each muscle and each item of clothing must be treated according to the light source. This is what will help you build the volumes in the piece. In addition, you won't become lost in your image, not knowing what to do next. You can see that I'm working in black and white here. I'll add colour later, but first I want to focus on the values of grey. Using this technique I have greater control of the full and empty spaces I have in my image. If I'd used colours from the beginning, they may have distracted me, and I don't want that to happen.

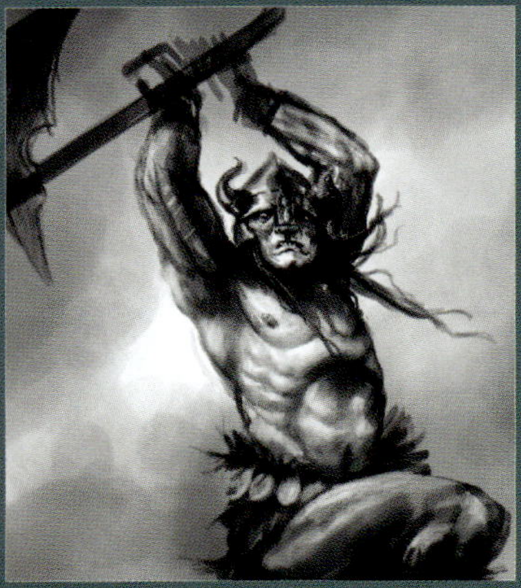

9 Make enemies

At this point my Conan looks rather stupid with his axe raised and not a single head to crush, in front of him. He screams for battle: "Crom! Where are my enemies?" To be perfectly honest, right now I still don't have a clue what his opponents will look like. But the composition seen from the abstract angle will help me in my task. Let's say that they're humanoids, reptile-like with long arms and maybe something of a toad or a lizard in their faces. I begin to draw their shapes very loosely – something between a reptile and a man. The good thing with monsters is that you don't have to worry too much about their anatomy; the more odd they are, the cooler they look!

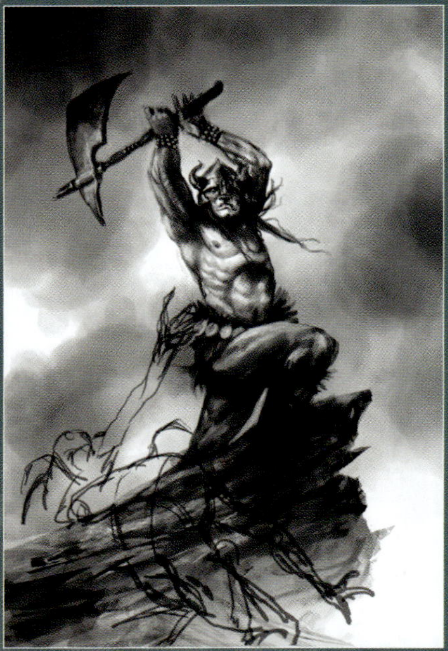

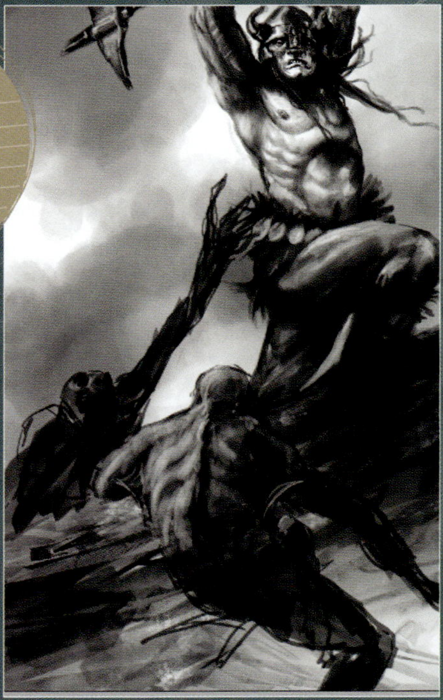

10 Keep to your composition

The main thing I want to focus on is my composition, so I try to sit the enemies on strong lines that complement my initial wavy composition, without breaking it. I first draw shadows and then build the lights slowly. As I paint, I decide on the necessary details. The ribcage of the first monster in the foreground is very defined; I want to see his bones under the skin. The arms are very long and the hands have only four hooked fingers. I flip the image horizontally to see where I've made mistakes.

11 Pay tribute to the master artist

The guy in the foreground is a tribute to Frazetta, in the way that he's bending his body over. I also chose to show his backside, which is something that you only see in Frazetta pieces. It reflects the freedom the creative minds had back in the 70s. Finally, I end up adding spikes on their heads and shoulders, and a thin carapace over their flesh. Not anything too Frazetta-ish this time, but more to my personal taste.

12 Separate shapes

While I'm refining the details, I decide to add a backlight to the monster in the foreground. This will help separate his shape from the texture of the promontory behind him. It's always good to add a second light source that comes from the back of the characters. It's used to outline the silhouette and make it pop to the foreground.

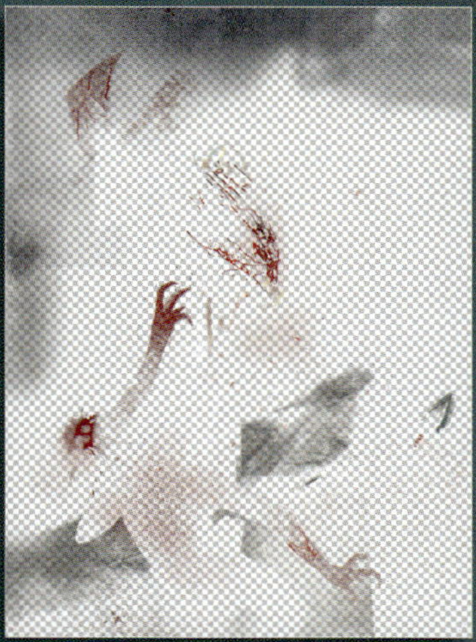

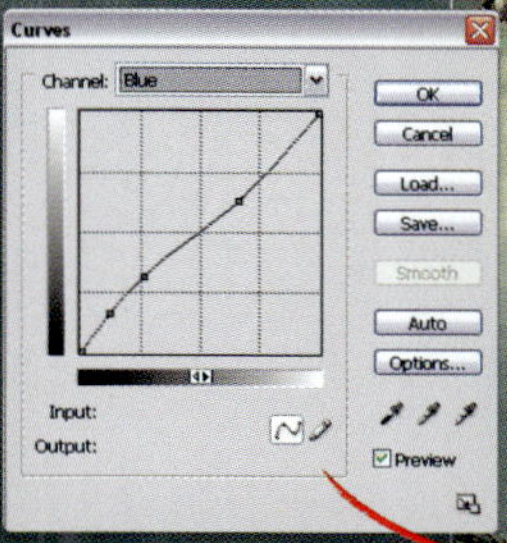

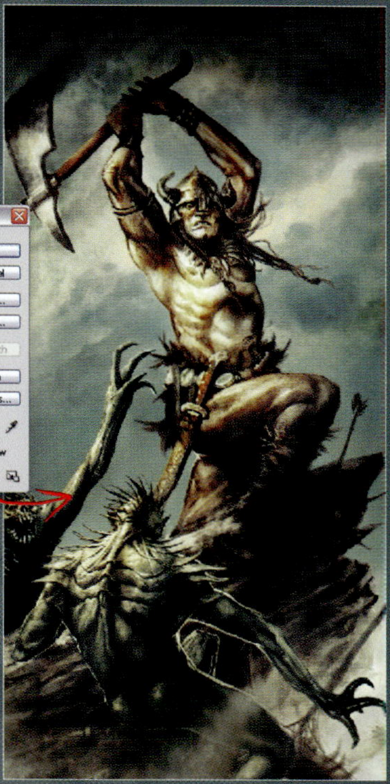

13 Add colour

There are many ways to colour an image in Photoshop. You can use the Colour Balance tool, create a Curves layer, apply colours with an Overlay layer and so on. I decide to use a handful of methods, starting with a coloured texture that I created earlier. I'm using it as an Overlay layer that enables me to add a painted texture to my image as well as some colour indications. After that, I use the Colour Balance tool to give a yellowish tint to the whole image. Usually, I use blue and cyan for the dark values, and yellow and red for highlights.

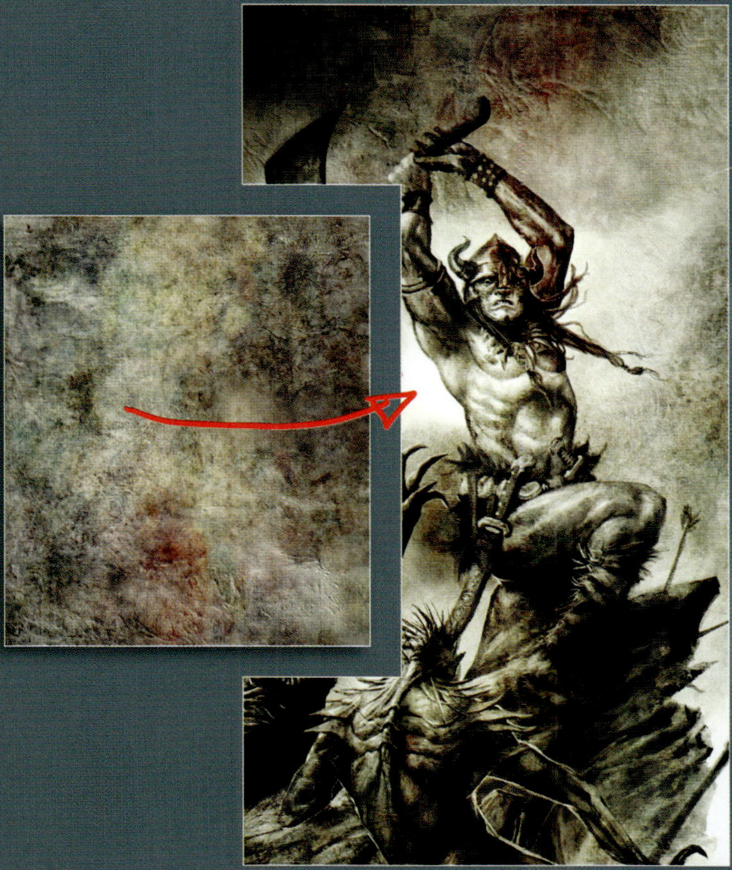

14 Celebrate curves

If, like me, you want to keep the fun flowing, try the Curves tool. I'm not too fond of the colours straight out of the tube – blue for the sky, pink for the flesh, that kind of thing. Using Curves is a great way to achieve results that you would never have imagined, because it acts directly on the RGB channels. And most of the time you'll produce interesting and surprising results. Finally, I'm adding colours on an overlay layer.

15 The painted touch

I've lost count of how many times someone has asked me what my secret is for making an illustration look like it's 'painted'. I do paint my images digitally, but of course they mean real oil paint! Again, there are a couple of simple techniques to achieve this. You can make a pass on Painter and add some digital varnish to your image, or you can also import it into ArtRage and paint over some areas to add the painted touch here and there (I do this sometimes). You can also search for painted textures online and apply them to your image on an Overlay layer, which is what I've done here. Don't hesitate to grab online textures for everything: clouds for the sky, rusted metal for the armour, fish scales for your dragons, concrete or stone for your mountains... Textures are a time-saver, but remember to use them only for the finishing touch, to add the kind of detail that will make a difference. Don't begin an image with the details – start with the overall composition!

PRO SECRETS

The Curves layer

At the bottom of the Layers bar is a round icon labelled Create New Fill Or Adjustment Layer. Select this icon, choose Curves and play with the red, green and blue values to achieve some surprising colour results. This Adjustment layer is also interesting because it acts like a mask, enabling you to erase unwanted areas with the Brush tool.

PRO SECRETS

Compose your image

I know, this sounds very basic, but even pros tend to forget this simple yet mandatory step. Don't be too quick – take the time to think about your composition. What big shape will you use to build your scene? A triangle, a square or a circle maybe? And inside this big shape, what lines of movement will you choose? Composition is the first step and the most important decision you will have to make.

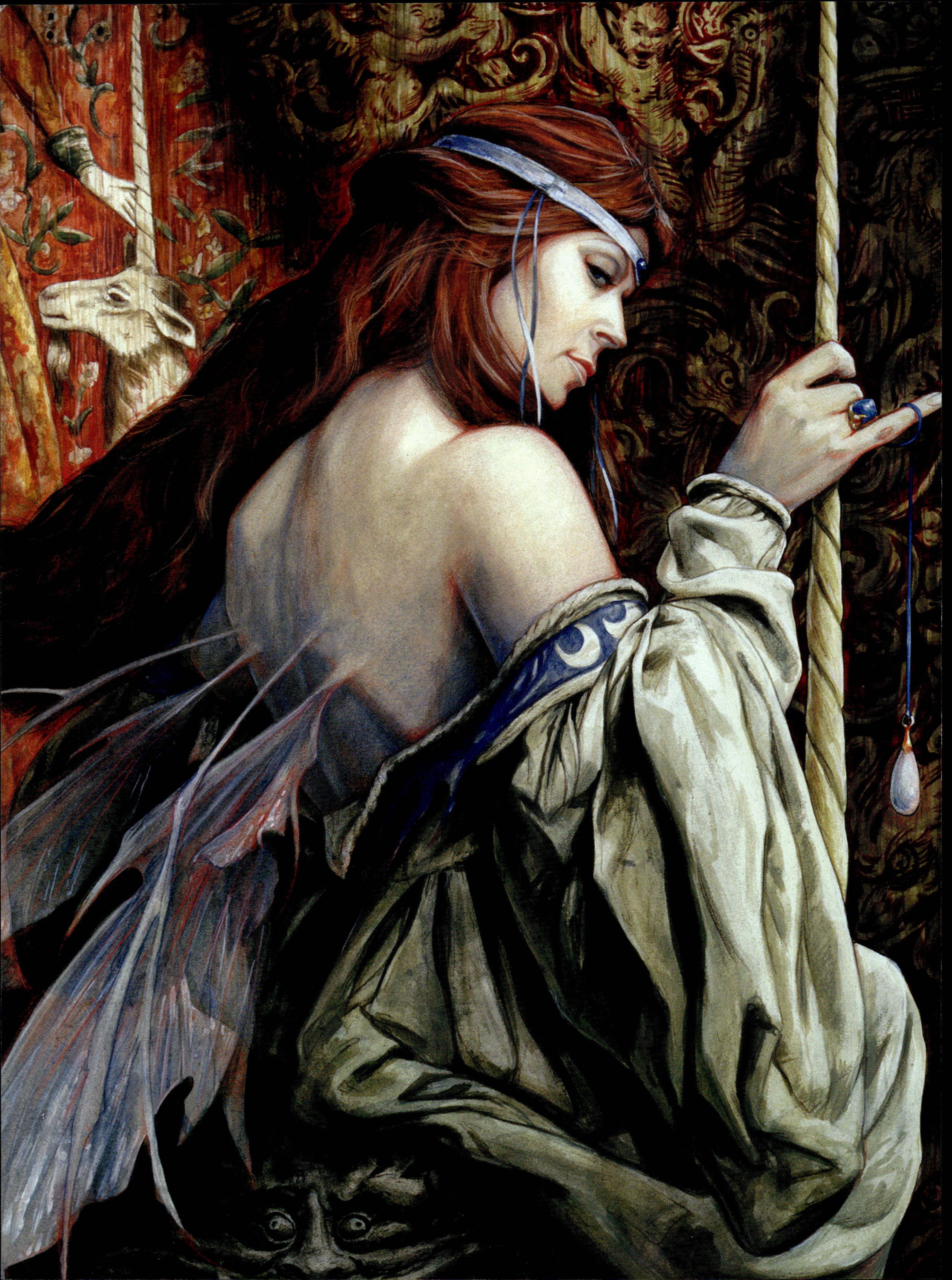

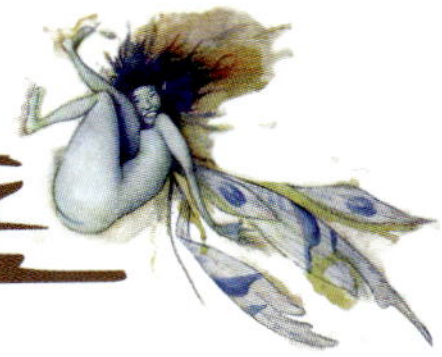

Interview

Brian Froud

With every painting, the artist **Brian Froud** brings to life characters and creatures from British folklore, reaching back thousands of years

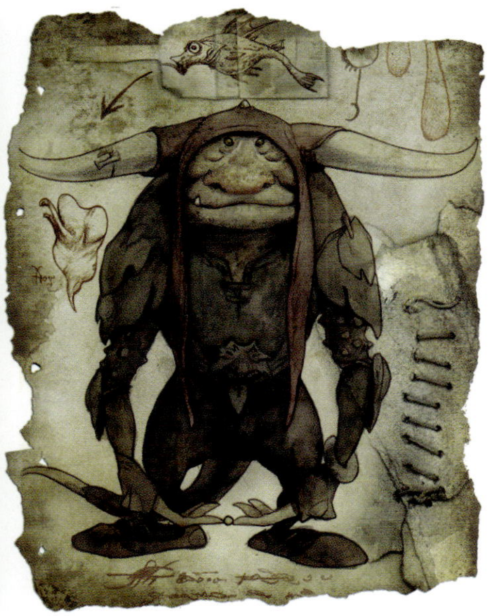

Don't believe everything you hear about faeries. They aren't always cute and kindly like a Disneyfied Tinker Bell. They're not made-up, fluffy nonsense that should be confined to the nursery. Instead of living in faerieland, they're inhabitants of this world, part of its fabric and spirit.

If you've had the chance to take in the artwork of the great Brian Froud at any time, you might have an idea of what we're getting at. For more than 30 years, this British painter has made himself an expert conduit between faerietale creatures and human beings. Faeries, trolls and goblins are some of his favourite subjects and he has a keen understanding of their characteristics and their meaning.

STRONG IMAGINATION

Brian has numerous books to his name – The Land of Froud, Faeries, Good Faeries...Bad Faeries and Lady Cottington's Pressed Fairy Book to name a handful. He's also worked with Jim Henson, bringing many wonderful creatures and characters to life in the films The Dark Crystal and Labyrinth. Here's a man with a huge and vivid imagination, which he's shared with his fans through paintings, books and the big screen.

Talking to Brian, though, it's clearly not just about imagination. He sees his work as being something that starts in reality, looking at the natural world. One of his

> **"Talking to Brian, it's clearly not just about imagination. He sees his work as being something that starts in reality"**

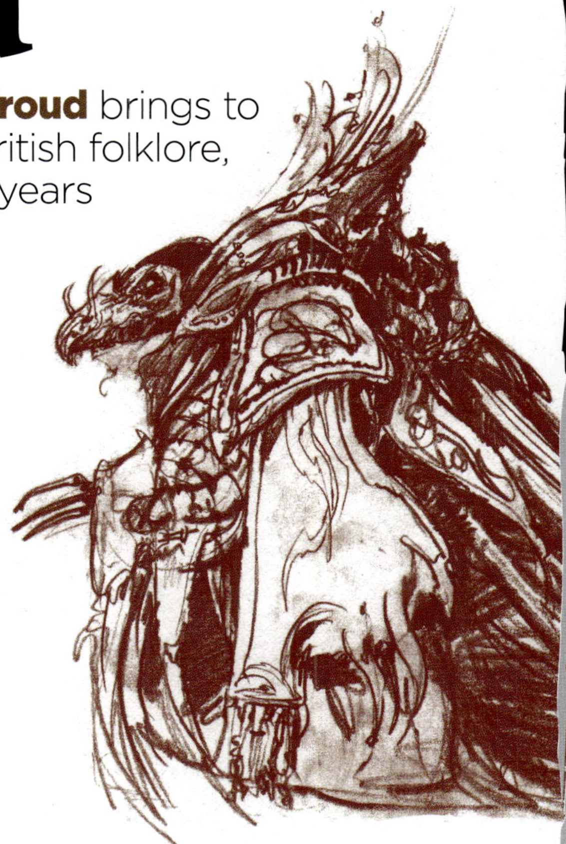

UNICORN
Faerie artwork has been a mainstay of Brian Froud's career and this illustration (left) is from his book Brian Froud's World of Faerie.

Artist **PROFILE**

Brian Froud

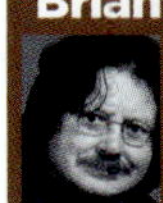

Brian Froud is one of the world's most respected folklore artists. His latest book is The Heart of Faerie Oracle, created with his wife Wendy, is on sale now.

Website: www.worldoffroud.com

THE DARK CHRYSALIS?

A funny thing happened on the way to the cinema

One of the many highlights in Brian Froud's career was his work with Jim Henson for the movie The Dark Crystal. Cited by many artists and fantasy lovers as an inspiring film, it could easily have been called The Dark Chrysalis.

"Fairly early on, he (Henson) had this idea of...well I didn't know quite what, because for a long time I was drawing these 'crystals'," says Brian. "He kept saying crystals and we did that and I said, 'It needs more drama.' So, I suggested 'dark' because that's a dramatic name. He thought it was great. I was drawing and drawing, and after a while he said, 'What's this crystal?' And I said, 'That's what you said. Crystal.' He said, 'No, I said chrysalis.' He was thinking the film was about transformation, which indeed it is, but I'd misheard him and was drawing crystals. We said, 'No, the crystal's good.'"

Brian's work on the film wasn't all happy accident, though. For five years he created the concepts for the bird/dinosaur Skeksis, the friendly dog-like Mystics as well as the Gelflings. It was while collaborating with the artists and puppeteers on The Dark Crystal that he met his wife Wendy, who helped create many of the physical puppets for the film.

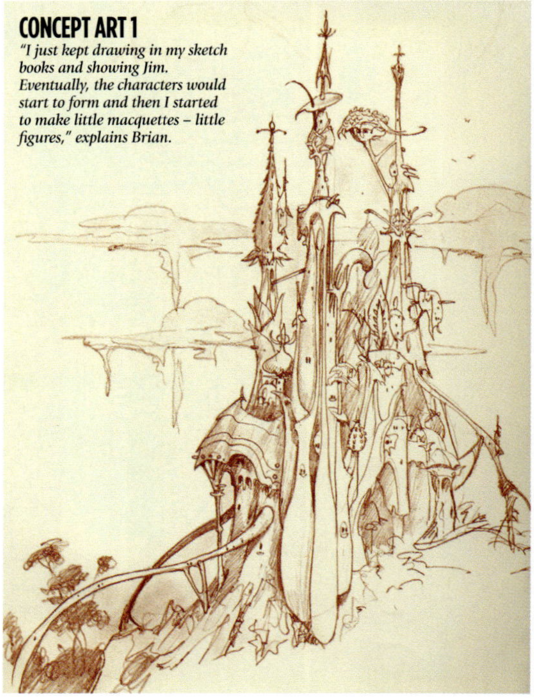

CONCEPT ART 1
"I just kept drawing in my sketch books and showing Jim. Eventually, the characters would start to form and then I started to make little macquettes – little figures," explains Brian.

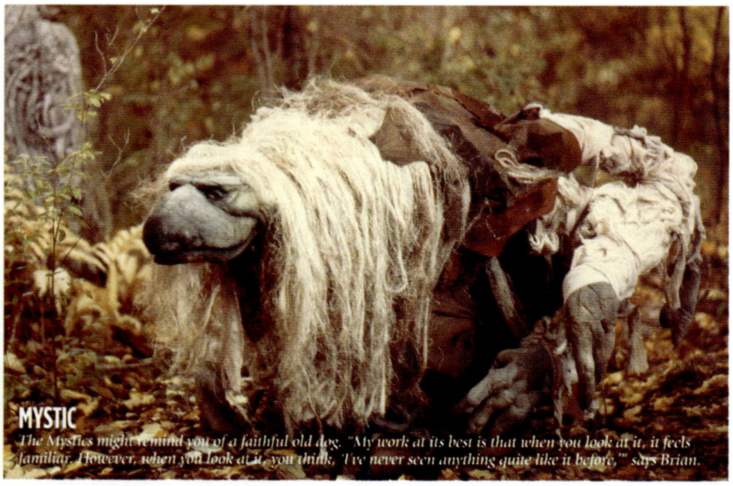

MYSTIC
The Mystics might remind you of a faithful old dog. "My work at its best is that when you look at it, it feels familiar. However, when you look at it, you think, 'I've never seen anything quite like it before,'" says Brian.

CONCEPT ART 2
Brian on The Dark Crystal: "We actually made the film we wanted to see ourselves. It never occurred to us that we were going to scare kids. Over the years, I've found out how many kids were scared."

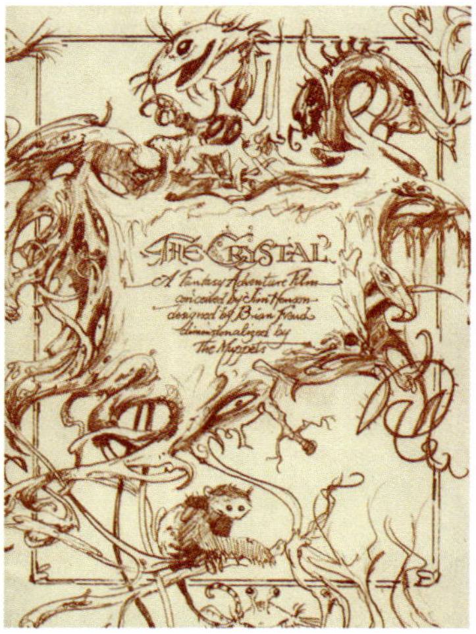

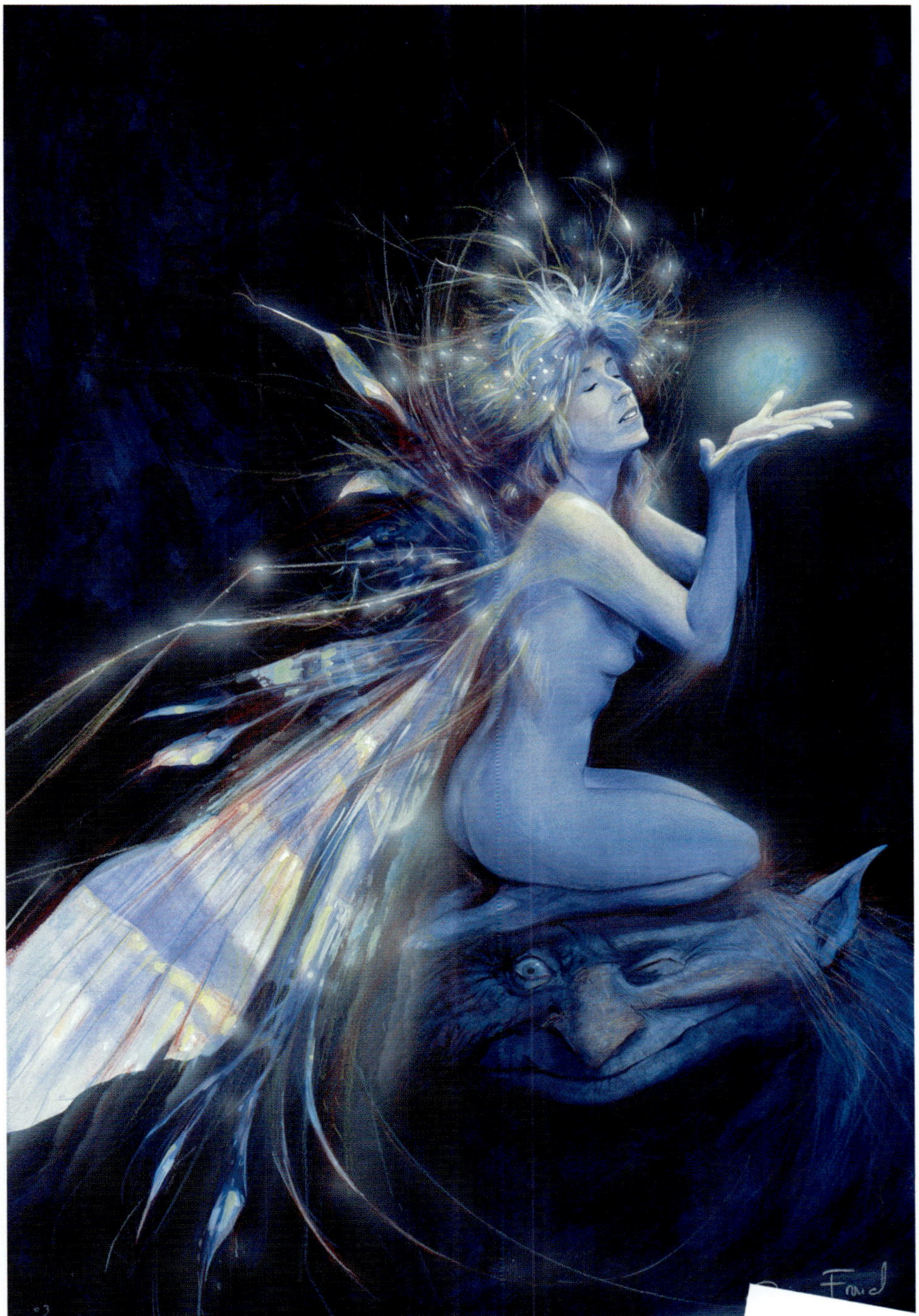

LIGHT AND DARK
Brian Froud's faerie paintings are layered with mystique, magic, emotion and hidden meaning. His compositions often employ classical proportions like the golden section which bestows them with cosmic geometry. There's usually more to them than meets the eye.

early influences was Arthur Rackham.

"I loved his drawings of trees," says Brian. "They were very expressive but they also had faces in them. It was a shock of recognition, because as a child I was always up a tree, always climbing trees, always exploring woods. When I saw Rackham's stuff it reminded me of how I felt about nature. I felt that nature had a hidden life to it, that everything had a soul, a personality."

PAINTING TROLLS

Brian moved to Dartmoor in the mid-1970s after spending several years as an illustrator in London. He began painting trolls and other fairytale creatures that appeared in books of British illustration. Soon he was asked to put together a collection of his own work, which was released as The Land of Froud, and then with fellow artist Alan Lee he worked on Faeries, a book released as a follow-up to the popular Gnomes.

Great lovers of folklore and mythology from around the British Isles, Brian and Alan retreated to their own libraries and researched all they could about fairies. By referring to Irish, Welsh, Scottish and English myths and legends, they seemed to get the real low-down on faerie creatures. Accurately following descriptions of these mischievous and sometimes rather dark-hearted creatures, the pair gave their publishers a bit of a shock. Characters such as Jenny Greenteeth – who dragged children off into rivers and devoured them – were not the expectation of publishers who thought faerieland meant cute, sweet, pink and fluffy.

"It was really a reinstatement of the power of faeries," says Brian. "It had been for a long, long time relegated to the nursery. It was thought to be a childish thing, the idea that they were fairytales and nonsense. Here we went back to the sources, such as Yates's The Celtic Twilight book, and tried to portray them as they really are, with their power. Faeries were dangerous beings that you had to placate. You had to leave little gifts of food, you had to live with them really and be nice to them. If you weren't, they'd do dreadful things to you."

This approach, of going back to folklore and then painting links Brian's work with people deep in the past, who saw faeries and various other creatures as part of nature and the land around them. Brian himself loves England for its history, the layers of old stories and the sense that there are mysteries beneath your feet. He connects to this and understands it through what he paints.

REAL-LIFE FANTASY

As you might have gathered by now, painting is not a literal process for Brian. Whatever he's working on, he wants to convey life, reality and feeling. "I'm always amazed when I look at American fantasy art. It's what I would call over-rendered. Every surface is shiny. It means to me that your eye skids off the art. But not only does your eye skid off it, your emotions also skid off it," says Brian.

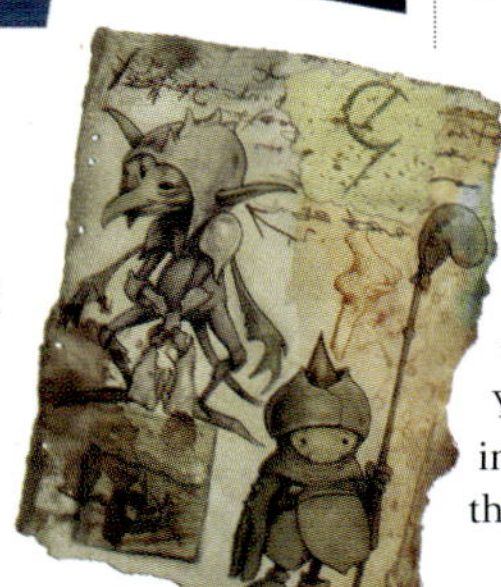

GOBLINS
Naughty they may have been, but Brian's goblins were never pure evil.

"What I try to do is I leave out certain bits of information, so when you view it you have to add bits to it to complete it. The completing of it, it imbues it with life, because it means that it has a little bit of you in it and each time you view it, you've changed and it changes. You enter into a relationship with the image. That's what we do in the art, and that's what we try to do in the graphics."

With his books, Brian has gone a stage or two further towards the goal of engaging the viewer or reader with the characters and the story. His secret is to make the book itself both a physical and an emotional ➔

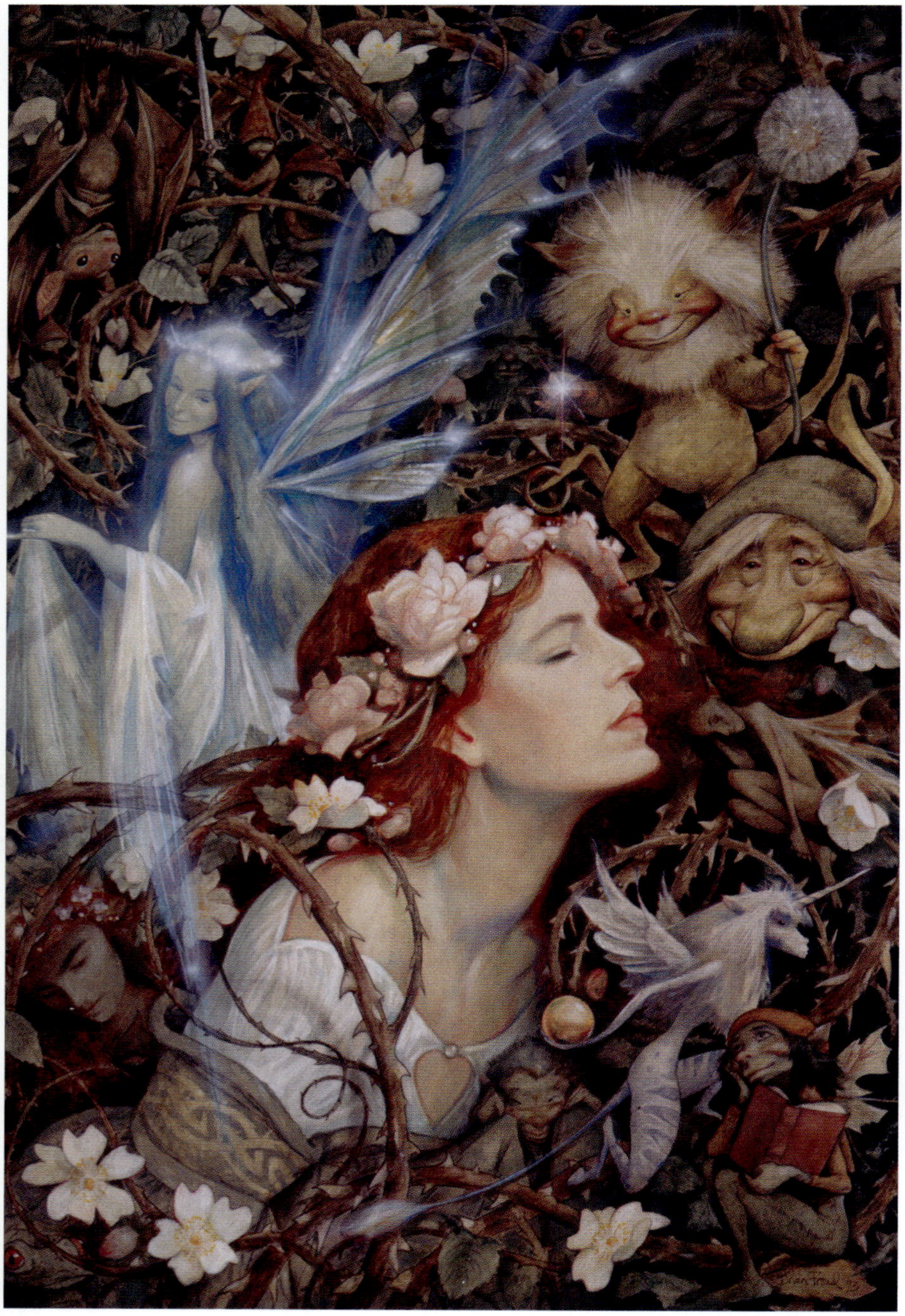

SLEEPING BEAUTY
Another illustration from Brian Froud's new book, this one captures the classic faerie tale.

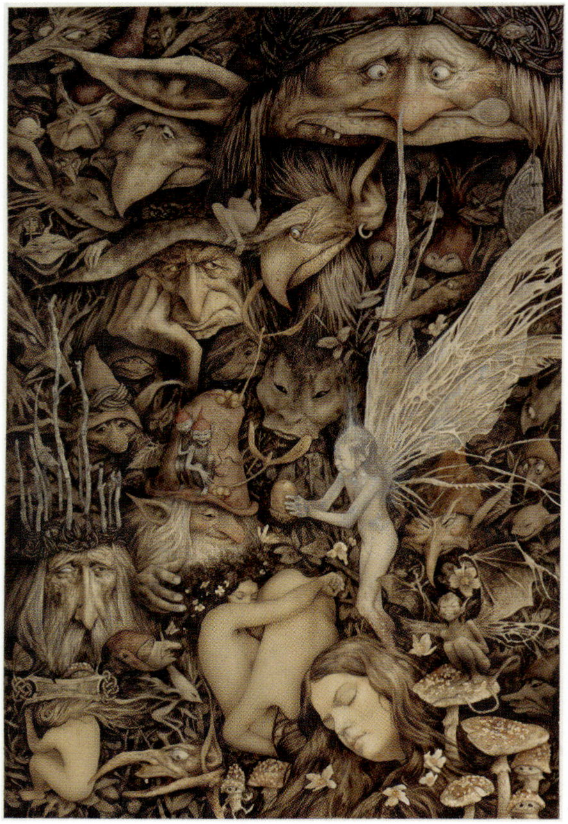

PAINTING
Some of Brian's creations are crammed with characters, faces and writhing forms from the World of Faerie.

experience. With a normal book, you pick it up, open it, page or read through it, reach the end and then close it. But Good Faeries...Bad Faeries, for instance, has two front covers. You can start by reading from the Good Faeries cover, then turn it over and flip it around and start reading about the bad ones. Your journey through it can start at either end.

PRESSED FAERIES

There's no better example of the physicality of a Brian Froud book than Lady Cottington's Pressed Fairy Book. First published in 1991, with Terry Jones of Monty Python fame (also Labyrinth, see the box opposite), it has become a successful series. The way it's painted and bound enables the reader to pretend to catch faeries by clapping the book closed and pressing them, just like the main character Angelica Cottington does throughout the book. This fun, physical idea is what helped Brian to convince Terry to write the book, and has played a major role in its popularity.

"The book was a huge success, but it's about belief," says Brian. "It's meant to be funny; the idea is that when you meet people who don't believe in faeries, as soon as you talk about squashing a faerie, and you bang the book closed, they cringe! And I say, 'See, you've changed! Now you're believing.' It's about allowing people to believe about faeries."

NEW BOOK

Brian released his latest book early in 2010, called The Heart of Faerie Oracle. This new book was illustrated by Brian but written by his wife Wendy. "Brian's work speaks to people," she says of the new book. "Each picture has something to say."

The book adopts the notion of faerie energy, with Wendy acting has a guiding hand to draw out the messages the faeries want to convey through Brian's paintings. It's a book that hones in on the spiritual aspects of Brian's work. But if you really don't believe in faeries, you could always simply admire the stunning art.

Brian and Wendy's work certainly has a magical touch. Is it charged with faerie energy or just that spark of genius all great art has? Perhaps you just have to believe?

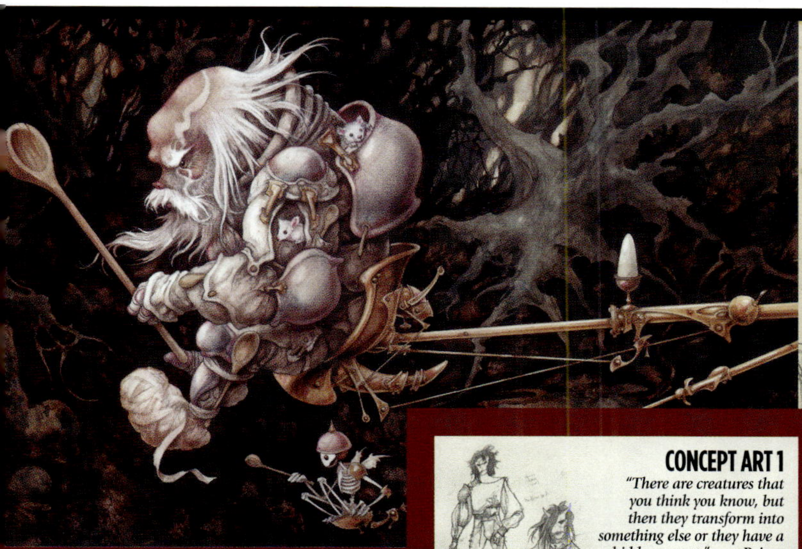

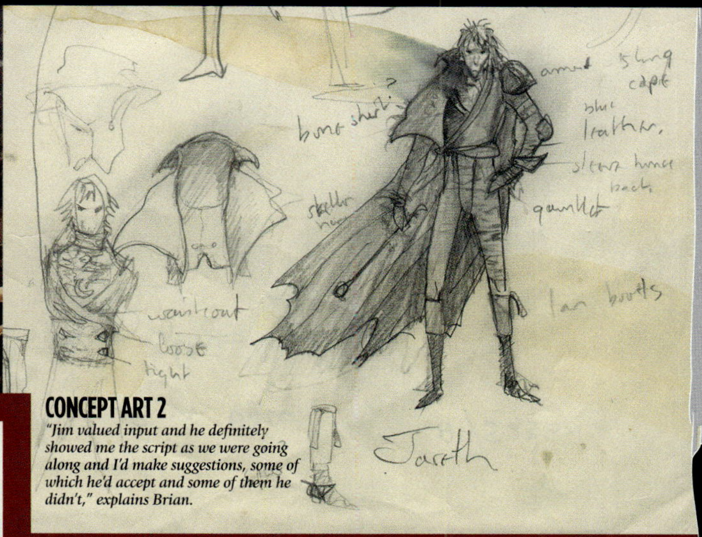

CONCEPT ART 2
"Jim valued input and he definitely showed me the script as we were going along and I'd make suggestions, some of which he'd accept and some of them he didn't," explains Brian.

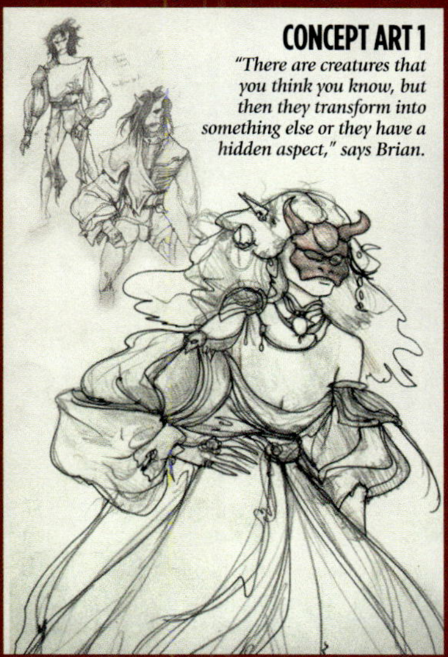

CONCEPT ART 1
"There are creatures that you think you know, but then they transform into something else or they have a hidden aspect," says Brian.

LABYRINTH

How Brian Froud gave Jim Henson the original concept for this fantasy flick

After a screening and gala dinner celebrating The Dark Crystal's launch, Brian and Wendy Froud found themselves in a limo with Jim Henson, who suggested they do it all over again and make another film. According to Brian, Jim had the idea of basing it on Hindu gods and beings.

Brian had other ideas and suggested one of his favourite topics: goblins. He went on to suggest the basic image of a baby surrounded by goblins. "I said it would be a great juxtaposition," says Brian.

Jim loved it and, once back in the UK, Brian painted a picture of a baby in the midst of a troop of goblins, which he passed on to his director. Soon he was painting further conceptual images for the film, they began building prototype creatures and the script was developed. Jim called on Terry Jones, of the Monty Python troupe, to tweak the script.

"Terry looked at my sketchbooks and kept finding little characters in the corner. He said, 'Hey, that's great, I'm going to write about that.' He sort of rewrote a lot of the script and introduced a whole host of new characters that we hastily had to build," explains Brian.

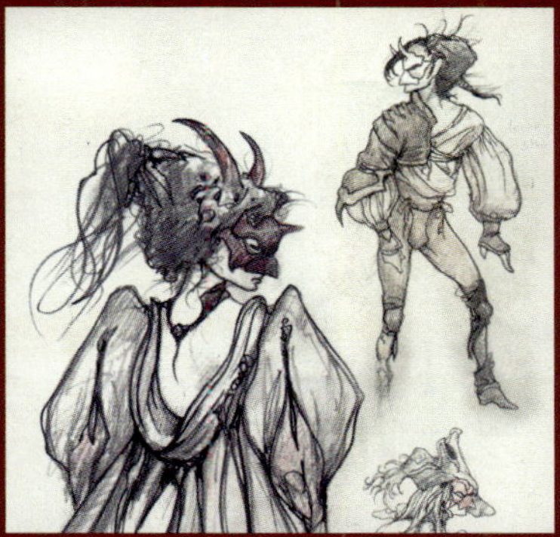

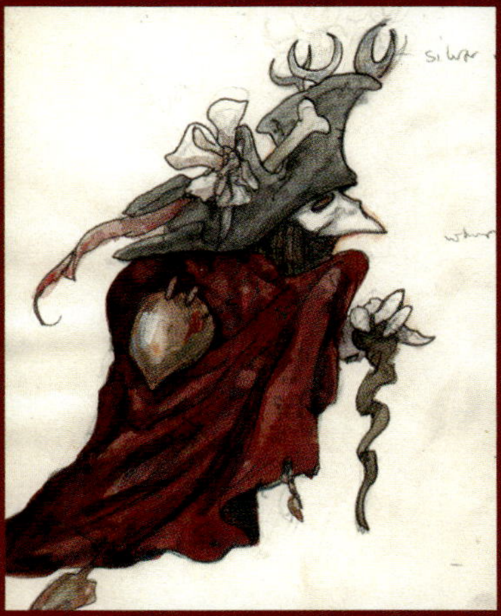

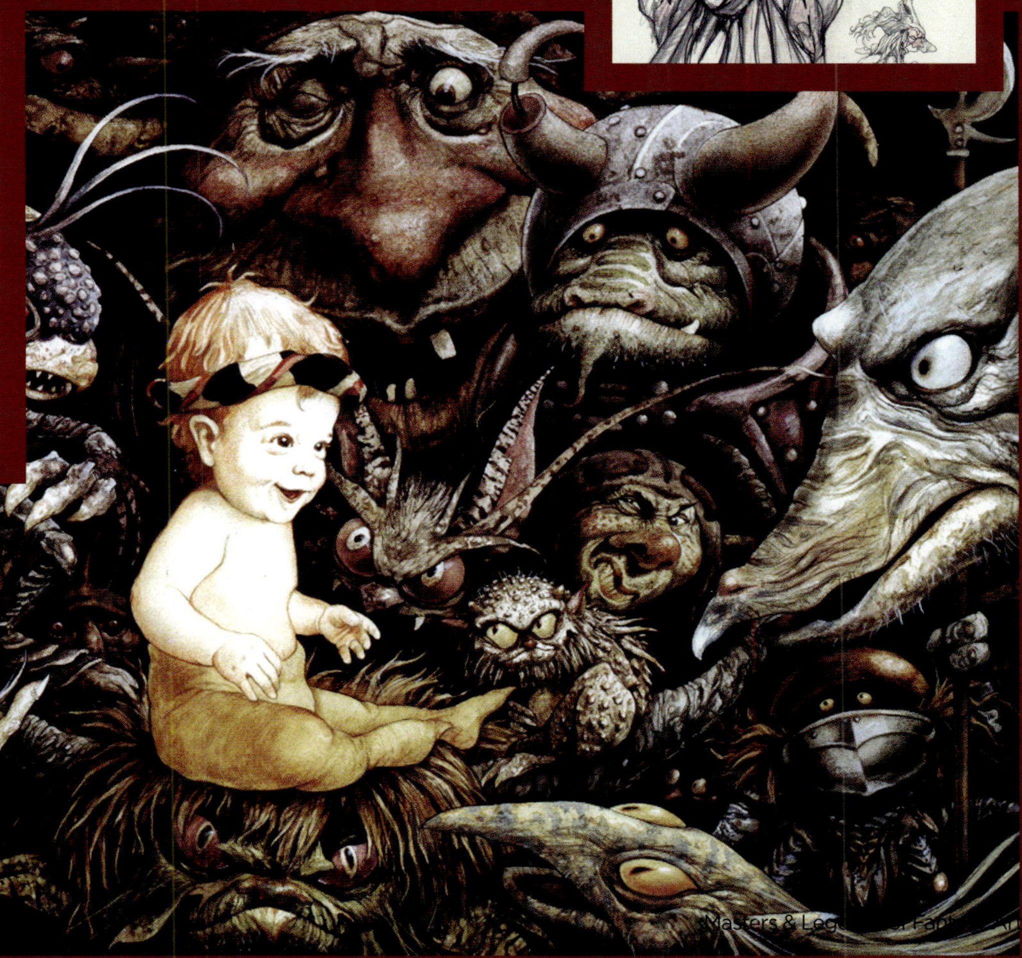

TOBY & GOBLINS
Juxtaposing innocence with gnarled, ill-willed goblins, this painting inspired Jim Henson to make Labyrinth.

Artist insight

THE NATURE OF FAERIE ART

Folklorist and faerie artist **Marc Potts** reveals his tips to get inspired, and admits that in his area of specialism it helps to be just the tiniest bit nuts...

Okay, so this isn't a workshop on how to paint faeries and it's certainly not a bunch of tips on artistic technique. I paint art based on folklore and mythology – witches, dragons, gods and goddesses – but I am mainly known as a painter of faeries. A bit of a girly subject? Not at all. Faerie folklore is steeped in pagan mythology, and if you look into it you soon realise that you could be reading about the pre-Christian deities of old. You'd also realise that faeries aren't all pretty and lovely. In fact, more often than not, faeries can be dark, sinister and sometimes plain nasty. I personally find it much more fun to paint the dark, the wicked and the downright bizarre.

The advice that follows is more about my inspiration, sources of ideas and how I approach my faerie art. I hope it helps to inspire you, too.

Artist **PROFILE**

Marc Potts

COUNTRY: England

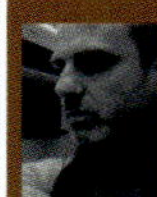

Marc is a UK based folklorist, occasional author and faerie artist, best known for his darker, pagan twist on faerie art. The elementals, nature-spirits, gods and goddesses of myth and the imagination are his main subjects.

www.marcpotts.com

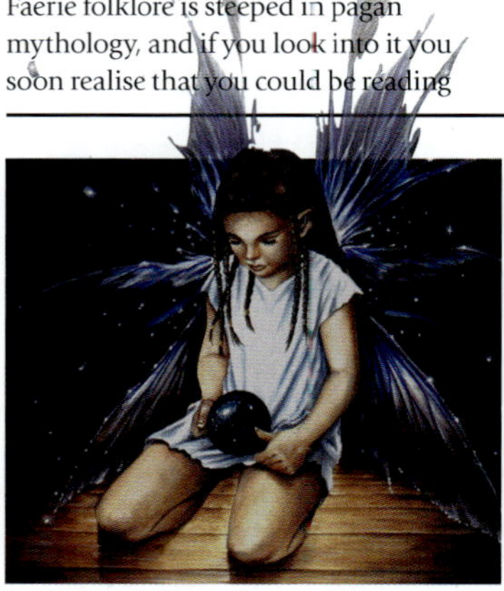

1 DO FAERIES WEAR STRIPY TIGHTS?

There's definitely a market for the pretty Victorian image of a faerie in a wispy, flowing dress, or even the modern punky-looking faeries in stripy tights, giving off a bit of an attitude. It's a convention and there's nothing wrong with following it.

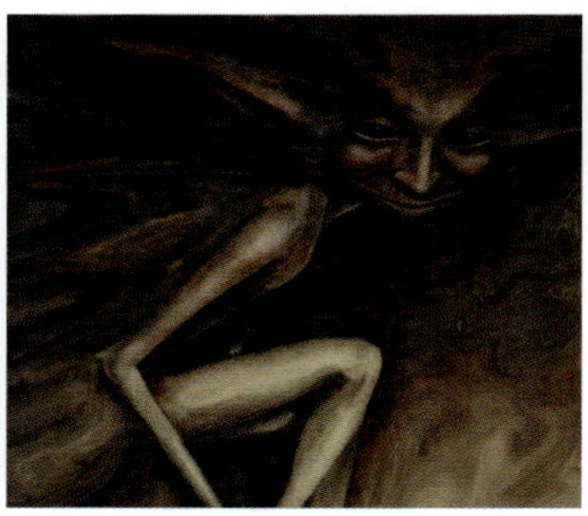

2 NOT ALL FAERIES ARE GIRLS

Don't forget the male of the species and the plain weird. A hedgehog could be an urchin – a faerie in disguise. Imps, goblins, brownies, pixies and elves are often considered to be male types of faerie. Titania is a popular subject, but Oberon and Puck shouldn't be forgotten. There's lots of scope for being unconventional, which I will elaborate on later.

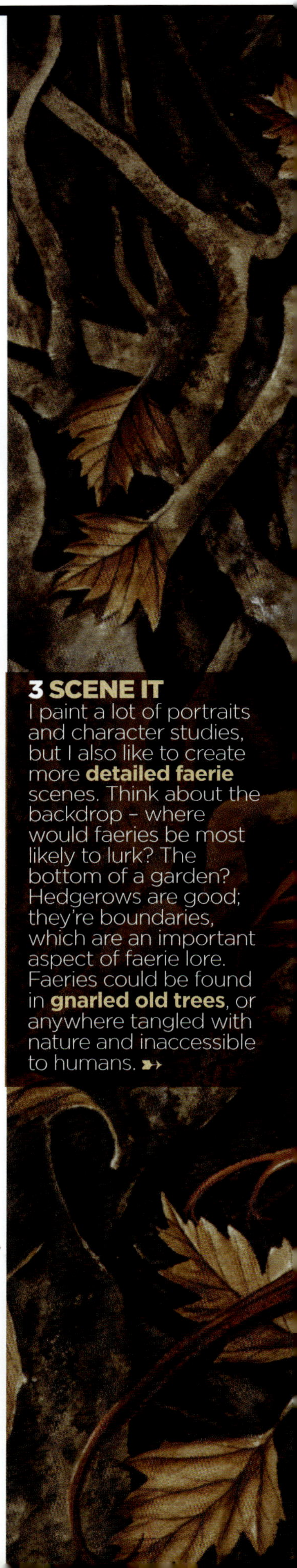

3 SCENE IT

I paint a lot of portraits and character studies, but I also like to create more **detailed faerie** scenes. Think about the backdrop – where would faeries be most likely to lurk? The bottom of a garden? Hedgerows are good; they're boundaries, which are an important aspect of faerie lore. Faeries could be found in **gnarled old trees**, or anywhere tangled with nature and inaccessible to humans. ➔

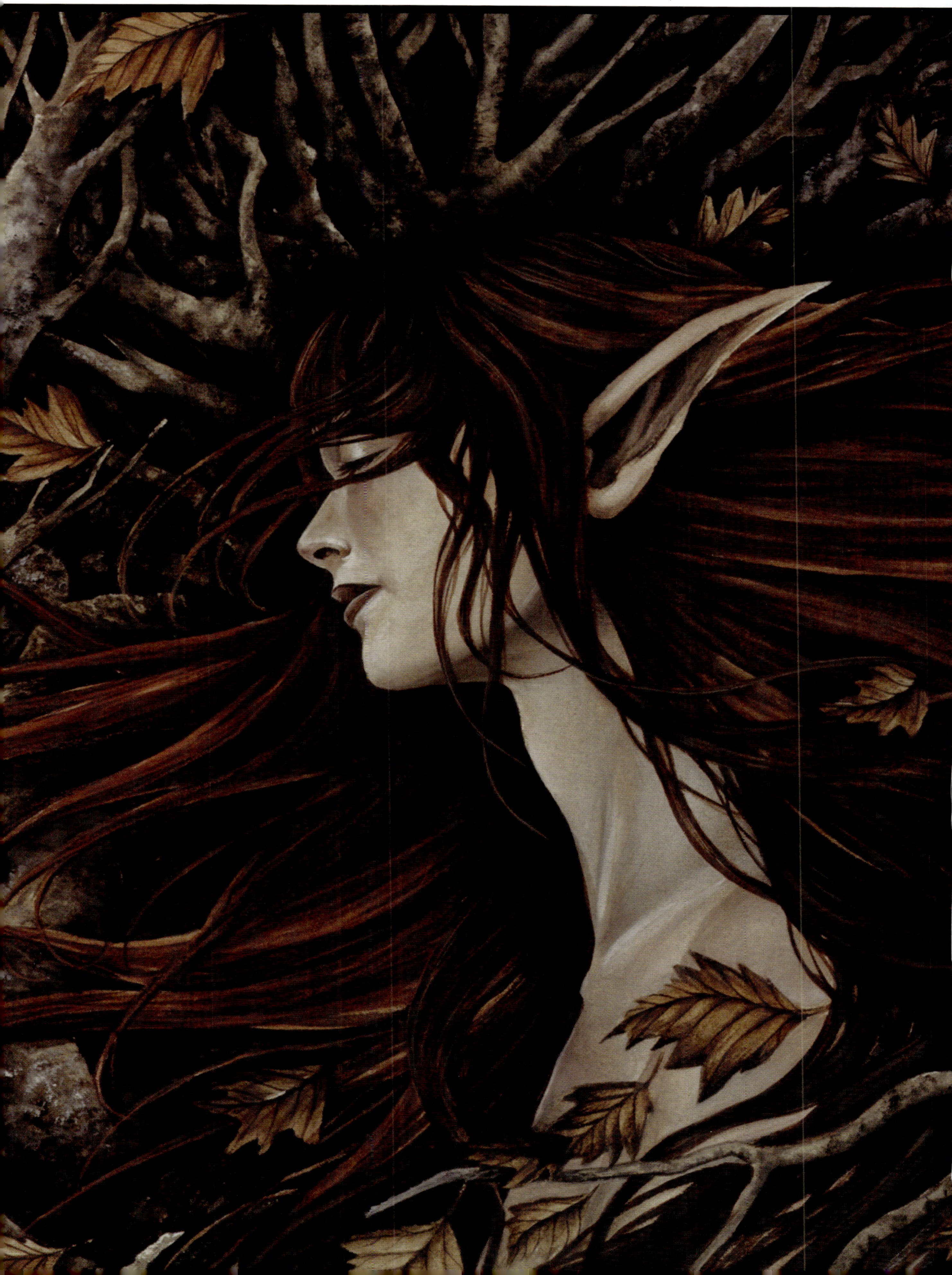

4 FOLKLORE

Get hold of some books on faerie **folklore**, then read and assimilate. A Dictionary of Fairies by Katherine Briggs is a great source of ideas, as is her Fairies in Tradition and Literature. The Fairy Mythology by Thomas Keightley is also a good resource. There are a lot of faerie A-Zs available, but one that must feature on your list is **Faeries by Brian Froud** and Alan Lee.

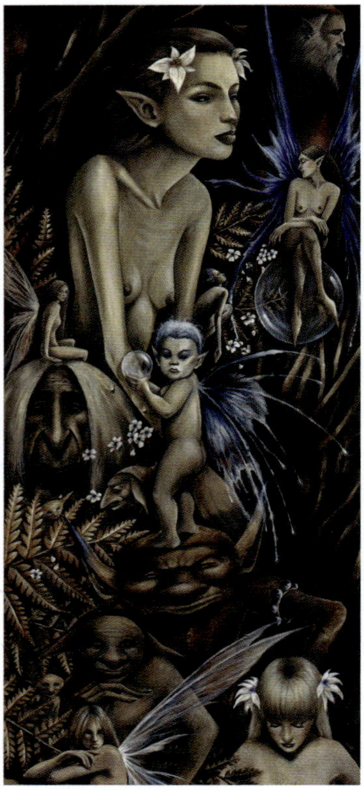

5 FAERIE TYPES

Here are just a few of the many faeries that can be found in ancient folklore: Asrai, Apple Tree Man, Abbey Lubber, Banshee, Barguest, Bogie, Brag, Brownie, Bwca, Changeling, Cob ynau, Derrick, Dwarf, Elf, Ellyllon, Fir Darrig, Faun, Firbolg, Ganconer, Gnome, Grindylow, Gruagach, Hag, Hedley Kow, Henkie, Hinky-Punk, Imp, Jenny Greenteeth, Killmoulis, Knocker, Leanan Sidhe, Lepracaun, Loireag, Lunantishee, Luideag, Mermaid, Muryan, Ogre, Pwca, Phenodyree, Pixie, Puck, Selkie, Skriker, Troll, Will O' the Wisp, Woodwose. Look 'em up!

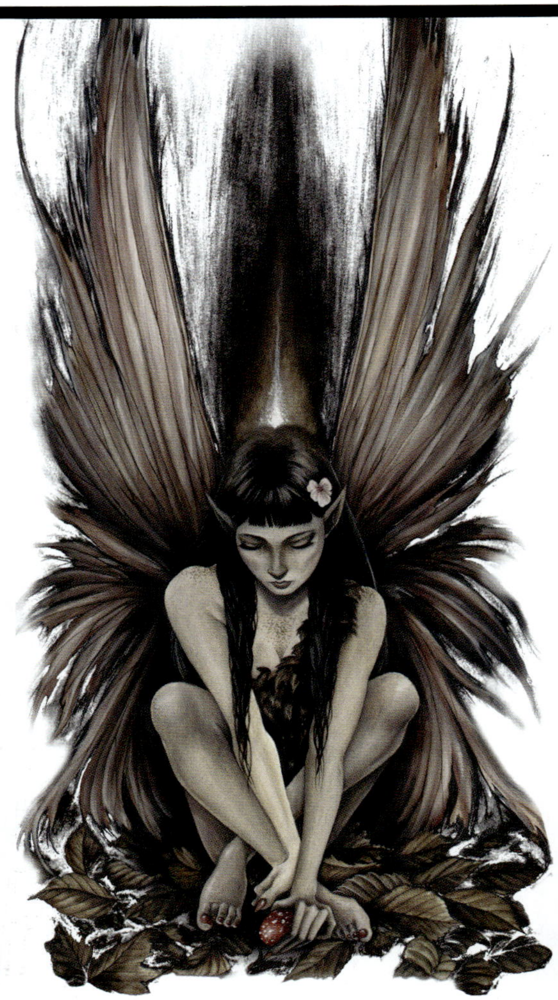

"Faeries can be sinister beings, with a peculiar wrongness about them"

6 MYTHOLOGY

A bit grander in scale than folktales. Poring over books of **world mythologies** will soon pay off, throwing up ideas for the weird and wonderful. This can be applied to all forms of fantasy art, but there are faeries here, too. Think of the Elves, Orcs and Trolls in Lord of the Rings – all mythologically inspired versions of the genre, but **faerie art** nonetheless. The Irish Mythological Cycle and the Welsh Mabinogion are good local examples.

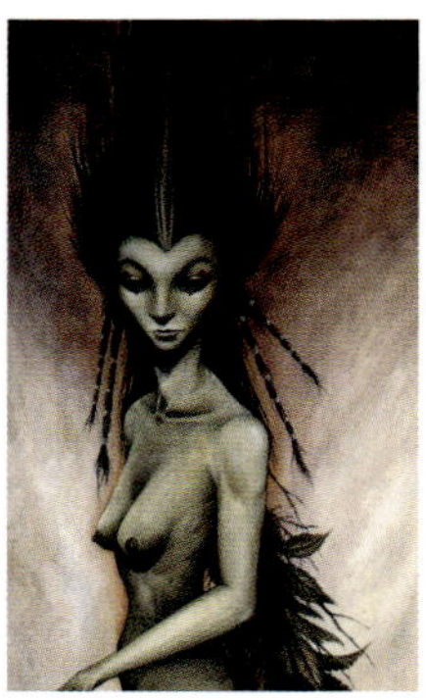

7 FAERIES AIN'T PRETTY

Faeries can be sinister beings, with a peculiar wrongness about them. Use this notion when developing a character – combine beauty with something odd, like a hare's foot in place of a hand, or twigs for hair. A faerie doesn't have to have wings, either. Simply making the eyes odd can set it apart from humans. Faeries often appear beautiful, but there will be something that gives them away.

8 THINK NATURE

I see faeries as nature spirits or elemental beings, so look to the natural world for inspiration. Leaves, twigs, feathers and bits of plants could all be incorporated into a faerie character. I often do this as part of the faerie itself – organic growths sprouting from the back or head, or from an arm or leg. And if you must clothe your faeries, apply the same approach to elements of faerie clothing – a dress made out of leaves or a mask of twigs and feathers. I'm always collecting stuff for reference when I'm out and about.

9 DO YOUR RESEARCH

This is an important one – it will make your character more believable and give it substance. The wealth of information in my mind can shape itself into an idea for a picture or character. I'm not suggesting that you hide yourself

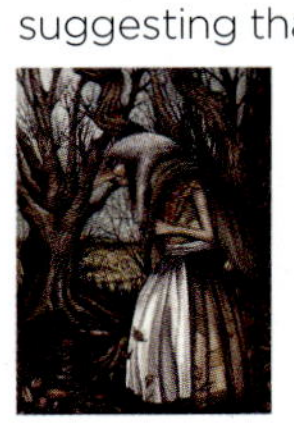

away for years and eventually emerge as an authority on mythology. Putting in a few hours' research is perfectly adequate.

10 SIMULACRA

Look with an artist's eye. Gnarled goblin faces could peer out from the bark or roots of a tree. Dragon heads could form in the shape of a **weathered rock**. If the morning light is just right, faerie creatures leer out at me from the pattern in my bedroom curtains. If you really want to see them, they'll appear.

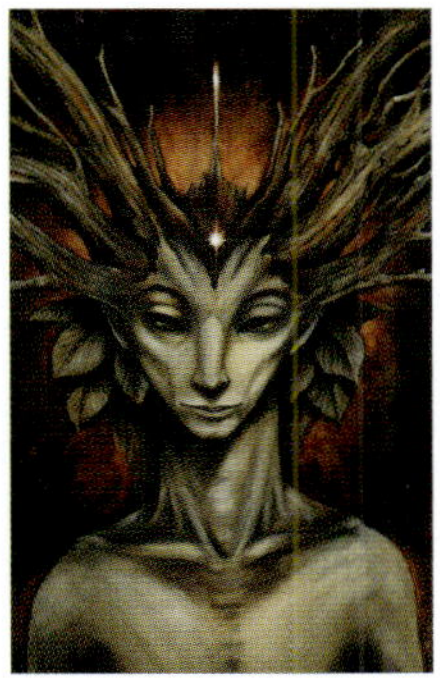

12 GET THEM TO POSE

If you're into the whole spirituality thing (and I am), try meditation or path-working to see them in your mind's eye. You could try this anywhere, but visiting a wild beautiful place, somewhere that faeries might lurk, could spark the imagination. Try to connect with the spirit of a place and you never know, a faerie might just pop out and pose for you. Of course, it helps to be a bit nuts as well...

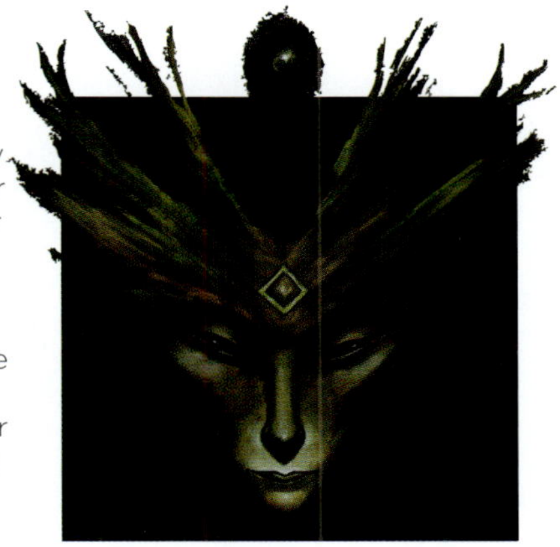

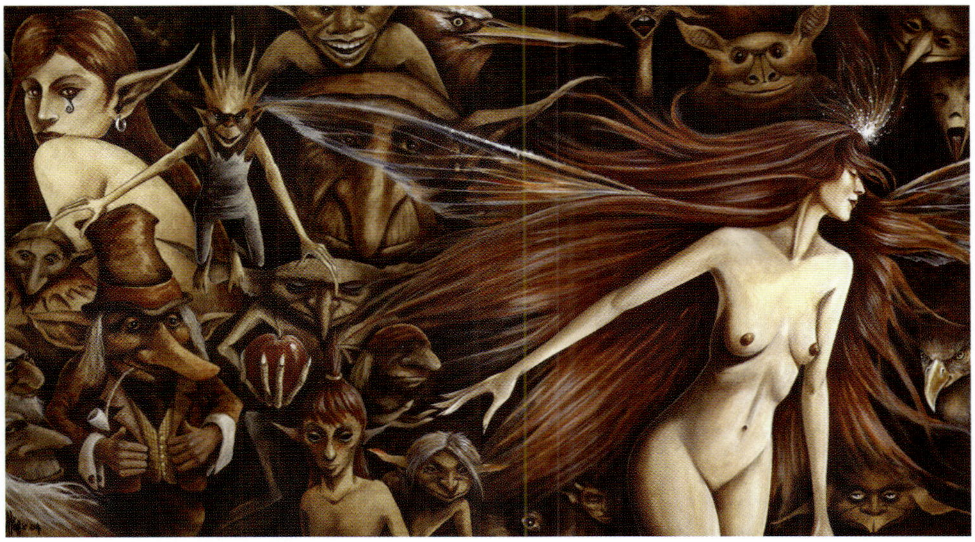

15 SUGGEST A NARRATIVE

This approach lends itself well to faerie art. Has something just happened? Or might it be just about to happen? Suggest a narrative and let the viewer's imagination do the rest. Allow them to involve themselves and create a story in their mind. This can really inspire, and can make a picture magical. I sometimes have a half-formed story in my head when I start a painting, and at other times a story might come later, from a finished piece. Either way, you're creating folklore.

11 COLOUR

The colours of faeries are the shades of nature – the greens and browns of autumn leaves and the delicate hues of flowers. The greencoaties and Green Lady are denizens of the faerie world, as are the brownies and brown men. The names all suggest their colours. Adding a splash of bright colour to the subdued tones can create a glow. I use mucky colours and build up translucent layers. Don't be afraid to experiment.

13 ANIMAL BITS

Faeries are said to be shape-shifters, so try incorporating animal parts that give this away. Faeries with gossamer insect wings are the obvious choice, but how about using moth wings instead of butterflies? Get a field guide and study the patterns. Paint faerie characters with frog legs or rabbit ears, horns or antlers. Some faeries could appear very insect-like – who's to say that a mayfly isn't a faerie?

> “If the morning light is just right, faerie creatures leer at me from the curtains”

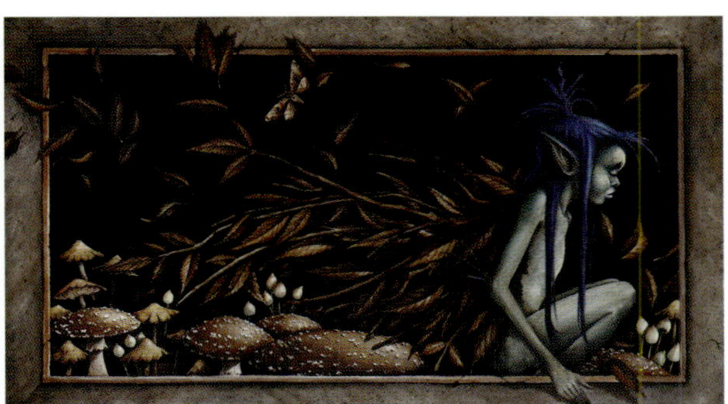

14 MAKE THEM GLOW

Faeries can be considered manifestations of supernatural energy, pulsing with light. You could suggest this energy with the flow of a painting, using sinuous lines to guide the eye. For instance, faeries don't need wings to fly, so they don't need to be structurally perfect. Instead of giving them solid wings, try impossible wings, constructed of light and colour.

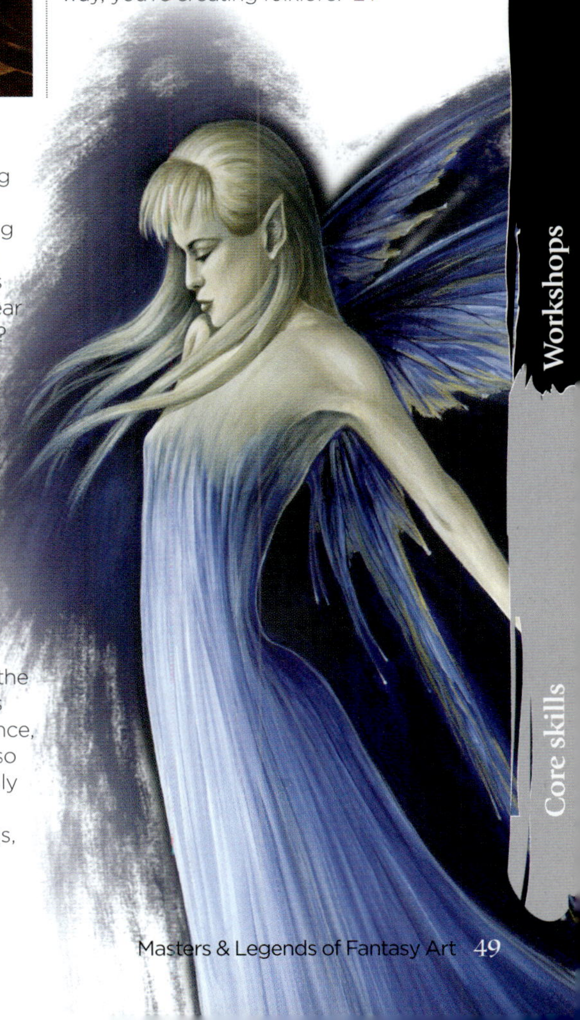

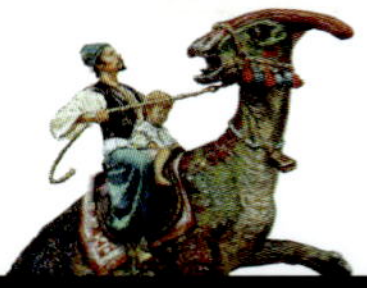

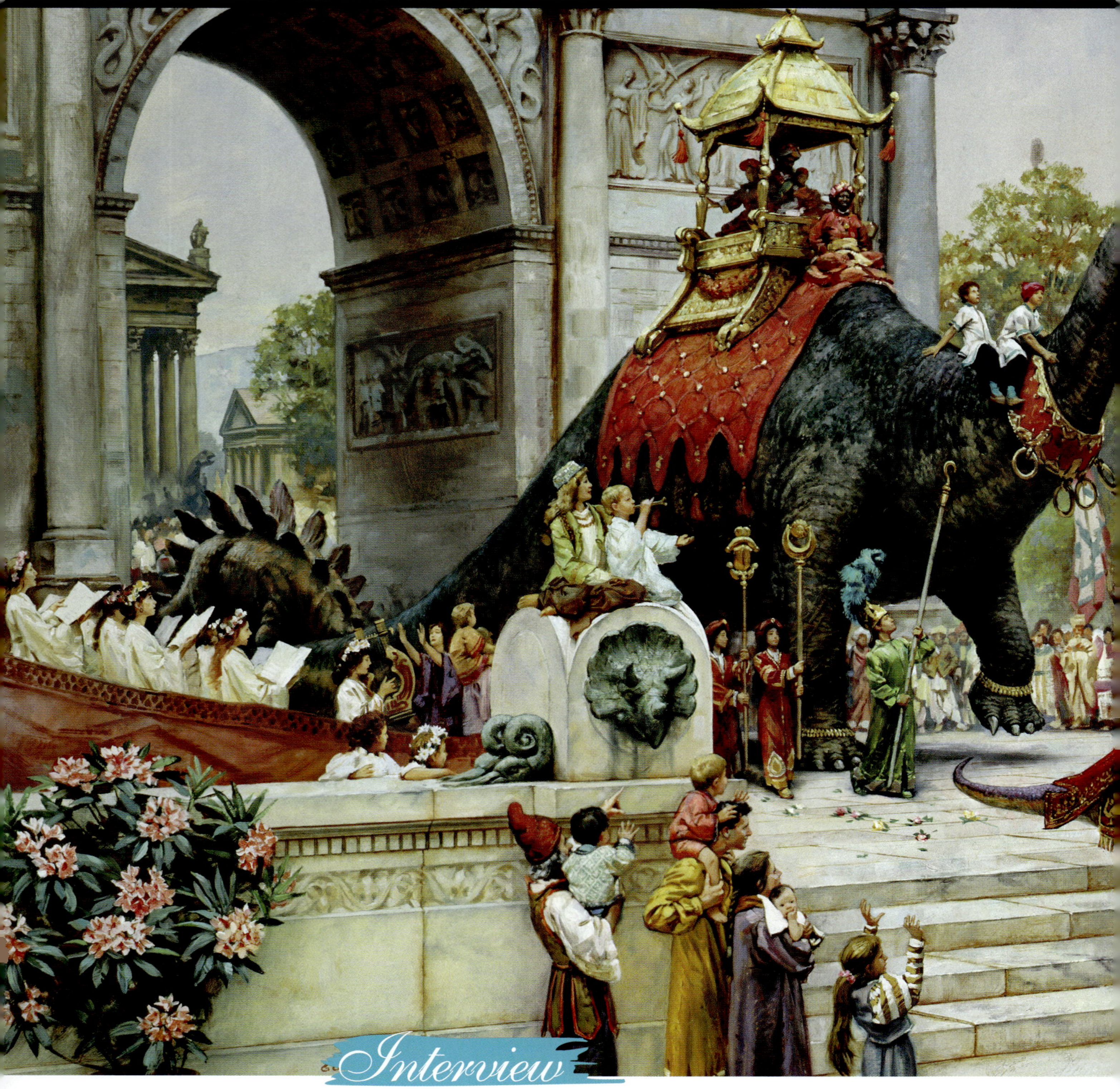

Interview

James Gurney

Dreams of mythical cities and a passion for dinosaurs come alive in **James Gurney**'s art

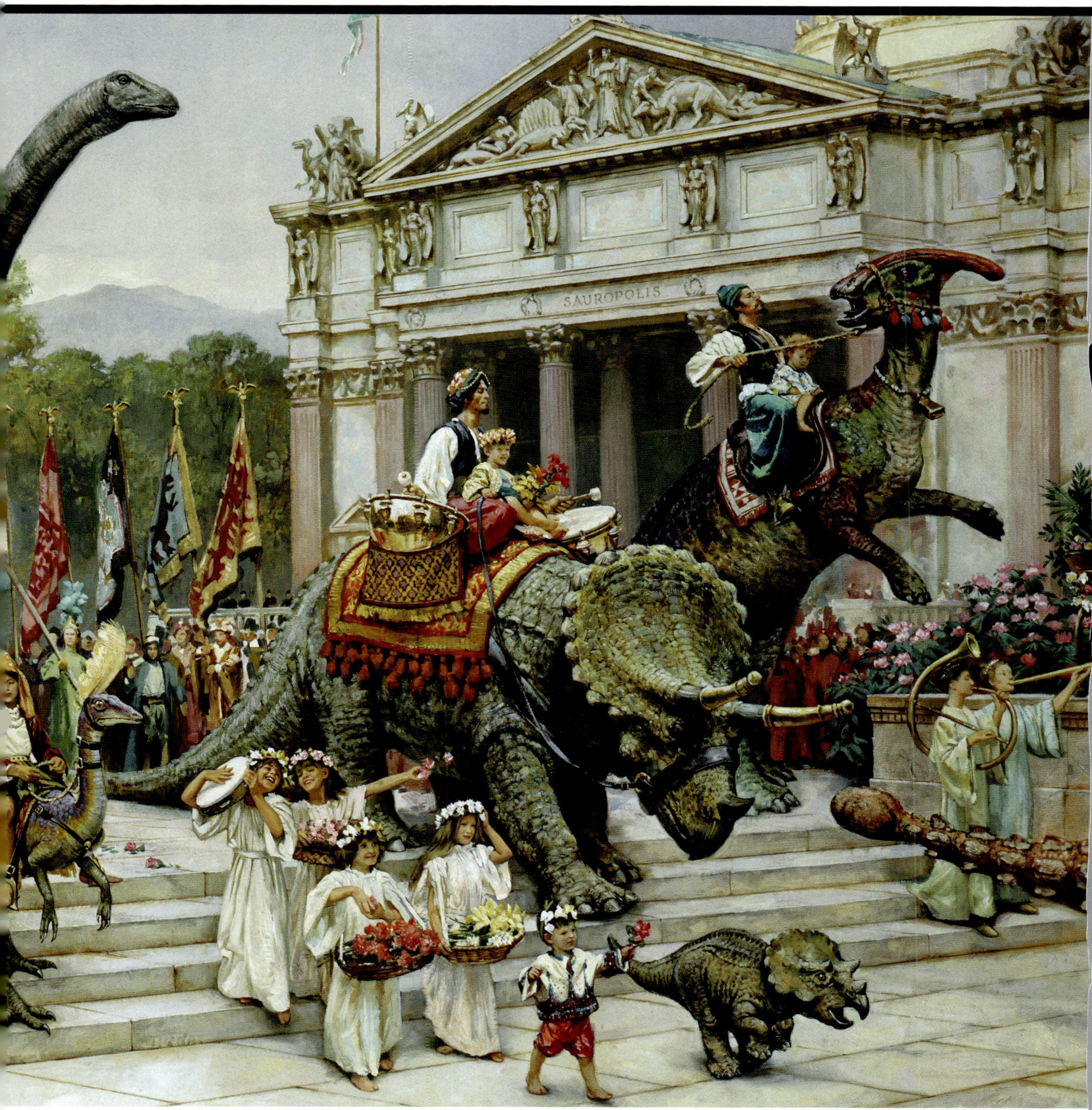

When Dinotopia: Journey to Chandara came out in November 2007 the artist behind it – James Gurney – was already the pre-eminent fantasy artist in the dinosaur genre. Extending the gloriously exciting travels of the Victorian adventurer, Arthur Denison, into realms of the Dinotopia world yet to be explored, the fourth book in Gurney's successful series, where dinosaurs and humans live in harmony, includes over 100 pieces of fascinating artwork, each meticulously painted in oils.

The press pack is enough to blow you away, but the book itself is an extremely lavish experience. Talking to James, you very soon realise that nothing other could result from his dedication to the artwork. "I'm a dinosaur myself in the way I approach picture making," he explains. "I work from miniatures, I build

DINOSAUR PARADE

The Dinosaur Parade is one of James's early Dinotopia paintings, setting the tone for what was to follow.

Artist **PROFILE**

James Gurney

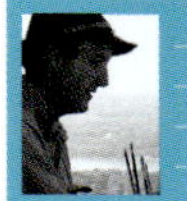

James Gurney is the multi-award-winning creator of the Dinotopia books, as well as a highly regarded fantasy artist and illustrator. He has a background in archaeology, with a particular interest in dinosaurs.

www.jamesgurney.com

WATERFALL CITY

Many of the creatures and settings in Dinotopia are modelled by hand first, and then hand painted.

Assignments for National Geographic took James Gurney to archaeological digs around the world earlier in his career. Drawing and painting visualisations of what early Etruscan tombs or first century Palestine would look like was one thing, but sitting around the campfire he'd hear the archaeologists talking about their dreams of discovering the next Machu Picchu or El Dorado. With this in mind James decided to paint imaginary lost cities in his spare time.

"The first painting I did was Waterfall City in 1988, a combination of Niagara Falls and Venice," he says.

The city has pride of place in the Dinotopia books. Before some of its vast intricacies were painted, James built models of parts of the city. He works from models for everything from dinosaurs to sand dunes: "I can see exactly where the light and shadow would be. One of the most difficult things to do when you're painting is to anticipate where the light and shadow will occur on a given form. It's not too hard on architecture but when you're dealing with complex forms like a dinosaur's body or a 3D art form, or something like that, the tendency is to go all towards the middle values and not commit to light and shadow."

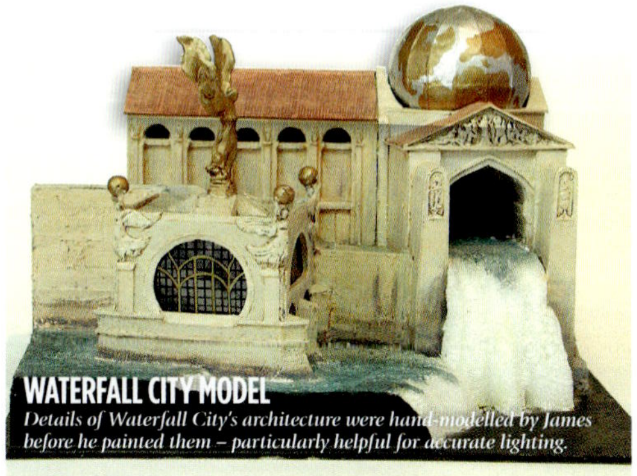

WATERFALL CITY MODEL
Details of Waterfall City's architecture were hand-modelled by James before he painted them – particularly helpful for accurate lighting.

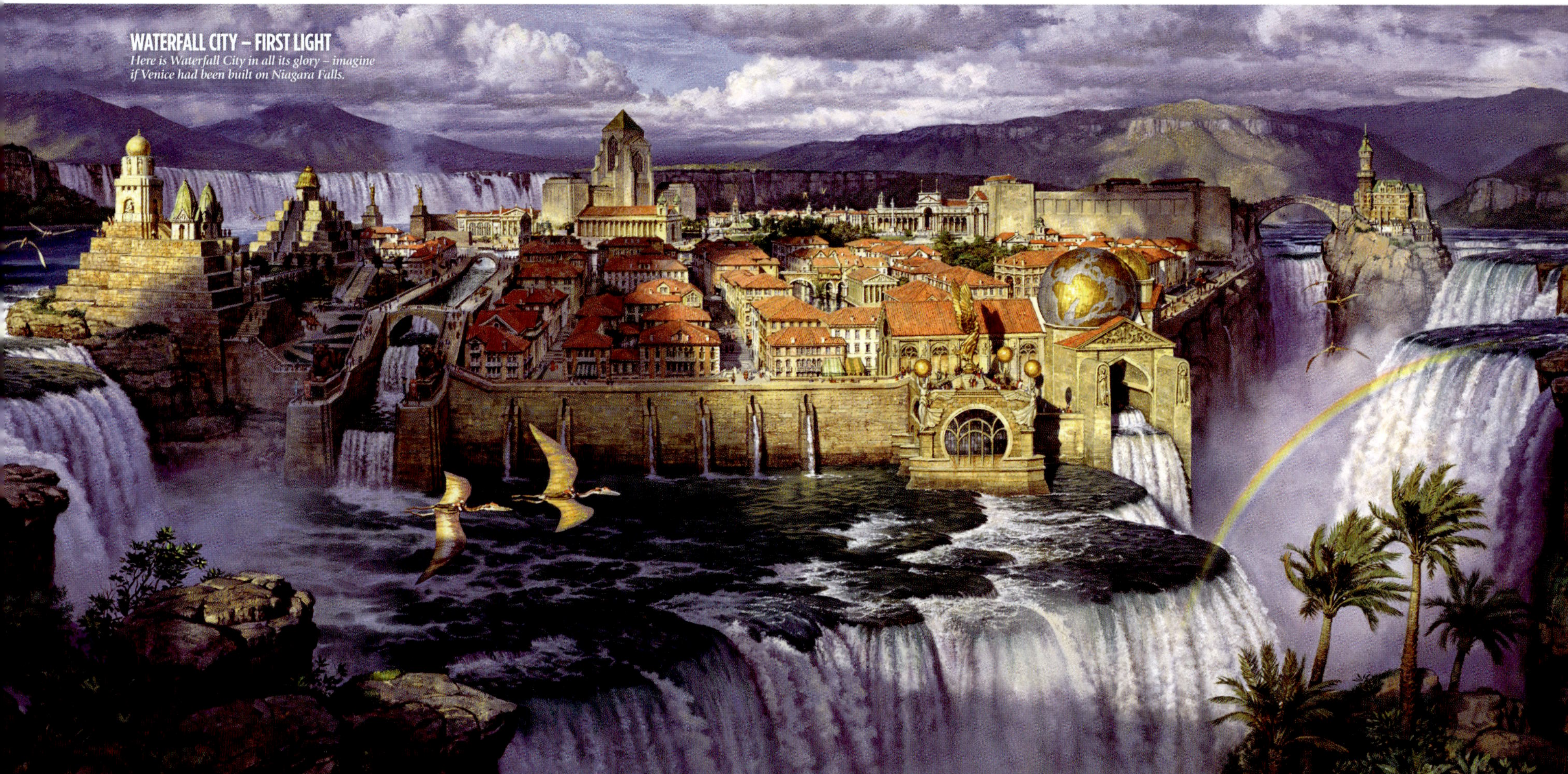

WATERFALL CITY – FIRST LIGHT
Here is Waterfall City in all its glory – imagine if Venice had been built on Niagara Falls.

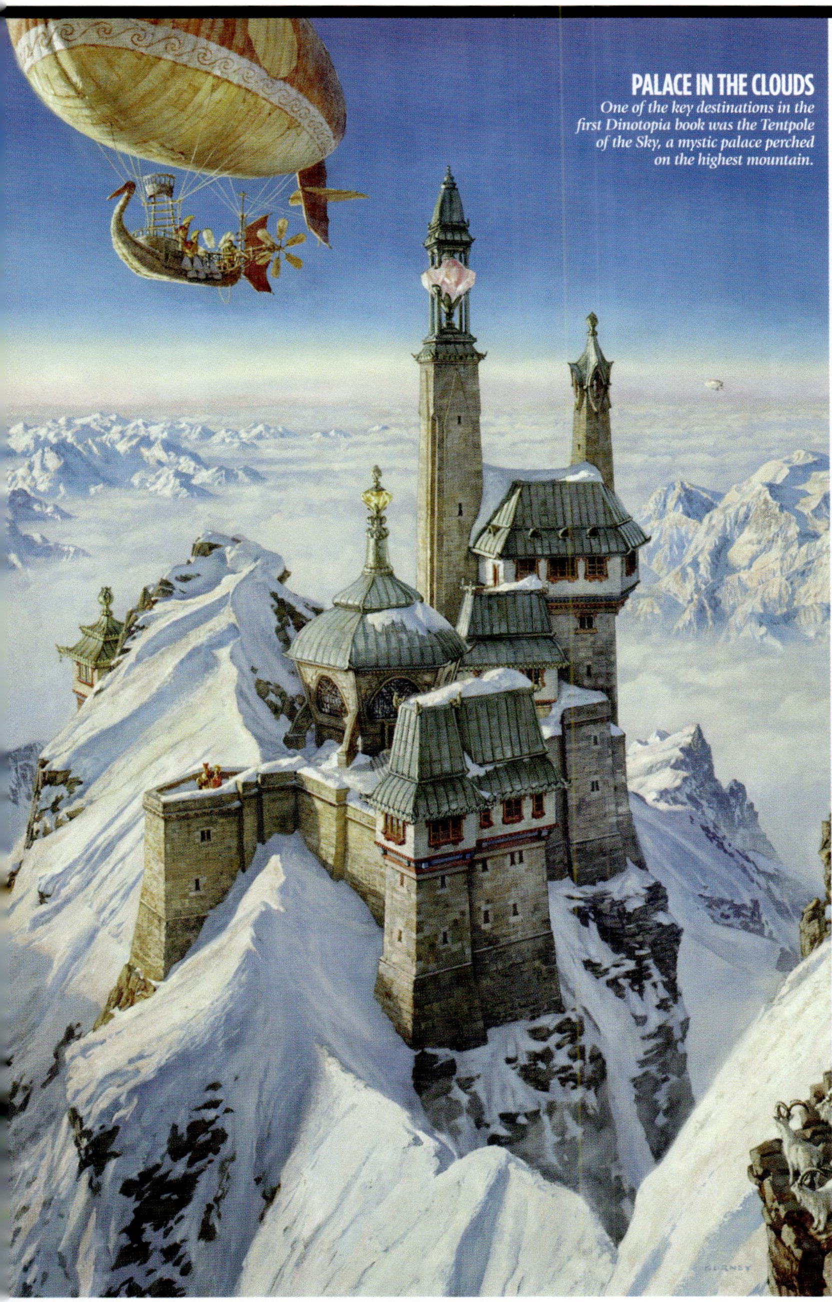

PALACE IN THE CLOUDS
One of the key destinations in the first Dinotopia book was the Tentpole of the Sky, a mystic palace perched on the highest mountain.

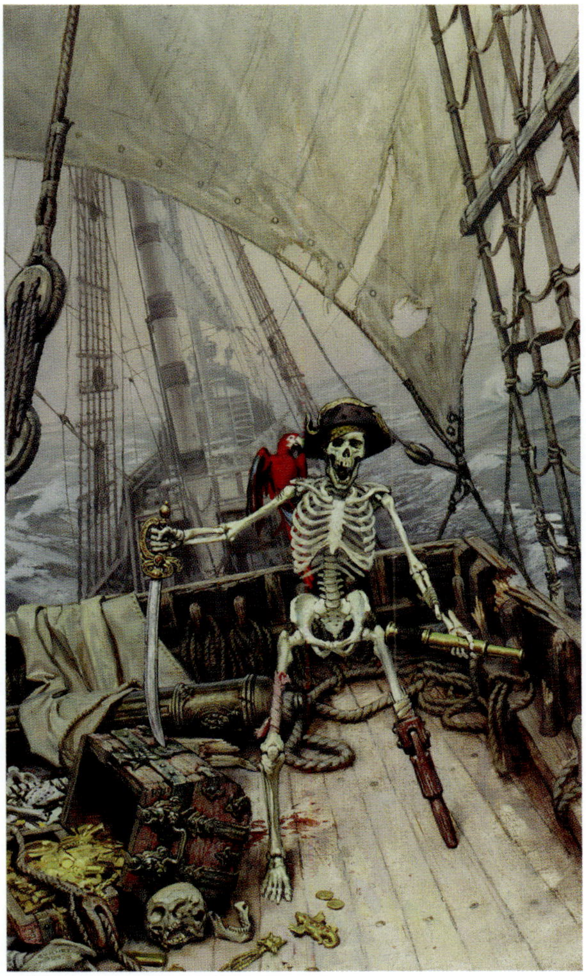

SHIVER ME TIMBERS
One of James's favourite book covers, this was created for On Stranger Tides by Tim Powers. The novel was optioned by Disney for the next Pirates of the Caribbean movie.

> **"I build models and macquettes and I get human models in costumes to pose. Sometimes I go the real traditional way where I do charcoal studies"**

models and maquettes and I get human models in costumes to pose. Sometimes I go the real traditional way where I do charcoal studies and work from those.

"The paintings are all done on an illustration board," he adds. "I start with a pencil drawing and then lay in washes of oil. Sometimes the transparent washes look like watercolour but it's an oil technique."

STORYTELLER

Not only does he create all the illustrations, but he also writes the stories for the books and is the creative force behind the entire Dinotopia world. On top of illustrated books published in 1992, 1995 and 1999, a TV mini series based on his world was made in 2002 with the CG dinosaurs designed by London's Framestore CCF, of Walking With Dinosaurs fame. In addition, Dinotopia novels have been published and his creation has sprawled beyond his dreams. Yet James still works in a very detailed way on his creations. The captions in Journey to Chandara are hand rendered with a steel ink-dip pen.

"On the second book, The World Beneath, we used a digital font because it was a lot easier, but I really love old-fashioned lettering and I love the feeling of dipping the pen in ink, so I went back and did it that way just because it's satisfying and because it really looks different when you do something by hand," he says.

Dinosaur science – palaeontology – has always been a huge part of the artist's inspiration. Named in 1841 by Sir Richard Owen, the 'terrible lizards' were for 140 years thought to be much like overgrown alligators. Kill. Eat. Sleep. Die off. Interesting creatures but ultimately a dead end. However, new discoveries in the field keep James busy.

NEW DINOS

The therizinosaurus, for instance, resembled a 2,000lb chicken with foot-long claws. It crops up as the pet of a hermit who Arthur Denison meets early in his journey. Further findings give him new ideas all the time: "There's been so much found

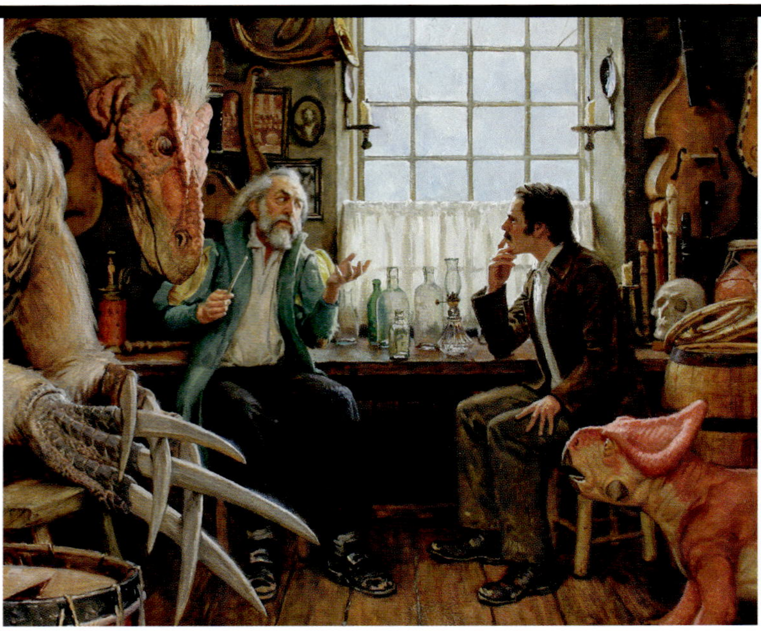

recently with some of the micro-data, of pollen, and a lot of footprints and track ways that weren't known about before and so many different types and forms of dinosaurs – polar dinosaurs, and just over the last couple of years, burrowing dinosaurs and a long-necked sauropod that was the size of a Great Dane. Every time you open a science magazine or newspaper there's always something revolutionary that comes along."

When considering how a world where dinosaurs live alongside people would work, one of the main points of contention was whether the creatures would remain true to science, or become a bit more anthropomorphic. James chose the former route to go down and has pretty much stuck with it up to now. Now and again they're seen wearing clothes or decorated in various unusual ways but in general they're painted accurately, albeit cleverly juxtaposed with some decidedly odd Victorian eccentrics.

OLD CONDUCTOR
Arthur Denison and his companion Bix meet an eccentric hermitic character along with his pet therizinosaurus, which resembles a two-tonne chicken.

> **I'm working on the next Dinotopia book and on another non-Dinotopia-related project that involves fantasy**

GIVING WORDS TO BEASTS

James is even careful about which dinosaurs can talk and which ones can't, and as the keeper of a pet parakeet, he came up with quite an elegant solution to the problem. "I just wanted to have a few of them that could speak in human-like languages," he says. "So the ones that I chose were the ceratopsians: the ones that have the beak and the frill like the triceratops and the protoceratops, because with that parrot-like bill you can imagine them vocalising just in the same way that a parrot would, and you don't have to deal with the whole issue of lips, which I thought could get kind of corny."

The original inspiration for Dinotopia came back in the 80s when James was

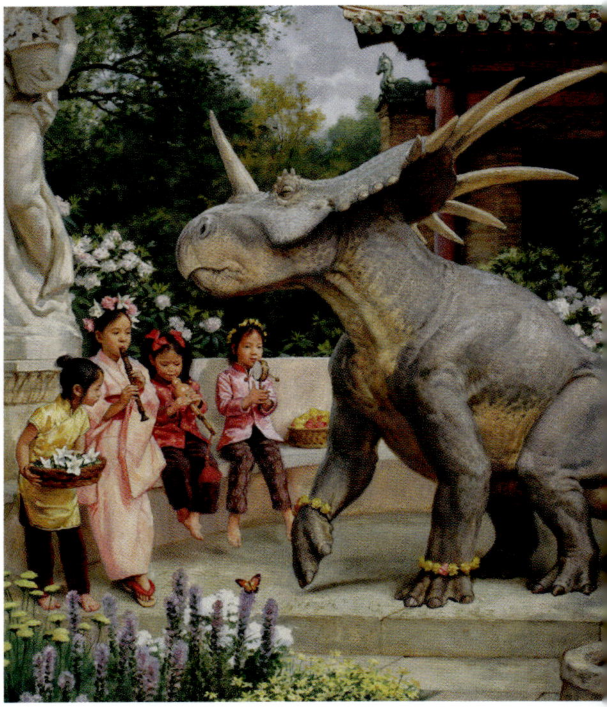

SONG IN THE GARDEN
Taking his cue from his pet parakeet, in James's world only the beaked dinosaurs can speak human languages. Here's a dinosaur that can sing.

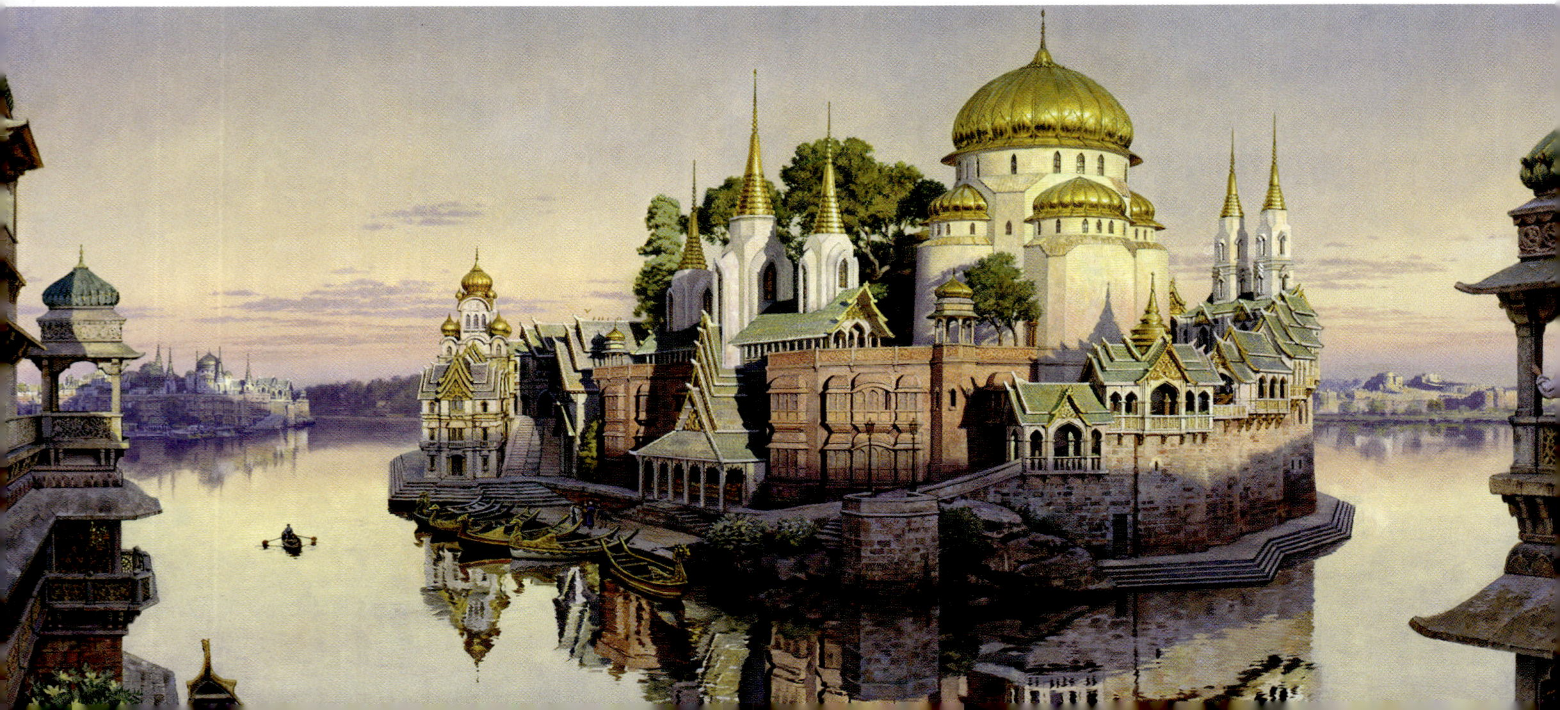

CHANDARA
Fascinated by lost civilisations and Eastern promise, James rendered this vista of Chandara, the city Arthur Denison seeks to visit in the fourth Dinotopia book.

working as an illustrator for National Geographic. Alongside art, he had studied archaeology and assignments for the magazine took him to digs around the world. The idea of lost civilisations waiting to be discovered inspired him to create his own imaginary one. The latest Dinotopia book draws influence from the caravan world of the Middle East and the Orient.

FACT AND FICTION

It seems like James has always applied his imagination to both fact and fiction. We can't overlook that he was also the artist behind over 70 science fiction and fantasy book jackets. One of his favourite pieces was for the story Quozl, written by his friend Alan Dean Foster. James created a flipbook animation for this project. He also mentions the cover of On Stranger Tides, a pirate-based story by Tim Powers. "It was kind of a realistic view of something that almost could exist in the real world. That's the kind of thing I like doing the most, to let my pictures be like a sideways elevator to bring people into other worlds, or to go where the camera can't go. It's really what you have to do for National Geographic," he says.

When you ask him which artists have influenced him, it's no surprise that the list includes some great illustrative painters, including John Berkey, Ralph McQuarrie, Norman Rockwell and Howard Pyle. Moving to Britain, Sir Lawrence Alma Tadema, Lord Frederic Leighton, John Singer Sargent and John Waterhouse. A trip to France brings in William-Adolphe Bouguereau and Jean-Léon Gerôme.

SELF-TAUGHT

After Dinotopia: Journey to Chandara James created two art instruction books, Imaginative Realism and Color and Light, both of which have become bestsellers.

Sensing there was a gap in the market James used material from his blog to create the books. "They focus on the thinking and the understanding that every imaginative artist needs to make a believable image, regardless of technique," says James.

"In the last few years I've also done several assignments for science magazines, reconstructing newly discovered dinosaurs," explains James. "For these pictures I try for a more photographic look, since the paintings have to share the pages of the magazines with wildlife photos. I suppose my specialty is painting realistically scenes that can't be directly observed, whether from the world of fantasy or actuality."

Turn the page to learn to paint like James Gurney

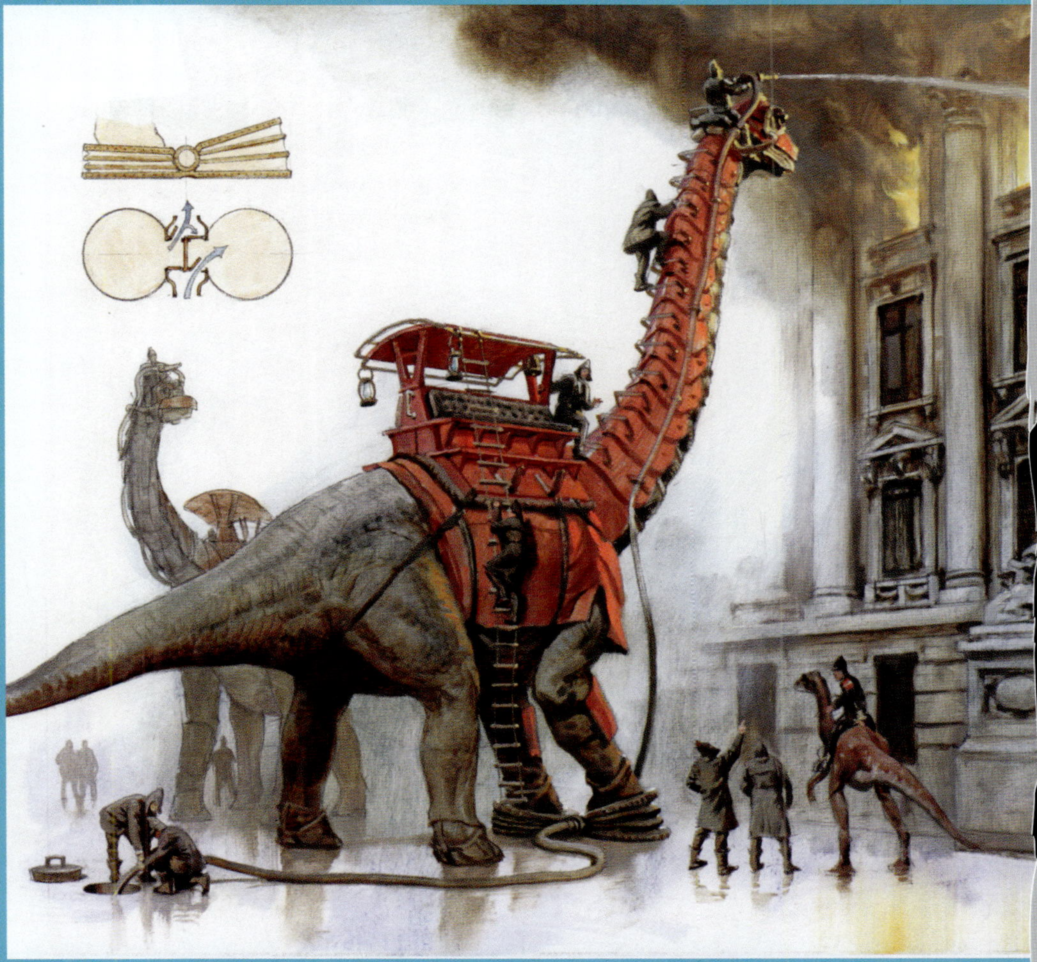

THE FIRE CHIEF

A foot-pump like you've never seen...

Always interested in juxtaposing humans and their activities with the dinosaur world, in Dinotopia: Journey to Chandara, James Gurney played with the idea of a joint fire department. He sketched some designs of the people, the dinosaurs and their devices and showed it to his friend Ernesto Bradford, a professional fire engine designer.

"I was very pleased with myself with the first sketch that I'd done until I showed it to him and he said: "Well that's very nice but it would never work." He explained all the reasons why my early sketches wouldn't function from an engineering point of view. And then he came up with some beautiful and simple solutions, including a pump that was to be operated by the dinosaur's feet."

In recompense, James included his friend in the book as the character Igneus Vinco, the fire chief who herds brachiosaurus with mounted water canons to the nearest burning building.

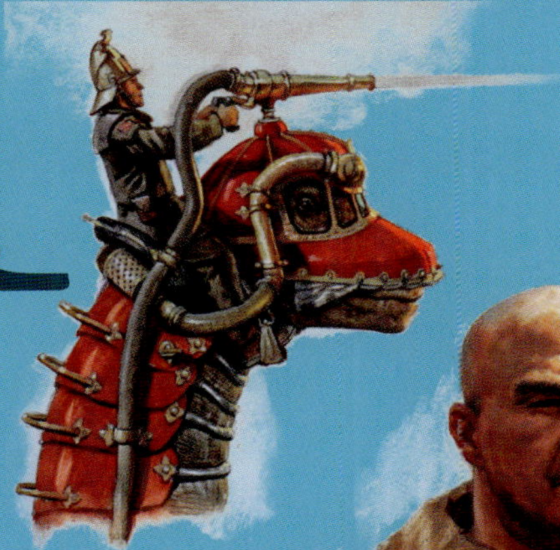

FIRE EQUIPMENT
Alongside a passion for creating the lost world of Dinotopia, James loves to design systems that might exist in this world, such as a dinosaur-powered fire engine complete with foot pump.

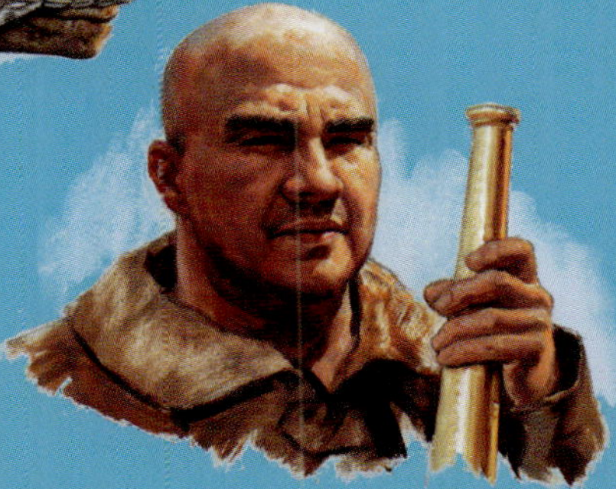

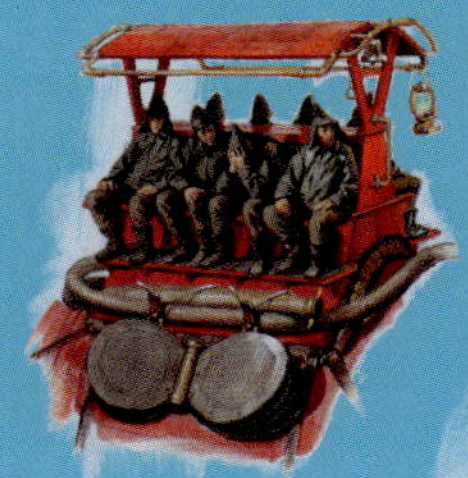

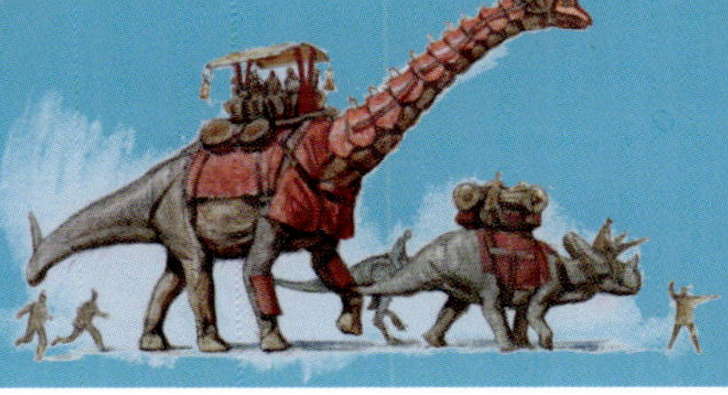

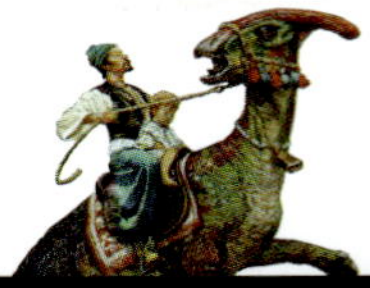

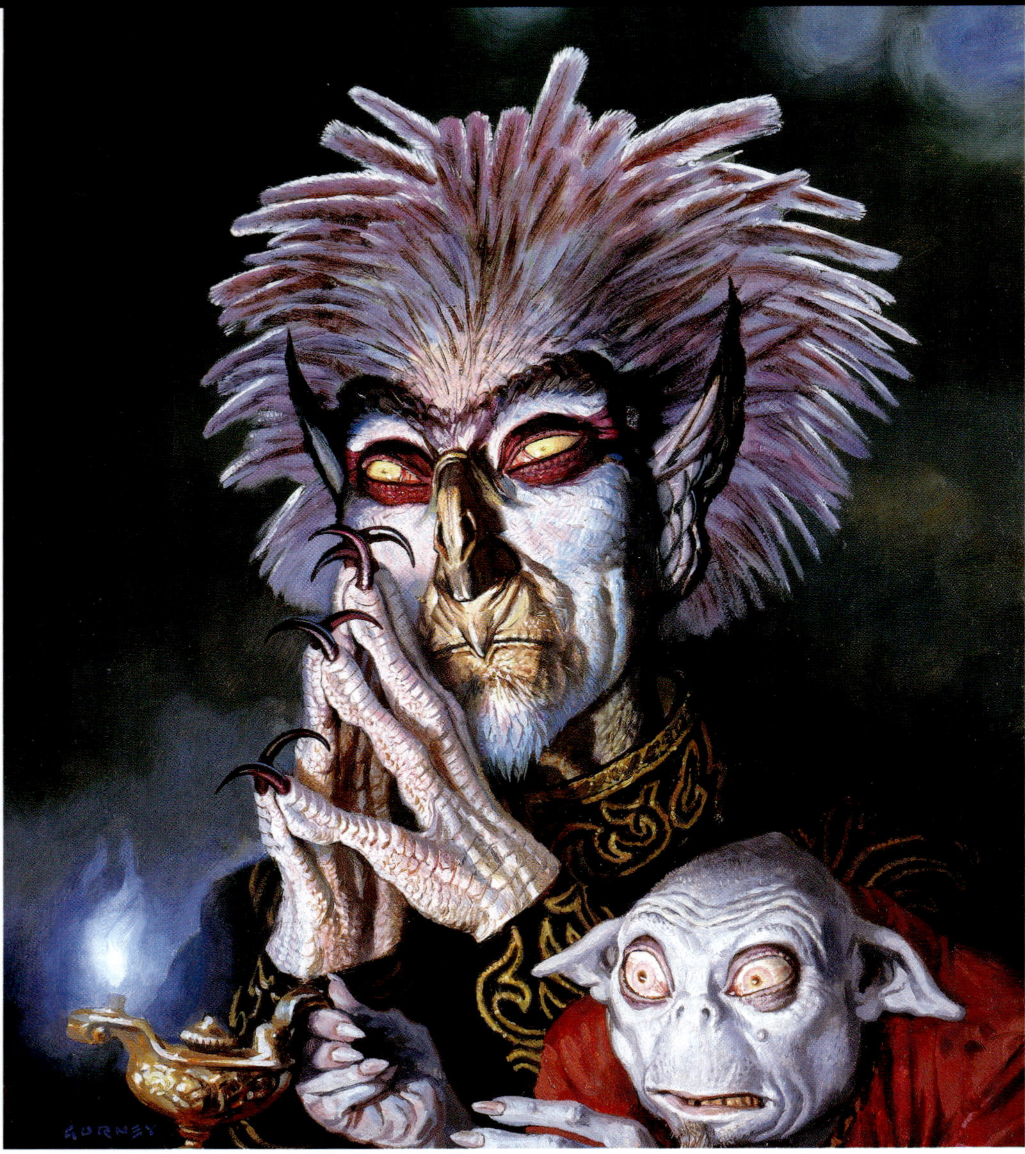

Traditional Skills

THE SCIENCE BEHIND VISUAL PERCEPTION

ImagineFX VIDEO WORKSHOP ON THE DVD

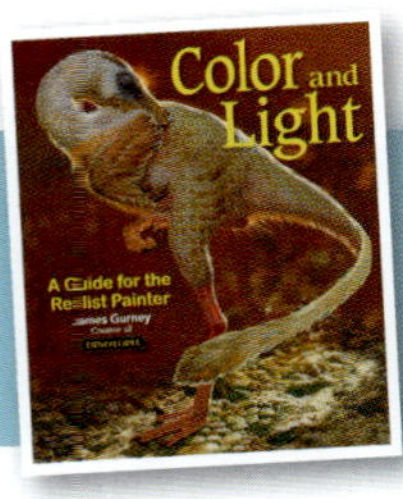

What we see has as much to do with our mind's eye as with what's out there in front of us. To paint something that appears real, you have to understand the weird quirks of visual perception, says **James Gurney**

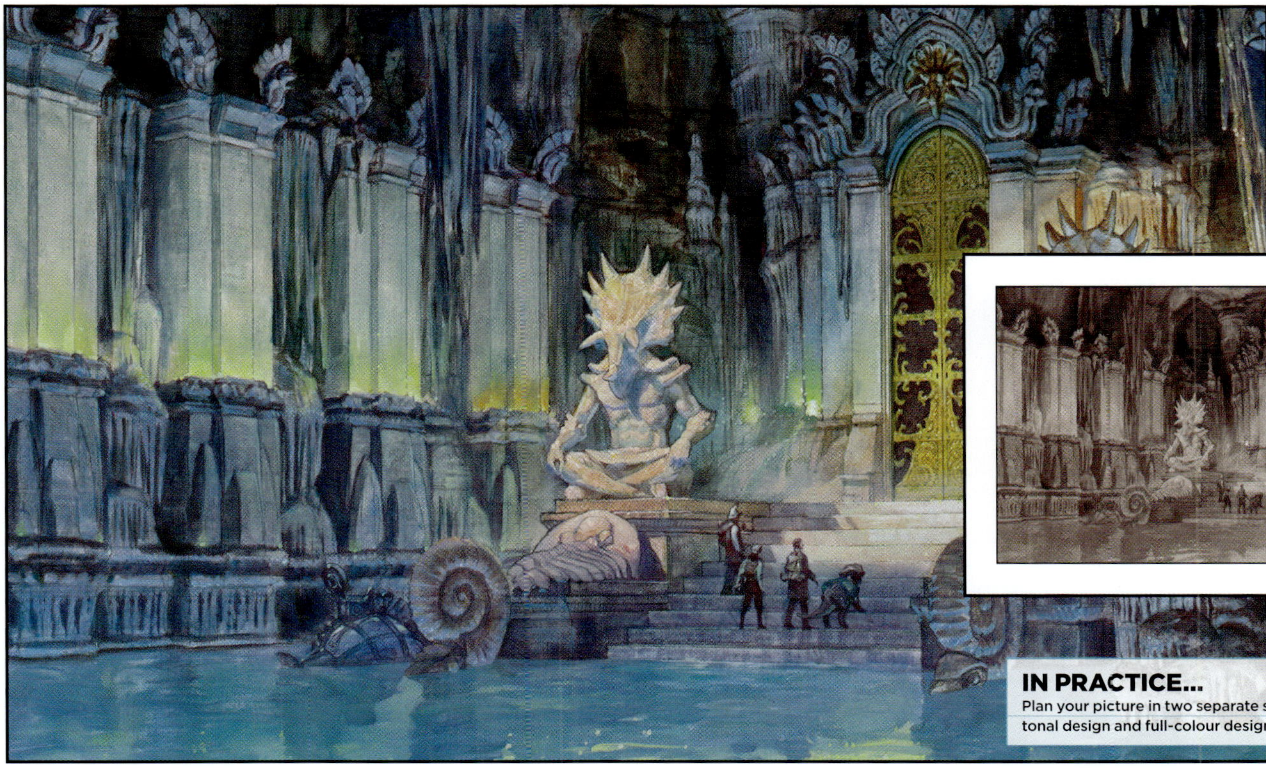

If you drain all the colour out of a scene, you can still understand what's going on, but the emotional flavour will be missing.

IN PRACTICE...
Plan your picture in two separate stages: tonal design and full-colour design.

COLOUR AND TONE ARE SEPARATE

We don't see colour in the same way that we see tone

Our eyes have two types of receptor: rods and cones. The rods detect light and dark, but they're colour-blind, and function better at lower light levels. The cones respond to colour and tone, and work at relatively high light levels.

Under normal light conditions, the rods and cones cooperate to create an interpretation of reality. But according to Dr Margaret Stratford Livingstone, a professor of neurobiology at Harvard University, the visual brain processes tonal information separately from colour. The two streams are kept separate from the retina all the way to the vision centres of the brain. According to Livingstone, the area of the brain that interprets tone is several inches away from the part that interprets colour, making tonal processing and colour processing as distinct anatomically as vision is from hearing. Neuroscientists characterise the tonal pathway as the 'where' stream. This capacity, which all mammals share, is adept at motion and depth perception, spatial organisation and figure–ground separation. The colour capacity is the 'what' stream, and is more concerned with object and face recognition, and colour perception.

ONCE IN A BLUE MOON

Moonlight isn't really blue – our visual system is just playing tricks on us

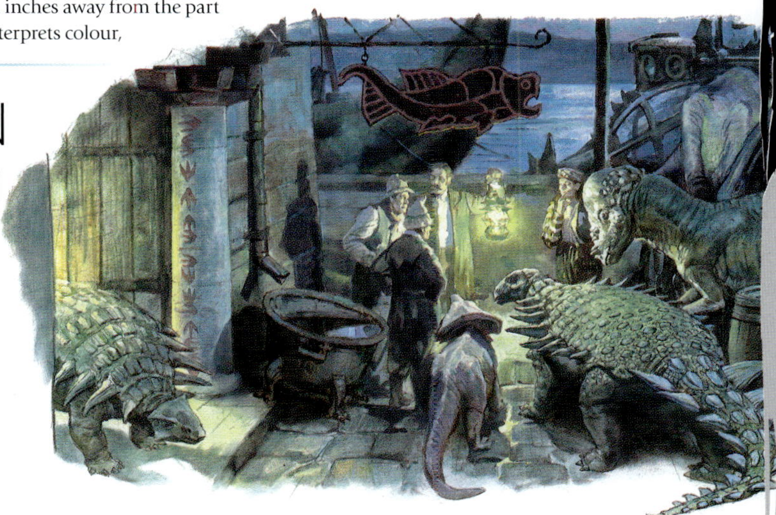

The light of the full moon is about 450,000 times weaker than direct sunlight. It's so dim that the colour-receptive cones can barely function. In moonlight, the colour-blind rods are most active. Moonlight is simply the white light of the sun reflecting off the grey surface of the moon. There's nothing to give the light a bluish quality. In fact, scientific instruments have shown that the light from the moon is very slightly redder than the average colour of direct sunlight.

You might ask, 'If moonlight is neutral or red-coloured light, and if it's close to the minimal threshold of our colour receptors anyway, why do so many artists paint moonlight with a blue or green cast? Do we really see it that way? Is it some kind of illusion, or is it just an artistic convention?' There's no way to be sure that you see moonlight the same way I do. Since we can't escape the prison of our own senses, paintings by artists are the best way for us to share our personal perception of moonlight.

Most observers agree that everything is not only cooler in colour temperature, ➜

IN PRACTICE...
Photos of moonlight are misleading. You have to observe the lunar view carefully, remember what it is you're seeing and later reconstruct the image you saw in a brightly lit studio.

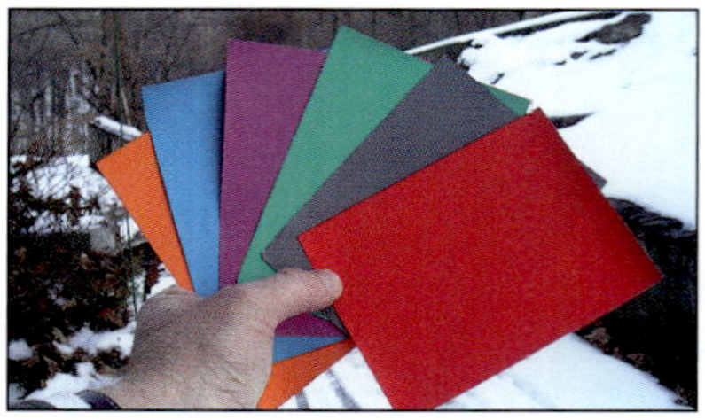

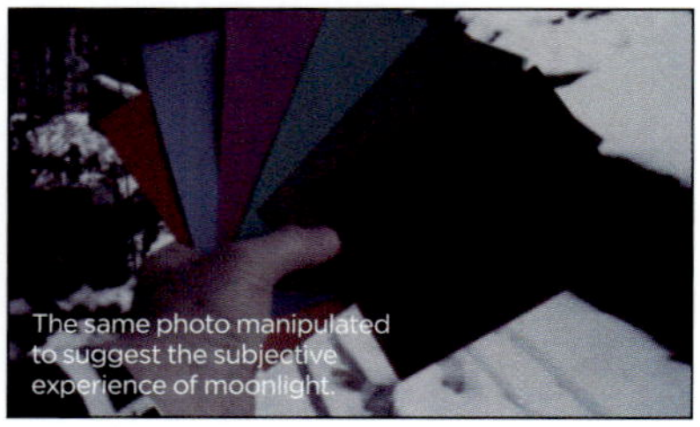

The same photo manipulated to suggest the subjective experience of moonlight.

but also duller, darker and more blurry. Contrary to what some authorities have claimed, most people can make some very basic colour judgments by the light of a full moon.

Moonlit colours

You can test it yourself by looking at bright paint swatches on a clear, moonlit night. However, when you look at the same swatches by a half moon or by starlight, most people's colour perception goes sub-threshold and shuts down.

Our retinas are made up of rods and cones. Colour vision comes solely from the latter.

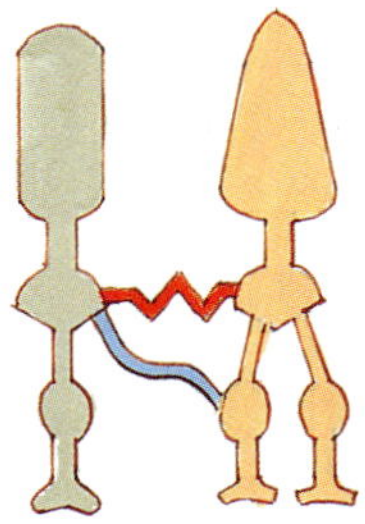

Saad M Khan and Sumanta N Pattanaik of the University of Central Florida have proposed that the blue colour is a perceptual illusion, caused by a spillover of neural activity from the rods to the adjacent cones. A small synaptic bridge between the active rods and the inactive cones touches off the blue receptors in the cones.

This influence of rod activity on the adjacent cones tricks the brain into thinking we're seeing blue-coloured light from the moon, even though we're not.

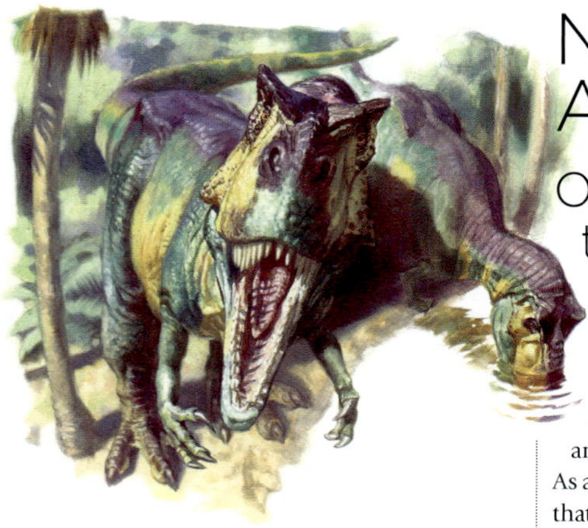

The focal plane is set to the dinosaur's eyes. Everything closer or further away is out of focus. If you're painting in oil, you can use larger brushes and a wet-into-wet handling in the soft areas to achieve this effect.

NOT ALL EDGES ARE SHARP

Our eyes constantly change focal length to create our impression of depth

A common mistake made by painters who are just starting out is one of over-sharpness. This is because our eyes adjust their focus to both near and far objects when we look around. As a result, we construct the impression that everything is equally crisp.

Cameras produce a shallow depth of field because they can focus on only one plane of distance at a time. Everything that isn't on the focal plane is blurry. The blur increases as objects get further away from the plane of focus. When one object sits in front of another in space, what happens where the contours intersect? How can you create a sense of space between the object in front and the one that's behind?

Blurring the lines in an image plays a big part in how we perceive depth in the scene.

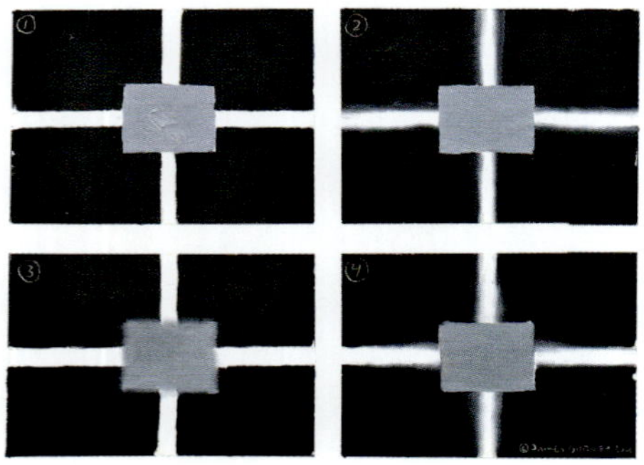

Intersecting lines

In the image (left), the top-left example shows a grey rectangle in front of a cross of white lines. All the edges are sharp and so the rectangle appears to be sitting on top of the lines, yet it's on the same two-dimensional plane. If you soften the edges of the white lines, as in the top-right, the rectangle floats up. This is how a camera interprets two objects on different planes of focus. The bottom-left example softens the edges of the rectangle and keeps the white lines sharp. It looks like the camera has shifted its focus to the back plane. This creates perceptual ambiguity. The grey rectangle still comes forward because it's superimposed, but the white lines also want to come forward since they're in sharper focus. The bottom-right example attempts to simulate human visual perception. It's similar to the photographic mode in the top right, but the lines get more out of focus as they pass behind the rectangle. This suggests the continual focal adjustment our eyes make while surveying a scene.

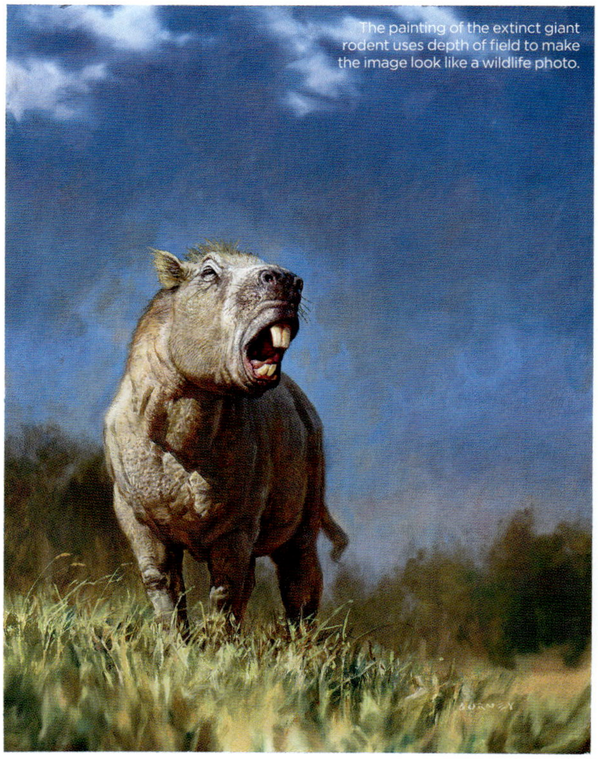

The painting of the extinct giant rodent uses depth of field to make the image look like a wildlife photo.

IN PRACTICE...

If you want to convey a sense of depth in your image, soften the edges just as they cross behind a subject.

The yellow-orange light streaming into the foreground pushes the reds toward orange. The red of the hanging carriage on the far side of the barn had to be greyed down to look right in the foggy light.

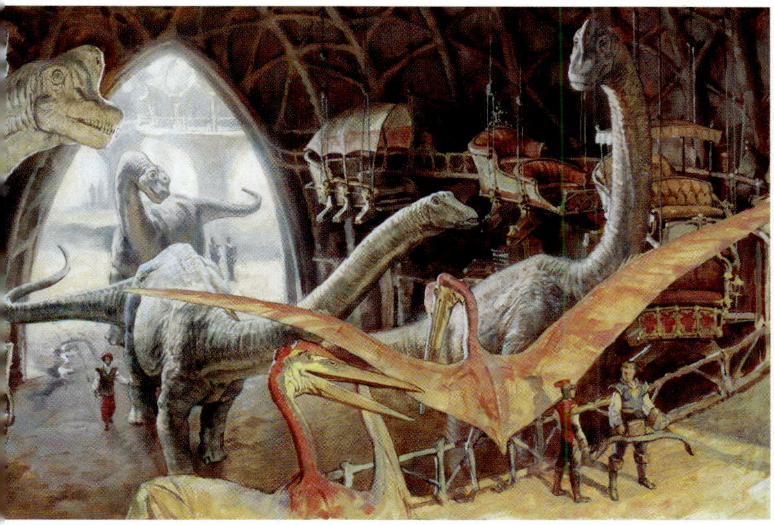

THE BRAIN'S AUTOMATIC WHITE BALANCE

Our brains make us believe that local colours are stable and unchanging

A fire engine looks red, no matter whether we see it lit by the orange light of a fire or the blue of the twilight sky. If it were parked partly in shadow, we'd still believe it to be a single, consistent colour.

Our visual systems constantly make such inferences. When we look at a scene, we don't see colours objectively. Instead, we construct a subjective interpretation of the colours based on context cues.

This system of processing happens unconsciously, and it's almost impossible for our conscious minds to override it. To demonstrate this, the coloured cube optical illusion shows how our brains alter what we see. The large cube with coloured surfaces appears consistent, despite being lit by red or green light.

The small red-coloured surfaces on the near corner seem to be the same from one picture to another, and it's distinct from the green-coloured square below it. But in fact, the paint mixtures used to render the green square (A) in the red-lit scene are the same neutral grey paints used to render the red square (B) in the green-lit scene. The context of each picture tricks us into thinking the actual colour notes are different. Is it possible to switch off the context cues so that you can see colours as they really are?

There are various methods for isolating a particular spot of colour. One is to look through the hole in a half-closed fist. Another is to look through holes in a card that's painted half white and half black.

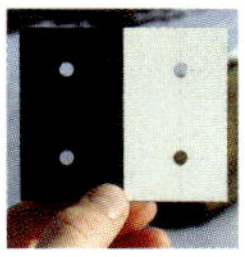

> **"To isolate a particular spot of colour, look through holes in a half-black, half-white card"**

IN PRACTICE...

For imaginative painting, you can't just match what you see. Instead, you have to create colours based on your knowledge of the colour of the light source and the colour of the object itself.

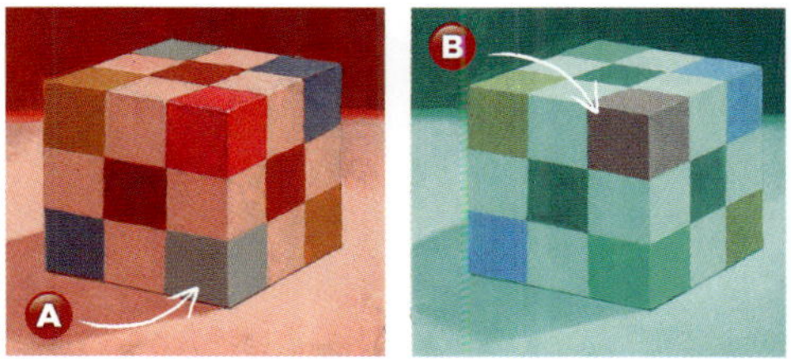

COLOURS, EMOTIONS AND CULTURE

Colour affects us at both an emotional and a physiological level

The neural pathway that processes colour is not only separate from our perception of tone, but it's also strongly tied to the emotional brain. Colours affect how we feel.

Social scientists tell us the division between warm and cool colours seems woven into the fabric of our human existence. Anthropologists Paul Kay and Brent Berlin have studied the evolution of colour terms in languages around the world. European languages have about 11 or 12 basic terms to describe colours. Yet some so-called primitive languages, such as the New Guinean Dani, have only two basic terms. Paul and Brent wrote: "One of the two encompasses black, green, blue and other 'cool' colours; the other encompasses white, red, yellow and other 'warm' colours."

Primitive peoples don't have poor vision. Rather, anthropologists suggest that as language evolved, it developed its first word concepts around the most psychologically important groupings. The cool colours seem to evoke feelings of winter, night, sky, sleep and ice. So the colour blue suggests quietness, restfulness and serenity. Warm colours such as red, orange and yellow make us think of fire, energy and hot spices. Advertisers use all these bright, warm colours to whet the appetite for fast food.

Complementary colours suggest an opposition of elemental principles – such as fire and ice – and they can suggest a feeling of conflict in a painting. The emphasis on the complementary oppositions of blue-violet versus yellow, green versus red, and light versus dark echoes the opponent process system of colour vision, where all colours we see are the result of interactions between opposing pairs of colour receptors.

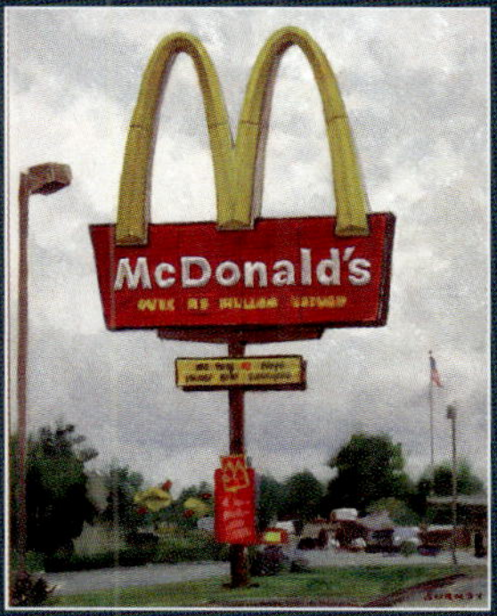

A plein-air study of a McDonald's sign. Would you stop for a burger if the logo were green and purple?

IN PRACTICE...

Make yourself aware of how you respond emotionally to different colour families, or even better, to different combinations of colour. Design your colour schemes to evoke the moods you want.

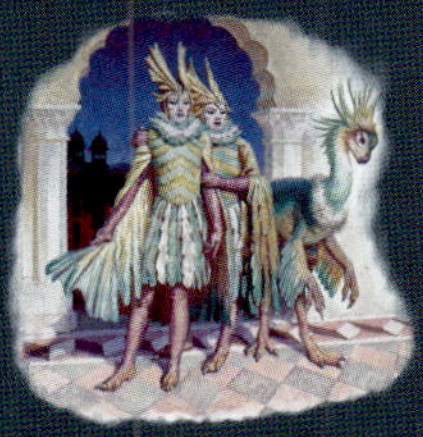

The relaxing colours of these figures suit their role: to guide you into your dream world.

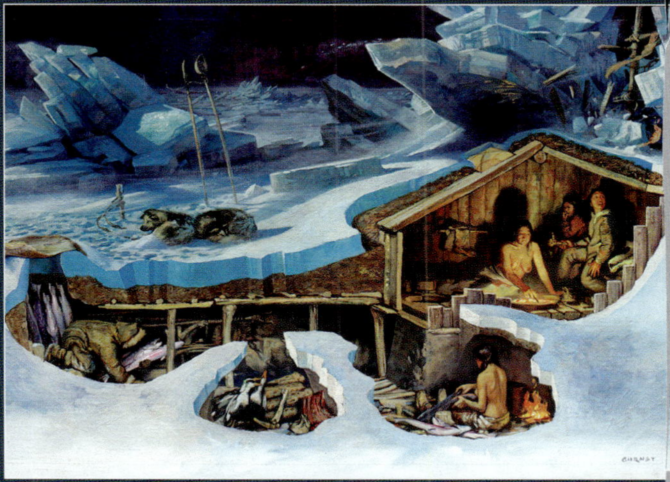

I used contrasts of warm and cool colours to help depict a true story: Eskimos in their dwelling 500 years ago, about to be buried by storm-driven ice.

AFTERIMAGES AND OTHER ILLUSIONS

When we look at a scene, the experience of one colour affects the way we perceive other colours

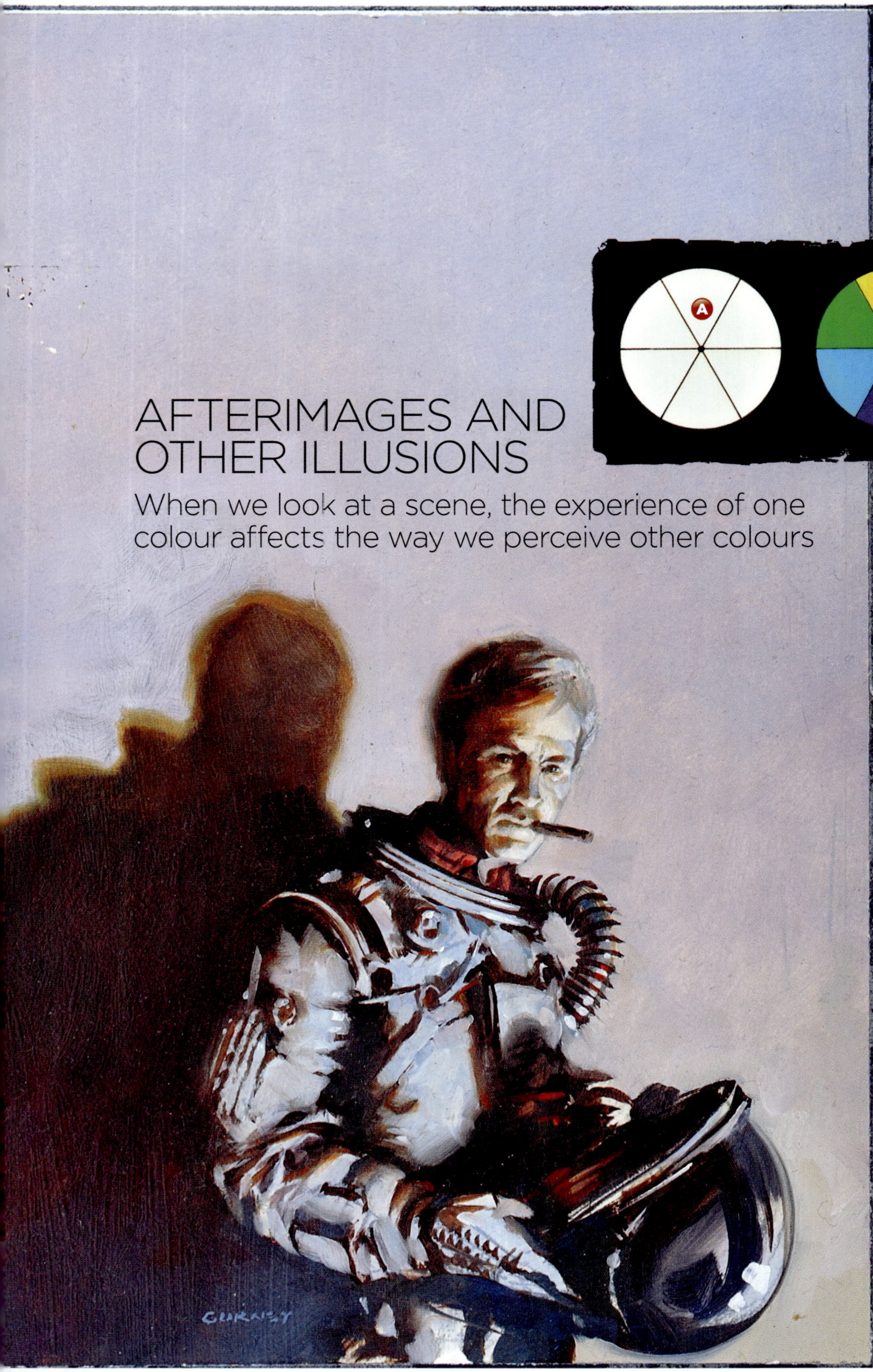

This is a concept sketch for a science fiction paperback cover using a cool key light. To emphasise the coolness of the light, the shadows have a warm hue.

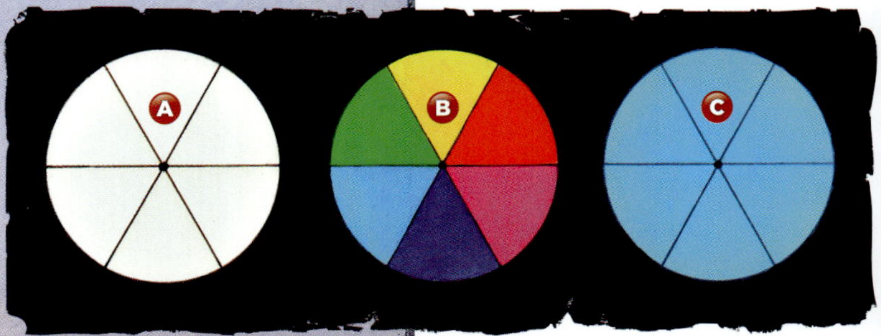

Stare at the central circle (B) above, under strong light, for about 20 seconds, then look at the centre of the white circle (A). Complementary afterimages should bloom on the white circle. The blue sector at the bottom becomes yellow. Green changes to magenta, and cyan to red.

Repeat the experiment, but this time shift your gaze from B to the cyan circle (C). Perhaps you'll notice that the afterimages now change your perception of each of the cyan sectors. Which sector appears the most intense version of cyan?

Most people report that the strongest cyan appears where the red sector had been. This is called successive contrast. When you look at an object of a certain colour, your eyes adjust or adapt to that colour. The resulting afterimage affects what you look at next. This is why

> **“Areas of complementary accents help enliven a colour scheme”**

providing a few areas of complementary accents helps enliven a colour scheme, and you can use this to enhance the illusion of your picture. As you look at a scene, try to isolate the colour, but also compare that colour to others in the scene. Is it different in hue, value or chromaticity? Always asking questions and searching for answers in this way will ultimately reward you.

IN PRACTICE...

The only way to know what colour you need to mix is to compare it to other colours in the scene, especially to a known white colour.

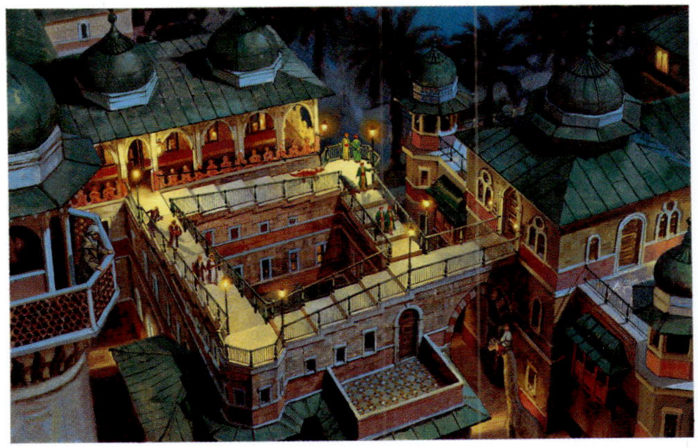

OUR EYES DON'T FLOW ACROSS PICTURES

Contrary to most compositional theory, our eyes look for figures and faces in an image, rather than following contours

I always wondered whether those old textbooks were accurate when they described how the eye moves through a picture. Do they follow golden section grids, or do they move in smooth circles or ovals around the picture space? Can we control the eye with abstract elements?

To find out, I asked vision scientist Dr Greg Edwards, president of Eyetools, to run some eye-tracking tests on some of my pictures. Eye-tracking technology uses sophisticated equipment to determine the exact pathway followed by the centre of vision throughout a composition.

Edwards had 15 people look at my pictures on a computer screen while a sensor tracked their eyes in real time. The thin blue line shows the track of the eyes, beginning at the green circle. The light haloed edge, around the pathway, suggests peripheral vision. The numbers in the black squares show where the eye travelled at each second of the 15-second session. Rather than moving in sweeping curves, our eyes move in jagged leaps, or saccades, resting very briefly at points called fixations. These happen at a rate of about three saccades per second.

I chose to have the subjects look at my painted optical illusion of an Escher-like stairway, because I wondered if people would move their eyes in a circuit around the stairs. But no one did. Instead, people skipped all over the image, grabbing an overall sense of the picture right away with big eye movements and zooming in to look at details as each session progressed. Another graphic shows an eye-tracking heatmap, generated by compiling the scan path data of all the subjects. The red areas show where 100 per cent of the viewers looked. Dark blue or black areas drew absolutely no attention. I was surprised that some areas of the picture I had rendered got no eye time at all.

The heatmap shows that people look at the centre of the picture. But what invariably grabs the eye is faces or people, no matter what design elements you use to try to influence eye movement. As Dr Edwards puts it, "Abstract design gets trumped by human stories."

> **“Faces or people grab the eye, no matter what design elements you use to try to influence eye movement”**

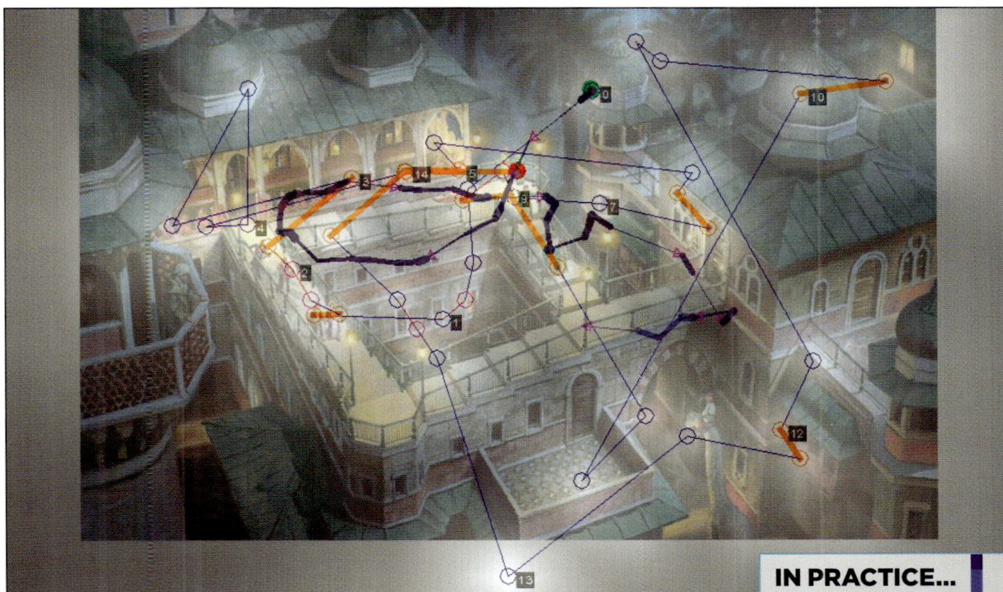

A scanpath image for my Scholar's Stairway painting from one test subject. We can't know for sure without a follow-up interview, but this observer probably didn't notice the optical illusion.

IN PRACTICE...

Because faces and people receive the most attention from the viewer, make sure that they're right, and downplay the other areas of the picture.

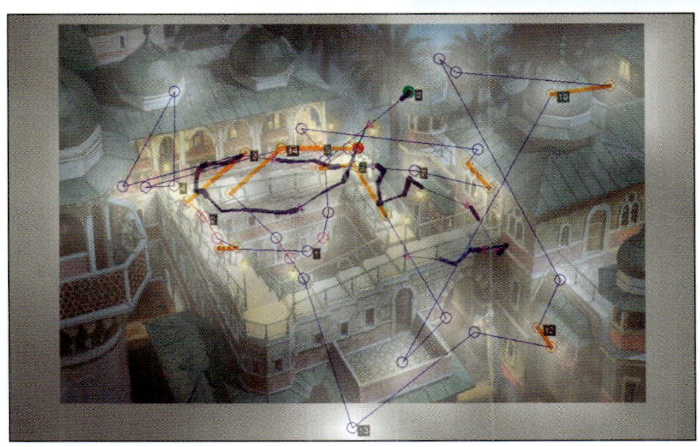

A heatmap for Scholar's Stairway. Interestingly, areas of the image where I had introduced a lot of detail failed to receive any eye time.

Interview

Rodney Matthews

"I encourage people to get on my wavelength a bit and, without being pretentious, travel to far-flung planets." Welcome to the world of **Rodney Matthews**

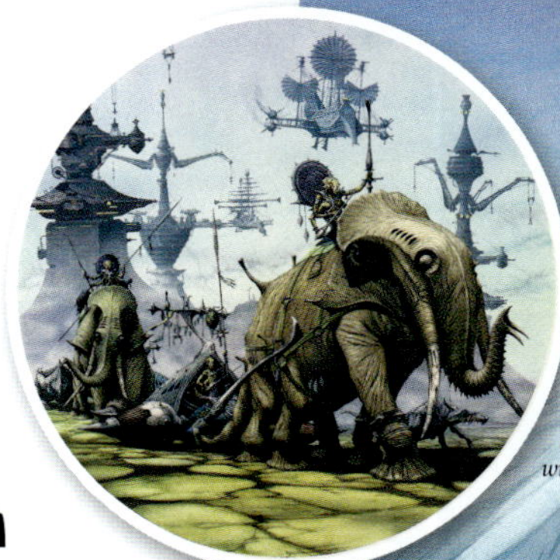

THE SACK OF ZODANGA
Depicting a famous scene from the writings of Edgar Rice Burroughs. Commissioned as part of a calendar based on the writings of fantasy authors.

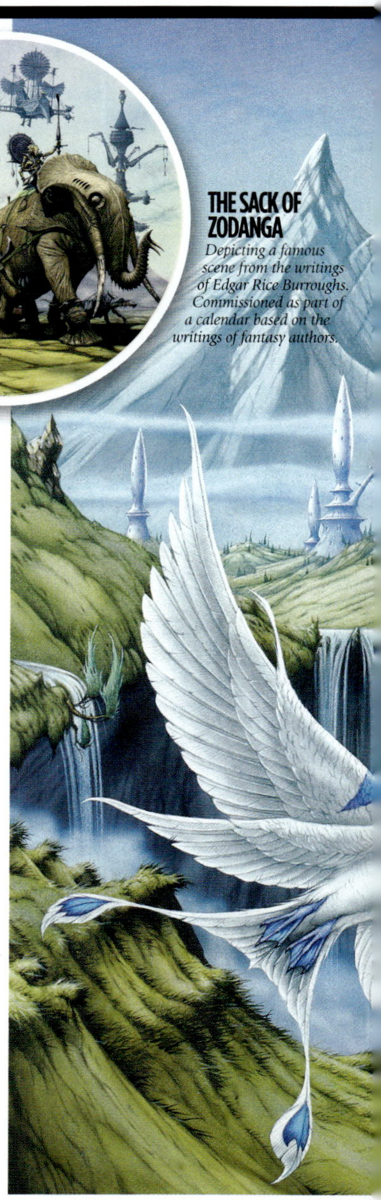

For more than 30 years Rodney Matthews has been one of fantasy art's defining figures. The style he characteristically downplays as "slightly organic, spiky stuff" has been used on countless book covers, record sleeves, posters and, in recent times, animation and video games. He maintains that his success is all down to fate: "Somewhere in the universe there's a stone pillar and chiselled on it is the legend, 'Matthews will be a fantasy artist'." Today, unflaggingly enthusiastic, Rodney is planning an assault on the world of animation.

SOMERSET BORN AND RAISED

Rodney was born in Somerset in 1945. A sensitive youngster, his parents encouraged his obvious artistic streak. Rodney recalls being a huge fan of cartoons, and of Disney in particular. "As a child I used to try and draw the characters," he says, "but I found after a while that I couldn't draw anything that was straightforward." Rodney seemed unable to draw simple copies; his creations struck a note of extremity. "I always liked to embellish," he explains, "which, I suppose, was the embryonic stage of being a fantasy artist."

As his education progressed, Rodney continued to work away at his fantastical side but, as ever, the practicalities of life came into play. "When I left school," says Rodney, "I thought, 'enough of this foolishness, I must earn a living'." This led to a job retouching photographic plates and film for a large Somerset print works: "A huge room of people lined up like slaves in a Roman galley." Suffice to say, Rodney didn't last.

LIGHT ENGINEERING

Still convinced he was destined for a life of hard graft, Rodney tried his hand in his father's workshop, which produced steel structures for the building trade. After six months, with his catalogue of injuries mounting up, Matthews senior, ever supportive, told his son: "You're not really suited to this industry. Why don't you go to art college?"

Rodney duly enrolled at Ealing to study design. This was where he discovered his love for rock music, played in numerous bands and in the process became a drummer of not inconsiderable talent. This, he kept up after leaving college and joining Bristol ad agency Ford's Creative, where he stayed for nine years.

Though Rodney readily admits he learned some important lessons at Ford's, it was clear he was being pulled in another direction. "I'd go off to play a gig at the weekend," he says, "then turn up at work on the Monday completely unwashed, and fall asleep at my desk."

His boss was surprisingly open-minded, but one day something happened to push Rodney out into the big wide world: "Someone came into the office carrying a portable commode and said 'Matthews, I want you to work on this' and I just thought, 'right, that's it'."

PLASTIC DOG

Eventually, Rodney settled into a loose partnership with another artist-musician, Terry Brace. The company, known as Plastic Dog, was based in Bristol and produced work for record labels such as MCA, Transatlantic and United Artists. It was during this phase that Rodney developed the distinctive style that his fantasy work is known for.

The record covers became increasingly fantastic and Rodney began to earn a reputation. "It took me a while to get into the style," he says. And, ever the pragmatist, Rodney sees the development of his 'spiky organic' style as a response to consumer demand, "That's what people seem to like best."

This all happened in the early '70s and, just as prog rock was really starting to go ballistic, Rodney was approached by Big O publishing and the poster years started. These were vintage Matthews. "In the seventies I lived from selling posters," he recalls with a wistful tone. "I sold millions." This was also the beginning of Rodney's fruitful collaboration with fantasy author Michael Moorcock.

Artist **PROFILE**

Rodney Matthews

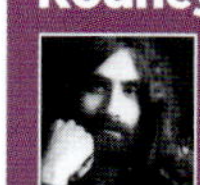

Born in Somerset, July 1945. Rodney Matthews has been a leading light of the fantasy art scene for more that 30 years. He's most famous for his work on album covers for the likes of Thin Lizzy and Asia. His vast body of illustration work has, in recent time, given way to animation and film projects, which he still pursues from his Welsh mountain hideout.
www.rodneymatthews.com

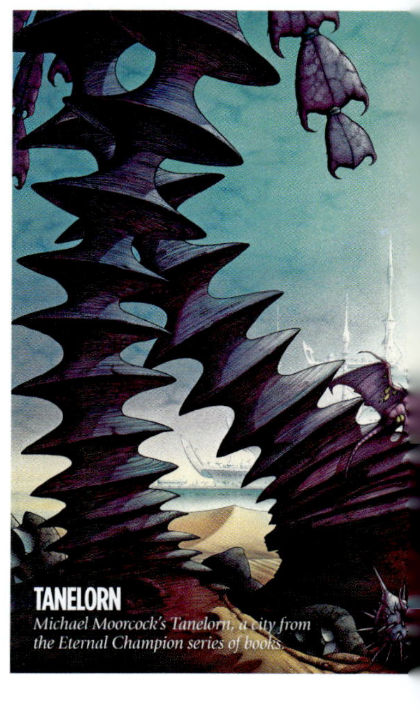

TANELORN
Michael Moorcock's Tanelorn, a city from the Eternal Champion series of books.

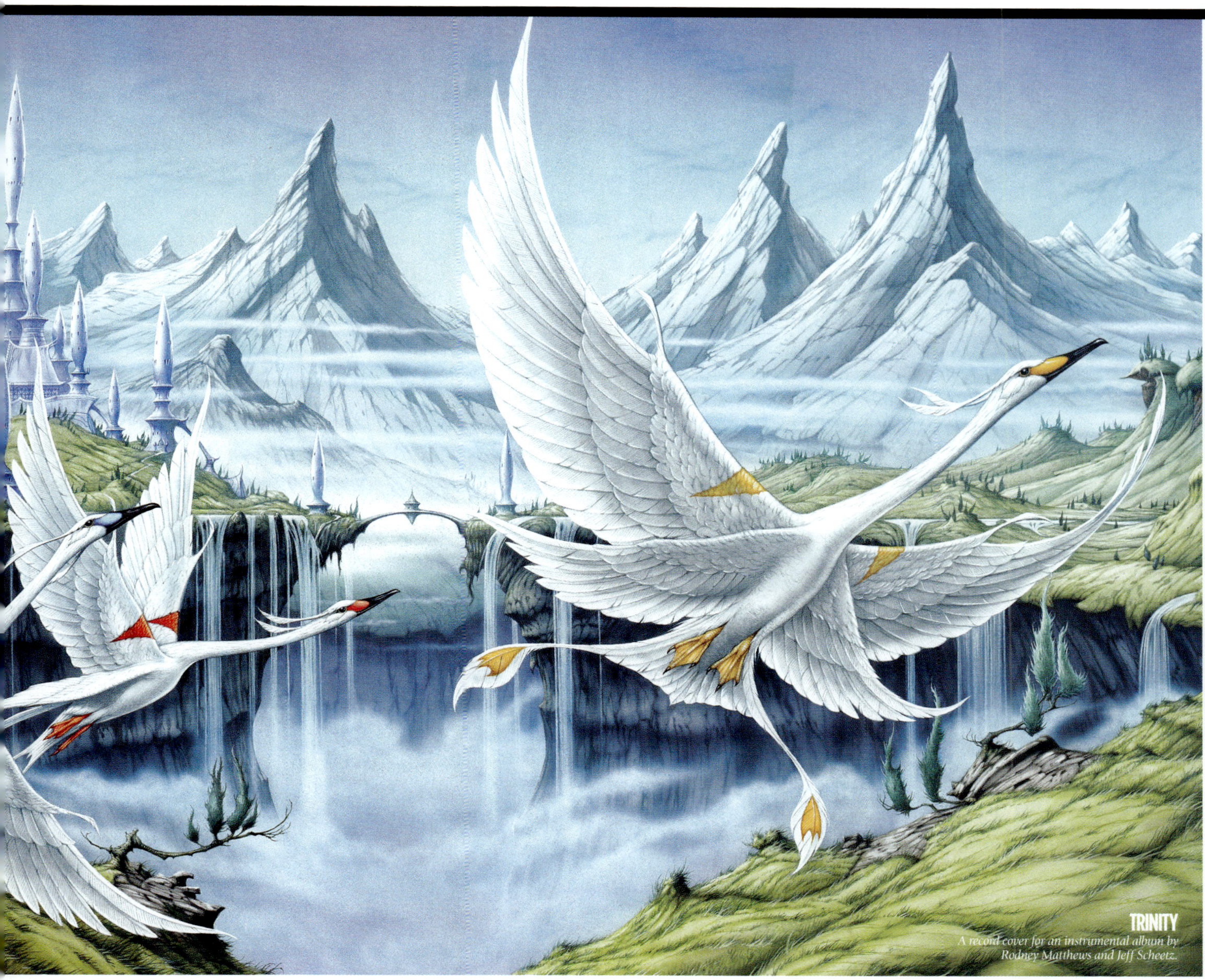

TRINITY
A record cover for an instrumental album by Rodney Matthews and Jeff Scheetz.

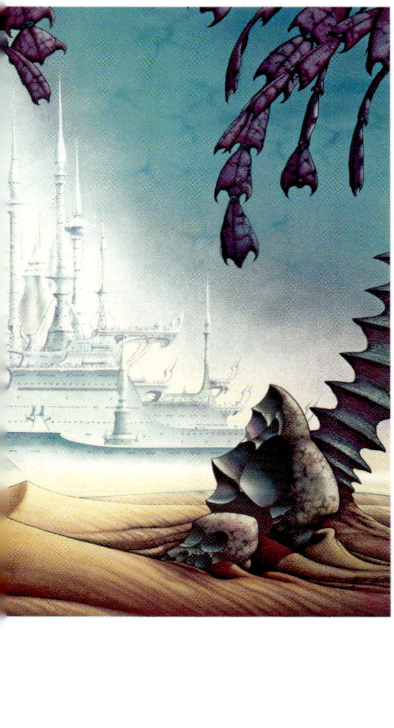

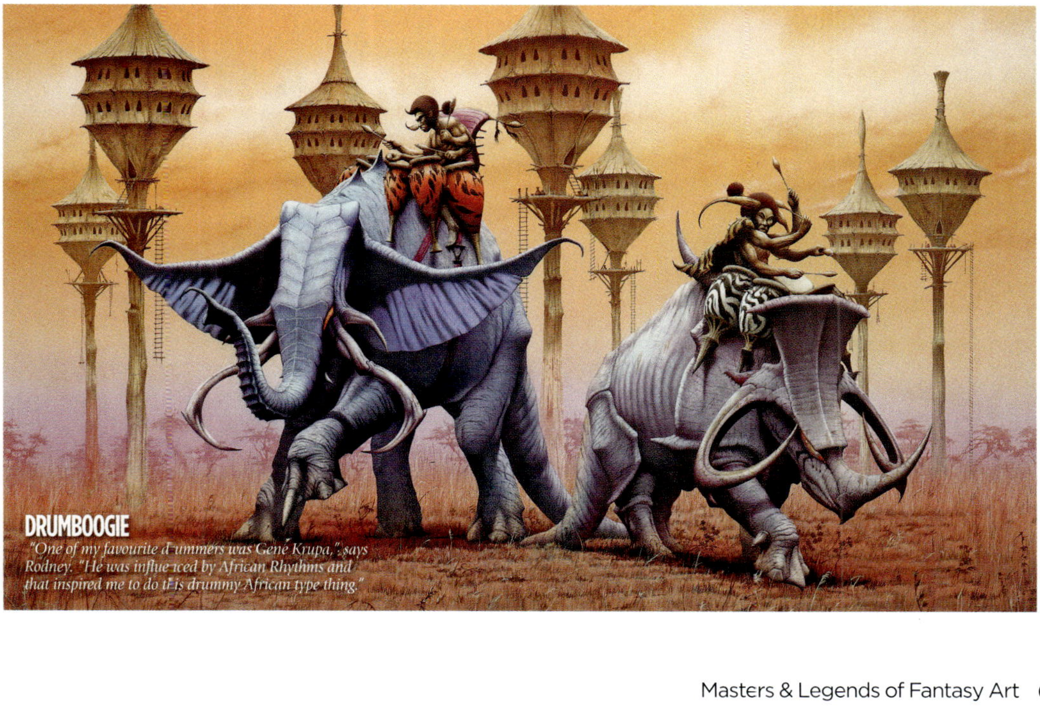

DRUMBOOGIE
"One of my favourite drummers was Gene Krupa," says Rodney. "He was influenced by African Rhythms and that inspired me to do this drummy African type thing."

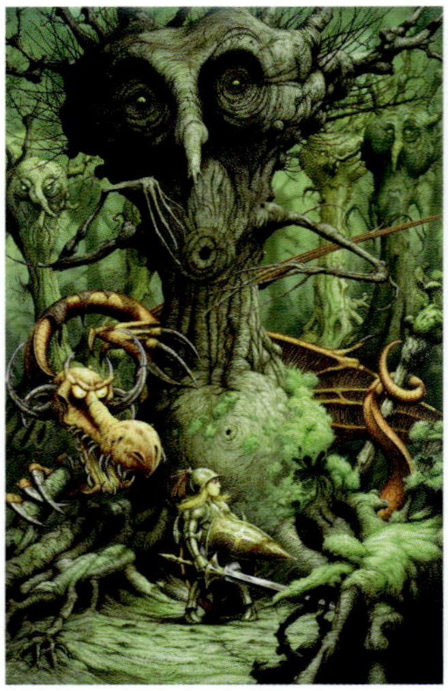

JABBERWOCKY
This was created for a poster based on the poem in Lewis Carol's Alice series.

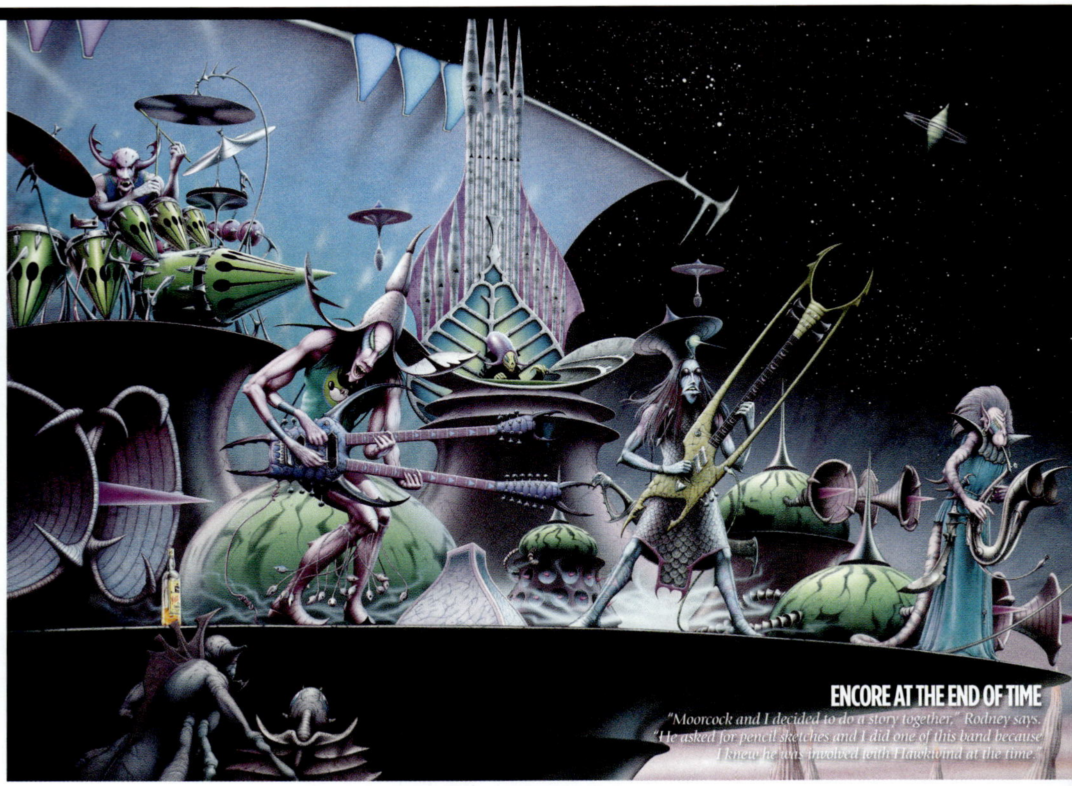

ENCORE AT THE END OF TIME
"Moorcock and I decided to do a story together," Rodney says. "He asked for pencil sketches and I did one of this band because I knew he was involved with Hawkwind at the time."

> **"I couldn't do anything that was straightforward. I always embellish, which I suppose is the embryonic stage of being a fantasy artist"**

From 1973 to 1980 Rodney produced more than 80 original poster designs and they sold around the world in their millions, but unfortunately the party wasn't going to last forever. "Everyone jumped on the bandwagon but the bandwagon couldn't sustain the weight. The whole thing collapsed in 1980." Rodney was genuinely grieved by the passing of this phase: "Almost overnight the whole thing fell apart."

PROG ROCK IMPLOSION

The bands that demanded Rodney's his work had become bloated and self-regarding and the quantity of poor imitations was increasing rapidly. Something had to give. The arrival of punk sealed the deal: "All of a sudden, my style was unfashionable."

What sustained Rodney throughout the '80s was the second wave of British heavy metal, "People such as Iron Maiden and Magnum." A decade of musical collaborations later and Rodney was still exploring that same consistently fantastical world. "What you've got to be asking yourself," he laughs, "is this: is there any one planet where all this stuff is going on?"

A NEW CHAPTER

"I was at a heavy metal event a bloke bought a load of my posters." It was 1992, he was from a video game company called Traveller's Tales. "He said they wanted me to design a logo for them." And so began Rodney's involvement with the digital world, a direction he's been pursuing with considerable vigour ever since.

The T T job led to more work, but this time Rodney collaborated with video game publisher Psygnosis where he helped to create its PlayStation game Shadow Master. "I went on to work on a couple of other games after that," says Rodney, "but the real bonus was getting involved with animation." The success of Lavender Castle, in 1998, produced by Gerry Anderson, gave Rodney the hunger for more.

Now Rodney's ultimate goal is to set up an animation studio and realise the numerous projects he has up his sleeve. "In an ideal world, if someone asked me what I want to do now it would be children's animation." Watch this space.

See the next page to learn to paint like Rodney Matthews

MATTHEWS AND MOORCOCK

A creative partnership bearing strange fruit

When Michael and Rodney got together, it was only a matter of time before something great was produced. That something was the illustrated fantasy classic, Elric at the End of Time.

Against his expectations, ("I thought he was going to be very intimidating, but he was a nice bloke actually"), Rodney became fast friends with Michael Moorcock and the two decided to work together. "He asked me if I could give him images, sketches that he could write into his story." So Rodney duly supplied his own brand of narcotic visions and Moorcock wrote the tale. One hundred and twenty pages later, Elric at the End of Time was born.

"This was when Moorcock was involved with the band Hawkwind," says Rodney. "He read his bizarre poetry on stage with them." Aware of the Hawkwind connection, Rodney decided to include the band among his images for the book. The result, Encore at the End of Time, has a strangeness, which is hard to top, and consequently one that is just now being rediscovered. "I've had people asking for it again lately," says Rodney. "Everything seems to be coming full circle."

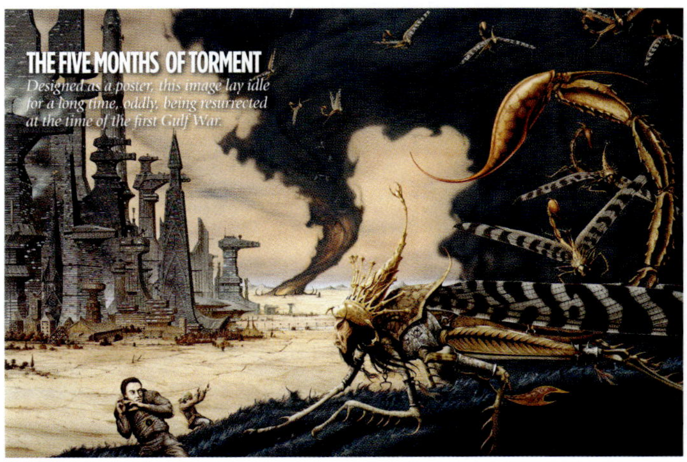

THE FIVE MONTHS OF TORMENT
Designed as a poster, this image lay idle for a long time, oddly, being resurrected at the time of the first Gulf War.

Traditional Skills

TELL A STORY

Legendary fantasy artist **Rodney Matthews** demonstrates how to create a painting that conveys a convincing story...

Even a simple fantasy illustration such as this one: Embarkation, needs to be properly considered before you even begin sketching.

Once you've visualised your idea, make bold thumbnail sketches on a tracing pad. Focus on the overall layout before concerning yourself with the detail.

When you're satisfied and know what ingredients will be included, you can work on a finished sketch.

Keep it simple. My image has just two points of focus: foreground (the child on the horse) and mid-distance.

You're now ready to paint. Use colour to convey a particular mood. Embarkation is gentle, optimistic; using key colours yellow and purple. Use blues to indicate distance to landscapes and red for energy. Don't throw in all you colours, this could dissipate focus and reduce impact.

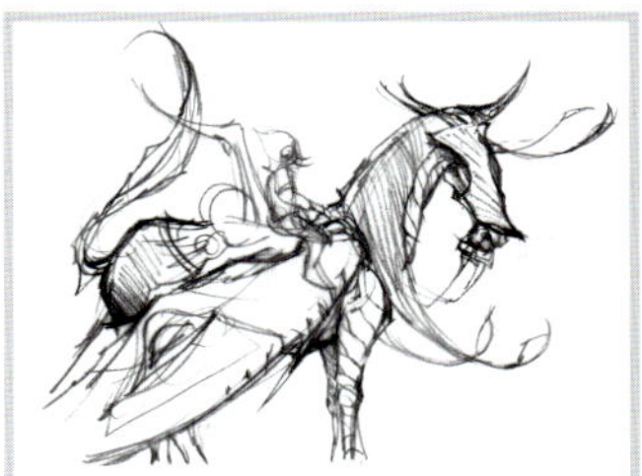

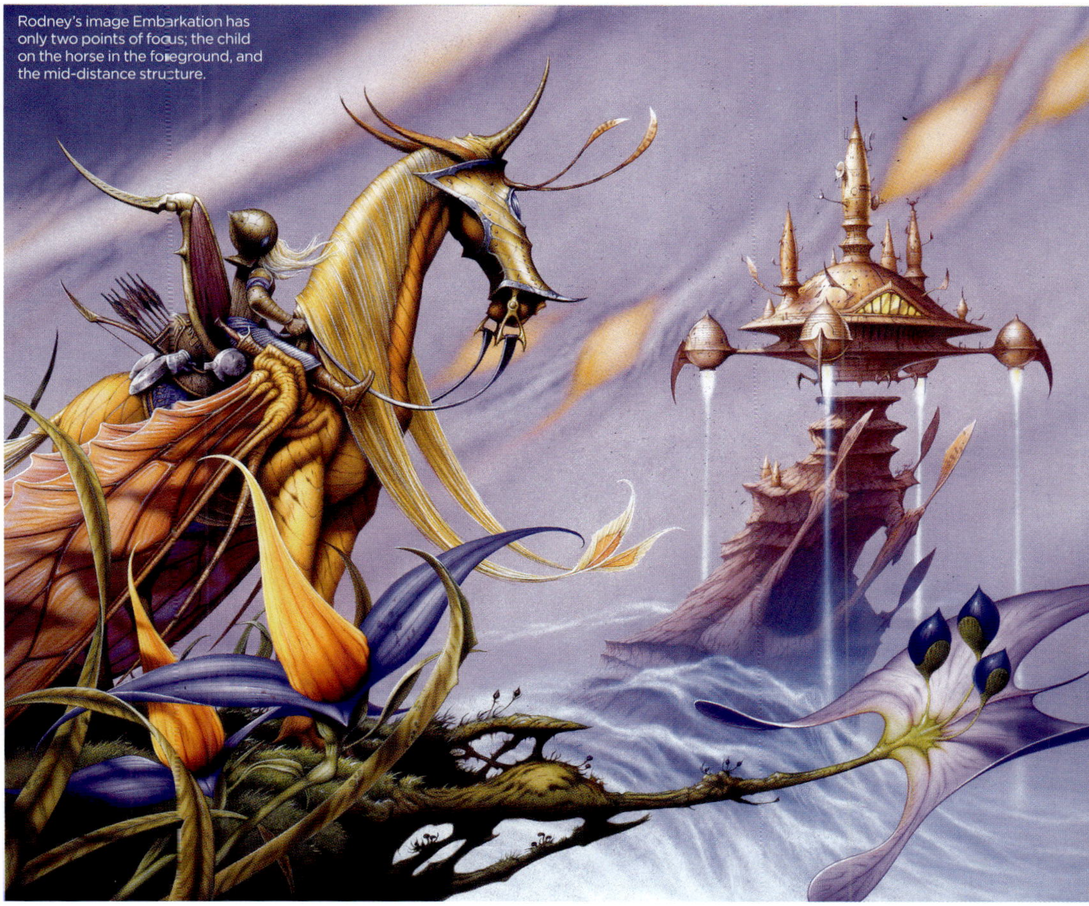

Rodney's image Embarkation has only two points of focus; the child on the horse in the foreground, and the mid-distance structure.

STEP-BY-STEP: Telling a fantasy story with your painting

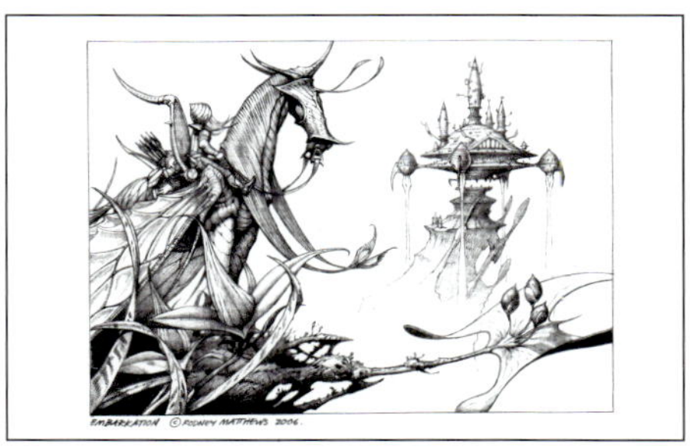

1 I start to scribble away at thumbnail sketches. I usually do up to six thumbnails. One of these will always shine out above the others because it's comfortable on the eye. You can't commence on your finished piece of work before you've sorted out the foundations – just like when building a house. Here's my finished sketch.

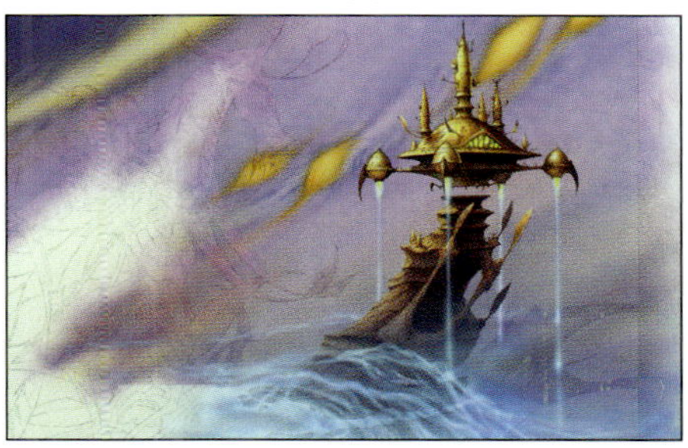

2 Having completed the pencil drawing to your satisfaction, trace it down to an art board and begin your colour work, masking for the airbrush area. Starting with the background, work forwards using airbrush for such things as skies and mists. The latter will help to give distance to remote objects within your painting.

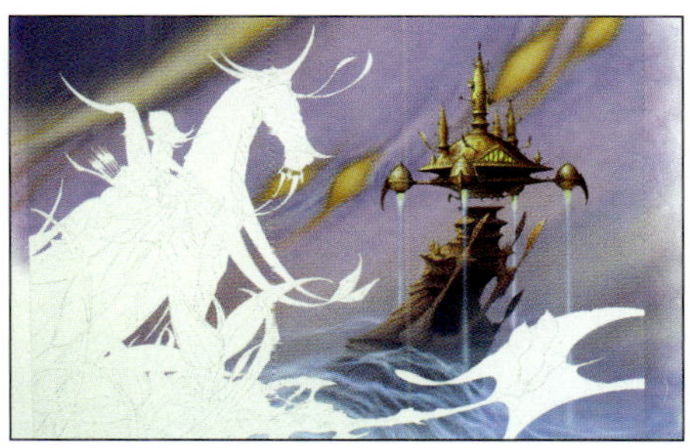

3 Use stronger colours and shadows for foreground features, remembering to establish your light source and direction. Study flora and fauna. The best fantasy has some factual elements that make it believable. You can now start on your main foreground character, remembering again to establish the direction of your light source.

Interview

Chris Foss

Chris Foss changed the future, drawing what didn't exist when film companies were feeling their way into sci-fi...

It's hard to overstate the influence Chris has had on our collective vision of the future. If you have any classic SF books, chances are you have classic Foss. If you're not big on print, you'll know his film work. Familiar with Alien or Superman?

Until he arrived on the scene, the future was a needle sharp, sleek-looking place that got less and less human. Chris introduced us to a human future, where spaceships were "rumbling bumbling bangy things with bits of metal hanging off." People responded with wide-eyed recognition.

FALSE START

"All I ever wanted to do was be an artist," Chris recalls. Like parents the world over, the Fosses were sceptical about the value of an art school education. "They fought me tooth and nail," recalls Chris. "Their argument was that once I had a degree, I could go and do my art stuff." He adds: "My parents were struggling school teachers. Then mum accidentally bought a Picasso in a draper's shop. She was terrific at rooting and ferreting."

The pressure was too much for young Chris, and just as the 60s started swinging he ended up in Cambridge studying architecture. This was a mistake though: "I went to two lectures in two years and by the end of the second year I was drawing cartoon strips for Penthouse."

ROOM WITH A VIEW

You see, Chris has more than one feather to his cap. "My first break was with erotic artwork," he says. "Because that's what they wanted at Bob Guccione's new magazine, Penthouse." And strangely, once you know of this 'other side' you can see that it somehow suffuses the SF images too.

It also explains something of the magic behind Chris's peculiar vision of the future: "For me a giant spaceship would have topless female stokers shovelling in nuclear nuts," laughs Chris. "Whereas for other people it was the Z-drive."

Artist PROFILE

Chris Foss

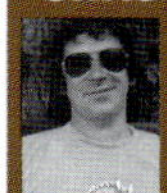

Chris set the world of science fiction alight with his covers for greats such as Harry Harrison, Philip K Dick and Isaac Asimov. Following success in print he moved to the silver screen with concept work for classics movies such as Superman and Alien.

www.chrisfoss.net

An intimate familiarity with the human shape, not just as an object but as a sexual form produces an organic way of seeing the world. Chris makes no attempt to imagine himself as a robot or an AI. "I'm perfectly aware that technology advances in leaps and bounds," he points out. "I'm just amiably waiting on the side lines for the most usable bits of technology."

OLD JUMBO JETS

Chris has produced covers for just about every classic SF author – Philip K Dick, Heinlein, and he was the Asimov man for a long time. Of the 1970s, Chris recalls: "JG Ballard too. I did a lot of his covers."

An editor at Penthouse guided Chris to recruit an agent, as he was being limited by the work he was getting on the magazine. "The first big job I got was for the Sunday Times, illustrating an article by Stan Kubrick on ESP (Extra Sensory Perception)."

Chris's unique skills was that he didn't need a photo reference; "The guy I went to see at Pan books was overjoyed. He said: 'Thank God, I can finally have spaceships!'" This ushered in a golden era: "The publishers were all located in and around Soho, we used to drink in a lovely little pub on Poland Street with the various art directors."

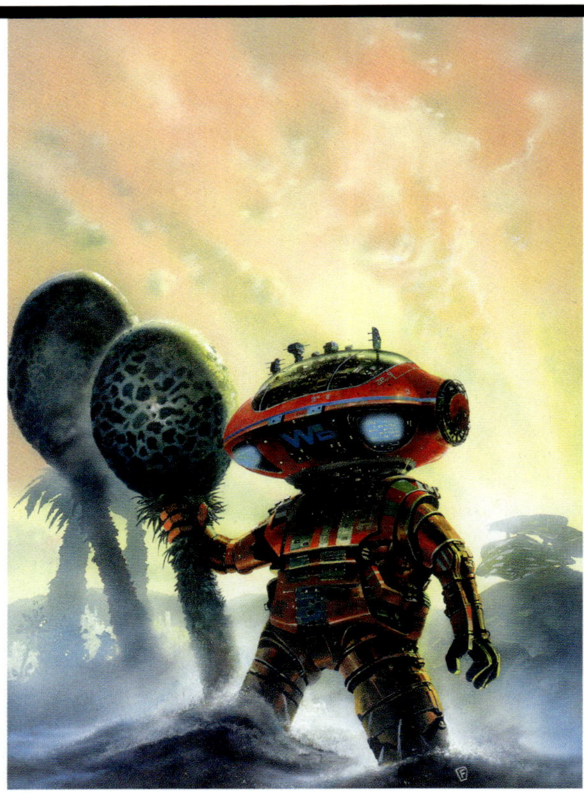

ROBOTS OF DAWN
Highlighting Chris's deft ability with character, this little chap looks as if he could turn nasty if he doesn't get his own way.

RAILRUNNER
From the elusive Chris Foss Portfolio, perhaps an example of the technology Chris is "waiting amiably for the world to develop."

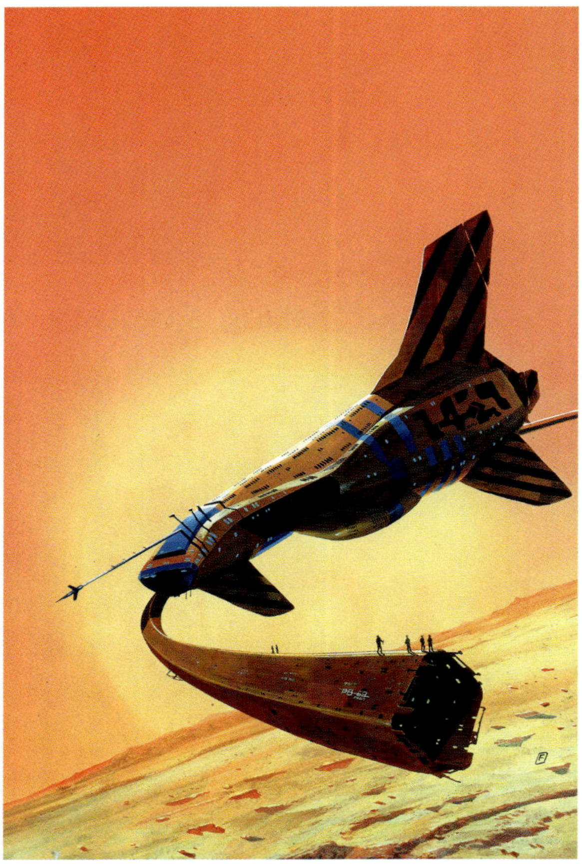

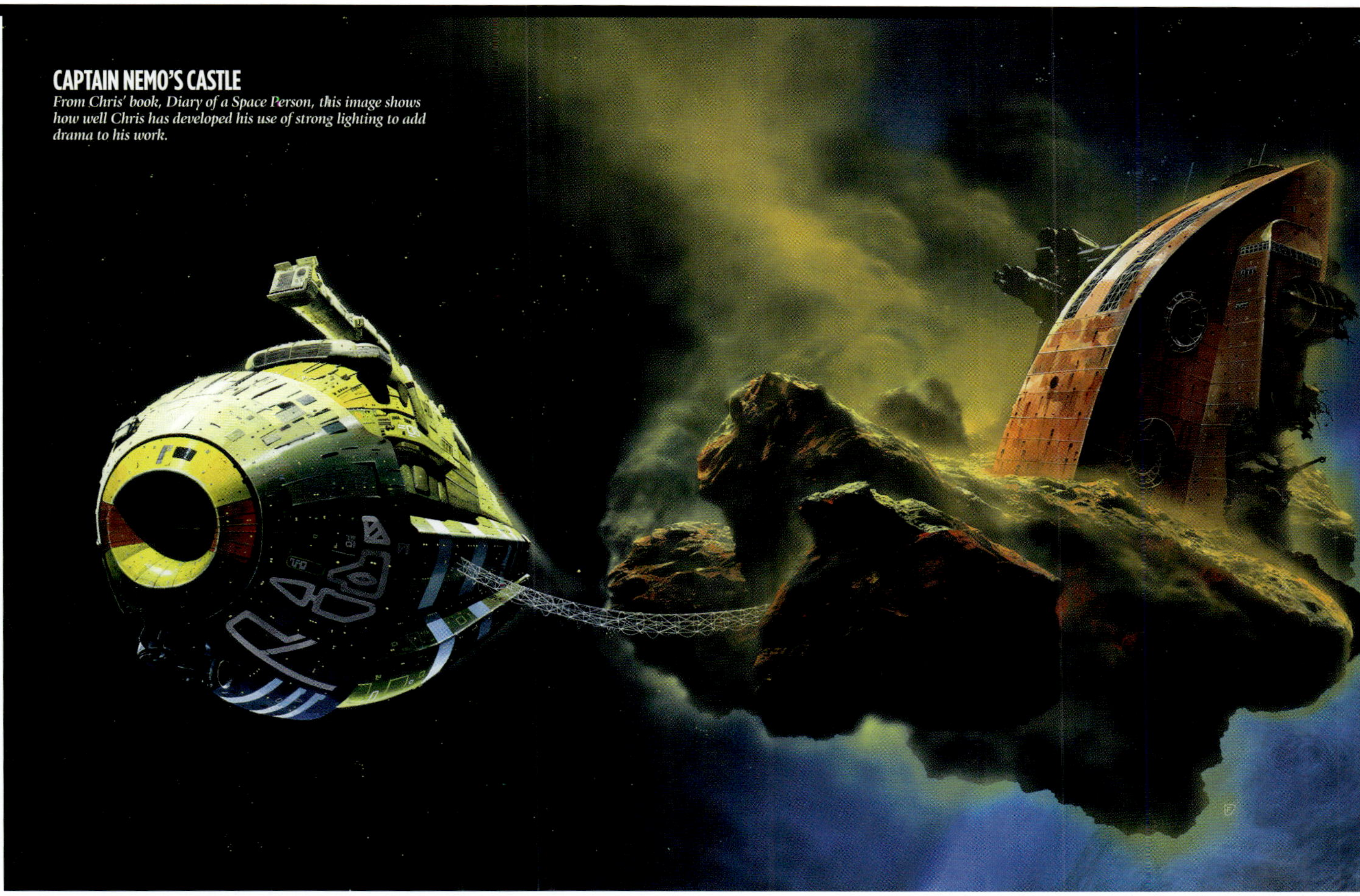

CAPTAIN NEMO'S CASTLE
From Chris' book, Diary of a Space Person, this image shows how well Chris has developed his use of strong lighting to add drama to his work.

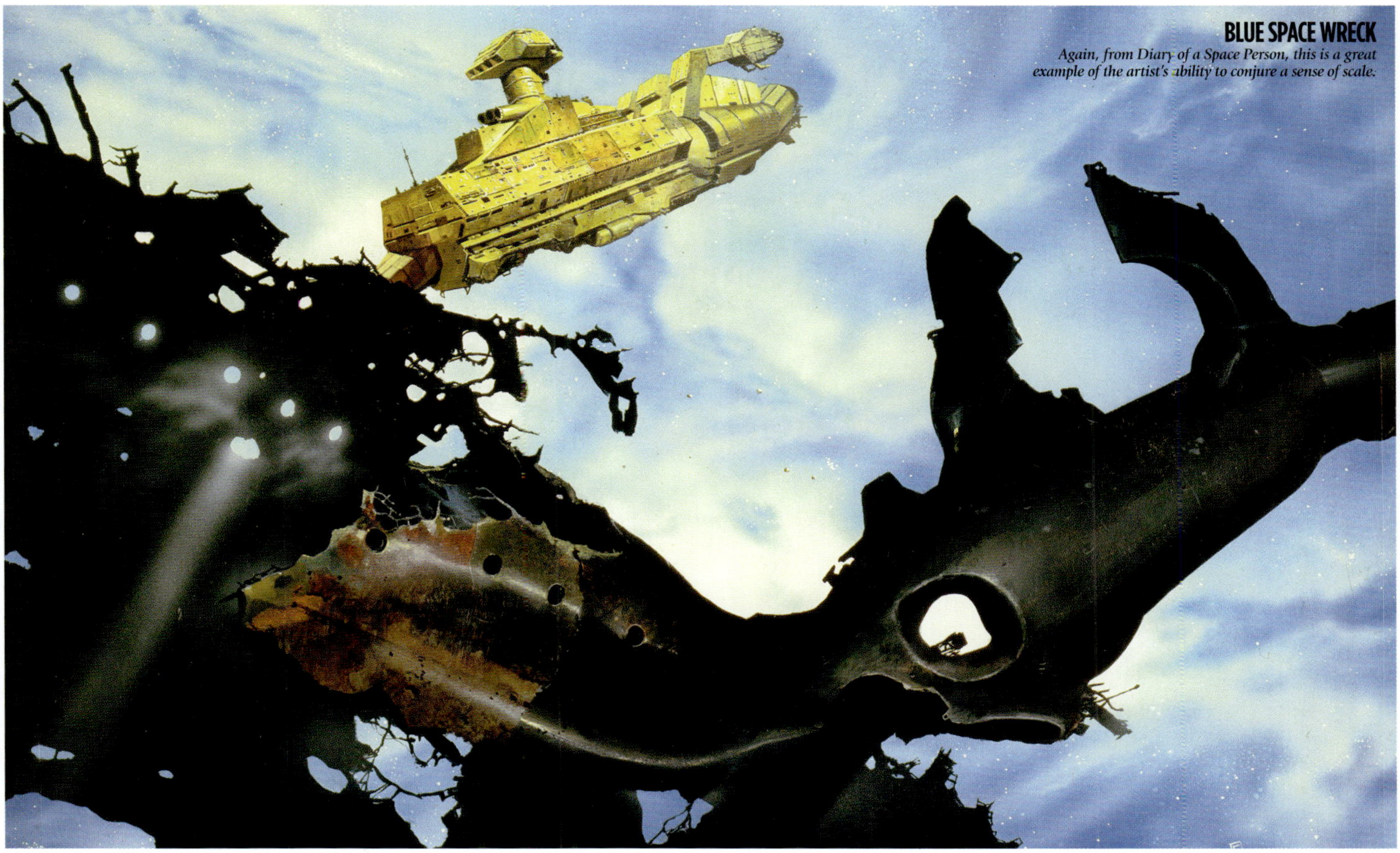

BLUE SPACE WRECK
Again, from Diary of a Space Person, this is a great example of the artist's ability to conjure a sense of scale.

FROM DUNE TO ALIEN

Chris began drawing for Penthouse while still at university, he became the cover artist to the SF aristocracy, so what next? "They were casting about for an artist to illustrate this book by Alex Comfort." So Chris drew the illustrations for The Joy of Sex.

Exciting as that was, it was not the zenith. "That began when I started on Dune with Alejandro Jodorowsky." This maverick genius had bought the rights to Frank Herbert's masterpiece novel and convinced French industrialist to make it.

"Somewhere out there is this huge book with the entire storyboard in it," Chris muses. When Dune was canned by shortsighted Hollywood execs, Chris didn't miss a beat; he had already been commissioned to do the artwork for another classic character: Superman.

While Chris was still on a high from his work on the caped crusader, Jodorowsky pulled a rabbit out of his hat: "The work we did for Dune ended up as the basis for Alien." Mr Foss, take a bow, your place in history is assured.

A prolific artist, Chris has a new book out in June this year, he continues to expand his universe in many directions while attempting to marry the two threads of his work – erotic and futuristic. "People like me are the filters," he ponders. "We take in everything around us and out the other end come these images."

Turn the page to learn to paint like Chris Foss

ALIEN

Chris Foss's evocative space scenes and craft soon caught the eye of film directors looking for inspiration. In 1975 Chris was hired to work on a film version of Dune, and though the film was never made it became the platform for more work. The following year Chris was commissioned to create spaceship designs for the film Alien, under the name Leviathan. Though they never made it to the screen, they still influenced the movie.

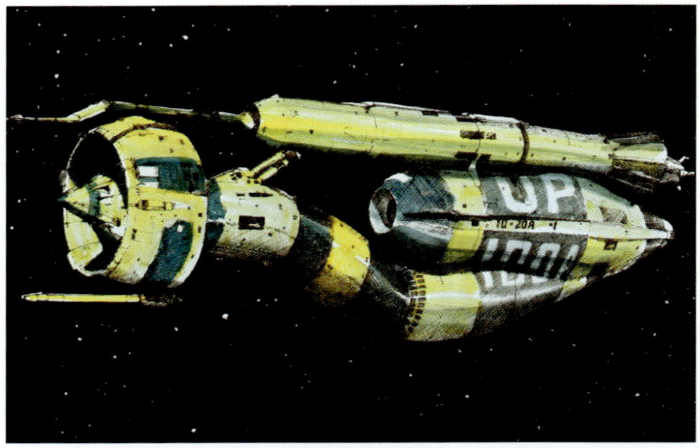

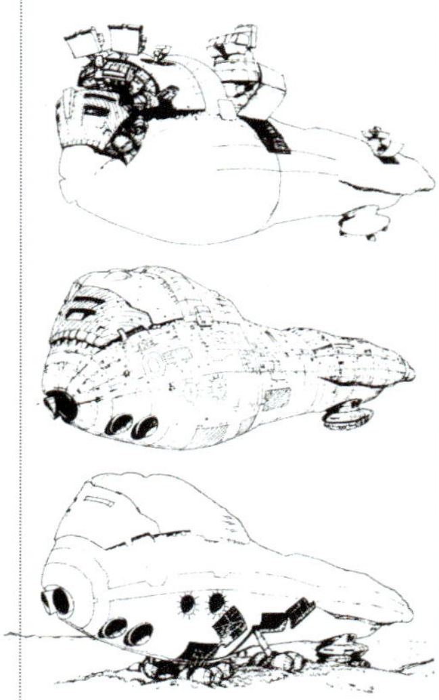

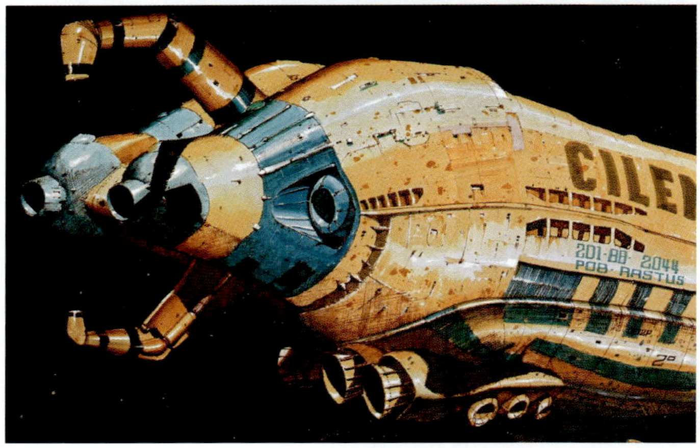

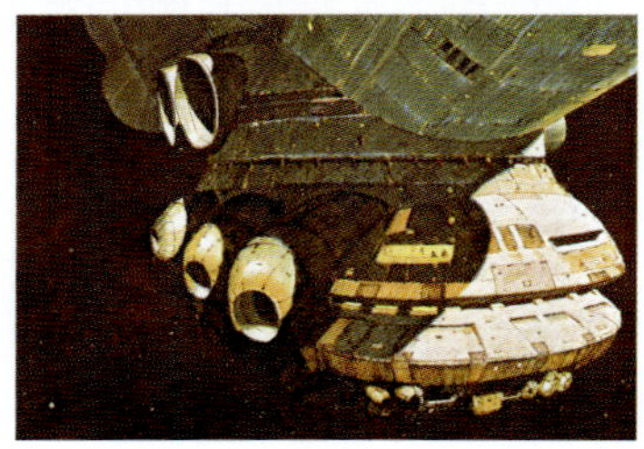

"The first big job I got was for the Sunday Times, illustrating an article by Stan Kubrick on ESP"

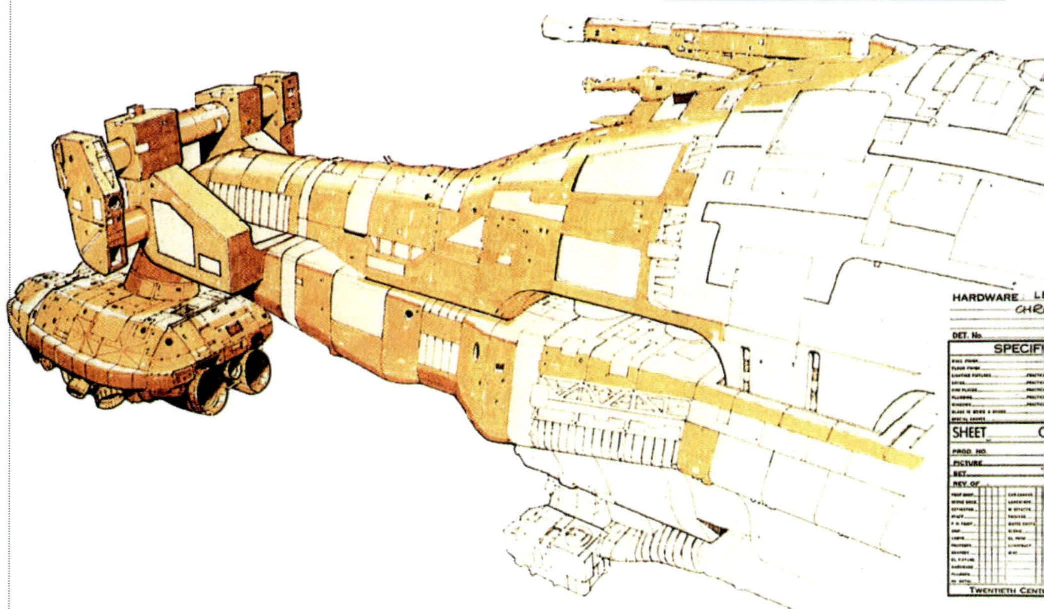

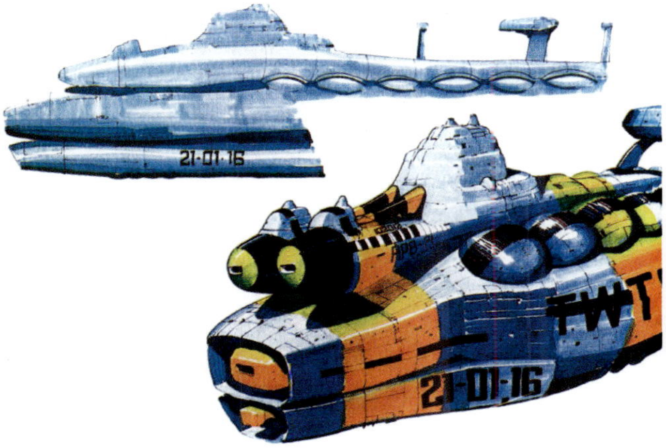
21-01-16
21-01-16

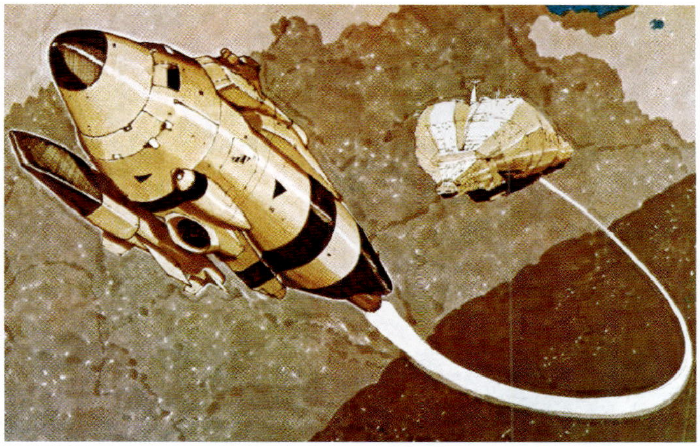

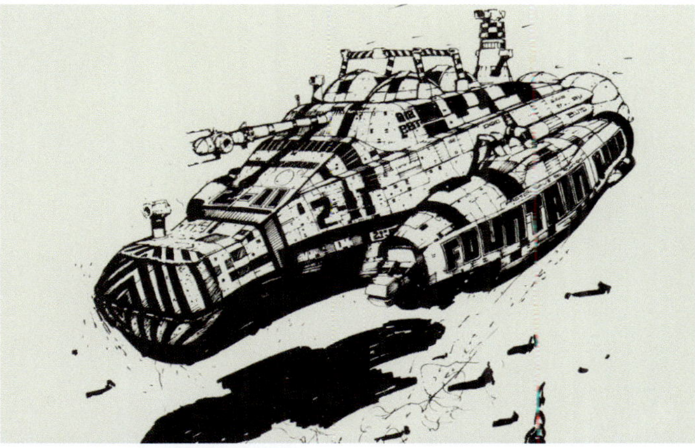

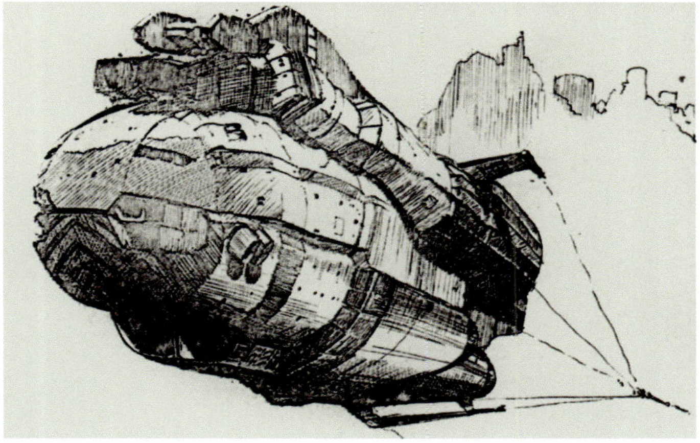

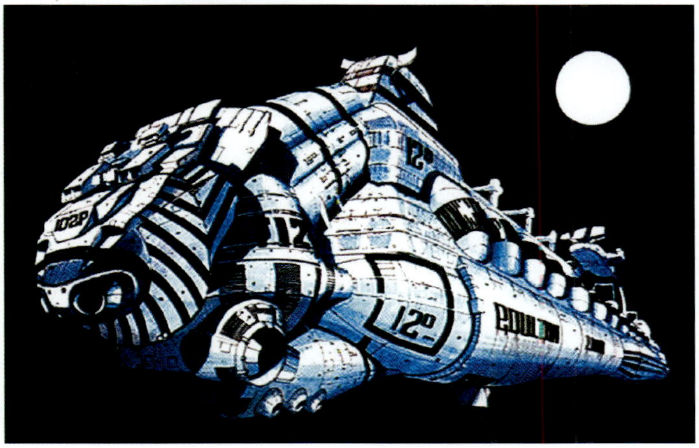

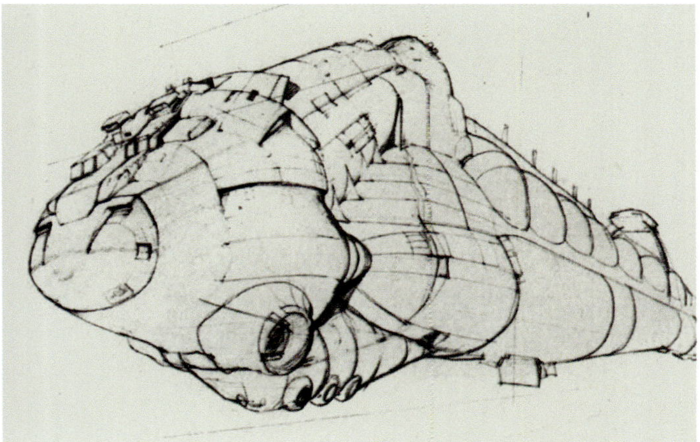

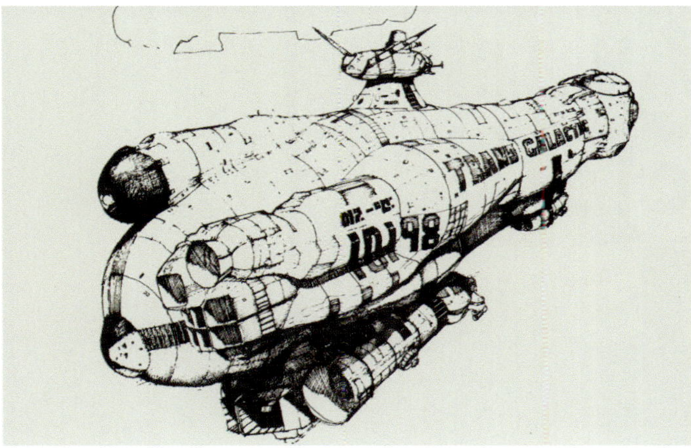

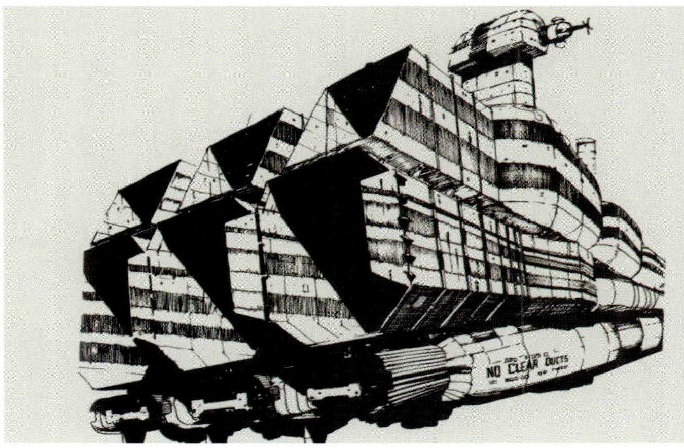
NO CLEAR DUCTS

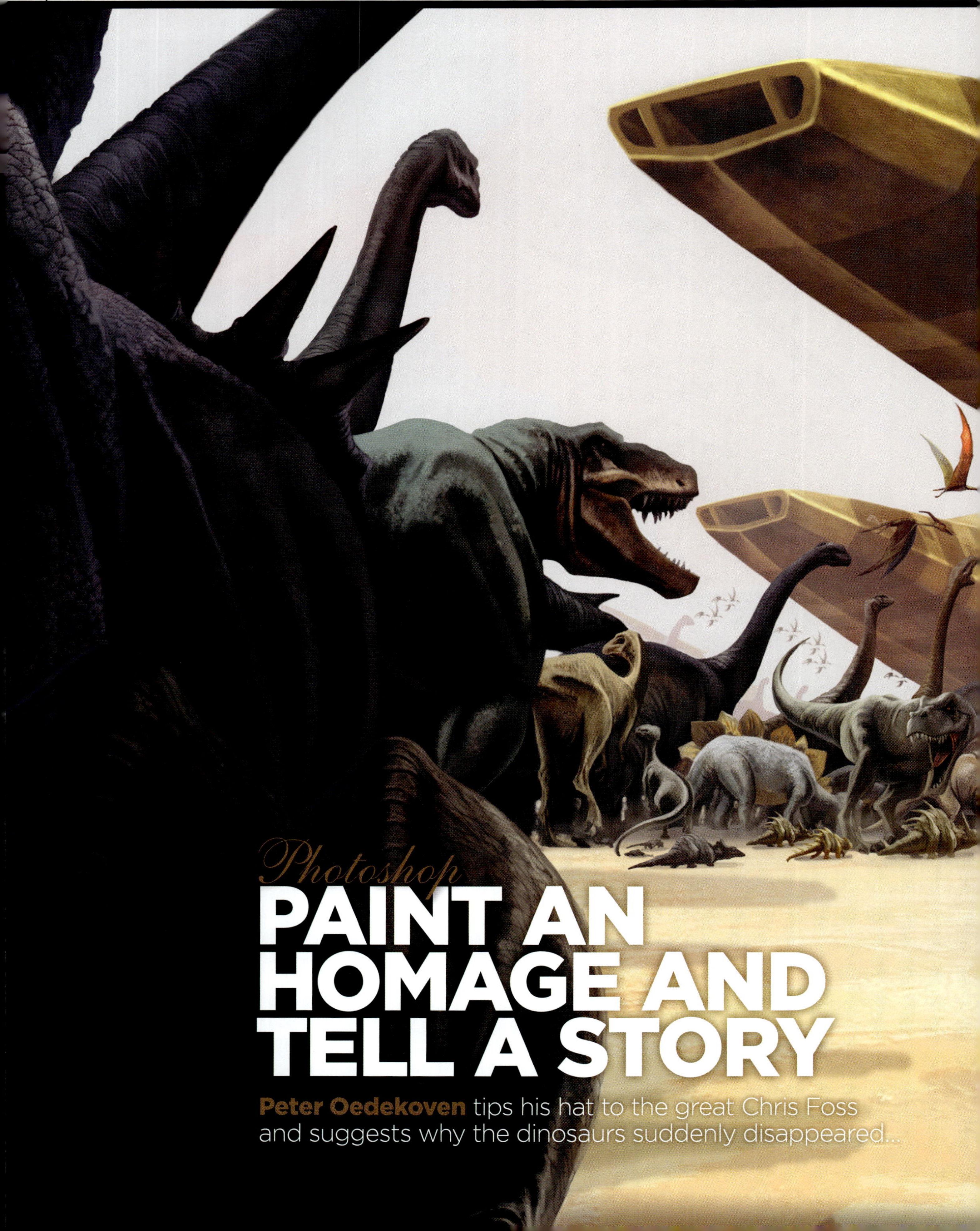

Photoshop

PAINT AN HOMAGE AND TELL A STORY

Peter Oedekoven tips his hat to the great Chris Foss and suggests why the dinosaurs suddenly disappeared...

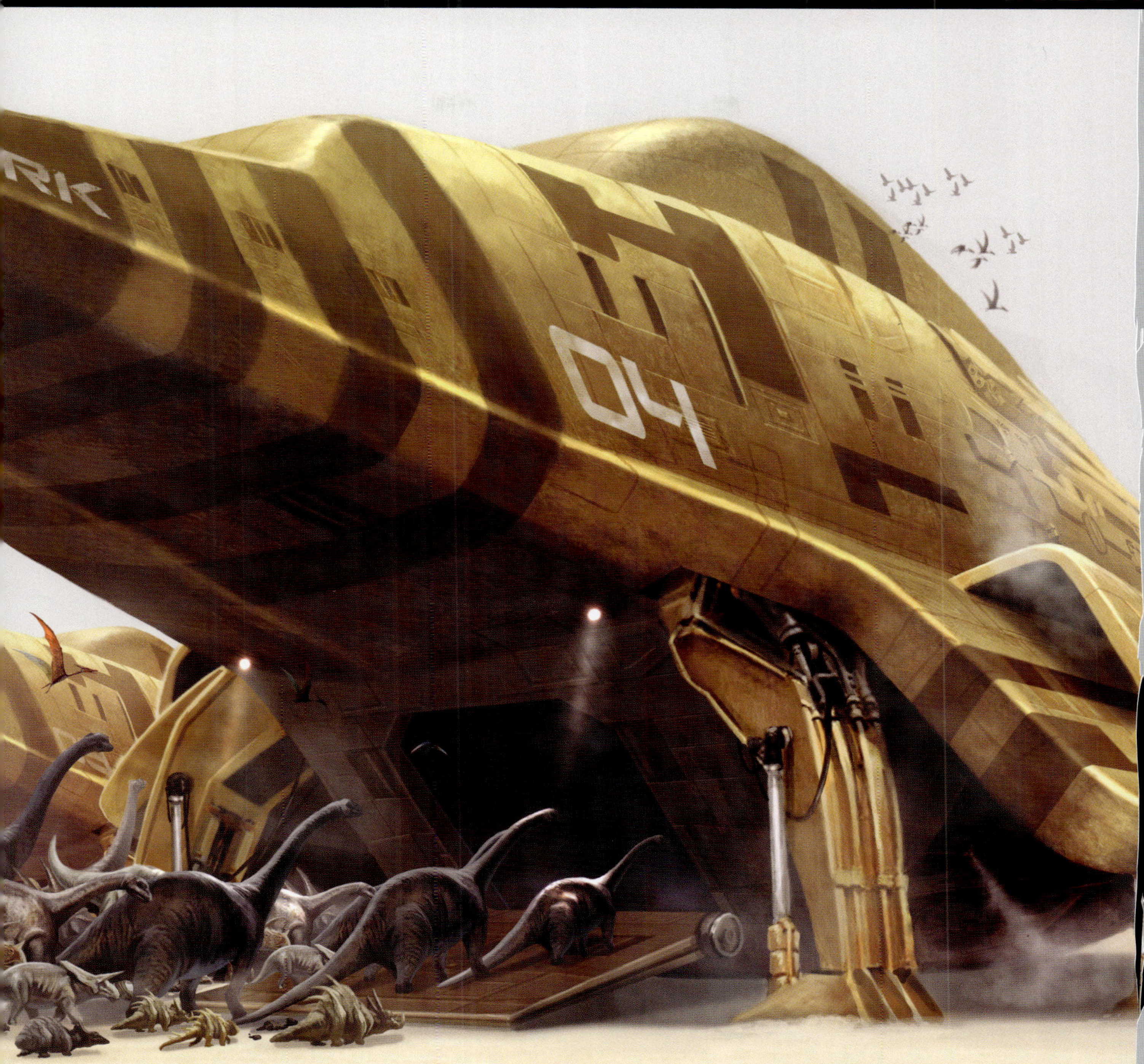

The first thing you create isn't on paper or on your computer screen, but in your head. It's the idea. There's no point spending an hour, a day or even a week perfecting an image when it doesn't grab the viewer's imagination. You can paint the most detailed environment, the most skillfully rendered creature, but if it's unable to tell a story or convey an idea then you'll have wasted your time.

Of course, to put your idea either down on paper or up on the screen, you must be able to visualise it. That's why the most essential tool – beside your software – is your drawing skill. You need to be able to draw to transform your idea into something of value. The drawing is the foundation upon which your finished piece of work will be based. No doubt there'll be lots of changes made during the process of painting, but in the end you'll create something that you're happy with, and will inspire the imagination of the viewer.

For this homage to Chris Foss I don't want to paint just a standalone "Foss-like" spaceship, but instead integrate it into a complete scene. In this workshop you probably won't find the best way to do such a task. It's just the way I paint, and should be taken as an example that with every image you create, you'll be confronted with fresh challenges, which in turn require new solutions. Remember that mistakes can help you to become a better artist. There's that old adage: learning by doing. Learning doesn't happen from the failure itself, but rather from analysing the failure, making a change and then trying again…

1 The idea

As I said in the intro, for me painting's all about telling a story. So the assignment of presenting an homage to Chris Foss narrows it down to sci-fi and spaceships. After some brainstorming and doodling I come up with a few ideas. The strongest one, for me, is of the alien spaceship that's arrived to evacuate the dinosaurs before a catastrophe befalls the Earth.

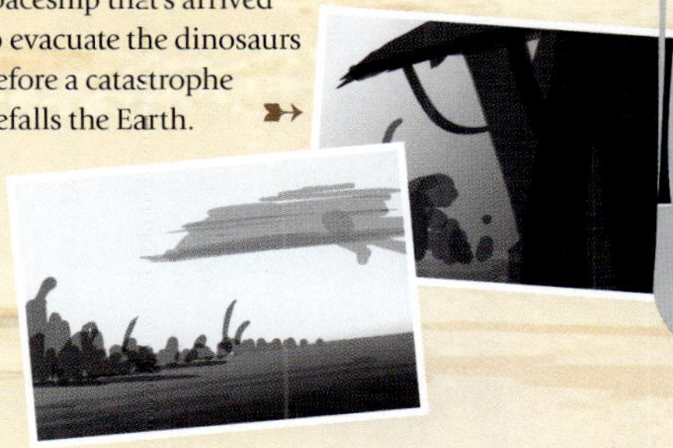

PRO SECRETS

Mood swing

Once you've finished your illustration and you want to change the whole mood, simply duplicate the layer and play with your colour channels. By erasing the top layer with a soft brush and low flow you can achieve soft colour gradients. You also can change your highlights this way.

2 Sketching the idea

Once the idea has been approved, I start sketching. For this I use a small canvas and a squashed round brush to block in my basic shapes. I use a grey colour palette to see how I can achieve the most readable layout. This is one of the most important stages, because once you decide which layout works best, your entire colour and lighting scheme will be based on it. I decide to use this layout, because it has the strongest readability and leads the eye through the picture very well. There's also a nice balance to it.

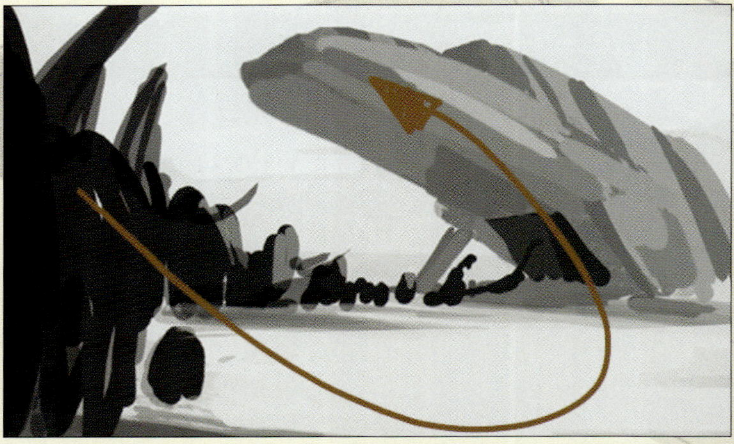

3 Creating the colour palette

Now that I've decided on my layout, it's time to introduce colour. I always search online for colour inspiration and in this case it was a collection of holiday photos, where a misty atmosphere provides depth and a desert-like mood. I pick some of the colours I want in my illustration by using the Eyedropper tool to create my own palette. I use these colours to turn my greyscale layout scribble into a colour guide.

4 Adding detail to the drawing

Now comes the part in which I make a more detailed image to work from. With my chosen layout in mind, I go back to the drawing board (or should I say, the Wacom tablet!) and make a line drawing of the illustration. Because I don't have a great knowledge of dinosaurs, I once again search online for some reference imagery. After I'm done with the drawing, I create a new layer underneath it and set the mode to Multiply. This enables me to block the colours in without erasing my line art.

Shortcuts

Select colour

Alt (PC & Mac)

This enables you to pick colours in your image, without having to select the Eyedropper tool first.

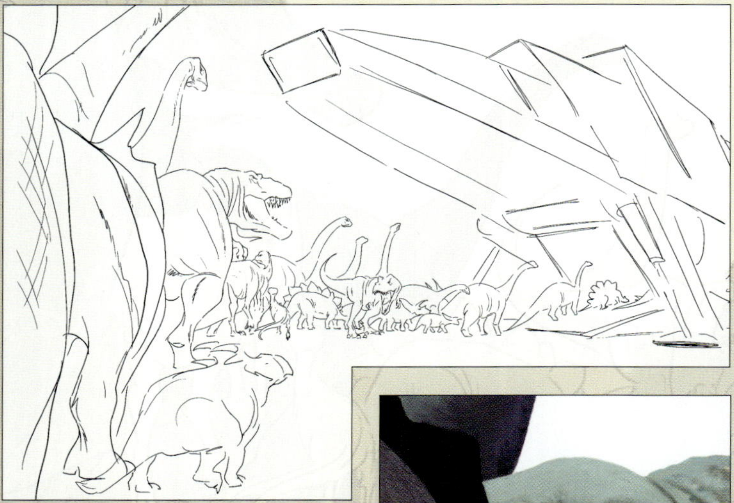

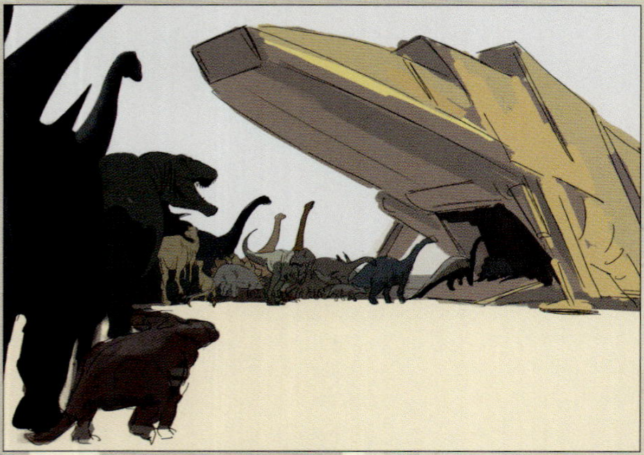

5 Blocking in the colours

With my colour sketch and my palette within easy reach I begin to block the basic colours underneath my line art. I use a thick brush for this. Naturally, the smaller the details in my drawing become, the finer my brush needs to be.

6 Texturing the dinosaurs

All my colours are now roughly in place, so I can now start to refine my dinosaurs. This is the most time-consuming part, due to the large amount of beasts I've decided to introduce in the scene. To achieve a realistic skin texture I vary my brushes in strength, size and form, and avoid using sharp-edged brushes. For the leathery skin I use a customised Photoshop brush, which you'll find on the DVD. During this step I regularly zoom out of the image to check that it's still readable. A good layout should be recognisable even if it's the size of a postage stamp.

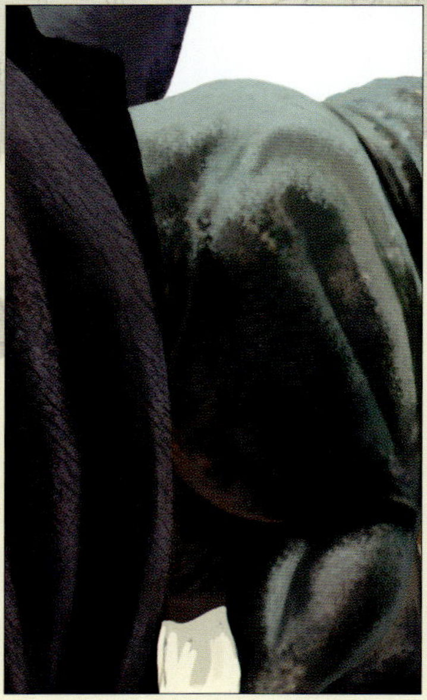

7 Real-world textures

I need some animal textures for my dinosaurs: crocodile and elephant skin seem to fit the bill. I drag the texture sample on top of my illustration and by changing the channel layer to Soft Light I blend the texture in, taking care not to change the colour tone. I use a soft Eraser to remove any sharp edges. Yes, it would have been easier to work from the background to the foreground, but it's just a mistake that needs to be dealt with now, and learnt from for future projects.

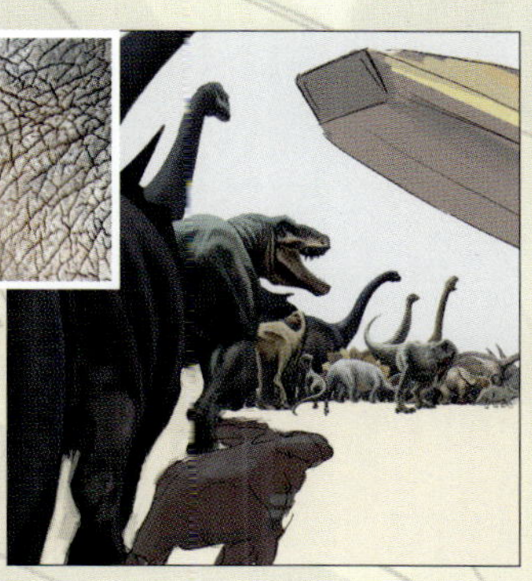

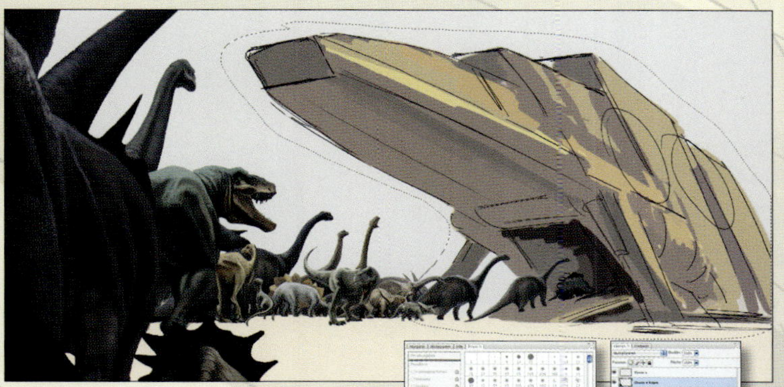

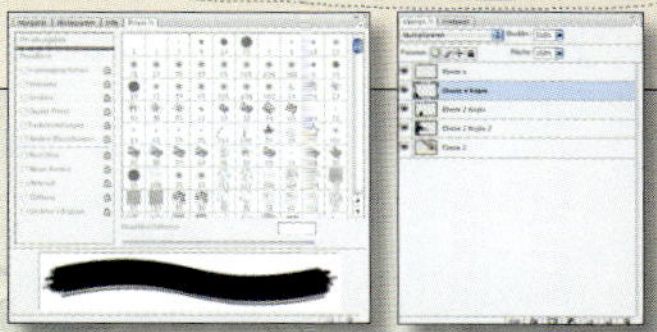

8 Making environment adjustments

After finishing the last dinosaur, I have a chance to fix my earlier mistake. I use the Lasso tool to separate my dinosaur layer from the background, making it easier for me to work on the different parts of the illustration. I have a relatively busy foreground so I keep the sky and ground very simple. It's tempting to put more detail into your image, but remember that it has to be clear enough to lead the eye of your viewer.

9 Tackling the Ark

Looking at the illustration, I'm not happy with the shape of the ship and so I start to adjust its form while I colour the exterior. I employ a brush with blunt edges to give it a more lived-in feel; some rusty metal textures come in useful here. I find an interesting excavator arm for the legs of the ship – I think this works really well. I paint over the photo so that it fits in with the rest of the ship, not only in colour value but also in shape.

10 Taking time off

It's time to have a break and freshen up my point of view. After staring at the same image, it becomes more difficult to focus and see the whole picture.

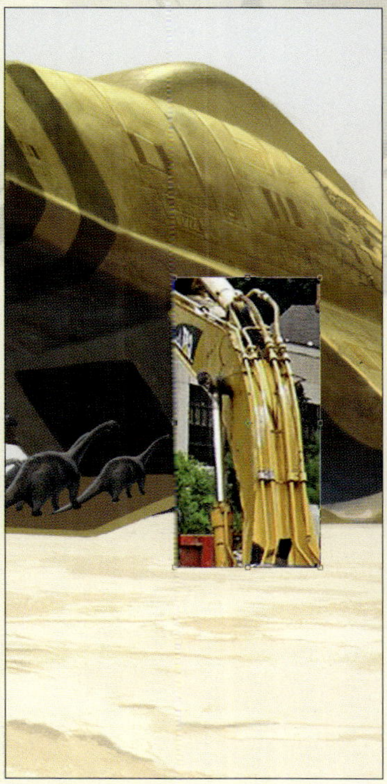

ON THE DVD

WORKSHOP BRUSHES

PHOTOSHOP

DINO BRUSH

I treat this brush like a stamp, which means that I don't have to paint the flock of pterodactyls over and over again.

SMOKE

I use this brush for the steam and the smoke, and also for the dust from the dinosaur march.

SKIN

The name says it all: I use it for painting the colour of the dinosaurs' skin, before I add the real-world textures.

11 Going into detail

So, after I've had my break and a fresh look at the painting, I begin tackling the details. I realise that adding a few more dinosaurs and one more ship would give more depth and scale. Because both elements are on separate layers, I can simply duplicate them. I also make a winged dinosaur brush, which means I save time when painting a flock of pterodactyls in the distance. They're another way to suggest that the rescue operation is taking place on a large scale.

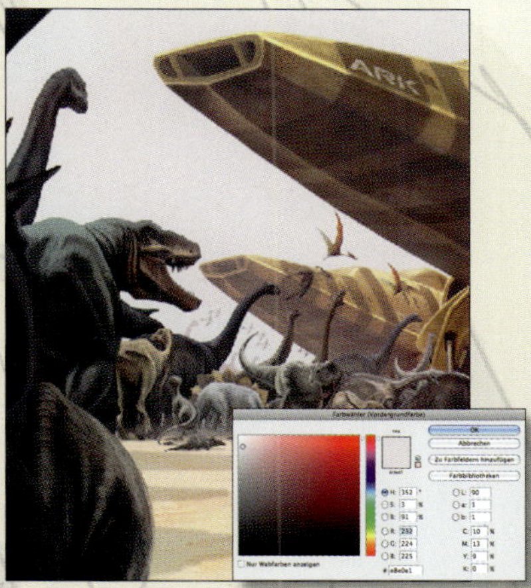

12 Adjusting mood and lighting

I'm almost done with the illustration and the time is right to introduce some atmosphere and depth. I want to give the whole setting a bigger scope. So, in the case of the ship in the background, I reduce its values and contrast slightly. I also take the colour of the sky and put it very gently and softly on another new layer, which I place between the foreground and the background on top of everything. I'm doing it carefully so as not to lose my highlights.

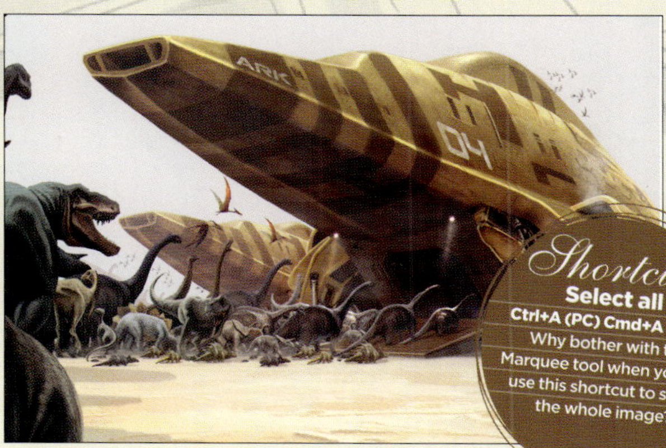

13 Making finishing touches

Everything is in place now and I can flatten the image. Now it's time for a few touch-ups here and there. For this I use the Blur tool to take away some of the hard edges. That's it... And it's almost the image I had in mind at the start of the project.

Shortcuts

Select all

Ctrl+A (PC) Cmd+A (Mac)

Why bother with the Marquee tool when you can use this shortcut to select the whole image?

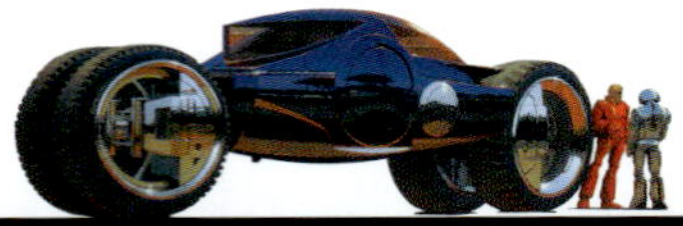

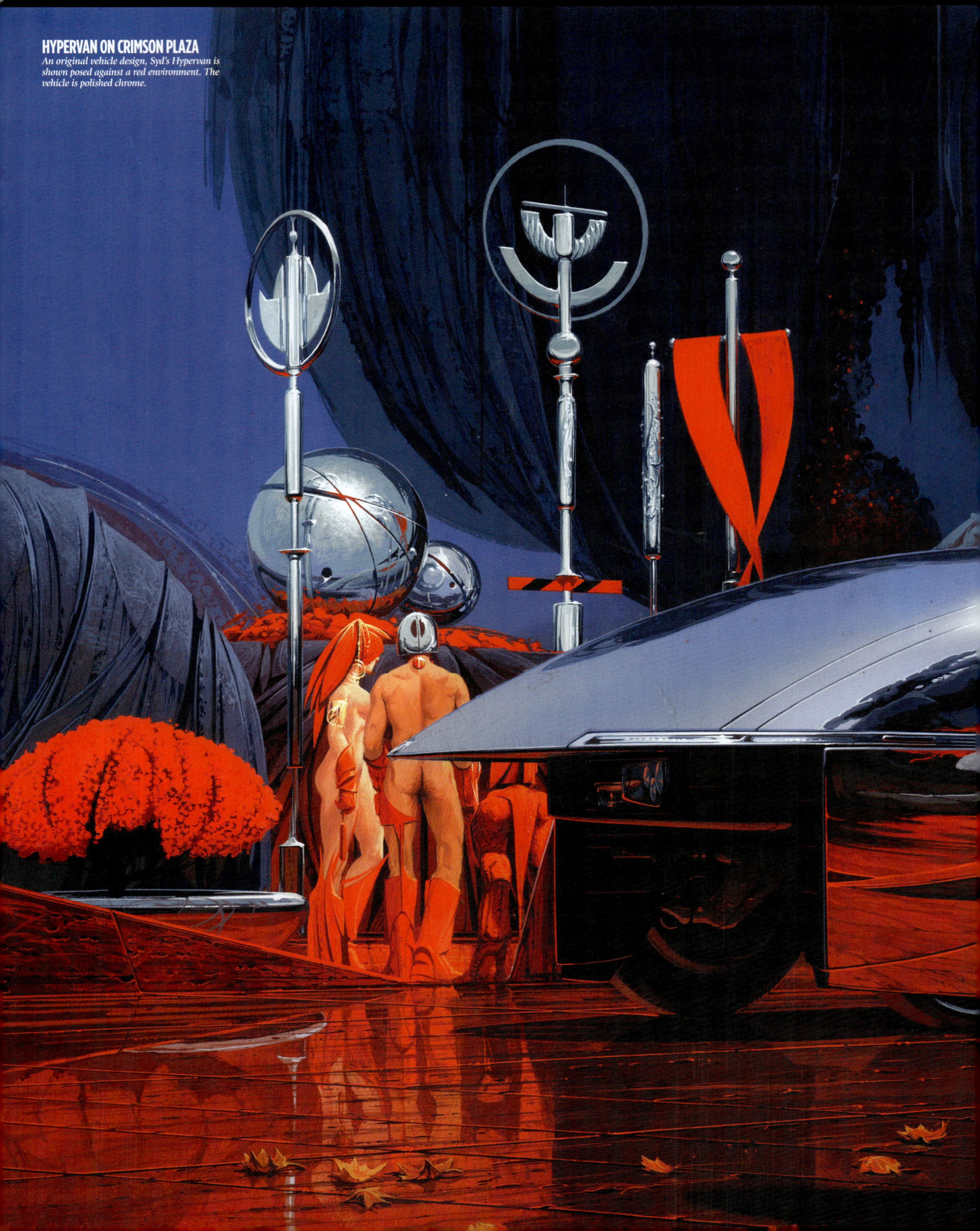

HYPERVAN ON CRIMSON PLAZA
An original vehicle design, Syd's Hypervan is shown posed against a red environment. The vehicle is polished chrome.

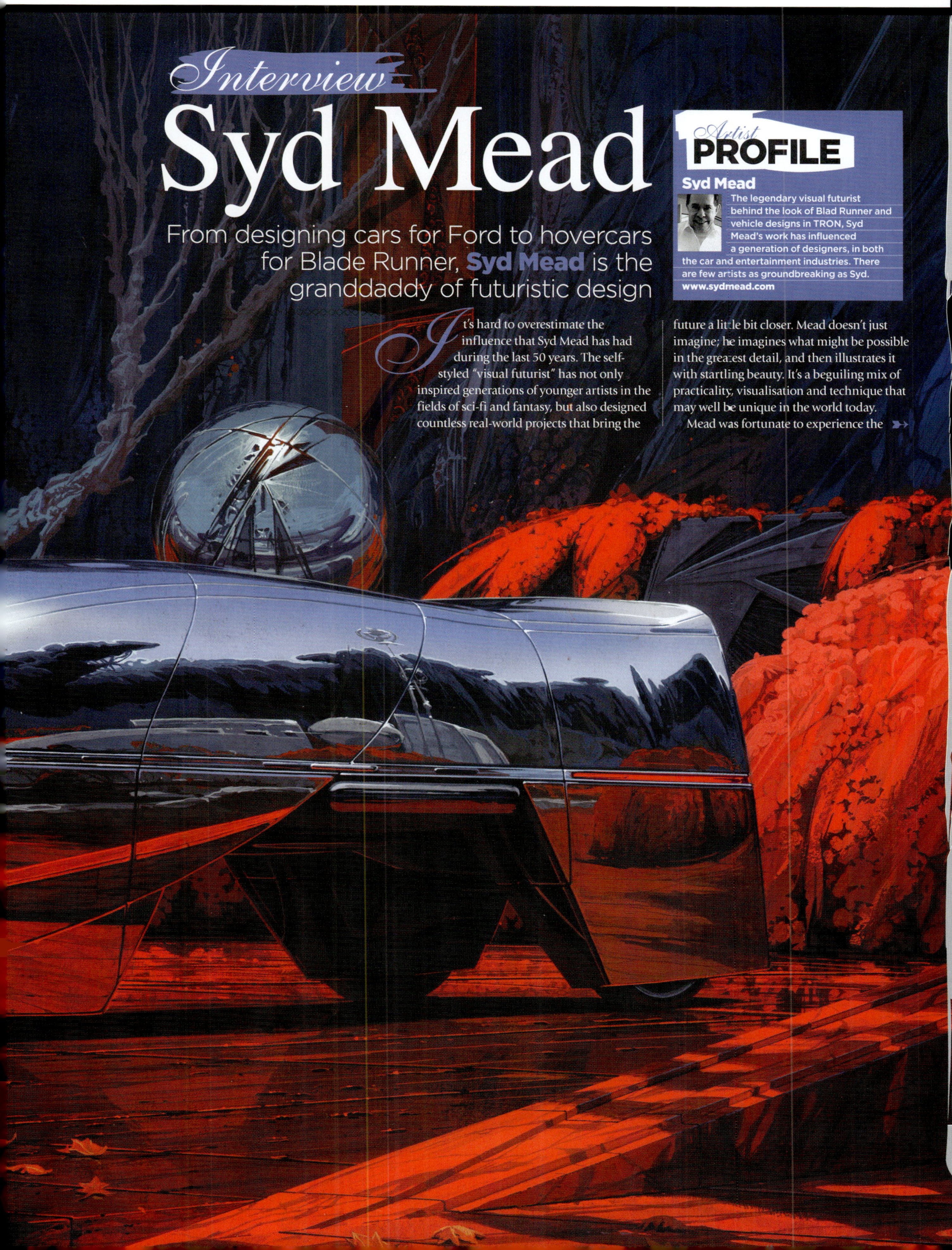

Interview

Syd Mead

From designing cars for Ford to hovercars for Blade Runner, **Syd Mead** is the granddaddy of futuristic design

Artist **PROFILE**

Syd Mead

The legendary visual futurist behind the look of Blad Runner and vehicle designs in TRON, Syd Mead's work has influenced a generation of designers, in both the car and entertainment industries. There are few artists as groundbreaking as Syd.

www.sydmead.com

It's hard to overestimate the influence that Syd Mead has had during the last 50 years. The self-styled "visual futurist" has not only inspired generations of younger artists in the fields of sci-fi and fantasy, but also designed countless real-world projects that bring the future a little bit closer. Mead doesn't just imagine; he imagines what might be possible in the greatest detail, and then illustrates it with startling beauty. It's a beguiling mix of practicality, visualisation and technique that may well be unique in the world today.

Mead was fortunate to experience the

Gallery
Interviews
Workshops
Core skills

buzz of postwar America while in the prime of his youth – a perfect time for a concept artist to be learning his trade. It was a era when new ideas in general and design ideas in particular were passionately embraced. Anything seemed possible.

"There was an ebullient belief that, collectively, we could imagine and proceed to create a beneficial future for all," he says of that period from 1950 to the late 1960s. "I was fascinated by the 'living room on wheels' idea for cars, whooshing along superhighways at high speed, completely auto controlled... We're pretty close to that now with the latest DARPA projects for autonomous vehicle operation."

CAR MAN

By the time Mead began his own company in 1970, he had a wealth of concept design experience. His first job, at the age of 19, involved animation cell inking, character origination and background illustration. After a stint in the army, he attended the Art Center in Los Angeles and went on to design concept cars for Ford, as well as working for US Steel and Hansen Co.

Such jobs mixed imagination with hard practicalities – there was no point designing a flying car for Ford that could never actually be built. His entire design process is built upon this idea of extrapolating from existing technology and imagining what might be possible in the future.

"My imagination is perfectly capable of inventing my own 'world view' to illustrate or use as an idea base," Syd explains. "When not on a job, I still do this all the time. Fortunately I am hired, and don't have a lot of time for my own stuff. In other words, happily – I guess, I can't afford my own time..."

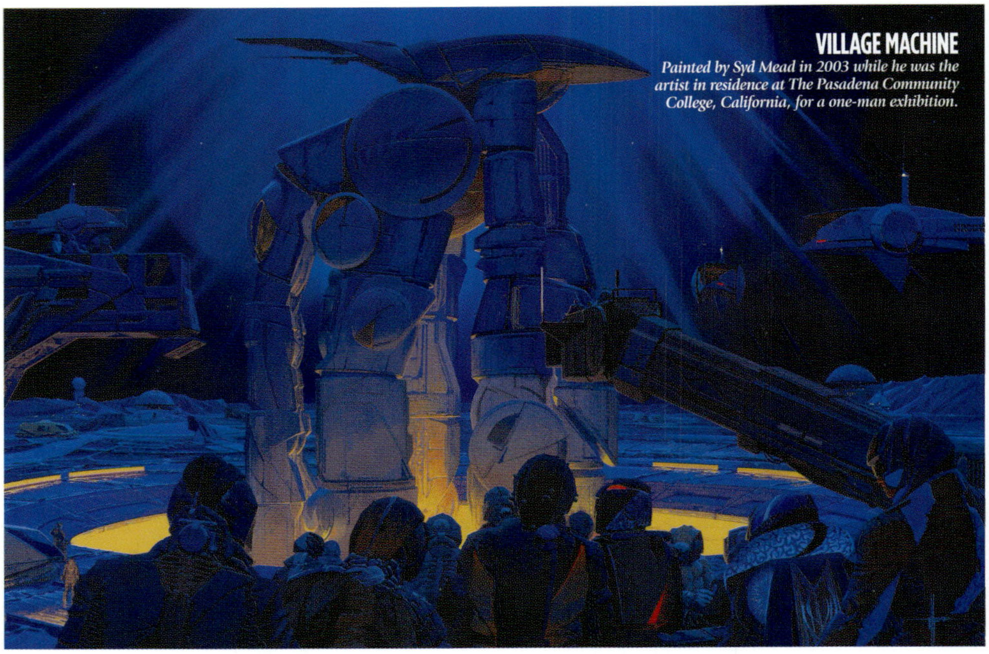

VILLAGE MACHINE

Painted by Syd Mead in 2003 while he was the artist in residence at The Pasadena Community College, California, for a one-man exhibition.

"Remember, a million dollar computer coupled with a dumb idea results in a million dollar dumb idea"

But it wasn't just Mead's capacity for practical imagination that set him apart; it was also his masterful ability to illustrate. Every design, no matter how seemingly insignificant, was lovingly detailed, becoming works of art in their own right. "Being able to expertly 'illustrate' your own designs [as a concept artist] is a tremendous advantage," he believes. "You can massage, shift, and change to suit *before* it goes out to the client or into general observation. And now, with 3D software, your idea can be rendered, rotated, duplicated, sent digitally – a seven-league-boots leap over what used to be the case."

Mead was really thrust into the limelight with his work on Ridley Scott's 1982 classic film Blade Runner. Initially he was hired to design a single vehicle, but Ridley was so impressed by his visions that Mead went on to design street sets and many other elements of the film.

The pair's creation of a believable, downbeat future LA also caught the attention of other Hollywood directors, and design work followed for Aliens, 2010, Short Circuit and many other films. These days it's unusual to find a big budget sci-fi film for which Mead hasn't been consulted at some stage, most recently he worked on TRON: Legacy. It doesn't bother him that many people might only know him for his film work, though. After all, "I can't afford 15 million dollars' worth of publicity," as he cheerily admits.

Establishing the thinking behind the design is particularly critical for him when working on films. "If I can't have a conference with the director, I decline to

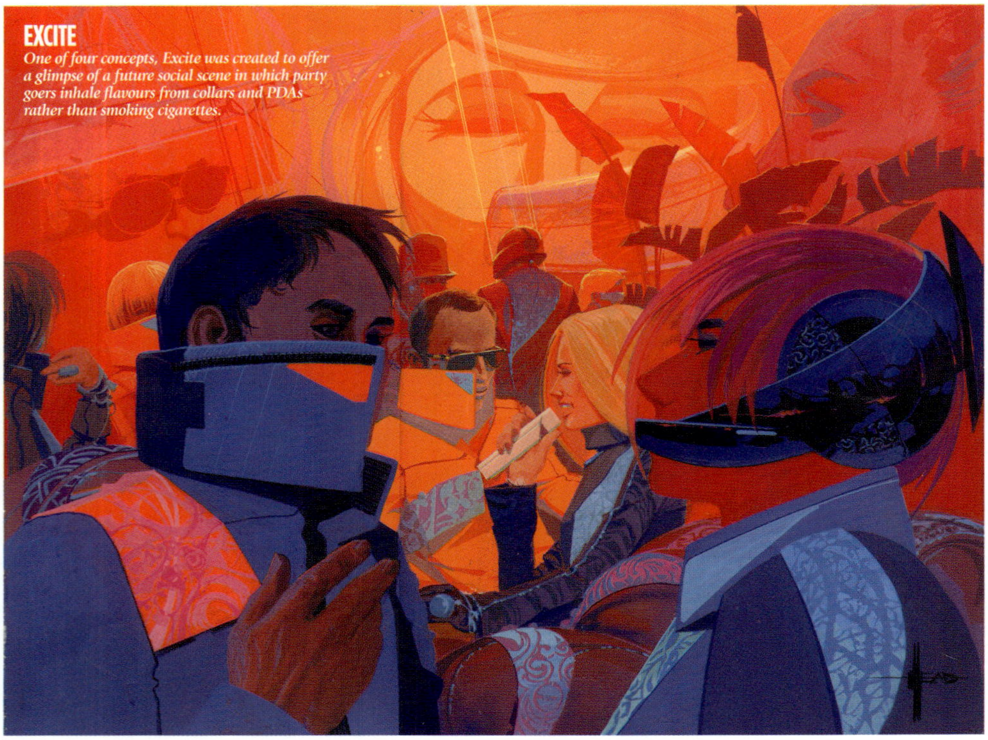

EXCITE

One of four concepts, Excite was created to offer a glimpse of a future social scene in which party goers inhale flavours from collars and PDAs rather than smoking cigarettes.

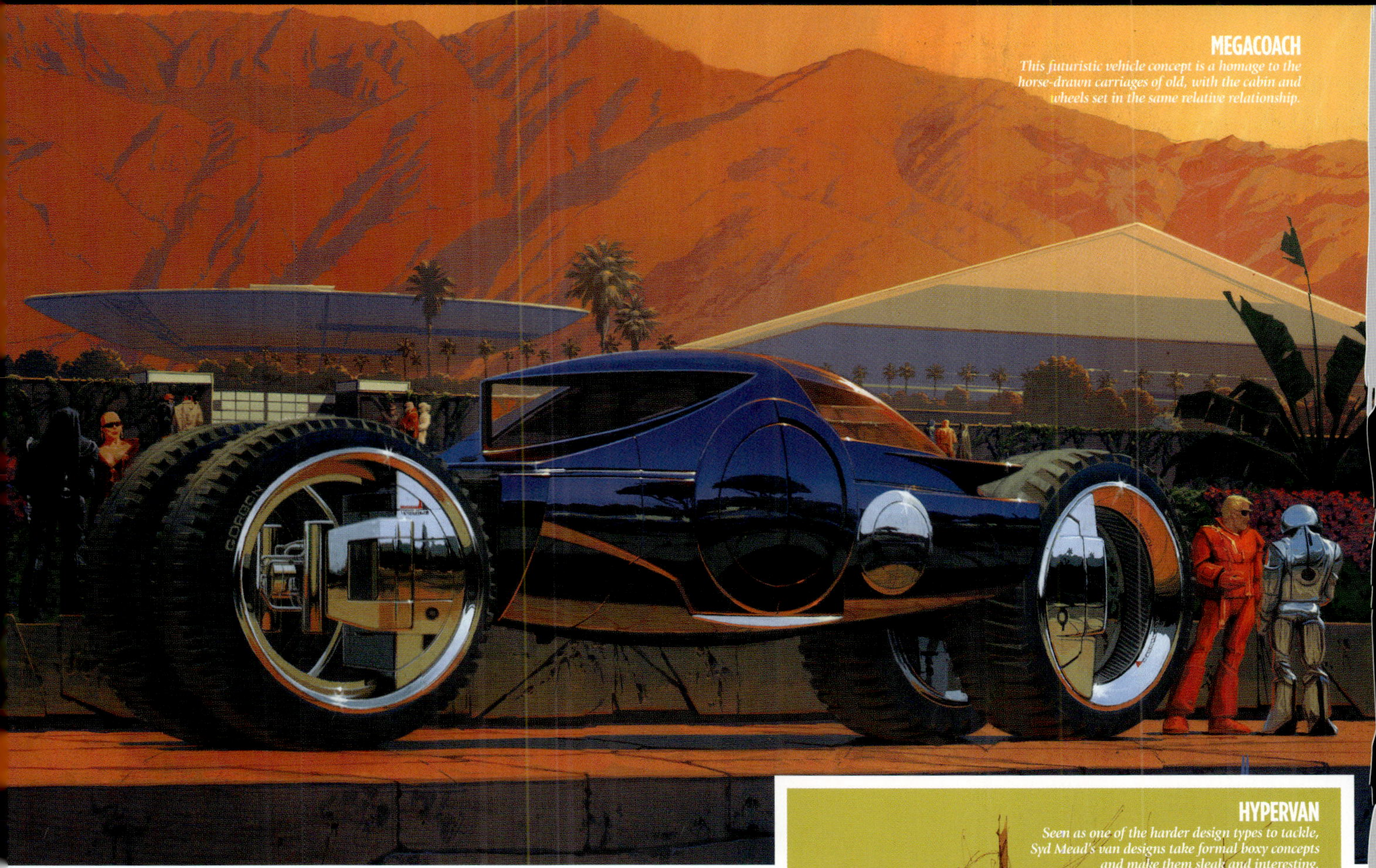

MEGACOACH
This futuristic vehicle concept is a homage to the horse-drawn carriages of old, with the cabin and wheels set in the same relative relationship.

work on the movie. Once the rationale has been established, then it becomes a 'backstory' and I simply illustrate the story." There's no room for wild design for the sheer sake of it in Mead's way of working.

ONGOING INFLUENCE

Blade Runner was so visually striking and original that it continues to influence the look of films even today – often as ill-conceived clones that show little real imagination. Are film concept designers simply becoming lazy and copying what has been proven to work? Mead doesn't necessarily think so. "The end product has to be profitable, otherwise it's a very expensive way to lose money," he says.

"The movie game is not a missionary effort; someone once said, 'If you want to send a message, use Western Union.'" he continues. "The end result in Hollywood is money. Along the way, depending on the director, the purity of vision and the appeal to a viewing public, great movies are made… few and far between."

The meat of all Syd's design work is still done with the traditional media of pen, paint and paper, because ultimately the medium in which he works really isn't important to Syd. "Repeat after me: *idea trumps technique every time*," he advises. "Remember, a million dollar computer coupled with a dumb idea results in a million dollar dumb idea. I'm mindful that all of the elaborate algorithms that allow electronically-enabled graphical production duplicate 'old school' techniques as much as is possible, by writing code – and the code is amazing," he says.

He does use a Mac extensively for "graphical accuracy," scanning and archiving his drawn and painted work, and sometimes for colouring, as well as adding typographical flourishes (another area over which he has complete control).

"I'm also now using SketchUp," he says, referring to the Google-acquired 3D package, "for massing architectural ideas into 3D ➳

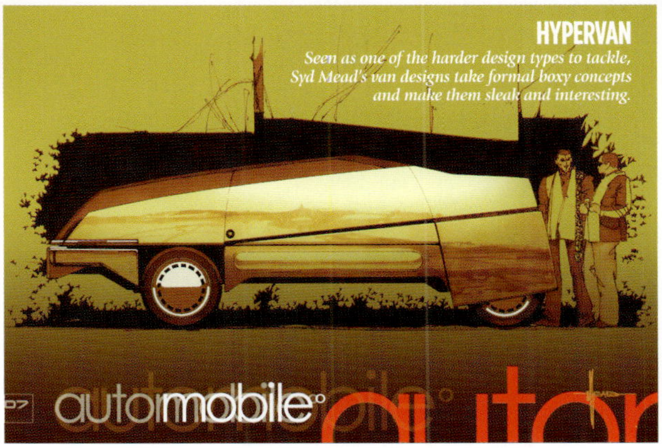

HYPERVAN
Seen as one of the harder design types to tackle, Syd Mead's van designs take formal boxy concepts and make them sleak and interesting.

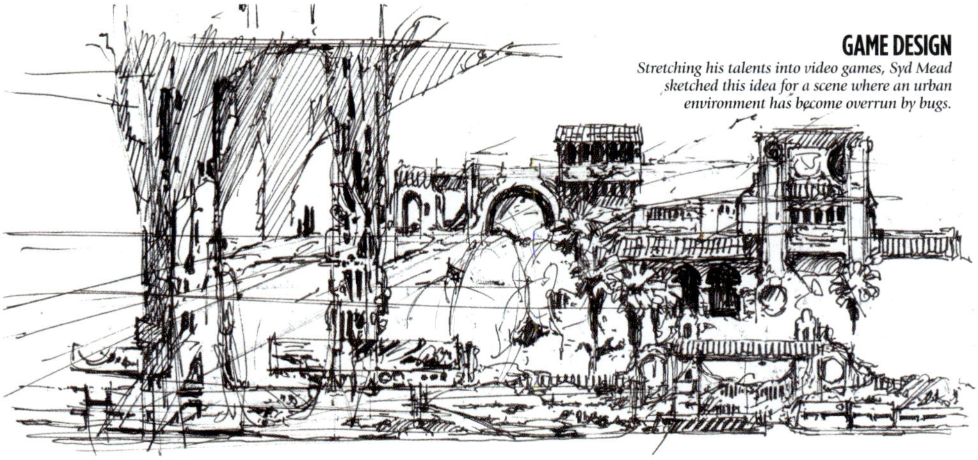

GAME DESIGN
Stretching his talents into video games, Syd Mead sketched this idea for a scene where an urban environment has become overrun by bugs.

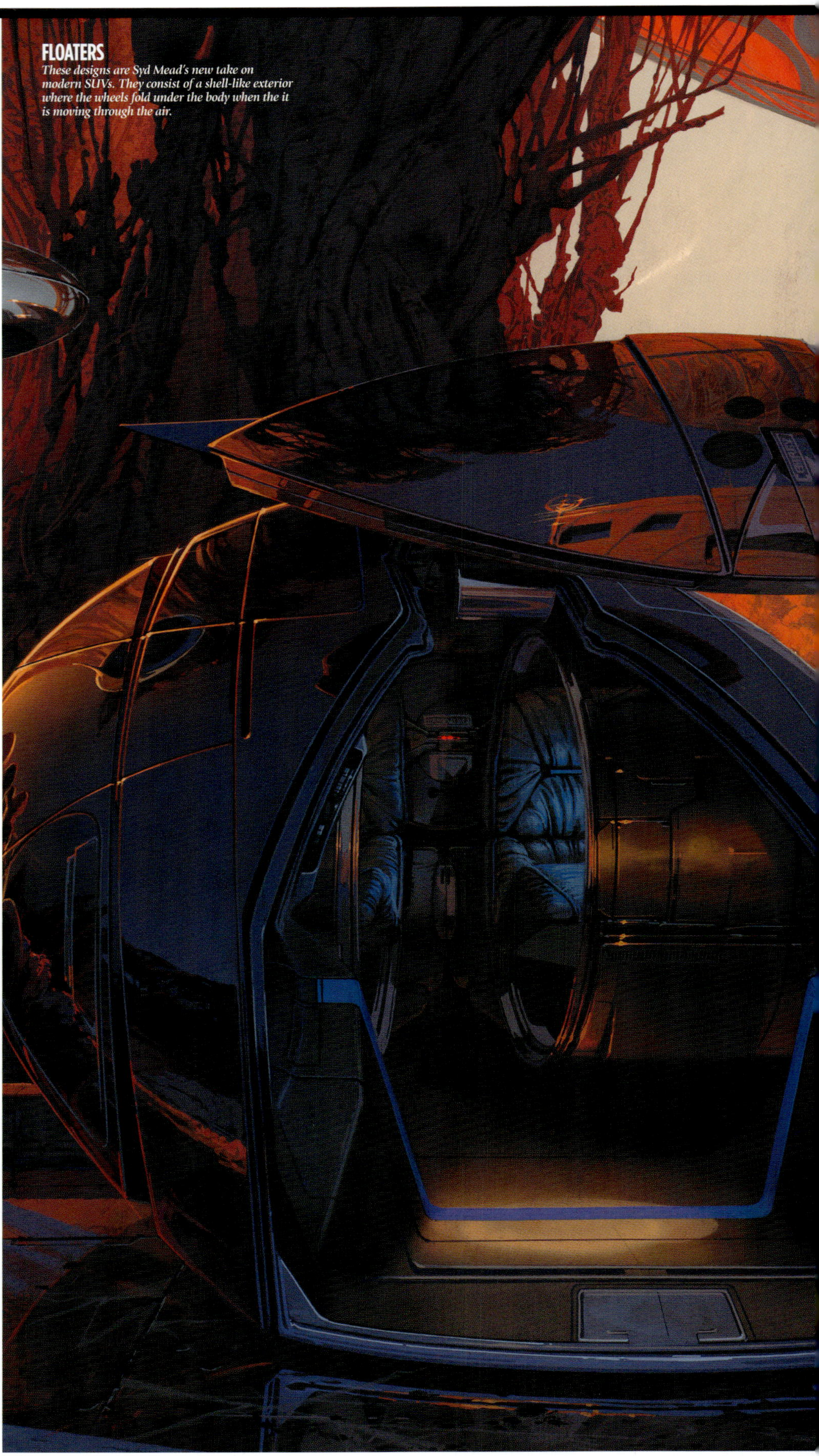

FLOATERS
These designs are Syd Mead's new take on modern SUVs. They consist of a shell-like exterior where the wheels fold under the body when the it is moving through the air.

“Designing and inventing concepts to order is what I do and who I am”

rotational and accurately scaled development. It is a huge advantage.”

At the age of 76, Mead continues to work in film, recently returning on TRON: Legacy, but he's also added to the astonishing range of projects on which he has worked. These include watches, television sets, theme parks and resorts, aircraft, super yachts, nightclubs, retail spaces, and an $87 million flying palace for King Fahd of Saudi Arabia, which he calls “the single most challenging and satisfying design project I've ever done.”

It doesn't come as much of a surprise, then, that he reacts with scorn to the idea that he perhaps might want to retire. “Retiring destroys one's sense of ‘who’,” he is quick to observe. “Typically, people who retire die within 10 years or sooner.” That's not for him – there's still the future to see, and too much imagining to be done.

“I will most likely die with a Windsor & Newton number two, series seven brush in my hand – or the digital equivalent,” he says. “Designing and inventing concepts to order is what I do, and who I am, I guess. So as long as my response to that challenge is viable, I'll keep doing it…”

Turn the page to learn to paint like Syd Mead

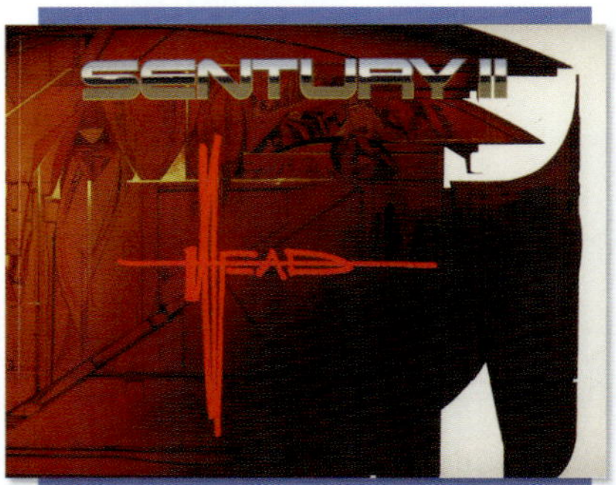

Sentury II
Published by Design Studio Press and distributed in the UK by Titan Books, Sentury II contains old and new sketches, concepts and finished paintings by Syd Mead. The book also offers an insight into the artist's thought processes, how he problem solves and arrives at his designs. A celebration of his career and new work all in one book, Sentury II proves no-one does it like Syd Mead.
www.titanbooks.com/dsp

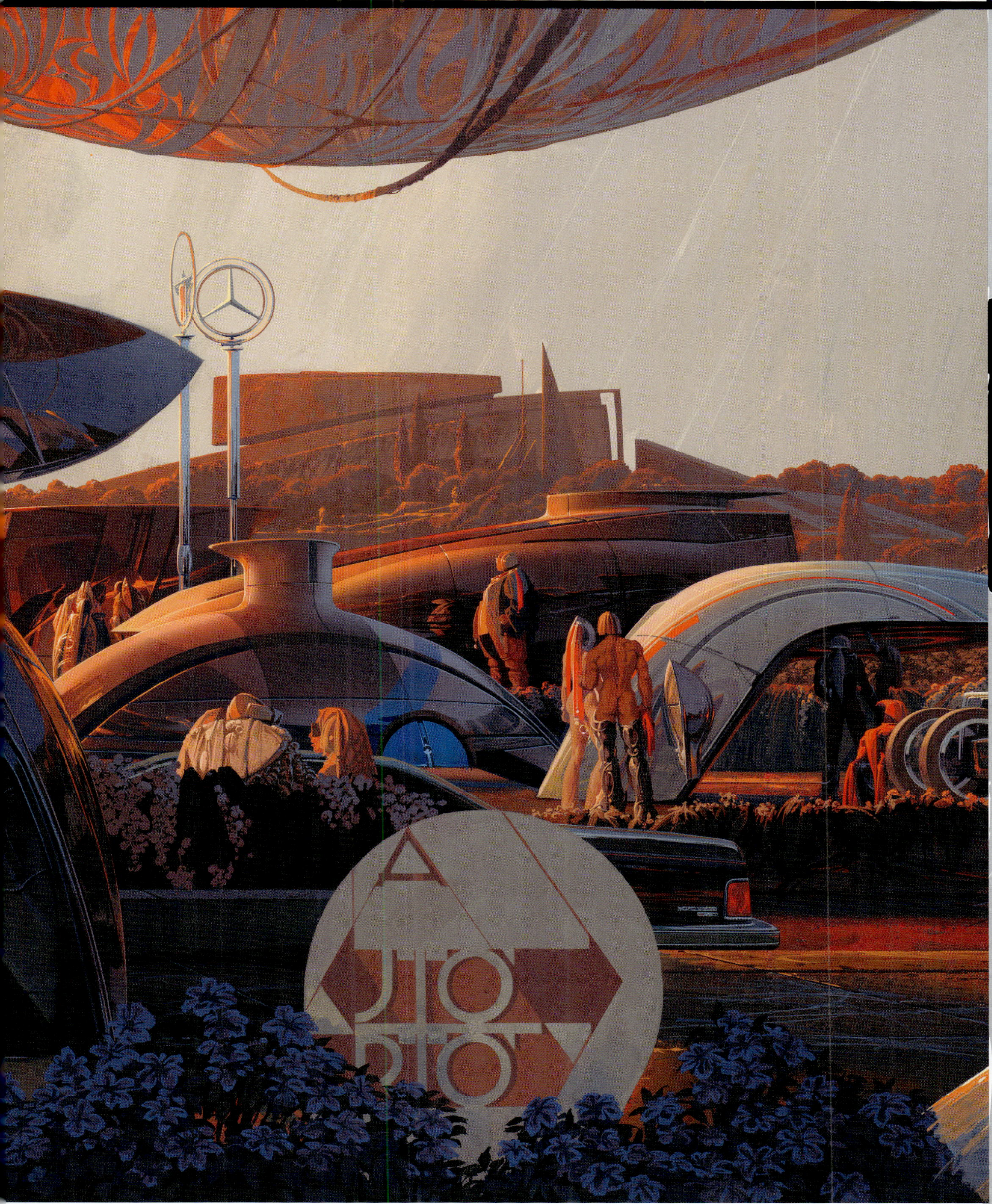

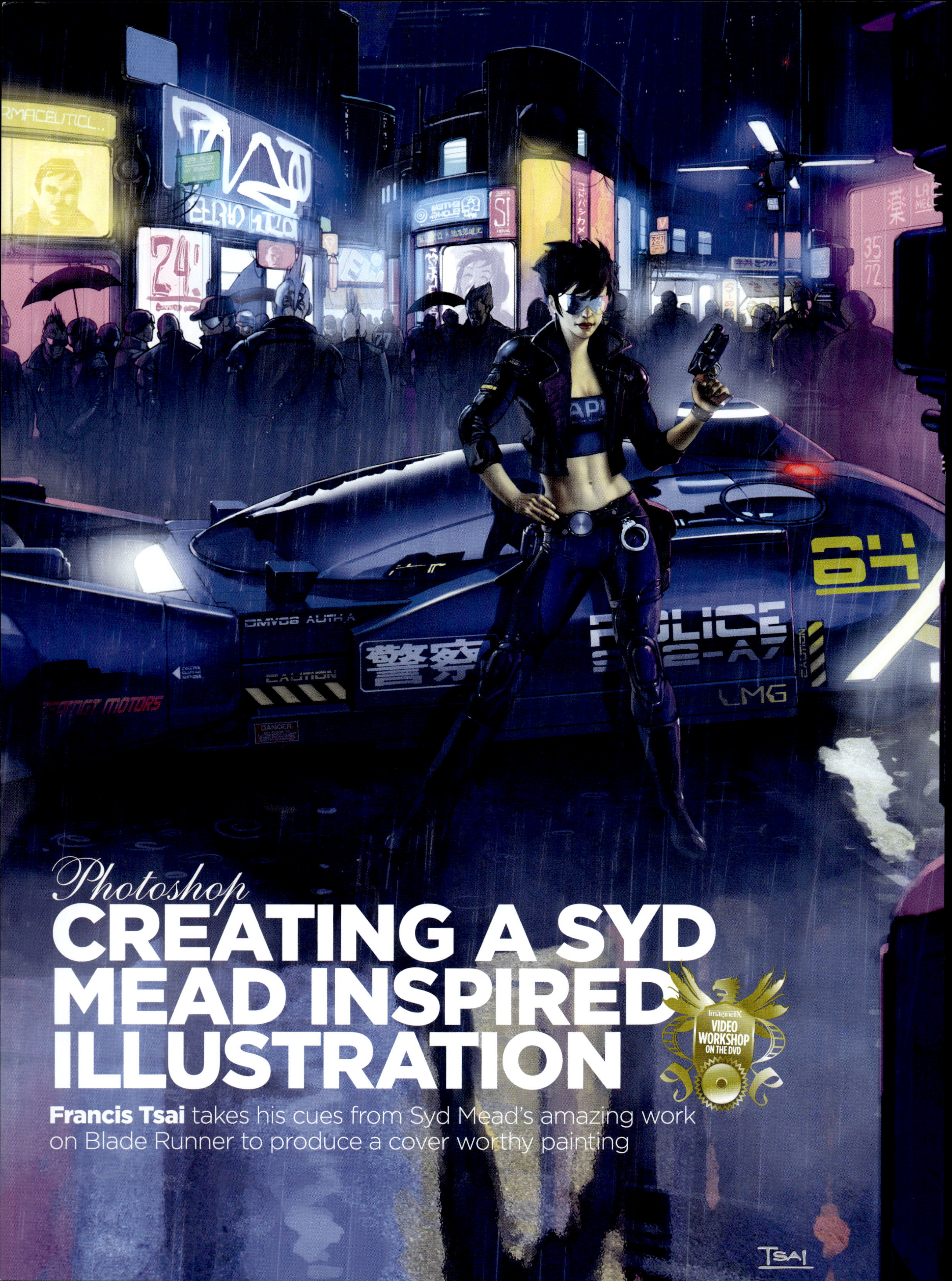

Photoshop

CREATING A SYD MEAD INSPIRED ILLUSTRATION

ImagineFX VIDEO WORKSHOP ON THE DVD

Francis Tsai takes his cues from Syd Mead's amazing work on Blade Runner to produce a cover worthy painting

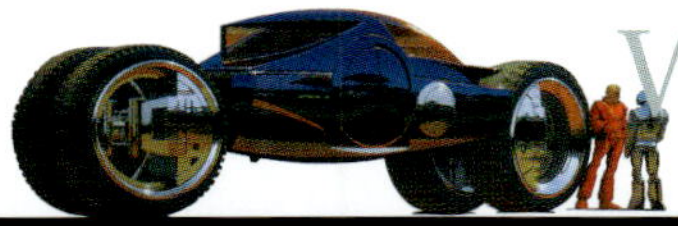

Artist PROFILE

Francis Tsai
COUNTRY: US

Francis is a freelance illustrator and concept artist living and working in Southern California. A roundabout career path beginning with degrees in physical chemistry and architecture eventually led to jobs in the video games industry. He currently works full time on a freelance basis for the games, comics, TV and film industries.
www.teamgt.com

Disc Assets
The files you need are on your disc in the Characters folder.

For me, as for many others in the entertainment design community, Syd Mead's work on Blade Runner has always been a huge source of inspiration. The designs for the sets, vehicles and props have a high-tech, science fiction vibe, but at the same time feel very rooted in reality. This is in no doubt due to his training and earlier career as an industrial designer (including designing cars for Ford), in which real-world concerns like budgetary and engineering constraints inform the design process.

For this workshop I'll be borrowing heavily from Syd's catalogue of designs and illustrations for the movie Blade Runner, and also bringing in certain influences from the movie itself, in terms of mood, lighting and character. I'll combine those elements with some of my own techniques in digital painting to create an illustration that pays homage to both the designer and movie.

> **For me and many others, Syd Mead's work on Blade Runner has been a huge source of inspiration**

My process isn't really as orderly as it probably could be. I have a definite end point in mind, and a few strategies that have helped me in the past with other illustrations – but there will be some back and forth along the way.

The overall look and feel of the world, and a significant prop design or two will come from Syd's work, while some of the mood and lighting will reference Ridley Scott's vision of the movie. Layered on top of that will be a bit of my own take on the Blade Runner world, along with my scattershot painting technique, which will hopefully tie all those elements together.

1 Initial thoughts

When Paul Tysall, ImagineFX's art editor, contacted me about doing a piece paying homage to the design work of Syd Mead to go on the magazine's cover, he had a few suggestions in terms of subject matter. Signature elements like the retrofitted architecture of 2019 Los Angeles, specific vehicle designs like the Spinner police car, the pervasive neon lighting, rain – these were just some of the things he mentioned that could highlight a police officer or replicant character.

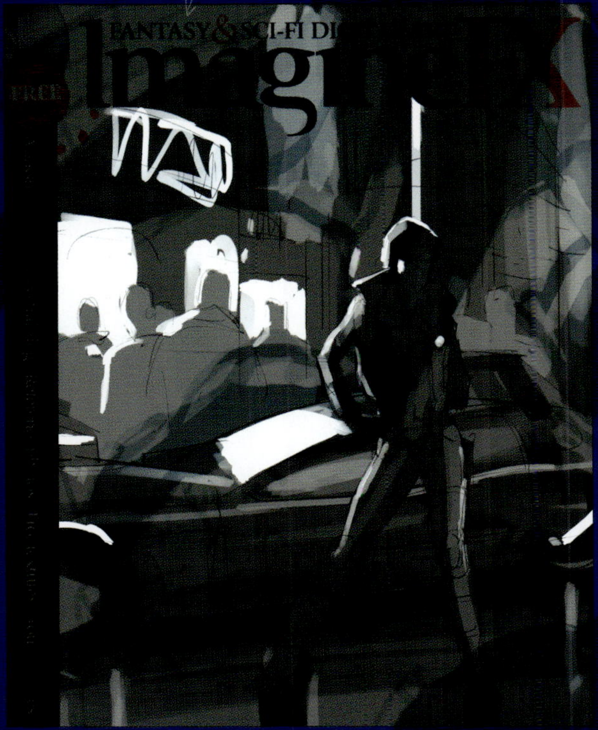

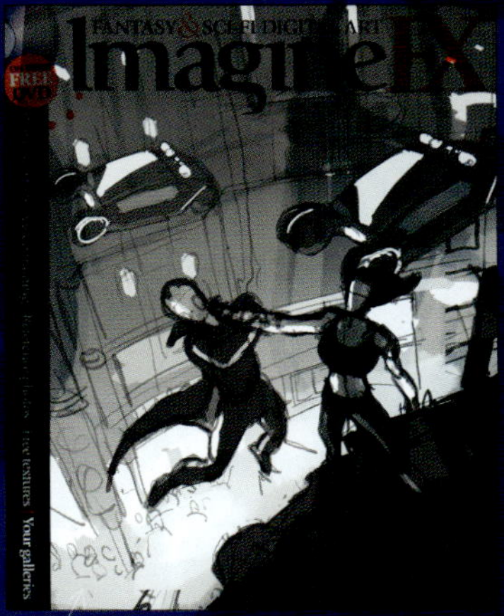

The two initial sketches (above and above right) incorporated similar elements – the futuristic street scene and the Spinner vehicle – but shifted the focus onto different characters. The female police officer was chosen over the action scene on the rooftop

2 Thumbnailing

After a bit of pondering, I do two thumbnail sketches. The first is a simple standing pose featuring a female police officer, or Blade Runner, in front of the iconic Spinner vehicle, with a backdrop consisting of a night-time, neon-lit, rainy city street. The second sketch is more of a re-creation or re-imagining of a scene from the movie, in which a rogue female replicant is dangling a Blade Runner policeman over the edge of a rooftop, with the city street and Spinner more in the background than in the first sketch.

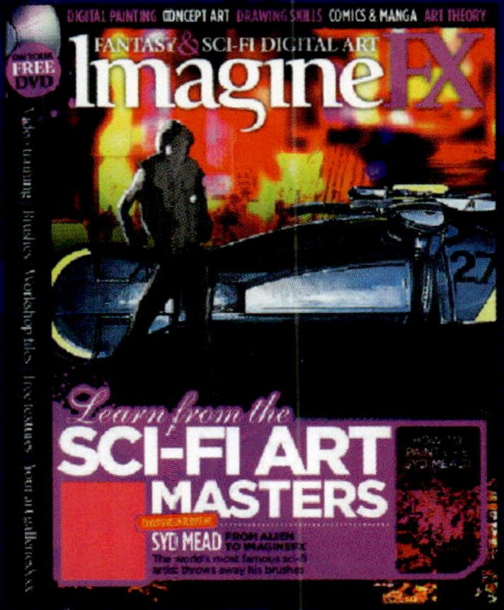

3 Sketch approval

Paul picks the first sketch, and suggests a scene from the movie for inspiration, showing star Harrison Ford reading a newspaper in front of a storefront window that's lit up with pink and purple neon. He also sends me a file containing the cover text and graphics, as well as a mock-up of the composition with the new cover elements. The text and graphics were done in a colour palette influenced by the scene from the movie, and provided a basis for the palette of the painting as well.

Gallery
Interviews
Workshops
Core skills

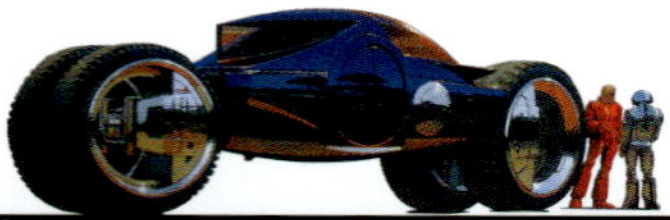

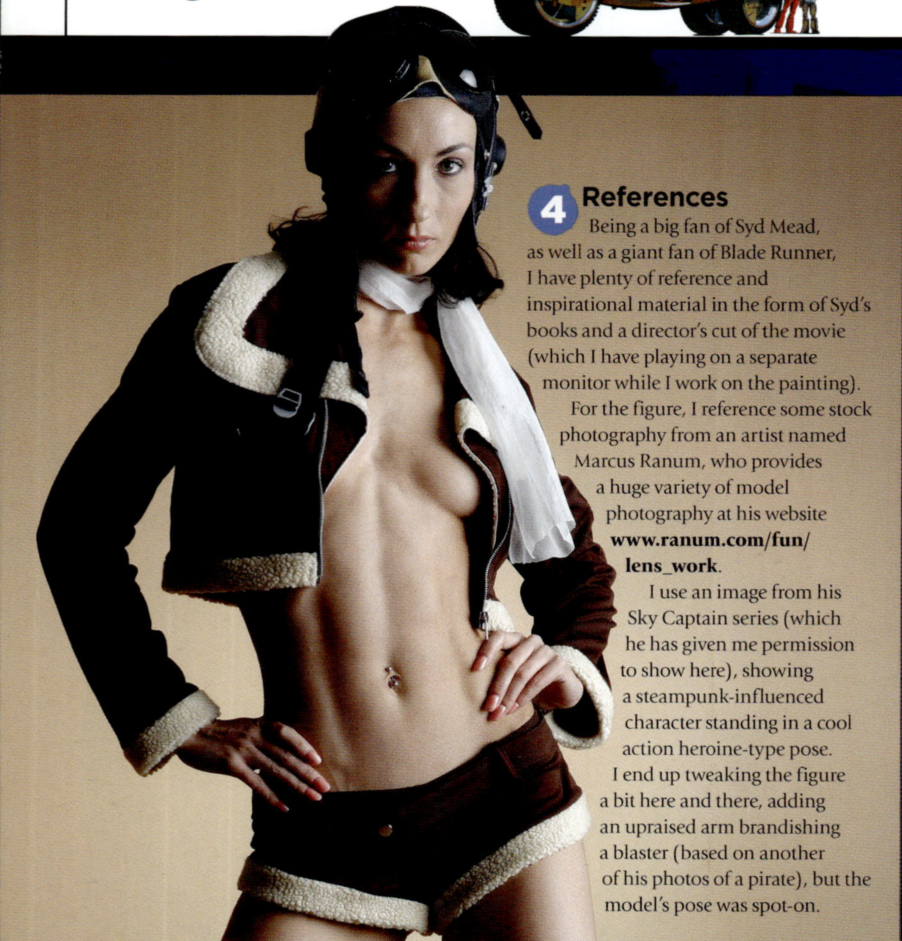

4 References

Being a big fan of Syd Mead, as well as a giant fan of Blade Runner, I have plenty of reference and inspirational material in the form of Syd's books and a director's cut of the movie (which I have playing on a separate monitor while I work on the painting).

For the figure, I reference some stock photography from an artist named Marcus Ranum, who provides a huge variety of model photography at his website **www.ranum.com/fun/lens_work**.

I use an image from his Sky Captain series (which he has given me permission to show here), showing a steampunk-influenced character standing in a cool action heroine-type pose.

I end up tweaking the figure a bit here and there, adding an upraised arm brandishing a blaster (based on another of his photos of a pirate), but the model's pose was spot-on.

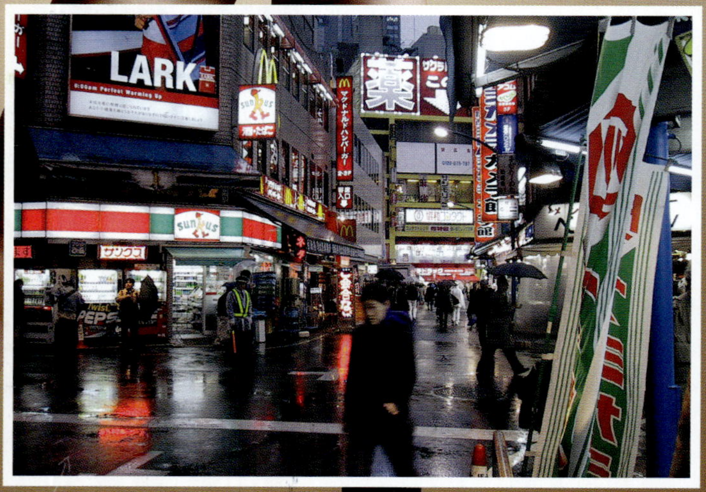

5 Location reference

I also pull a few photos from my own collection, from a recent trip to Japan. This is a shot of a neighbourhood in downtown Tokyo, taken right after a rainstorm. The scale and density of the street, as well as the interplay of lights and signs in the wet surfaces, were elements I wanted to include in the environment.

PRO SECRETS

Fast fingers

My left hand usually rests on the keyboard so I can quickly hit various hotkeys and shortcuts. I noticed recently that I was using the base of my thumb to pushdown the space bar so I could quickly pan around the image. This also enables me to easily hold down the space bar and press Ctrl/Cmd with my pinky, which brings up the Zoom tool without having to select it from the toolbox.

6 Colour palette

For the next phase, I refine the illustration a bit, establishing a colour palette based on the cover graphics and the screen grab. I also add a few elements that I wouldn't ordinarily add until late in the process, including rain and glow effects. I put these on separate layers, including them at this stage to give the editor a more accurate impression of what the final art would look like.

7 Back story

At this point a bit of back story is already forming in my mind for the character. I want her to have a certain level of sex appeal, but not in such an over-the-top way that she'd have no credibility as a futuristic street cop. It is important to convey a sense of power and confidence. I feel some wraparound shades will serve a number of purposes – invoking the visual of the typical American cop's mirrored sunglasses, referencing the cyberpunk mirrorshades aesthetic and providing a reflective surface that echoes some of the colours in the environment. Obscuring the character's eyes also heightens the sense of mystery, subliminally adding to the "is she a replicant?" factor.

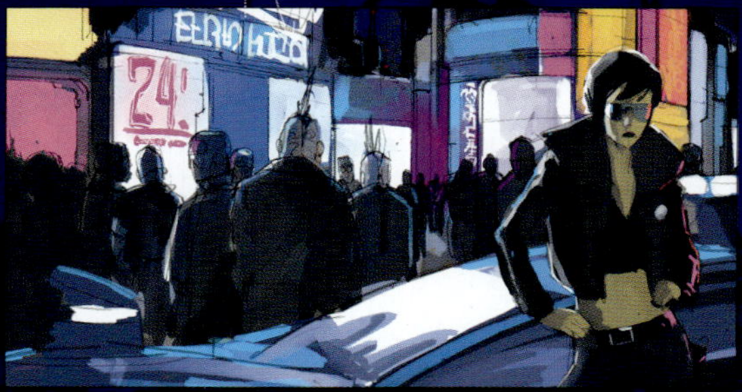

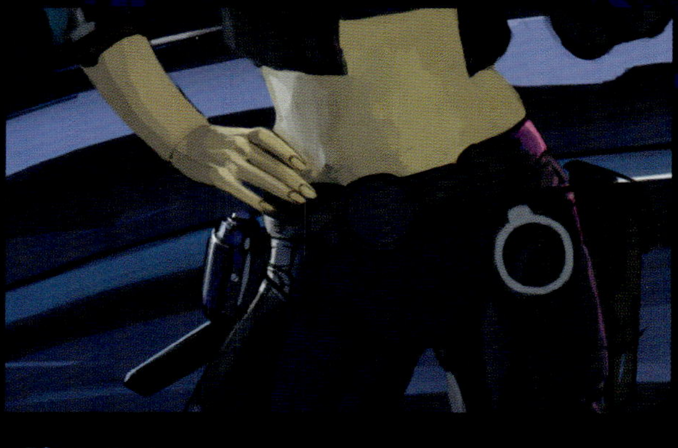

8 Refining

I keep a layer on top of the painting containing the cover text and graphics so that I can easily see what will be obscured by it in the final art, and then turn it off once all the major elements are blocked in. I feel pretty confident about the background environment, but know the Spinner will require a fair bit of attention, as it's kind of the co-star of the image. The curvy, bulbous form proves to be a challenge to correctly portray in terms of perspective, and I end up eyeballing it into shape, with a lot of tweaking and adjustments.

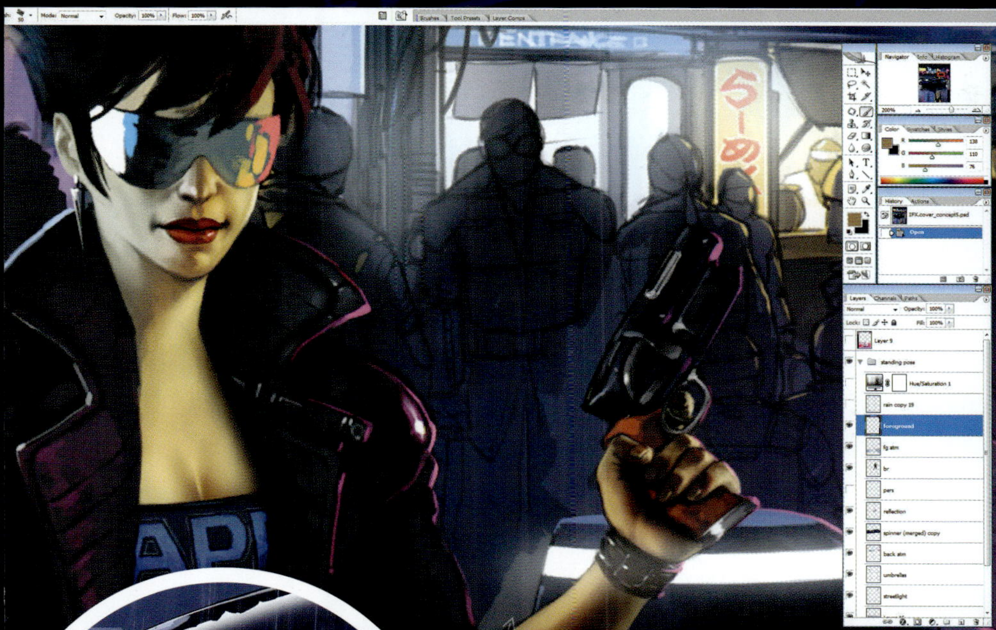

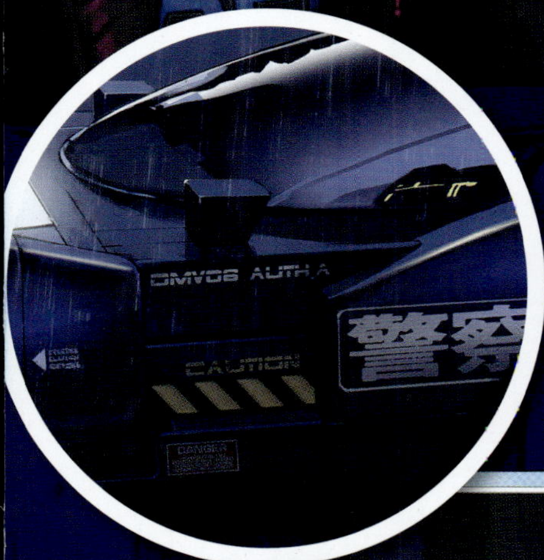

9 Reflective surfaces

Aside from the car's form, the reflections in the metallic surfaces present another mix of challenge and opportunity. Accurately rendering vehicle highlights and reflections is a whole other aspect of industrial design that almost seems like alchemy to me, but it provides another chance to echo the environment colours. As a bit of a car fanatic I've looked at a lot of vehicle renderings, but for some reason I've rarely been called upon to produce one. Luckily, I have the benefit of adding logos and graphics on the car to distract the eye a bit!

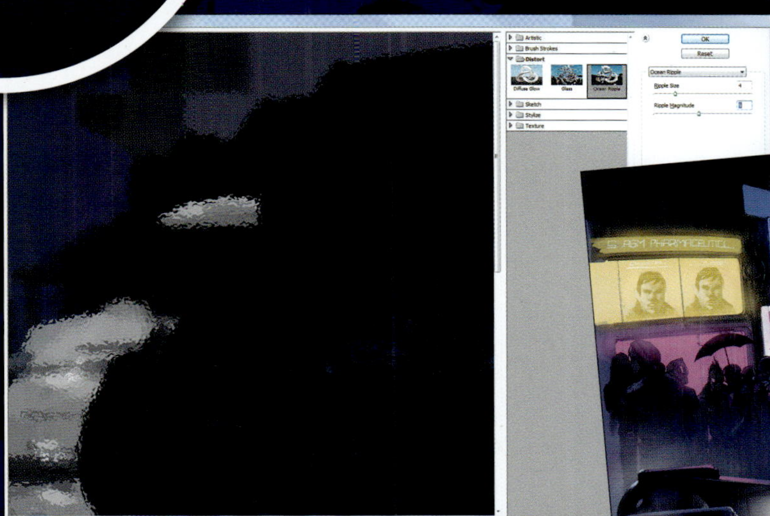

PRO SECRETS

Quick new layer

Although it kind of feels like I'm trying a Vulcan mind meld on my keyboard, I'll sometimes use the Ctrl/Cmd-Shift-Alt/Option-N combination to quickly create a new layer in a Photoshop document.

10 Filter effects

Ordinarily I don't use a lot of filter effects. This isn't necessarily because of some personal prejudice against them, but more because I haven't really figured out how to use a lot of them in a way that seems natural. Having said that, one effect I do find useful in this particular case was the Ocean Ripple effect in Photoshop, which helps to add a bit of the distorted reflection feel to the wet street surface.

11 Last five per cent

It's been my experience that the last five per cent of an illustration tends to take at least 50 per cent of the time. That's the case with this image as well, and there was plenty to work on. One bit of useful feedback that my friend and former boss Farzad Varahramyan gave me was to add some separation between the various layers in the scene, to increase the sense of depth. Adding some mist behind the Spinner but in front of the crowd helps push them back a bit. Some atmosphere also pushes the storefronts and noodle stands further back in the middle distance. Finally, massive high-rises are implied in the far distance, their scale established by the tiny pinpoints of light indicating lit windows.

12 Final touches

I also want to keep the rendering a bit looser on the background characters and environment. The graphics and logos on the Spinner are pretty closely based on the movie vehicle, although I do take some personal liberties here and there. The main character's outfit is totally made up, and has much more of a motorcycle cop aesthetic than Deckard's outfit had in the movie. The choice here again is made to take advantage of the wet and reflective feel of the image, and some of the same colours and graphics from the vehicle are incorporated into her outfit. Finally, a subtle colour adjustment layer, some indication of rain splashes on the ground and some texture on the road surface are the last things I add before shipping the final art off.

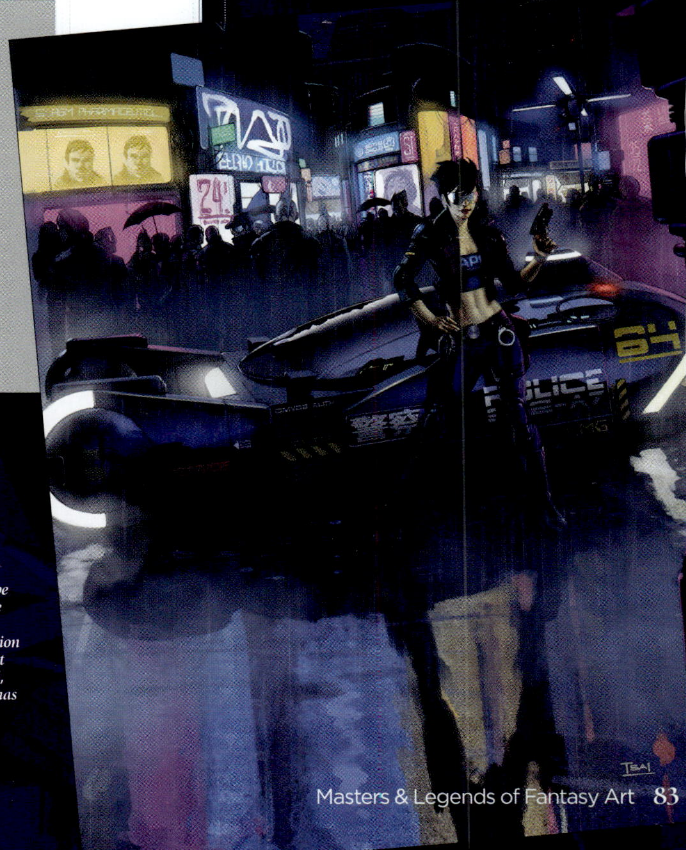

The finished image. The foreground will be covered by text on the front cover, but the policewoman's reflection isn't the only way that a moody, rain-soaked, neon-lit atmosphere has been conveyed.

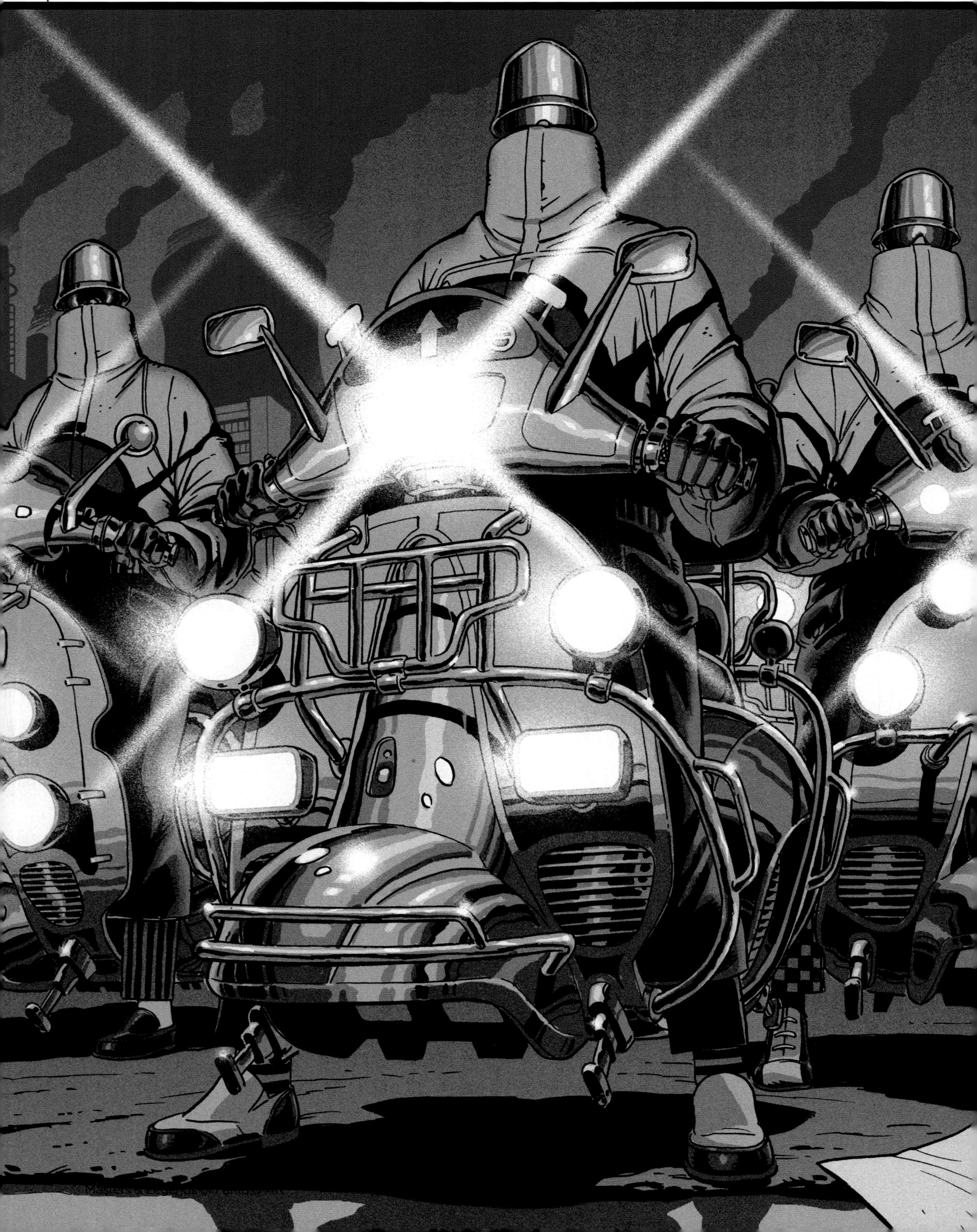

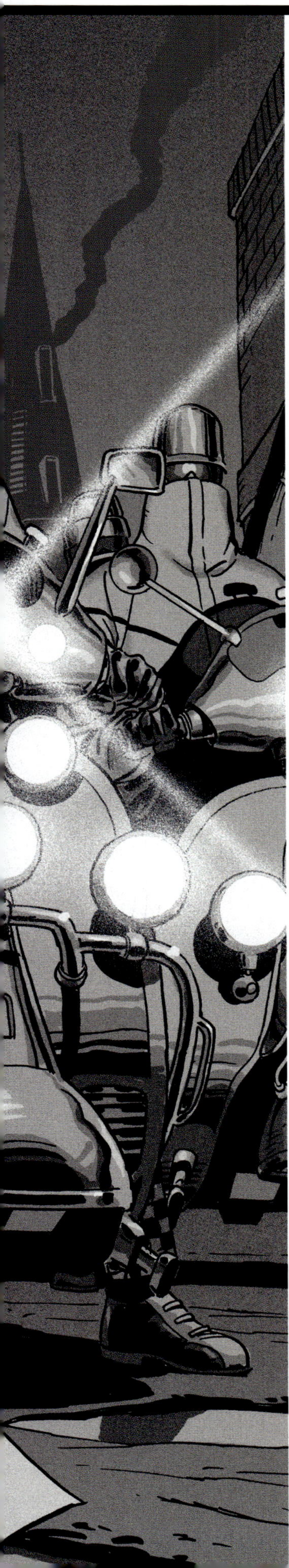

Interview

Dave Gibbons

A modern comic innovator and co-creator of the groundbreaking Watchmen, catching up with **Dave Gibbons**, godfather of the comic industry...

There are only a handful of contemporary British illustrators to whom the term groundbreaking can accurately be applied. Dave Gibbons is one of them. His CV reads like a roll call of the great and the good within the world of comic books: co-creator of the revered Watchmen series with the legendary Alan Moore, collaborator on US comic giant Frank Miller's Martha Washington projects, lead artist during 2000 AD's UK heyday and scriptwriter in his own right on Batman Versus Predator and his own creation, The Originals. These are just a few projects to which Dave has turned his inimitable style, not to mention his pioneering digital technique, which hauled comic book illustration from the sketchpad and pencil into the computer age.

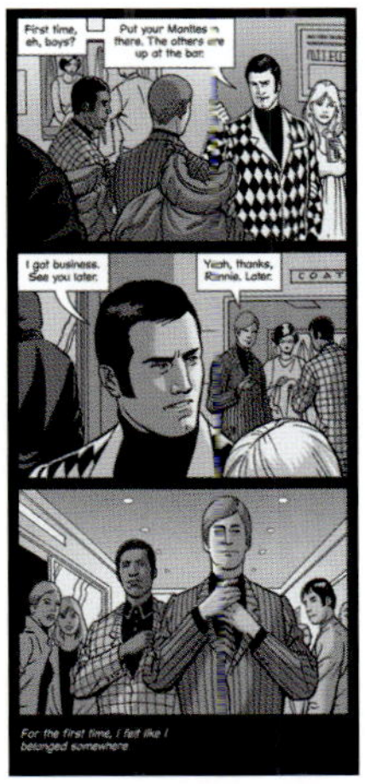

For a man who's been working on comic books for several decades, Dave remains exceptionally enthusiastic about the medium. "It's only ever been comics that I've wanted to do," he admits. "Not general illustration or artwork, but storytelling through pictures."

THE FORMATIVE YEARS

For as long as he can remember, Dave has sketched out characters and scenes. As a trained architect his father would work into the evenings under the glow of an angle-poised lamp, with the tools of his trade

Artist **PROFILE**

Dave Gibbons

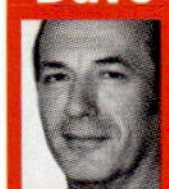

Dave Gibbons is a comic book giant, famous for his work with Alan Moore on Watchmen. He started out with DC and was original art director when 2000 AD was launched

www.davegibbons.net

ORIGINALS

The Originals was scripted and drawn by Dave, and takes the Mods and Rockers battles of the 60s into an alternate future, dealing with the violence of youth cultures.

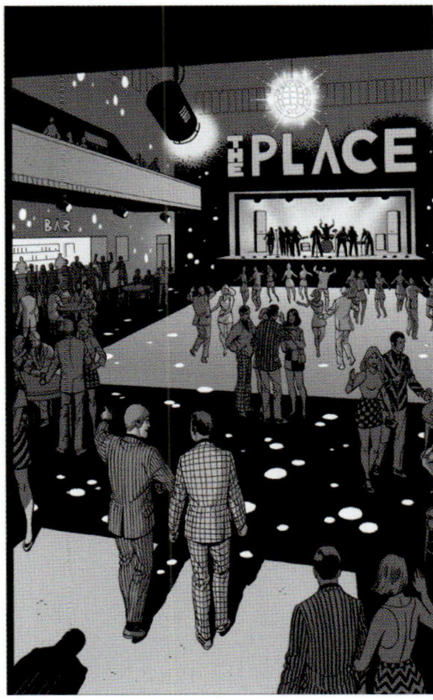

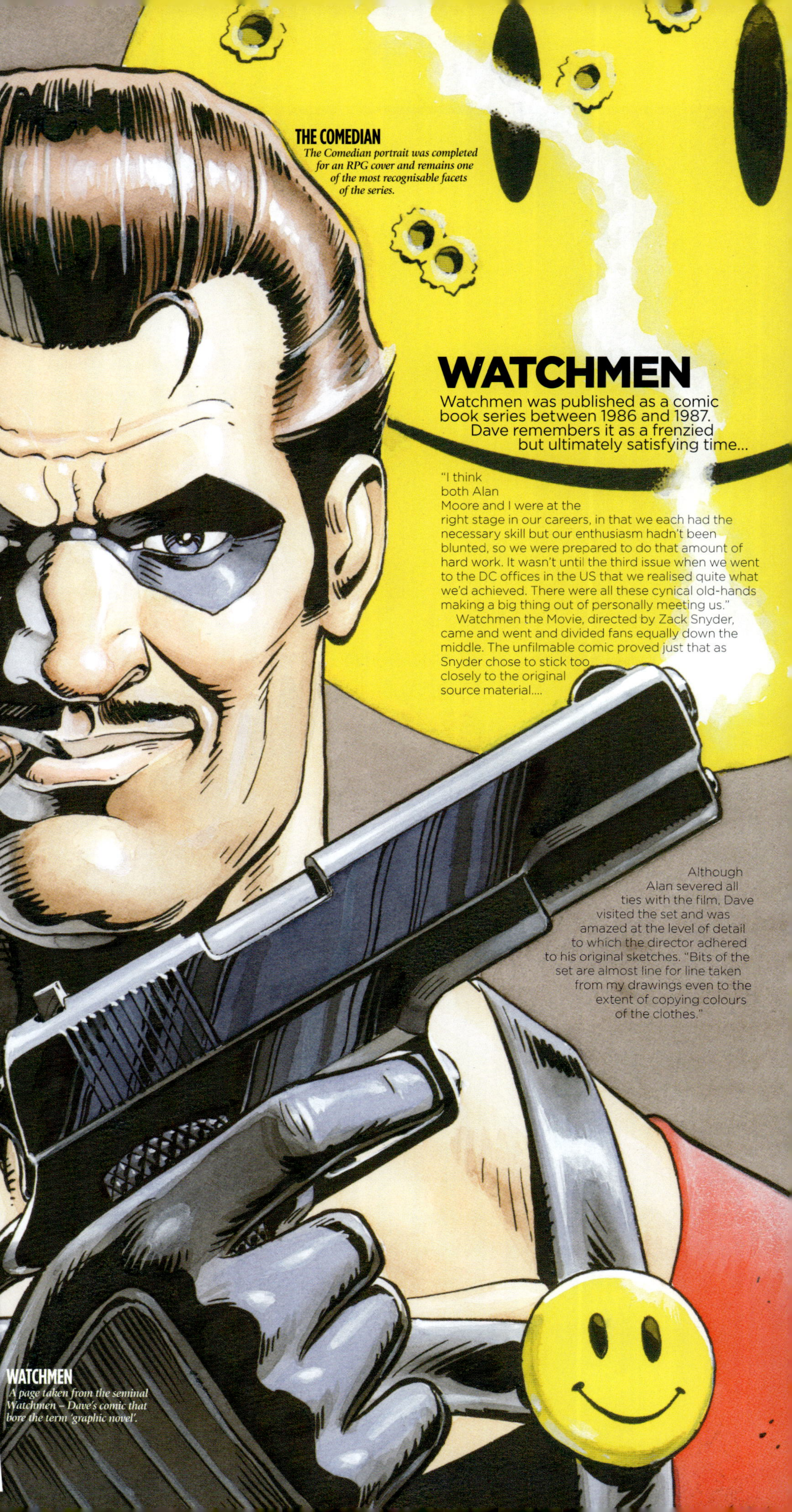

THE COMEDIAN

The Comedian portrait was completed for an RPG cover and remains one of the most recognisable facets of the series.

WATCHMEN

Watchmen was published as a comic book series between 1986 and 1987. Dave remembers it as a frenzied but ultimately satisfying time...

"I think both Alan Moore and I were at the right stage in our careers, in that we each had the necessary skill but our enthusiasm hadn't been blunted, so we were prepared to do that amount of hard work. It wasn't until the third issue when we went to the DC offices in the US that we realised quite what we'd achieved. There were all these cynical old-hands making a big thing out of personally meeting us."

Watchmen the Movie, directed by Zack Snyder, came and went and divided fans equally down the middle. The unfilmable comic proved just that as Snyder chose to stick too closely to the original source material....

Although Alan severed all ties with the film, Dave visited the set and was amazed at the level of detail to which the director adhered to his original sketches. "Bits of the set are almost line for line taken from my drawings even to the extent of copying colours of the clothes."

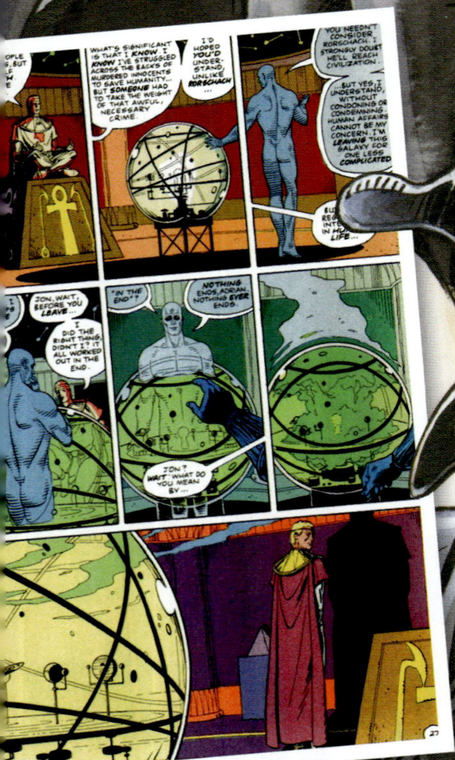

WATCHMEN

A page taken from the seminal Watchmen – Dave's comic that bore the term 'graphic novel'.

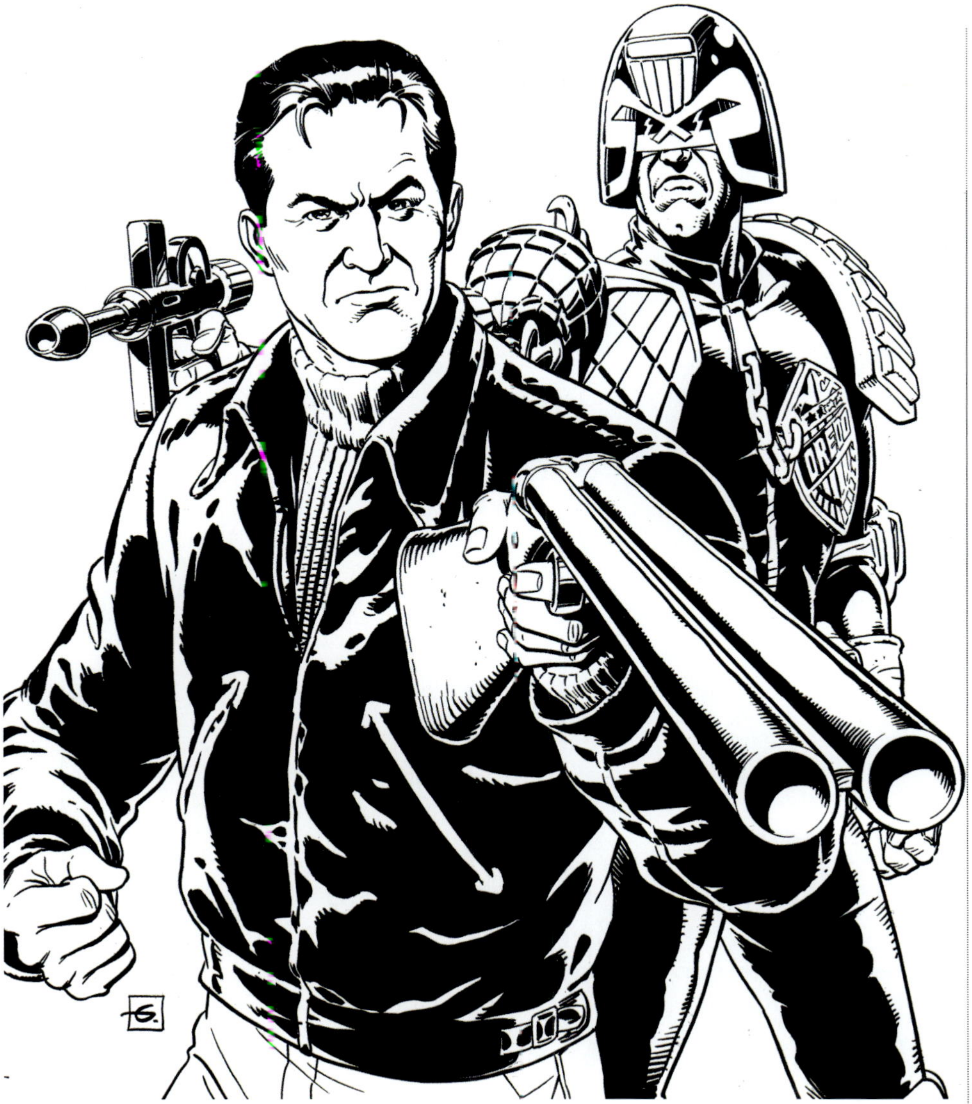

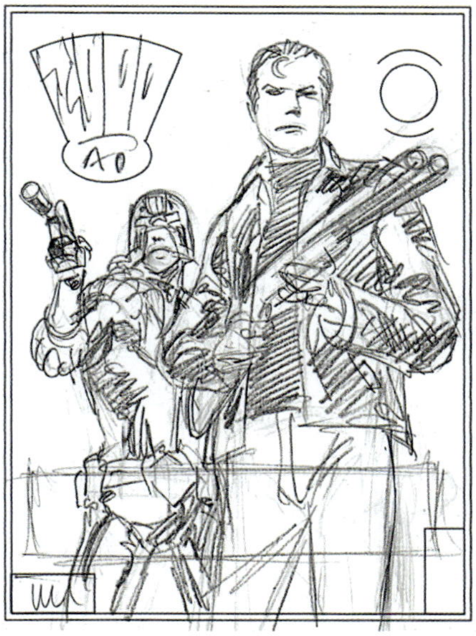

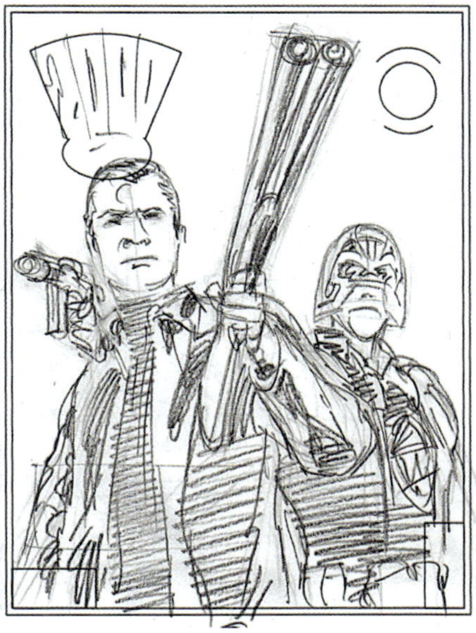

“It’s only ever been comics that I’ve wanted to do, not general illustration or artwork, but storytelling through pictures”

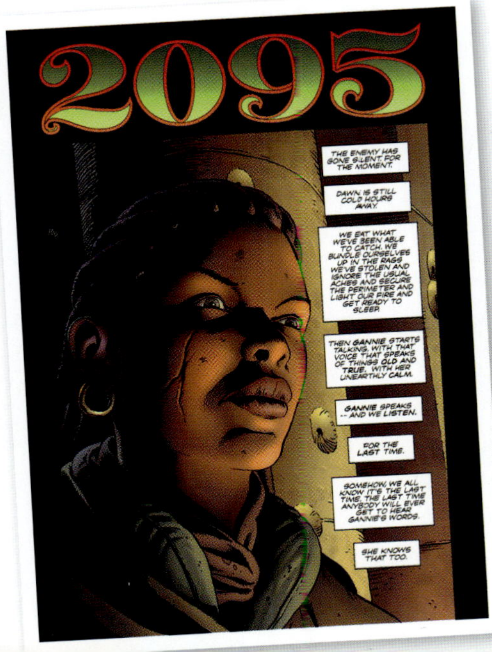

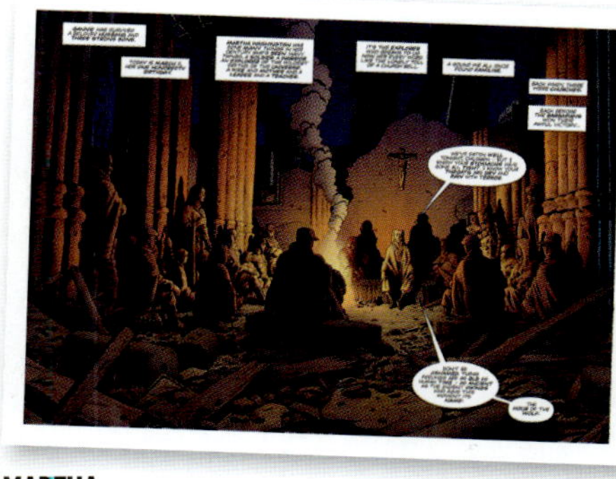

MARTHA
Pencils, line and colour for the final issue of Martha (Martha Washington Dies), on which Dave collaborated with US comic book giant Frank Miller. Colour by Angus McKie.

scattered across a drawing board. Accordingly, Dave was well stocked with drawing paper, Indian inks and watercolours, and would often help his father colour his designs. But while his artistic leaning was no doubt nurtured by his dad’s profession, it was the world of comic books that struck him deeply.

“I have a crystal-clear memory of picking up my first Superman comic when I was in Woolworths with my granddad,” recalls Dave. “After all these years I’ve still got it. It’s got Superman on the cover in a cave with a big chest of diamonds and gems and Lois Lane saying, ‘Superman, you’re also a super-miser.’ I remember thinking, ‘Well, being Superman and having all the girls after you and all that money is the kind of thing I could be interested in.’

“It was the combination of the storytelling and the drama that I loved. It went beyond being a single picture;

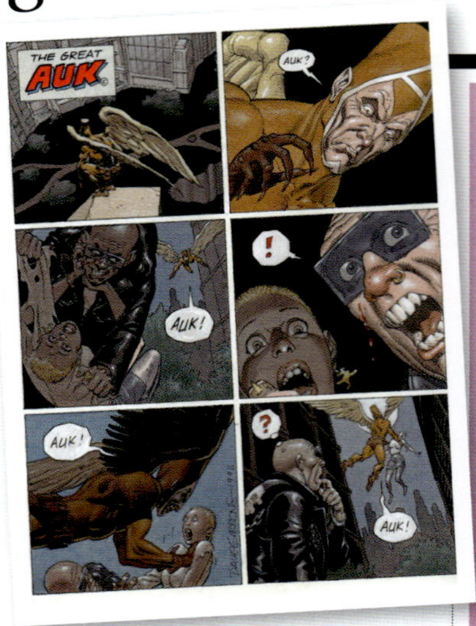

GREAT AUK
A page Dave created for a German magazine. The bad guy's ear-ring became the magazine's logo.

there was a narrative – something where you'd have an experience and see something unfold in front of you, whether that was a joke or a story. It was the nexus of the writing and the pictures that grabbed me and that's still very much my thing."

CAREER PATH

After training as a building surveyor, Dave soon tired of the daily grind of a 'proper' career. His sole highlight was time spent away from the office, during which he'd visit as many comic book shops as possible. After approaching an old friend who worked at IPC Publishing, Dave managed to acquire some lettering work for a Beano-style comic called Cor!! This led to more and more regular lettering work for IPC, and during that time he was careful to take on board all the little nuances of comic book style.

Dave got himself an agent through his IPC work, who set him up with the seminal DC Thompson in Dundee. The work didn't pay that much, but importantly was regular and, according to Dave, imperative in his artistic training.

"I used to send DC my roughs and they'd send them back with very practical changes and comments – things like, 'Make sure you show the character's reaction' or 'We need to see the key going in the lock' and so I soon realised these seemingly minor things were actually incredibly important. That was really my formal education in comic drawing."

With a portfolio of work under his belt and a growing connection with IPC, Dave's agent put him in touch with the formative 2000 AD. Editor Pat Mills was searching for a new talent that didn't rely on the heavy European influences that were permeating comic work of the time. Stumbling upon Dave's style, he offered him a job.

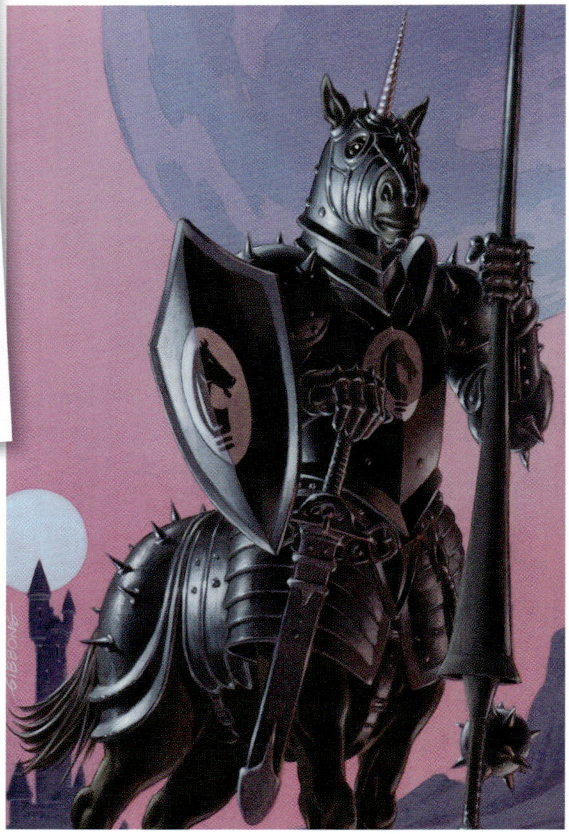

CHEVAL NOIR
Completed for the Dark Horse anthology comic Cheval Noir, this shows Dave's talent at turning away from his famously detailed comic style and applying the same principles to fantasy art.

"I'd learned the ropes and was young, hungry and ready to go," recalls Dave. "People like Mick McMahon and Kevin O'Neill who I'd known from fandom were about to work there and it was very much a case of right place, right time.

"It really was a case of the lunatics taking over the asylum. What you had prior to 2000 AD were people working in the comic book industry who'd ended up there; people who had aspirations to be illustrators or painters. But what we had at 2000 AD was people who'd grown up, like me, solely wanting to work in comics, so it had that mix of influences and a tremendous enthusiasm."

> **"At 2000 AD were people who'd grown up, like me, solely wanting to work in comics, so it had a mix of influences and tremendous enthusiasm"**

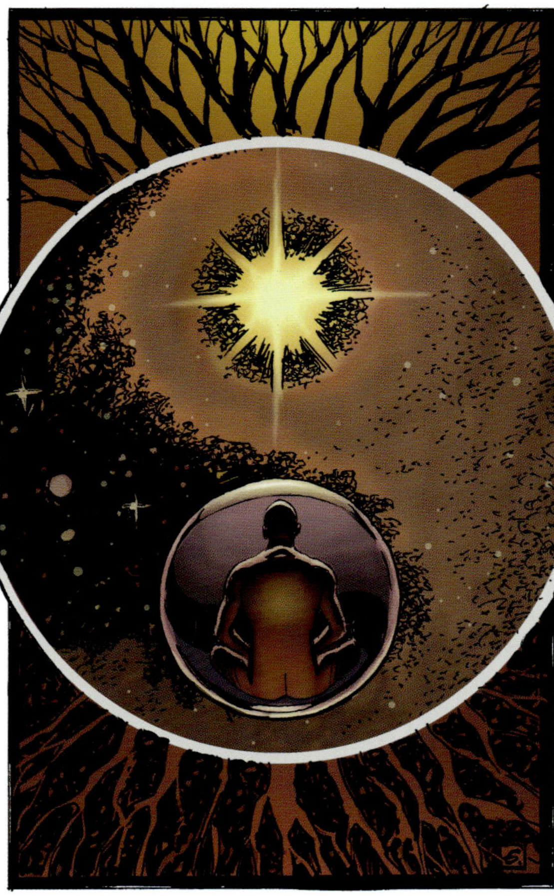

THE FOUNTAIN
Completed roughs and finishes for an illustration to promote Darren Aaronofsky's movie The Fountain.

This heralded the golden age of the UK comic industry, which Dave readily admits was aided by the growing mainstream influence of sci-fi – particularly in wake of the first Star Wars film – and the influence of punk, with adult themes and the anti-authoritarian leanings of the likes of Judge Dredd drawing on punk's pop culture.

WATCHMEN COMETH

In late 1985 Dave teamed up with Alan Moore, the writer who he'd first worked with during a spell drawing Superman. They both set about creating a comic that they, as comic fans themselves, would want to read. Published in 12 single-issue magazines over the 1986 and 1987 period, Watchmen was a revelation, both in terms of sales and structure.

By taking a modernist approach to the traditional comic book hero, Dave and Alan were widely credited with shifting the comic book genre into the realms of high art. The publication of the complete 12 issues as a single volume heralded the birth of the graphic novel. Stan Lee described it as his "all-time favourite comic book outside of Marvel," while in 2005, Time Magazine added Watchmen to its list of the 100 greatest novels in the English language.

"I can remember the day that Alan came to my house and we kicked ideas about and started thinking, 'Well, this is unlike anything we've ever worked on before, this really could be something…'" Dave reminisces. "Not in an arrogant sense, but we felt it was very interesting and I suppose we knew that, as comic book fans ourselves, we were on to something that could be a little bit special."

FROM SKETCH TO SCRIPT

Following the incredible success of Watchmen and a stint as lead artist on Doctor Who Magazine, Dave turned his hand to a number of projects, including a collaboration with the legendary Frank Miller on Give Me Liberty and the ensuing Martha Washington series.

But Dave is a creative soul, and his interest in scriptwriting led him to penning storylines for artist Andy Kubert on Batman vs Predator, as well as for Steve Rude on World's Finest.

Dave's move into scripting culminated in his self-written and drawn series, The Originals. Published in 2004 by Vertigo, The Originals is set in a Judge Dredd-style future, drawing on the imagery of the mods and rockers' pitched battles of the 1960s.

"I think of myself as a storytelling artist as well as a scriptwriter," says Dave. "It's where the two intersect that my interest really lies. In a way I've only ever wanted to draw well enough to tell the story, so that I can convince people what's going on."

HISTORY REPEATING

Though Zack Snyder's Watchmen movie split opinion, possibly because it stuck too closely to Dave and Alan's original comic books, there's no denying that it put the artist back in the public gaze and reminded everyone why he's so special.

"I'm amazed, and I am sure Alan is as well, at the longevity and the status that Watchmen has achieved," he admits. "I look back on it very, very fondly. As a life-long fan of comics, I'm just really pleased to have been involved in something that's had such an influence on the development of comic books."

Looking to the future Dave is working on an eagerly awaited new spy-themed comic series with Mark Millar, writer of Wanted, Kick-Ass and creator of Kapow! Comic-Con and CLiNT. Mark is following in grand footsteps, as past writers who have worked with Dave include the great Frank Miller and of course, Alan Moore. The future looks bright for Dave Gibbons.

Turn the page to learn to paint like Dave Gibbons

HOW DAVE CREATED THE COVER FOR ALBION

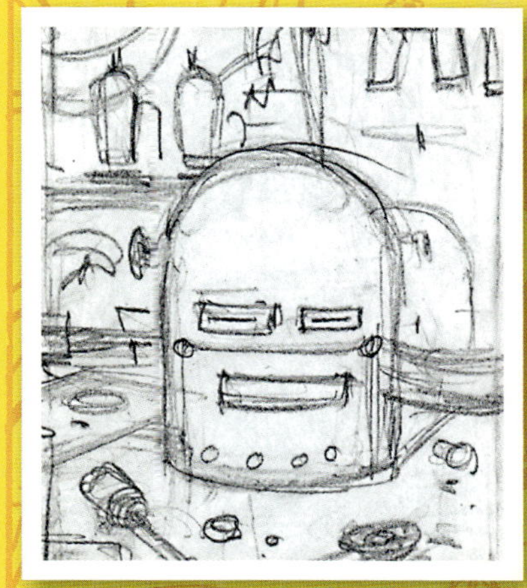

1 A quick pencil rough is enough to nail down the basic composition of the cover image.

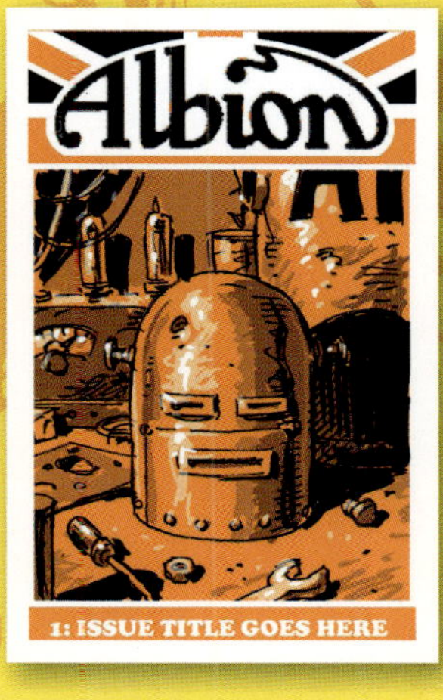

2 Scanned into Photoshop, the rough is loosely inked and combined with a logo, flat colour and tone to give a better idea of the finished piece for editorial approval.

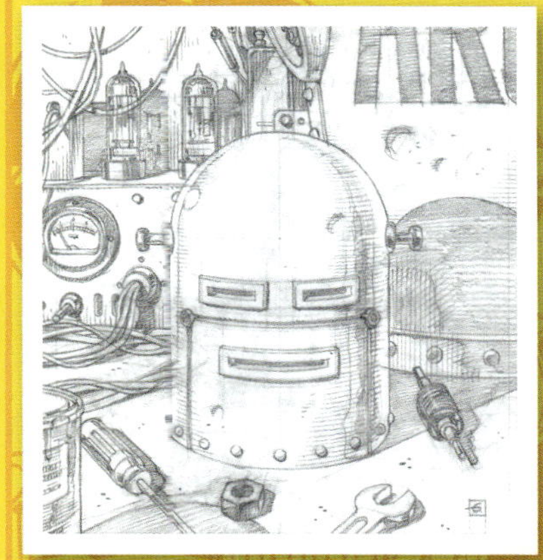

3 Using an artwork-sized printout of the original rough as a trace, the image is tightly drawn in pencil on layout paper.

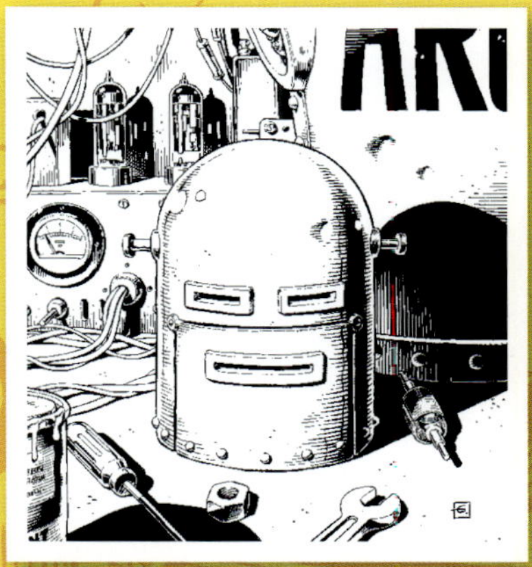

4 Scanned into Photoshop, adjusted and printed out in light blue on to Bristol board, the image is rendered in ink.

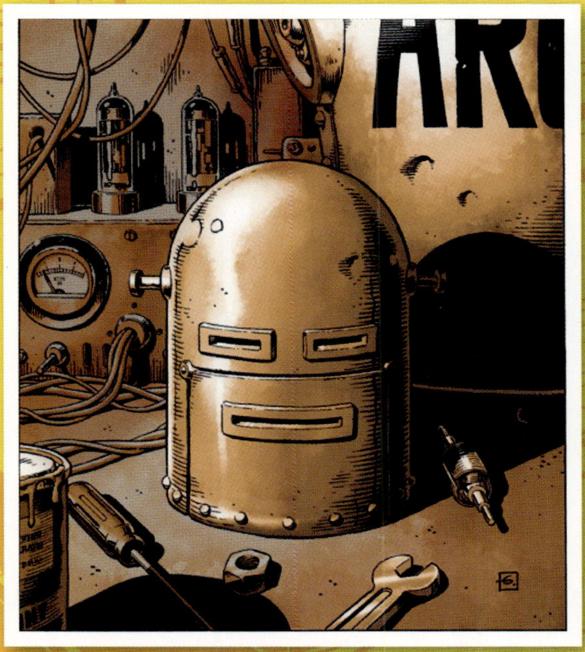

5 After scanning and removing the blue lines, the ink drawing is coloured in Photoshop by Wildstorm's in-house colourist Randy Mayor.

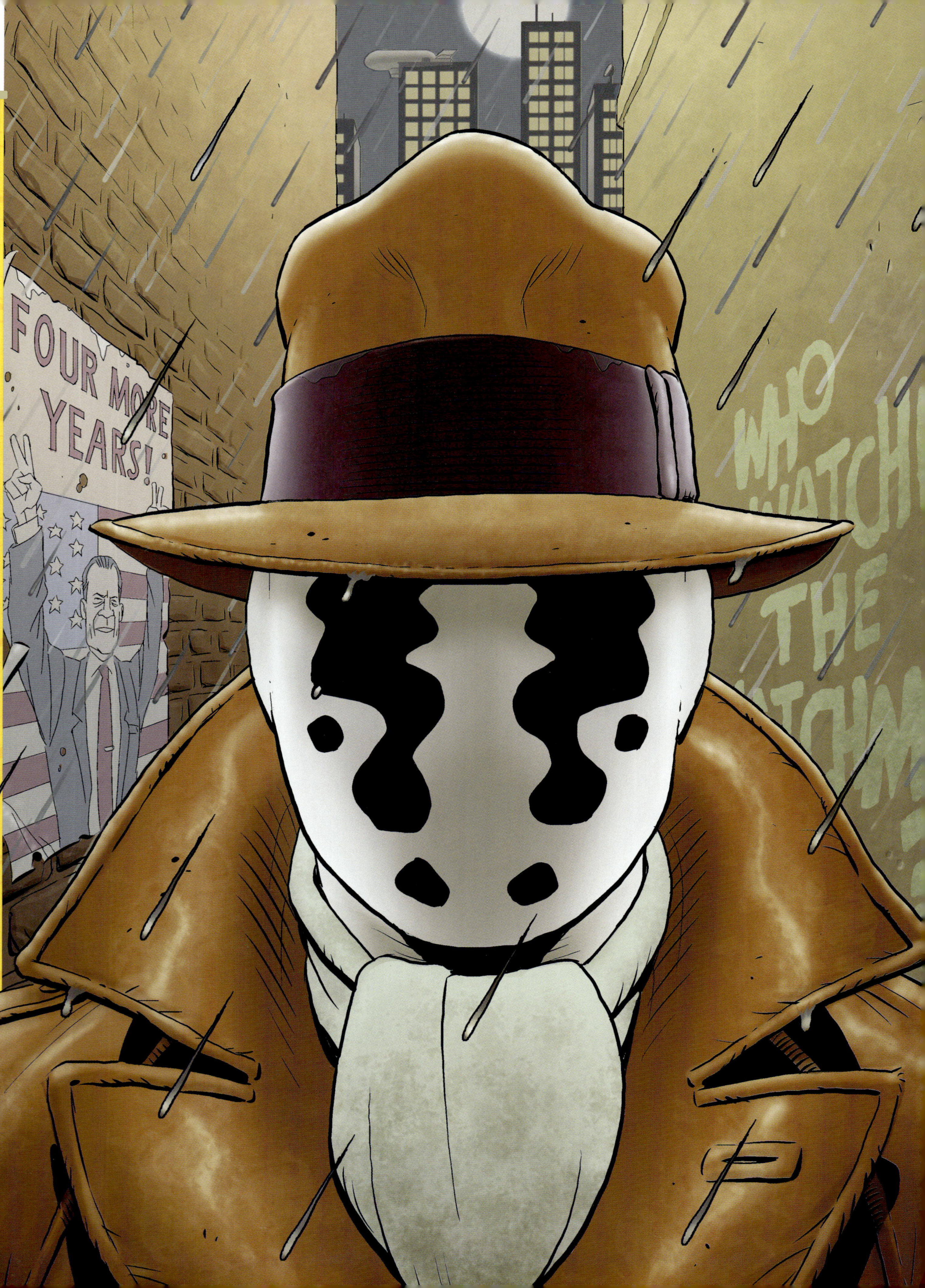
FOUR MORE YEARS!
WHO
THE

Manga Studio & Photoshop

HOW TO PAINT RORSCHACH

Watchmen legend **Dave Gibbons** shows us how he created our exclusive Rorschach cover image

Welcome to my walkthrough on how I created the April 2009 Rorschach cover for ImagineFX. On the left-hand page is the finished thing, more or less as it appeared on the magazine cover. So I'll step back in time, return to the very beginning and try to show you how I got there. As you can see, we went for a straightforward straight-on symmetrical headshot of Rorschach.

I think that he's the character who most people would associate with Watchmen and he's got a really interesting abstract design on his face – which is hopefully quite arresting.

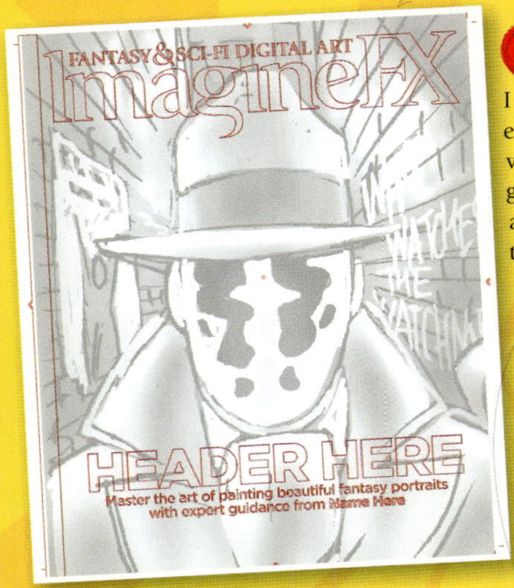

1 Roughing it out

This is the rough sketch that I originally agreed with Paul, the art editor of ImagineFX. This was done very quickly in Photoshop, just in greyscale, to give an idea of how all the cover elements might work together in the end.

2 Getting perspective

Here's the same rough, placed into Manga Studio – which is a really useful piece of kit for doing the equivalent of comic book work in. It's got some wonderful pencilling and inking tools. It also has a very nice feature that you can use to quickly establish perspective, drawing lines that radiate from a point. I use this tool to begin setting up the perspective on the brick wall.

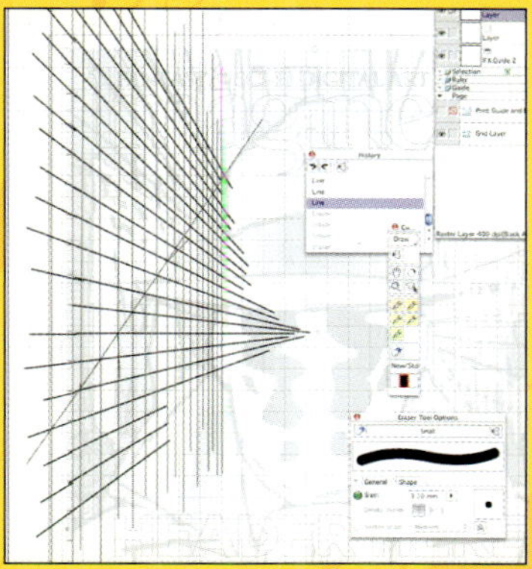

PRO SECRETS

Keep it simple

I pencil fairly loosely early on. You can zoom in to do details, but generally with a pencil drawing it's probably best if you keep more or less at the same scale and don't get too lost in details at an early stage.

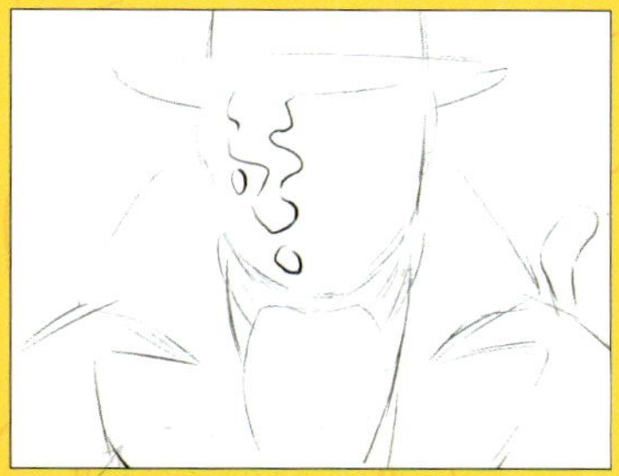

3 Retracing steps

I use the Manga Studio Pencil tool to trace over the original rough, just to get a slightly cleaned up, better-proportioned version of it. It's still loose and, I think you'll agree, looks like real pencil.

4 Symmetrical sketch

This is done using Manga's Symmetry tool, which enables you to draw symmetrically on an axis. I only had to draw the left-hand side of Rorschach's hat and it drew the right-hand side for me automatically – pretty useful.

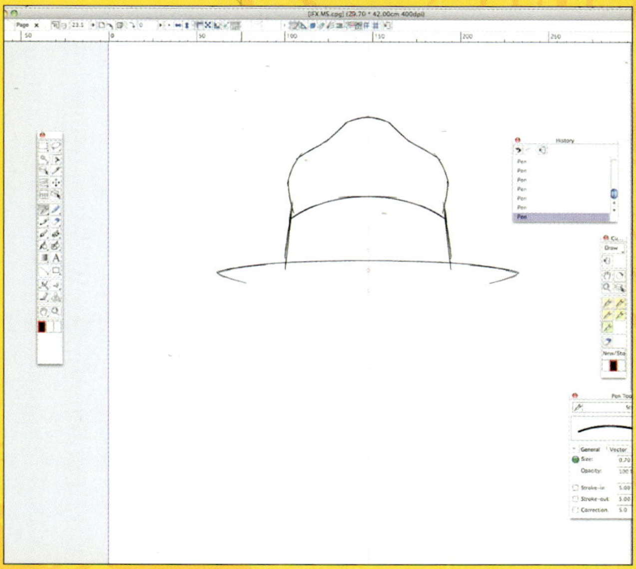

Shortcuts

Copy layer
Ctrl+Alt+T
This makes a copy of the layer that you want to transform.

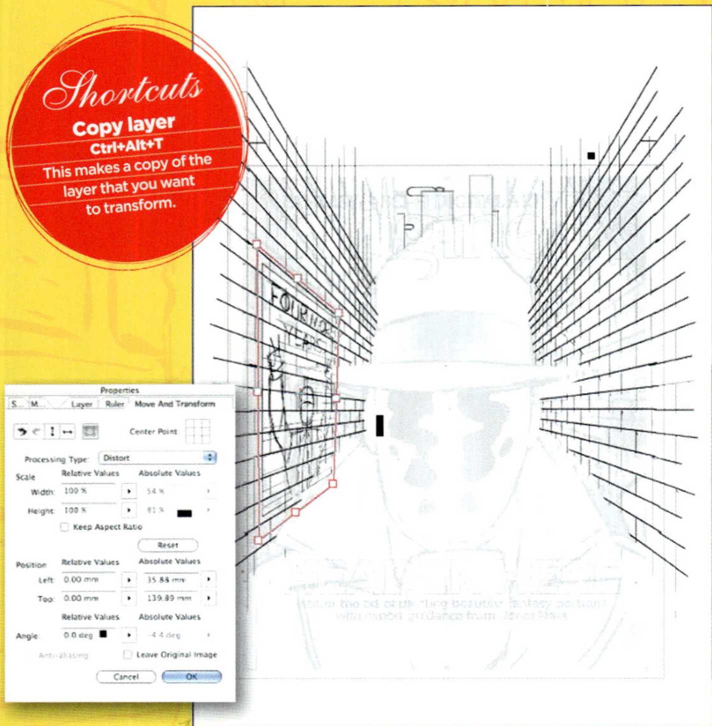

5 Getting the background convincing

I'm working a bit more on the walls, here. Although we only see a little bit of the wall on the right, I wanted to make sure that it fitted with the other side, which is quite simple if you're drawing symmetrically. You can also see the poster on the wall, which, again, I drew quickly in Manga Studio, then did a Perspective Transform on.

All this kind of work is mechanical, but it's really necessary if you want to get background elements to look convincing. It's always worth a bit of preparation here, particularly if you're using software that very easily enables you to get certain effects.

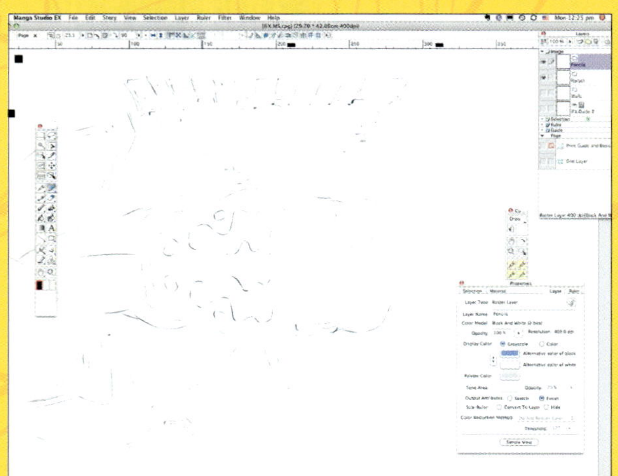

PRO SECRETS

Make it grubby
Use Hue/Saturation as a useful method of globally adjusting elements in the picture. I used it to add effects like the grunge on Rorschach's scarf.

6 Expand with freehand

As well as being drawn in Manga Studio, this image was drawn on my other new toy – a Wacom Cintiq tablet – which is a screen where you actually draw on the image with a pressure-sensitive pen. Because of the size of the Cintiq tablet and the fact that it will rotate to any orientation, I actually turn it so that it's in portrait, rather than landscape format. Then it's exactly the same as drawing on a piece of illustration board and it gives precisely the same sensation. Here I'm just pencilling freehand. I've already got the symmetrical sketch underneath, but it would be too much to do the pencil sketch symmetrically as well – it would look far too mechanical. So I'm just using this drawing as a guide.

7 Begin inking

Next I begin the inking process, which is done on a separate layer in Manga Studio. I've knocked the Opacity of the pencils back a bit I think (although I may have actually brought them forward here for the sake of clarity) and I'm just inking as I normally would. The fact you can rotate the working surface mimics the conventional painting process.

8 Adding detail

I could have done the lettering on the poster by distorting some typeset of the words 'four more years'. But I did it the way that I did all lettering in Watchmen – by hand. The easy way to do this is to rule top and bottom lines, fill in the letters in between them and then erase lines when you don't need them. This helps to keep everything nicely lined up.

9 Switch to CMYK

Okay, now we're in Photoshop, where I've turned the black and white Manga Studio image into a CMYK document. It's useful to have the black line in a separate channel – particularly if you have to make a selection. This is handy if you want to turn the black line into a different colour, and it's also a good standby in case everything goes terribly wrong later on.

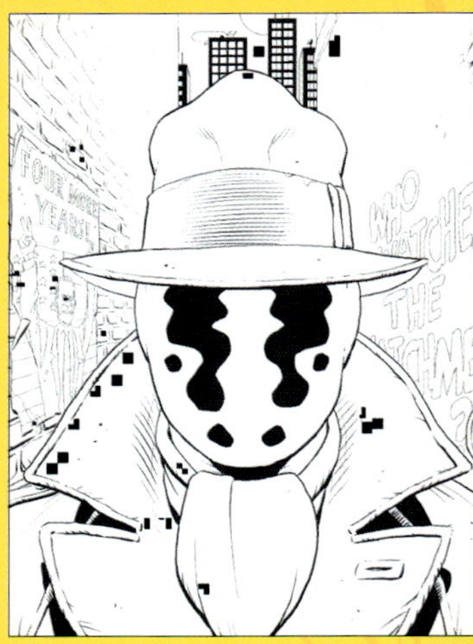

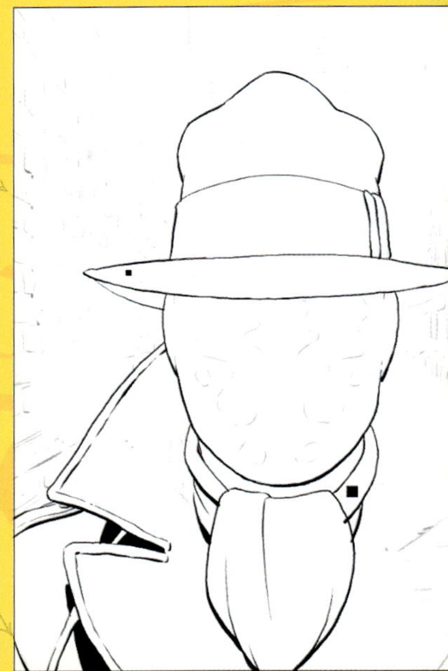

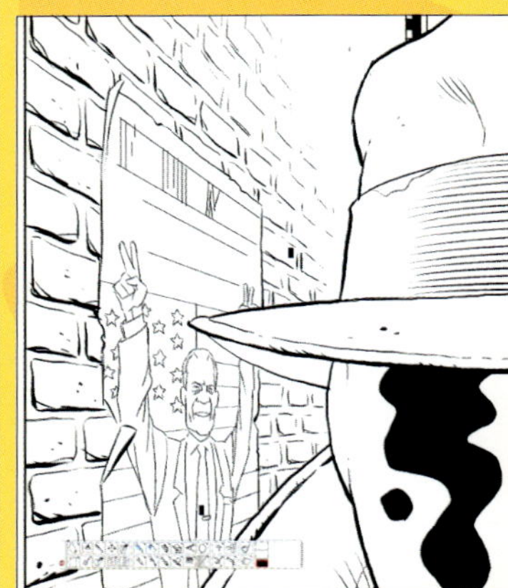

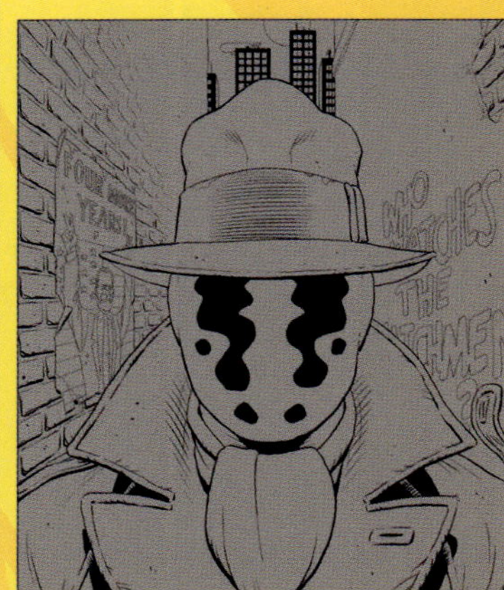

10 Beginning to add colour

This is the first stage in doing the flat colours – anything I do in colour with line art, I always make sure that I have a flat version of it. It's also always a good idea to work from large to small. As you can see from the screenshot above, I've covered the whole image area with a kind of darkish, middlish tone.

11 Shading the figure

Now I separate out the next big element, which is the figure of Rorschach. I've done the whole thing in one colour, making it very easy to separate out the hatband, for instance, with the Lasso tool. You can click round the hatband, but you don't have to worry about selecting the edge of it again, because you can go beyond that into the background colour and then fill the colour in – not by using Opt+Del, but by clicking with the Paint Bucket tool. This will only fill in the colour that you've got on your foreground object, which saves selecting edges twice – and this can be a real time-saver in the long run.

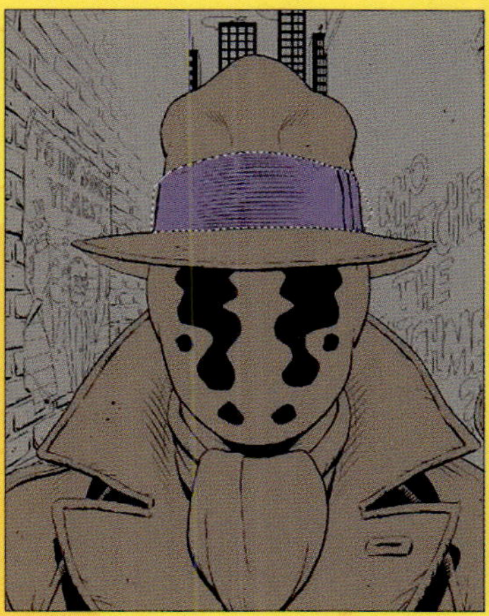

12 Create channels

Once I've got the flat colour in, I copy the whole Colour layer, then paste it into a channel. I've called this channel Flat. Now that you have it saved seperately you can back to that channel at any point later on, with the Magic Wand tool and select any area. So even after you've rendered an area, you can still get back to the whole flat area.

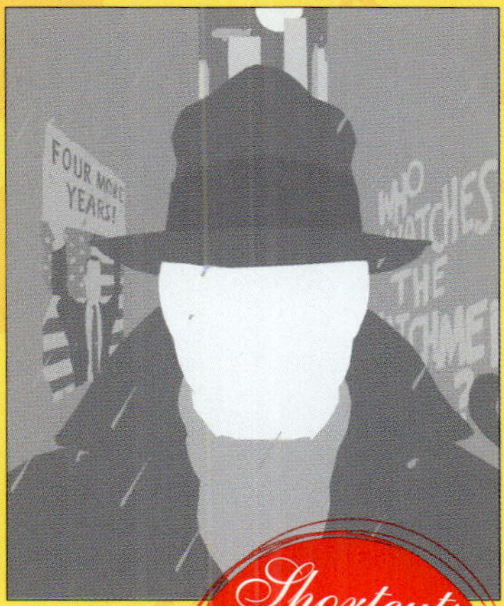

13 Colour hold

This shows what's known in the trade as a Colour Hold; where you turn an area of black line work into colour line. It's useful for knocking a background back. Use your Line channel to select the Line layer and delete the areas that you don't want, then fill those areas with the colour of your choice. If you select Preserve Transparency on the layer you can do it without recourse to the channel. This is an easier way of ensuring you only select exactly the area you want to change.

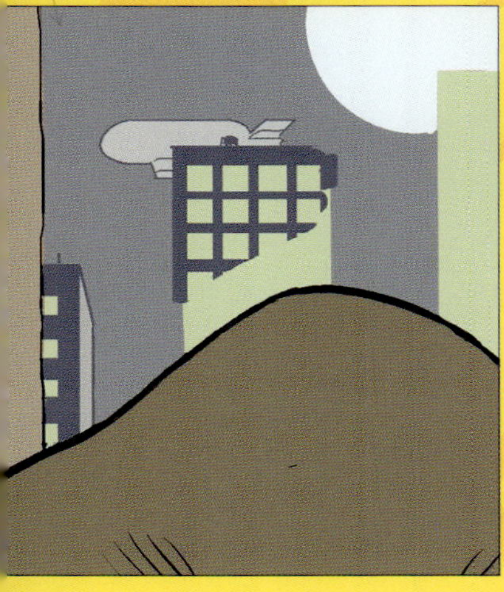

Shortcuts
Undo lasso
Backspace
When using the Polygonal Lasso tool, Backspace will undo a lasso step each time you press.

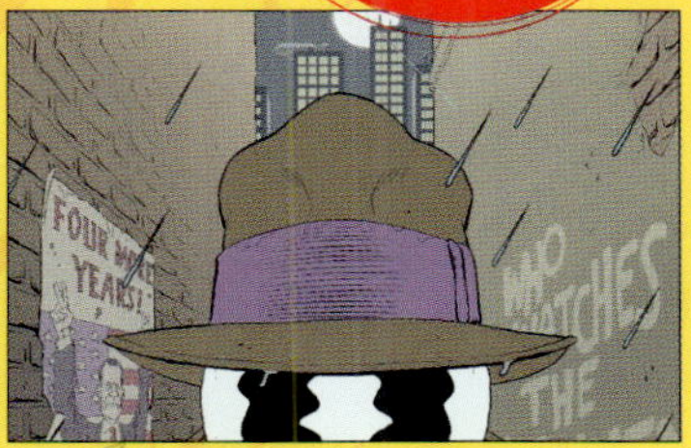

14 Creating distance

This is the gradient going on to the background walls. As you can see, I've dragged out a gradient from the centre of the moon and also put a little blur around its edge. It's actually just a feathered selection that I've filled in. I've used this to make the moon look distant – and as if you were looking at it through the damp of a rainy sky.

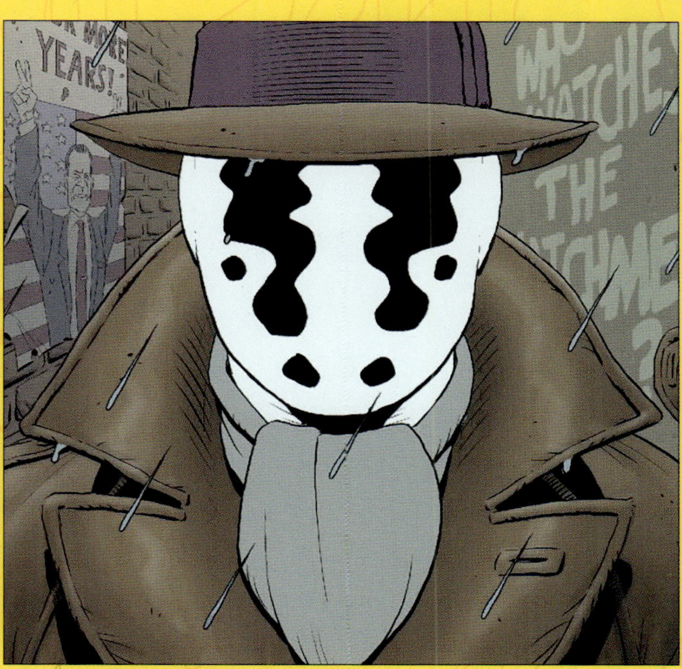

15 Rendering the tones

I'm now rendering on top of the Colour layer. Although I sometimes like to render straight onto the Colour layer, it can be useful to have a couple of layers – one set to Multiply and one set to Screen. You can use the Multiply layer to darken and the Screen layer to lighten. If you always lighten with the same colour and darken with its own colour, this can help to give a sense of consistency to the lighting throughout the scene. Set your Brush, your Airbrush, or your Pencil at a fairly low Opacity so that you can actually build up the lights and darks on it.

16 Getting dirty

Here we're coming in a little closer to show you a brush that I've used to add a bit of dirt and texture to the image. I'm not sure where I got this brush – it was probably off an ImagineFX DVD – but it's a texture brush that you can use on one of the Screen and Multiply layers, just to add a bit of character and interest to the subject matter.

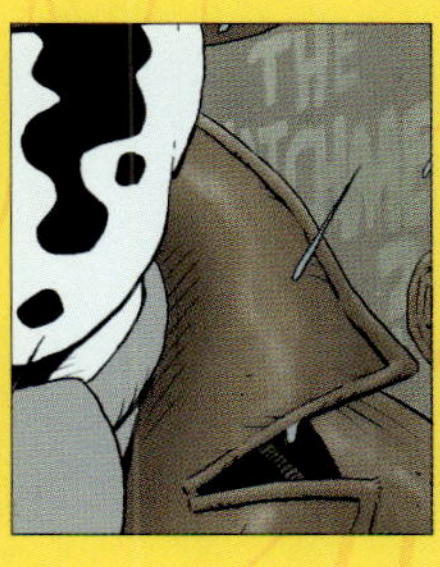

17 Raining (Watch)men

I've put a frame on a layer showing me where the trim of the cover will be. As you can see, I've got some layers here for the rain. We've got the rain that I drew in my line art layer and another that I've called Tiny Rain, which I made by putting random dots on a layer and using Motion Blur. The More Tiny Rain layer is the same again, but smaller and again using Hue/Saturation and so on. At this point I've just done it all over the whole image and later, using the Flat channel, I'll delete bits of rain that are in the way. So this is the end – I hope it's been of interest.

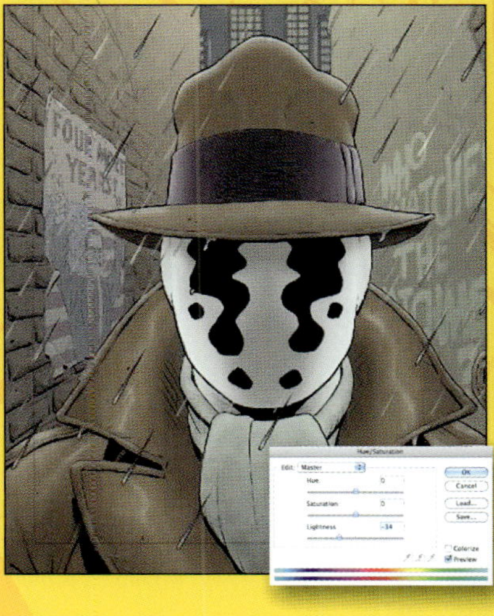

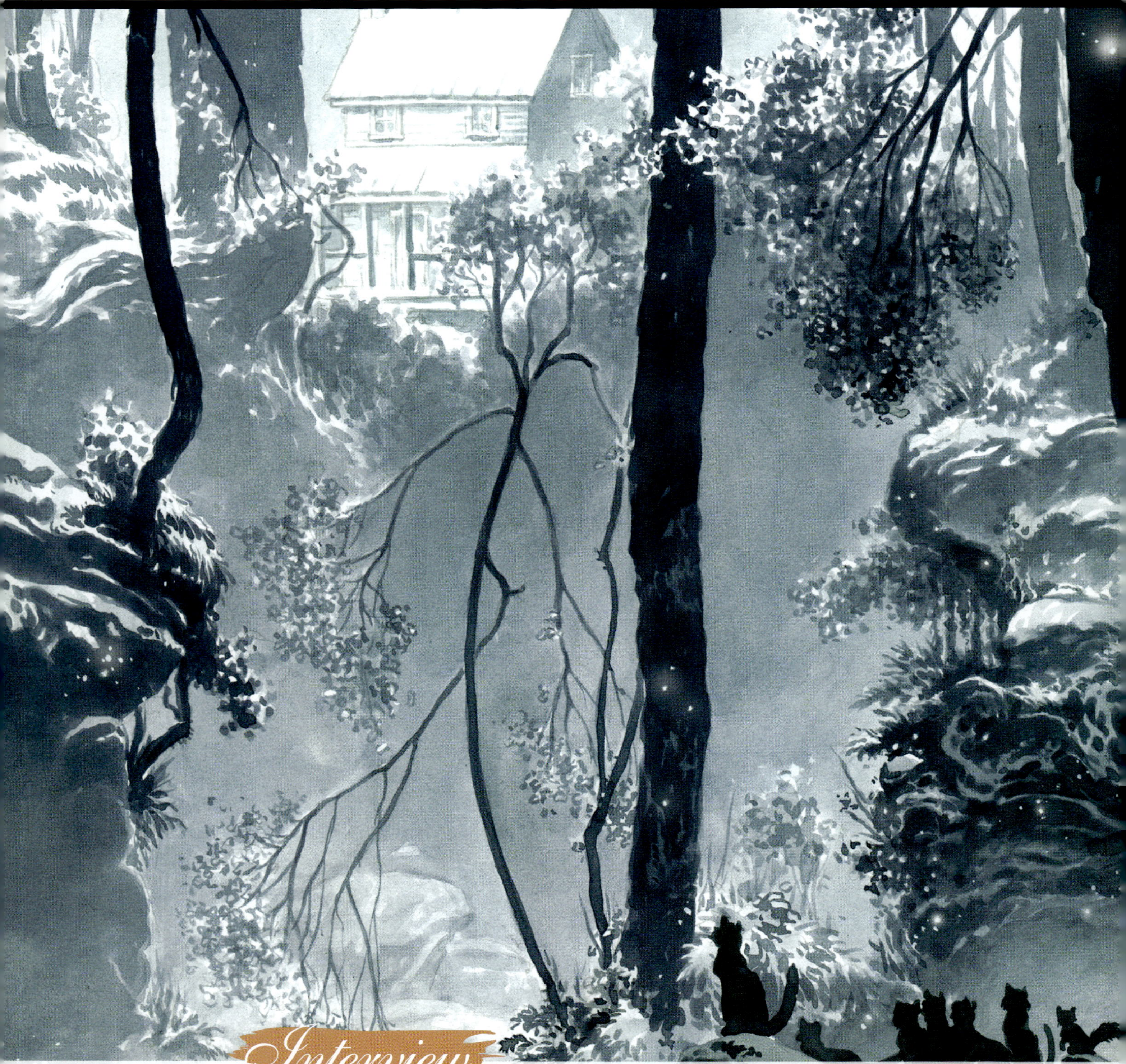

Interview

Charles Vess

The creator of one of the most iconic 80s Marvel covers, **Charles Vess** always wanted to run from the world of the superheroes into the land of the fairies...

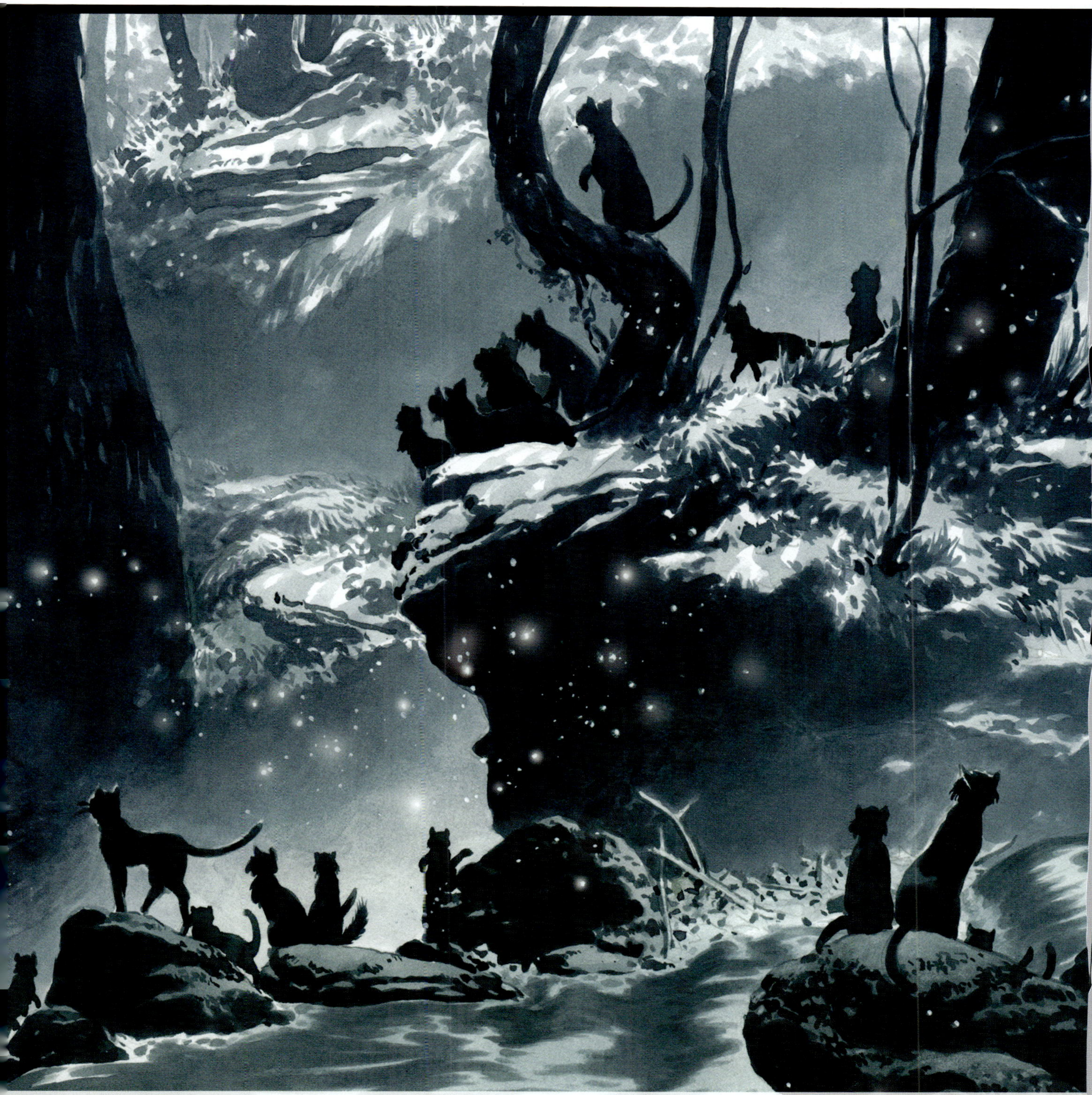

A CIRCLE OF CATS
The fascinating endpapers for Charles de Lint's book of the same name.

Charles Vess is laughing. Having just arrived home from a trip encompassing two conventions and an exhibition at the Galerie Daniel Maghen in Paris, he has plenty of cause to feel happy. "It was right on the Seine," he says. "You could walk outside the gallery with a glass of champagne and toast Notre Dame down the way. It was gratifying, as an artist, to be there. Then, when I came home, I found out I'd won the World Fantasy Award for Best Artist."

It's the third time he's been recognised by the body, and the prize is just one of numerous accolades he's collected over a career in fantasy spanning four decades. But he doesn't like to describe his style as fantastical. For him, that equates to large men in armour fighting dragons. The Vess approach is more subtle.

"When I was first trying to break in, I tried to develop paintings that had those aspects in them," he says. "After a while, I began to realise that I was just flat-out

Artist **PROFILE**

Charles Vess

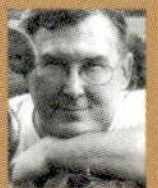

After training in fine art at Virginia Commonwealth University in Richmond, Charles escaped to New York in 1976, establishing himself as a comic artist and fantasy illustrator. He later returned to his home state of Virginia, where he now lives.
www.greenmanpress.com

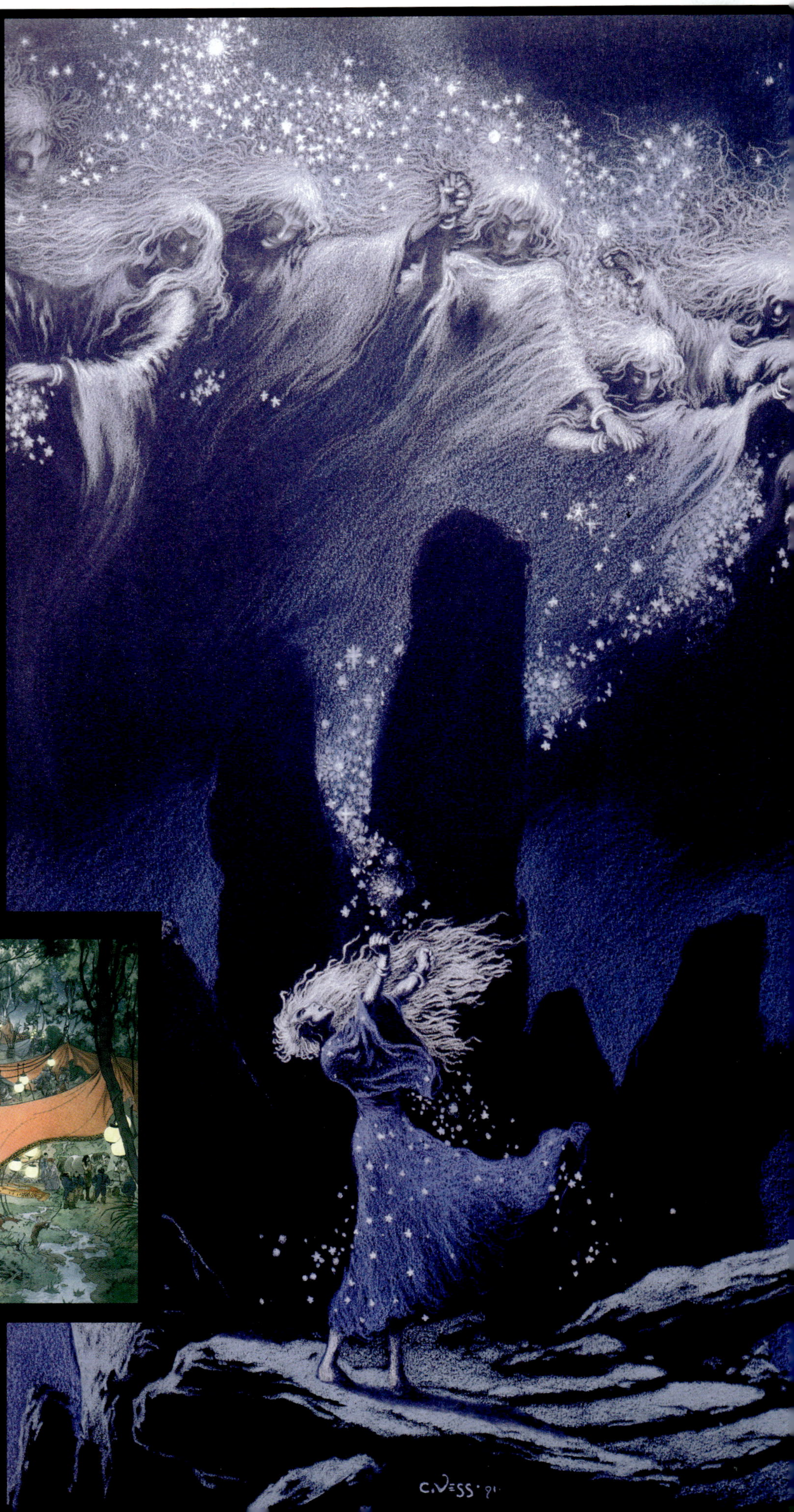

THE SLOW DANCE OF THE INFINITE STARS
This image from Stardust is imbued with the kind of subtle and poetic undertones that Charles loves.

A SPRINKLING OF STARDUST

Charles Vess looks back on a magical tale that swept him into the realm of fantasy

Arguably the finest fantasy illustration works in the Charles Vess portfolio are the 175 illustrations that he did for Neil Gaiman's story Stardust. The book was released in 1998 and is set in the 19th century, but it also takes the reader over into the ethereal world of fairies.

Charles more or less thrives on the influences of artists like Arthur Rackham and Alphonse Mucha and, fittingly, the story opens in a faerie market. "Neil is quite good," says Charles. "He doesn't just write for the artist involved; he might also write something that'll pull you out of what you're used to and challenge you a bit. It's quite fun working with him.

"Stardust really changed people's perception of my work, and I sort of crept out of the comic book direct market into the world of illustration with the book," he goes on. "I've been moving that way every since."

The collaboration between Charles and Neil has been mutually beneficial over the years, and a film version of Stardust came out in 2007, which credited Vess for his artwork and also renewed interest in the print version. "The movie did really well in Europe, but not too well in the US," Charles says. "It made the book sell like crazy, though, so that was good. I'm proud of the work, and still love looking at it."

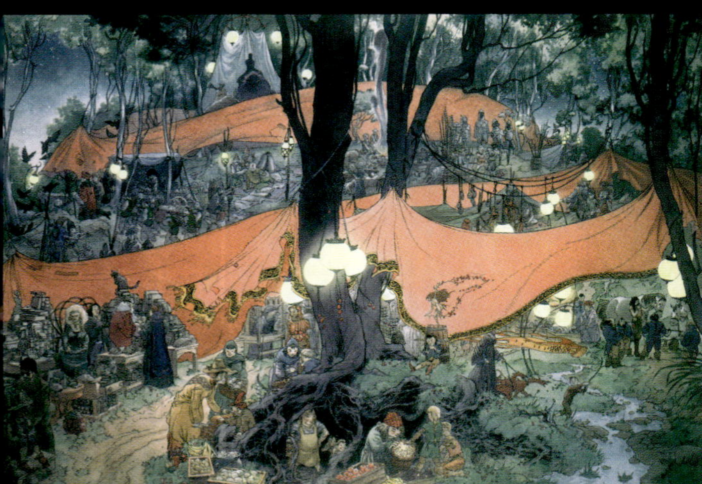

THE FAIRY MARKET
Neil Gaiman's storyline for Stardust gave Charles ample opportunity to indulge his passion for Rackham-esque painting. It's a particular favourite of the artist's and he's never bowed to pressure to sell it to collectors.

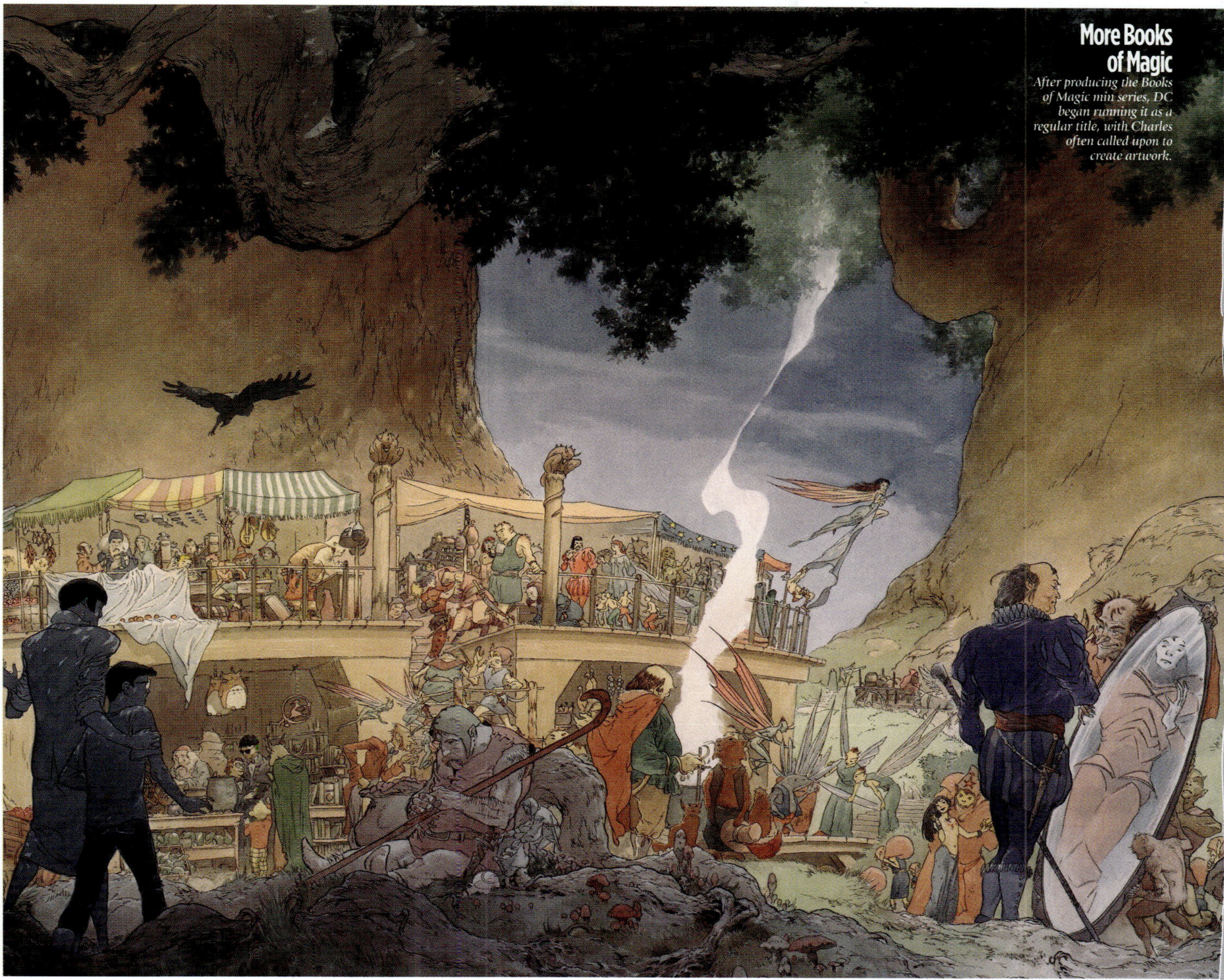

More Books of Magic
After producing the Books of Magic min series, DC began running it as a regular title, with Charles often called upon to create artwork.

“I love the way the words and pictures collaborate to make a third world that neither one of the words nor pictures can make by themselves”

bad at it. So I tend to keep to the woodland scenes with elves and fairies.”

THE COMIC CONNECTION

That's not to say he excludes heroes and drama. Take the Spider-Man painting used on the front of Web of Spider-Man issue one (see page 110). The superhero's black suit couldn't look more vivid, yet Charles managed to project a moody, Gothic setting that Marvel readers weren't used to in 1985. Alongside artists like Bill Sienkiewicz, he brought an arty approach to comics that would set the market on fire.

Aside from painting in liquid inks, he also uses watercolour and oil. And as well as painting, he writes, sculpts and designs stage sets. Charles often refers to a nebulous borderland he likes to inhabit: “I love the interaction between words and pictures, and that can be done with an illustrated book, comic book, picture book for children, or movie. I just love the way the words and pictures collaborate to make a third world that neither one of the words nor pictures can make by themselves. Playing in that borderland is what I really enjoy in all my art.”

The popularity of the Web of Spider-Man cover boosted his reputation, leading to more high profile work. Spider-Man: Spirits of the Earth was a graphic novel he wrote and drew that came out in 1990. Then he had a fantastic run of Swamp Thing covers, working with the writer Nancy Collins.

“That was blissful, drawing all the roots and branches I ever wanted to draw,” says Charles. “He's basically a green man, like the old pagan, nature archetype. I applied a lot of techniques to the painting of those images. I learned a lot doing a painting a month, and trying different techniques, different applications and different ways to produce an interesting cover.”

During the same period, Charles began doing artwork for the Books of Magic series. This brought him into contact with one of his most important collaborators, Neil Gaiman. They produced the award-winning Sandman #19, an adaptation of A Midsummer Night's Dream. Further projects surfaced, and the comic world began to lose its grip on both of them. ➔

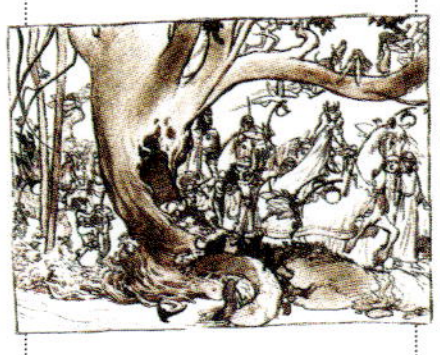

Charles Vess workshop
Discover the thought processes and ideas behind one of Charles's classic faerie images, Companions to the Moon.

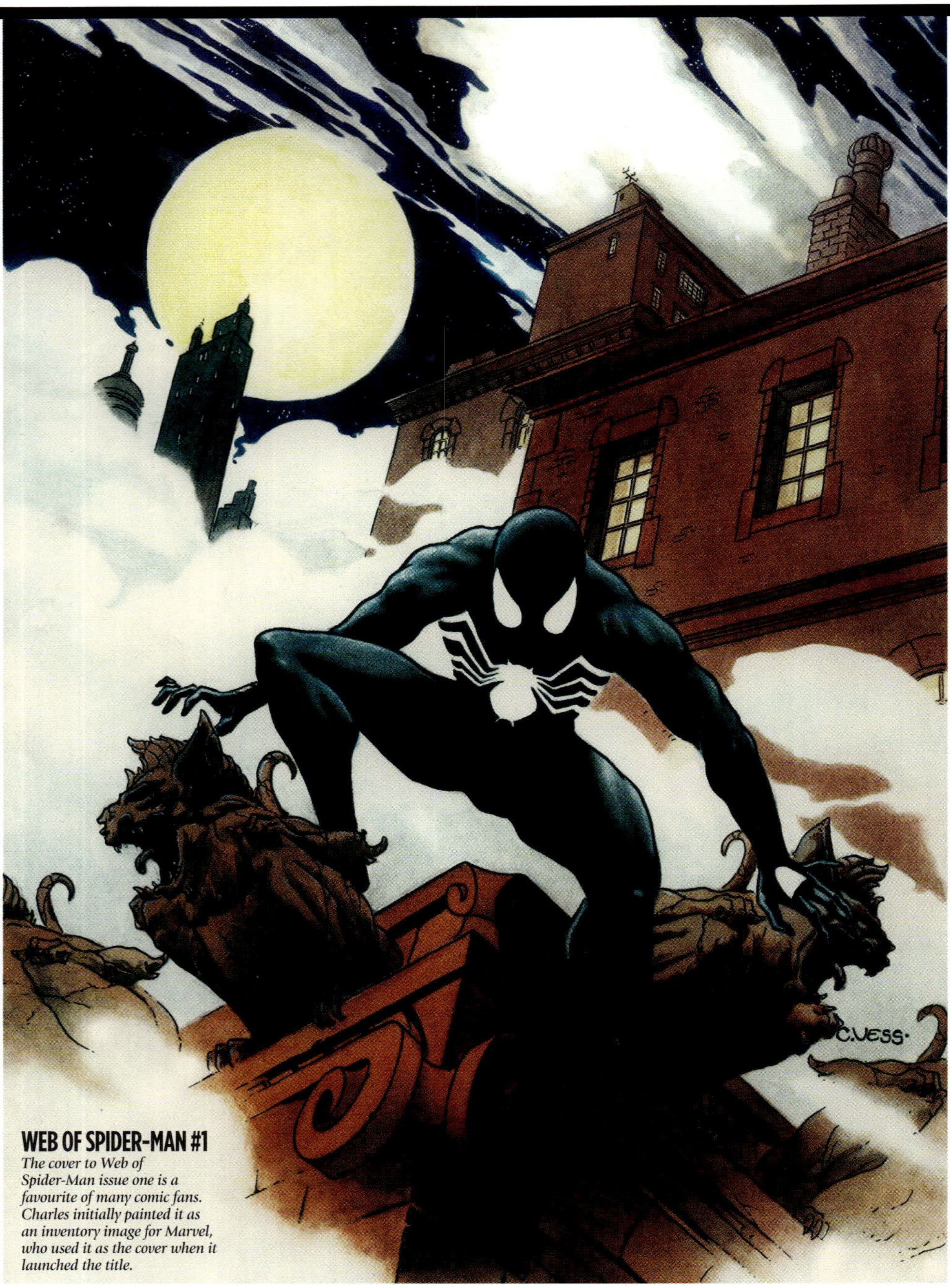

WEB OF SPIDER-MAN #1
The cover to Web of Spider-Man issue one is a favourite of many comic fans. Charles initially painted it as an inventory image for Marvel, who used it as the cover when it launched the title.

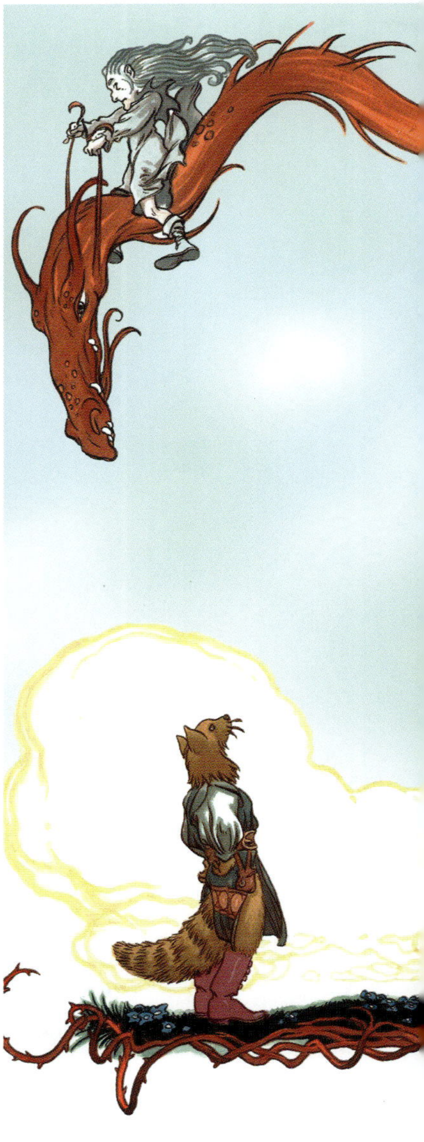

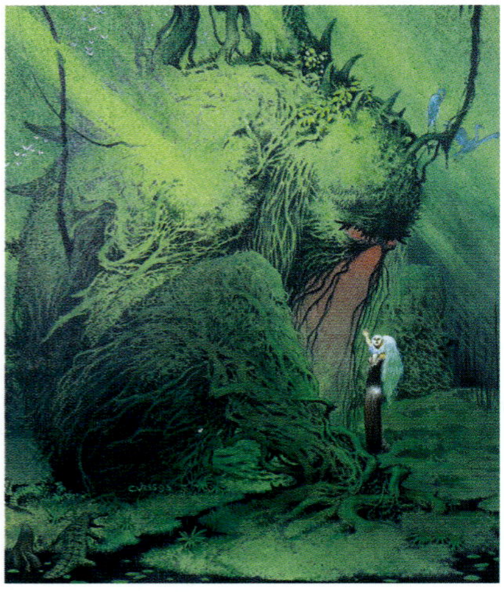

SWAMP THING #135
Charles loves the mystical, paganistic, Green Man aspect to the Swamp Thing character, but also used the opportunity to paint these covers to experiment with his techniques.

"With superheroes, whoever has the biggest fist wins. It's not the way I think of life. I want work that's subtle, suggestive and poetic"

"With superheroes, whoever has the biggest fist wins." says Charles. "It's not the way I think of life. I want work that's subtle and poetic; that leaves room for the reader or viewer to participate in the story."

In 1997 and 1998, Charles and Neil worked on perhaps their most important project. The four-part story, Stardust, included 175 paintings and won numerous awards. More recently, Charles has illustrated Gaiman's Blueberry Girl poem, which was released in 2009. Early last year, Instructions, in which they created a children's guide to faerieland, came out.

Shortly after Stardust appeared, Charles's wife Karen suffered spinal injuries in a car accident. They didn't have insurance to cover the treatment they needed, so Charles looked for ways to raise funds. Gaiman suggested asking artists to contribute to a follow-up to Stardust. Charles invited 30 artists, including Mike Mignola and Brian Froud, to get involved with A Fall of Stardust. For legal reasons it wasn't published as a

INSTRUCTIONS

Charles's latest collaboration with Neil Gaiman is Instructions, a book that guides the reader through the realm of fairies.

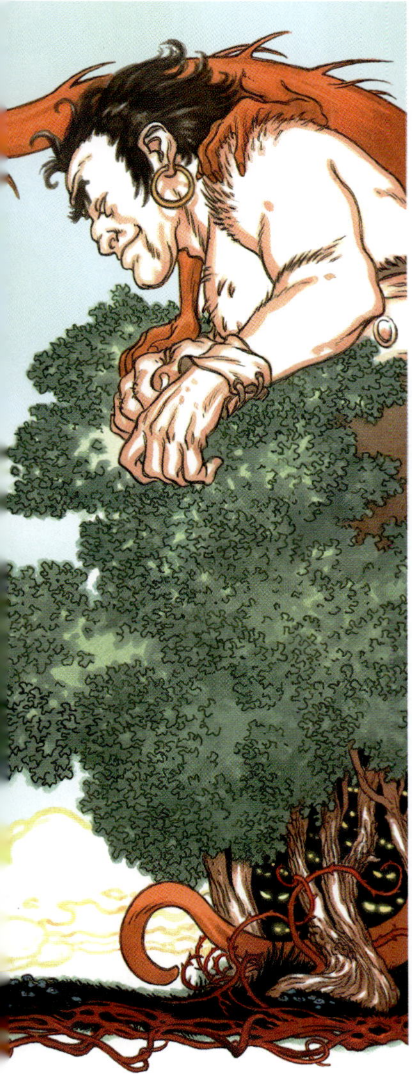

book, released instead as a portfolio with two Stardust story pamphlets.

"It's a really interesting, creative way to deal with a devastating incident," says Charles. "Just doing the footwork on this was quite a bit of work. Any time you're getting a bunch of artists doing one thing, you're herding cats."

Today, he's as busy as ever. While a 4x8 foot watercolour sits on his easel, he's also painting 50 images for an expansion to Charles de Lint's A Circle of Cats. And there's more. "I'm working on a project called The Greenwood, and it has sections of graphic narrative, pure text and illustration. There I am in the borderland again, playing with all these different things, and that's exciting."

Turn the page to learn to paint like Charles Vess

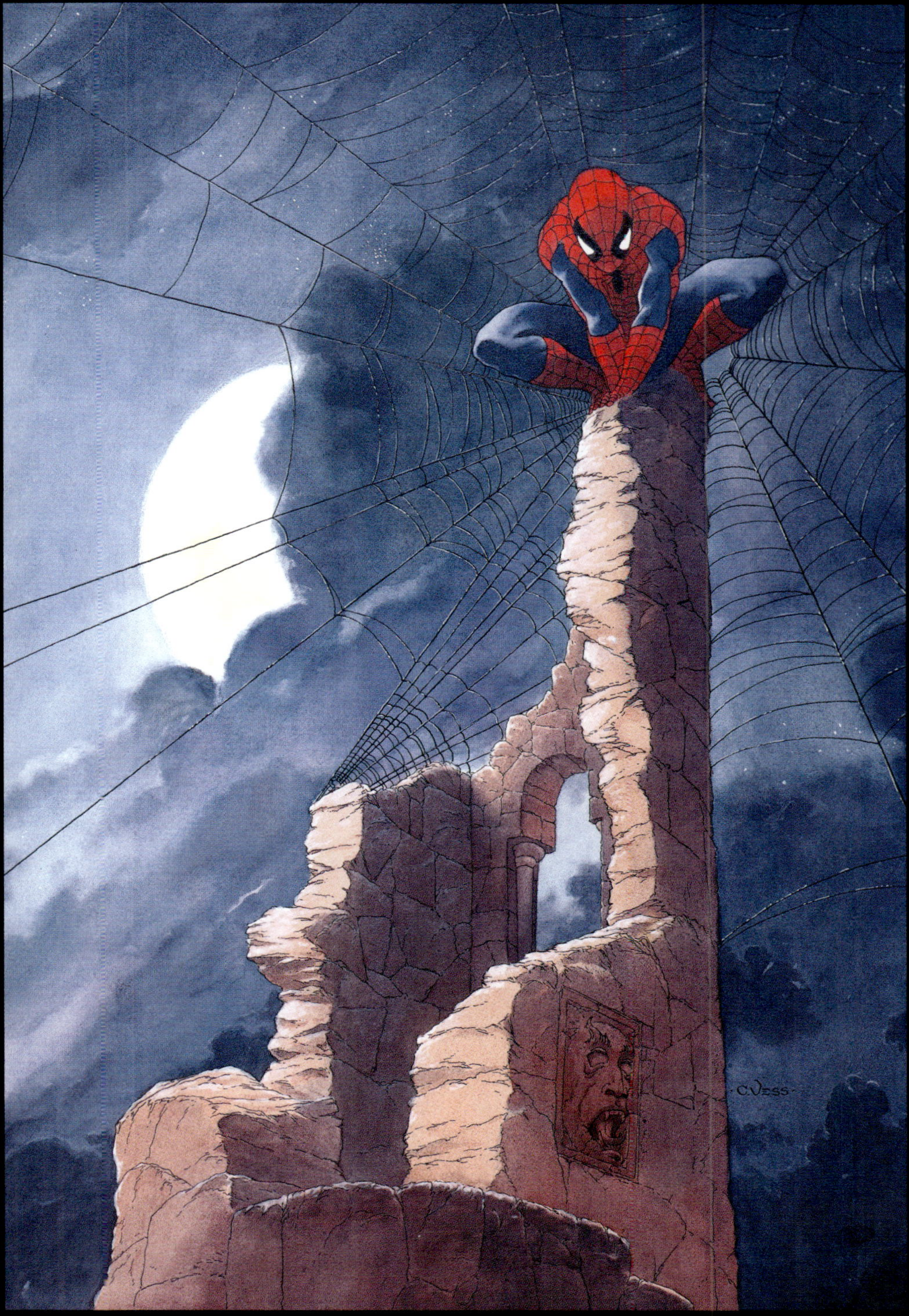

SPIRITS OF THE EARTH

What happened when Charles took Peter Parker and Mary Jane to the Highlands

Charles Vess regards Spider-Man: Spirits of the Earth, his 1990 graphic novel for Marvel, to be one of the key breakthrough pieces of his early career. "I took him out of New York City and sent him to Scotland, so he couldn't react the way he usually does in a story because he couldn't simply swing away from a villain," he explains.

Charles wrote and illustrated the book, and it contains many of his favourite subjects, such as fairies, ruins and castles, as well as equally Celtic elements – pubs and windswept grasslands.

Although it had been drawn earlier, Spider-Man: Spirits of the Earth came out at roughly the same time as Sandman #19, the Midsummer Night's Dream adaptation Charles worked on with Neil Gaiman. He feels that the two works really gave his career a jolt, within comic art at least.

"Both of those titles came out within a month of each other," he says. "So, suddenly, I was on the map. Retailers were aware of what I did, and a lot of other people were too. I still have very, very good memories of both of those works."

Traditional skills

DELVE INTO THE MIND OF A MASTER

Acclaimed fantasy artist **Charles Vess** lifts the curtain and reveals what he thinks about when producing a piece of art for a private client

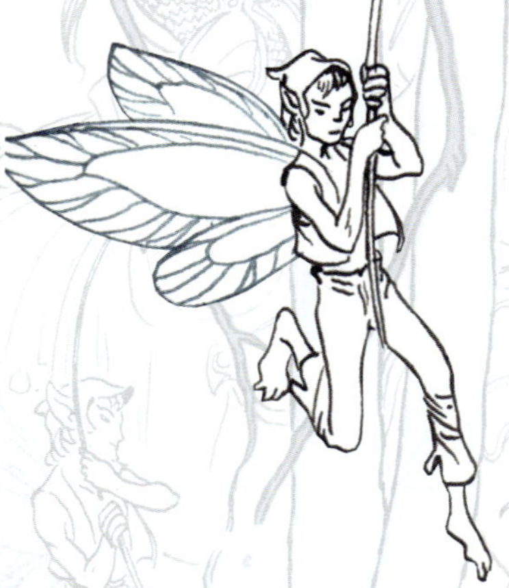

This image, Companions to the Moon, was my first fully fledged commission. It began with an inquiry from an art buyer, who asked me if I'd consider painting a piece like my iconic Stardust image for him, which depicts Yvaine, the fallen star, kneeling in a forest glade. He'd seen the picture at a previous San Diego Comic-Con and been disappointed when he was told that it wasn't for sale. I love that painting and, knowing that I might be tempted to sell the piece, had given it to my wife as a gift. We were displaying it over our table.

Initially, I declined the offer. Over the years, I've been asked numerous times about commissions but had never felt like I had the time in my work schedule to pay proper attention to such a piece. Furthermore, I'd never wanted to just be a hired hand, producing whatever a client dictated. Ideally, what I wanted was to be paid to do art from the heart.

In fact, I'd been thinking about several images that had been floating around in my head for some time, wondering if they might never be painted because of constant deadlines with my book publishing work. So I wrote back to this particular client and described one of those art-from-the-heart pictures. I quoted a price that would give me the time to lavish the attention on the image that it deserved and still be able to pay the bills. I also gave a timeframe that was flexible enough to work such a painting into the present workload. There was a quick reply saying, "Yes, sounds great to me."

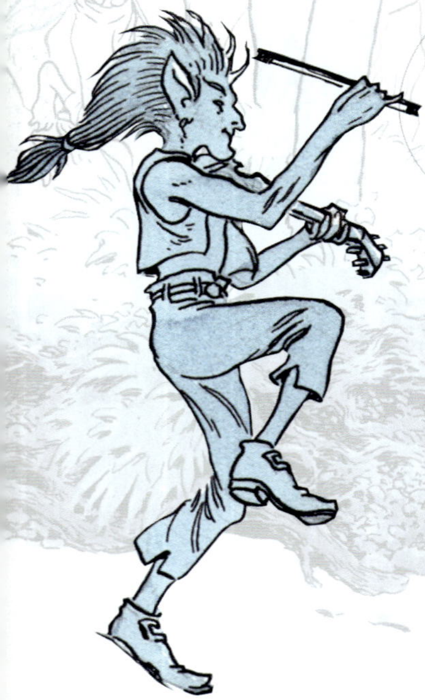

1 Sketch the idea

Here's my initial rough pencil sketch – done on 8.5x12-inch copier paper – of that idea. The image does share some similarities with the Stardust painting. Both are set in the deep, moonlit woods, and are filled with all sorts of faerie life. This preliminary drawing is rendered more elaborately than I would normally do for a simple concept sketch; I generally like to work out all my finished ideas on the board that I'll actually be working on.

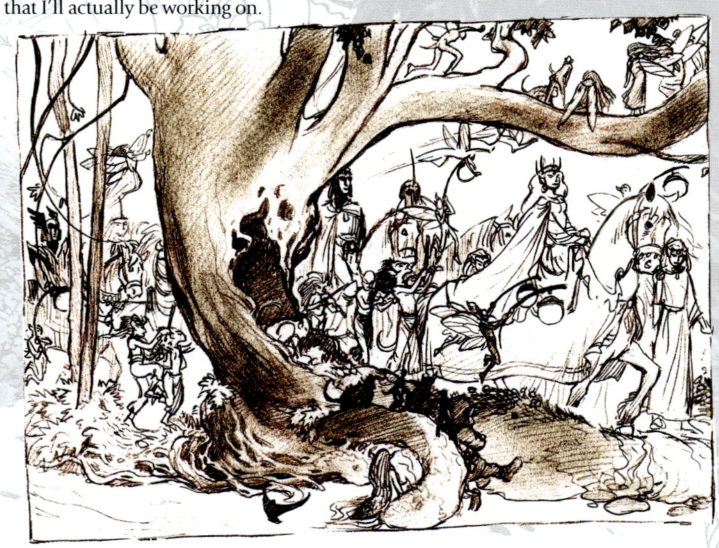

2 Establish the composition

At the sketch stage I'm still just trying to establish the overall composition, as well as attempting to convey the general mood of the piece. There's no practical sense in adding all the countless details that will be necessary to achieve a painting's finished look until after the client says that they like it. And of course, it's extremely tedious to have already worked out all the details at an early stage and then have to redraw them all onto the actual working illustration board.

3 Transfer the image using tracing paper

After the sketch is approved, I enlarge it on my copy machine to the actual size (16x23 inches) that I'm going to paint the final piece. With the aid of a sheet of transfer paper, I trace the enlarged image onto my preferred paper – Strathmore Series 500, 4ply. After hours and hours of redrawing later, I arrive at this finished pencil drawing.

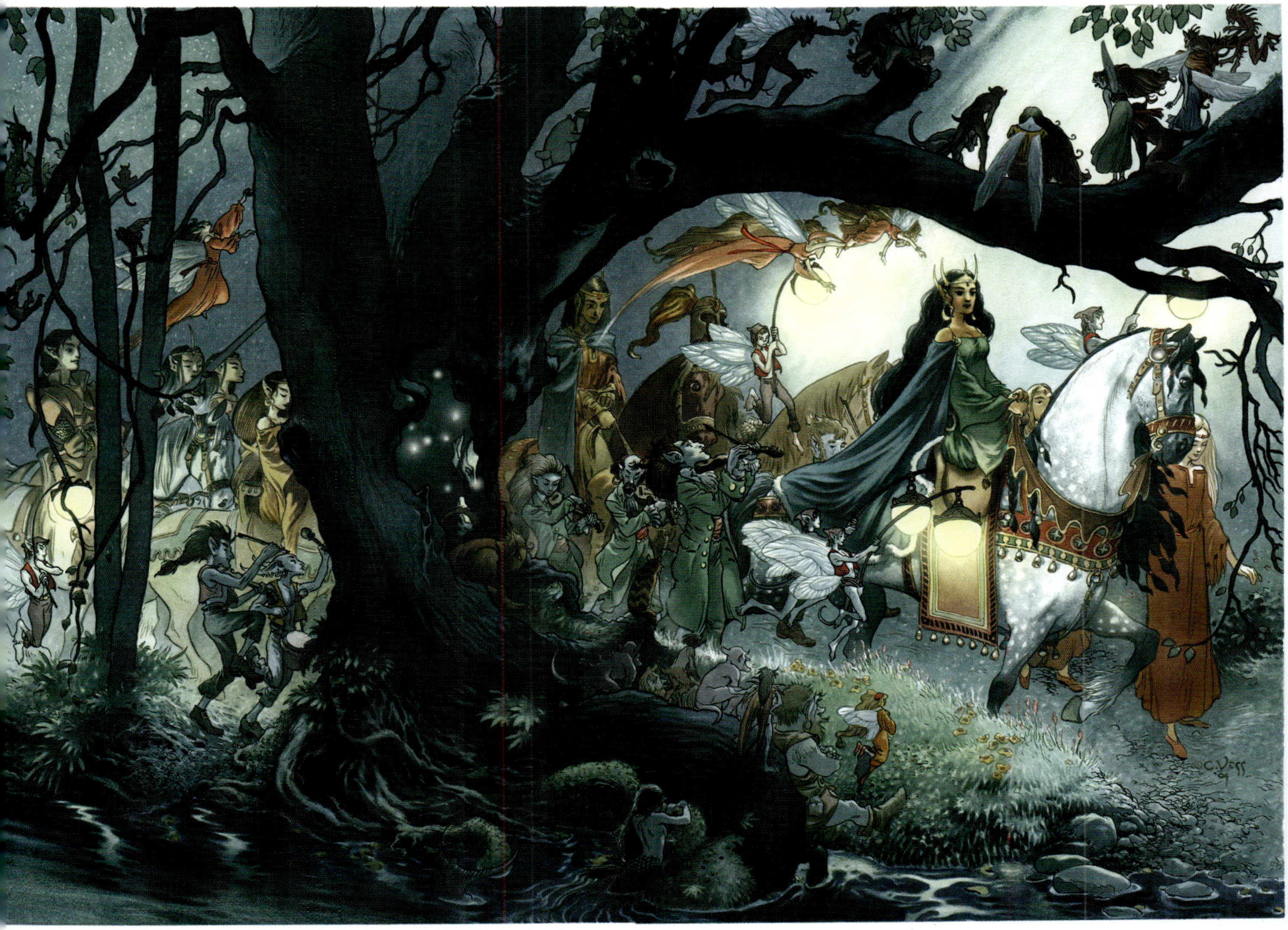

4 Search for ideas

For me, the process of drawing involves looking through the art and reference books that fill my studio. This isn't so much looking for how someone has already done the same idea and trying to copy their approach – where would the fun be in that? – but seeking random visual inspiration. What I might be looking for is a particular colour of moonlight that a certain artist has used in a painting; the toss of a horse's head; an interesting pattern in a dress; the peculiar twist of a tree branch. Hopefully, my subconscious will store all these details, and when I begin it'll be able to access that information.

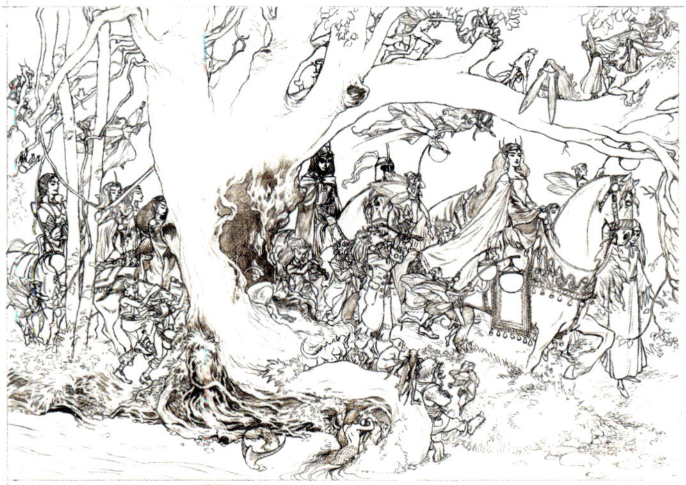

5 Introduce characters

As you can see, I've also added lots of new characters into the drawing, placing details into all the costuming as well as specific facial characteristics for all the denizens of my faerieland extravaganza. I find that it also helps if, as I draw each of these characters, their particular story plays out in my thoughts. This mental process seems to add a certain reality to each elf, faerie, dragon, mermaid, or cat. But you have to be careful and not allow any of these faerie inhabitants to steal the spotlight for themselves. Every character, be they humanoid or rock or tree, needs to be integral to the picture as a whole.

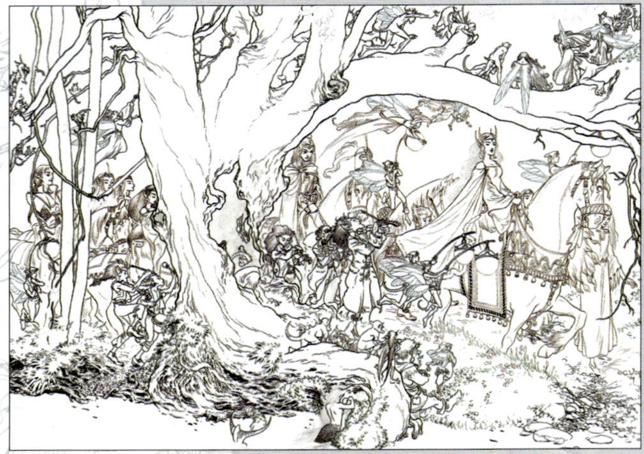

6 Decide on the mood

Choosing which of these pencil lines to ink and which to leave in their graphite state is dependent on the overall mood I'm looking for. Early on, I decided that this image was going to be drenched in moonlight with a strong, diagonal beam flooding down onto the Faerie Queen herself. Therefore, I ink most of the piece with a sepia tone rather than a harsh, solid, black line. The light brown of the sepia ink makes it easier to dissolve certain forms back into the moonlight-and-shadow mood that I'm seeking.

7 Tackle the wings

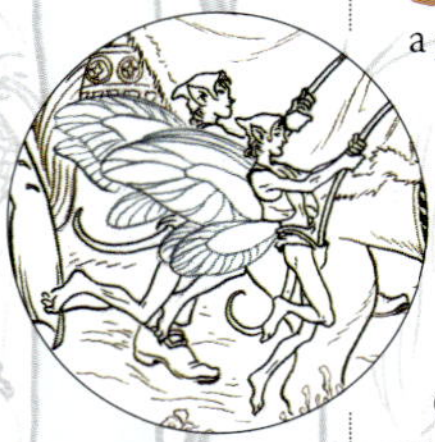

All the faerie wings are rendered in a pale blue ink line. This makes it easier to suggest their translucent look. After years of painting with a transparent medium – FW Inks – I've found that you can leave out many of the hard pen outlines and replace them with pure colour for a better effect. Of course, only experience and patience will tell you which of those lines to leave in and which to take out.

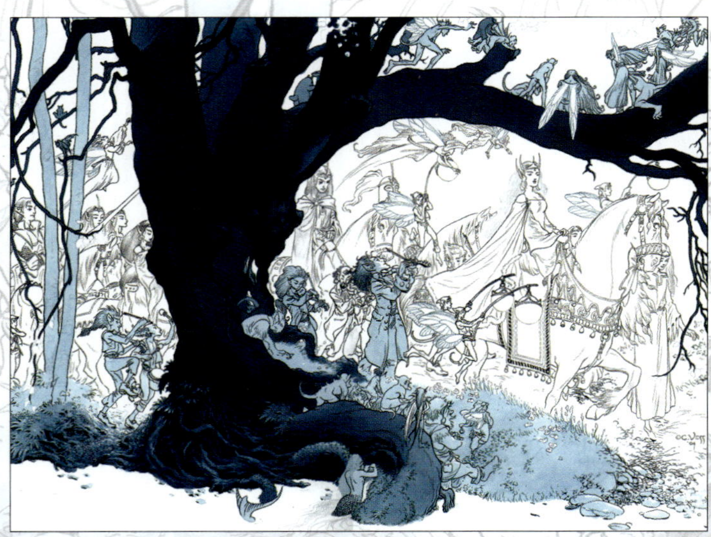

8 Step up to colour

Painting the first washes of colour onto a detailed piece can be exceptionally scary. I keep putting off applying those initial layers and procrastinate with work on other projects for a week or two. At last, I finally decide that I can't delay the process any longer, and so I have to jump right in and start painting.

9 Unify the elements

I mix up a pale blue-grey colour and wash it over most of the image, except for those areas that will be directly around the glowing lanterns and the interior of the Queen's moonbeam. A monotone sweep of colour like this will help to unify all the disparate pieces of your image. In addition, if applied properly, it'll give you a good sense of where your light source is going to come into play throughout your image.

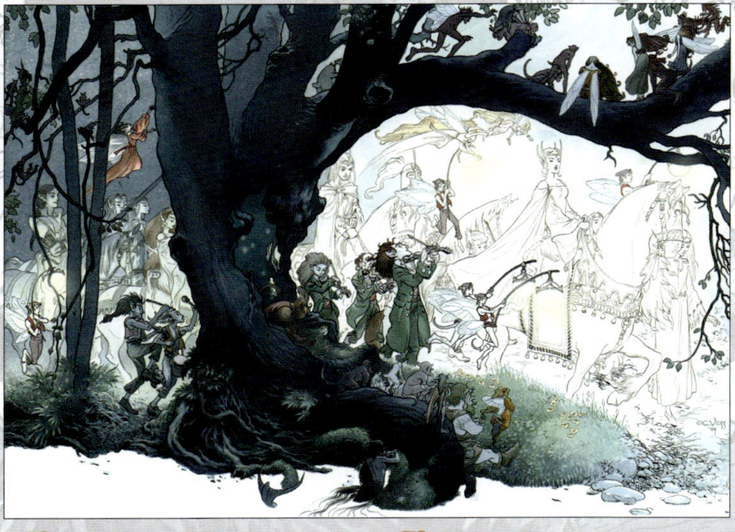

10 Work up the tree

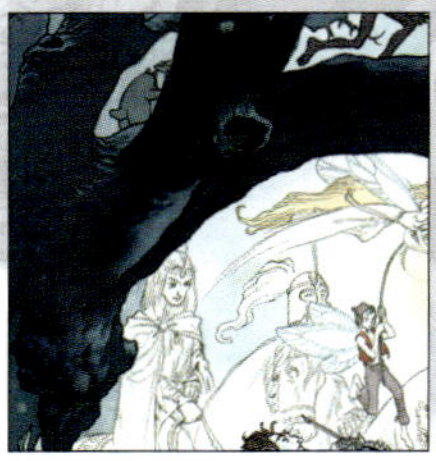

At this stage of the painting process I'm simply trying to solidify the form of the tree because it's so central – literally and figuratively – to the success of the finished image. Most importantly, I have to establish the depth between the tree and various other pictorial planes that are present in the picture.

11 Tease the viewer

Like I said earlier, with so many large and small characters occupying the same composition, you have to be careful to choose which ones to spotlight and which to render in such a way as to make them part of a pattern of secondary discovery for the viewer. The diagonal moonbeams help me do this by throwing the multitude of faerie creatures cavorting through the limbs of the tree into colour silhouette. All those beasties are still there but don't distract the viewer's attention from the central character of the Queen.

12 Establish a rhythm

The secondary light sources from the multiple lantern-carrying elves that fly throughout the piece help to establish a visual rhythm into other areas of the piece. They're also subtle enough to not distract the viewer from that moonbeam and its lovely inhabitant. This kind of piece, filled – as it is – with so many characters, is fun to produce because you can layer in lots of hidden stories among the multitude.

13 Place Easter eggs

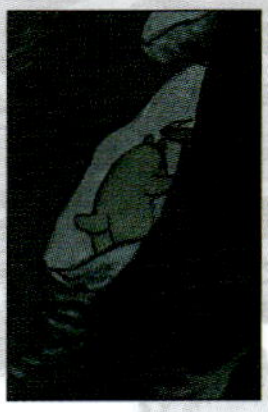

With a patient eye, you might happen upon the Japanese anime character Totoro, a favourite film of mine, as well as the dragon Balsaad from the Rose series I did for Cartoon Books. I'll leave the rest of these hidden stories for your curious eyes to discover for themselves…

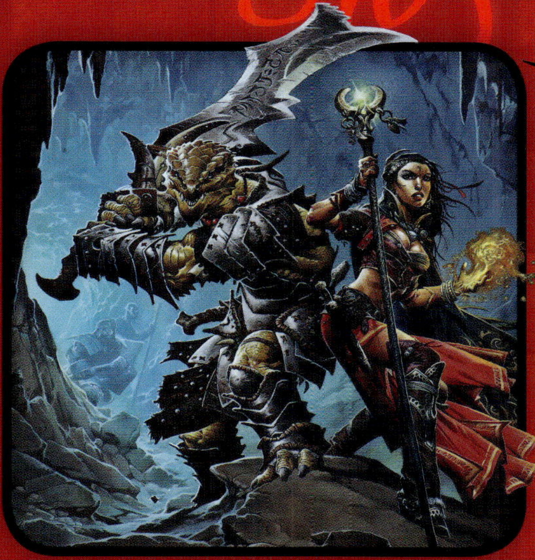

The Art of Dungeons & Dragons

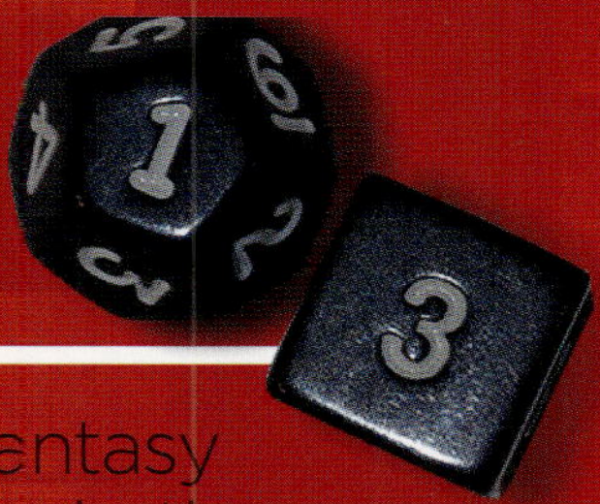

Without a doubt, the D&D phenomenon defined fantasy artwork. We take a trip back to D&D's early era of inspiration and find out how its look has been reinvented...

THE CURRENT LOOK
The cover of the current Player's Handbook, created by Wayne Reynolds. One of today's leading D&D artists, he's closely associated with the Fourth Edition rules.

"Paladin in Hell. Talk about setting a scene. Can you imagine being the only paladin in Hell? So much butt to kick, so little time to live," says Jon Schindehette.

He's referring to an iconic line drawing by David C Sutherland III, which appeared on page 23 of the Player's Handbook in 1978. A glowing knight in platemail hacks at a spike-tailed demon with his sword, while numerous other denizens of darkness close in around him. In the late 70s and early 80s, versions of this image and others like it were doodled in countless school books as thousands of young players took up Dungeons & Dragons. Not only did it set the scene for a worldwide craze in gaming, it also formed a starting block for a whole generation of fantasy artists.

Jon was an avid gamer back then, and today is living the dream: he's the senior creative art director for Dungeons & Dragons, at Wizards of the Coast. Although it sounds like the perfect job, it can't be easy. As with that paladin back in 1978, the denizens of darkness have been closing in on D&D itself.

With card games attacking from the right, hyper-real computer games lunging in from the left and competing RPGs rushing head-on, the game that started it all has required reinvention. With well over 30 candles on its last birthday cake, these days D&D is played under the complex Fourth Edition rules. Now, Jon and the team at Wizards have come up with a lighter introduction to the game that comes in a very attractive red box. ➳

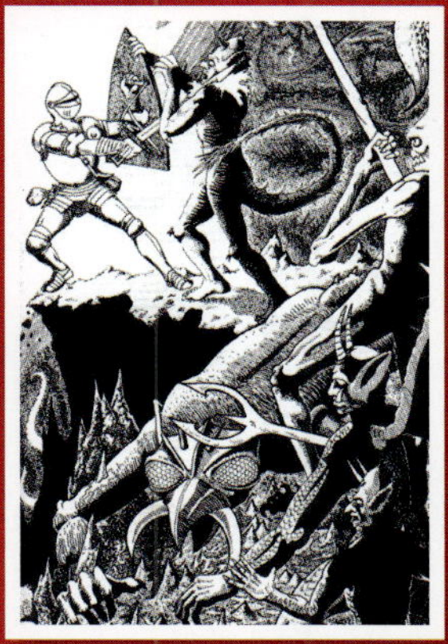

A PALADIN IN HELL
This 1978 line drawing by David C Sutherland III inspired a generation of D&D players and young fantasy artists.

Photo credit: Jeff Salzer

Tamer of the Amazons
Clyde Caldwell

BORN 1948.
EXPERIENCE POINTS: The original Ravenloft artist, painted the covers of the D&D Gazetteer series and numerous TSR calendars from 1985 to 92.
LOCATION: Originally from North Carolina, moved to Wisconsin to work at TSR.
D&D ERA: 1982-92.
MEDIA USED: Oils on illustration board.
MAIN CREATIVE INFLUENCES: Sci-fi and fantasy literature, comic books from the 1950s-70s.
FAVOURITE D&D TOPIC: Strong, sexy female characters and monsters.
HIGHS: Just being a part of the whole thing.
LOWS: Making deadlines.
I WISH I COULD PAINT... I look forward to finding the time to do some painting just for myself.

www.clydecaldwell.com

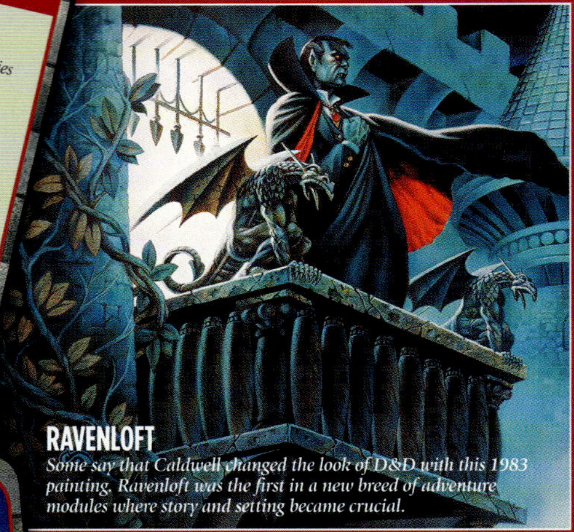

RAVENLOFT
Some say that Caldwell changed the look of D&D with this 1983 painting. Ravenloft was the first in a new breed of adventure modules where story and setting became crucial.

UNEARTHED ARCANA
Jeff Easley was part of the in-house team that defined D&D artwork. This image adorned the first edition of Unearthed Arcana, a guide book about spells and magic.

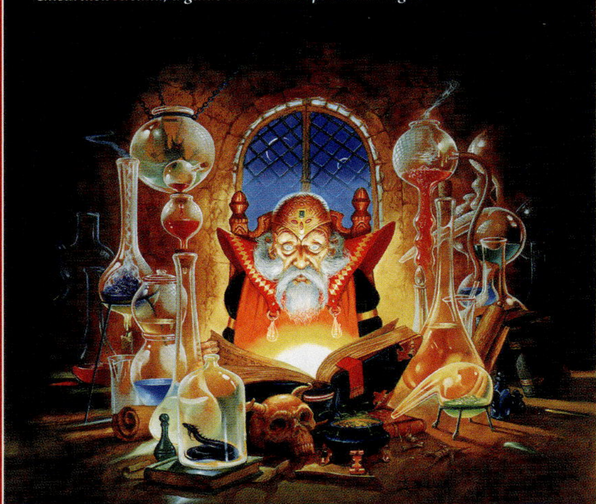

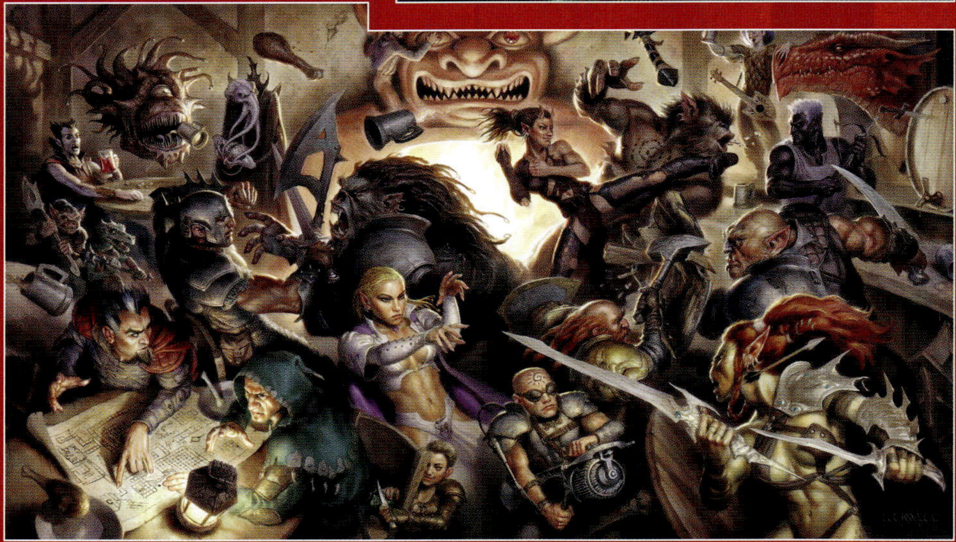

ARELENE
"I was into focusing on a central character with less emphasis on the background, so wanted to show Larry and Keith that I could paint a landscape too," says Clyde Caldwell of his Dragon magazine image.

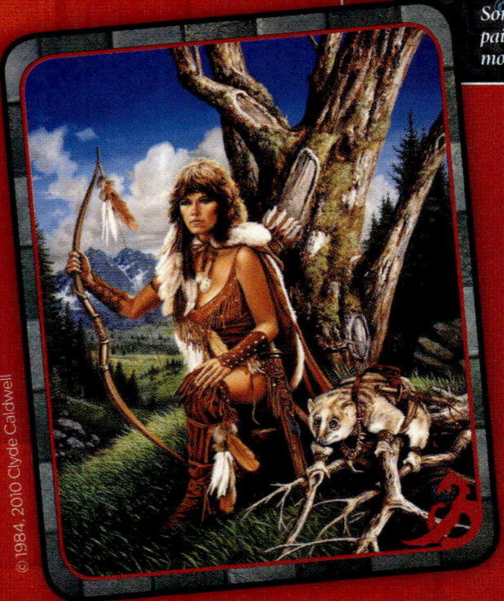

MONSTER MELEE
Todd Lockwood painted this scene for the game's 30th birthday back in 2004. Note the homage to the old Player's Handbook in the background.

Hero in battle
Ralph Horsley

BORN 1966.
EXPERIENCE POINTS: Guidebook covers in the red box Starter Set; interior spreads in the current Dungeon Masters Guide, Monster Manual and Players Handbook; cover for D&D Fantastic Locations: City of Peril.
LOCATION: Leeds, West Yorkshire.
D&D ERA: 2003-present.
MEDIA USED: Acrylic on board.
MAIN CREATIVE INFLUENCES: Todd Lockwood, Mark Schulz and Angus McBride.
FAVOURITE FANTASY/D&D TOPIC: Scenes of multiple characters and monsters battling.
HIGHS: Revisiting the classic red box artwork.
LOWS: Making changes is always irksome.
I WISH I COULD PAINT... Campaign covers.

www.ralphhorsley.co.uk

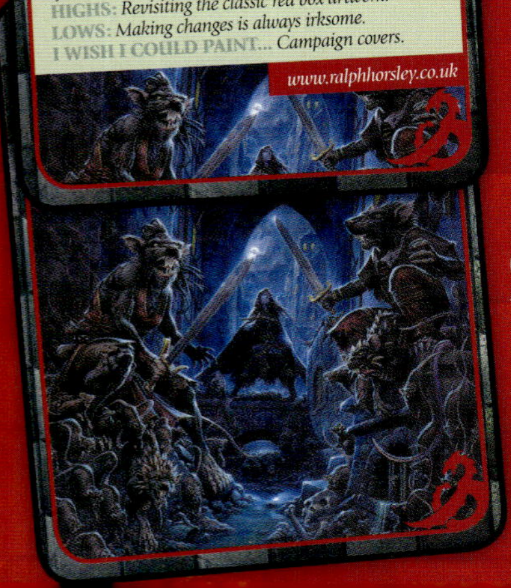

CITY OF PERIL
Enter the world of the wererats. Ralph Horsley painted this dark and threatening image for a recent D&D adventure cover.

If this sounds familiar, maybe you remember 1983's Basic rules? Bursting from its red box were a fierce red dragon and a barbarian warrior in combat. That very image, by legendary artist Larry Elmore, appears again on the front of last year's D&D Fantasy Roleplaying Game Starter Set, along with the old Dungeons & Dragons logotype. It's a touch of class for which Wizards should be commended. But employing one of the game's most enduring images isn't just a nod to nostalgia; the new red box hopes to attract new players, too.

> **"A favourite piece of art or an artist's style was one of the things that kept the fans coming back"** *Jon Schindehette*

Although there are character sheets, dice and maps, D&D is played primarily in the imagination. Yet art has always been at the heart of it. The covers of the modules, internal drawings and lead miniatures used to represent characters were all starting points for how players envisaged their fantasy world. "Countless times I've had discussions with D&D fans whose game experience either began with, revolved around, or related to, a favourite piece of art or an artist's style," says Jon. "And that's one of the things that kept them coming back."

Today he works with an established freelance stable including Ralph Horsley, Wayne Reynolds, William O'Connor, Steve Prescott, the partnership of Zoltan Boris and Gabor Szikszai, among many others. He looks for a distinctive style that brings something unique, but fits with his vision for the game. Back when D&D was first

D&D FOR THE FUTURE

We asked senior creative art director Jon Schindehette what his vision of the Dungeons & Dragons world entails...

What look and feel do you want Dungeons & Dragons art to have?
My personal take on the brand of Dungeons & Dragons is one of heroic adventure, where even the lowliest of characters can be bigger than life. Every villain can become an arch-enemy. Each monster brings the promise of the thrill of victory... or the agony of defeat.

What goals do you set for the D&D artwork?
I'm always striving for the art to get gut-level responses like: "That guy is so cool! I want to be him!" When I can illicit an emotional response to our heroes, villains, monsters or environments, I win!

What are the challenges you face from today's leisure markets?
Hyper-realism in today's games and movies has removed the need for imagination to fill in the blanks. How do we live in a world of hyper-realism, and yet inspire imagination? I believe we need to make decisions about what and when we choose to illustrate.

What do you think has been the most memorable D&D art?
D&D and its related worlds have historically been defined by its artists. Dragonlance by Elmore, Dark Sun by Brom and Ravenloft by Caldwell. They defined a look. Heck, they didn't just define it, they owned it.

Wayne Reynolds is one of several artists on the team today who bring a distinctive style to the D&D brand. As an art director, I like to find artists who have a defined artistic style. Why? Because they're memorable. Weren't we just talking about Elmore, Brom and Caldwell?

For you, what does an artist need to become the next hero of D&D artwork?
I may not know what it takes to become a hero, but I do know what it takes to work your way to the top tier of fantasy artists.

First off you need a commitment to excellence, always striving to produce a personal best. Second, nurture the desire to improve – be open to critiques and suggestions, and always look to improve your hand drawing skills.

Third, always try to exceed your expectations, rather than simply meeting them. Forth, expand your core art skills, refine your vision and nurture your ability to tell a story. Finally, you have to develop your own look or style. It's not enough just to be a great painter. You must have an edge – something that makes your work stand out from the crowd.

DARK SUN
Gerald Brom – usually known only by his surname – joined TSR in 1989 and became strongly associated with D&D's Dark Sun campaign setting. This image was the cover for Dragon's Crown and appeared in 1993.

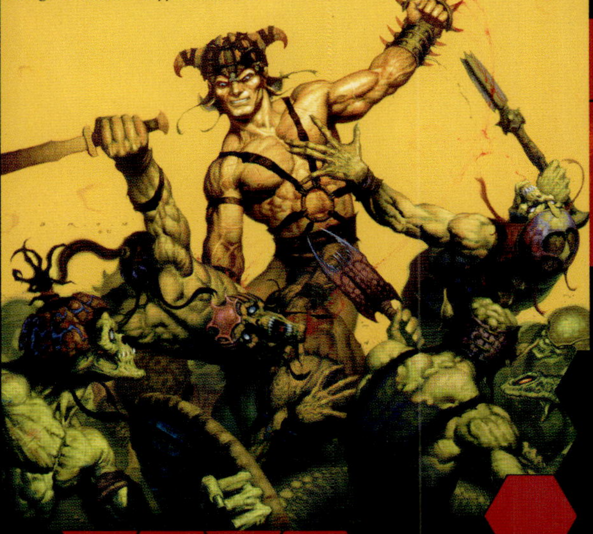

CHARACTERS AND RACES
William O'Connor was a lead concept artist for the latest version of D&D and his styling for the character classes and races can be found in Fourth Edition publications.

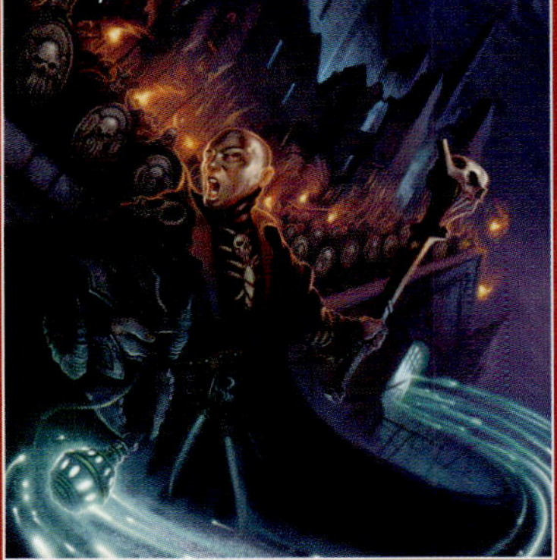

established, the art direction wasn't so strategic. The earliest D&D artists like David Sutherland, Erol Otus, David A Trampier and Jim Roslof set the tone for the game in a range of styles. Shortly thereafter, TSR decided that an in-house team of trained artists could take it to a new level.

During 1981 and 82, Larry Elmore, Jeff Easley, Clyde Caldwell and Keith Parkinson joined to paint cover artwork for new releases. "I didn't know it when I was doing that box cover, but me, Parkinson, Easley and Caldwell were setting a look for games," recalls Larry Elmore. "We were just sort of painting the way we wanted to and there wasn't much fantasy art around at the time. So we didn't have a lot to build on."

All eyes on TSR

This in-house dream team hadn't only stepped into an undefined area of fantasy. They were with a company that was enjoying tremendous success. Just about every kid in the English-speaking world was enjoying D&D. Gamers and budding artists all wanted to work at TSR's HQ in Lake Geneva, Wisconsin. "I won't forget the first time I saw a book with one of those guy's art on the cover. It was Jeff Easley's painting of the hill giant on the cover of the AD&D Monster Manual II. Here was something professionally crafted, with focus, story and power. I was blown away," says Todd Lockwood, now a well-known D&D artist himself.

That book was published in 1983 when demand for the game was going through the roof. In the same year, TSR launched Ravenloft, a module that became a campaign adventure and remains an important franchise for Wizards today. ➔

Wizard with a paintbrush
Larry Elmore

BORN 1948.
EXPERIENCE POINTS: *Painted the Basic Rules, Expert Rules and Master Rules Compendium box covers in 1983, the first three Dragonlance covers.*
LOCATION: *Originally from Kentucky, moved to Lake Geneva, Wisconsin. Then back to Kentucky.*
D&D ERA: 1981-1987.
MEDIA USED: Oil on masonite.
MAIN CREATIVE INFLUENCES: *Frank Frazetta, the Hildebrandts, NC Wyeth, Howard Pyle.*
FAVOURITE D&D TOPIC: *Big scenes with armies, an epic look and dragons.*
HIGHS: *Seeing the success of Dragonlance.*
LOWS: *Worrying that TSR would go under.*
I WISH I COULD PAINT... *Portraits of all the main Dragonlance characters.*

www.larryelmore.com

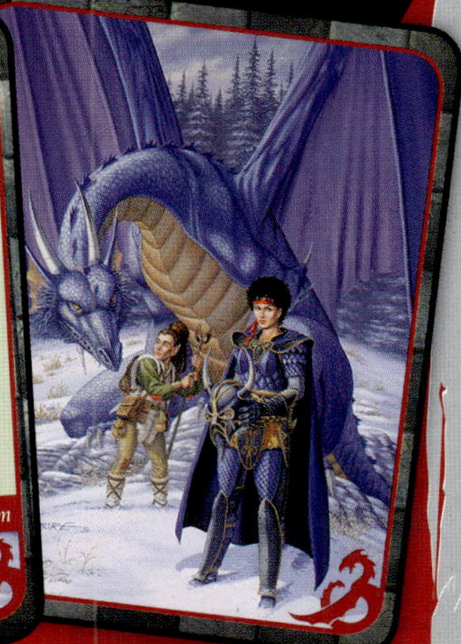

DRAGONS OF WINTER NIGHT
Even when the first series of Dragonlance books were reprinted in 1992, Larry Elmore was invited back to paint the covers. This image was for the third book in the series.

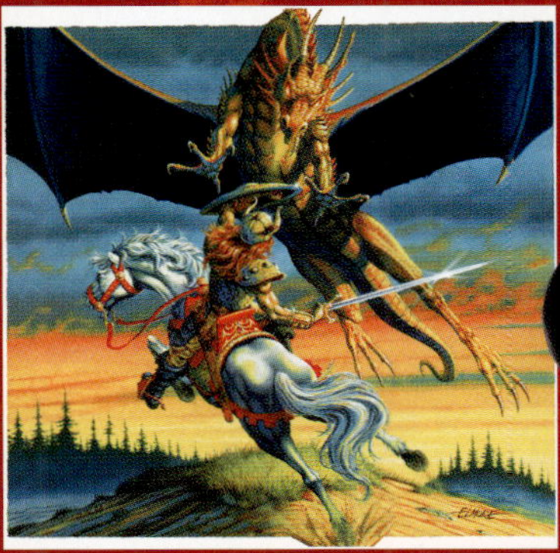

AIR ATTACK
Another early classic by Larry Elmore, this painting appeared on the Expert Rules Set 2, a blue box, published in 1983. Perhaps we'll see it again soon on a new D&D product?

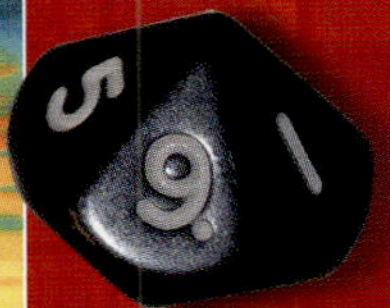

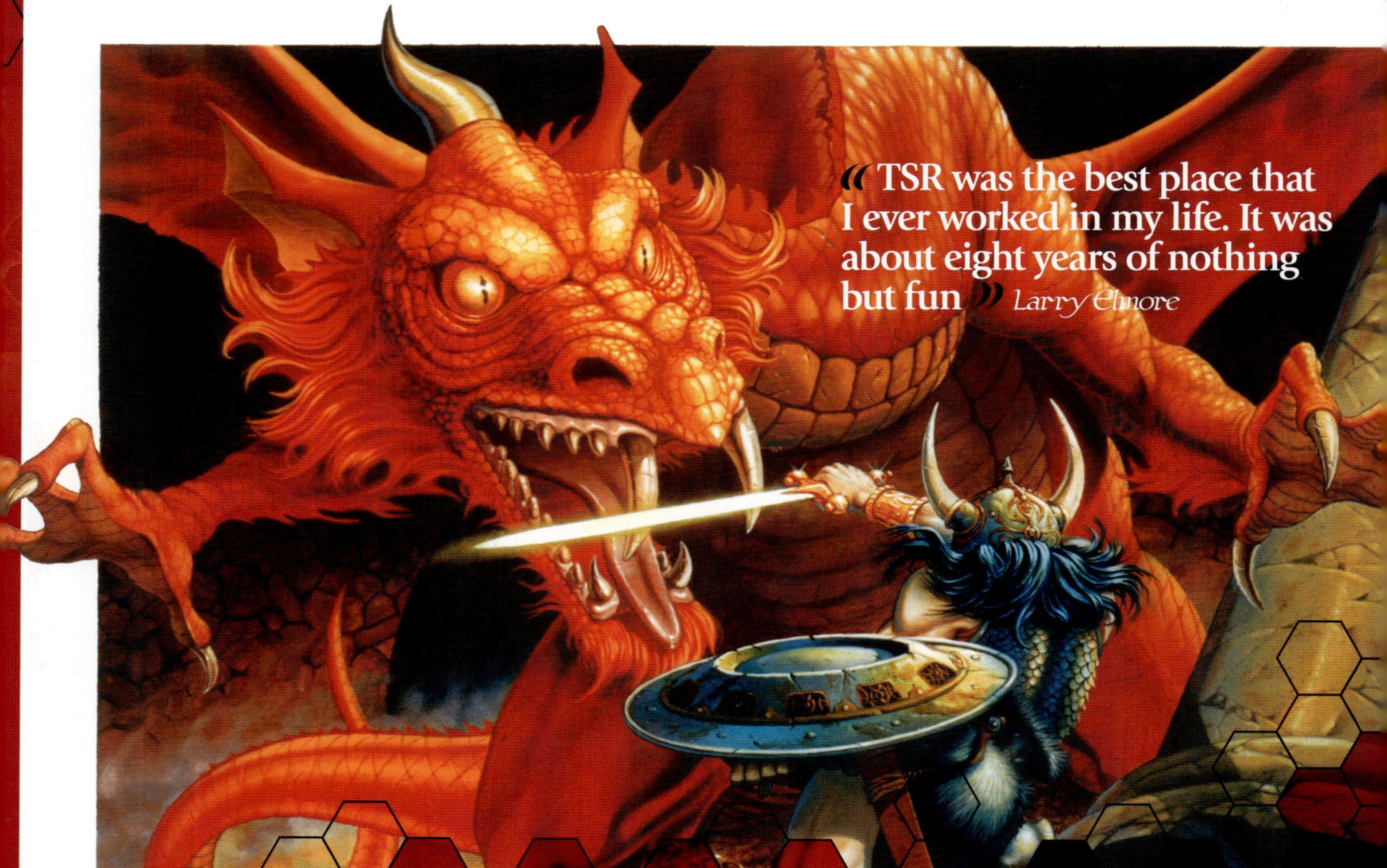

> "TSR was the best place that I ever worked in my life. It was about eight years of nothing but fun" *Larry Elmore*

VENTURE INTO THE LAIR OF ANCIENT RED

Larry Elmore recalls how he created the iconic artwork of the latest D&D Fantasy Roleplaying Game Starter Set released by Wizards

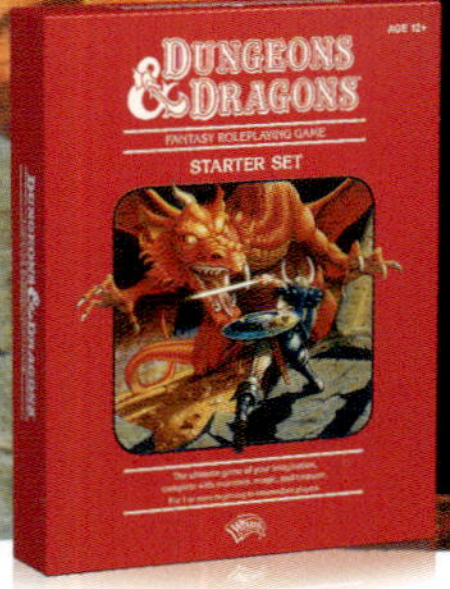

In 1981, Larry Elmore joined TSR, as one of the first really experienced illustrators they hired to work in-house. He'd previously been in the US Army, but as an artist his work had already been published in sci-fi magazines. One of his key assignments was to paint new artwork for the D&D rules box sets, which TSR revamped in 1983.

His initial sketches were rejected by Gary Gygax. As head of TSR and one of the founders of D&D, Gary was god-like to other TSR staff, but Larry marched down the hall and demanded to see him. A secretary tried to stop him, but eventually he gained admittance.

"So we discussed it, and I did some sketches, and I understood what he wanted," he says. "I thought it was a good idea – he wanted it to jump out at you, and I'd been doing some stuff for the Army two years before that, where we'd have tanks bursting out of a frame, like bursting out of the page, trying to get more impact. So I said, 'I know what you're talking about.'"

The result was a painting called Ancient Red, and a good working relationship with Gygax. Air Attack followed for the Expert Rules box, then Dragon Blade on the Master Rules Compendium. He also did the covers for the first three Dragonlance novels.

"TSR was the most unique and best place that I ever worked in my life, and it was about eight years of nothing but fun. You'd go in to work and you'd work there until nine or ten at night sometimes. You didn't want to leave," Larry says.

He did leave in 1987, as it turns out, but Larry has never given up on fantasy art, painting hundreds of images for various other game systems, books and magazines. Today, he teaches painting and does private commissions. "They'll have to prise the paintbrush out of my cold, dead hand, before I'll stop," he adds.

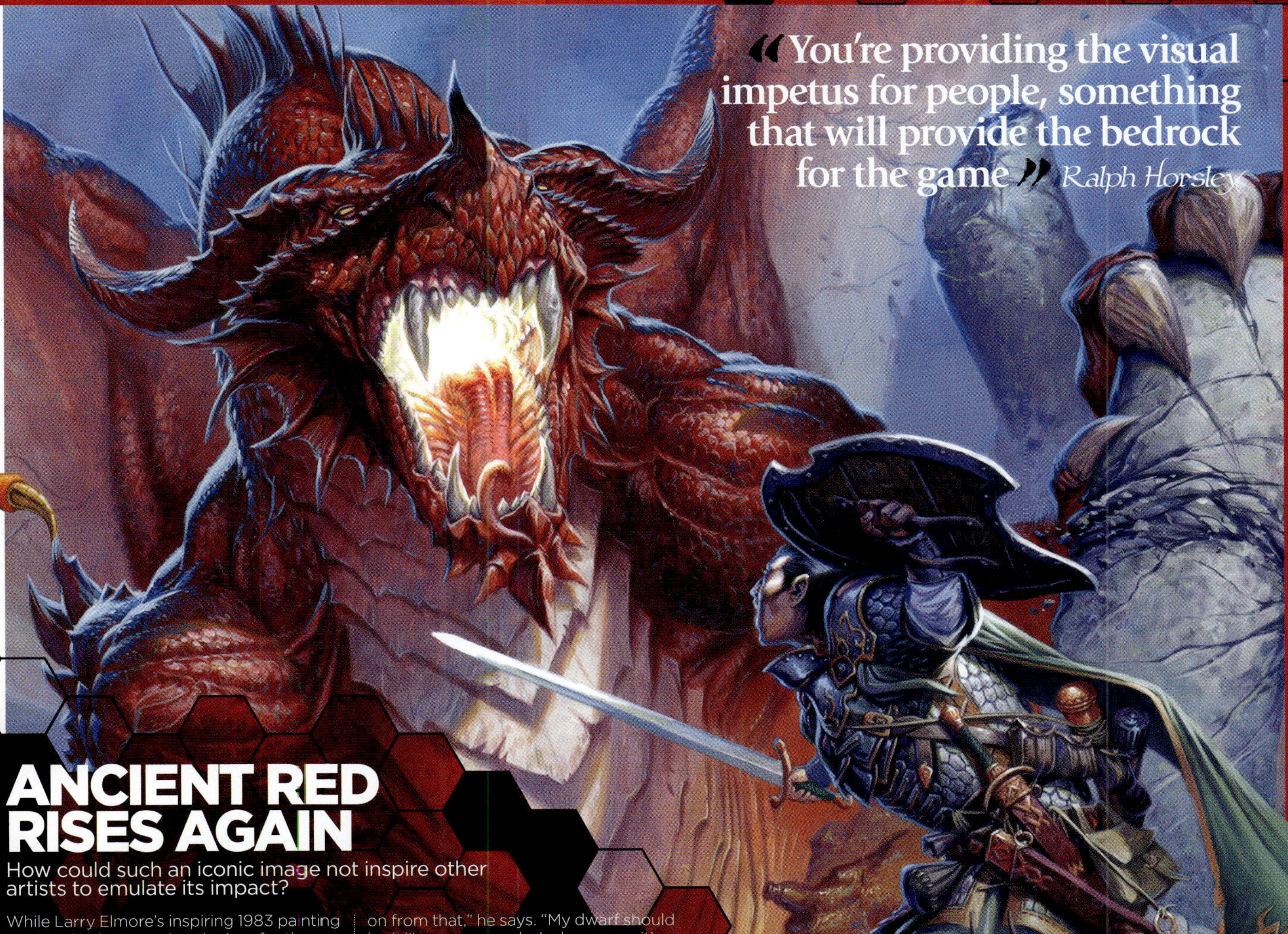

> “You're providing the visual impetus for people, something that will provide the bedrock for the game” *Ralph Horsley*

ANCIENT RED RISES AGAIN

How could such an iconic image not inspire other artists to emulate its impact?

While Larry Elmore's inspiring 1983 painting Ancient Red returned as the box for the D&D Fantasy Roleplaying Game Starter Set, the Player's Book and Dungeon Masters Book inside the box featured a new red dragon painting by current D&D artist Ralph Horsley. Alongside fellow British artist Wayne Reynolds, Ralph is recognised as a defining artist for today's D&D style. This work has been described as an homage to Larry's original piece.

“Growing up, I never thought that I would end up working on the product and being associated with Larry Elmore and that generation of artists in such a direct way. It's very satisfying and very rewarding.”

Although Larry Elmore, Keith Parkinson, Jeff Easley and Clyde Caldwell were art directed, in their day the game world was far more open to their interpretation. With everything that competes with D&D in 2010, artists like Ralph have to fit in with a style guide. “If I'm doing a dwarf it'll follow on from that,” he says. “My dwarf should look like everyone else's dwarves, with a certain amount of leeway. It's very much, 'This is what our dwarves are like, we'd like you to do an exciting variant on that.'”

Certainly there's more pressure on D&D artists now than ever before. The game has an incredible heritage to live up to, while so many other things are competing for the RPGer's pound. For Ralph, it's important to consider the breadth of contemporary fantasy work and move forward. “Maybe I'm aware of video games and whatever else, but I'm not trying to mimic them. You're aware of the same dynamism that's out there in comic art and so on,” he says.

“You're providing the visual impetus for people, something for them to easily pick up on and that will provide the bedrock for the game. There's a responsibility to make the game look exciting, the characters look interesting, and create a world that you'd want to immerse yourself in.”

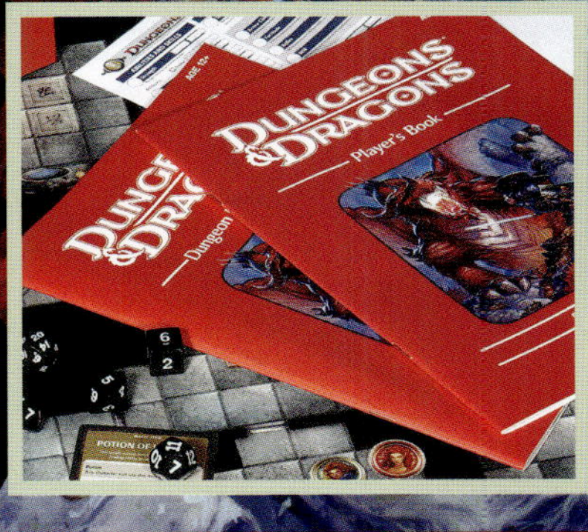

Ralph Horsley's homage to Ancient Red adorns the books inside the new D&D Fantasy Roleplaying Game Starter Set.

Gallery
Interviews
Workshops
Core skills

Grand illusionist
Keith Parkinson

BORN 1958, passed away of leukaemia 2005.
EXPERIENCE POINTS: Dragonlance module covers for Dragons of Desolation and Dragons of Hope, and the first Forgotten Realms campaign cover.
LOCATION: San Diego, California.
D&D ERA: 1982-1987.
MEDIA USED: Oil on canvas/oil on masonite.
MAIN CREATIVE INFLUENCES: Norman Rockwell, Frank Frazetta, NC Wyeth.
FAVOURITE D&D TOPIC: Human wizards and dragons.
HIGHS: Getting to work in the TSR "art pit".
LOWS: Failed a saving throw versus a Beholder in the Fall of 1986. Spent three months encased in stone.
WOULD HAVE LOVED TO PAINT... Maybe just a few more dragons.

www.keithparkinson.com

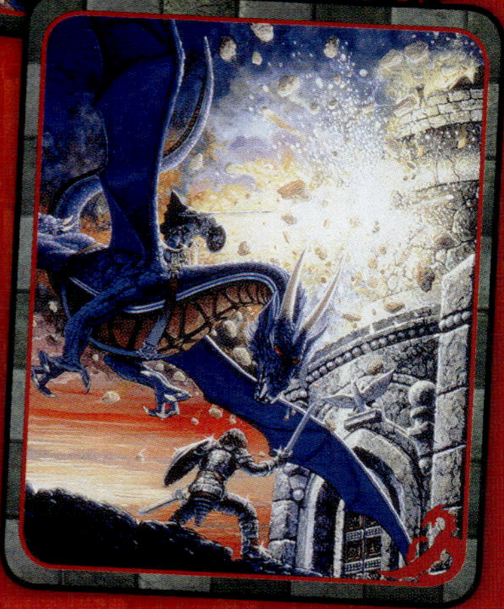

DRAGONS OF WAR
Awesome energy explodes from this painting by Keith Parkinson for the eighth module by Tracy Hickman and Margaret Weis for the Dragonlance series.

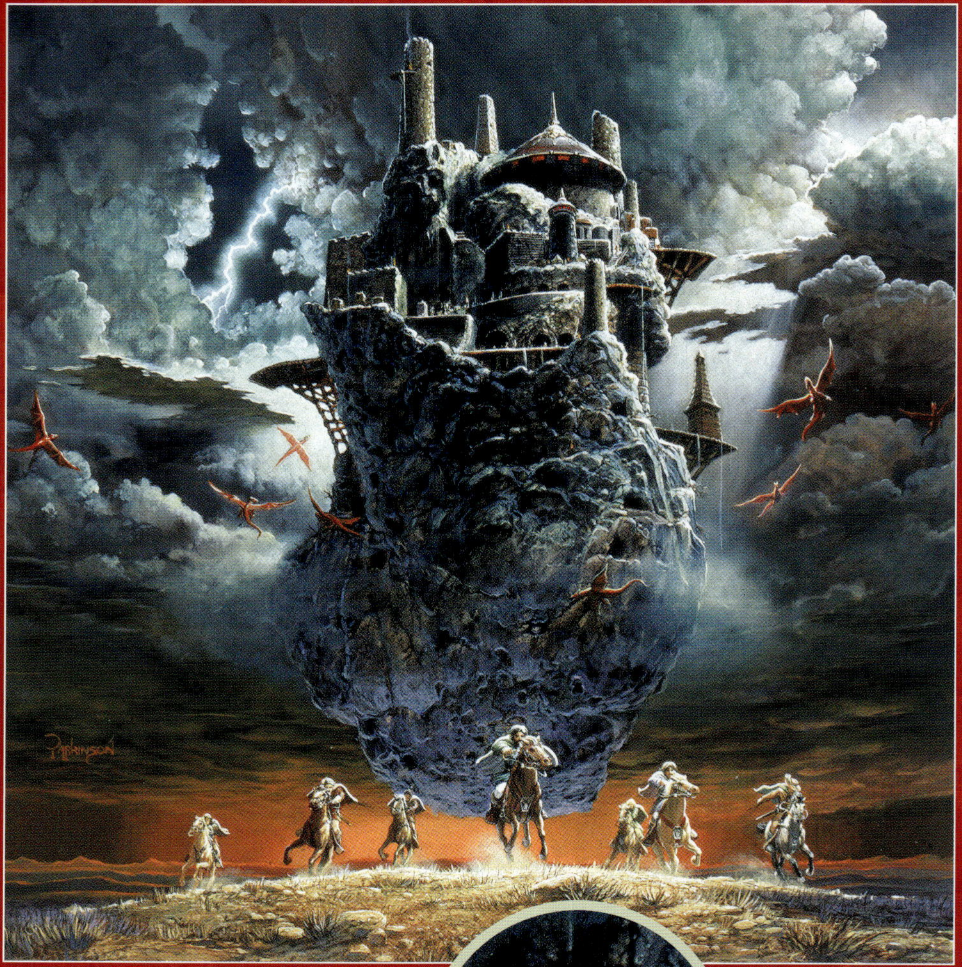

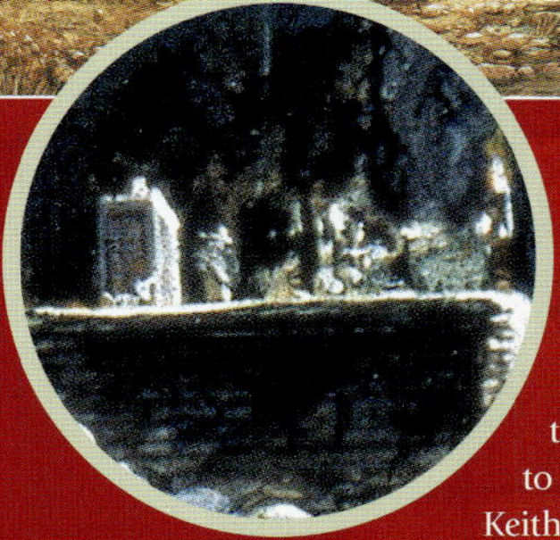

DRAGONS OF DESOLATION
The citadel floats up out of the earth in Keith Parkinson's painting for the fourth Dragonlance module, Dragons of Desolation. The insert reveals Keith's nod to Doctor Who.

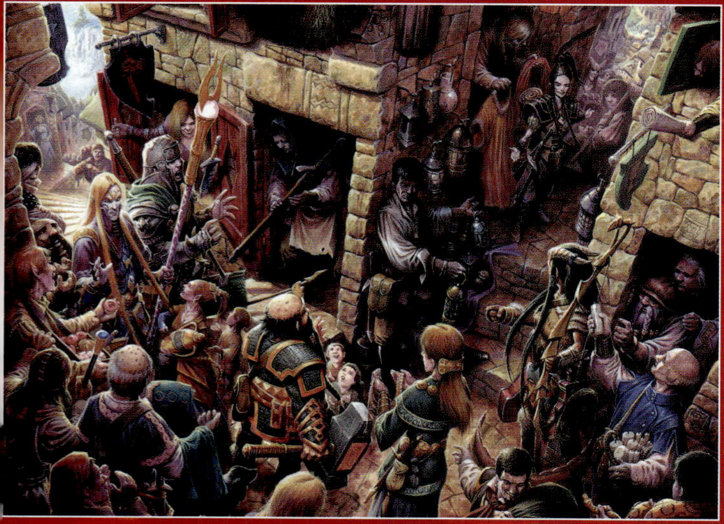

FELLCREST
Ralph Horsley loves to create settings that involve multiple characters and lots of action. This depiction of Fellcrest appears in the latest Dungeon Master's Guide.

A large part of its success is down to Clyde Caldwell's chilling image of a vampire surveying the lands around his keep.

"Ravenloft was one of my early pieces as a staff artist," explains Clyde. "That was my first exposure to Tracy Hickman. I had a lot of fun doing the art for that module, since I was ready for a little horror in my artistic stew, and I got to do all of the interiors for the module as well as the cover, which let me put my visual stamp on it. Tracy was heading up the Dragonlance team and all the artists were excited about it. It was a chance to create a whole new gaming world from the ground up."

The team created illustrations for the Dragonlance Chronicles, which consisted of game modules and novels. Authored by Tracy Hickman and Margaret Weis, it allowed the young Keith Parkinson to shine as a cover artist.

Keith passed away in 2005, but his son Nick recalls how his father had fun painting Dragons of Desolation: "The reason that was a favourite has more to do with a joke than the actual subject of the painting. My dad was a big Doctor Who fan, and if you look carefully, on the ledge on the citadel you can see the Doctor, K-9 and the TARDIS."

By 1987, two million Dragonlance novels were sold, along with another half a million D&D modules. The art team had now become mainstream. However, as Larry points out, that wasn't the aim. Like everyone at TSR, they were gamers at heart. Playing every lunchtime, their campaigns

TAKING ON THE MANTLE

One artist talks of his time in the world of D&D

The Fourth Edition rules and D&D Essentials range bring new opportunities for artists like Tyler Jacobson. Graduating from the Academy of Art University in San Francisco two years ago with an MFA in Illustration, he's already had his first handful of commissions.

"My first important image was my first commission. It was for an elf woman casting a spell in a candle-lit dungeon," he recalls. "I used my traditional painting skills and painted the image in oils. I wanted to do more but because of the oil drying time I didn't have enough time to complete the image in oils. So I turned to completing the image digitally."

Like many artists before him, he's also developed his skills and ideas working for Dragon magazine. Today it's an online publication, but it still nurtures new talent. One of Jacobsons biggest inspirations growing up was Jeff Easley, whose covers jumped off the page, yet he's developing his own style and approach.

"I really enjoy the darker characters in D&D. I love the imagery of a dark, moonlit world where there are magical beings lurking in the corners. I also like the more animistic characters. I'd really love to see a world full of more alien-like creatures that are very unlike what we normally get to see," he says.

Young turk

Tyler Jacobson

BORN 1982.
EXPERIENCE POINTS: Cover image for Dragon issue 384, and a range of internal images for recent and upcoming D&D-related publications.
LOCATION: Renton, Washington.
D&D ERA: 2009-present.
MEDIA USED: Oil on board, Photoshop, Painter.
MAIN CREATIVE INFLUENCES: Frank Frazetta, Dean Cornwell, JC Leyendecker, NC Wyeth, Alex Ross, Craig Mullins, Donato Giancola, Greg Manchess, Jaime Jones, Jon Foster, Todd Lockwood, Jeff Easley, John Howe and Alan Lee.
FAVOURITE D&D TOPIC: Shifters and wilden.
HIGHS: My first commission and my first cover.
LOWS: None so far.
I WISH I COULD PAINT... Dragons.

www.tylerjacobsonart.com

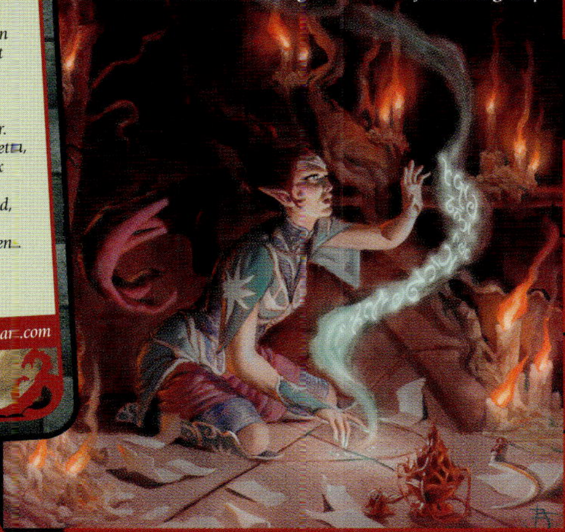

PLANAR DESTINIES
Many D&D painters include their first image for the game among their favourites. Tyler Jacobson is no different. Planar Destinies was begun in oils and finished digitally.

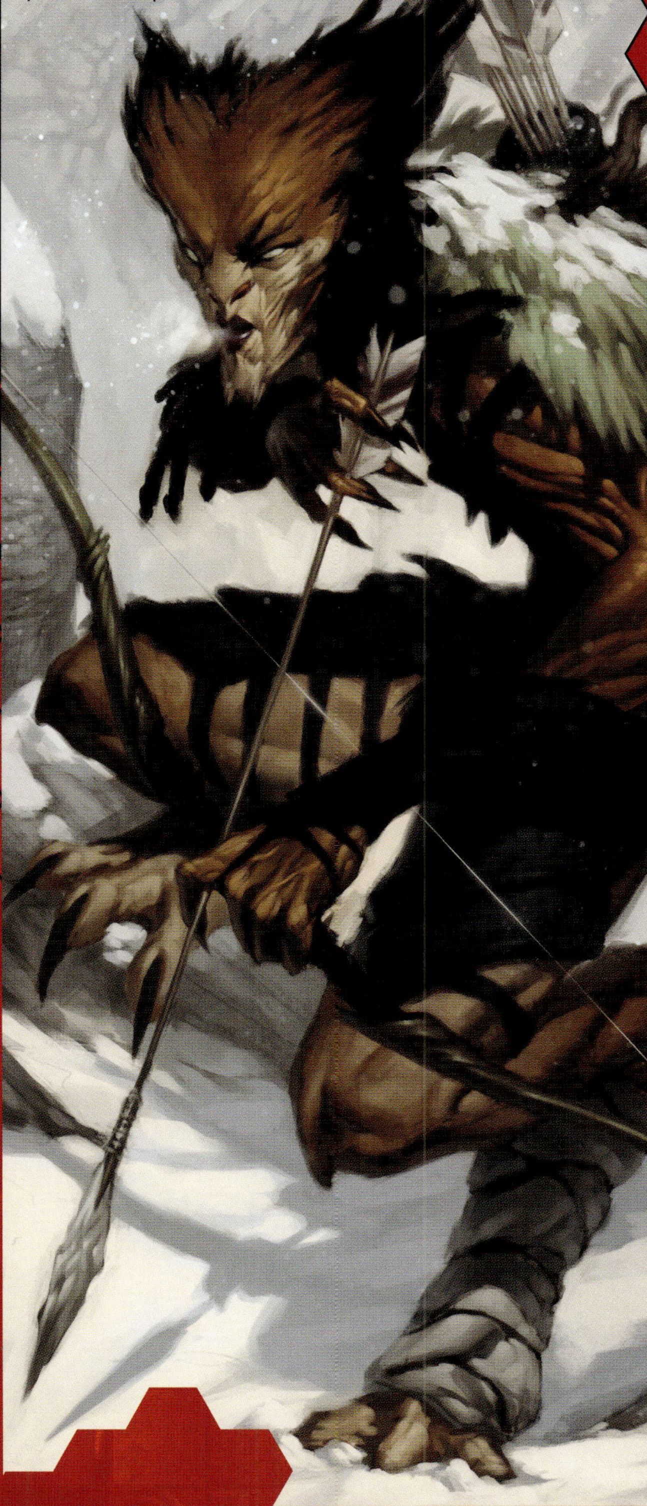

WILDEN
Here, up-and-coming D&D artist Tyler Jacobson depicts a wilden – one of D&D's newer and more mysterious races that your character can be.

lasted for years, feeding their art with authenticity. Experienced artists from advertising firms got in touch, hoping to illustrate for D&D. Although some of them could produce great fantasy imagery, the details of the game were missing.

"We knew that everything in the scene was important to the game – the weather, the time of day, you name it," says Larry. "Like when we did a fighter or an adventurer, he would usually have pouches and, if we had to, we'd show a backpack. We'd put ropes and maybe a hook or something to climb walls. We gave him armour that looked functional."

A gentle flame of competition flickered in the campfire of D&D art, fanned by the opportunity to work for Dragon magazine. Published by a separate division of TSR and edited by Kim Mohan, Dragon covered new developments in role playing and fantasy art; early editions had articles on Boris Vallejo and the Hildebrandts. The in-house artists enjoyed more freedom with Dragon commissions, as did other freelancers such as Den Beauvais. His popular Bridge of Sorrows painting for issue 92 was made into a model set by Ral Partha.

"I think what attracts me most about Bridge of Sorrows is the classic dragon

> **"All the artists were excited about Dragonlance. It was a chance to create a world from the ground up"** *Clyde Caldwell*

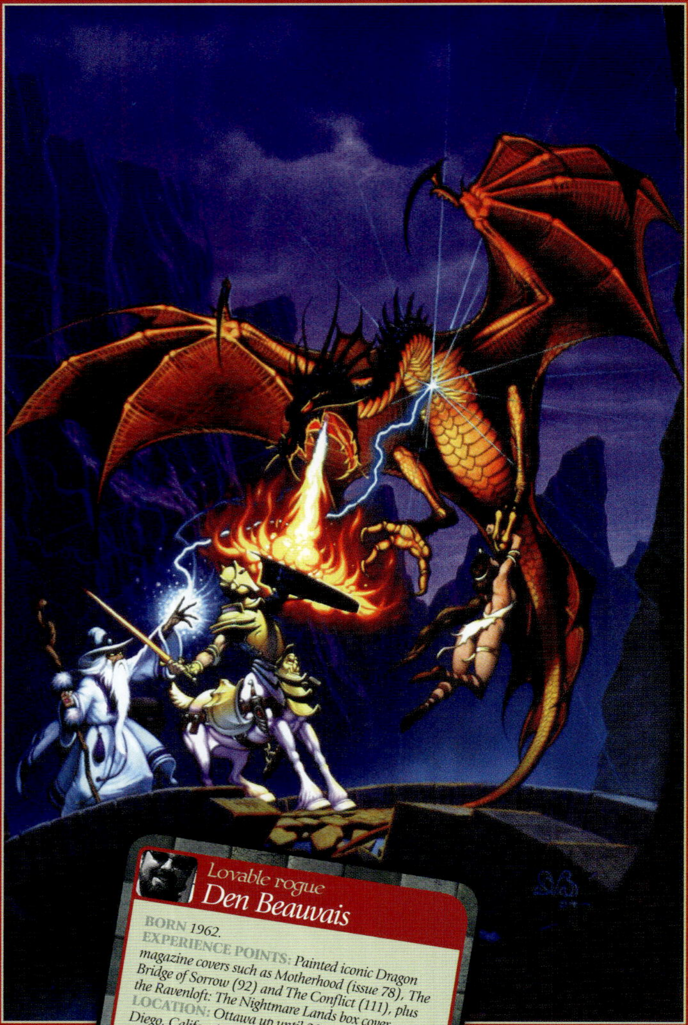

Lovable rogue
Den Beauvais

BORN 1962.
EXPERIENCE POINTS: Painted iconic Dragon magazine covers such as Motherhood (issue 78), The Bridge of Sorrow (92) and The Conflict (111), plus the Ravenloft: The Nightmare Lands box cover.
LOCATION: Ottawa up until 2003, then San Diego, California. Just moved to Vancouver.
D&D ERA: 1980-1996.
MEDIA USED: Acrylics and air brush on board.
MAIN CREATIVE INFLUENCES: Frank Frazetta, Syd Mead, Roger Dean and Keith Parkinson.
FAVOURITE D&D TOPIC: Dragons. What else?
HIGHS: Money, inspiration and weed.
LOWS: No money, uninspired and out of weed.
I WISH I COULD PAINT... A new race of Hemp Elves that I'd make up myself.

www.denbeauvais.com and www.conspiracycards.com

THE BRIDGE OF SORROWS
This stunning cover for Dragon magazine issue 92 by Den Beauvais sparkled in the imagination of many young players. So popular was the image that Ral Partha made it into a fantasy model kit.

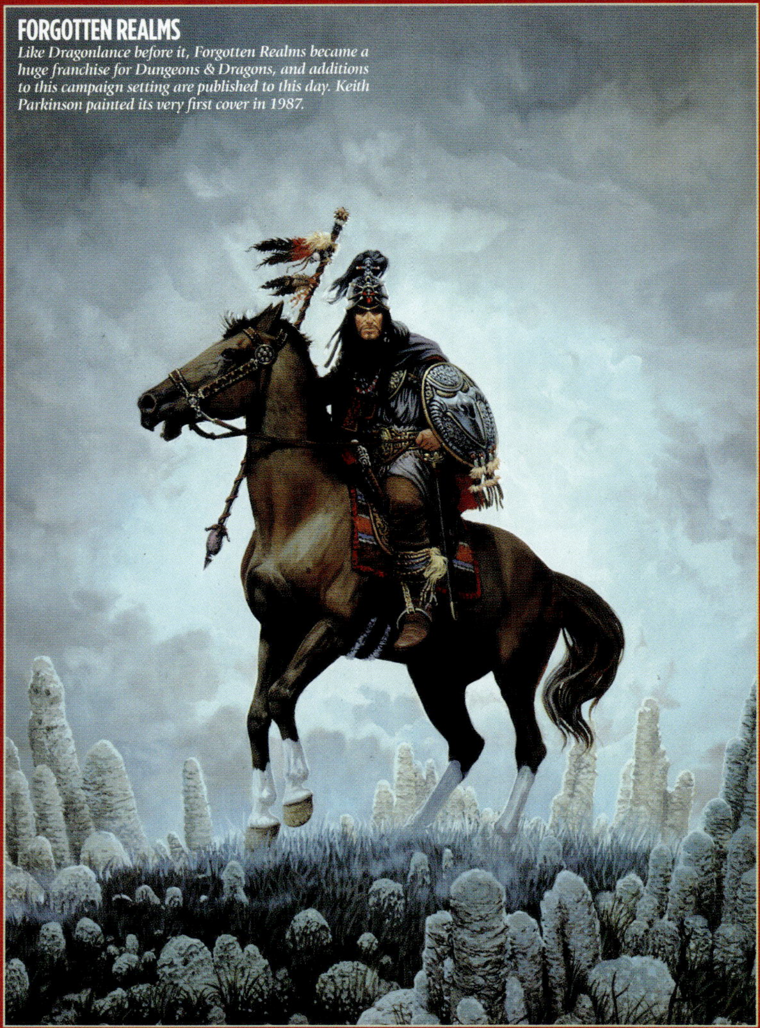

FORGOTTEN REALMS
Like Dragonlance before it, Forgotten Realms became a huge franchise for Dungeons & Dragons, and additions to this campaign setting are published to this day. Keith Parkinson painted its very first cover in 1987.

pose," he says. "Back then we were all competing to get these classic poses and we were all racing to do these images first, especially dragons. They're the icon, the top fantasy creature there is."

No party of adventurers stays together forever. Having made a defining impact on fantasy art, eventually the in-house artists began going their separate ways. Clyde stayed with TSR until 1992. Jeff Easley stayed even longer and saw in a new generation of in-house heroes like Fred Fields and RK Post, both now legends in their own right. And who can forget Brom's work for the Dark Sun campaign setting?

> **"Back then we were all competing to get these classic poses and we were all racing to do these images first, especially dragons"** *Den Beauvais*

In 1996, Todd started at TSR just in time to experience D&D's huge revolution. The company was bought by Wizards of the Coast and moved to Renton, Washington. Undoubtedly influenced by D&D's imagery, its Magic: The Gathering cards had usurped TSR's hold on fantasy gaming. The new management decided to tear it up and start again, and work began on the Third Edition rules. Todd, a keen gamer and an experienced graphic designer, pushed for an opportunity to give D&D an overarching visual style from the get-go. Art director Dawn Murrin agreed and, working with Sam Wood and the other in-house

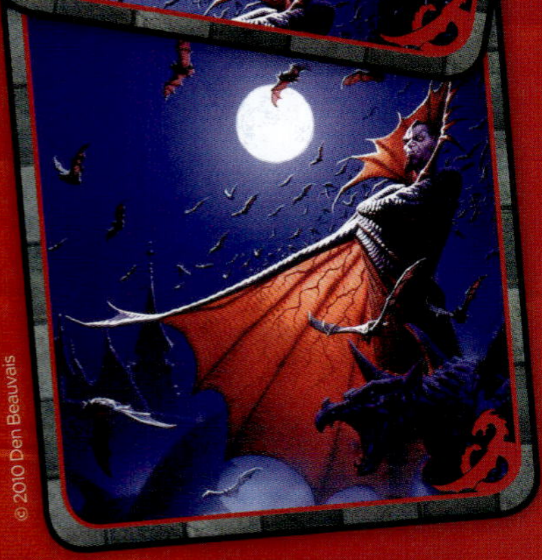

SOUL SEARCHING
In addition to magazine covers, Den Beauvais contributed paintings for D&D modules in the 80s and 90s. Soul Searching was used for an adventure in the Ravenloft series.

artists, they moulded a new look. Styling the dragons was a good place to start.

"That was certainly one of the highlights of my career: designing dragons for Dungeons & Dragons! You really can't have more fun than that. We were given pretty wide latitude to envision the game as we saw it," explains Todd. "Working on the Third Edition was a thrill not just because I got to see it the way I really always had, but because what we were creating was a centre rail, not the whole railway, passengers and all. In D&D, every player gets to imagine his or her characters exactly as they like."

Debate continues over the merits of the Third Edition, but from the late 90s the game was in a new milieu. Competition for real world gold pieces was stiff. The card

"Designing dragons for Dungeons & Dragons – you can't really have more fun than that!" Todd Lockwood

game Magic: The Gathering gave fantasy addicts something quick and easy to play. The Lord of the Rings film trilogy brought unprecedented special effects. Computer games were becoming more realistic, immersive and social. Was there still room for an imagined game?

D&D GOES FOURTH

In 2002, toy giant Hasbro purchased Wizards of the Coast. Wizards still operates as a fantasy games company, but the in-house D&D painters were let go. A design team headed by Jon Schindehette now works with freelancers, currently forging ahead with Fourth Edition products. Successful sub-brands such as Forgotten Realms, Dark Sun and Dragonlance are still going, and the Eberron campaign world has become a successful online game.

Last year the red box Starter Set led the way for D&D Essentials, a brand aiming to introduce the game to new players and lapsed dungeoneers alike. In today's artwork, swords are bigger and poses more expressive. Manga, game graphics and contemporary fantasy styles are now influencing D&D. New artists such as Tyler Jacobson, Slawomir Maniak, Eric Belisle and Eva Widermann are leaving their own distinctive marks on the game.

"It's very neat to see it evolve now to the look it has today," reflects Larry. "We might have influenced the younger guys, but now you look at some of the stuff those artists do, and that influences me. It's like a big circle." ●

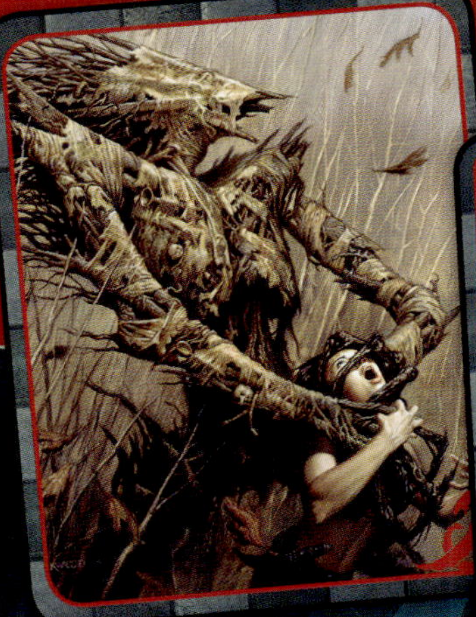

WOOD GOLEM
Each creature needs to be defined visually for the many rulebooks. Todd Lockwood's artwork has been key in that process.

Lord of the dragons
Todd Lockwood

BORN 1957.
EXPERIENCE POINTS: *Painted covers for The Silent Sentinel and Forge of Fury, the first two D&D Third Edition modules.*
LOCATION: *Bonney Lake, Washington.*
D&D ERA: *1996-2002 (end of Second Edition AD&D, to the birth of Third Edition).*
MEDIA USED: *Painter, with bits of Photoshop.*
MAIN CREATIVE INFLUENCES: *Walt Disney, Frank Frazetta, Michael Whelan, Boris Vallejo, Jeff Jones, all the great D&D artists past and present.*
FAVOURITE D&D TOPIC: *Dragons.*
HIGHS: *Partying in Amsterdam with Kenny Baker.*
LOWS: *The arrival of the corporate mindset.*
I WISH I COULD PAINT... *I always wanted to do a portrait for each of the Third Edition dragons.*
www.toddlockwood.com

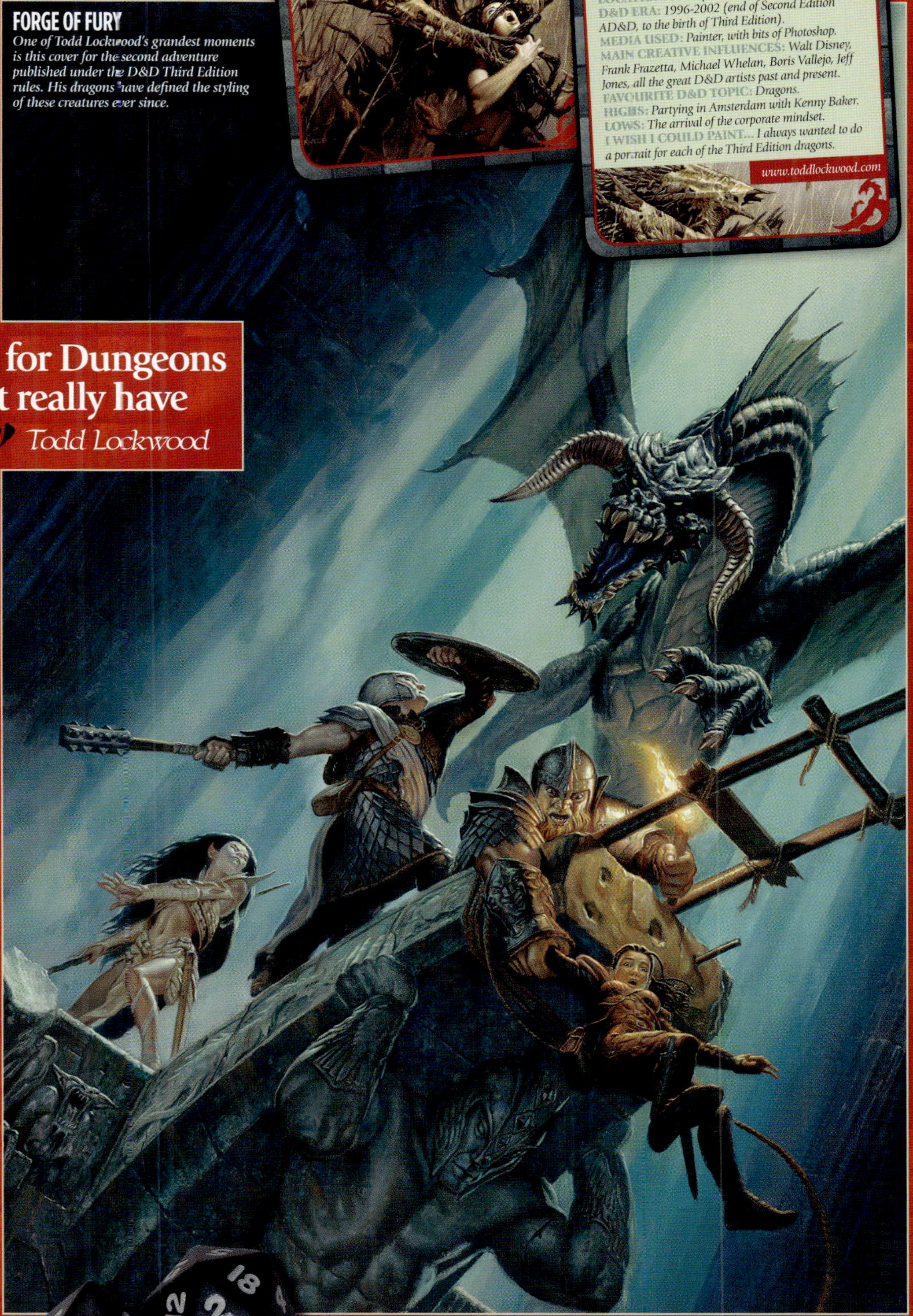

FORGE OF FURY
One of Todd Lockwood's grandest moments is this cover for the second adventure published under the D&D Third Edition rules. His dragons have defined the styling of these creatures ever since.

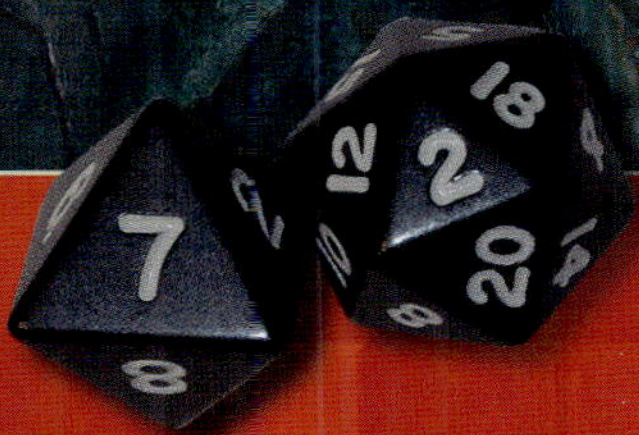

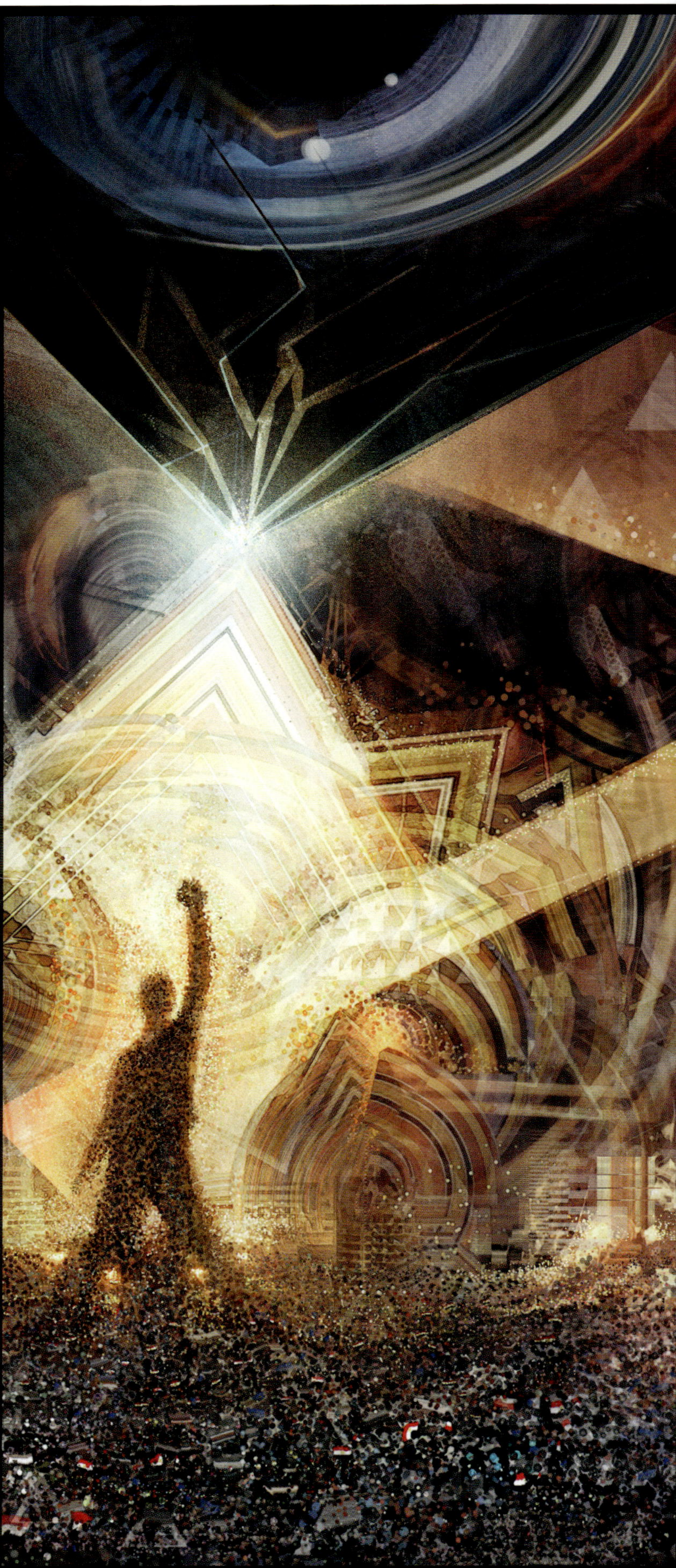

ART MASTERS

Inspiration and tutorials from today's pro artists...

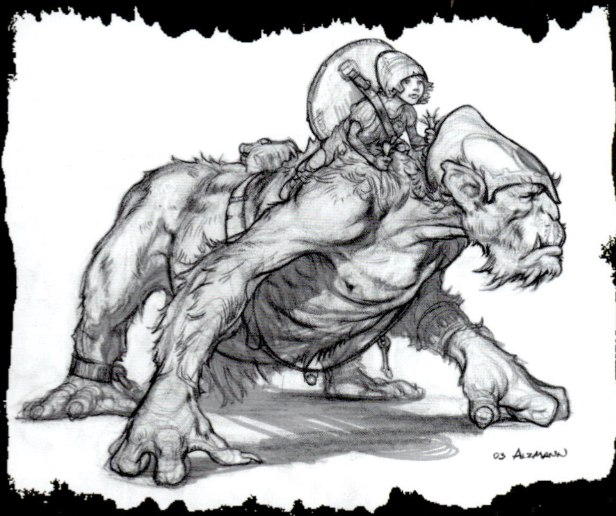

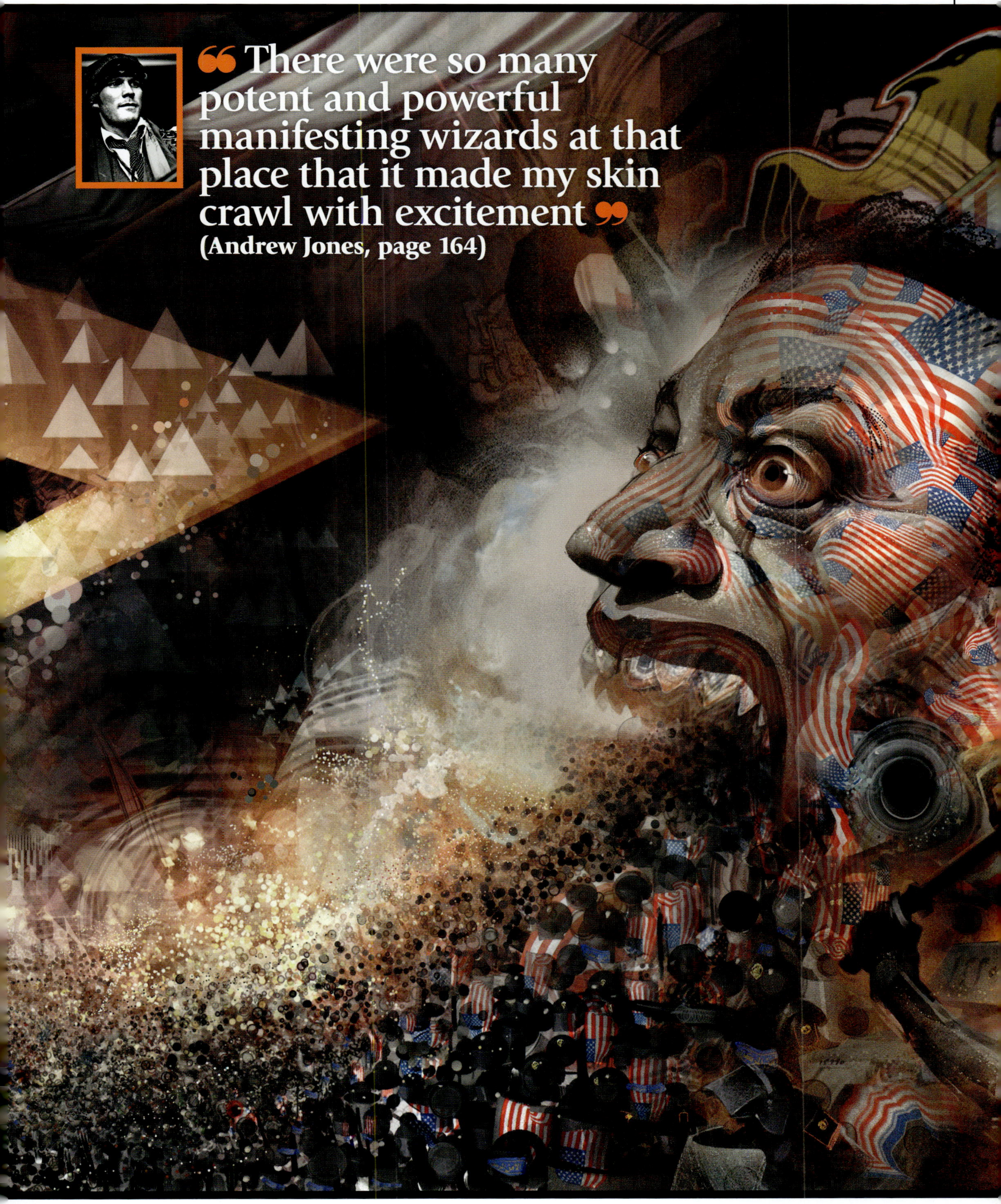

> “There were so many potent and powerful manifesting wizards at that place that it made my skin crawl with excitement”
> **(Andrew Jones, page 164)**

Interview

Mélanie Delon

In the guise of Eskarina, **Mélanie Delon** creates enigmatic fantasy portraits, each with their own rich mythologies

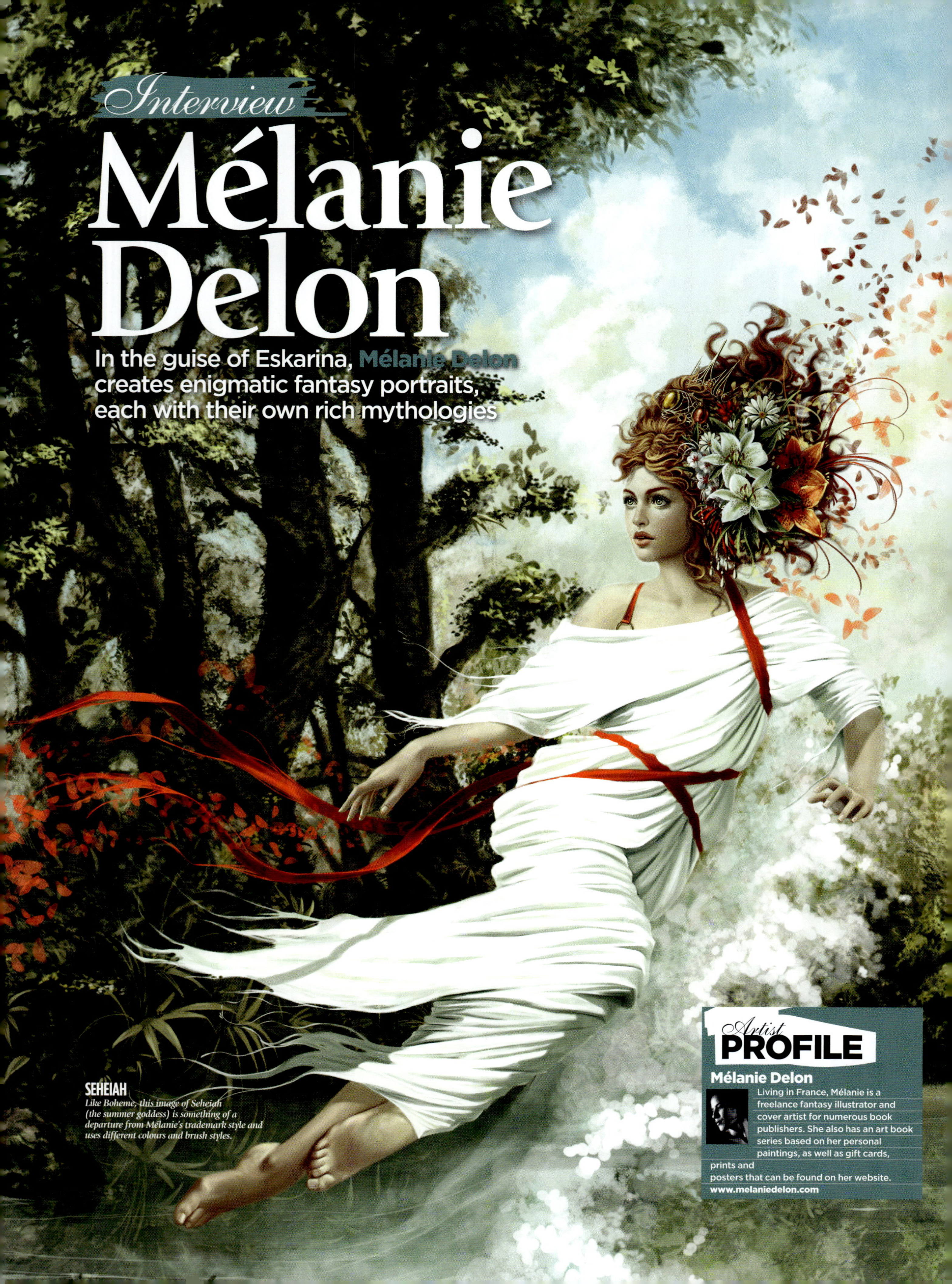

SEHEIAH

Like Boheme, this image of Seheiah (the summer goddess) is something of a departure from Mélanie's trademark style and uses different colours and brush styles.

Artist

PROFILE

Mélanie Delon

Living in France, Mélanie is a freelance fantasy illustrator and cover artist for numerous book publishers. She also has an art book series based on her personal paintings, as well as gift cards, prints and posters that can be found on her website.

www.melaniedelon.com

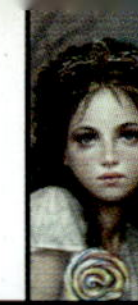

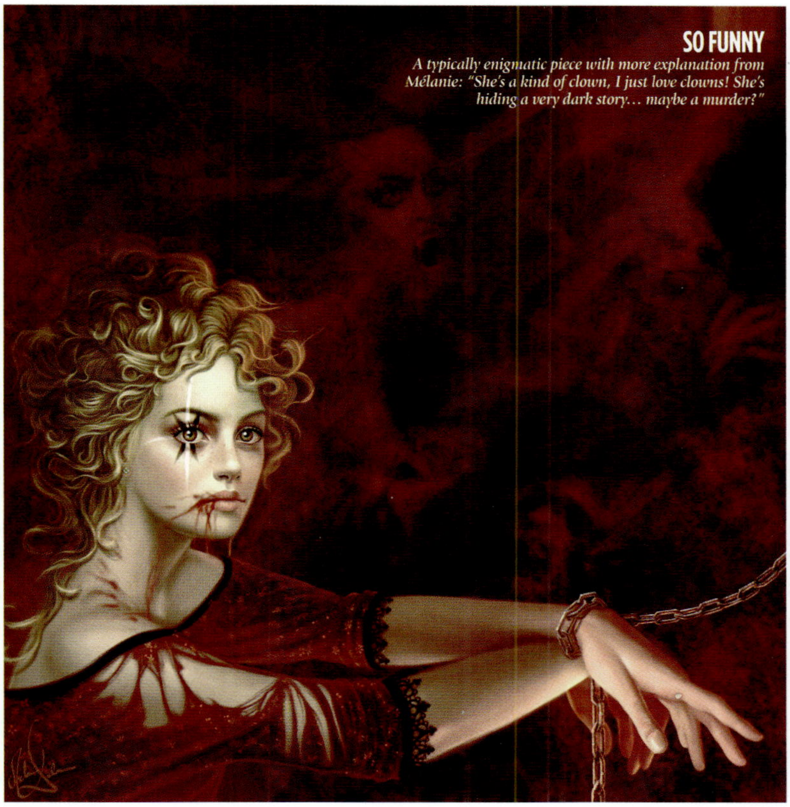

SO FUNNY
A typically enigmatic piece with more explanation from Mélanie: "She's a kind of clown, I just love clowns! She's hiding a very dark story... maybe a murder?"

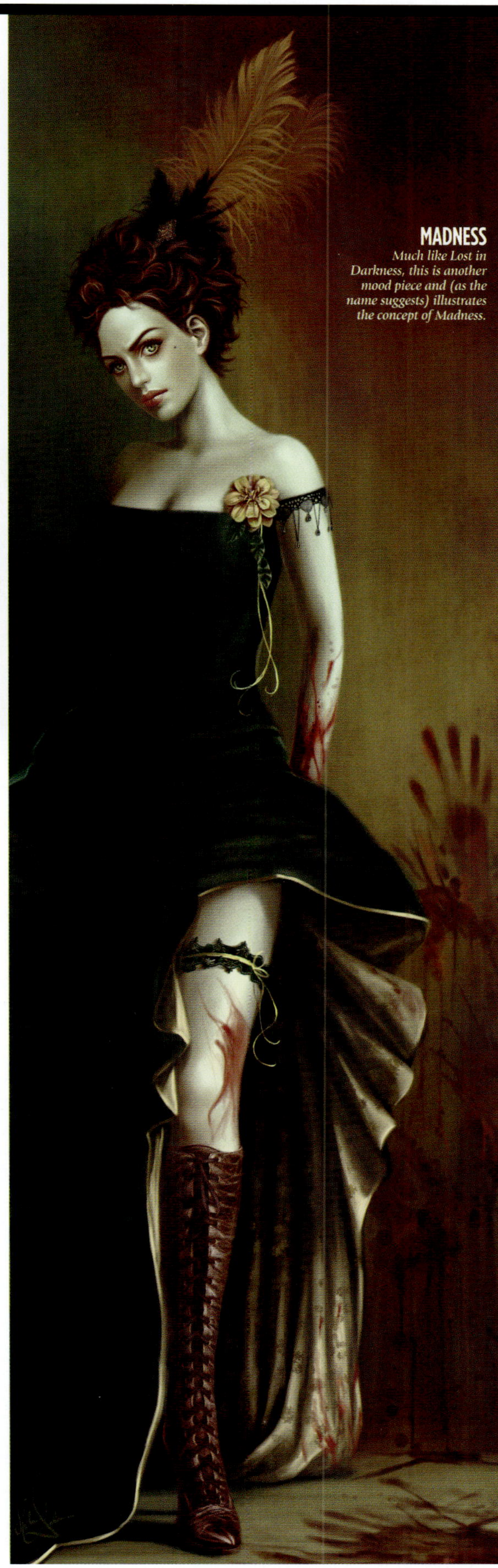

MADNESS
Much like Lost in Darkness, this is another mood piece and (as the name suggests) illustrates the concept of Madness.

"Feelings like sadness or solitude are pretty strong and even violent," enthuses Mélanie, who works under the moniker of Eskarina – a name taken from a heroine in one of Terry Pratchett's Discworld novels. "It's the story of a little girl who wants to became a wizard," she explains. "It's a kind of tribute I make to that author."

Mélanie is well known for creating otherworldly portraits that are mysterious and often emotionally charged. Images with titles such as Madness and Lost in the Darkness show her attempts to try to capture the power of these feelings on a digital canvas. "I try to re-transcribe what I am feeling when I have an idea, and to paint them I often contrast colours," she says, describing the starkly juxtaposed reds and greens of these images.

Brain teaser

But not all of Mélanie's paintings deal with such morbid subjects – images like Boheme and Sucre d'Orge show she has a much lighter side. "They are all a part of me," she says, "kind of like a puzzle."

In many ways, Eskarina's paintings are indeed a part of her. Look closely at her work and you'll notice they share some similar features, as much of the reference material comes from her own image: "For everything that concerns anatomy or posture, I use myself and a mirror," she explains. "I have a little one next to my computer for painting faces and a big one in my room for the whole body."

Like many fantasy artists, Mélanie is an avid reader and she draws on literary references from Philip K Dick, Tolkien and obviously Terry Pratchett. "Some drawings are inspired by music, other drawings, movies and everyday situations. All my characters have their own stories – it helps me to create them and to give them life," she muses.

But Mélanie leaves some room for ambiguity and wants the viewer to infer their own stories from the images: "When I post on forums, I don't go into much detail in my descriptions," she says. "I prefer the reader to make up his or her own mind."

One day she hopes to publish a book of her images and set the record straight: "I think it will be fun to compare the stories they thought of with mine," she says.

Down with tradition

One of the most surprising things about Mélanie is how quickly she has developed her style, particularly as she only started using Photoshop in 2005. What is even more remarkable is that her technique has been developed entirely using digital tools, having never worked on a traditional canvas. "I never painted," she confesses. "I drew a lot, mainly with pencil and markers, but it was for fun; until I discovered Photoshop."

Rather than seeking professional training or reading manuals, she learned entirely ➔

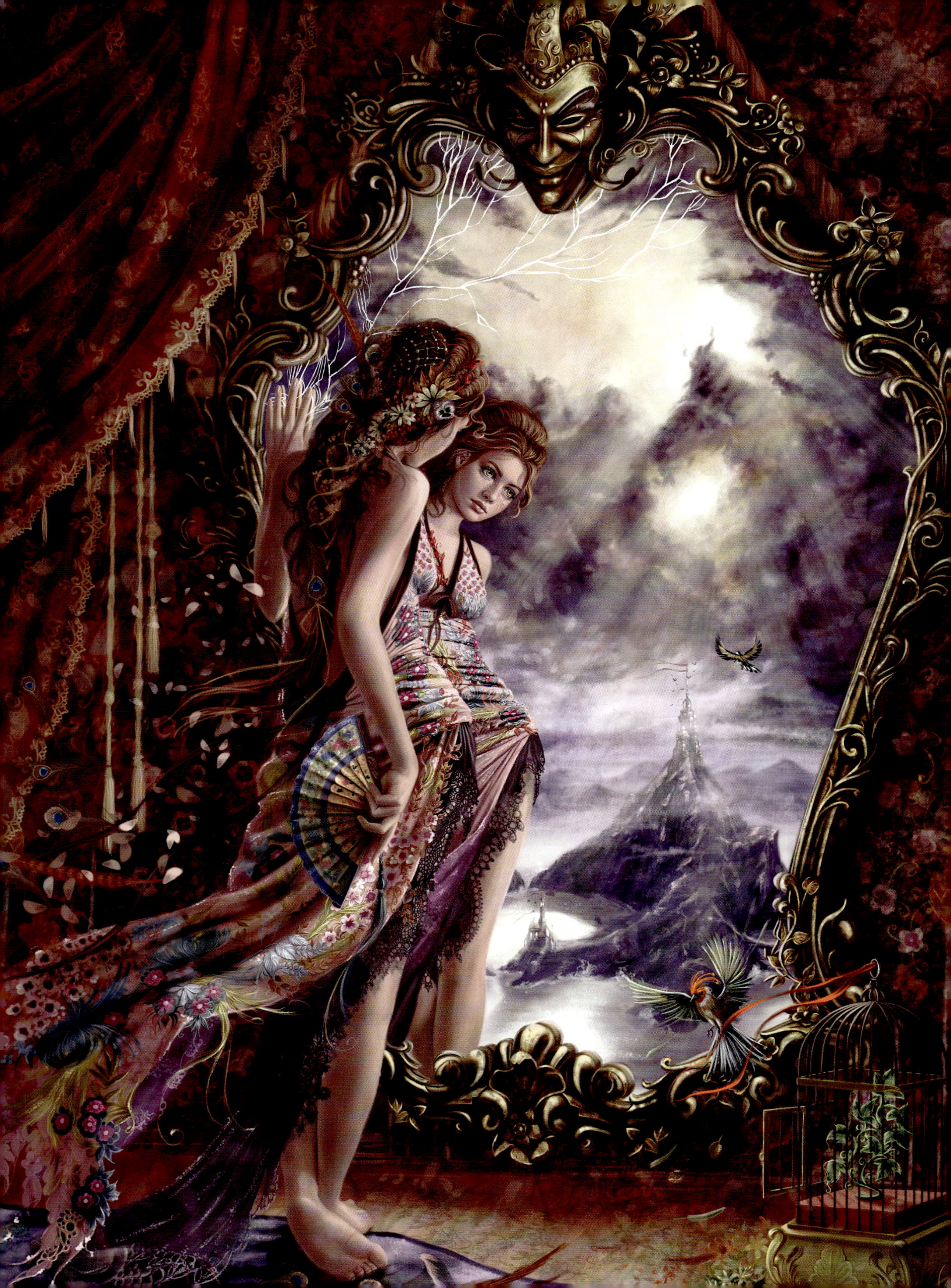

HOPELESS REFLECTIONS

A typically melancholy image, Hopeless Reflections is where Mélanie illustrates the feeling of imprisonment. "She's here, alone," Mélanie explains, "watching her birds fly away..."

PEARL

Mélanie explains Pearl's backstory: "She is Myrhaelle, the last descendant of the lords of this earth. She lives alone on an island, in the ruins of the ancient city."

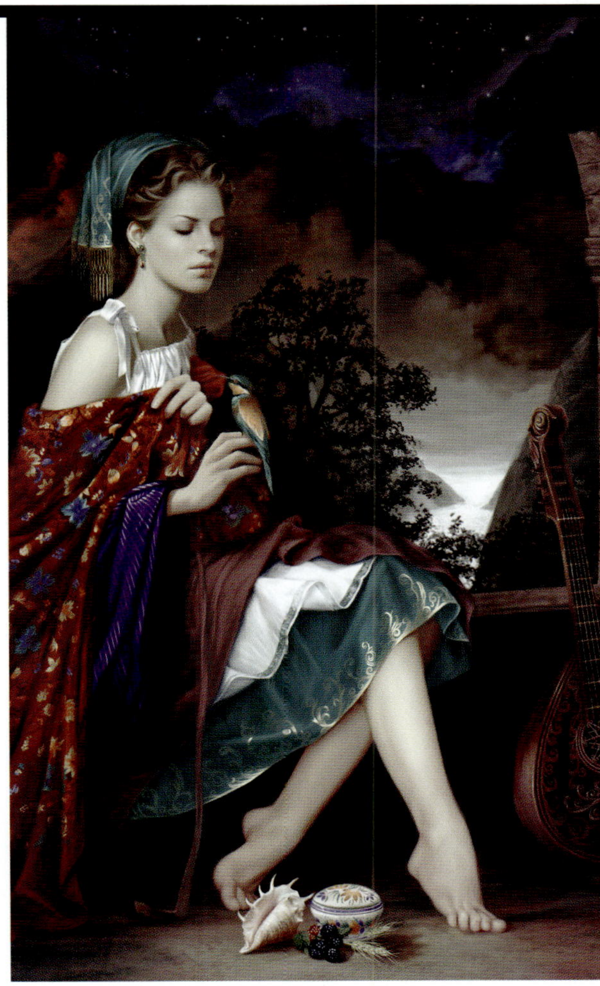

through experimentation. "It wasn't easy at first, I didn't know which way to go, but I kept on working and working, and the more I painted the more I tried to surpass my last work while learning new things," she enthuses.

Mélanie combines Photoshop CS4 with Corel Painter, taking advantage of the relative strengths of the two packages: "For my rough sketches and quick colouring, I find Painter easier to work with, but the biggest part of the painting is done with Photoshop and a Wacom. I do sometimes switch back to Painter for certain textures."

She's enthusiastic when talking about her tools: "I use my own brushes, two in particular: a basic Hard Round edge that I use for almost everything, and a Spackled, which is great for blending colours and bringing life to texture. Then all my custom texture brushes, the Blur tool (never the filter one), which is extremely useful and adjustable, and finally, layers. I love layers," she grins.

History of art

But while she may not have painted traditionally, she has developed a unique and self-confident style that owes a lot to her university studies on the history of art. "Those two years of studies helped me discover many artists and to understand the evolution of art," she explains. "It's also, culturally speaking, a big help. I think that's why my works can't be tagged as pure fantasy, there are always historical elements that blend in with the ones I create."

Look closely at the detail of Mélanie's paintings and the historical influences become clear. She references Turner, for example, as an influence on her background painting technique. But the artist she draws on most heavily is the 19th century French academic painter William Adolphe Bouguereau, who painted mythological themes. Mélanie is humble in acknowledging her debt. "I think he has influenced – and keeps on influencing – me on all levels," she says. "Moreover, the way he deals with lights and colours, it's incredible. Bouguereau's characters are so alive. I would like to have his talent!"

Mélanie has clearly thrown herself into her artwork since going digital. "Drawing has become more serious for me and more than just a hobby," she says. "I usually spend about 10 hours a day on my painting – even more sometimes! I paint all day long, for my work and for fun. I'm trying to learn more and more with each painting."

Turn the page to learn to paint like Mélanie Delon

> **"It wasn't easy at first, but I kept on working and the more I painted, the more I tried to surpass my last work while learning new things"**

BOHEME

Mélanie shows her lighter side: "I wanted to paint something different. She's a gypsy, walking the streets with her beloved cat."

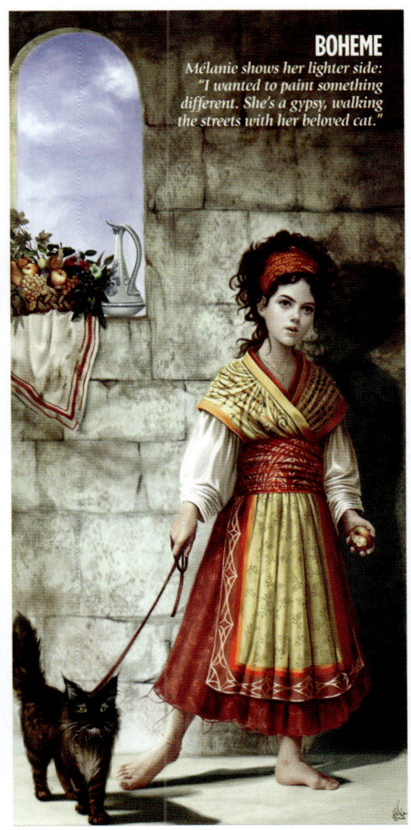

SUCRE D'ORGE

The sweeter side of Eskarina

While much of Mélanie's work deals with the darker side of human emotion, she shows a lightness of touch in some of her more whimsical images, like Boheme and Sucre d'Orge.

In these images, Mélanie shows a markedly different style to her more morbid portraits – gone are the starkly contrasted reds and greens, in favour of an altogether calmer blue pastel palette.

"I painted Sucre d'Orge for Exposé 4," she explains. "I wanted to create something really fresh, without darkness, so I decided to illustrate the innocence of childhood – she's a kind of little fantasy princess." While it's one of Mélanie's most accomplished images, it was actually one of her shorter projects, taking her only a week to paint (painting Pearl – see the image top-right – however took a full three weeks to complete).

What this image does share with her darker images is the model; again the facial features are taken from her own visage. According to Mélanie, the hardest part was getting the detail on the lollipop: "I added this because all children love them. I studied a lot of pictures to create the texture, and I must admit I'm pretty satisfied with the result." And so you should be, Mélanie.

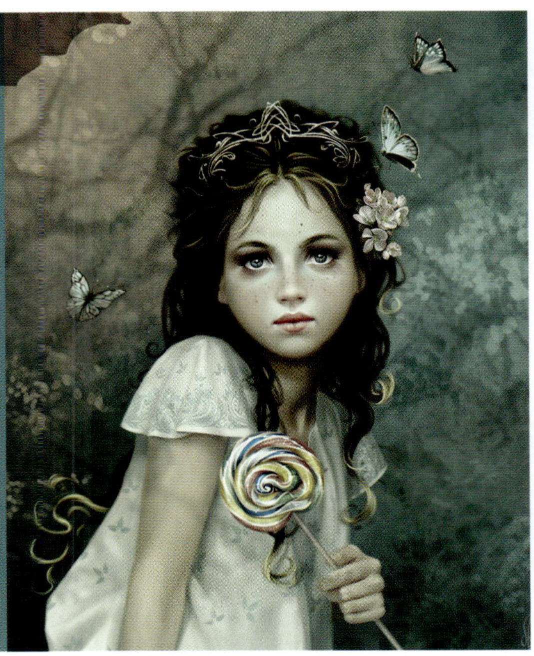

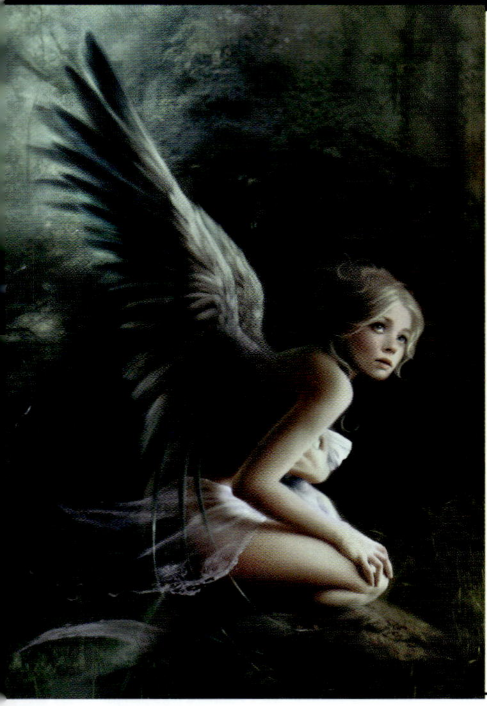

Painter & Photoshop

FEATHERS AND ANGEL WINGS

Wings and feathers can be tricky to paint. **Mélanie Delon** explains her technique for creating a realistic look…

Painting wings is quite similar to painting hair: the first time you do it seems impossible, but in fact it's not, and there are little tips that can help a lot.

Before I start painting, I always do some photo research; in this case I looked at a lot of bird pictures to understand the feathers and decided what kind of design I wanted. Then I did a little concept sketch to test out a few colours.

When I paint wings, I think of them as a block; I never paint feather by feather, always as a whole element. I add in details later, once the lightning and the shape are okay. Working on them as a block helps to unify the wings and stops you getting too wrapped up in minor details.

Wings can also reflect the character's mood or attitude: you can do this with colour, or by making the wings lighter or heavier. Here, I want to avoid the image coming across very clean and pure: she's not an angel, so her wings will be more like a bird's – a bit dirty and old.

When painting wings and feathers, I usually use two brushes. For the base and the shape of the feathers, I use one that's very smooth and quickly gives me the kind of lightness I want. Then I use a spackled one for adding the details.

Now let's look at how to paint the wings and feathers, step by step.

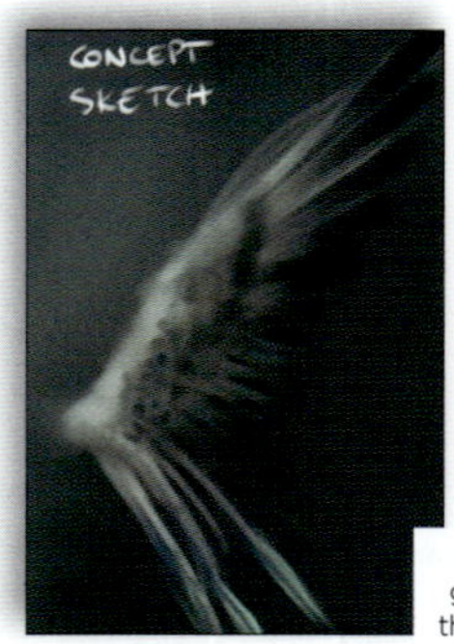

The concept sketch doesn't go into detail but establishes the general shape and colour

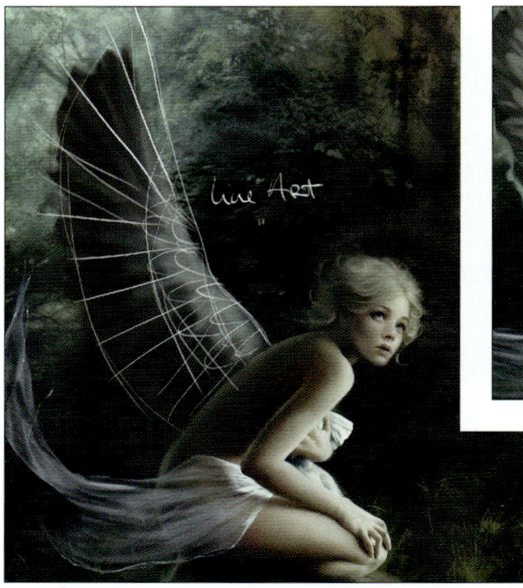

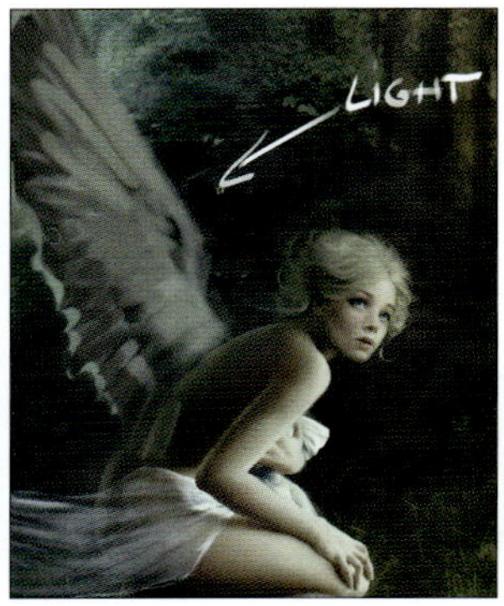

Once you're happy with the general shape of the wings you can start sketching in the feathers.

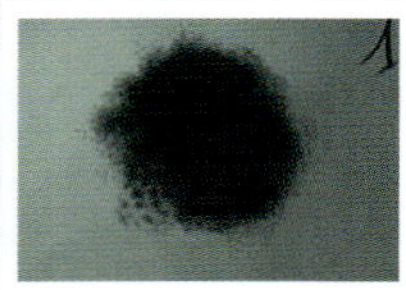

Custom brush, with Spacing set to 10 per cent and Opacity set to Pen Pressure.

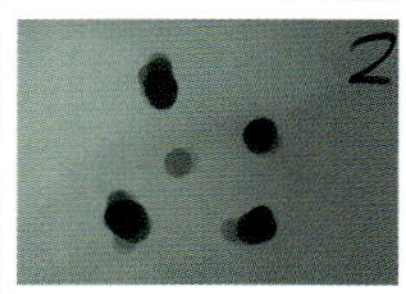

Spackled brush with Spacing set to seven per cent and Opacity set to Pen Pressure.

1 The base

I usually start by doing a basic sketch of the general shape of the wings. I also do a little research on another canvas. I use a large-sized custom brush to work the general look and to set the base of my future wings. I don't need to go into details, I just choose my colours – which are basically the same as the background – and paint in huge blocks of colour.

2 Sketching the feathers

I start to sketch the first feathers, still using the same brush as in the previous step. I flip the canvas horizontally quite often at this stage to correct any little issues. Once the base is okay I can start to look at light: for this I pick the same colour I use for the background.

3 Detailed part

Now comes the fun part. I lay down the colour of the feathers, which are very dark at the extremities and brighter at the base of the wing. I use brush number one again, and paint huge blocks of colour – no need to start on the details here, it's only the base for future feathers. The extremities also need to be more defined, so I erase some parts and add more green here, because the second light source (which is more diffuse than the main one) will affect the feathers.

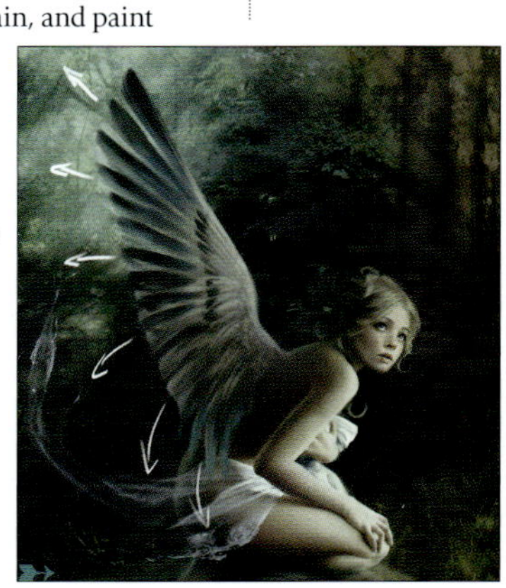

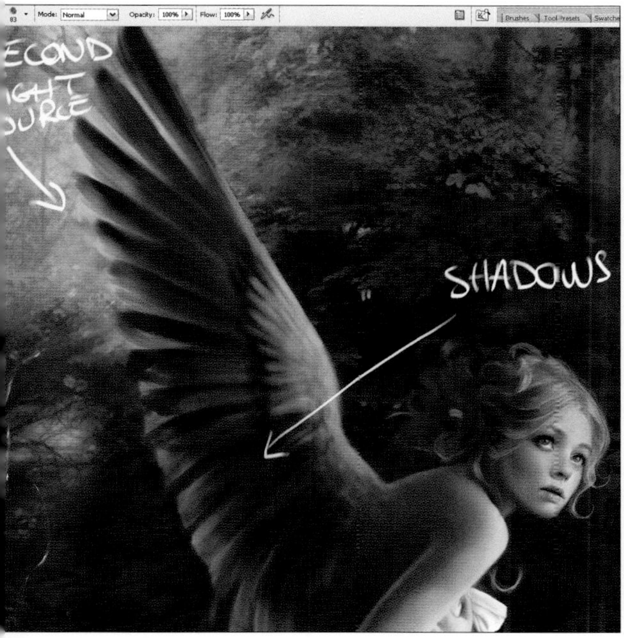

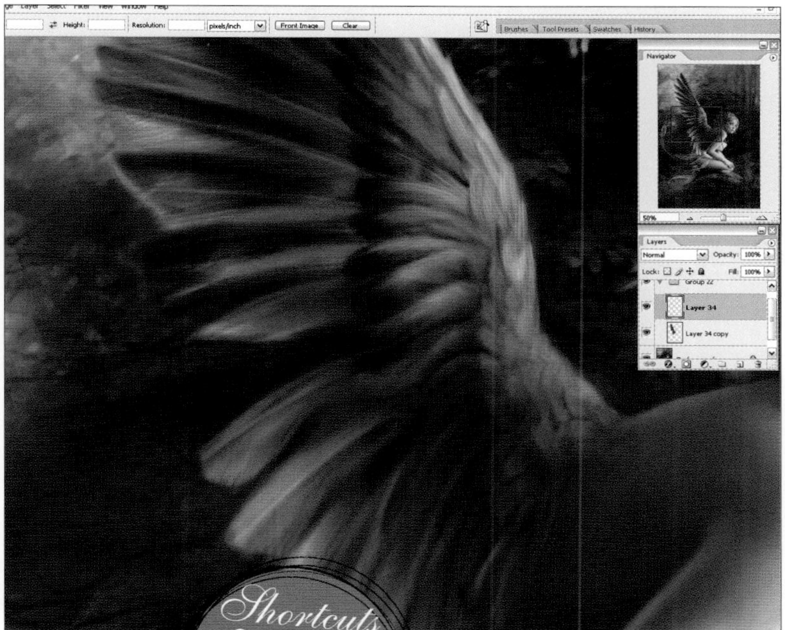

4 Light and shadow

They're lacking volume so I have to add more contrast. I select a dark green tone for the shadows, and with brush number one I bring more darkness to the middle of the wing. I also add extra green from the second light source at the top of the wing.

5 Blurring

Now I switch to Painter, which is more appropriate for this stage. I create a new layer and with the oil palette knife I slightly blur the wing. I'm following the arrows below, to unify the feathers and to bring more movement and lightness to them. If you don't have Painter on your computer you could use Motion Blur on Photoshop with a very low distance (around 10 or 15 pixels) instead.

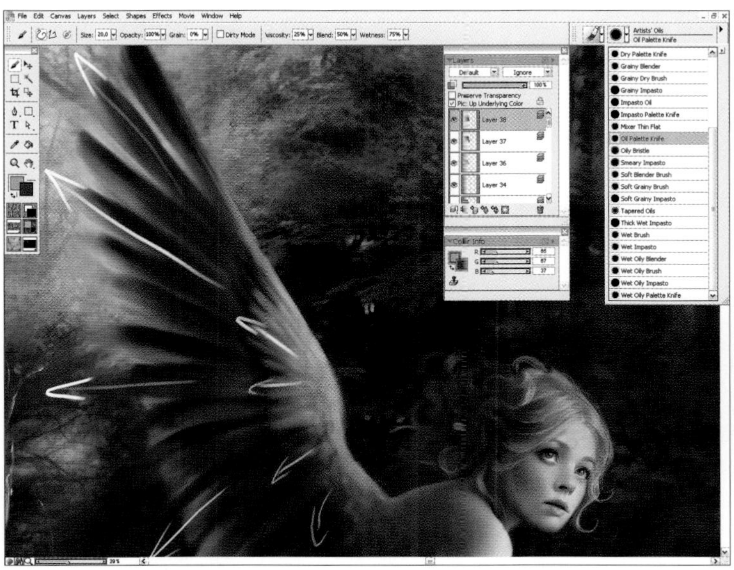

6 General refining

Here I decide to give the feathers more definition. I don't need to paint them one by one, just a few of them where the light source affects the wing. I also add more blue and more texture with the spackled brush. I do this several times, then I duplicate the layer and set it to soft light with a low Opacity; this will bring more volume to the wing.

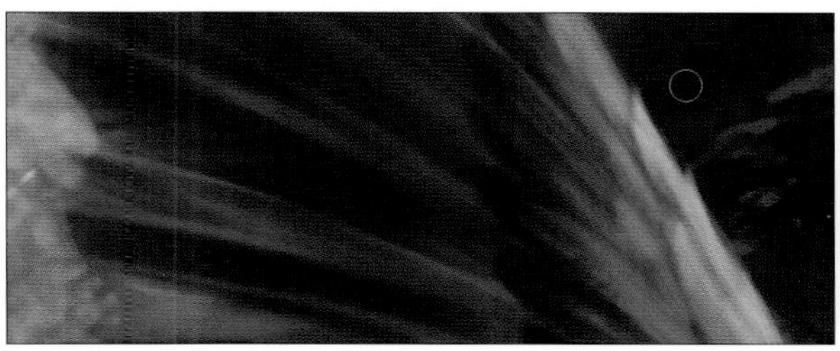

Shortcuts
Screen mode
F
Use this shortcut to switch from standard screen mode to full screen mode quickly and easily while you work.

PRO SECRETS

Add extra movement

Once my wings are finished, I duplicate the layer and add a little blur filter with a very low Opacity. This is pretty useful when you want to add more movement or increase the feeling of lightness. You can also do this in Painter with the Oil Palette Knife, which is better than the filter in Photoshop. Also don't forget to blur each feather's extremities with the Blur tool, setting strength to 50 per cent.

7 Special FX

I erase some parts of the extremities of the feathers to increase the realism. With the spackled brush I start to add more details to the feathers, picking a very saturated green (from the background) and painting some little rays of light on the extremities. I repeat this step a few times until I'm satisfied with the result.

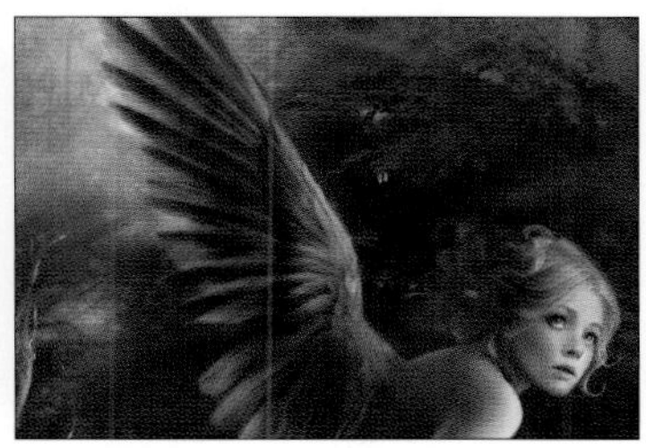

8 Final touches

Now I only have to add extra light and some little colour variations on the biggest feathers. I usually switch to Painter one last time to fix some minor mistakes, and to unify everything.

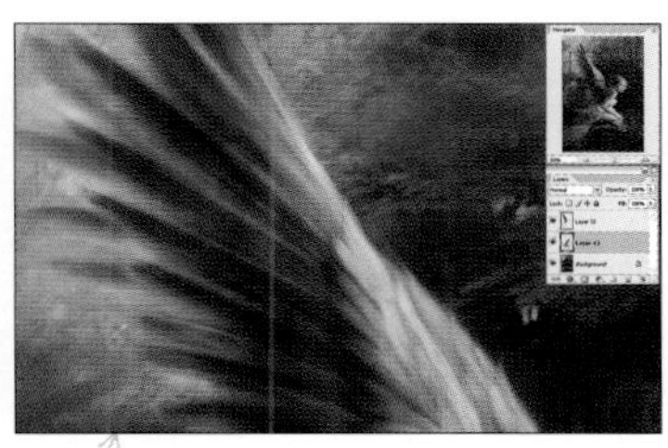

9 Second wing

The first wing now finished, I duplicate the layer and place it under the main wing. I slightly modify the shape, add more light and blur the final result.

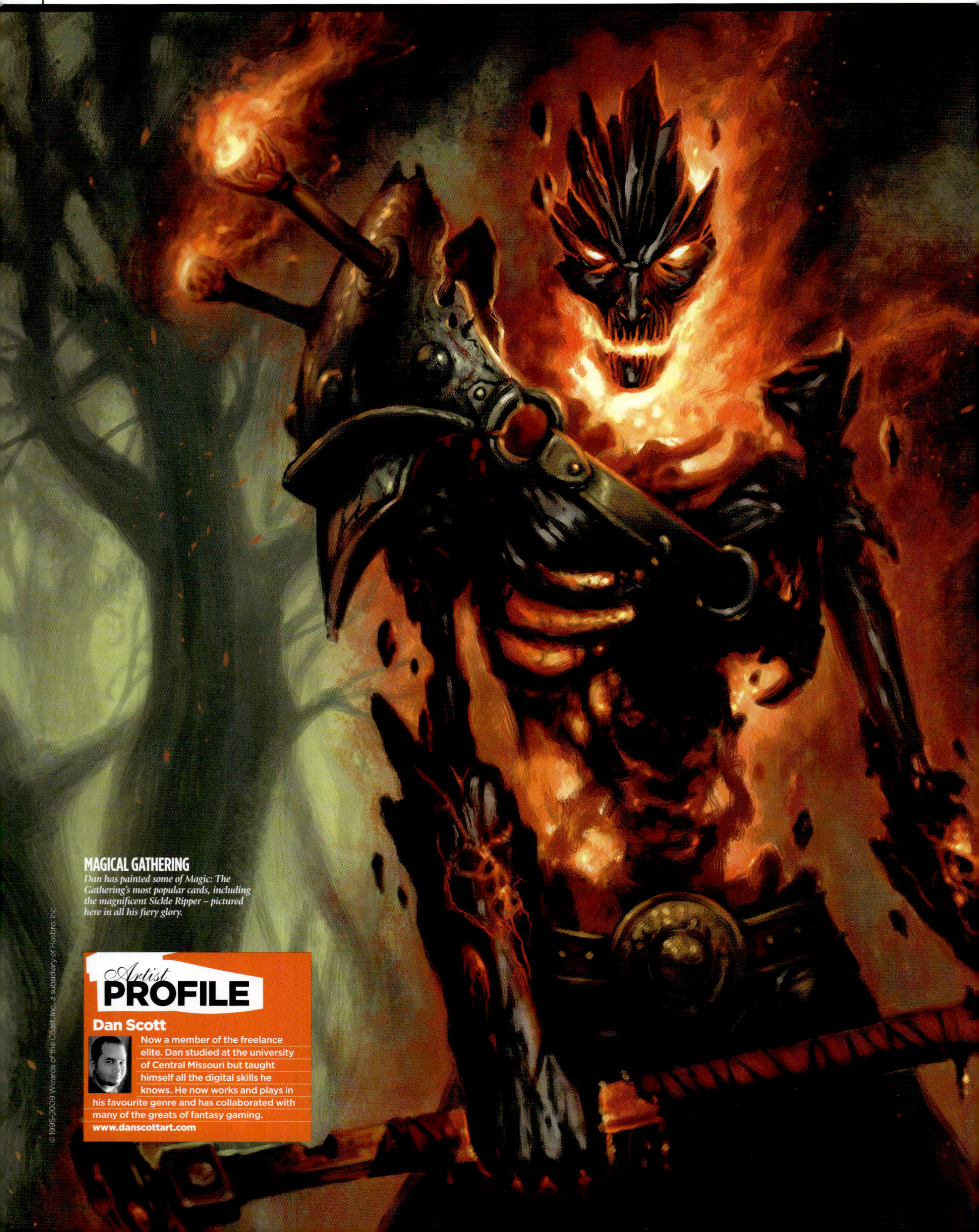

MAGICAL GATHERING
Dan has painted some of Magic: The Gathering's most popular cards, including the magnificent Sickle Ripper – pictured here in all his fiery glory.

Artist **PROFILE**

Dan Scott

Now a member of the freelance elite. Dan studied at the university of Central Missouri but taught himself all the digital skills he knows. He now works and plays in his favourite genre and has collaborated with many of the greats of fantasy gaming.

www.danscottart.com

Interview

Dan Scott

Fantasy fan **Dan Scott** has managed to turn his passion for the genre into his career. It helps to have talent, too...

Chances are if you love fantasy gaming you'll have thumbed through hundreds of dragons, druids and decomposing corpses painted by Dan Scott. He's he man trusted by the planet's elite fantasy publishers to make their worlds spark into life; just check out his speed dial list: World of Warcraft, Magic: The Gathering and Warhammer.

Dan's depictions of classic fantasy have inspired a fanatical following among many role-players. "I was completely surprised and a little flattered," says Dan, as we raise the spectre of two devoted fans. "I've had people ask me to personally design a tattoo for them, but these guys actually got tattoos of art I'd already done for game products." Dan reveals that the first man had a full-colour image of his art from the

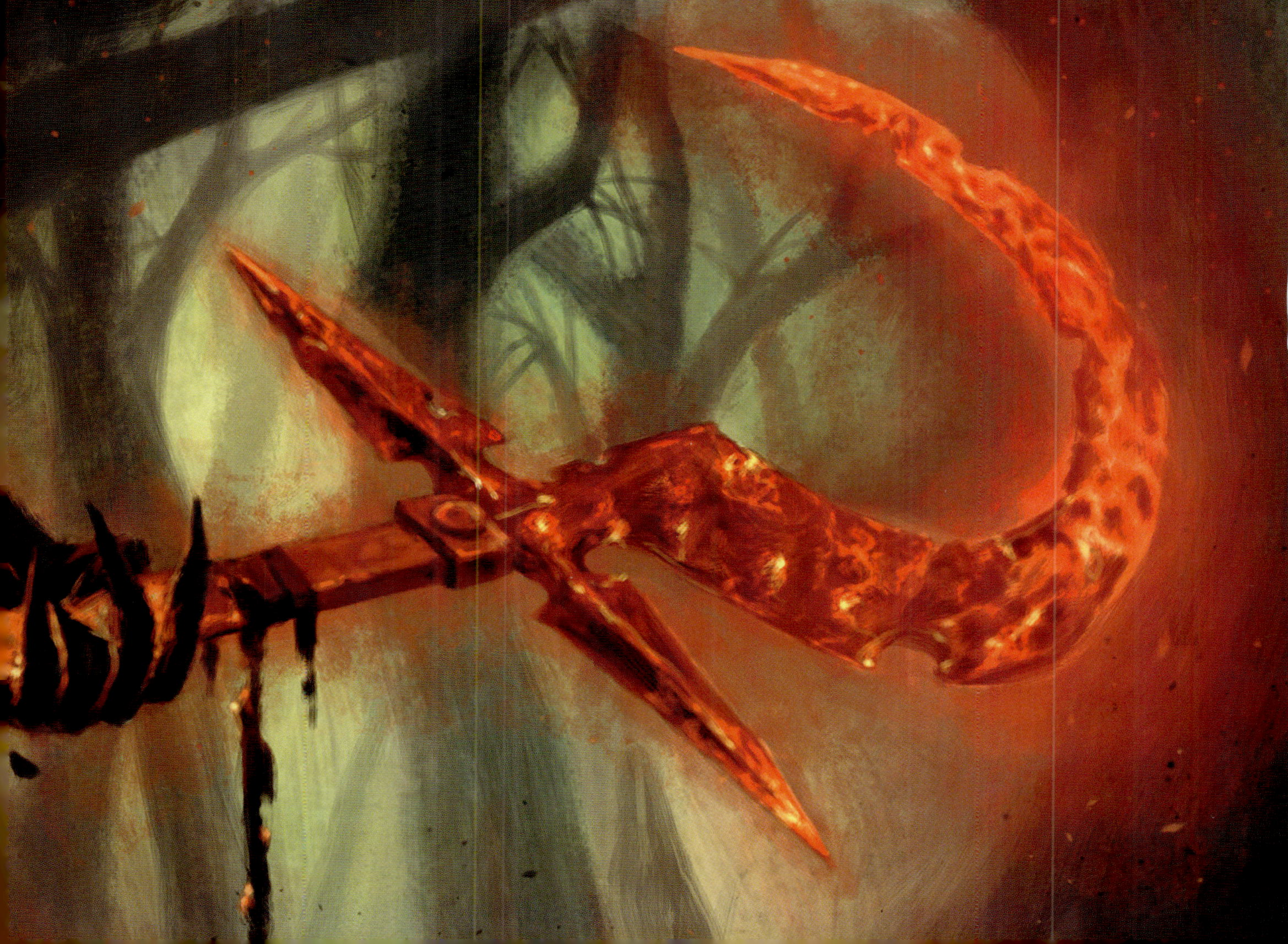

ARTIST TIP

ACTION KEYS

"Use hotkeys as much as possible to save time, but to really speed up your workflow, assign action keys to repetitive tasks. I have action keys assigned to bring up my Image Size and Canvas Size menus, expand and contract selections, flatten an image and much more."

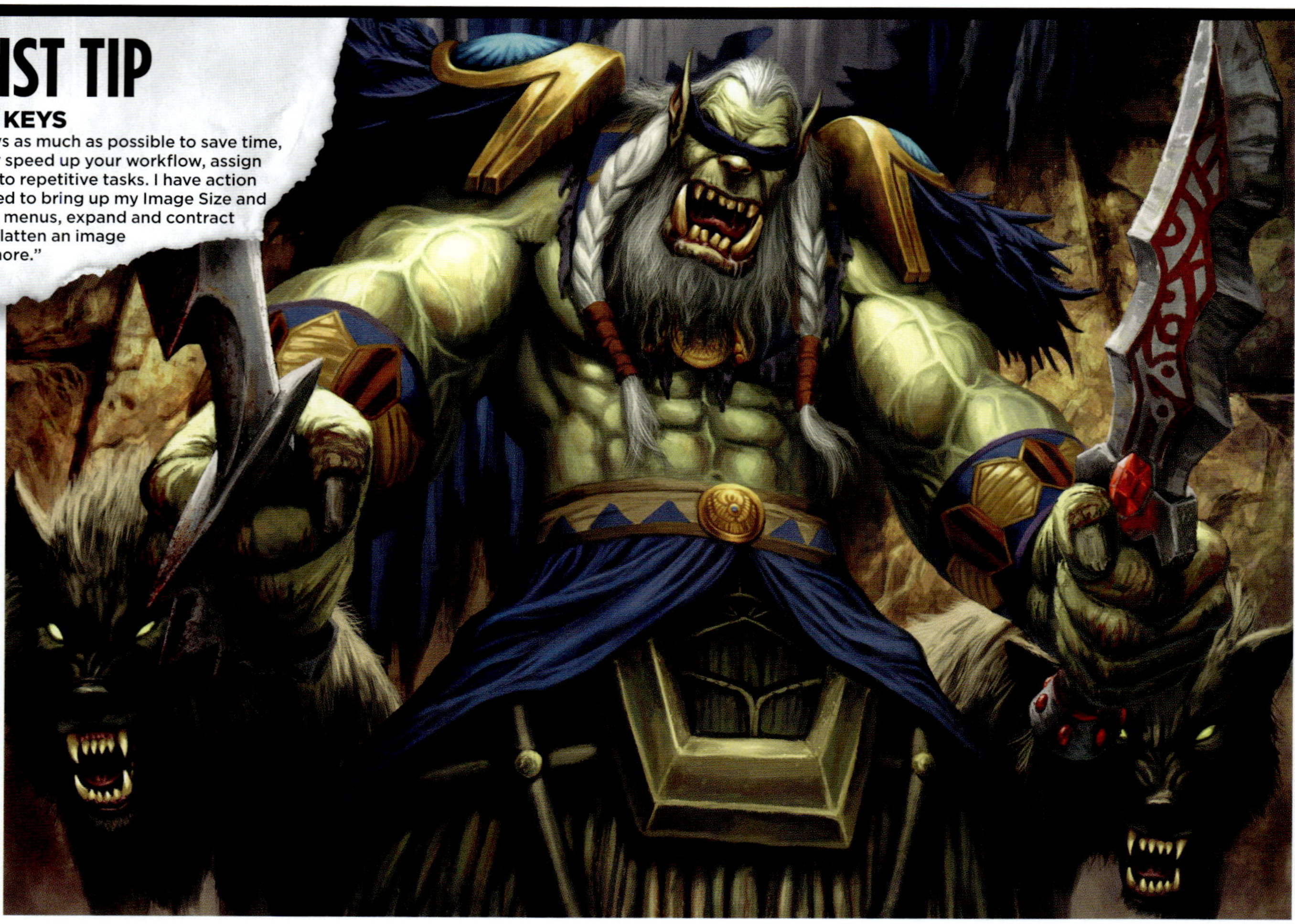

POWER PLAY
World of Warcraft's blind shaman Drek'Thar displays elements of both power and wisdom.

"I remember discovering the Official Handbook of the Marvel Universe series and trying to redraw every character"

Magic: The Gathering's Memory Plunder card across his back. The other had WarCry card Fast March on his upper arm.

FAN FAIR

"I spend so much time by myself in my studio, toiling away for hours on end with very little human interaction," says Dan. "It's easy to forget that people actually get to see and enjoy the art I'm producing, so it's really cool to get out and get to meet some of those people." Dan has accepted that developing some kind of fandom is part of the game with the type of art he's creating, and he admits it's something he enjoys. "It's a really nice side-benefit of doing this type of art. I know artists in a lot of other fields don't ever get to interact with or meet fans of their work."

What's refreshing about Dan is his devotion to fantasy art and role-playing-game illustration. Like the two fans who had his work inked forever across their bodies, Dan is a fantasy fanatic. Before turning pro, his interest in fantasy art was spiked by the comic Dragon Slayer, which led him to play Dungeons & Dragons – and from there to discover the art of Keith Parkinson, Larry Elmore and Fred Fields. "Early on, though, it was definitely comic books that were the biggest inspiration," he says. "I was a big Marvel comics fan and would draw all the characters. I remember discovering the Official Handbook of the Marvel Universe series as a kid and trying to redraw every character in it in my own version of the books."

At school, Dan was a dreamer, his head stuck in Marvel art books while his maths notes were fodder for doodles (what is it about squared paper that's just so hard to resist?) – and, like most boys, Star Wars turned his head. "It sounds clichéd but I've always drawn, as far back as I can remember," he says. "I just never stopped. Most people do as they grow up." Putting down his graffiti-strewn maths books, Dan attended the University of Central Missouri for five years, where he majored in commercial art and illustration. As well as introducing the basics The Official Handbook of the Marvel Universe couldn't teach, the course opened the door on digital art – and Dan jumped through.

SOFTWARE SUCCESS

"It turns out digital ended up being the best fit, but I learned almost nothing about it in college," Dan explains. "I was there in the early- to mid-90s, so digital just wasn't used by artists nearly as much as it is now. Almost everything I've learned digitally has been self-taught, through

INSANE ART
Dan's rendition of Salia from World of Warcraft shows off his eye for provocative poses.

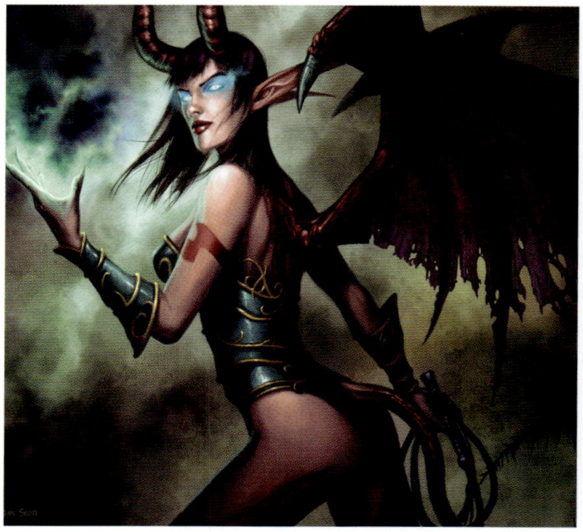

PAINTING OUT YOUR DEMONS

Dan Scott explains the pros and cons of fighting the fantasy style sheets

Dan has more than a decade of experience in painting licensed products. His client list includes DC, Marvel and giants of fantasy gaming like World of Warcraft and Magic: The Gathering. The need to paint within strict style guides has some good and bad points.

"There are going to be style guides and established characters and settings with just about any licence you work on, so it's part of the territory," says Dan. Some commissions have strict guides, but some offer wiggle room to be creative. "As an artist, you want to be free to create your own vision for an image," Dan says. "There are other times when it's fun to portray an established character everyone's familiar with. Not having to design a character can make the painting go faster and cause fewer headaches."

That's not to say Dan doesn't bang his head against creative brick walls just like everyone else. Trying to devise new compositions at the sketching stage can be a pain, as can conjuring up a new colour palette. "These are the most intellectually challenging times of any painting," he says. "I'm sure I can be difficult for my family to be around when I'm struggling with these parts of a painting. When you finally solve the problem, though, it's a wonderful feeling."

CARRION HILL

This gruesome bug-eyed monster adorns the cover of Carrion Hill – a dark module from the Dungeons & Dragons off-shoot game, Pathfinder.

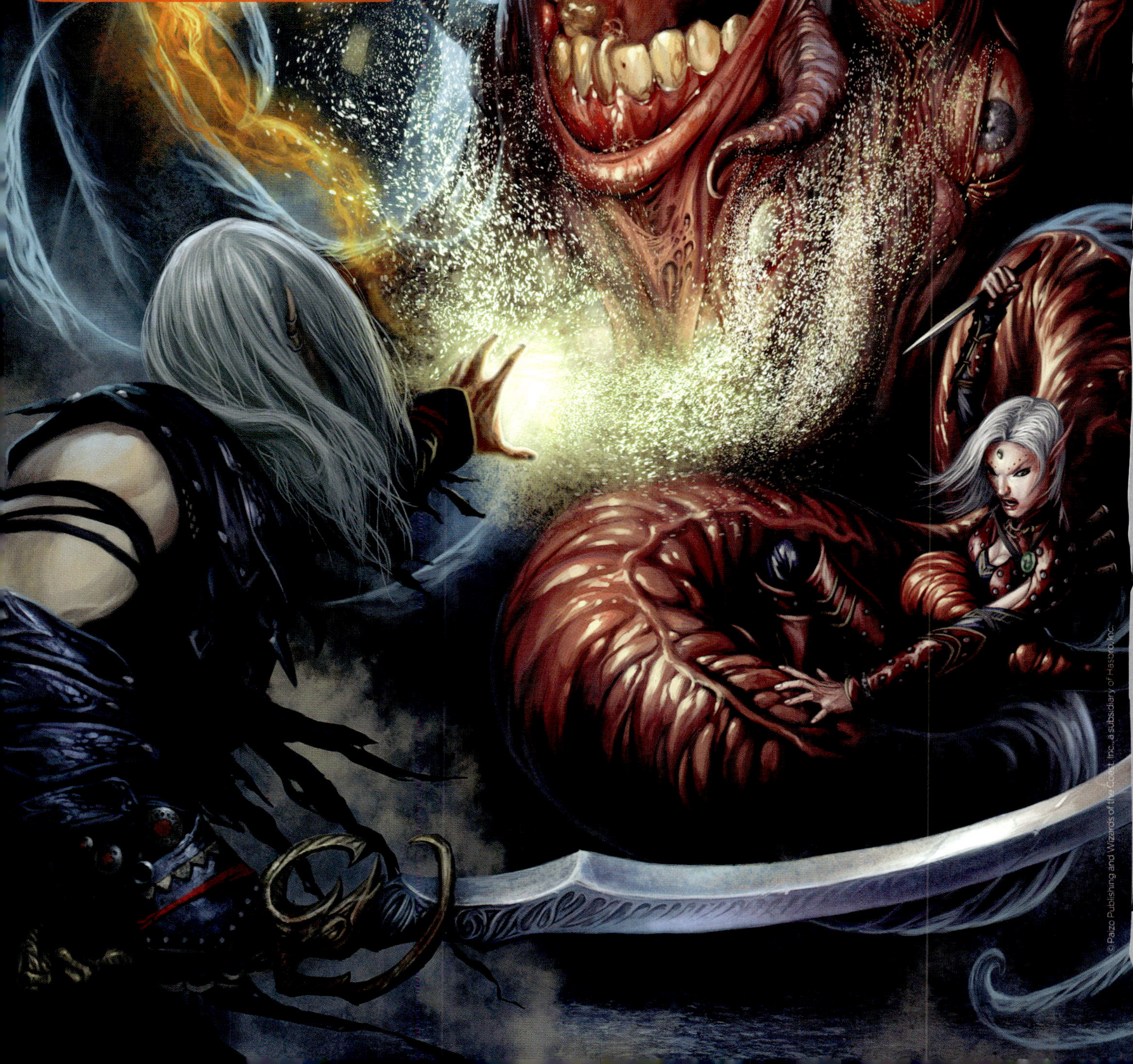

ARTIST TIP

SET GOALS

"Give yourself small, realistic and achievable goals, like 'work for (fill in the blank) company', and large lifetime goals like 'write an art book'. Achieving your ambitions gives you a sense of progress and having goals you haven't achieved keeps you motivated to always improve as an artist."

trial and error, examining others' work and instructional videos, books… and great magazines like this one."

Working in Photoshop and Painter, Dan sings the praises of both software packages, but admits that in the early days Painter was a bewildering option. "The interface was confusing and nothing seemed to work the way I expected," he says, offering a tip for first-timers: "It helped me to pick one brush I felt comfortable with and use it for a while. Over time I branched out to using more and more brushes." Photoshop was more intuitive, but Dan confesses that it's been an easy-to-learn, hard-to-master journey for him, which has thrown up its fair share of hideous filter and lens flare experiments. Not that you'd find them in his finished paintings. "It's absolutely amazing all the things you can do with both of those programs. I learn something new at least once a week. The trick is remembering everything you've learned and when the best time is to apply it."

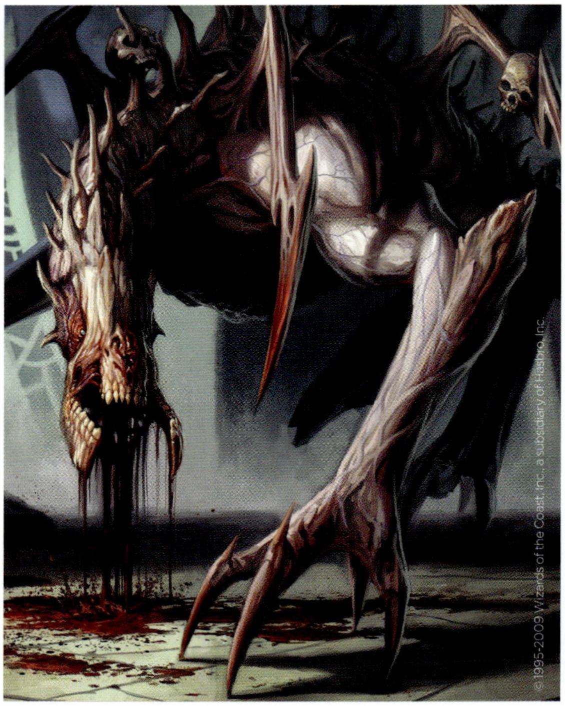

SKULL & BONES
An unusual creature, the Kederekt Parasite from Magic: The Gathering oozes acid. The skulls of its victims are a neat touch, hanging from its bony body.

> "I'd played Magic since college, so it was kind of a lifetime goal to do art for that game. It was such a thrill"

Skill with the stylus is important, and Dan says he now uses it more than a traditional pencil. "It's become second nature," he explains, "even to the point that it sometimes takes me a while to get used to sketching with a pencil when doing conventional sketches." However, in his mind there's no excuse for not mastering the basics. Learning colour theory, proportions and composition were Dan's bedrocks, and he reminds us that research is crucial too. "It ensures your image is accurate, but can also serve as inspiration," says Dan. "Whether you've painted horses dozens of times or you're doing it for the first time, you probably have some preconceptions in your head about what they look like. Doing a little research may make you try a different skin pattern, muscle structure, colour, pose, angle or even how the light interacts with the skin. It can help keep you from falling into the same patterns every time."

BIG BREAK

Armed with traditional training, self-taught digital artistry and a fan's eye for fantasy art, Dan embraced the world of freelance illustration. There wasn't much work straight out of school, but his first commission, from an internet-published collectible card game called Chron X ,was invaluable in offering him a taste of deadlines, contracts and working with art directors. Then the big boys came calling.

Dan's break came with a commission for Warhammer 40K. "It was the first work I'd done for a major licence and paid much better than anything else I'd done at the time," he says. There's a sense, though, that he considers his first commission for Magic: The Gathering to be the moment his career took off. "I'd played Magic since college, so it was kind of a lifetime goal to do art for that game," he says. "It was such a thrill to finally get to do it."

Dan's career seems to be driven by his love of the fantasy genre. The first cover he painted was for Dragon magazine, a D&D bible for many (including Dan himself). "Growing up playing Dungeons & Dragons, I was familiar with Dragon magazine," Dan explains, "so it was very exciting to get to do a cover for them."

His current commissions only serve to secure his place in the fantasy genre elite. He's continuing to work on Magic: The Gathering and World of Warcraft, but his well-thumbed copy of the Official Handbook of the Marvel Universe is still coming in handy, since he's about to begin painting an issue of What If? for Marvel, with Dave Ross pencilling. "It would be nice to paint over my own pencils but I know I could never make the deadline if that were the case," says Dan.

Asked about life as a freelancer, he says: "If you're a workaholic personality then it can be very difficult to have any sort of personal life." Dan lists the troubles of a jobbing artist, including the health insurance nightmare in the US, irregular paychecks and the lack of formal benefits – so don't expect bulging pension pots, bonuses or sick pay if you take up the stylus. "Despite all these pitfalls," says Dan, "it's a deeply enjoyable job and I really hope I'm able to do it for the rest of my life."

Turn the page to learn to paint like Dan Scott

COVER STORY
This lavish painting was commissioned for the cover of BradyGames' World of Warcraft Dungeon Companion III and showcases Dan's talent for storytelling.

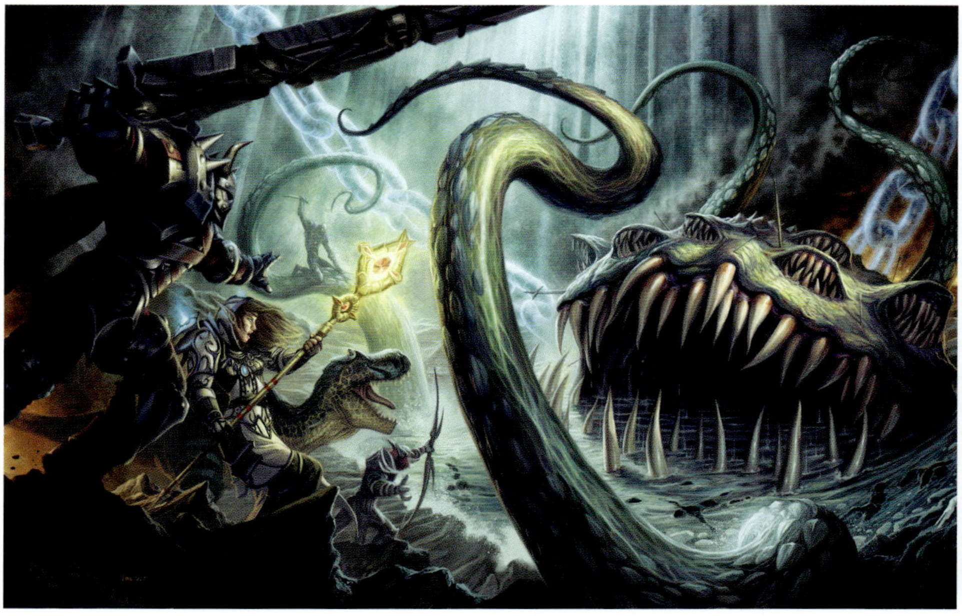

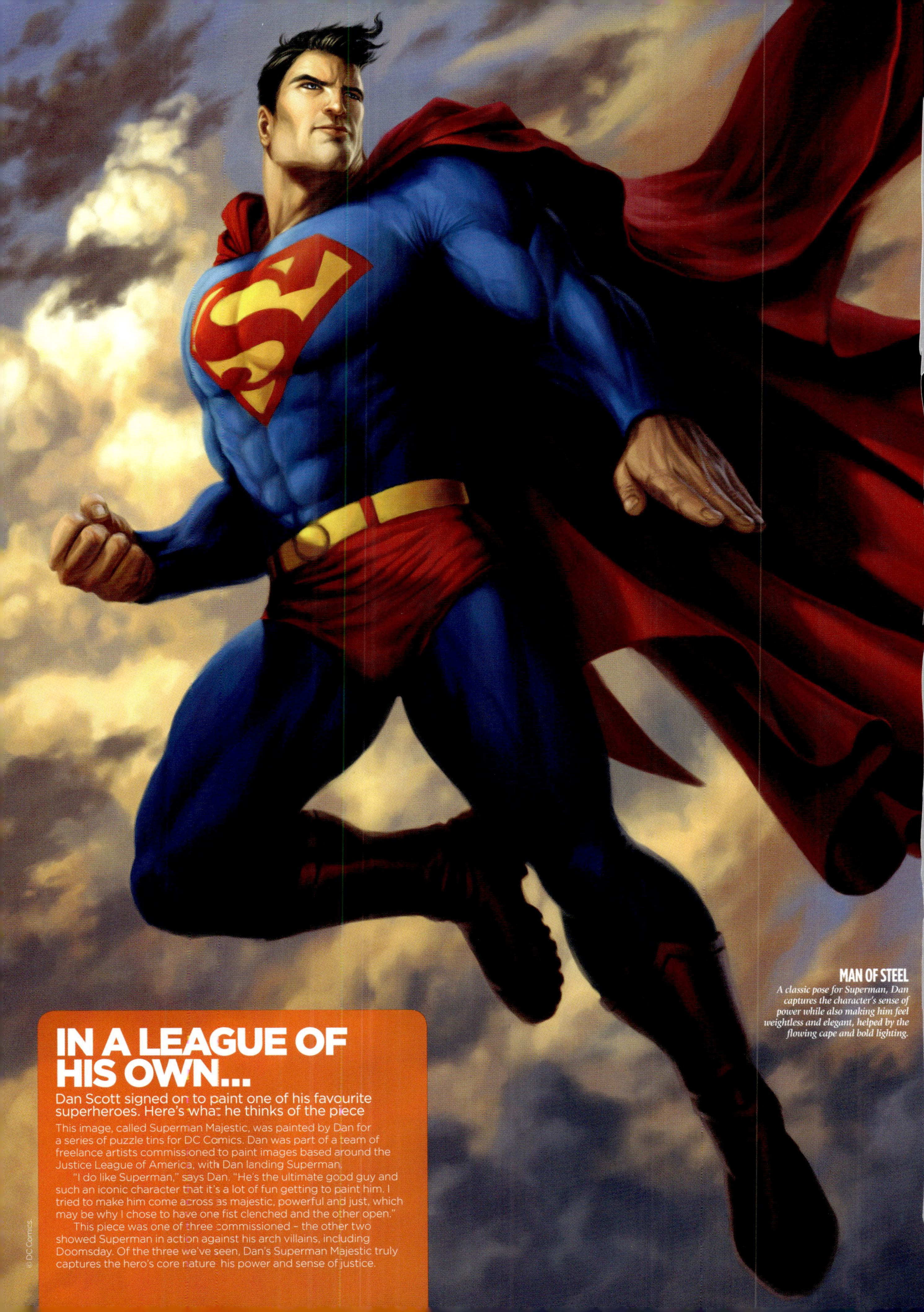

MAN OF STEEL
A classic pose for Superman, Dan captures the character's sense of power while also making him feel weightless and elegant, helped by the flowing cape and bold lighting.

IN A LEAGUE OF HIS OWN...

Dan Scott signed on to paint one of his favourite superheroes. Here's what he thinks of the piece

This image, called Superman Majestic, was painted by Dan for a series of puzzle tins for DC Comics. Dan was part of a team of freelance artists commissioned to paint images based around the Justice League of America, with Dan landing Superman.

"I do like Superman," says Dan. "He's the ultimate good guy and such an iconic character that it's a lot of fun getting to paint him. I tried to make him come across as majestic, powerful and just, which may be why I chose to have one fist clenched and the other open."

This piece was one of three commissioned – the other two showed Superman in action against his arch villains, including Doomsday. Of the three we've seen, Dan's Superman Majestic truly captures the hero's core nature: his power and sense of justice.

Photoshop

CAPTURE THE ESSENCE OF A D&D CHARACTER

A strong D&D image is always a crowd-pleaser. **Dan Scott** takes aim at a classic character class...

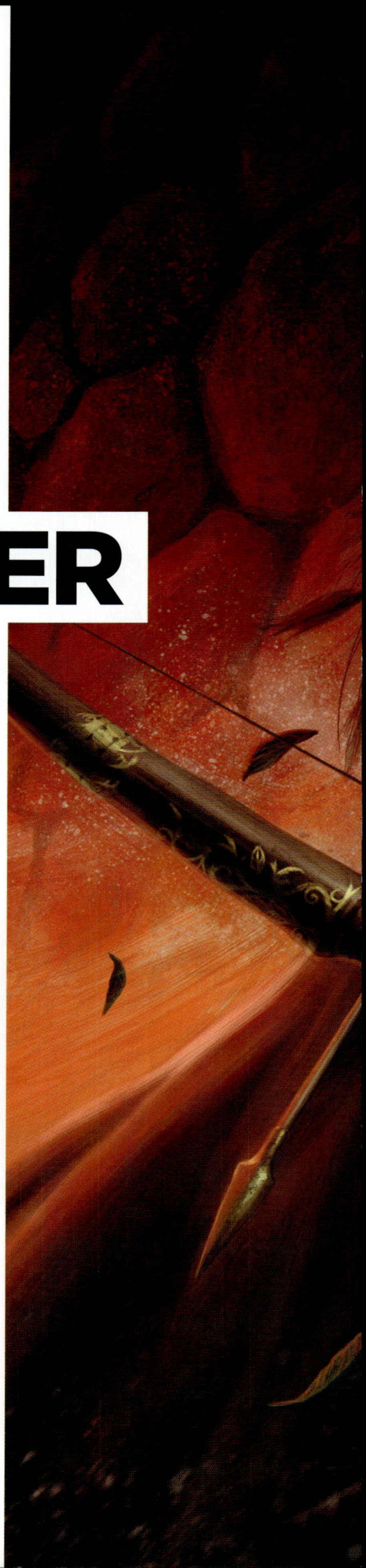

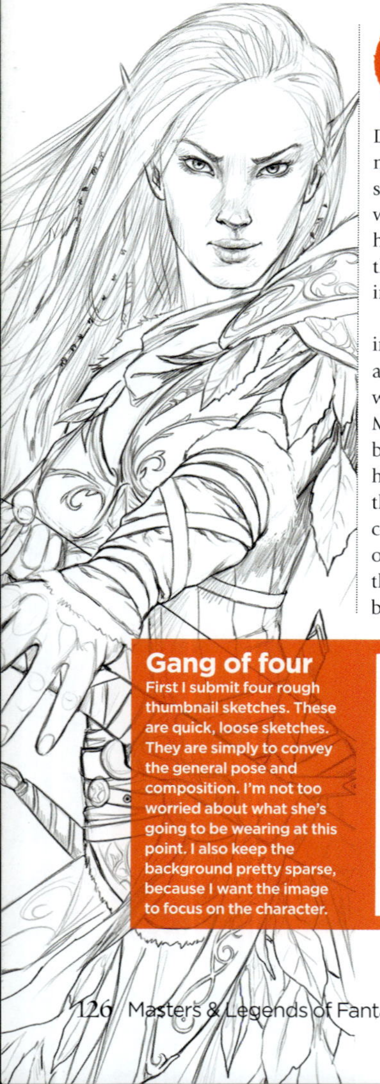

Art editor on ImagineFX, Paul Tysall contacted me, to ask if I'd like to do a cover image focusing on Dungeons & Dragons imagery. I'm a big fan of the magazine, owning every published issue, so I was excited to work with the team. I was comfortable with the subject matter, having played my fair share of D&D through the years and painted several interiors and covers for D&D products.

The art brief was for a female Elf Ranger in a snowy setting with some sort of red and green colour scheme, because this was for an issue coming out at Christmas. My main goals were to make her beautiful, powerful, confident and hopefully have some connection with the viewer. I also know that a red-green colour scheme could easily look garish or cartoony if handled too harshly. With these aims in mind, I set out to create the best image I could muster.

Gang of four

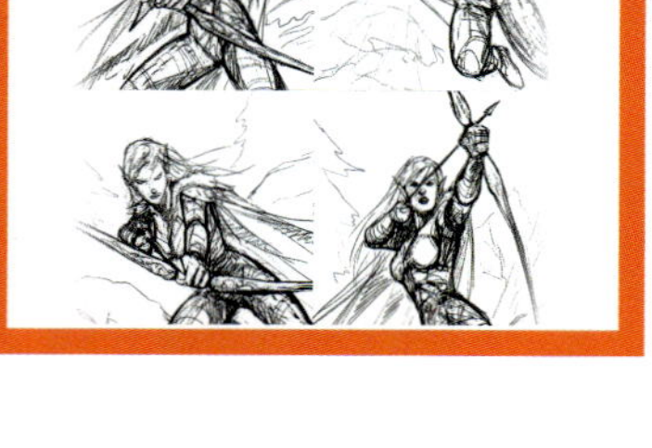

First I submit four rough thumbnail sketches. These are quick, loose sketches. They are simply to convey the general pose and composition. I'm not too worried about what she's going to be wearing at this point. I also keep the background pretty sparse, because I want the image to focus on the character.

Down to two

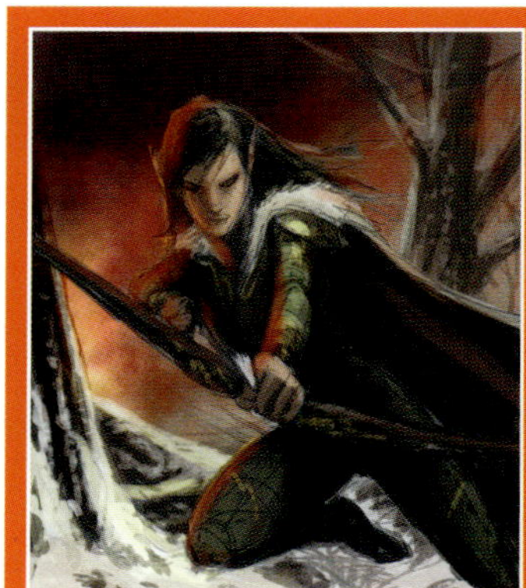

I usually do a tight sketch and add greyscale values before I start working in colour, but Paul, wants to see two of the rough sketches in colour before deciding on which of the images to go with. This image, featuring the Elf Ranger in an action pose, is eventually rejected on the grounds that her body angle would look awkward on the cover. In addition, the snowy background might obscure the text that will eventually be superimposed onto the scene.

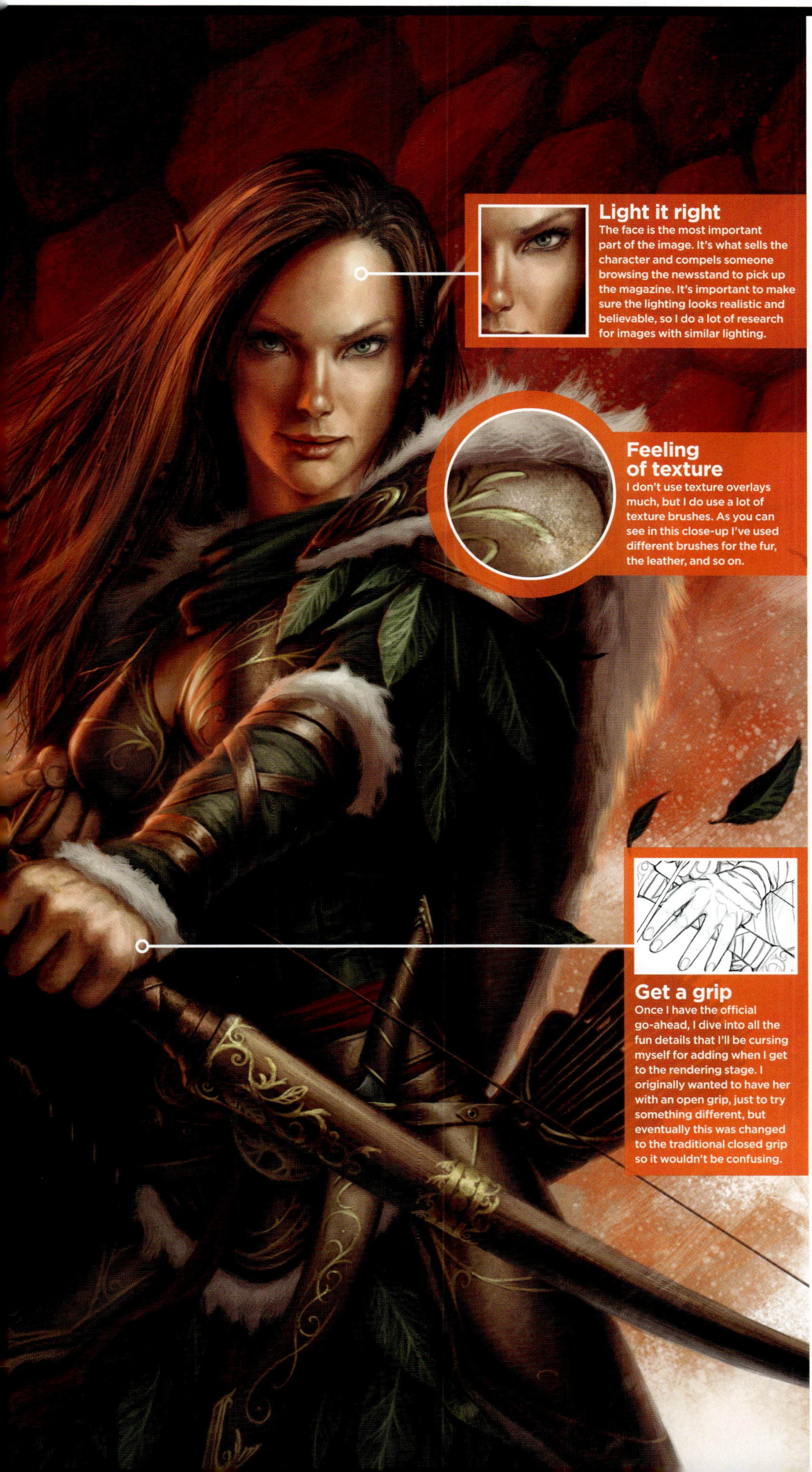

Light it right

The face is the most important part of the image. It's what sells the character and compels someone browsing the newsstand to pick up the magazine. It's important to make sure the lighting looks realistic and believable, so I do a lot of research for images with similar lighting.

Feeling of texture

I don't use texture overlays much, but I do use a lot of texture brushes. As you can see in this close-up I've used different brushes for the fur, the leather, and so on.

Get a grip

Once I have the official go-ahead, I dive into all the fun details that I'll be cursing myself for adding when I get to the rendering stage. I originally wanted to have her with an open grip, just to try something different, but eventually this was changed to the traditional closed grip so it wouldn't be confusing.

How I create... AN ELF RANGER

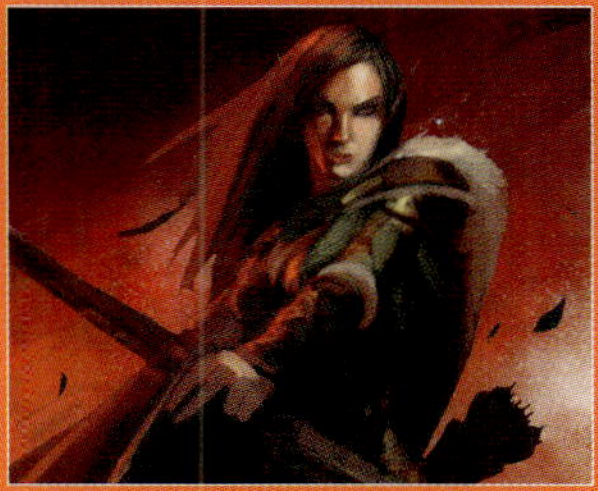

1 Surface tension

I now apply colour to my tight sketch. All the linework can still be seen and the basic colour scheme is all intact. I can't mess it up too badly at this point, so it's now time to render out all of the different surfaces and details.

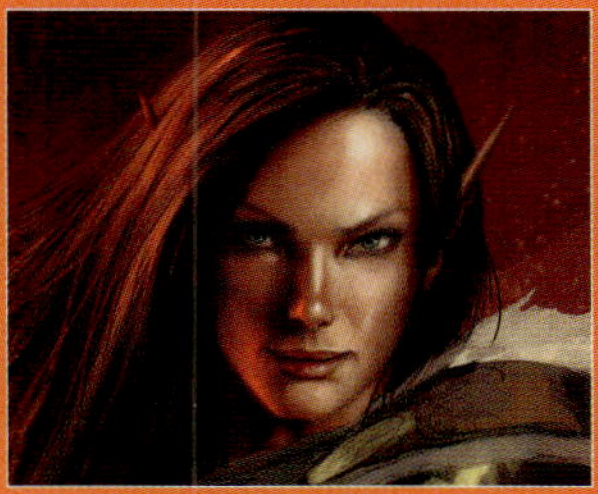

2 Face the facts

I start defining the face. I spend a lot of time trying to get the lighting and expression just right. Other parts of an image can be less defined if need be, but the face is what's going to grab the viewer's attention.

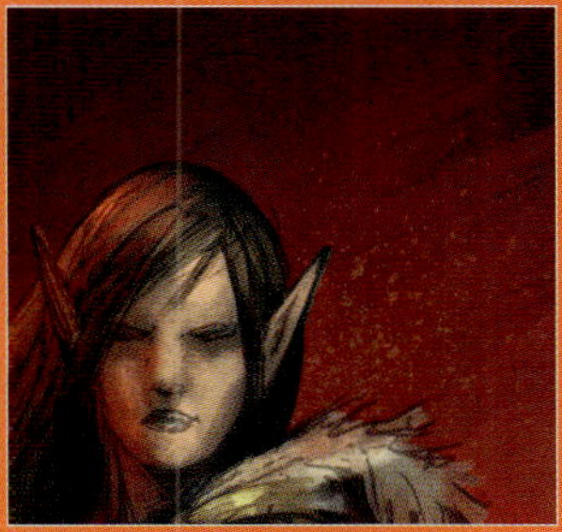

3 Scaling it up

All of the rendering is now done. At this point, I step back from the piece as a whole and see what areas need tweaks in values, colour, detail, and so on. I try a version with dragon scales in the background, as if she's standing in front of an enormous red dragon that she's just conquered. Paul likes this version and decides to go with it.

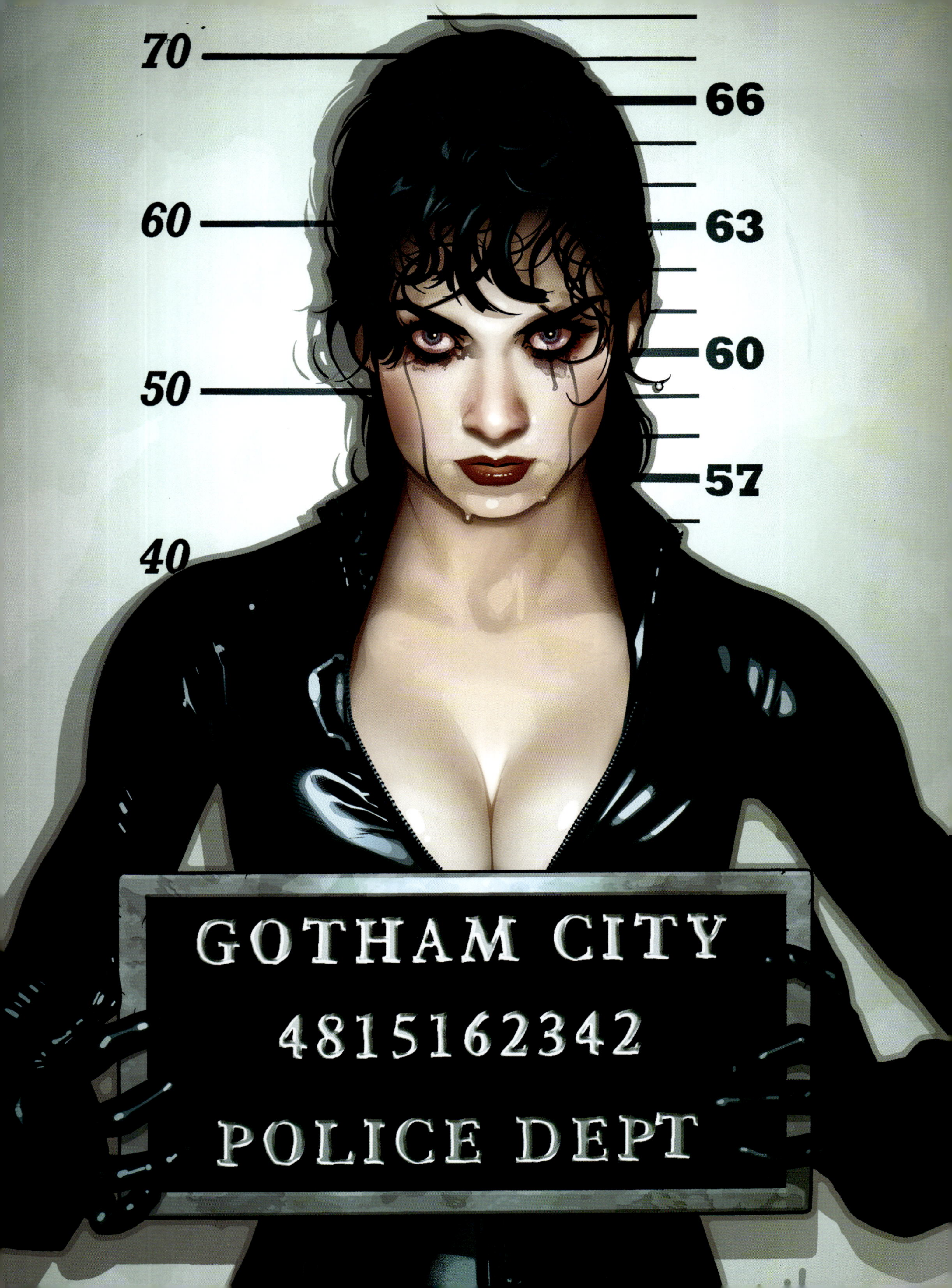
70
60
50
40
66
63
60
57
GOTHAM CITY
4815162342
POLICE DEPT

Interview

Adam Hughes

One of comics' hottest artists reveals the inside story on a voluptuous career

"One day I can do no wrong, the very next I draw like a retarded chimp with a hangover. I wish I could find a happy middle ground," says Adam Hughes. He's been a superstar comics artist for over 20 years, made famous by drawing heartbreakingly beautiful women with power and grace. He got to work on his dream assignment, creating a smash-hit miniseries starring his beloved Wonder Woman. Just imagine where his career would be if he ever reached his own high standard of being consistent.

Adam was brought up in New Jersey, in a town called Florence. "It's just like the one in Italy, except that it's completely devoid of art and culture," he tells us. His love of comics began with a 1968 issue of Fantastic Four, and he's been inspired by artists from many fields, including George Pérez, John Byrne, Michael Golden, Norman Rockwell and film-poster legend Drew Struzan. However, despite his passion, he didn't go to college – he's artistically self-taught.

LOST KITTY
Recognise the numbers? The Dharma Initiative should know better than to cross a black cat's path.

Artist PROFILE

Adam Hughes

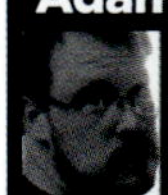

Pin-up art specialist Adam was born on 5 May 1967 in Riverside, New Jersey, USA. He has worked for everyone from DC to Marvel to Lucasfilm, but Adam is perhaps best known for his long run of stunning Wonder Woman and Catwoman covers.
www.justsayah.com

"I had no other recourse," Adam explains. Of the university system in the US he comments: "I had to make lemonade out of the fabulous lemon of being too dumb to get a scholarship and too middle-class to get financial aid." But he wouldn't recommend going it alone. "Formal art courses offer plenty to anyone with an open mind and the ability to apply personal experience to their particular craft."

> **"Art courses offer plenty to anyone with an open mind and the ability to apply experience to their craft"**

Fortunately for Adam, the 1980s were a boom time for US comics and also for the artists that drew them; it was a golden age when "anyone with a pencil and a dream could get into the industry". Adam broke in at the end of 1985, when a successful portfolio review at a convention earned him a pin-up for a local publisher.

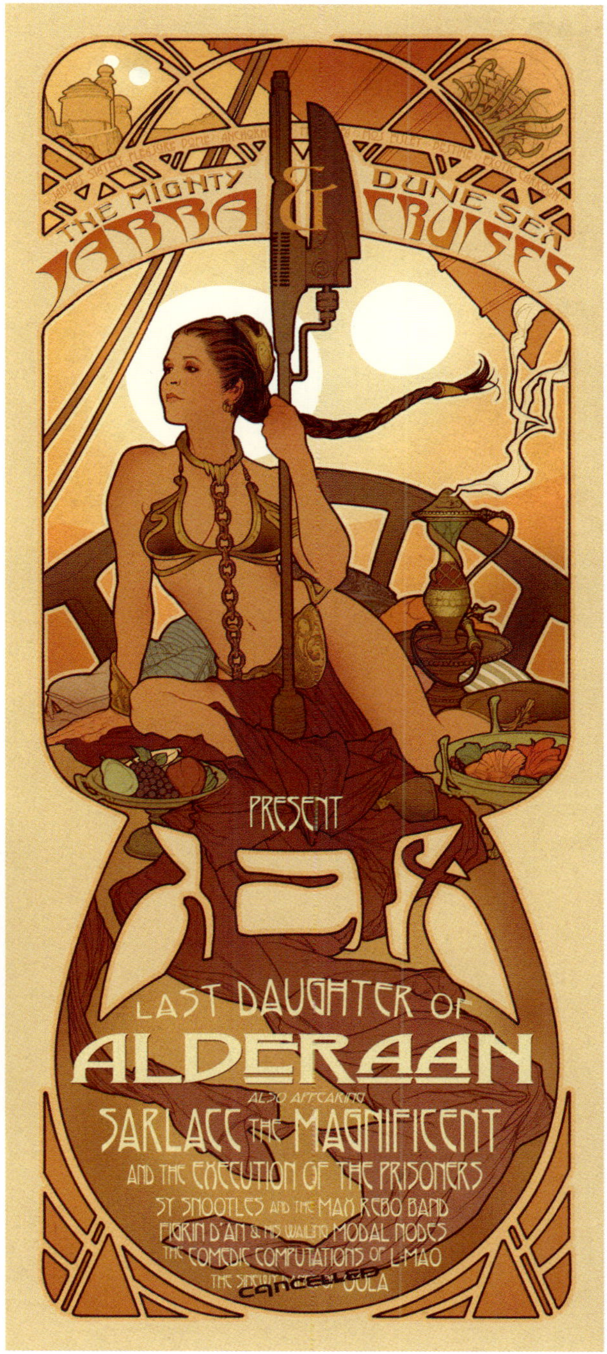

HUTT PROPERTY
Limited print for the 2007 convention Star Wars Celebration IV, commemorating the 30th anniversary of the film's release. "I love Art Nouveau, I love the poster art of Alphonse Mucha and my DNA has Star Wars written on it," says Adam.

COPING WITH CLUES

Various work for small companies led to Adam's first major assignment in 1988. He worked on a mystery series known as The Maze Agency for 18 months, which challenged readers to solve each issue's whodunnit before the detectives. The ➔

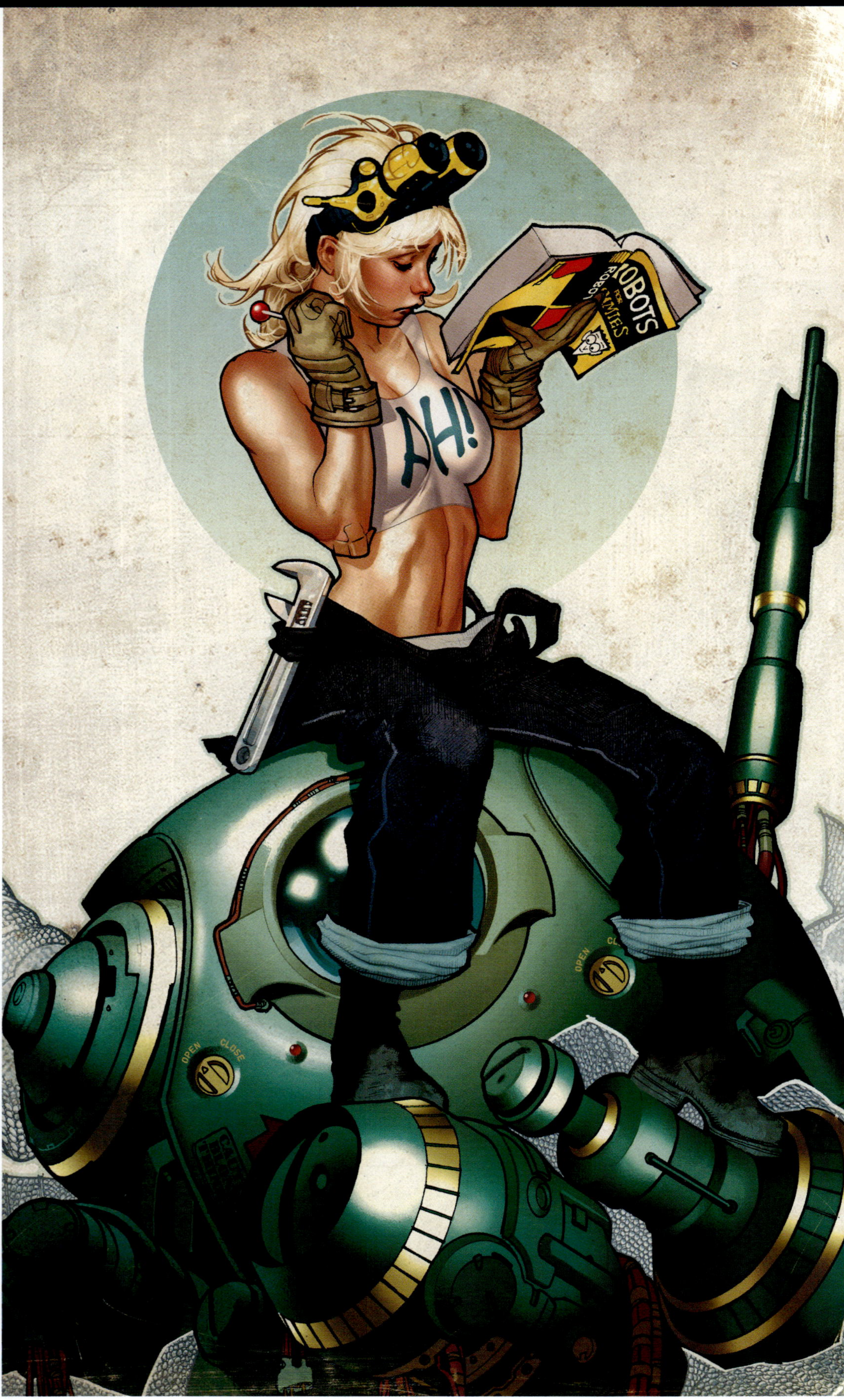

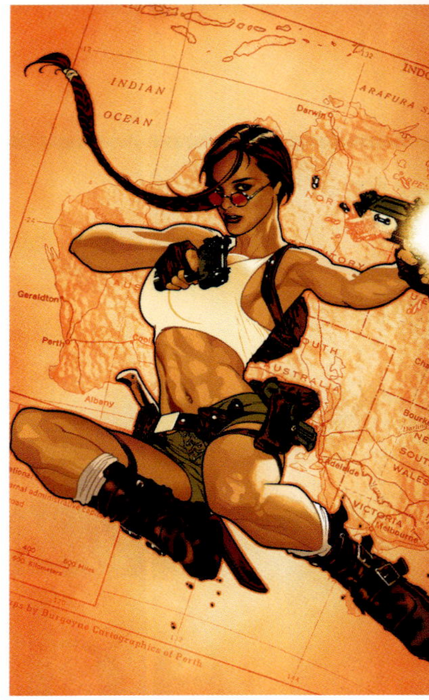

MOVE OVER, INDIANA
Pop culture's second-favourite archaeological adventurer starred in her own comic from the late 1990s to 2005.

scripts by occasional Batman writer Mike W Barr also stretched the artist with their unique storytelling demands. "DIY colonoscopies would have been easier," Adam recalls. "I was all about doing a superhero book. The Maze Agency made me work too hard, too early on."

At a convention in 1988, Adam met the editor of DC's superteam book Justice League of America, which is still, one of the highest-profile titles in comics. "When Maze was put on hiatus in 1989, I was out of work for a good 45 minutes before Andy Helfer called and asked if I would do JLA," Adam remembers.

So, how did he successfully juggle such a large cast on covers, interior pages and sometimes both in the same issue? "Many would argue that I did not, in fact, handle all those characters that well," he responds. "I actually wanted to work on League member Mister Miracle instead."

MIXED MEDIA

After the Justice League came the final frontier. Adam drew the 1992 Star Trek graphic novel Debt of Honor. Since then, Adman has frequently illustrated characters from other media, including Lara Croft, Star Wars and Buffy the Vampire Slayer. But how does this differ from his usual comic book assignments? "Sometimes you have to go through extra editing, thanks to the licensors getting approval," Adam says, "and sometimes the chimps in charge of approving art have no art in them at all!"

Three years later, Adam helped launch the Dark Horse superheroine Ghost. The series gave him an opportunity to explore an Alphonse Mucha influence. "Art

SILVER SNAIL
Adam Hughes plays with the conventions of pin-up portraiture in his work to create new, fun glimpses of familiar heroines.

CHARITY CASE
Illustration for the 2008 Wonder Woman Day charity event in Portland, Oregon. "I like to use these pieces as a way to experiment with different or better ways to draw Diana," says Adam.

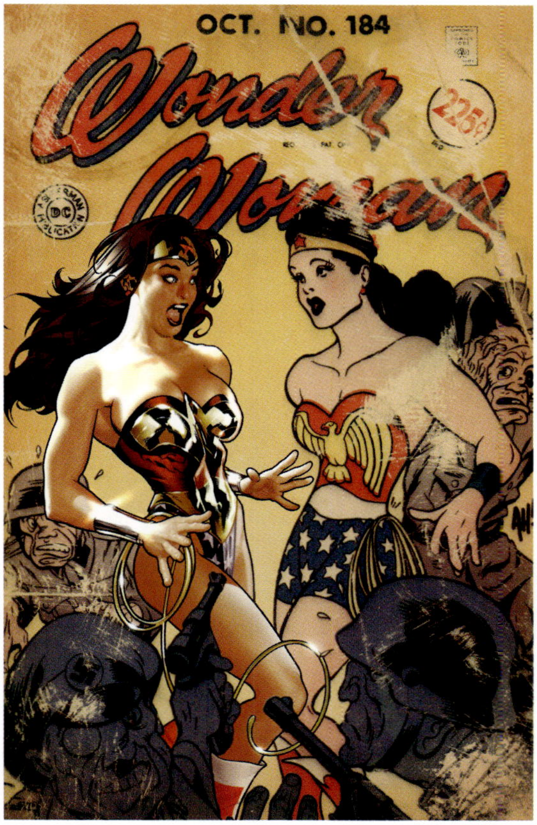

ARTIST TIP

REACH OUT

"Join online communities like ImagineFX.com and deviantART. The contacts they give you are invaluable. It's great to get feedback and take the pulse of the audience. Also, being able to see what others are doing with their crayon boxes is a tonic."

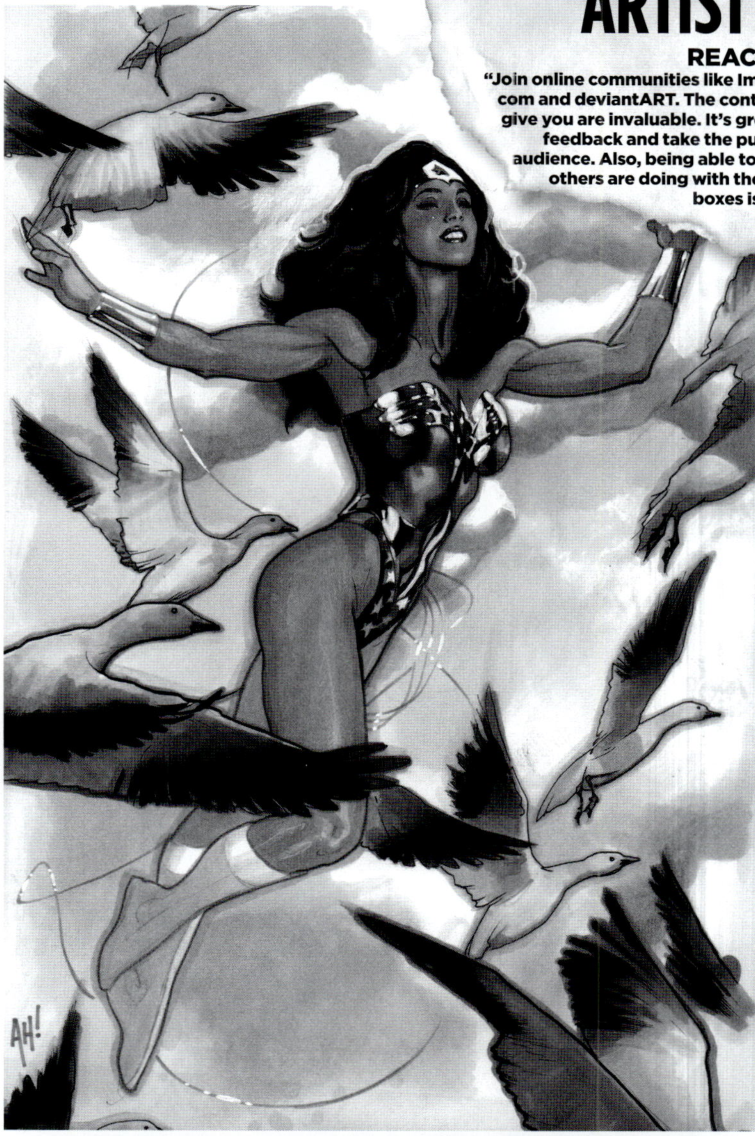

Nouveau poster art is a classier, older cousin to comics. There are similar graphic sensibilities," he says.

His career started to head in a slightly different direction in 1995 when he wrote and drew a miniseries starring the teenage superteam Gen13. Writing wasn't a particular ambition for Adam. "I ended up doing that by accident. I liked Gen13 because of how different the five kids were and the potential for interaction. I especially liked the idea of Fairchild," he says. Appropriately, Fairchild is a bright-but-plain girl transformed into a drop-dead-gorgeous superheroine. He also wrote a second miniseries in 2000 where the team met Superman.

SPOT THE DIFFERENCE
The modern-day version of comics' own Princess Diana confronts her 40s self, in the rather idiosyncratic style of penciller HG Peters.

> **"Art Nouveau poster art is a classier, older cousin to comics. There are similar graphic sensibilities"**

Until recently, Adam spent the majority of his time creating covers for two of DC Comics's strongest female characters. The Wonder Woman assignment lasted four years (from 1999) and Adam also illustrated covers for Catwoman for three years until the book's cancellation. How did he stay fresh? "Did I stay fresh?" he asks. "I wonder… But there's so much room for extensive creative exploration with those characters."

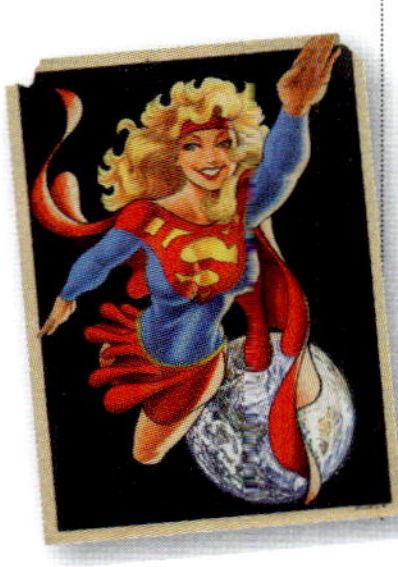

BACK TO THE 80S
Adam's 1986 take on Supergirl, created in Berol Prismacolor pencil on typing paper: "I was 20. Hopefully there's been some improvement!"

That hard work has paid off, giving Adam the freedom to experiment with his covers more than ever. "When you do your best work for the same company for years, people start to trust you," he explains.

His process is admittedly a little odd. After sketching ideas, he submits a ➛

SECRETS OF SUCCESS

Adam shares the tricks of the comic art trade – and reveals what he really hates to draw…

There's no typical working day for Adam Hughes. "I sleep when I'm tired, and I get up when I'm done sleeping," he says. "Structure and discipline make me claustrophobic. It took me years to figure that out!"

"I work on a wooden drawing table, so that I can use push pins as vanishing points for my perspectives," he adds. When pencilling he uses a standard lead holder with a lead from B to 6B, depending on the humidity. "I like Strathmore Series 500 illustration board, 3 to 5 ply, cold-press finish."

Is there anything Adam hates to draw? "Today, I hate drawing rocks. Clifts. It's killing me!" At least he knows where to go for inspiration: 'Whenever the well runs dry, the work of my favourite artists is always the perfect remedy."

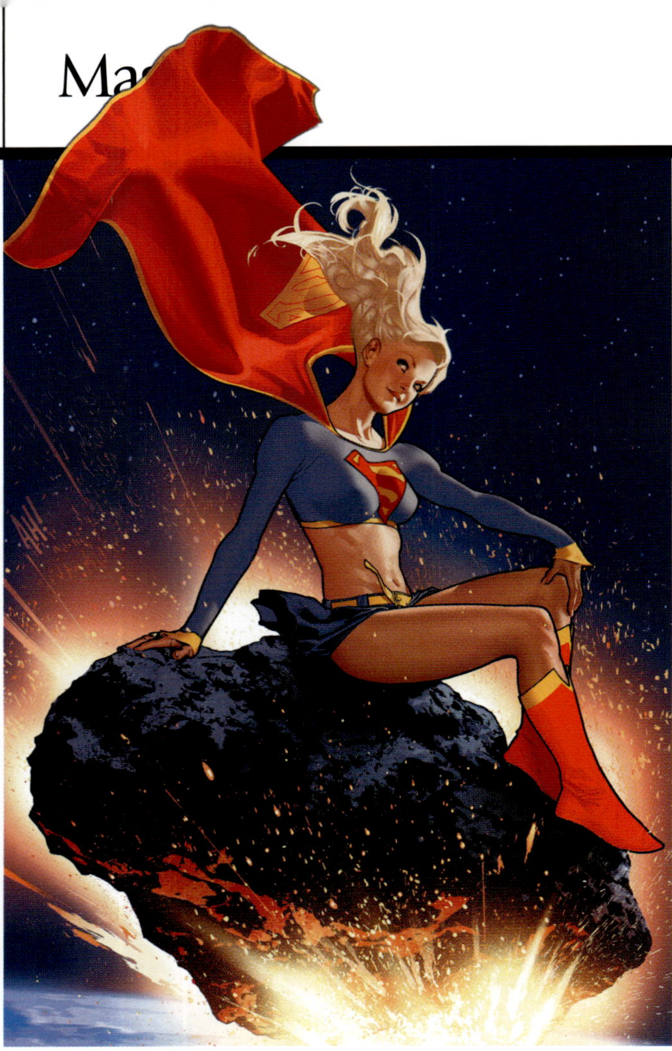

SITTING PRETTY

"My tribute to pin-up king Gil Elvgren," says Adam. "I wanted Supergirl to look like a pretty girl sitting on the rocks by the sea under a starry sky, and only afterwards do you notice that she is riding a meteor into the atmosphere."

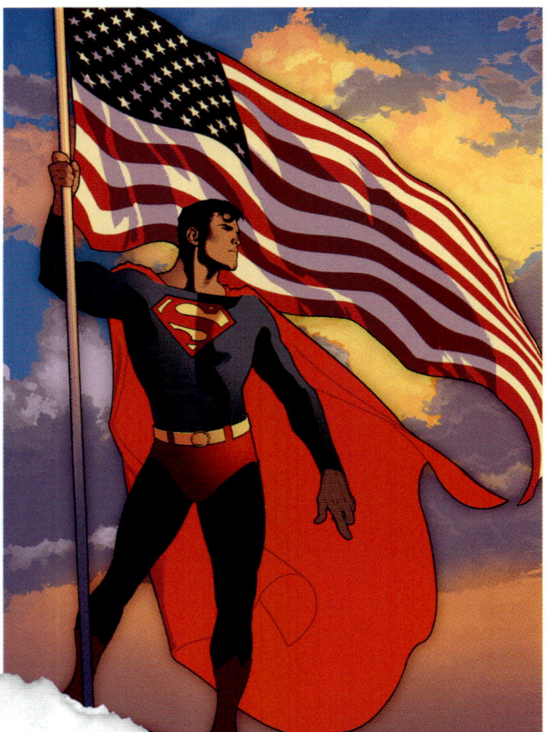

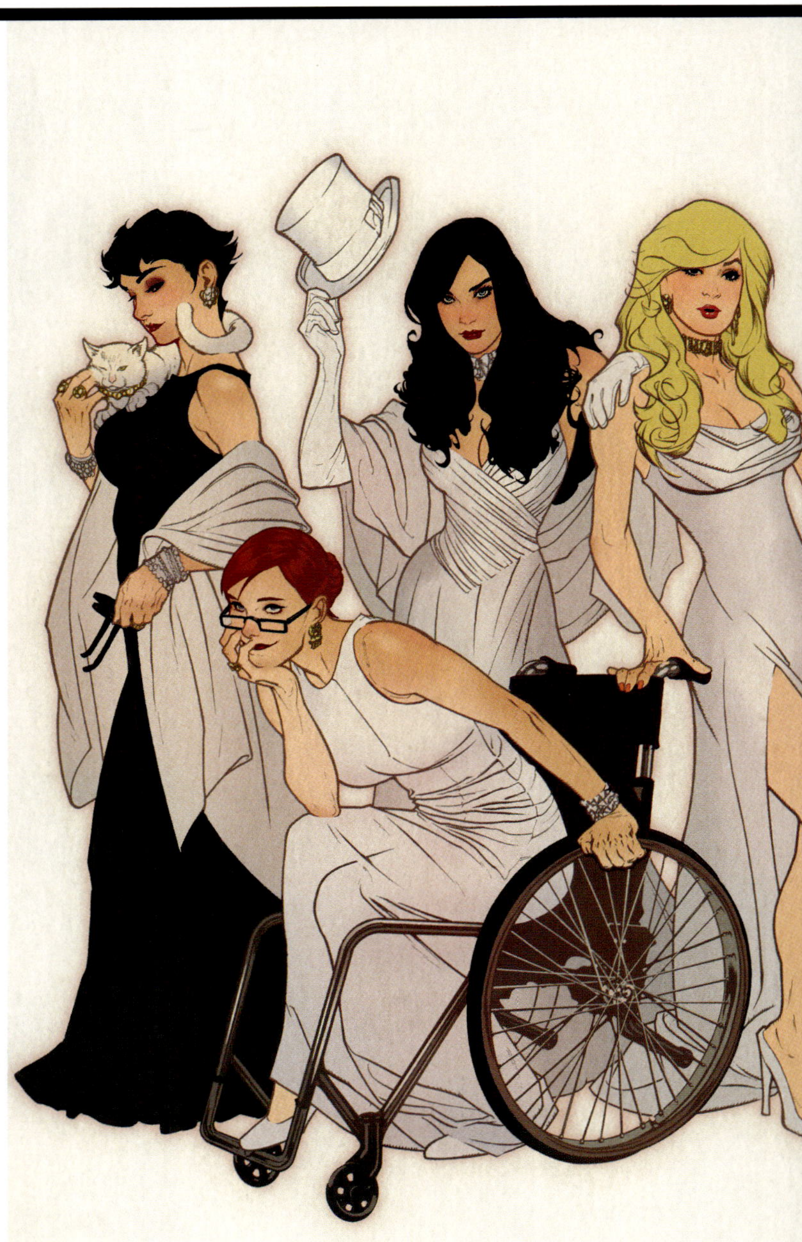

KRYPTONIAN COOL

DC released four prequel specials coinciding with Bryan Singer's film Superman Returns in 2006. Adam illustrated each cover.

thumbnail for approval before pencilling in a sketchbook or on scrap paper. "I make a lot of mistakes and corrections (because I don't know how to draw, shhh), so I really mess up paper," he reveals. "Once the art looks passable, I make a copy and transfer it in pencil to a piece of virgin art board. I can then ink it without thinking about how I ruined the paper with my constant erasing." Finally, he scans the inked art onto his computer and colours it in Photoshop CS2.

He wrote, drew and inked the six-issue All Star Wonder Woman, which launched in 2009, and relished the assignment. "She's Dorothy Gale from The Wizard of Oz, she's Captain Kirk, she's Luke Skywalker. She comes from a perfect place, a paradise on Earth, yet all she yearns for is to see what lies over the next hill and beyond the farthest star," he said of his muse.

Although the character was originally created in 1941, Adam rejects any suggestion of irrelevance. "Because Diana's an outsider looking in, stories about her can reveal a lot about our world," he explains. "Things we take for granted can be seen fresh through her eyes."

WRITING AN ICON

He admits he found it intimidating to write as well as draw one of the most famous superheroines in comics. "The fans deserve the best Wonder Woman," he says. "More often than not she's portrayed as a strident bitch, which says to me that the writer doesn't know how to write about a powerful woman other than to make her pushy. I'm not saying my take on Diana is a

ARTIST TIP

IT'S A HARD LIFE

"Photo reference can help you fix a bad bit of anatomy, or get the folds in clothing right. I shoot my own, or find a picture in a book or online. I also use life models. Getting a babe in a bikini to loiter in your studio all day for art? Best. Scam. Ever."

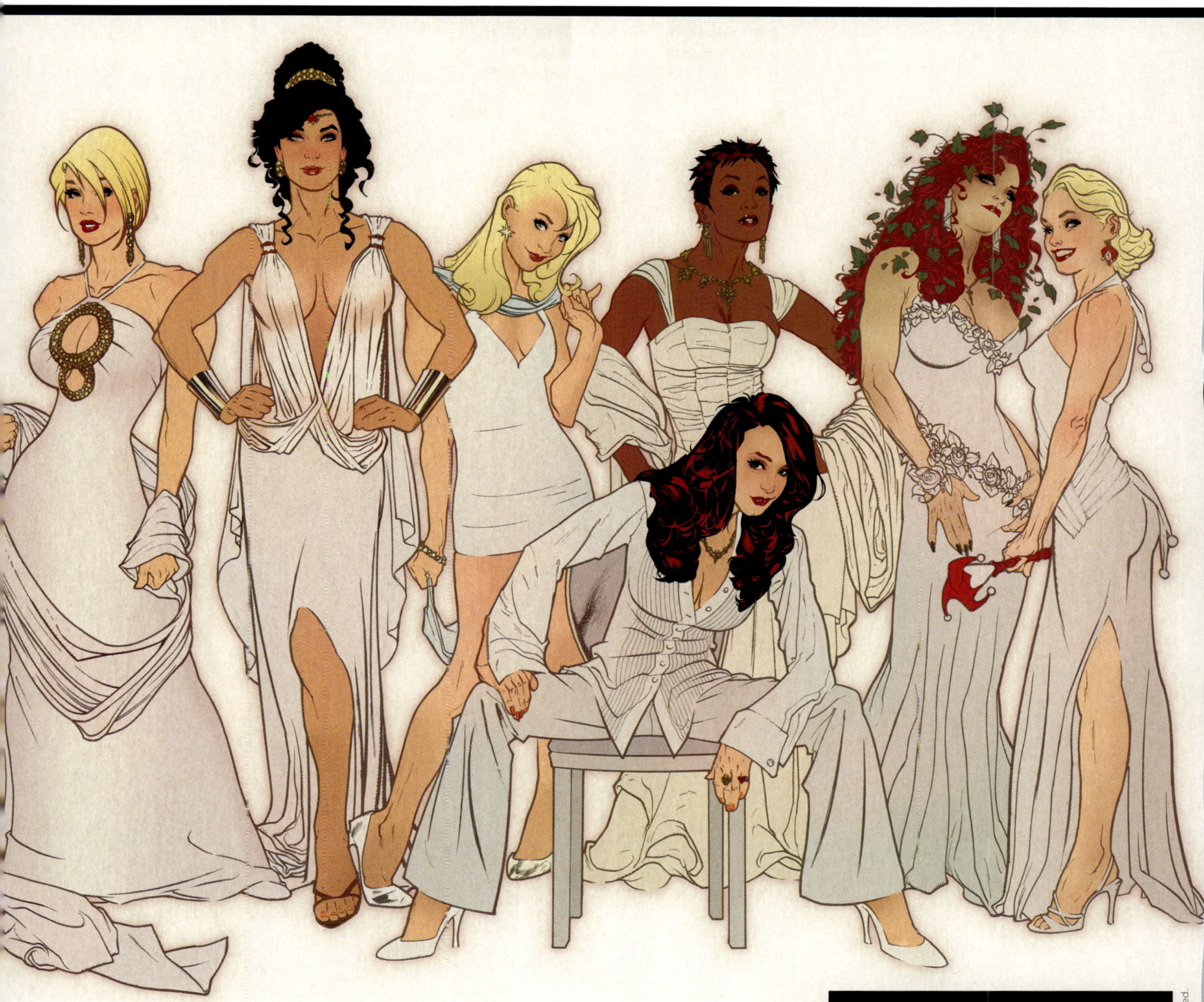

STRENGTH IN NUMBERS
A showcase for some of DC's female stars, from heroines such as Vixen to villains such as Poison Ivy. Then there's Catwoman, who's a bit of both.

"The fans deserve the best Wonder Woman I can deliver. More often than not she's portrayed as a strident bitch"

better way of presenting her. I just think I have an angle."

So, did he enjoy working on internal art? "It was hard! Juggling that with other assignments created delay after delay. I'm not the fastest guy to begin with," he says.

Though work can be tough and daunting, even for Adam Hughes, and even after more than two decades as one of the industry's most sought-after cover artists, he still finds comics fulfilling. "I get tons of creative freedom, more so than in any other commercial-art field," he explains. "I get to meet and have positive experiences with people who enjoy what I do. The question really is: do comics want me working in them for the rest of my life?"

His creative ambitions seem more than achievable for an artist who has defined how DC's biggest heroines should look for a generation, after all his recent book, Cover Run, is a best-seller beyond the comic community, yet it goes to show how modest and grounded Adam is. All he wants is "to be a better artist. I'd like to draw a woman so achingly beautiful, you want to avert your eyes. That'd be a nice achievement." Please nobody tell him that he accomplishes this on a daily basis. We need all the Adam Hughes art we can get.

Turn the page to learn to paint like Adam Hughes

GROUP DYNAMICS

Despite Adam's experience and popularity in the comic industry, not every project is plain sailing

Adam created this stunning promotional illustration (above) featuring DC's major female characters in evening wear. "About as basic an assignment as it gets," he says. "Except for the part where they didn't want Catwoman in the piece."

"I think Selina Kyle is such a fabulous femme fatale," says Adam. But executive editor Dan Didio felt otherwise. Nevertheless, Adam included Catwoman in the final image in case he changed his mind, but at the side for easy Photoshop removal.

"I slapped them around and made them see the light," Adam jokes. "That's why Selina has that great bitchy look. She's pissed, thinking, 'Oh, now I'm good enough for your little-white-dress cocktail party?'" Naturally the party crasher got her way.

Photoshop

DRAW AND PAINT A SEXY CAT BURGLAR

Explore one of the methods **Adam Hughes** uses to colour his comic covers. Here, he focuses on the face of Catwoman – and who wouldn't?

If you can follow my unstructured methodology when focusing on the face, you've pretty much grasped how I do the entirety of my illustrations.

I normally use one of two methods: Photoshop colouring of pen and ink lineart (traditional comic-book-style colouring) and Photoshop colourisation of greyscale marker or pencil art. The second method is what we'll be dealing with here. It's a pretty simple way of working: we treat the greyscale illustration like a black-and-white photograph; in traditional painting terms, you'd call it the under-drawing.

The basic idea of the under-drawing is that you start with a tonal illustration – charcoal, pencil, markers, whatever you like working in! The under-drawing pretty much establishes the values of your piece, especially the darks. If it's done properly,

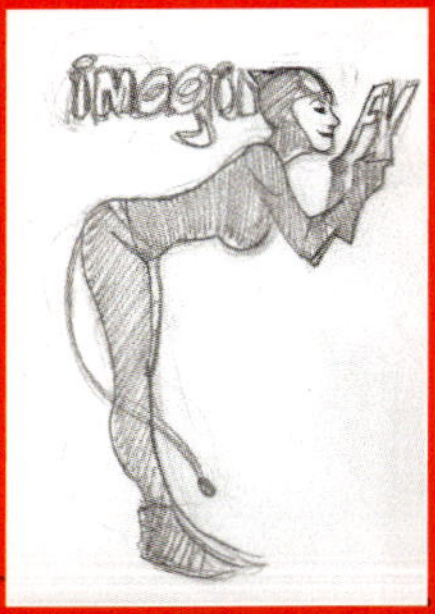

you won't be messing with your darks once we've coloured them up; you'll just be working on the lighter values.

The nice thing about doing this style in a program such as Photoshop is that the more work you do in the traditional greyscale phase, the less work you'll have to do during the colouring stage. I rendered this piece completely in that stage, so that the colouring steps wouldn't be too arcane.

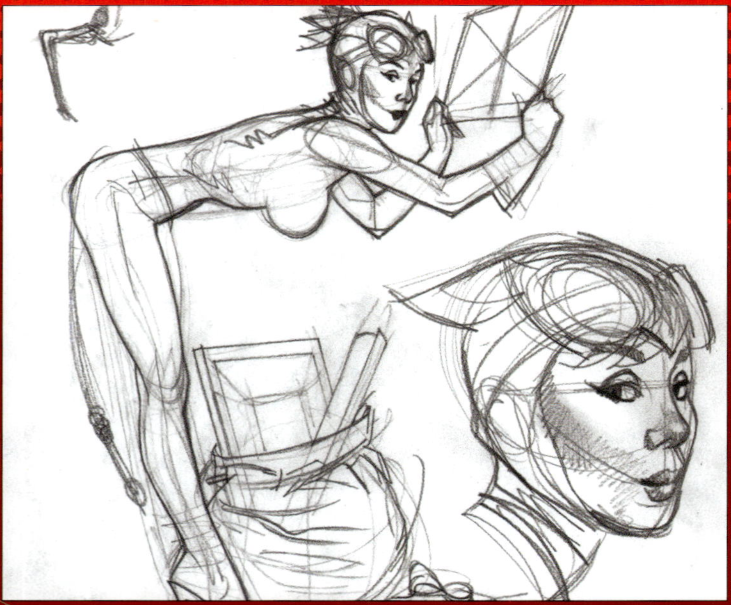

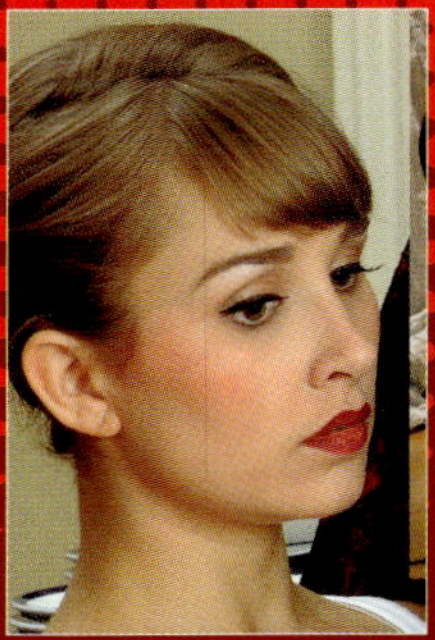

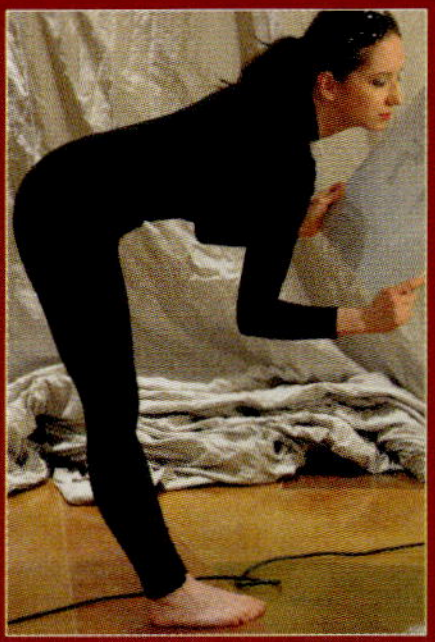

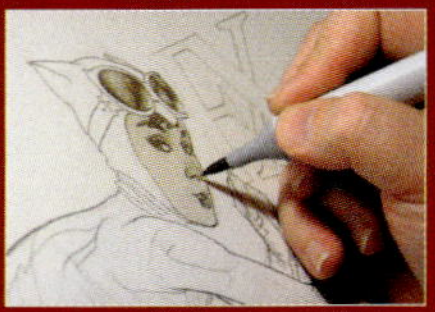

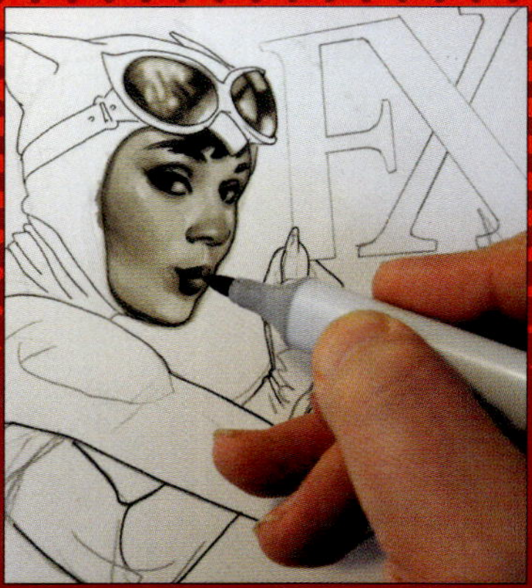

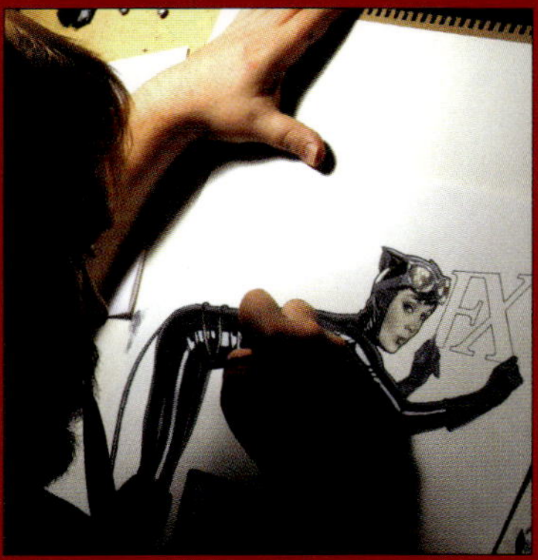

1 Draw something!

Once I've got the approved concept sketch for the illustration, I do a few sketches to work the bugs out of the drawing and get it looking the way I want. I try to avoid doing this on the final art paper, because I tend to erase a lot, and this really chews up the surface. Once I get a layout that I'm happy with, I transfer it to a fresh, virgin piece of art board or paper. I then render the piece in whatever medium I think works best for the assignment.

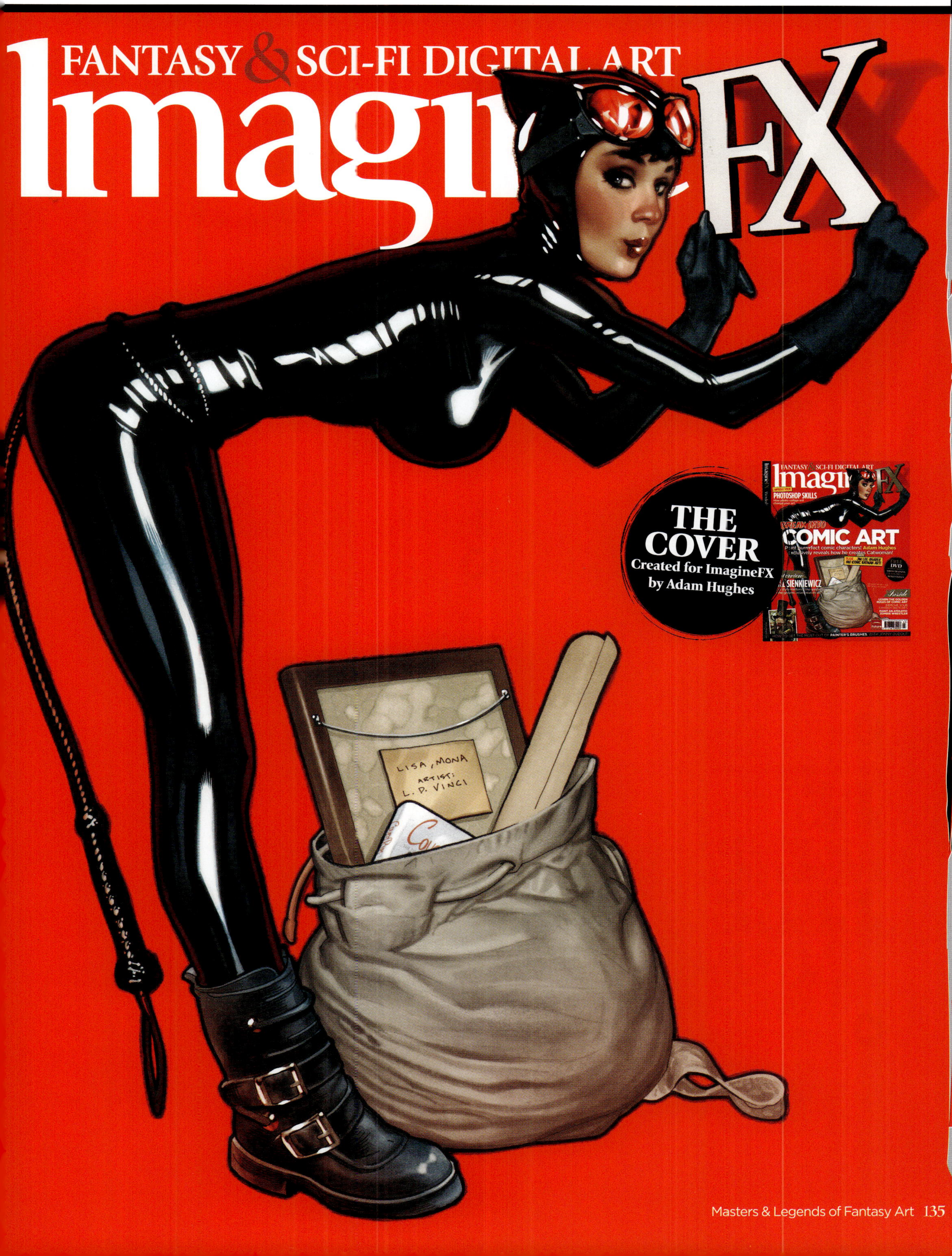

THE COVER
Created for ImagineFX by Adam Hughes

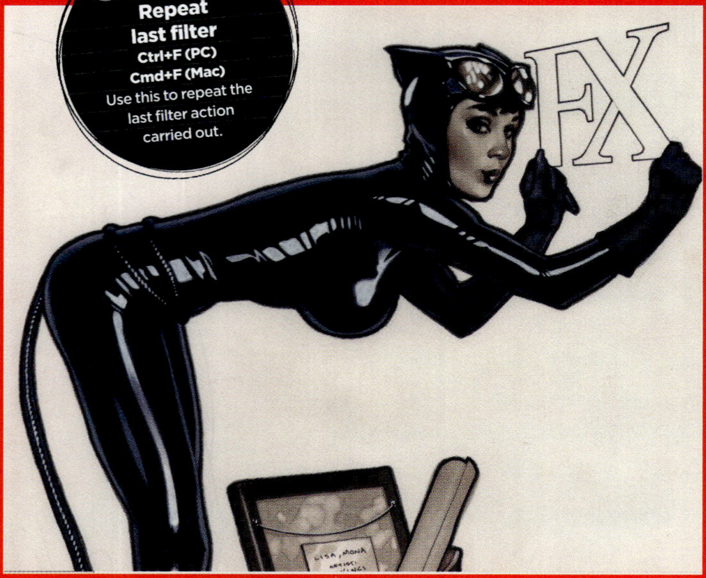

Shortcuts

Repeat last filter

Ctrl+F (PC)
Cmd+F (Mac)

Use this to repeat the last filter action carried out.

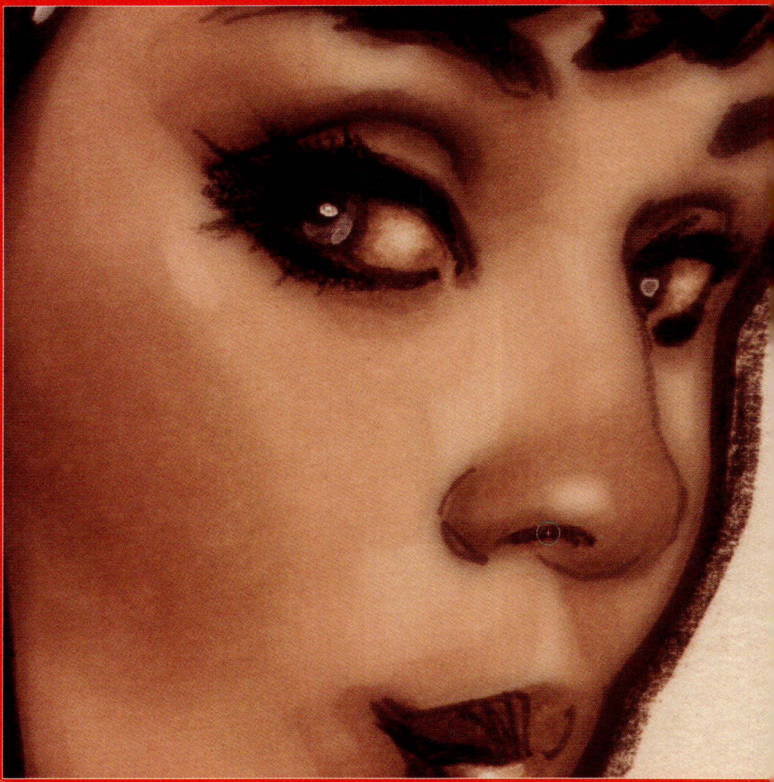

PRO SECRETS

All filters in CMYK

You can use filters in CMYK mode if you apply them one channel at a time. Every individual channel is just a greyscale one, combined with others to make a colour image. Click a channel, run your filter, repeat, and so on...

2 Prepping your scanned art

I scan the original art at 400 dpi and at original size – a much higher resolution than ImagineFX needed. It's always a good idea to work bigger than necessary, if your computer can handle it. I did the original using warm and cool grey Copic markers, so I scan in Color mode. You can work monochromatically and scan in Grayscale mode, though, if you like. Convert to CMYK mode before we begin: Image>Mode>CMYK Mode. Clean up the scan at this stage if it needs it!

3 Getting colourful

You can use many different Photoshop methods to get the under-drawing to the initial colour stages. One I like to use is Image>Adjustment>Variations. This is nice, because you can get a real-time preview of what it is you're doing. Image>Adjustment>Channel Mixer can give some great results as well.

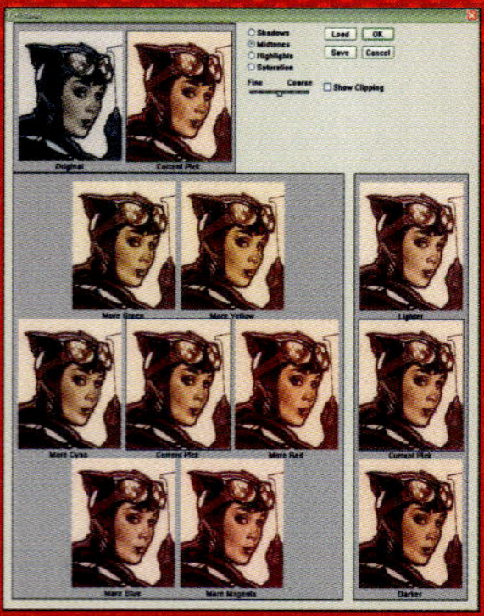

I use these processes because you can play with the saturation levels of the grey pixels, preventing that dirty pixel look you can get if you just use an adjustment layer set to Multiply. I like to copy any area that I work on to another layer, just to be on the safe side.

4 Eliminate unwanted texture

If the face is grainier than you'd like, perhaps thanks to the texture of the art board, here's what I like to do. Make another copy of the face layer, then run it through Filter>Blur>Gaussian Blur and make it as soft as you want. Whenever I do anything like this, I always immediately go to Edit>Fade>Filter. You can change the opacity of the action you just took, as well as alter the Color mode! On faces, you can get some really lovely effects if you set the mode to Lighten. Try all of the modes – experiment to see what works for you.

5 Erase to restore

Now that the whole face is soft and blurry, you'll want to get the sharpness of the features back. Using the Eraser tool, I just erase the blurry bits I don't like – usually the eyes, the mouth and the rest of the facial features. Once I get my face back, I go to Layers>Merge Down to combine the two layers, and suddenly I've eliminated the dirty pixels that Selina had on her cheeks. A face is starting to emerge!

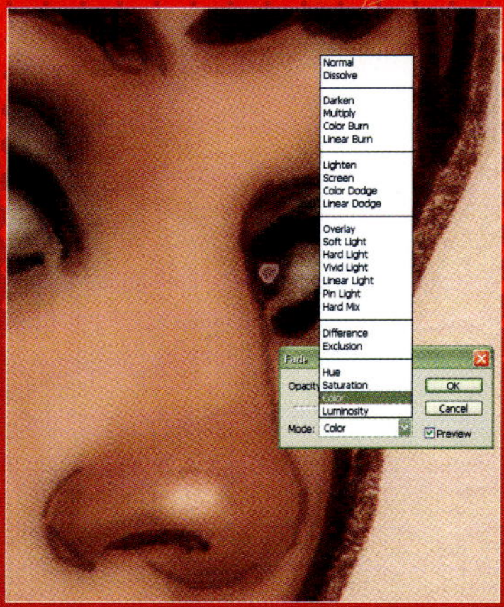

6 Adding colour to the face

Due to the presence and absence of blood under different parts of the skin, the face will usually have more or less colour in certain areas. Most people tend to have less blood – and so less colour – around their eyes, so I use a soft feathered selection around the eyes and make some changes. I'll use Image>Adjustment>Hue/Saturation and lower the saturation a little. Sometimes, sliding the hue away from magenta/red and towards yellow/green does a nice job, too. If the luminosity changes, use Edit>Fade>Filter and set the mode to Color.

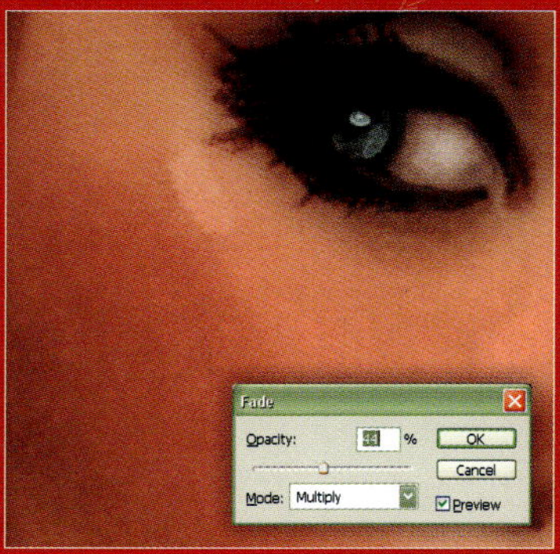

7 Make a girl blush

You can use the same method to establish the colour of the eyes, as well as their whites. My favourite part is adding blush to the cheeks and nose; it really brings the face to life. One method is to make a very feathered selection (value: 30-60) on the cheeks and apply a light pink (such as C:0 M:40 Y:20 K:0), using Edit>Fill set to Foreground Color in Normal mode. Then use Fade>Filter and set to Multiply. You can then play with the opacity until you get a nice blush.

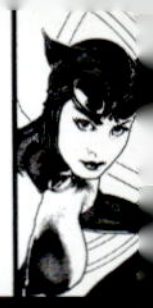

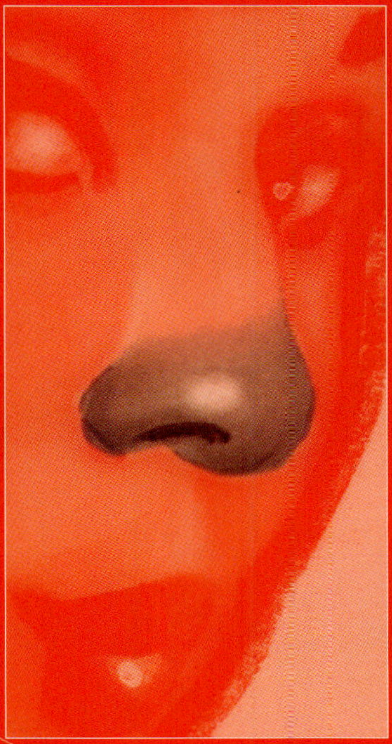

8 A rosy nose

Do the same for the nose, this time using a more subtle selection. You want a soft fade going up the nose, but you also want the rosiness to end under the nose and on the sides. Make a nose selection and then go into Quick Mask mode (hit [Q]). Using the Gradient tool, stroke down to make a really nice vertical fade in your selection. Revert to Standard mode ([Q] again) and do the colour application from Step 7, or use Image>Adjustment>Variations again. There are 13 different ways to get there in Photoshop…

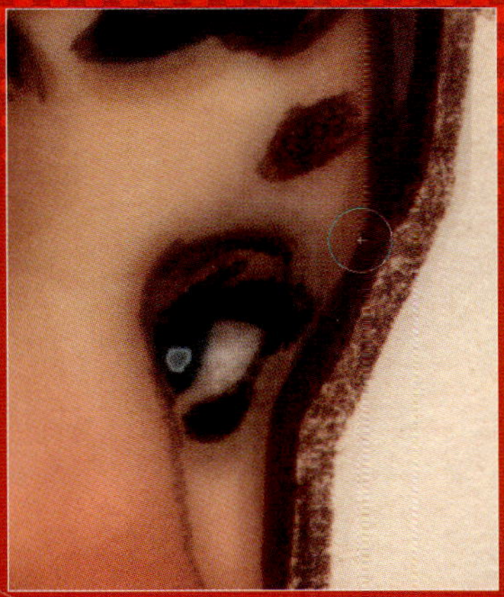

9 A dash of mascara

Using the soft feathered selection again, I add a hint of colour to her upper eye area using the methods we've already discussed. The nice thing about doing so much of the rendering in the traditional art is that you only have to push some hues around at this stage to get your face looking really great.

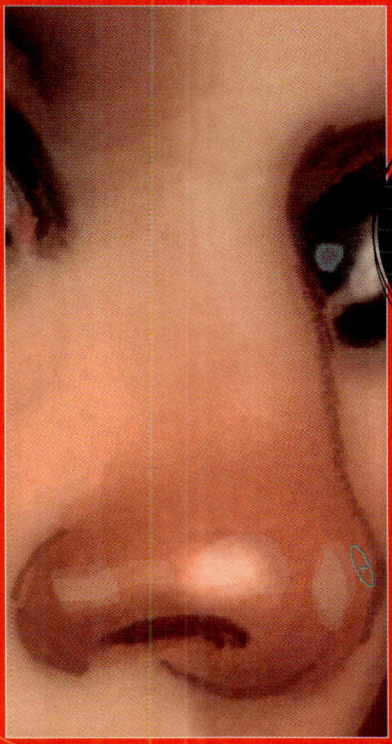

10 A few opaque highlights

I then take the Pencil tool, squashed into a brush-shaped ellipse, to add the final highlights. In a traditional painting, oil paints would be used. Here, I set my Pencil tool opacity to a low percentage, and the mode to Lighten. I then stroke in the highlights slowly: the tip of the nose, the lips and the eyes. If you absolutely love this part of the process, you can do less in the traditional phase and paint to your heart's content here.

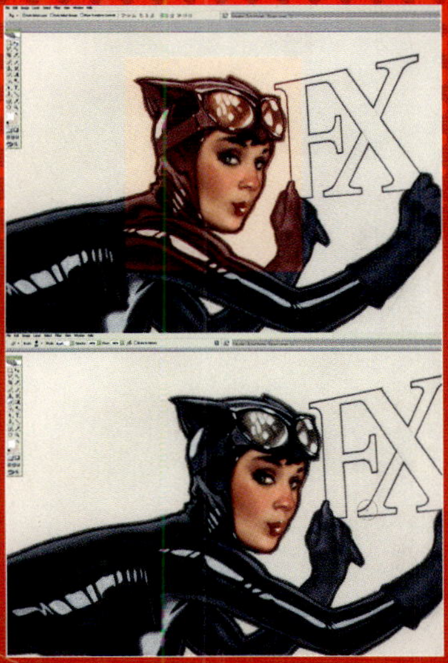

11 Re-applying the face

I then take my finished face layer back to the master illustration and erase all of the unwanted extra bits, such as the cowl, the goggles and so on. I then have the finished face and I'm ready to attack the rest of the piece. You can do this for any section of your illustration – simply isolate it on its own layer, focus your artistic attentions, and then return it to the piece when you're happy.

> *Shortcuts*
> **Fade filter**
> **Shift+Ctrl+F (PC)**
> **Shift+Cmd+F (Mac)**
> Use this to change the opacity of the last filter performed, as well as change modes.

12 The rest of Catwoman

If I had another 10,000 words, I could discuss the rest of the piece in detail. Once the face is good enough, I can mess with my levels and get the values to where I want them. I know it sounds backwards, but with the high-contrast nature of her costume, it's easier this way. I shift the colour temperature of her outfit to more of a teal, to complement her facial hues – this also goes nicely with the red background.

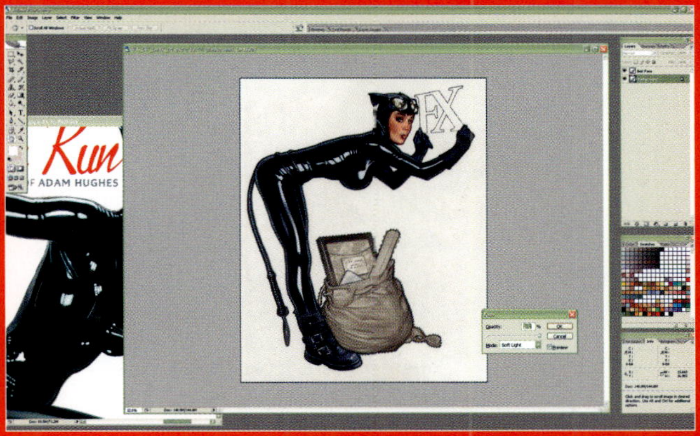

> **PRO SECRETS**
> **Eliminate history**
> Only use one History state; too many of them will mean that your computer has a hard time running large graphics files. It's art: if you need to have the ability to undo a brushstroke from 20 actions ago, maybe you aren't making great decisions to begin with. Half of art education is what you learn from painting yourself out of mistakes.

13 Red all around

One of the last touches is to get the character looking like she's actually in the space, and not just a cut-out. This means that the red of the background needs to show up on her. Adding some red via the Gradient tool or the Airbrush tool, either set to Multiply or Color, adds some nice red bounce light to the forms. ●

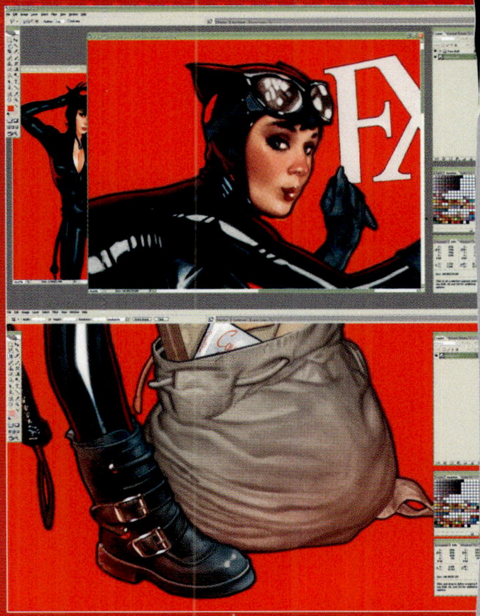

Interview

John Kearney

A glimpse into the world of the former games industry artist John Kearney, who isn't adverse to a bit of creative masochism to develop his considerable talents

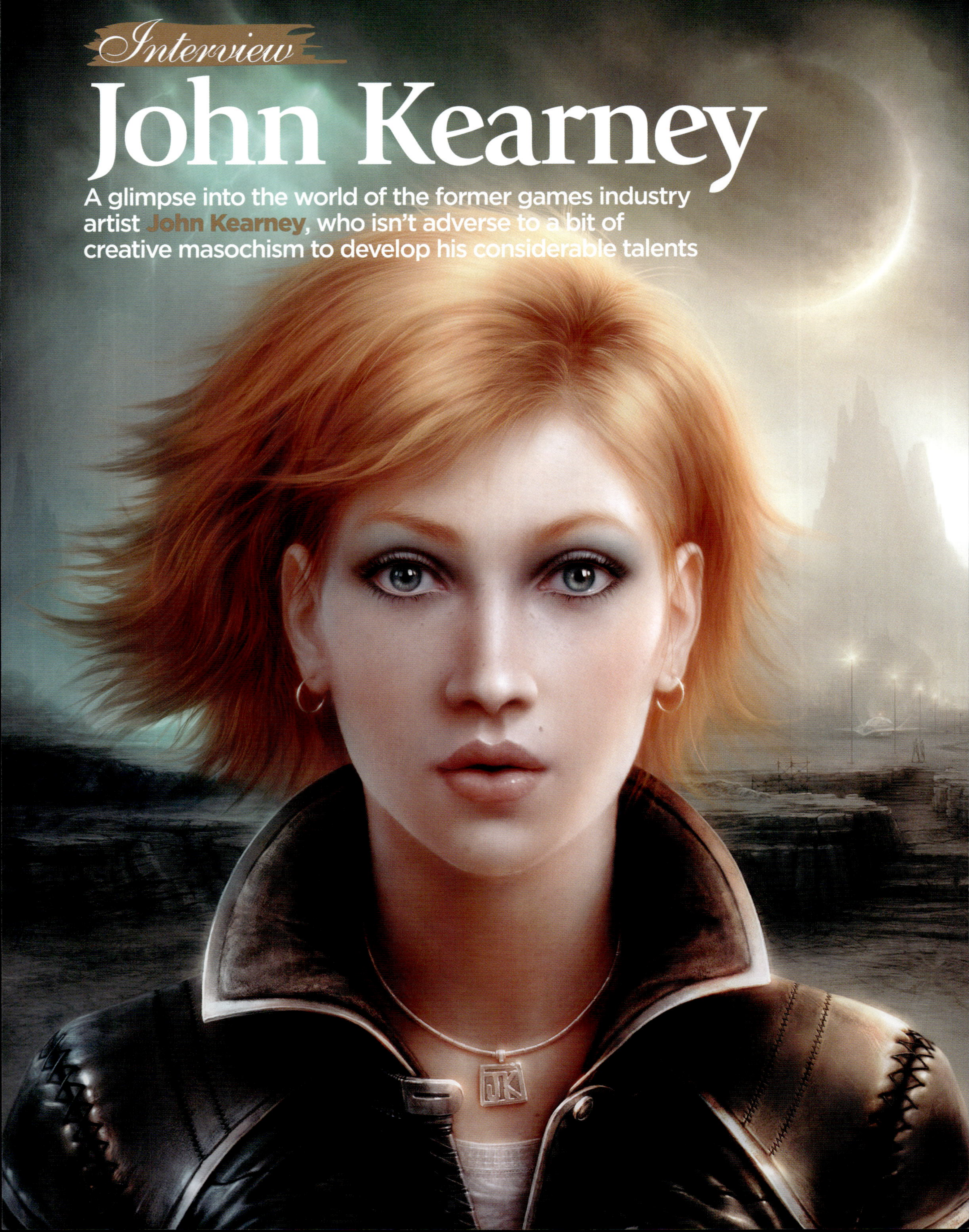

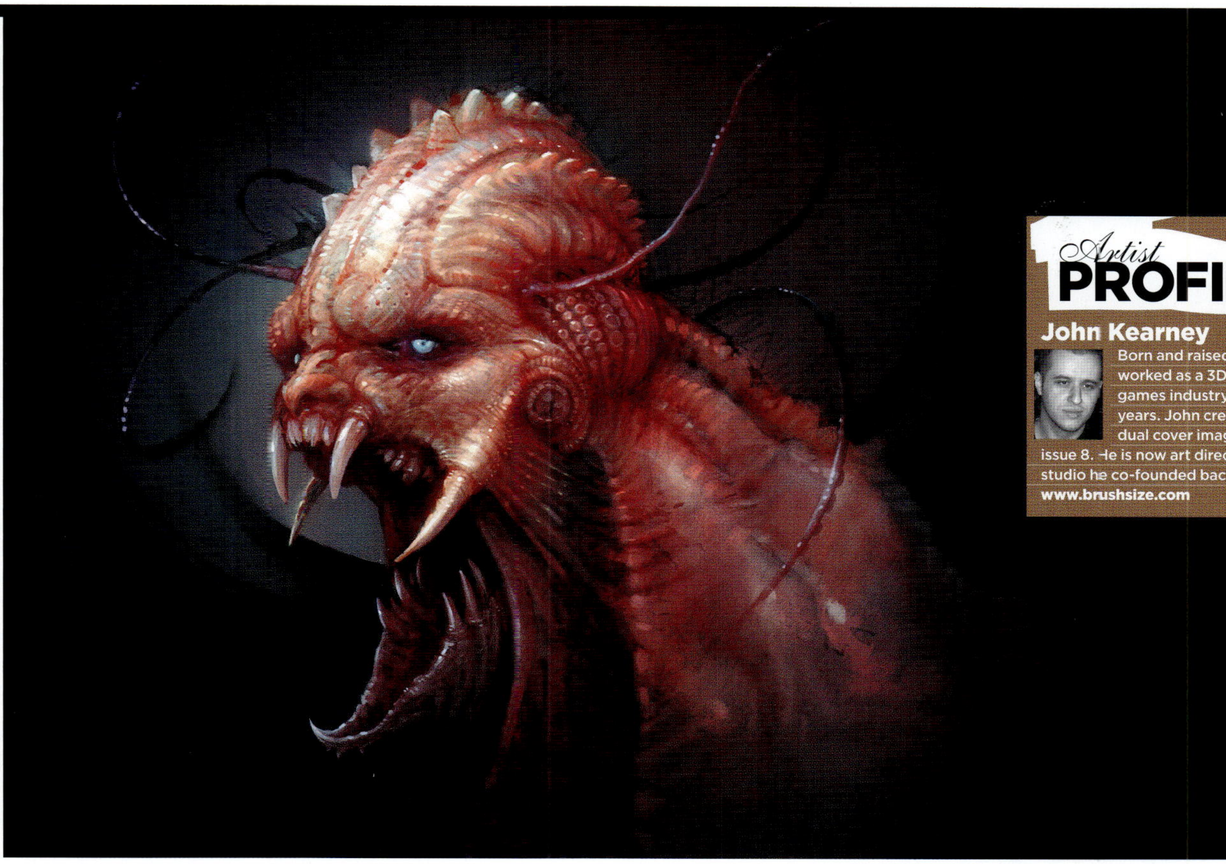

ALIEN
John used multiple reptilian references to create this piece.

Artist **PROFILE**

John Kearney

Born and raised in England, John worked as a 3D graphic artist in the games industry for over seven years. John created the famous dual cover images for ImagineFX issue 8. He is now art director at VooFoo, the studio he co-founded back in 2006.
www.brushsize.com

Talking to John Kearney, it's clear that John's somehow unearthed something remarkable within himself; a natural ability that has enabled him to create work that ranks alongside the very best fantasy art.

"I remember reading about the artist's 'First Fire'," he enthuses, "a sudden flash of inspiration that all artists experience at some point. It's a moment of crystal clarity and vision, a tantalising glimpse at something exceptional in your subconscious. Whatever it is, it's important to try to capture the essence of that intensified moment of perception by sketching down all you can before it's gone."

QUICK LEARNER

While this kind of inspirational epiphany might be a common stage in artists' development, what is unusual in the case of John is how quickly he has developed the associated technical skill to commit his visions to canvas. "Bizarre as it may sound now," he says, "for many years I'd never completed a 2D digital painting. I'd dabbled and messed about, but I never had the opportunity to take it further than that in a professional capacity."

BOUDICCA 3060AD
John's most ambitious work so far, this is a futuristic version of the flame-haired Celtic warrior queen. John didn't use any references, creating this iconic character image from scratch.

For the first part of his career, John had been employed full-time as a 3D texture artist in the games industry, which didn't offer him the opportunity for expression he needed. He describes it as "soul destroying."

"I completely lost all of my creativity and passion for the job," he says. "I started out like most young artists do, with a romantic vision of how great it would be to create art professionally. After realising how cynical and disillusioned I'd become, I quit my job and decided to go freelance as a 3D/2D artist to try and recapture my motivation."

Freed from the constraints of the 9-5, John set about developing his portfolio. He completed a number of paintings and posted them to the 2D art site ConceptArt.org, and quickly garnered praise.

"I was unbelievably surprised by the support I received," he says. "I had offers of work almost immediately and it enabled me to continue expanding my portfolio and improving my ability at the same time."

It was through his work on ConceptArt.org that he came to the attention of this magazine, and he has become a regular contributor, a highlight of course being painting the stunning Beauty and Beast dual covers for issue 8 of ImagineFX.

John works primarily in Photoshop, though he dabbles with Painter occasionally. The hours he put in at his first job using Photoshop have meant it has become second nature to him.

"I know the program and it's tools well enough to forget I'm actually using software

"I had offers of work almost immediately, and it enabled me to expand my portfolio and improve my ability"

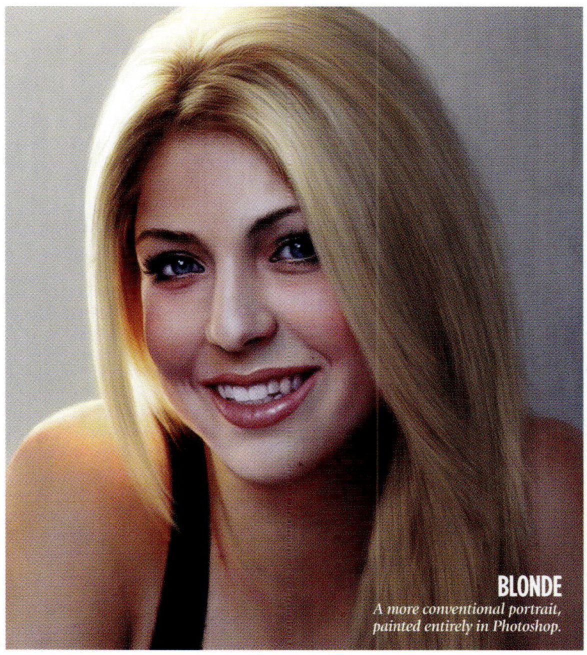

BLONDE
A more conventional portrait, painted entirely in Photoshop.

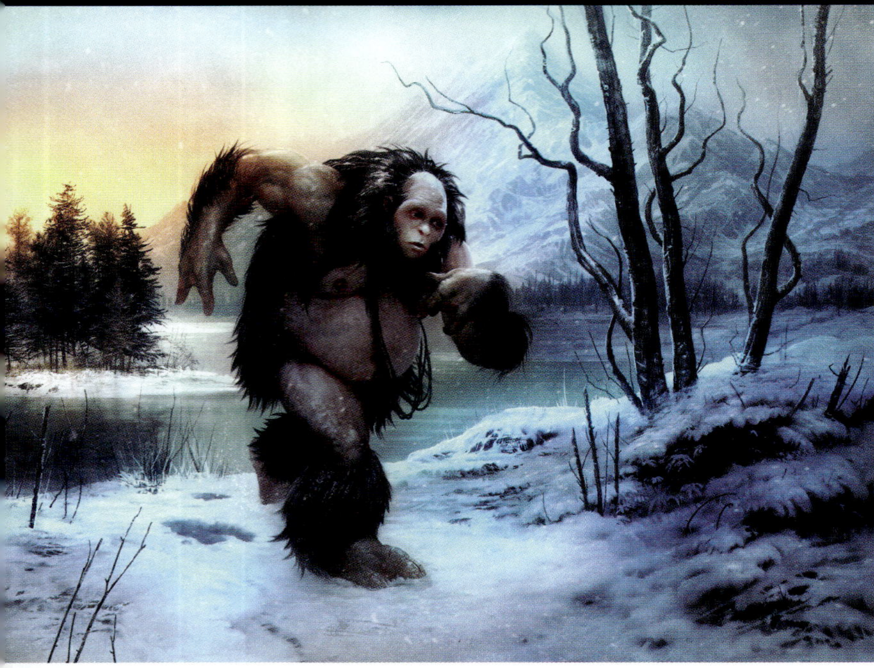

“At no point do I have to stop and work out how to do something, which means I'm able to get into the flow and paint at my full potential”

BIGFOOT
John used this in a Photoshop Q&A for ImagineFX about creating realistic snow.

when I'm painting,” he explains how much of an advantage that knowledge is: “It becomes like a traditional pencil or a paintbrush, at no point do I have to stop and work out how to do something, which means I'm able to get into the flow and paint at my full potential.”

Though the majority of his work is created digitally, John doesn't think the tools are all that important. “I feel I could do whatever I do digitally to a similar level with traditional media,” he assures us. “It's crucial to improve your eye and judgement for any art related discipline, digital is just another outlet for that fundamental ability.”

NATURAL MEDIA

So while many Photoshop artists create their own custom brushes, John opts mainly for Photoshop's default Natural Media brush set and would rather try to paint details than let snazzy brushes do the work.

To keep up the momentum, rather than slavishly working on a single, big project John often works on several paintings at the same time, using reference material for one, while another will be created entirely from his imagination.

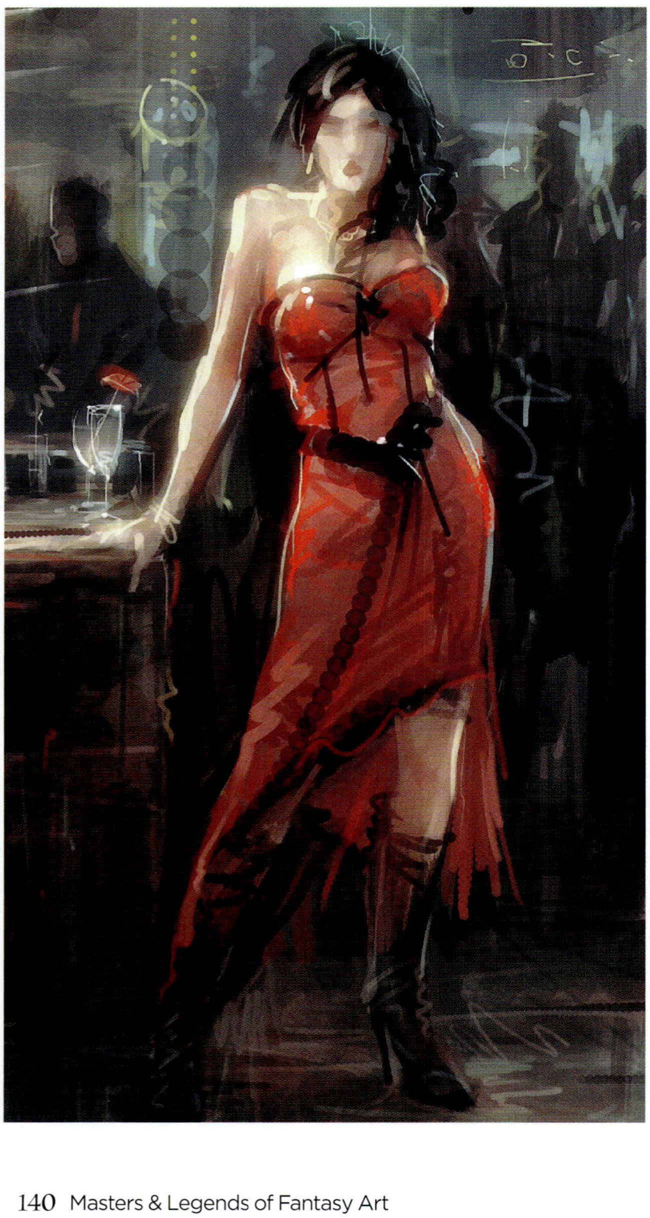

BAR GIRL
A more loose style, created with Hard-edged brushes.

“In the long run, I feel it's going to benefit me and improve my overall technical ability,” he says. “I'm certainly not sure whether it's the best approach, but I don't really care – I feel it works for me and it's a personal challenge that motivates me.”

John is self-taught for the most part and admits his formal education hasn't really been relevant to his eventual career path.

During his studies John undertook a placement at game studio Elite Systems and, impressed by his portfolio, they offered him a job immediately. At the tender age of 18, John describes his move in to the world of work having been “a baptism of fire”, but it was clearly a formative experience.

“The professional experience I gathered through working full-time with other artists helped me immensely,” he says. “There's nothing like milestones and deadlines to get your arse into gear.”

Right now, John's art director at VooFoo, the studio he co-founded in 2006. It was always Jon's dream to return to the collaborative atmosphere of the design studio; “I love being part of an art team with a lot of potential and ability,” he says. “Film work would also be of huge interest to me, designing creatures for the movies would be a dream come true.

“I'll keep my options open, continue doing the best work I can and see what arises. Whatever I do, I'm going to grasp it with both hands and see how far I can push myself.”

QUEEN TRIFFIDIA

A tale of two covers, nine days and 70 hours...

In July 2006, John received a call from ImagineFX offering an ambitious commission, with an even more ambitious deadline. John accepted, and the idea for Queen Triffidia soon materialised. John turned around the concept sketches for the then untitled image in a matter of days. John explains further, showing the investment each of the images needed.

“The paintings took me around 70 hours over nine days,” he says. “The majority of the time was spent on detailing the paintings, which can feel like forever when working at large print resolutions. The most critical period is always the first two or three days when the concepts have to be nailed.”

As for his favourite out of the two: “Definitely the monster version! The beautiful version might be just as aesthetically pleasing, but the real creativity and challenge came in designing the monster which had to look just as realistic and believable. Finding a balance between the quality of the cover images was imperative, otherwise it would have been a pointless exercise to offer readers a choice.”

Turn the page to learn to paint like John Kearney

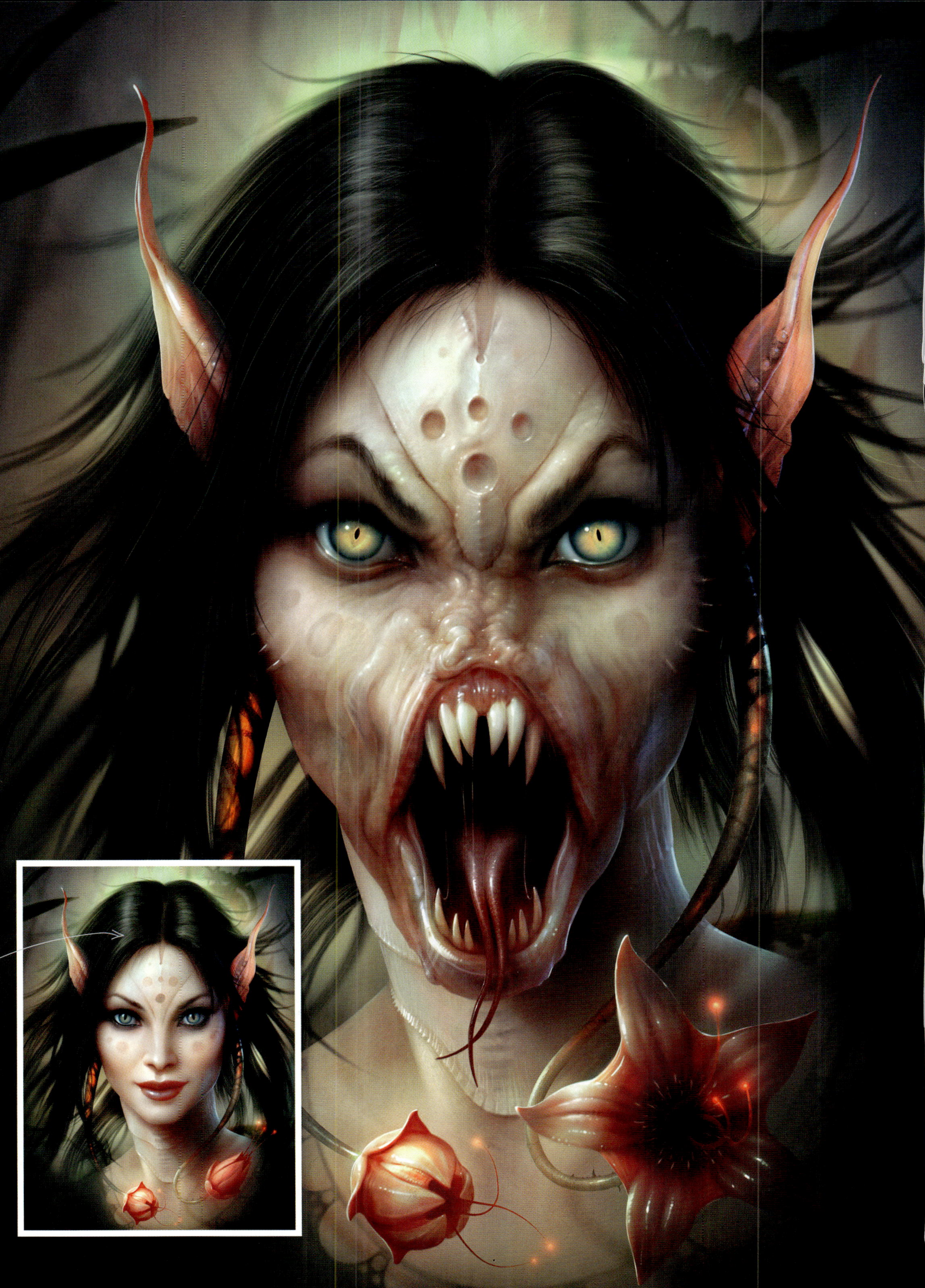

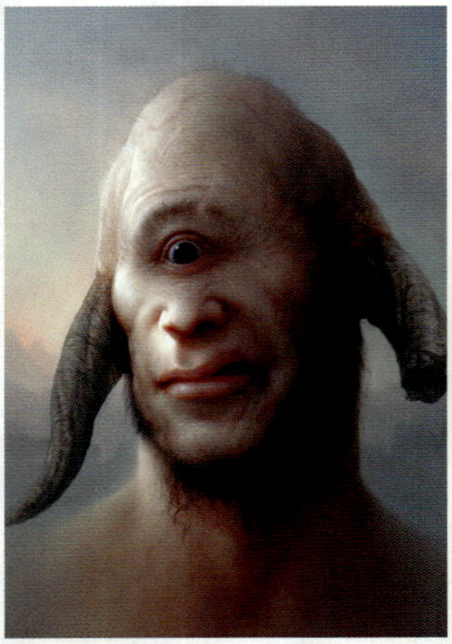

Photoshop

BEAUTY IS ONLY SKIN DEEP

Discover how to give your fantasy characters realistic skin using Photoshop. **John Kearney** fleshes some ideas out

Of all the surfaces an artist can paint, skin is traditionally one of the hardest to get right – and it becomes even trickier when your character is not human! Through experience, I have realised that there are no gimmicks, tricks or Photoshop hacks that can be used to make life easier when it comes to painting convincing flesh. I believe the key to improving is investing some time and effort into the subject matter, so that you can gradually train your eye to solve problems without reference. It may be worth doing this in the hope that when the stabilisers come off your bike, you're able to ride it without falling off.

Luckily, there are some things you can do to help improve your ability to render skin, it's less about your painting style and the tools you use, though, and more about what's in your mental library. With that in mind, I'd like to share some observations that may help.

Like most materials, skin colour is relative to the light conditions that are taking place around it. All light illuminating your character's skin will directly affect its colour and its properties. You can have any colour as skin, still recognisable as such because of its fleshy attributes. Therefore, the base colour of the skin is only as important as its inherent properties and the surrounding light. What are its properties, I hear you say? It helps to think of the surface in a more complex way, so that you're thinking a little deeper than just surface colours.

1 Skin properties

Flesh is one of many materials capable of absorbing and scattering light rays (other examples include wax and soap). The effect is commonly known to 3D artists as sub-surface scattering (SSS), an essential quality that should be taken into account when attempting to paint believable skin.

It sounds complicated, but it isn't if you consider this practical example: press a torch under your fingers and look at the way the light has penetrated your flesh and made your blood visible. Although it may be an extreme example of SSS in action, the same effect is visible in human skin even when the light is less intense. It may not be immediately recognisable in the same way, but it is there to some degree, and forms one of the properties that's responsible for giving flesh a radiant glow.

Another significant attribute of skin is its capacity for reflectivity, which results in specular highlights picking out details such as wrinkles, furrows or natural bumps on the surface. The reflectivity of skin can vary greatly, and the amount depends on how oily or wet the skin is. Generally, dry skin tends to be matte, with highlights being very scattered and diffused. On the other hand, oily or wet skin is a lot more reflective – highlights appear much sharper, more focused, and more intense. Keeping these things in mind help me approach the next stages with more confidence and assurance.

2 Concept and foundations

To start, I like to nail my character concept. I rough out some thumbnails using a pencil, and then choose one that works best. After this, I will either draw a refined version, or scan my thumbnail directly into Photoshop. With the ideas in place, I am a step closer to visualising the finished character, minimising the chances of something going wrong.

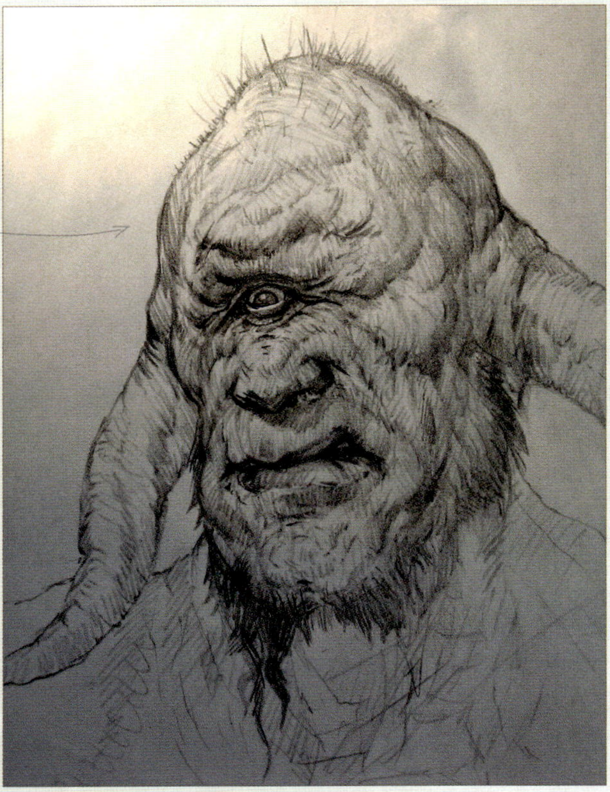

3 Lighting considerations

Lighting is a key factor. I think carefully about what I want the painting to achieve and then work out my light directions. In this case, I wanted to show a close-up of my Cyclops character with his flesh clearly exhibiting the properties of SSS. To achieve this, I decided that a key light and some reflected ambient lighting would illustrate things clearly.

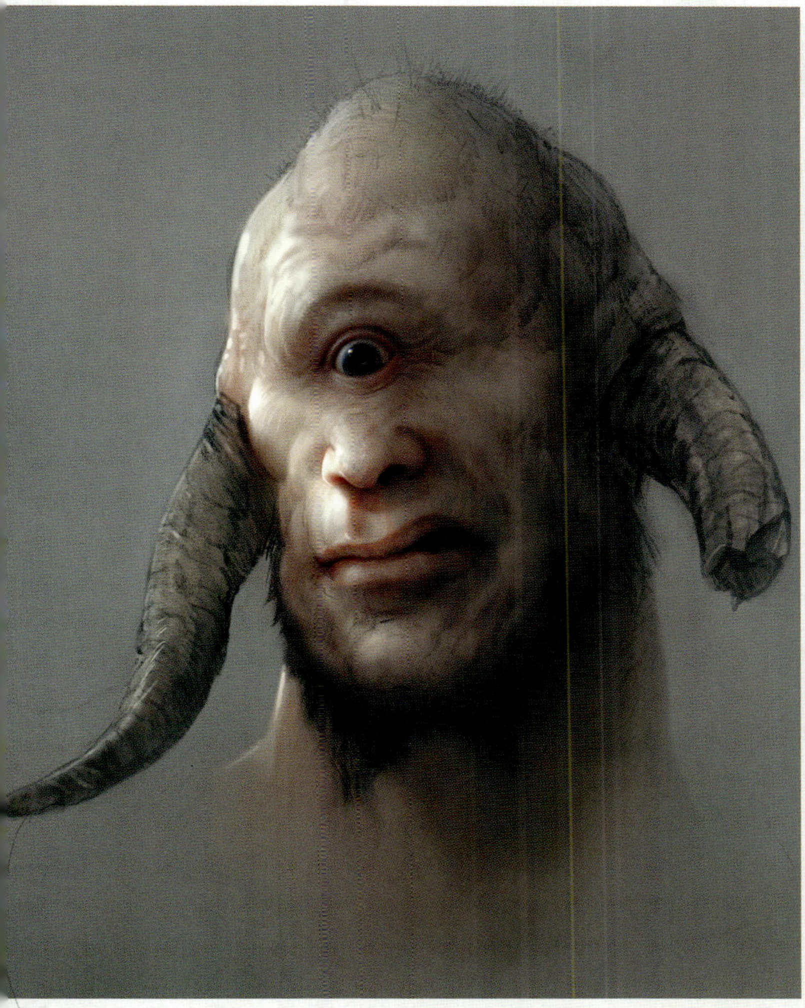

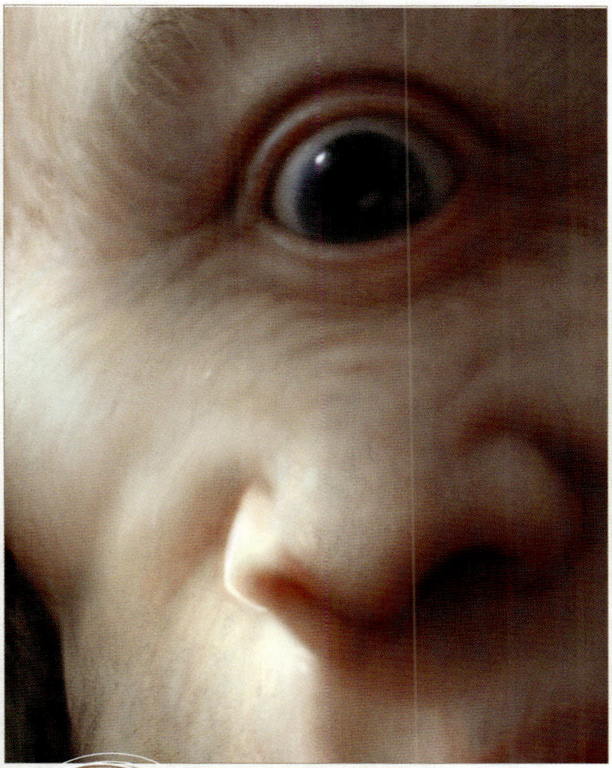

4 Blocking it in

Starting with a rough concept sketch will often mean little or no direct reference material, so it's time to rely on research and preparation. The stabilisers are off, and I'm all too aware from previous accidents that the best approach is usually to start simply. If my intention is to paint a lot of detail, then I am prepared to do it in several passes. I start in a way that gets the core foundations down so that I have something to build on. Initially, I use the Soft-edged and Hard-edged brushes for the base colours and values. They enable me to paint the first pass without having to think too much about texture or detail. At this stage, my focus is on light direction, colour, intensity, and shadows.

5 Rendering the skin

After blocking in the basics, I begin to think about injecting more life into the flesh by carefully using colour and tone. Because colours are relative, I always think of them in terms of warm and cool. On thinner parts of his flesh (such as eyelid and nostrils), I tried to show the penetration of light by painting the transition into shadow a little warmer. I also do the same for any raised areas of flesh that would catch the light. The shadow side of the full head would be virtually impervious to light penetration, which means the skin colour will be tinted by the ambient light.

Shortcuts
Sample colours
Alt (Mac or PC)
Use Alt to interactively sample colours from your base layers as you paint the finer details on your character's skin.

PRO SECRETS
Tweak colours
If part of your concept sketch isn't working as well as you would like then don't be afraid to change it for the better. Allowing yourself to continually improve what you're working on is all part of the process, and helps to fine-tune your artistic judgement. One example is to colour correct your painting. I regularly tweak the colours as I go along, or I do it right at the end by adjusting the Levels or using a photo filter for a particular mood.

6 Skin details and refinement

If you like painting macro details, there are other things you can do to take the realism of the surface even further. Although not for the faint of heart, pores, scars, moles, spots, hairs, veins and other natural occurrences and irregularities will make it look highly refined and lifelike. I usually paint them once I am happy with the way the light is reacting to the skin's surface. I utilise Photoshop's natural media brushes with a low Opacity setting for roughness and texture. I hope you found this mini-workshop useful and I wish you the best of luck with future creations!

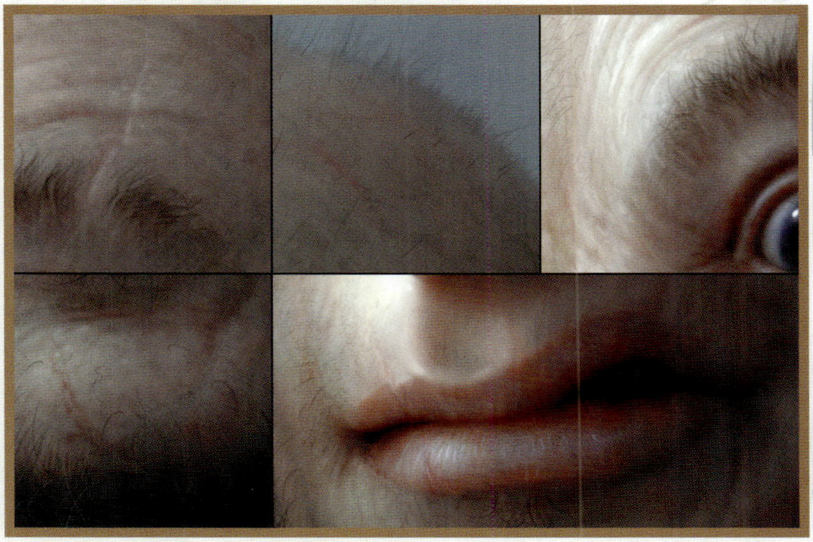

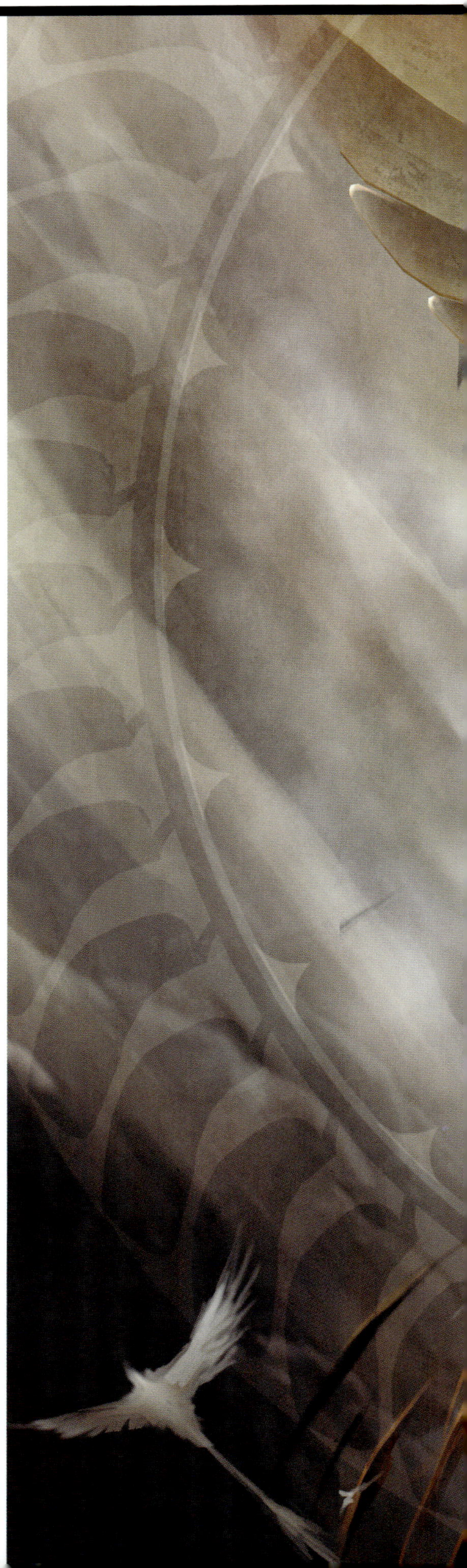

Interview

Raymond Swanland

Established artist **Raymond Swanland** is busy working on films and writing fantasy. Is there anything he can't do?

"Part of the intensity, freshness and action that people say my work has, has come out of the desire to loosen up," Raymond Swanland tells us. Intensity is the right word indeed; the swirling, dynamic images that he creates look – at first glance – as if they've been painted in a frenzy, yet their gorgeous detail and technical mastery suggest many hours of dedication and careful craft.

Raymond is the perennial example of an artist who was always drawing; right from childhood – pictures, posters, you name it you'll find it in his earliest portfolio – but his big break came much sooner than he could ever have dreamed.

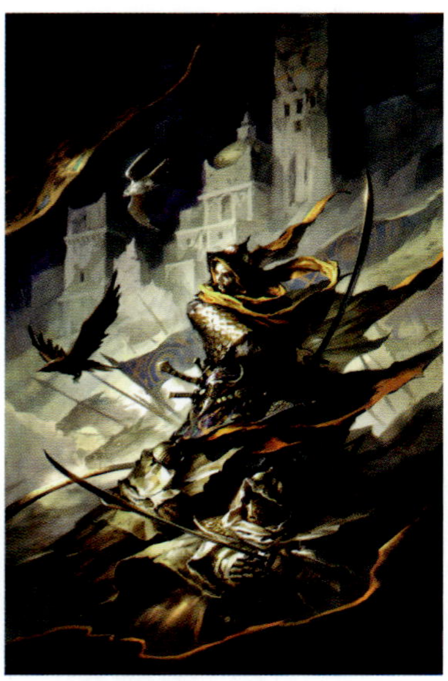

A FORTRESS IN SHADOW
This scene was created for Night Shade Books and demon-strates Raymond's great ability for storytelling.

Artist **PROFILE**

Raymond Swanland

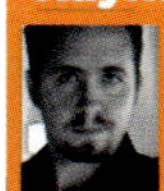

Raymond started at video game company Oddworld Inhabitants, and has been involved on many book, comic, advertising and film projects. His career, so far, has also included work for the diverse worlds of tattoo and snowboard design.
www.raymondswanland.com

CAREERING AHEAD

As soon as he left high school, he applied for a job at Oddworld Inhabitants, a video game company that had created an entire fantasy universe for its prospective games. And somewhat to Raymond's surprise, they took him on.

"I think I'd just turned 19 when I got the job," he explains. "I'd just gotten into college a few months before that. So I did the job and the first year of college at the same time. By the end of that, I pretty much decided I wanted to be an artist for a living, and didn't do any further education."

Not that there was any need for formal education, as Raymond learnt his skills on the job from the talented artists at Oddworld. Over the course of about eight years, Raymond worked in various design roles for all four Oddworld titles, most of which were critically acclaimed. At the same time he began picking up freelance illustration work, setting him up perfectly for his current job as a full-time freelance illustrator. He has combined numerous

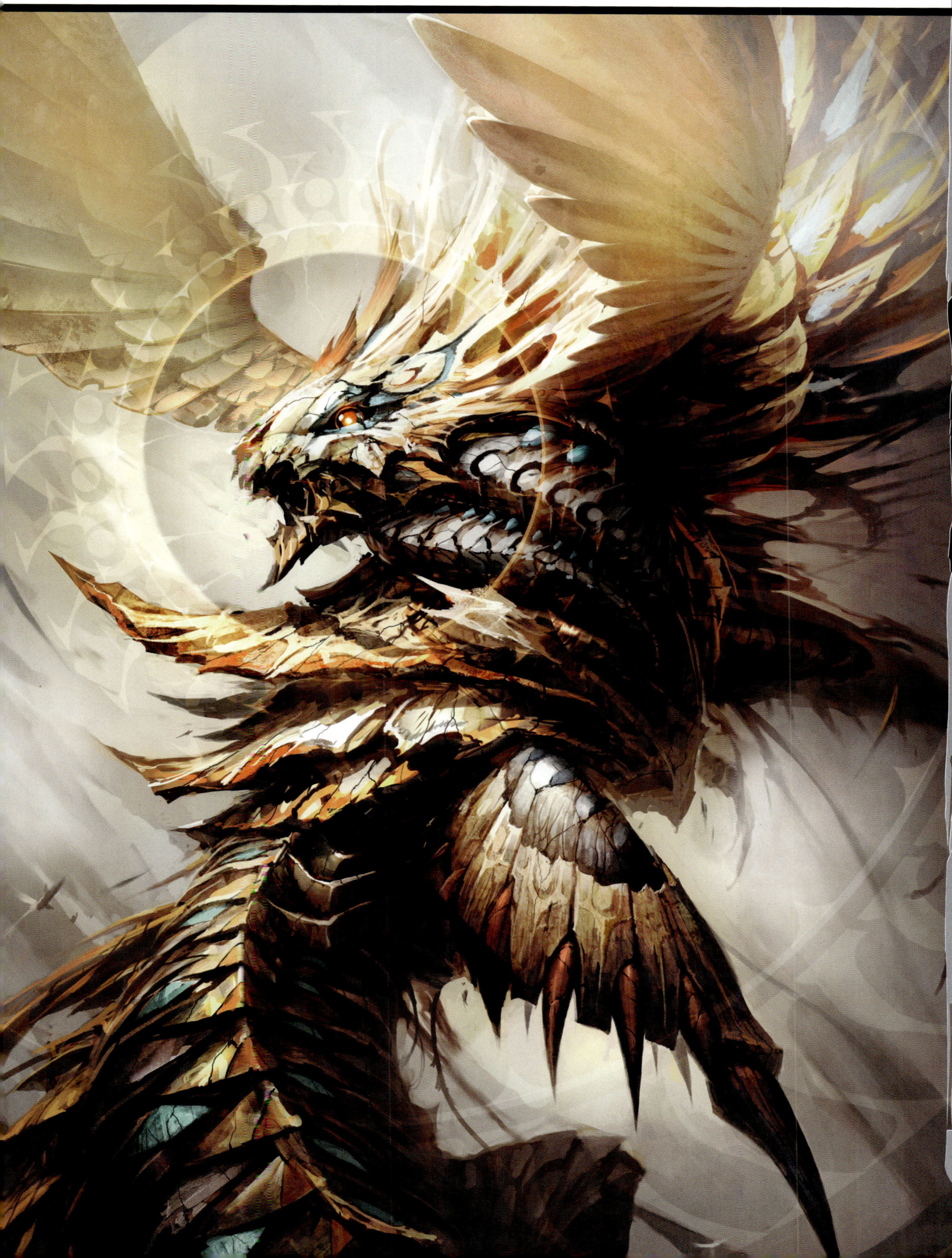

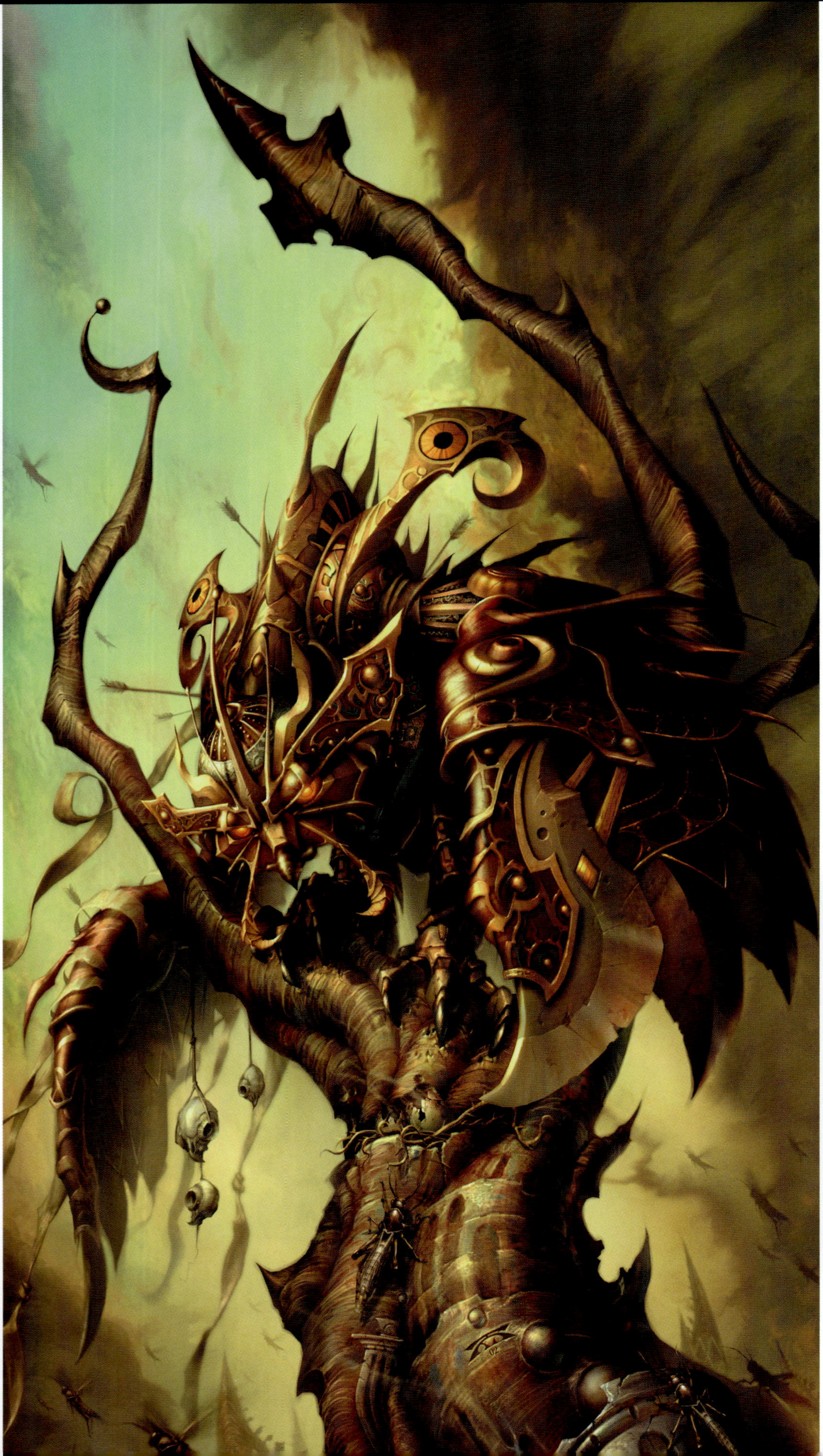

THE OWLS: BED OF ASHES
Part of the Owls series of animals. This is one of the first that Raymond painted.

fantasy and sci-fi book covers, as well as the US covers for the Korean comic book Priest, with extensive personal work.

Going freelance wasn't a planned career move. "I'm actually a pretty big believer in collaborating, and really my ambitions are to work in film as a director," he says. "That is definitely a collaborative process. Video game production is not too dissimilar; there are directors, managers, art directors, and I've been fortunate to play at some of those roles for a while. So it's a surprise that I've become an independent artist, but there's still plenty of work, I'm enjoying the freedom it offers."

That freedom enables him to take several trips abroad every year – he's just spent a month travelling around Spain, for instance, and is even considering moving there for a while. The trips are a mixture of holiday and inspirational sources; as he says, "At the very least, I can take a sketchpad with me and explore ideas."

INSPIRATION AND DEDICATION

For Raymond, that initial composition stage, when the ideas run freely, is the most exciting part of the artistic process. "The initial stage is very abstract and is something that I still can't tie down to a technique. I look at my past work and my sketchbooks for reference. I also listen to certain types of music and read specific books to access the part of my brain that's wild and intuitive."

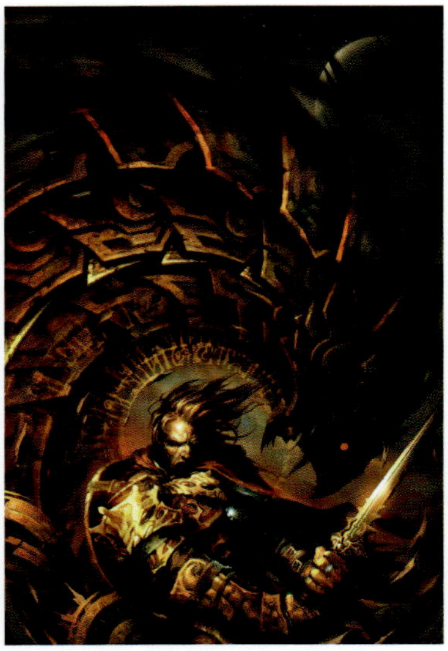

LORD OF THE SILENT KINGDOM
Created for Tor Books in 2007 this piece illustrates Raymond's unique blend of fantasy with his own unique stylised techniques.

EYE OF THE HUNTER

Adding another string to his bow, Raymond goes back in time to design a tattoo for a top bodyart company

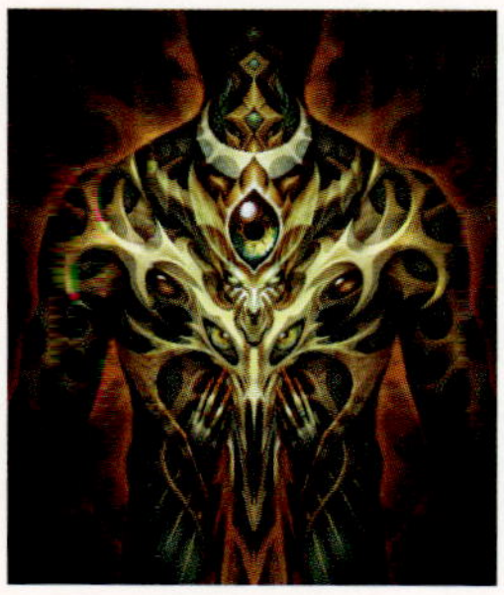
© 2006 Bullseye Tattoos

When Bullseye Tattoos approached Raymond early in 2005 and asked him to create a full-back tattoo design for them, he was both excited and nervous. "The tattoo was a welcome chance to exercise my very intuitive graphical art side that rarely finds its outlet in my freelance work," he explains. "But the blessing and curse of the piece was that I could create anything I wanted."

At that time Raymond had just returned to his native California after living in Hawaii for a while, and it was the natural splendour of that state which eventually inspired him. "I did my research and soul searching and focused on the part of human history when we were still very much part of the wild, but had also taken a step outside of it – I could relate to that."

After completing a myriad of sketches, he approached the painting in a free-form way, allowing his feelings to guide him. "I called the final image Eye of the Hunter as a homage to some of the first hunters known. History reveals they had just as much respect for the spirit of their prey as the food it provided for them and their families. They felt the pain of the animals they killed and loved them for that sacrifice – a life of balance that we might do well to remember."

But the actual rendering process of fleshing out his incredibly detailed and textured illustrations also has its appeal. "I find the whole creation part soothing. You become more and more confident in your technique and it becomes something like a reflex. Once I've made a solid composition, filling in the details is fun."

While all of his current colour work is created digitally in Photoshop, Raymond is from a background of canvas, airbrushes and charcoal, and he still sketches profusely using traditional media. It's something he'd like to explore in greater depth.

"I feel like that's the next stage for me – not to go 100 per cent traditional, but to start, at least, including some of that to the process; even if it's not part of the finished piece. There's a bit of romance to being a [traditional media] artist, and there's also something very powerful about having an original. When you put that time and energy into one thing as an object, it absorbs that and adds electricity to it."

“I find the whole creation part soothing. You become more and more confident in your technique and it becomes something like a reflex”

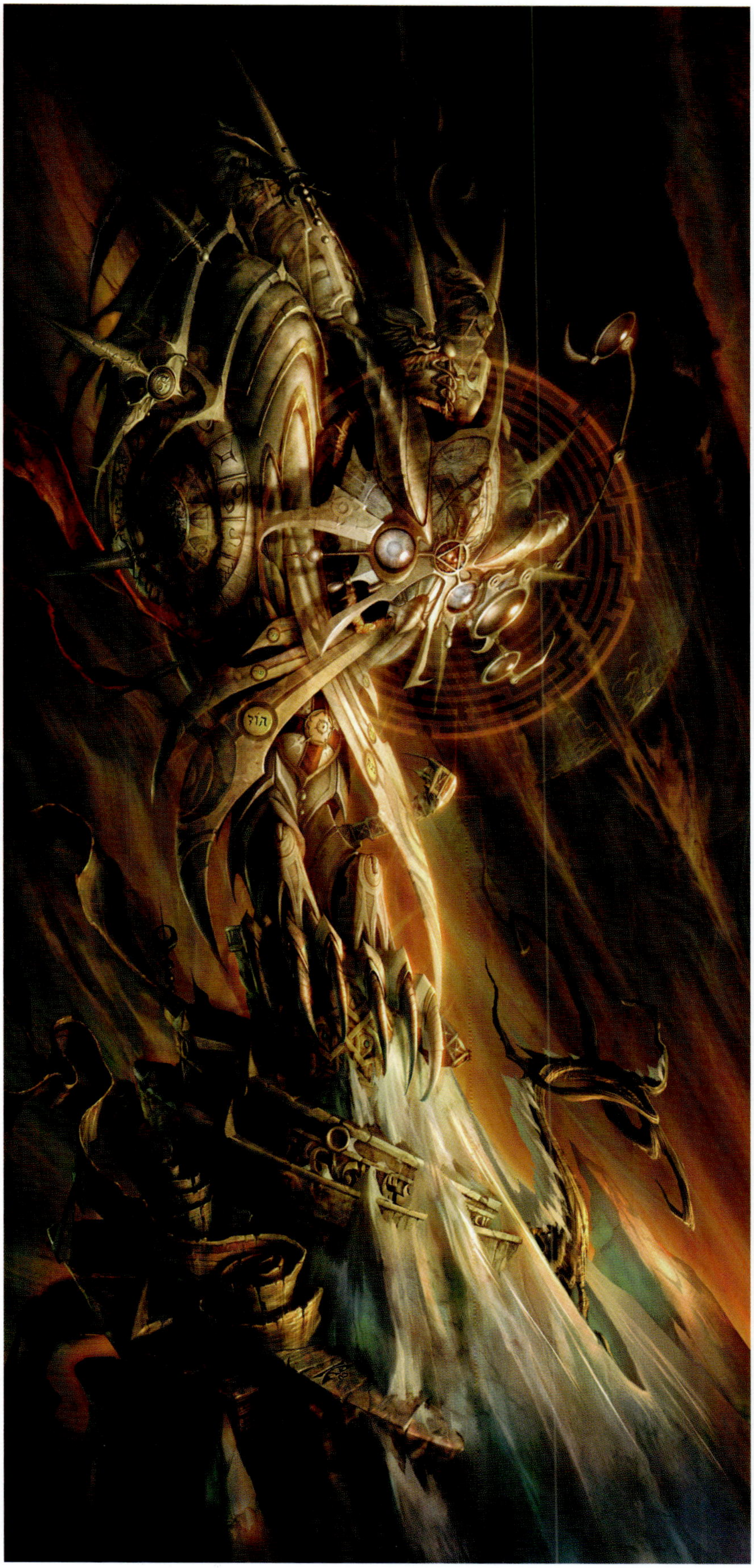

THE OWLS: THE FORGOTTEN MOUNTAIN

The Owls are one of Raymond's paintings of animals symbolic of elements of the human psyche.

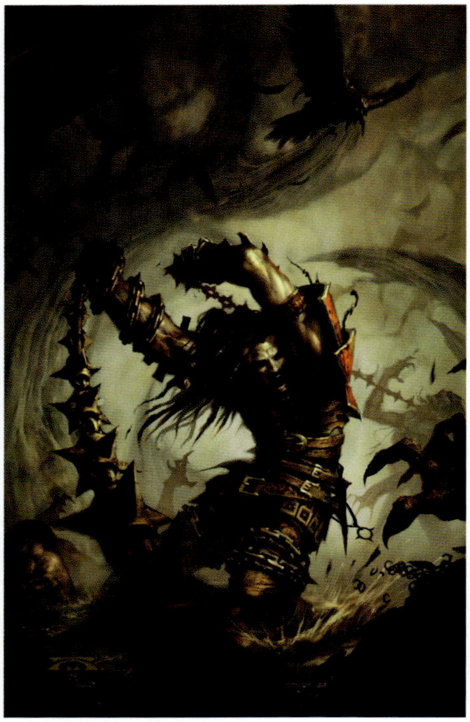

THE FIGHTERS: MASTER OF CHAINS
A 17th century pirate and a traditional Samurai were combined for this character, who graced a book cover.

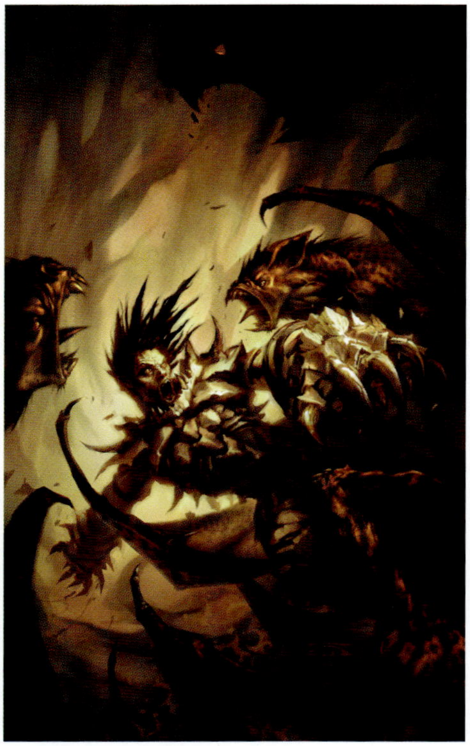

THE FIGHTERS: SON OF THUNDER
Another fantasy novel cover, this time featuring a warrior who is covered in dinosaur bones.

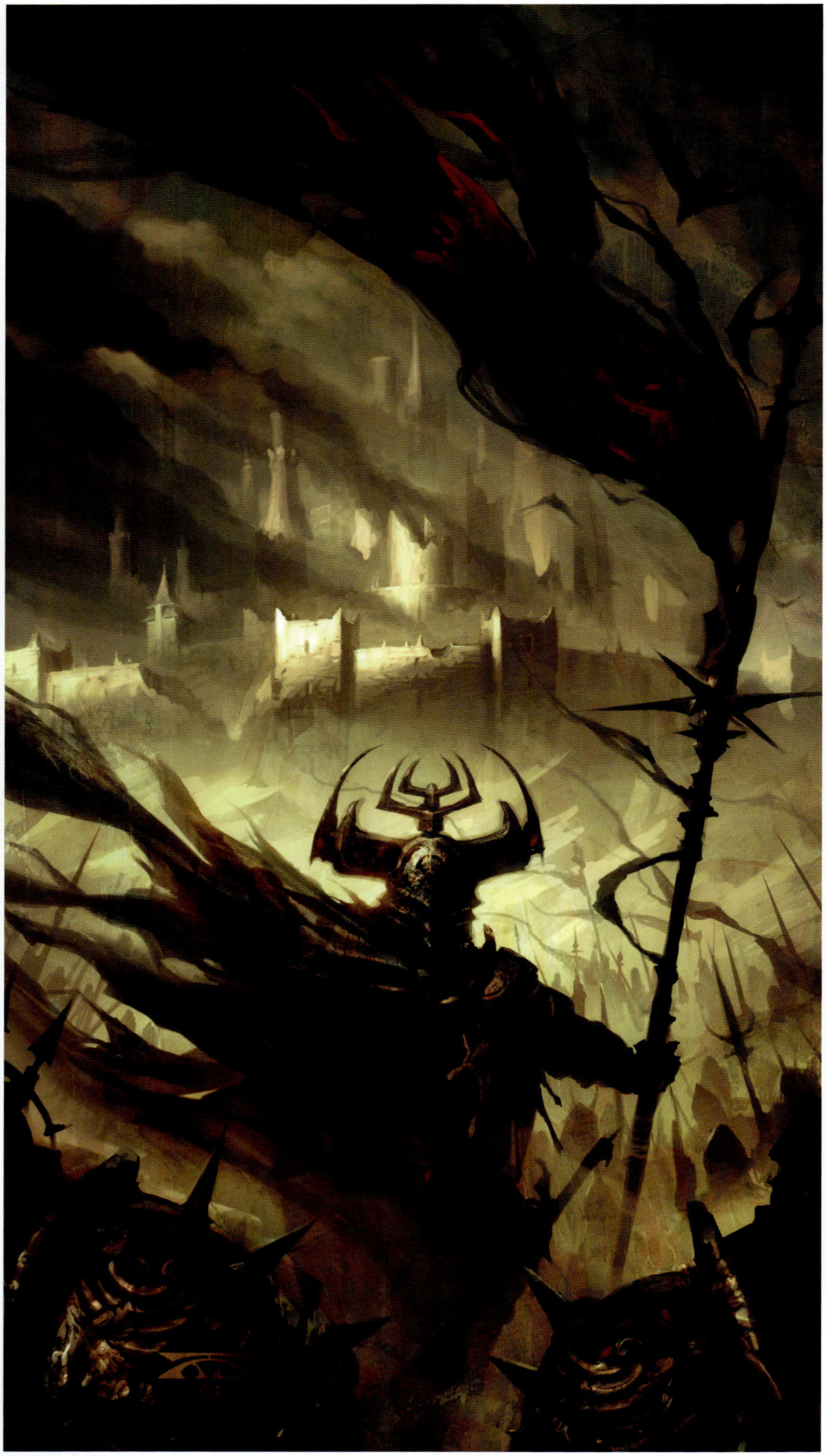

A CRUEL WIND
Raymond created this powerful image as a cover for a fantasy war epic by Glen Cook.

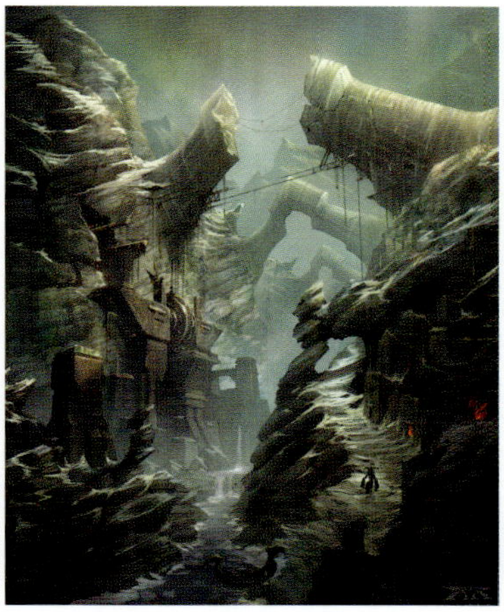

CANYON FORT
Oddworld: Stranger's Wrath was the basis for this piece of concept design.

Whatever the medium, storytelling is vital – creating an image for its own sake does nothing for him. "The image and the story come in unison," he says. "There's no doubt my personal pieces in particular are just a slice of a much bigger story. They're part of a universe and you're only seeing part of it. That's what comforting in making those pieces. In all those hours rendering, I'm exploring that universe."

LIFE IN PICTURES

In recent years Raymond has been very busy, now he's one of the most sort after fantasy and concept artists in the industry. His client list spans comics, films, books and board games, with Darkhorse Comics, Magic: The Gathering and World of Warcraft earning him a reputation for innovative art within tightly controlled formulas.

He's often said commented in interviews that he considers himself more of a sci-fi fan than a fantasy artist, so it was no surprise that he would eventually marry the two when he created the cover art for the Aliens Vs Predator series. These aren't Raymond's only book projects, he was also invited to create the cover for the Towers of Midnight by author Robert Jordan.

A highlight in recent years, and one that truly matched his love of sci-fi with fantasy, was a contribution to the Star Wars Visions art book. Artists were personally picked by the book's editor in collaboration with George Lucas. Raymond's piece, called Shadows of Tatooine, depicts Han Solo and Chewbacca rendered in his unique style.

Look out for more from this exceptional artist in the coming years.

Turn the page to learn to paint like Raymond Swanland

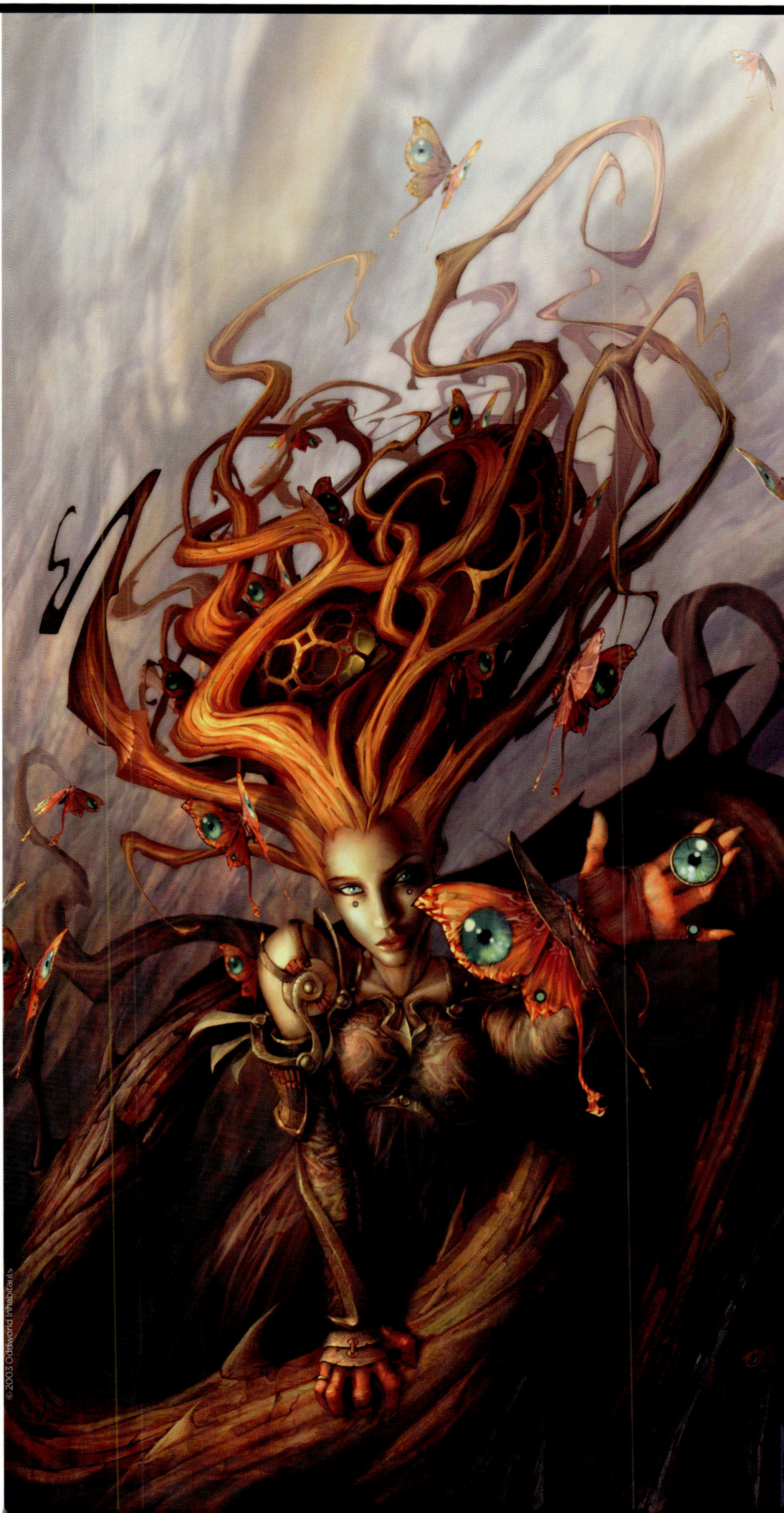

MIMIC
This stunning image focuses on a recurring theme in Raymond's work: the relationship between human beings and nature.

Photoshop

FACE THE WRATH OF MEDUSA

Raymond Swanland used a perfect blend of traditional methods in Photoshop and created this monstrous gorgon...

Greek mythology possesses a wealth of visceral adventures and moral conflicts that resonate with the human condition to this very day. It also taps into the purest depths of our imaginations to provide us with experiences, places and characters that indulge our most extreme fantasies. Medusa is one such fantastic character; she embodies the essence of myth by combining many archetypes that represent our darkest fears. In this workshop, I'll be designing my own take on the classical look of Medusa, with homage to the familiar past, but also an eye for contemporary pop culture and a new, fresh edge sprinkled in.

Though I often sketch using pencil and paper to kick off a design, this piece was created entirely in Photoshop with a Wacom tablet. Although I take advantage of tools that don't exist in the physical world of painting (such as layers and colour adjustments), I still approach the process of digital art in a fairly traditional way. I tend to paint from dark to light with simple brushes, and I flatten my image on a regular basis to keep it cohesive. Ultimately, my process is more about the basics of colour, lighting and composition than it is about digital tools. Having said that, the computer is the best artistic tool I've ever laid my hands on.

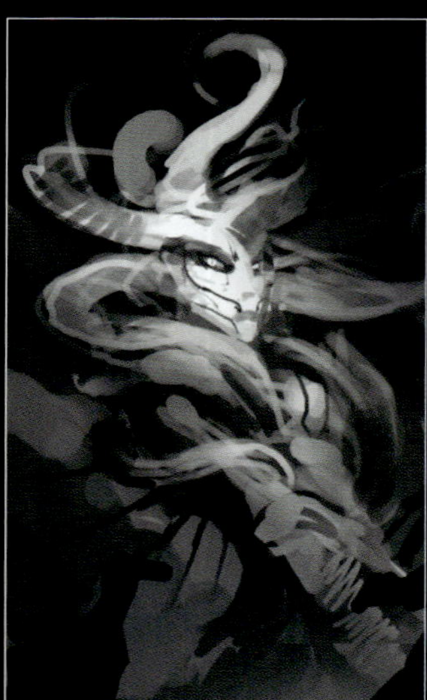

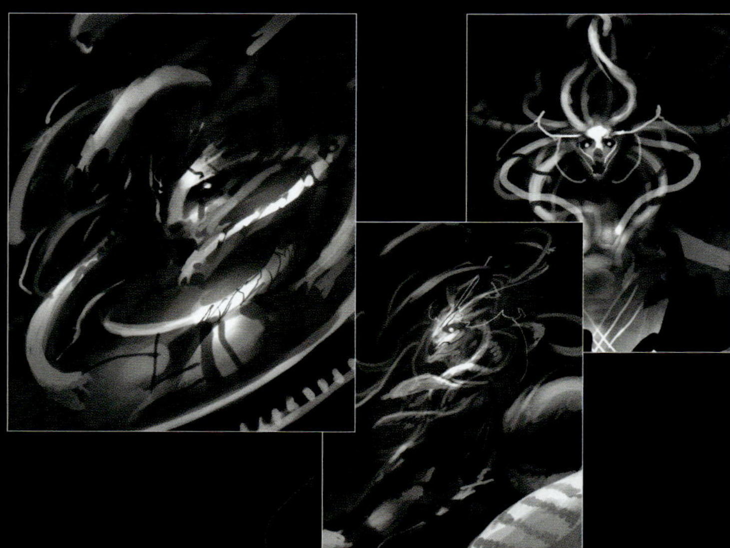

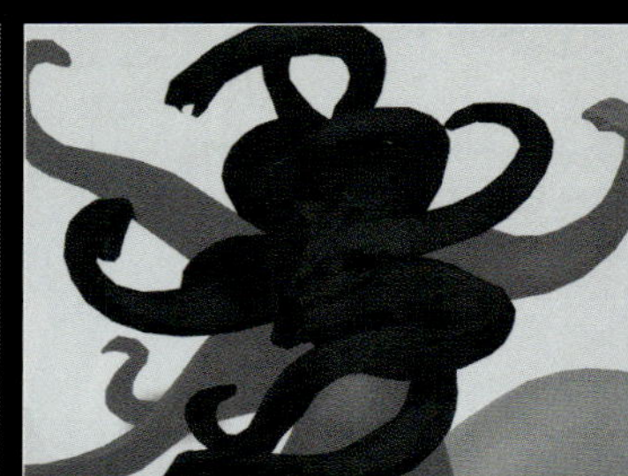

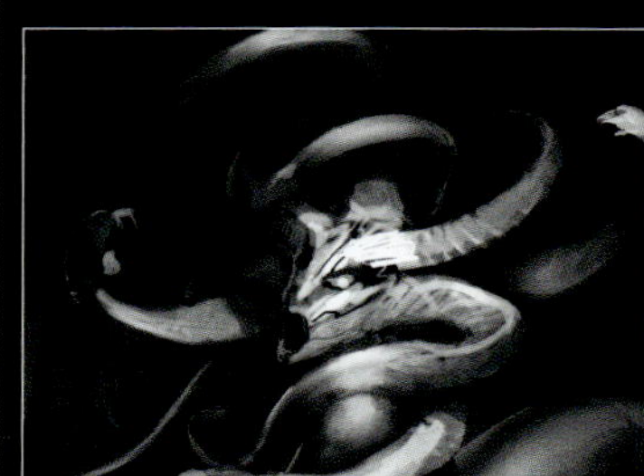

1 Inspiration and concept

When I was asked to paint my own take on Medusa, a fairly clear image appeared in my mind right away. While I'm familiar with many of the previous representations in books and films, I knew that I wanted to create something more ghostly and alien. As she was cursed to guard her subterranean lair, I imagined her as one of those cave-dwelling creatures that never see the light of day and gradually evolve to lose all their pigmentation. An ancient albino guardian could be as beautiful as porcelain and as frightening as a wraith.

2 Black and white

Although I often start straight in with colour, the ghostly nature of this piece enabled me to work in simple black and white. Rather than sketch each piece as a line drawing, I dived right in to pick up where the light illuminates Medusa's form as she emerges from the dark recesses of her home.

3 Separating layers

I separate the image into layers, and grade them from darkest in the foreground to lightest in the background. I get a sense for how the graphic reads and the how well the positive and negative space is balanced. This creates a fog-like atmosphere, which confirms the physical weight of Medusa is correct.

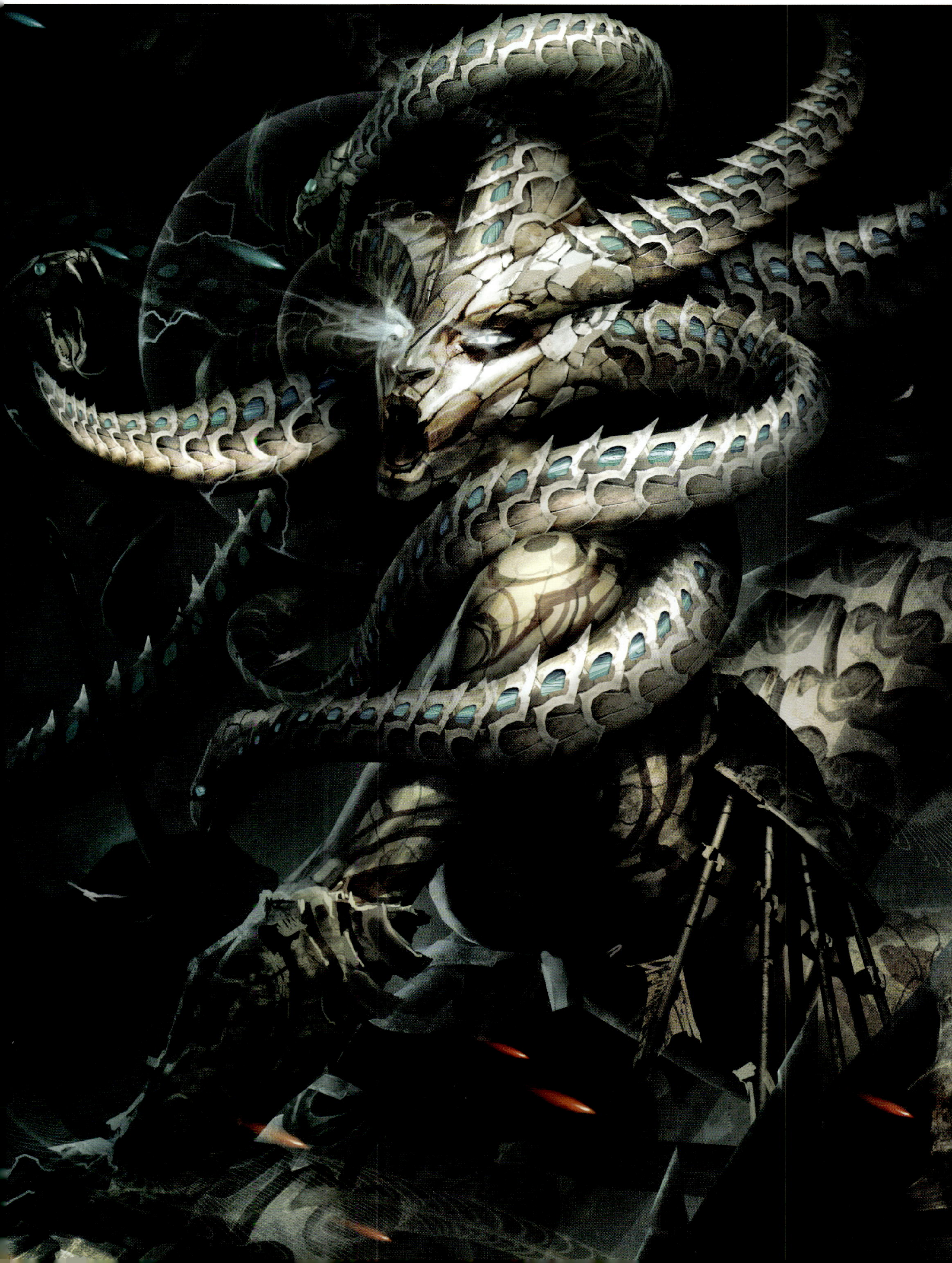

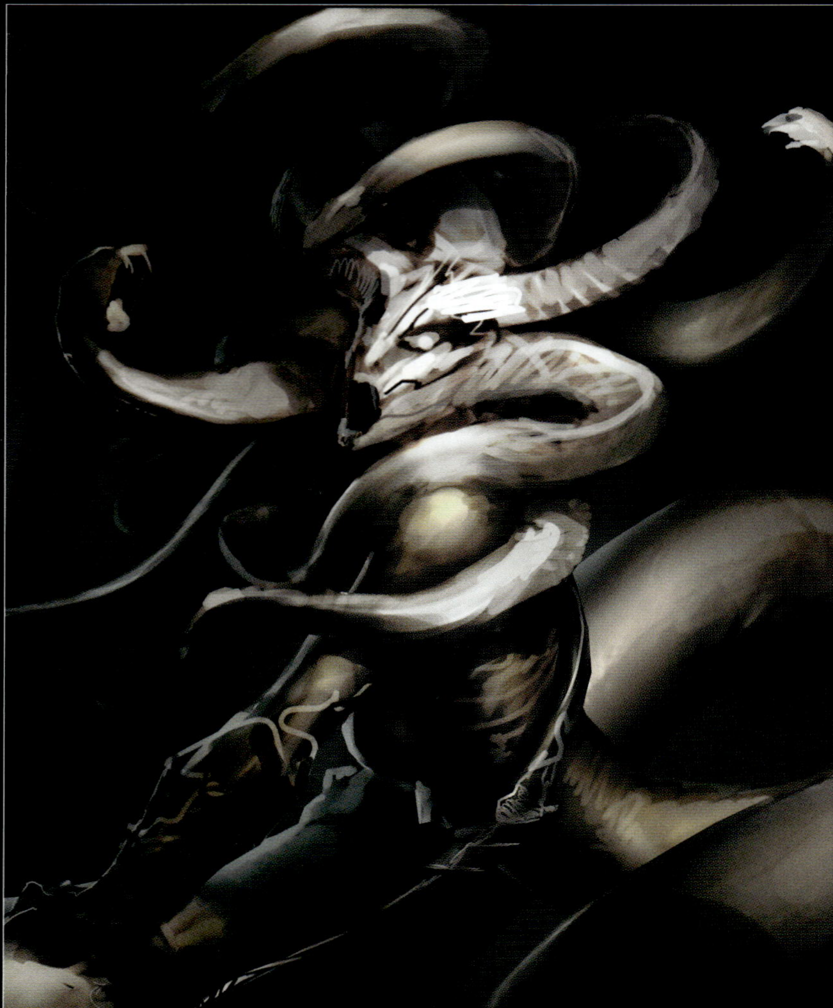

4 Adding colours

With the layers separated, it's now easy to drop in some colour division between the materials. Because of my take on Medusa as an albino cave-dweller, her coloration is of bleached bone and dingy porcelain. The background is a complementary blue-green to contrast with her subtle warmth. I'll keep the colours fairly desaturated for the time being, because I want to paint the details in the intended material colour, before layering in a stronger colour for the mood.

5 Focal details

As with most creatures and characters, the focus of the whole design and composition of the piece is the face, and this is particularly true of Medusa. Ultimately, this is where I'll paint the greatest amount of detail; so as to draw the eye and connect with the viewer. As I move away from the face, the detail becomes looser and more impressionistic to give a sense of movement and life, without detracting from the character.

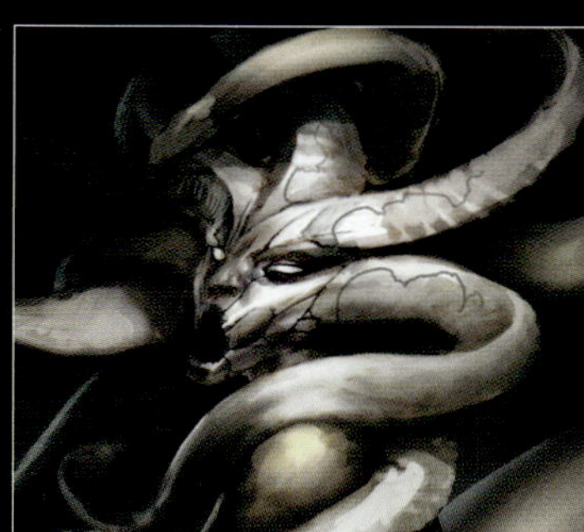

6 Killer's physique

Although she was once beautiful and graceful, Medusa has become a hardened, merciless killer, and her physique reflects that. I keep her proportions feminine, but refine the muscular details, particularly in her arm, to highlight the strength and tension in her character.

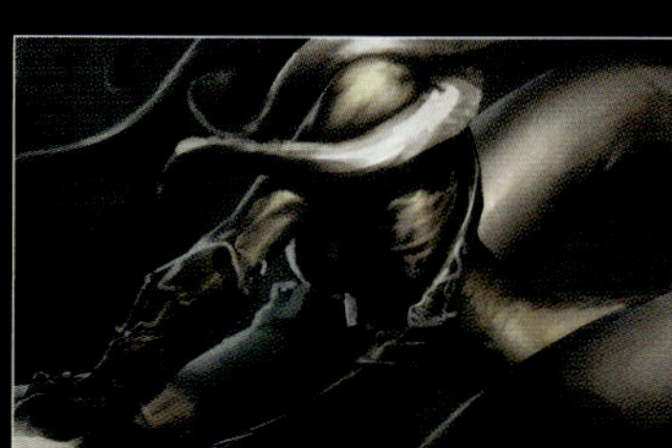

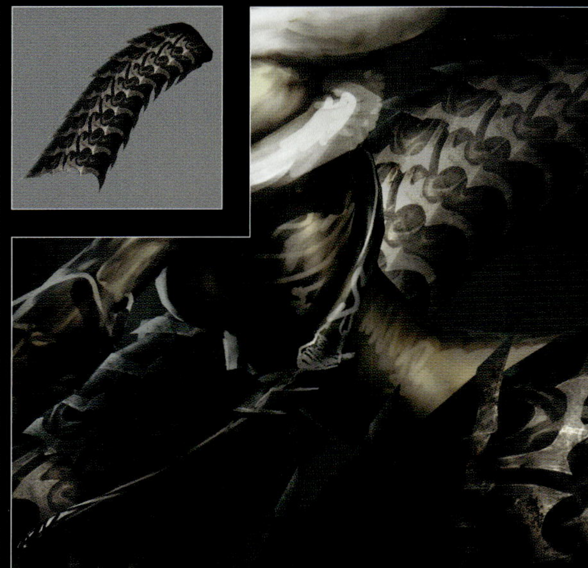

Shortcuts

Liquify

Shift+Ctrl+X (PC)

Shift+Apple+X (Mac)

Photoshop's Liquify tool is helpful if you need to sculpt and adjust organic forms.

7 Armour-plated

Part of my take on Medusa was to step away from making her a literal snake with simple scales, and to bring a sense of artistry to her structural details. I've covered her long serpentine body with segmented plates. They are part of her, but also finely carved pieces of armour. When the Gods changed Medusa into her cursed form, they built her destiny into her very skin by giving her the organic armour of a warrior. To do this, I create one well-rendered segment of the carapace, and repeat it to form the structure. I use the Transform and Liquify tools on each segment to bring it into the proper orientation and perspective.

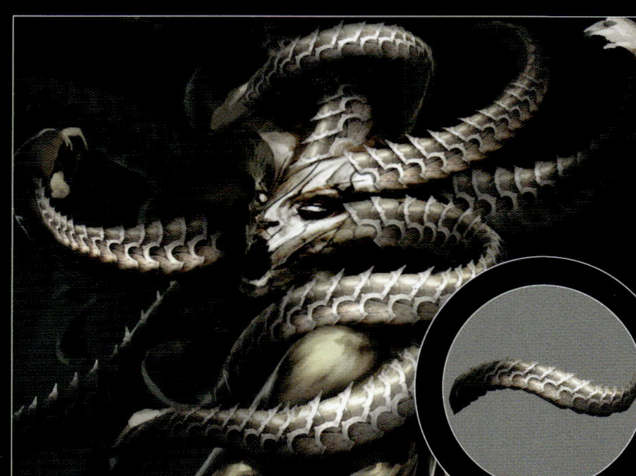

8 Biomechanical patterns

The armour-like segments of Medusa's body carry into the design of the snakes on her head as well. This biomechanical look of the snakes gives her an alien or futuristic feel that truly steps out of time and into fantasy. This process of repeating a single segment into the entire length of each snake body is even more heavily dependent on the Liquify tool. Plenty of subtle finessing gradually massages the segments into nicely rounded shapes. Shading with the Dodge and Burn tools does the rest.

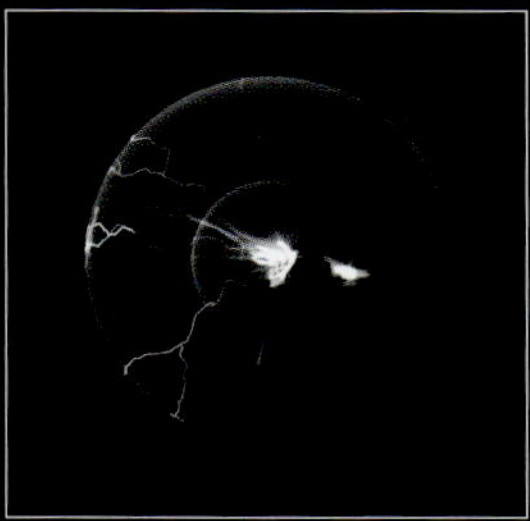

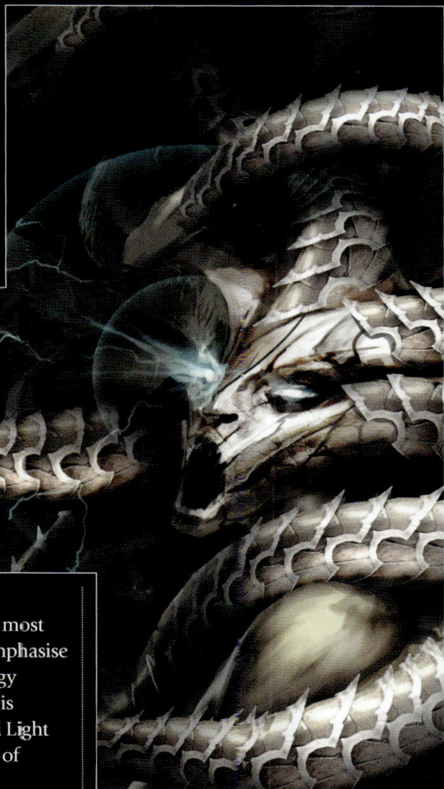

9 Graphic overlays

Medusa's stare is one of her most legendary characteristics, and I emphasise it with translucent halos and energy emitting from her eyes. The effect is painted in a few overlapping Hard Light layers that gradually build a sense of electric luminosity.

10 Functional design

At this stage, it's time to nail down the rest of the designs in the image, particularly the weapons. Although I originally painted her bow slung across her back with the string wrapped around her chest, she wouldn't actually be able to remove it over the snakes on her head or her tail unless she were to un-string it – that would just be thoughtless design. For the sake of functionality, I've moved the bow to her hand and given her a side-facing quiver of arrows that would snap into place to prevent them falling out or getting tangled up with the snakes. This is a small, but important example of thinking about the design of the character beyond the moment of the painting.

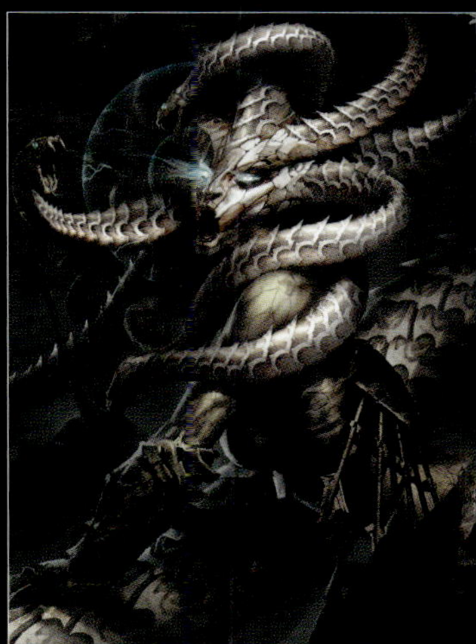

11 Atmospheric colour

With many of the details in place and the overall composition slightly reframed, it's time to emphasise the ominous mood of Medusa's lair. I'm shifting and saturating the overall colour into reptilian greens. I do this with an image-wide Overlay layer of green, then paint in areas of slightly warmer gold and red to bring out the face and upper body.

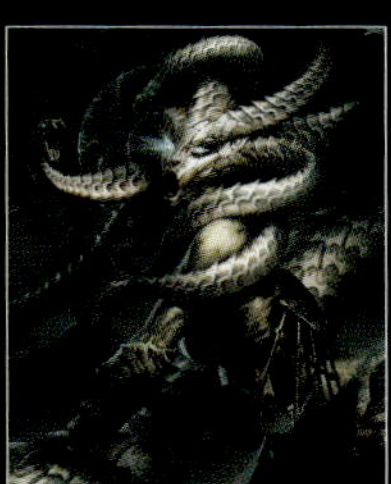

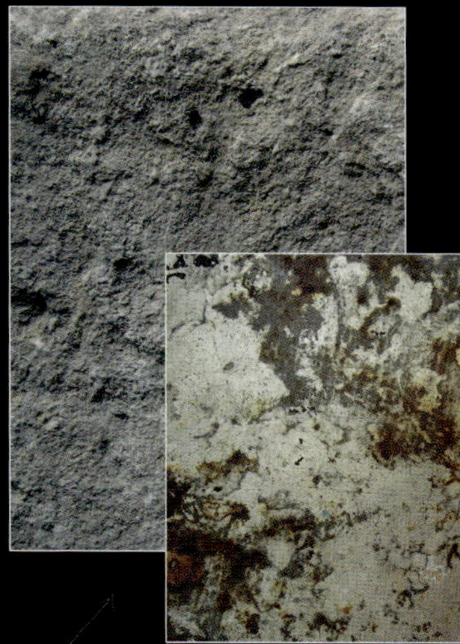

12 Texture overlays

Ever so slightly, I drop texture details from **http://texturez.com** across the different materials within the piece. With this Medusa design, much of the texture is already in the repeated plates of the snakes and her tail. However, I drop in even more texture as an Overlay layer set to a very low opacity, just to break up any artefacts of the digital brushes and to give a sense of texture to the whole piece.

PRO SECRETS

Experiment

When using multiple layers in one illustration, it's easy to fall into the trap of not wanting to alter details or layer placements because it would mean having to change all the layers. Sometimes, this can cause the overall composition to become a little stiff. Throughout the process, break out of complacency and occasionally flatten the image (perhaps in a separate file). Then play around and adjust the image, without fearing changes you can't undo. This allows to open-minded experimentation that will keep the piece constantly evolving.

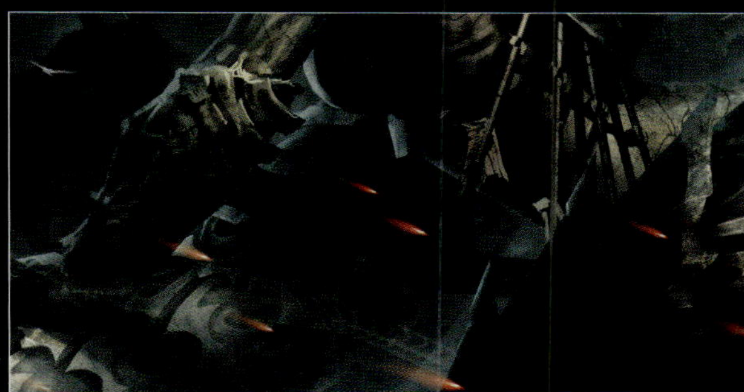

13 Motion and scale

As the image nears completion, it's time to add small hints of detail that give a sense of life, motion and scale to the final image. Indications of flying insects, blowing embers and wisps of smoke fill out the environment and remind the eye that we're looking at a mere moment of a larger story.

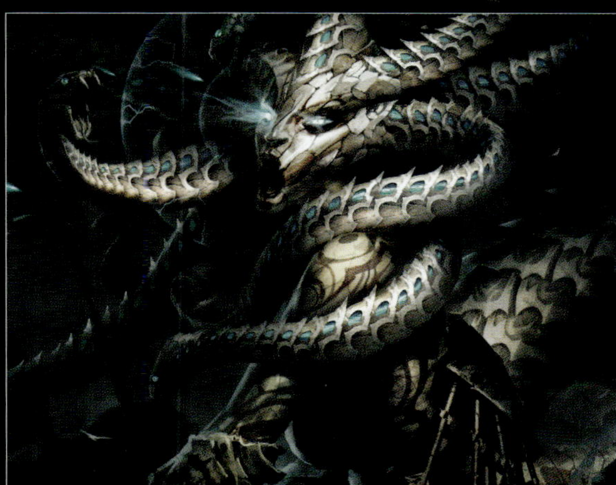

14 Final touches

Lastly, it's time to step back and add the finishing elements. I bring in accents of blue-green to the segments of her snakes, both to complement the rather monochromatic warm colouration and to connect her with the background. I add one more touch of culture by tattooing her skin with tribal patterns, which provides a sense of history and self-adornment. Medusa has survived as a symbol of fear in the deepest recesses of our psyches for millennia. It's an honour to provide an interpretation of a character so ancient and still so potent. I'm sure her deadly stare will continue to gaze deep into artists' imaginations for generations to come.

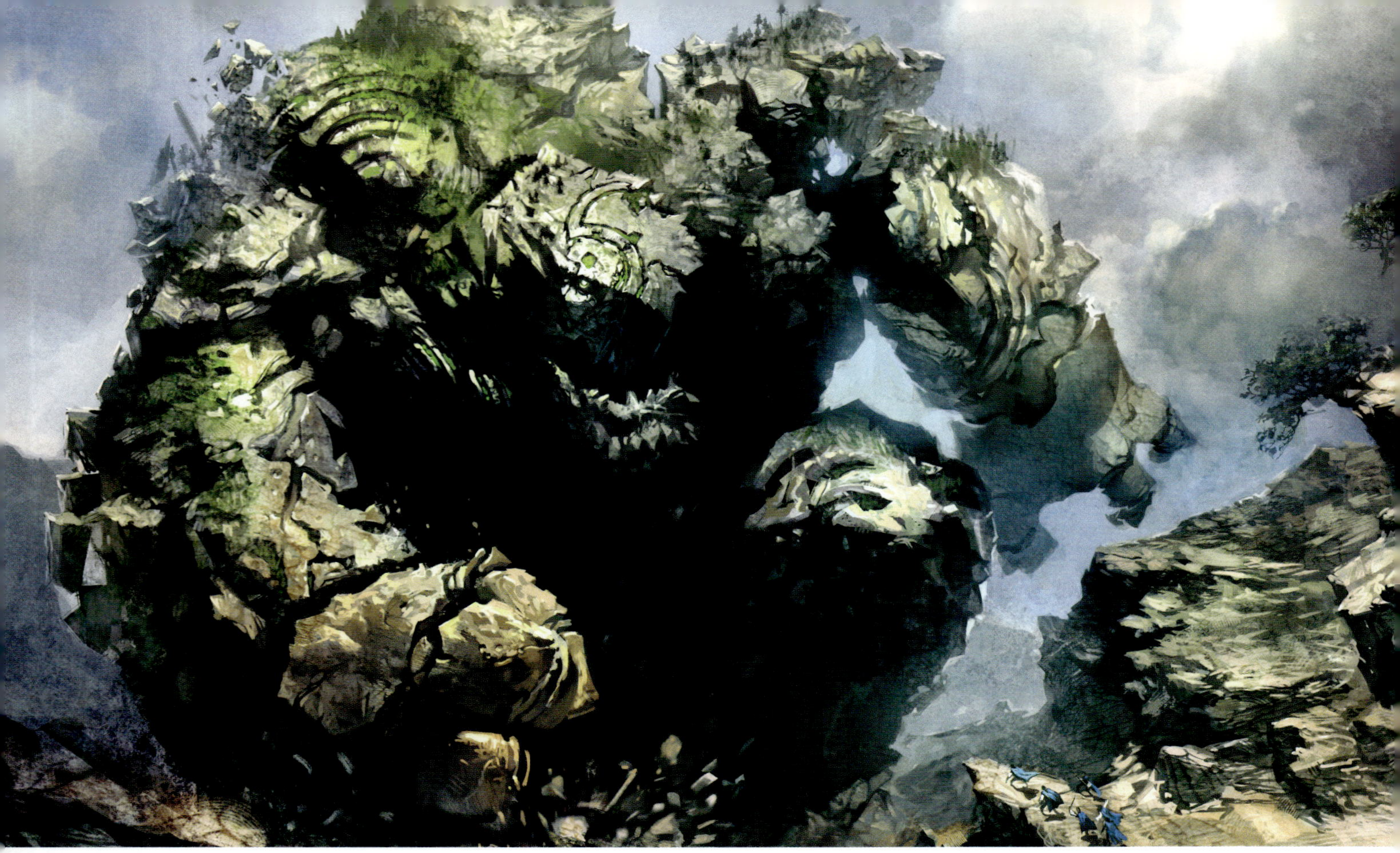

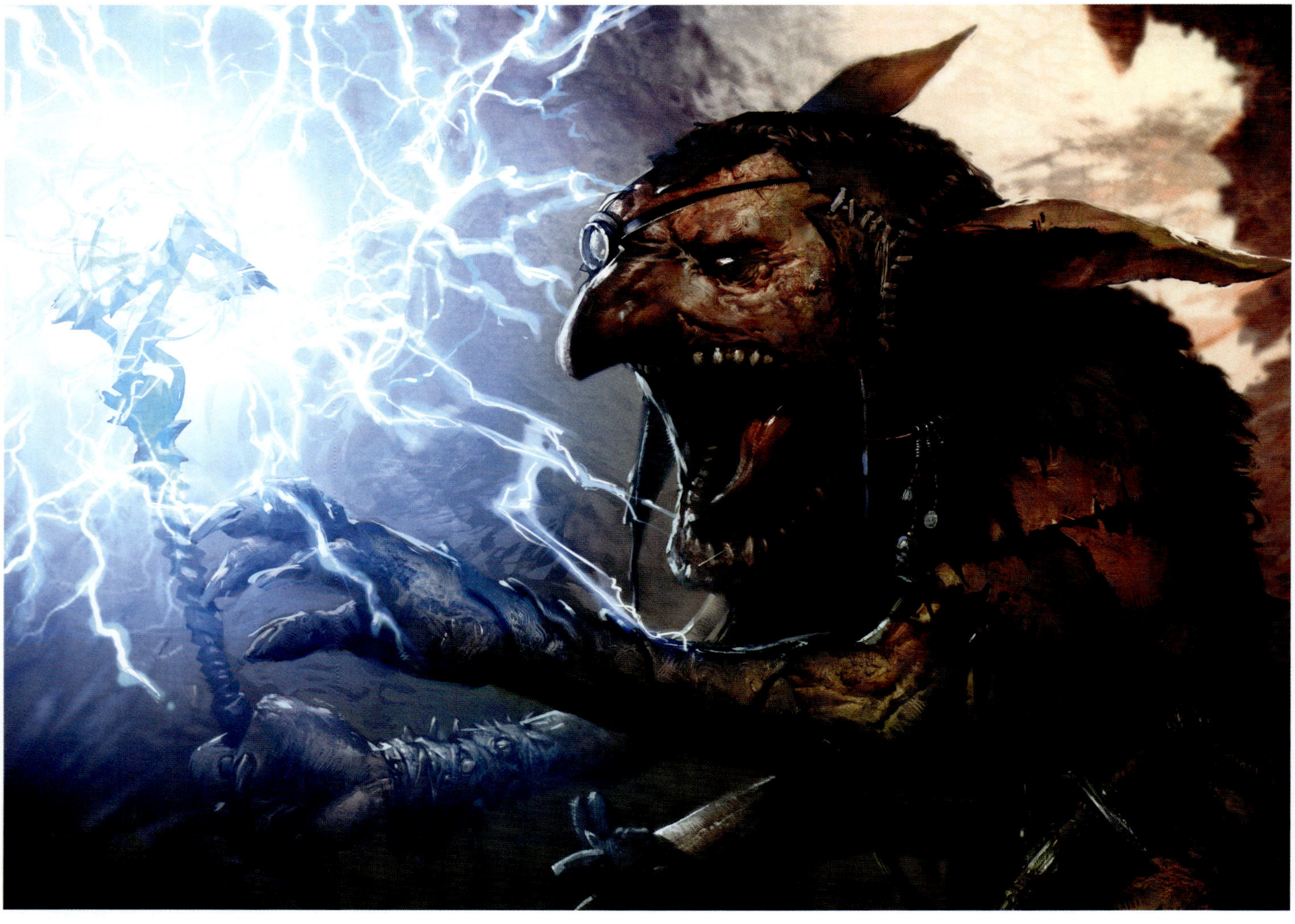

EARTH ELEMENTAL
Svetlin's subject matter has remained similar to when he started but his technique has developed. Looser shapes and lines as well as light tones prove powerful.

Interview

Svetlin Velinov

Illustrator, animator and comic artist, **Svetlin Velinov** uses dramatic colour and even more striking characters to convey the emotions behind his artwork

To those who instructed Svetlin Velinov in his formal art studies, the fact that he creates graphics on a computer is pure heresy. The 31-year-old Bulgarian artist, however, whose comic art and distinctive fantasy artwork has been wowing fans for years, now says that he uses nothing else.

"My professors, educated in the staunchly academic tradition, felt that painting is all about getting dirty with paint and materials," he says. "However, for good or for ill, I knew my own mind and followed my own path."

Instead of indulging in his early aptitude for painting and continuing his education at the National Academy of Arts, Svetlin chose instead to study animation in the New Bulgarian University in Sofia. It was here that he was exposed to then new digital techniques and discovered an enduring love for the comic art form. From the these early experiences Svetlin new where he wanted to take his career.

But, just like any other student, Svetlin needed to earn a living from his chosen path, so he found a job at one of the most prestigious advertising agencies in Sofia, where he worked for three years as their creative designer. These early years proved pivotal for the fresh artist.

Artist **PROFILE**

Svetlin Velinov

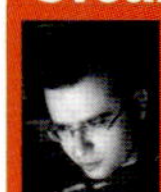

One of the most sort after fantasy artists currently working, Svetlin is the new breed of artist who has embraced digital techniques and isn't afraid to incorporate them into his workflow. With a client list that includes various video game companies as well as Wizards of the Coast, it doesn't seem as if Svetlin's star is going to wane any time soon

www.velinov.cgsociety.org

GETTING STARTED

"Over time, my interests expanded," he recalls. "I found myself drawn to fantasy illustrations, character design and concept design. The lively and dynamic drawing style, typical of the comic genre, impacted on my general approach to art and helped me build an individual graphic style."

In 2003, Svetlin quit his job and dedicated himself to drawing. He now works as a freelance artist, a role that enables him to work on a variety of projects.

Svetlin doesn't pretend that his background is grounded in the comic

BUG BOLTER
There's still room for some traditional goblins for trading card games in Svetlin's new and numerous freelance projects.

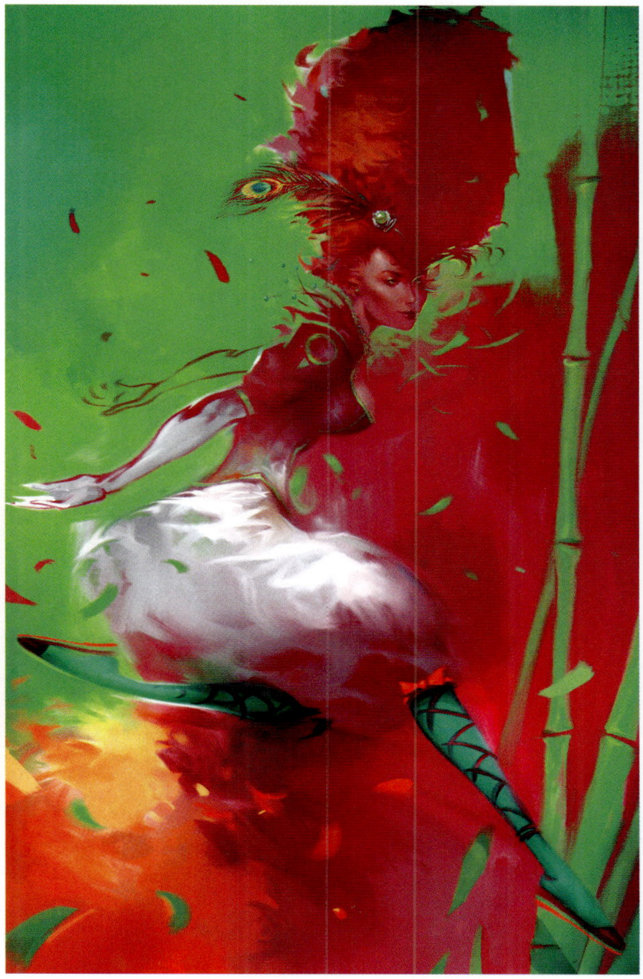

JUMP GODDESS
This personal project showcases Svetlin's eye-popping use of colour, it's quite different from his freelance work.

> "The lively and dynamic drawing style, typical of the comic genre, impacted on my approach to art"

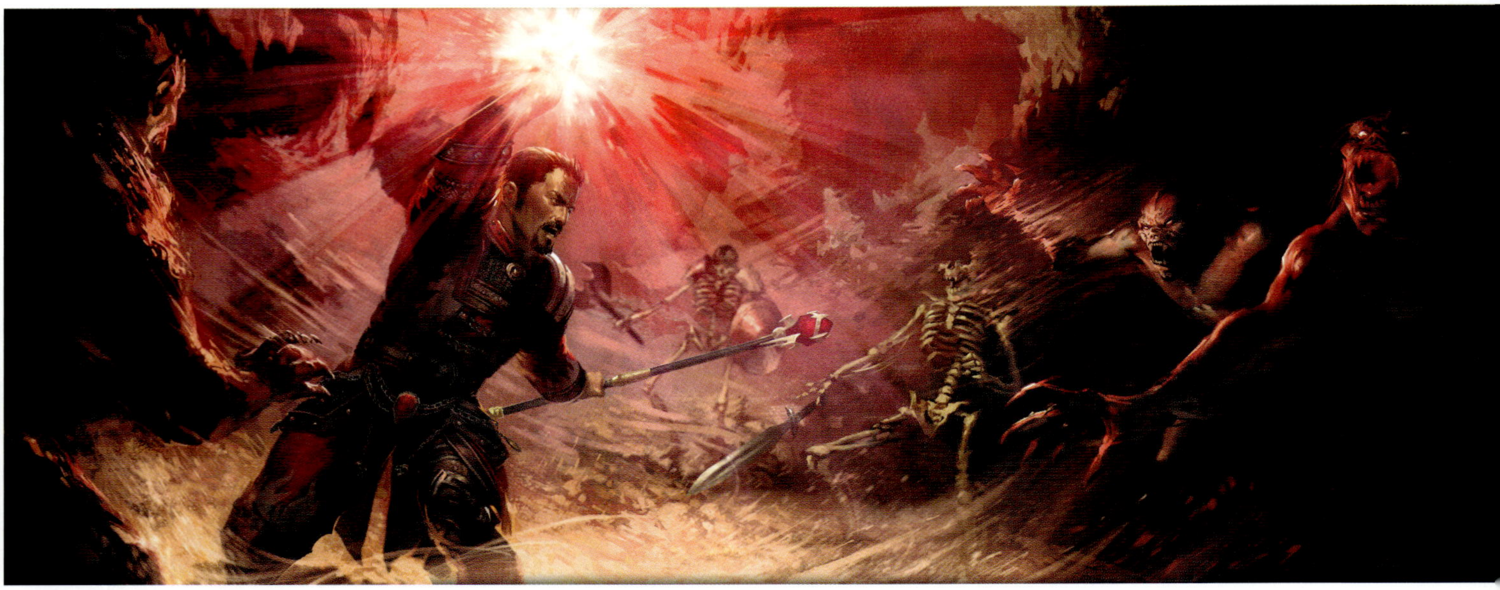

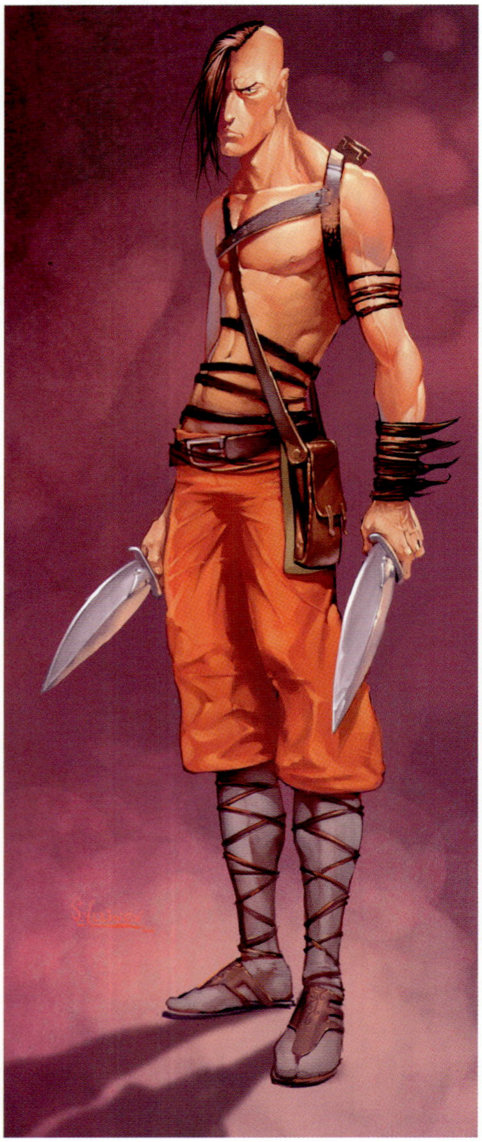

“To be really good at 3D art, it's not enough to just have talent. You need to think in a 3D way”

HELLBREED
Stunning use of colour and contrast highlight why Svetlin is one of the world's best new fantasy artists.

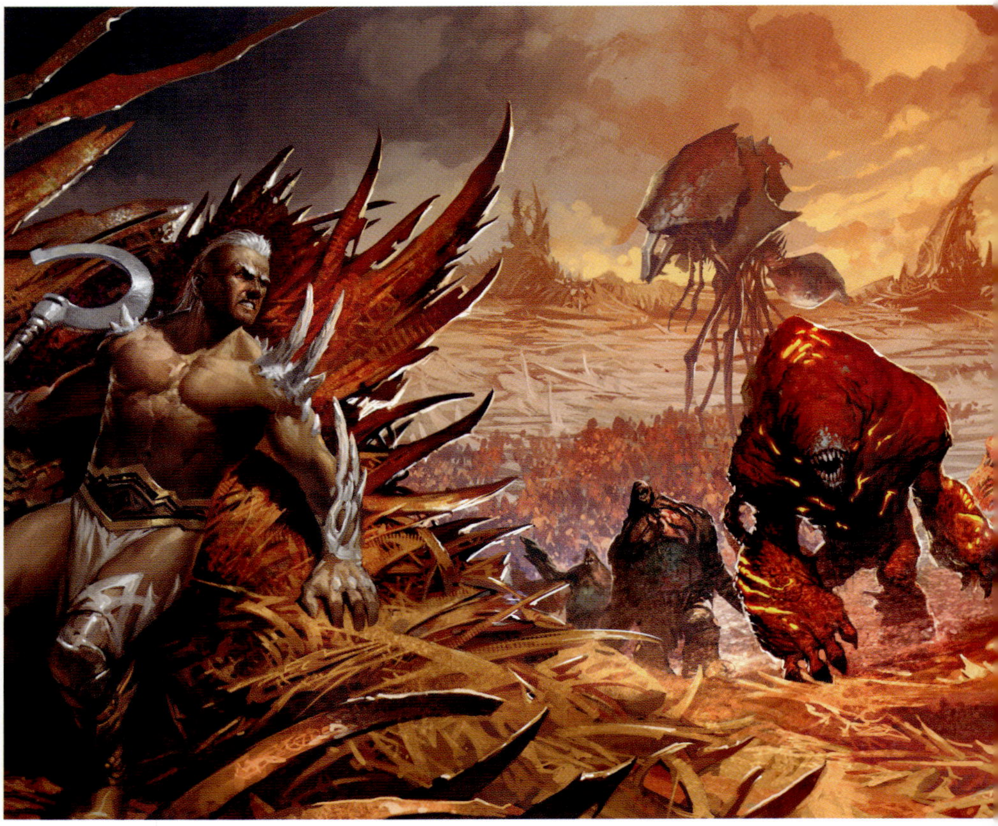

BONE KILLER
Though not created for any special project or client, the colours in this piece and the strong characterisation bear all the hallmarks of Svetlin's distinctive style.

UNCONTESTED INVASION
Overtures to the late, great Frank Frazetta in this beautiful new painting from Russia's Svetlin.

art and fantasy genres, rather he says he was influenced by the classicism of Bulgarian and Russian art. "Only when I discovered artists such as Luis Royo, Brom and Simon Bisley, did I decide I wanted to experiment in this aspect of painting," he explains.

Running concurrently with Svetlin's journey into the world of comic graphics was his departure from the analogue world of art production. "In time, I was totally turned off from using paper," he continues. "The scanner became useless. I now do everything with the computer."

DIGITAL MAN

For this digital approach, Svetlin prefers to use Photoshop. "This is the program I feel most comfortable using, and with which I feel I can best develop my artistic potential," he says. "I use Painter, too, but unlike Photoshop, my confidence with this program is much weaker, and so the environment feels less intuitive."

On the 3D side of things, Svetlin says he's a big fan of ZBrush. "I really fell in love with this software," he says. "To be really good at 3D art, it's not enough to just have talent. You need to think in a 3D way. That's why there are so few artists who are really good at both 2D and 3D art. ZBrush provides the 2D artist with an accessible way to get in touch with this 'unknown domain' and really takes the fear factor out of manipulating 3D objects."

THE PROCESS

After taking the plunge and going freelance, Svetlin honed his style and improved his drawing techniques. He says it's difficult to generalise when describing how he creates his unique artwork, however, he reveals the basics: "I begin by roughly sketching with the brush."My approach depends on whether I have a concrete idea or I'm just looking for an outline or another form to provide inspiration. After the rough sketch, I try to clear up the composition, working on specific sections. I lighten and flesh out the dark silhouette, then set the form in stone, designing the character and background, and further developing the colour. Applying the right lighting is very important in my pictures. It gives life to the drawing and creates the necessary ambience. Then comes the fine detailing stage and the addition of any important accent colours."

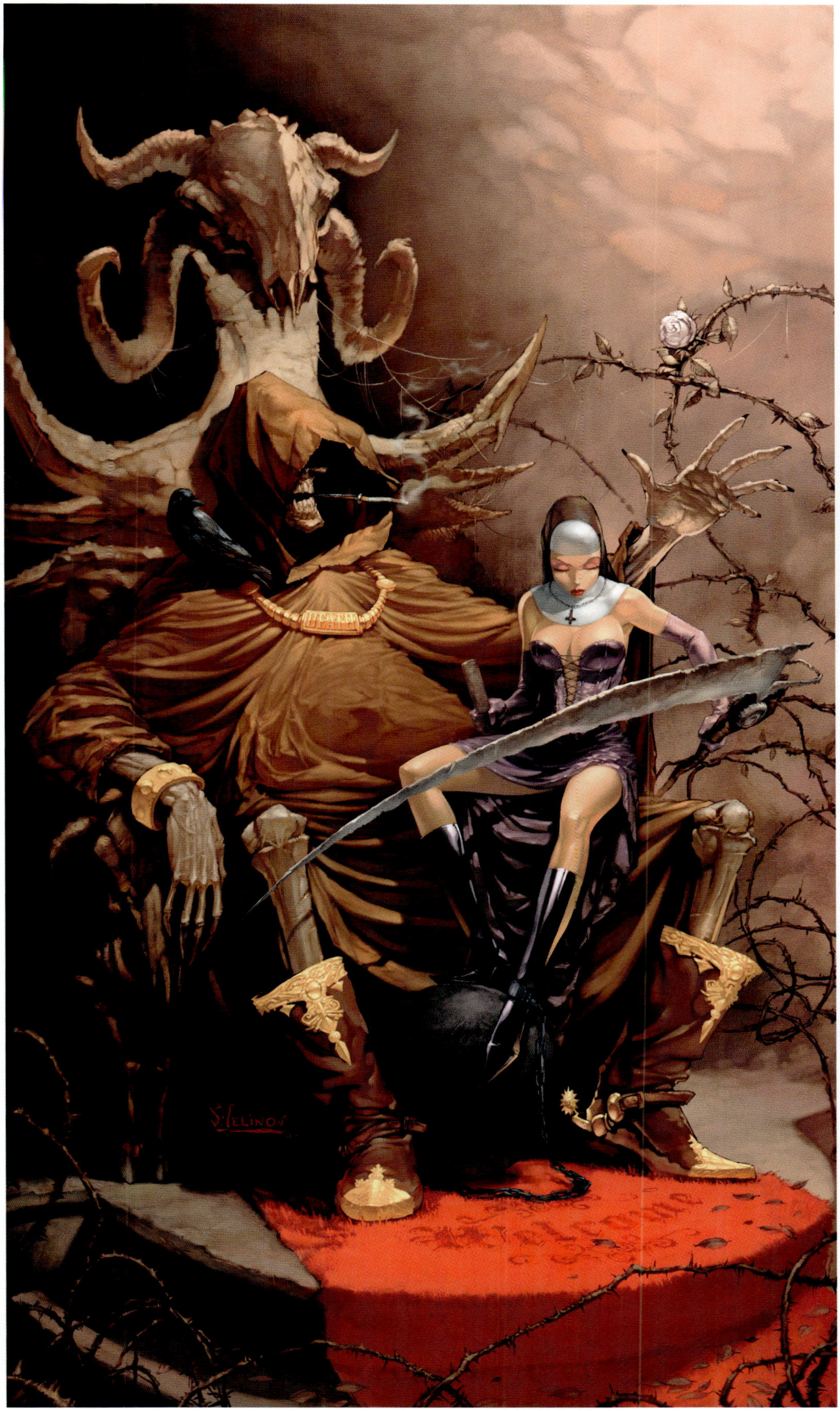

MASTER AND SERVANT

One of Svetlin's favourite pictures, this was created for his participation in a CGTalk competition. "Could there be the slightest hint of love between these characters, or are they are damned to be master and servant?" he says.

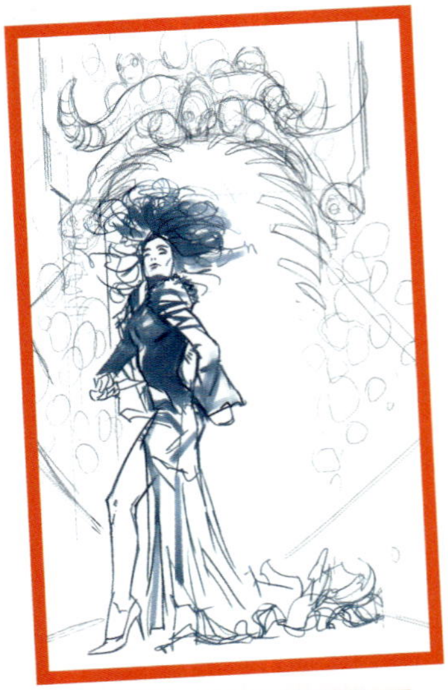

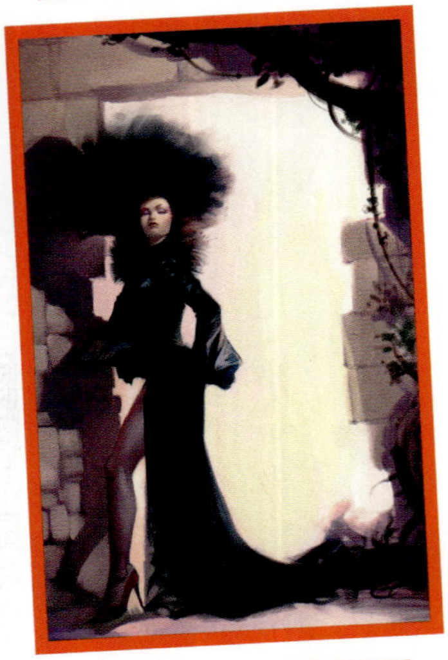

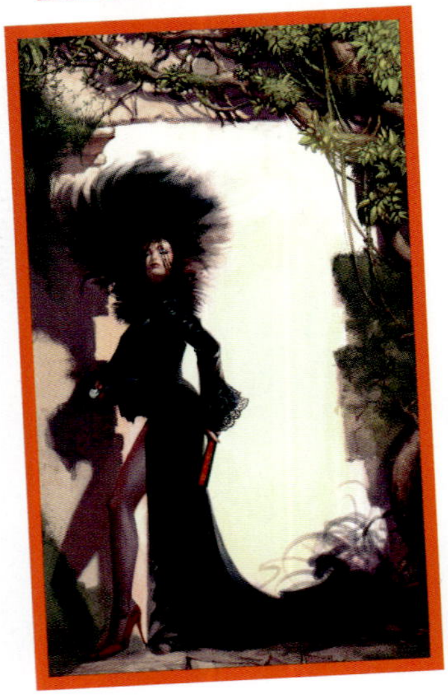

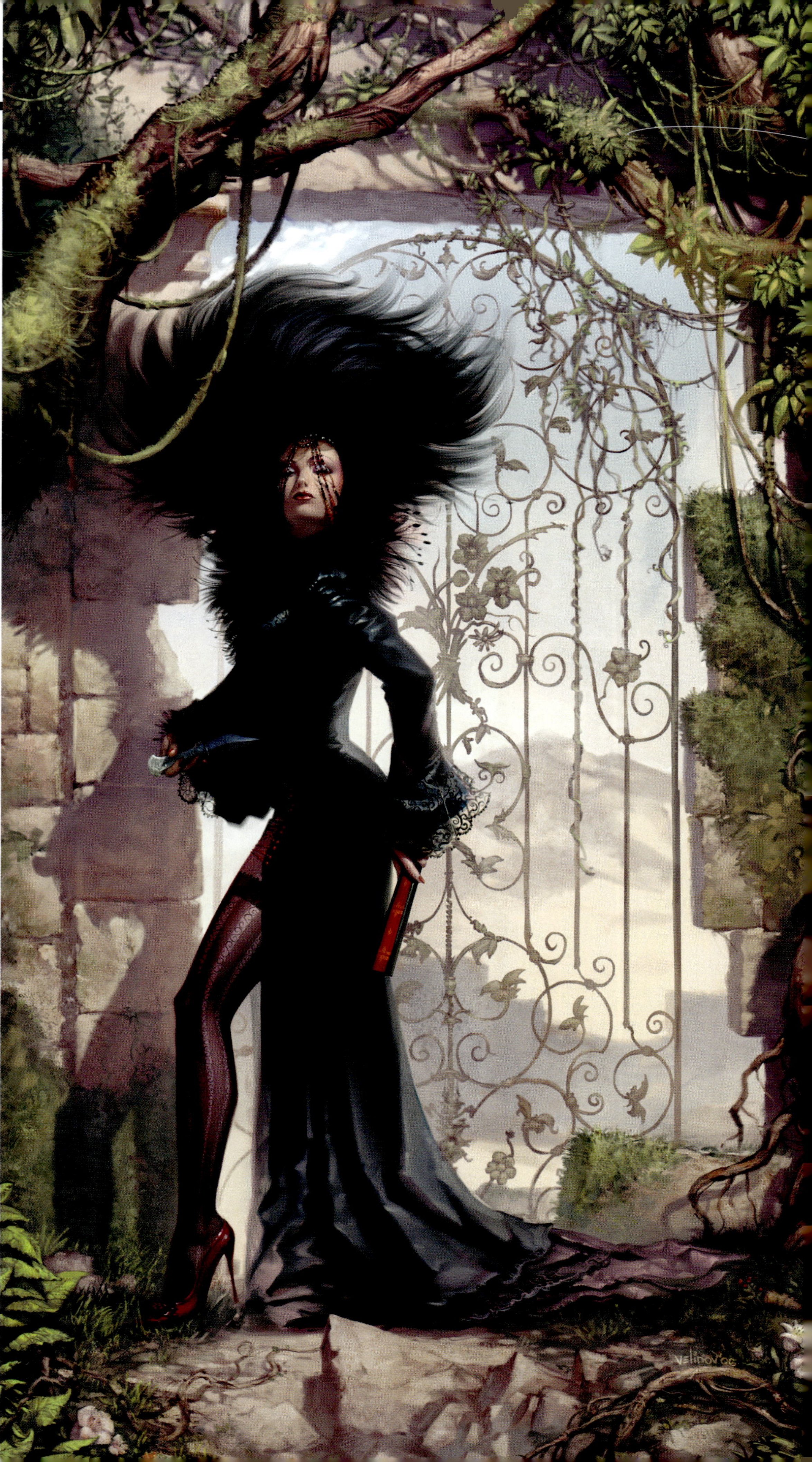

SOUL DANCER:
Svetlin's greatest achievement: "If I had to describe my art, I'd say it is a mess of vibrant feelings, full of pain thoughts and suicidal happiness, and that all is The Soul Dancer."

SOUL DANCER

Svetlin looks deep into the character

"I've always wanted to create a picture with a deeper and enduring feeling," says Svetlin. "I hope that with this one I've conveyed the hidden emotions under the heroine's haughty mask. I wanted people to understand the loneliness of her solitary reign in this 'lost world' kingdom and the hidden despair on her stony face."

Svetlin started with a rough drawing and explored some ideas for the setting.

"I wanted to show contrast between the character and the background using colours, and also conveying contrasting ideas, such as good and bad, life and death," he explains. "The demonic door symbolised a lost soul. The knife in her hand is the link with the dead. The entry door leads to her ultimate salvation, though what's hidden behind this door may be worse than before."

The next step changed the whole concept and idea behind the piece. Svetlin decided to express contrast through the internal conflict of the character. "I used the fan as a link with life, a counterbalance to the deathly radiation of the character," he says. "I decided to replace the demonic door with a neutral environment. I now wanted the background to be melancholic, a place where time has no meaning, it's just waiting to be rediscovered."

The last step was to pull everything together. "This was the key moment where I harmonised and balanced the whole drawing," says Svetlin. "There were many 'busy' areas that I had to calm so that important accent colours could emerge. I scattered the plants and gave the environment a much more intense feeling.

"The loftiness of the character and the sense of superiority was the best way to show that behind this stone mask, which lacks emotion, there's a desperate and hurt, but also a strong and definite, woman."

Svetlin isn't sure that he achieved his initial goal with Soul Dancer, but says it's enough if it manages to provoke some feeling and emotion in the viewer.

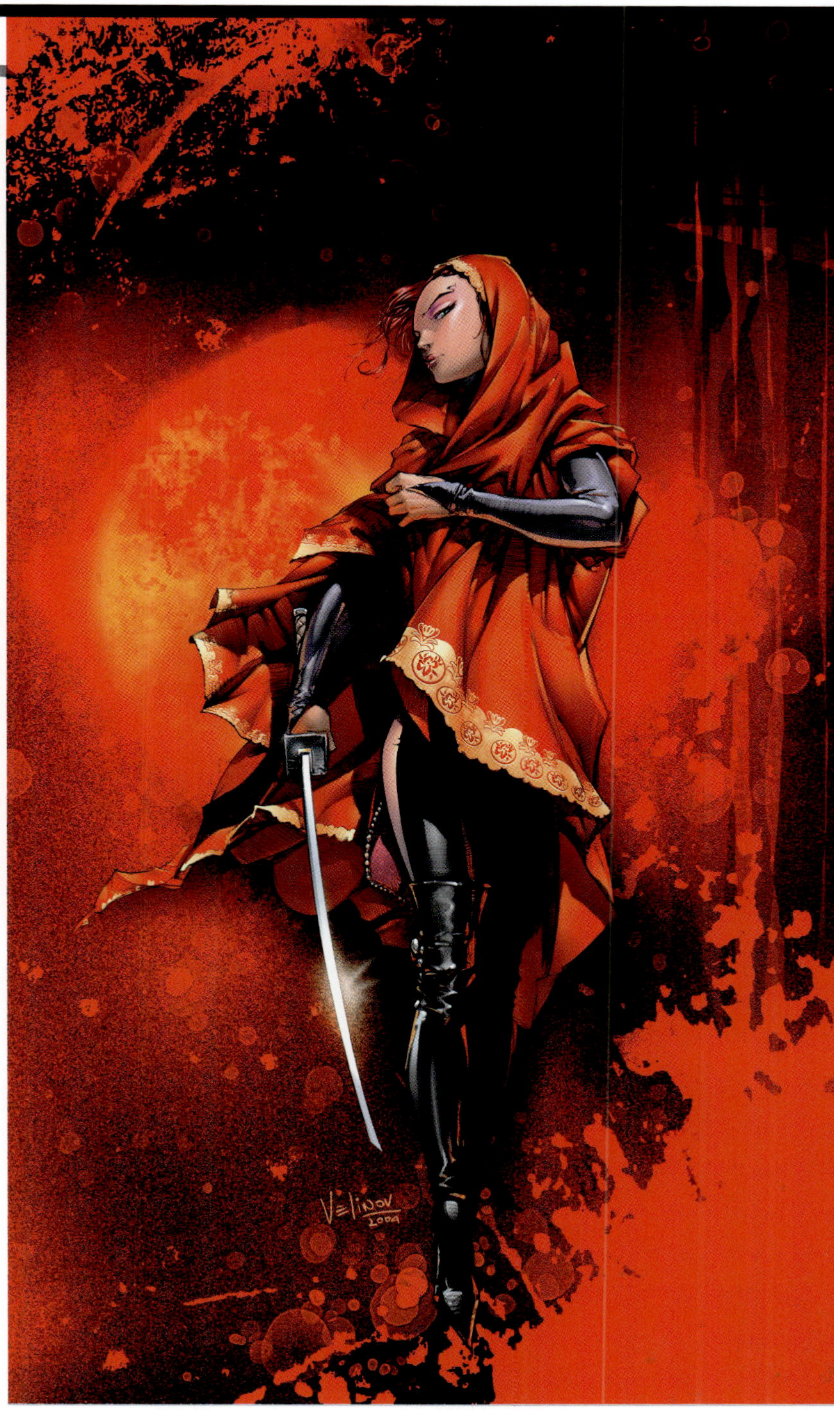

RED MOON
"This was created when I worked as a designer," says Svetlin. "I didn't expect the impact this illustration would have on my development as an artist. Maybe this piece marks the beginning of the dream."

Red Moon was the first piece of work that Svetlin published online, at the CGTalk forum. It garnered huge interest and received good feedback. "I know that the forums aren't objective enough and one can often receive praise," he says. "However, this feedback made me believe in my capabilities and my potential. It made me look seriously at becoming a digital artist."

In the early days Svetlin says his biggest challenge was his time spent working on the environmental concept work for video game Death Jr. 2 by Konami. "This was probably my first brush with the professional market and it defined my working style," he reveals. "It taught me a lot and made me more disciplined, because I had to be exact and work to a tight deadline. I succeeded because I just couldn't afford to fail."

During the last few years Svetlin;s career has taken off dramarically. he has worked on illustrations for leading products such as Warhammer 40K and Warmachine. "The work on the projects was a real challenge, but fun," he says. Since then Svetlin has worked on a video game project for the Nintendo DS and a character concept for an MMO video game. He has also become a regular World of Warcraft illustrator and worked with Darkhorse on one of their editions."

"I have a stimulating and interesting work schedule, which provides me with real pleasure and satisfaction," he says.

Since his early success Svetlin has gone on to refine his digital art, creating more stylised images and experimenting with the toolset. In 2009 Svetlin created a series of impressive digital paintings for the Facebook App Castle Age.

> "In the future, I hope to produce a book showcasing the best of my work"

At the same time Svetlin has become a regular illustrator for Wizards of the Coast, creating card art and illustrations for Magic the Gathering, with his recent illustrations for the Scars of Mirrodin game set showcasing his skills.

That's not to say Sevtlin is content just yet. "In the future, I hope to produce a book showcasing the best of my work and including previously unseen artwork," says the artist. We can't wait to see what else this artist has to offer.

Photoshop

CREATE A CLASSIC FANTASY SCENE

Svetlin Velinov takes staple fantasy ingredients – a band of heroes, an evil lair and an unspeakable horror – and brings them to life with ease...

The starting point of every illustration is the story, which needs to be told as objectively and clearly as possible. In this case, it's a timeless fantasy scene, which made choosing what to draw fairly easy. I took the classic ingredients – a pretty and gutsy heroine, her trustworthy companions and a stalking, insidious evil – and combined them in an exciting setting.

At first glance, the beast has the advantage, hiding in the darkness of its lair, preparing for a surprise attack. However, the selflessness and strength of the heroes should enable them to gain the upper hand – unless one of them makes a mistake. I try to emphasise the calm moments before the storm when I put the characters in an environment. For example, the danger present in the dark cave contrasts against the light from the outside world, which is mirrored in the brave hearts of the three friends as they prepare to confront their adversary.

Because it's a classic approach to the subject that's been done countless times, I attempt to inject suspense into the story. The struggle between good and evil is an ambiguous affair and it's the shades of storytelling in a painting that catch the viewer's eye. After all, he or she may not always side with the forces of good...

ImagineFX VIDEO WORKSHOP ON THE DVD

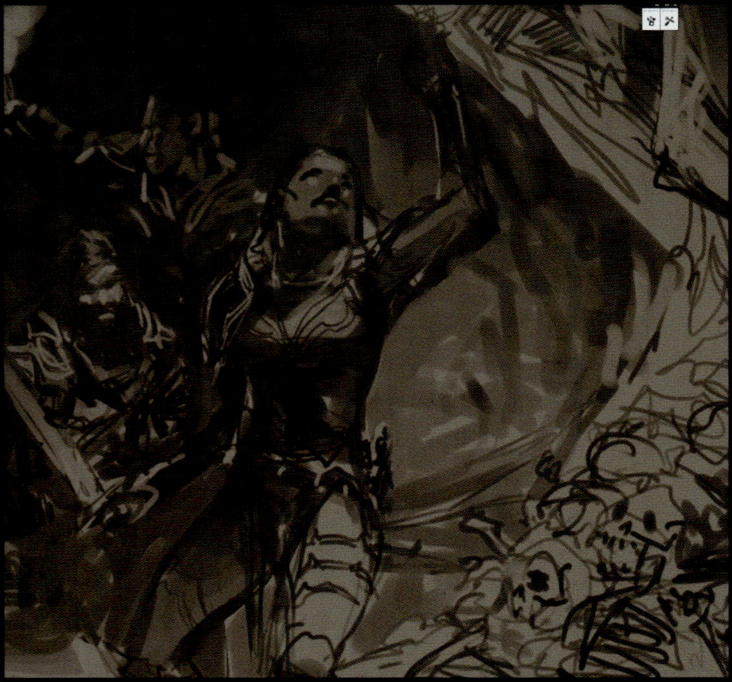

1 Covering the basics

I do a quick sketch that enables me to check that the concept and composition are clear. There's no need to make it a detailed drawing. Many artists do an intricate sketch – an accomplished drawing in its own right – only to overpaint it later on.

PRO SECRETS

Quick colours

Once you've created a monochrome image, you can easily select the tone you want to work with using the Colour Range option. Furthermore, use the slider to define the range of undertone colours. This is useful when you're colouring or overpainting.

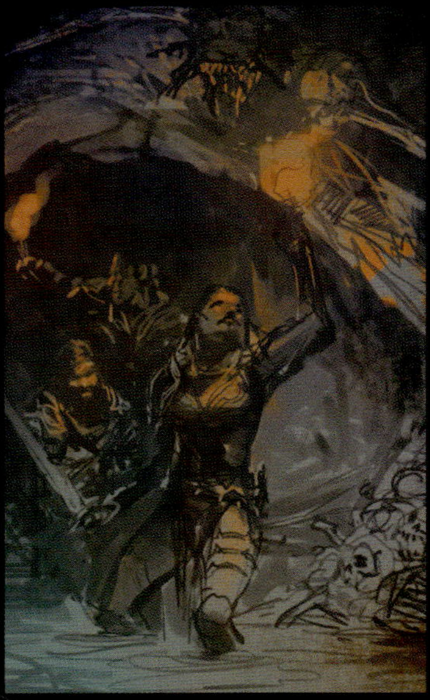

2 Colour choice

The right colour scheme will support the mood, content and ideas of the drawing, so it's crucial to sort this out sooner rather than later. I mark the various areas of colour on a new layer, set to Color mode, and regularly refer to this until the painting is complete.

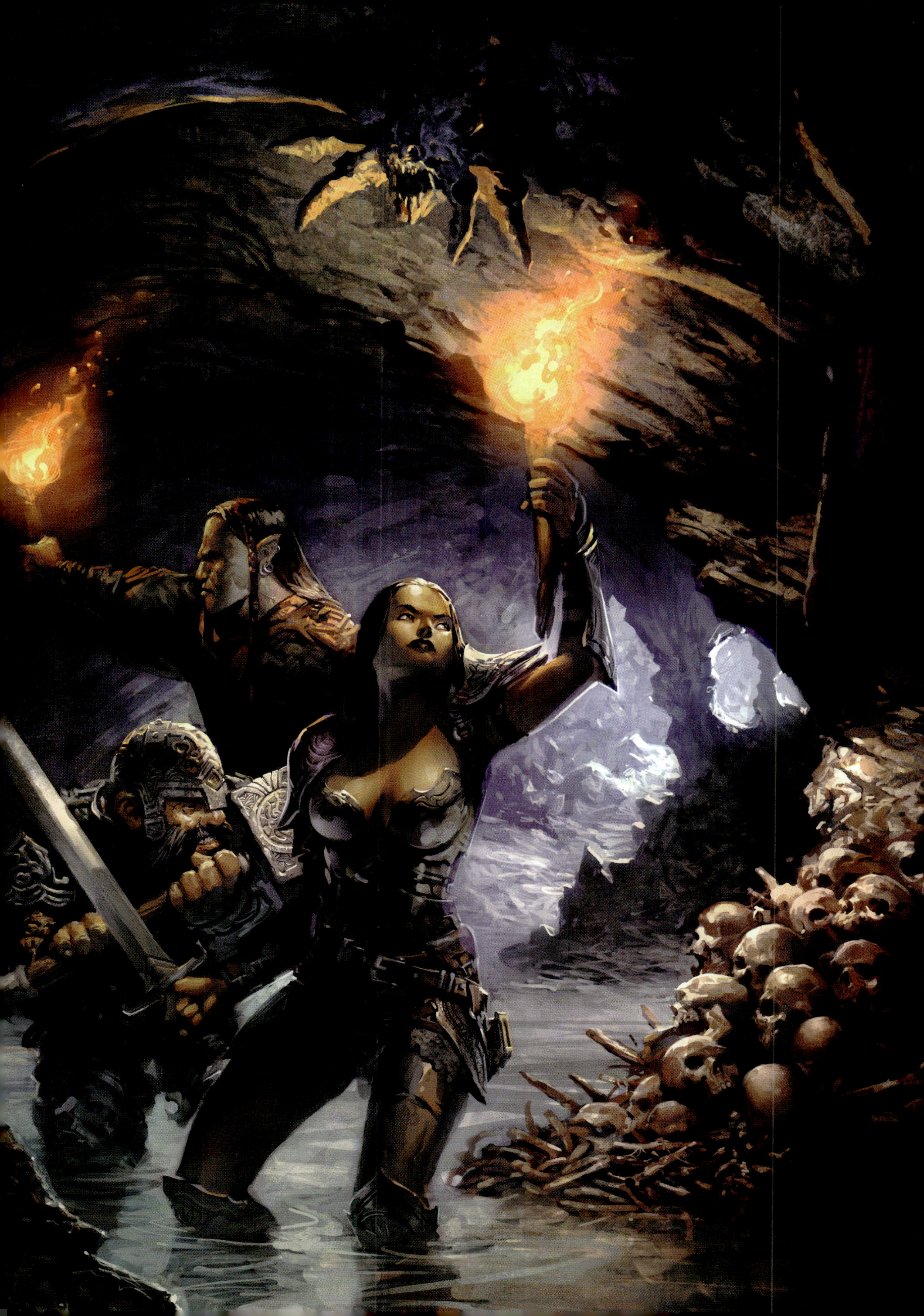

Shortcuts
Quick invert
Shift+Ctrl+I (PC)
Shift+Cmd+I (Mac)
Invert your selection, handy for separating a subject from its background.

3 Laying the foundations

I develop the colour scheme further at this stage, and add more details to the scene, making corrections to the figure and environment where necessary. Everything's now in place for me to start work on the painting in greater detail. If I find myself deviating from the foundations that I've laid here, then something's gone wrong!

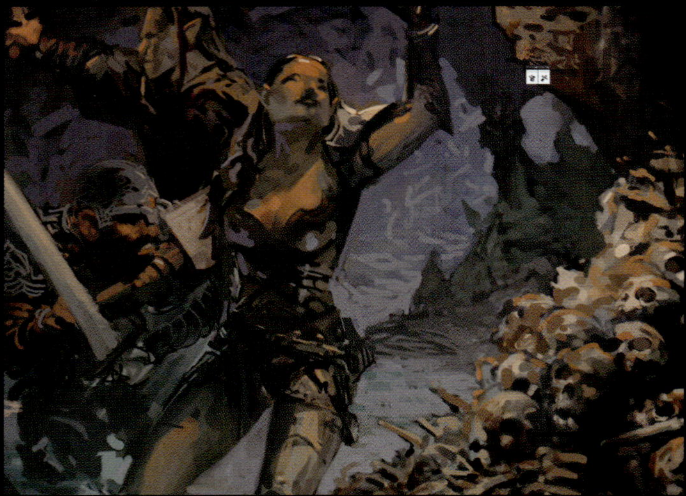

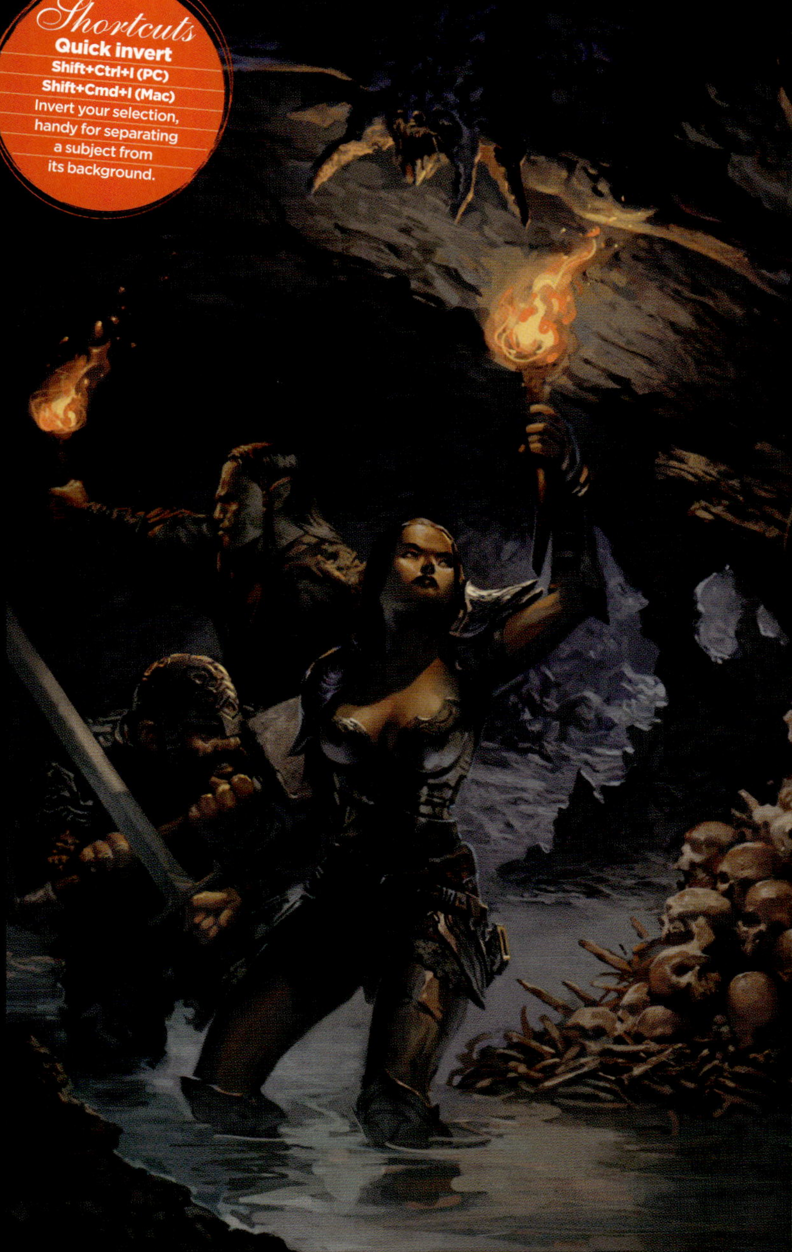

PRO SECRETS

Brush sizes
If you use a Wacom Intuos 3 or 4 tablet, the touch pad can be used to control the size of the brush. You can set this feature up in the tablet's control panel.

4 Colour values and light sources

Next, I create a Multiply Layer and start drawing in it, while determining what the lighter areas of the composition would be, based on where the various light sources are, such as the entrance to the cave. Once this important step is out of the way, then the real work on the illustration can begin.

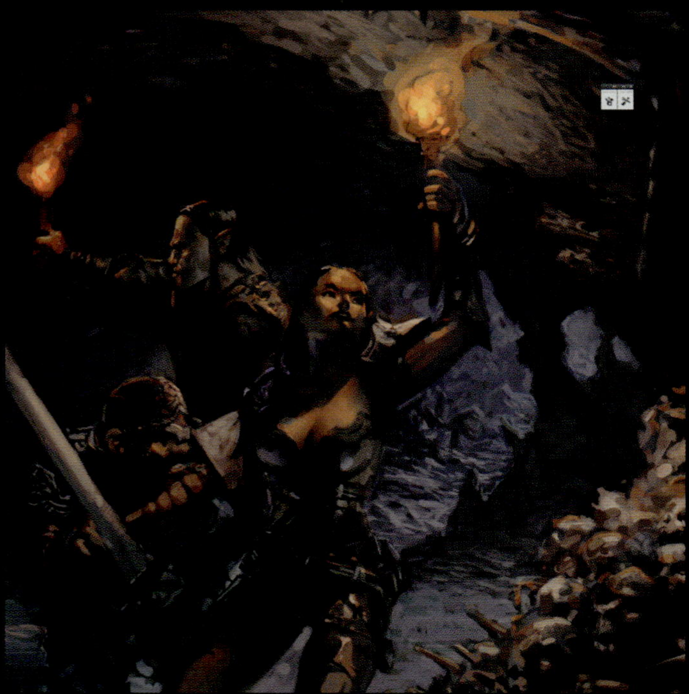

5 Overpaint the image

The painting's elements are defined and its concept as a whole is evident. Although there's a lack of detail, a clear message is sent to the viewer: "You're looking at a critical moment in a classic fantasy adventure." It now needs me to strengthen and focus the visual script. I start by overpainting the elements to create the necessary emphasis.

6 Refining the details

This is my favourite stage; it's like putting the cherry on the cake. Skipping this bit would result in a perfectly acceptable painting, but there would be a sense of incompleteness. It's now that I have fun defining the character of the three heroes by embellishing their armour and weapons, as well as this, I'm improving the figure detail in general.

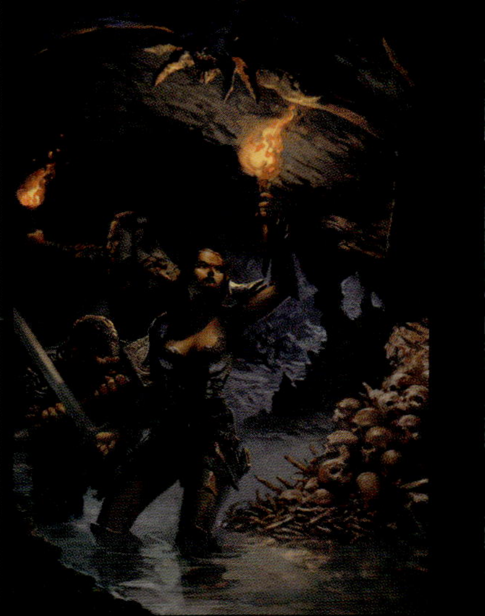

7 Define the surfaces

I can use one of two methods to make the surfaces of the environment look more realistic. I could apply a Gaussian blur, or alternatively use different colours. In the latter case, I can apply a sense of warmth and cold, and add appropriate colours to the foreground and background. This helps to convey the idea that our small band of heroes is the only source of heat in an otherwise chilly, waterlogged cave system.

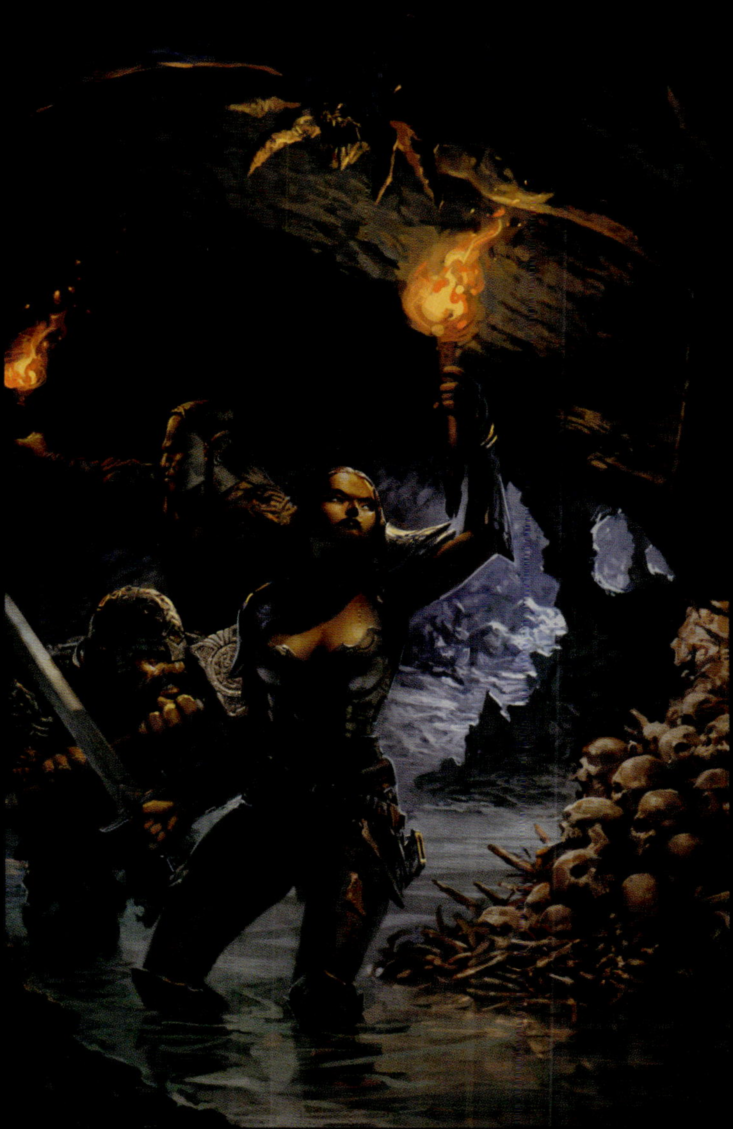

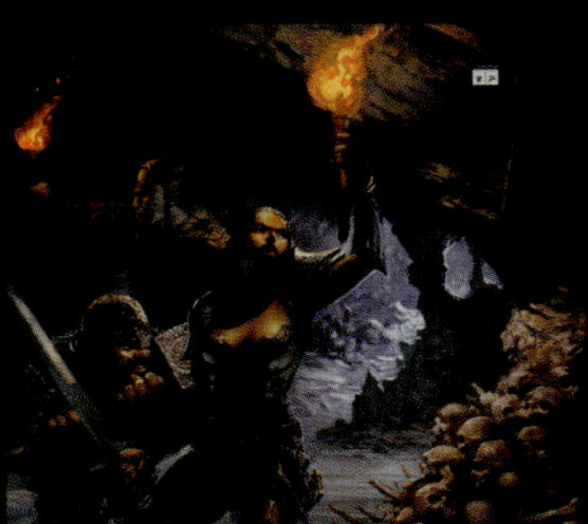

8 Add some subtle textures

Applying textures is usually an important stage in my work. However, in this particular painting, there was no need to go overboard on textures. In order to add substance and completeness to the various objects in the composition, I have used some textures, but these are barely noticeable. I've added a subtle degree of noise, as well as some gentle textures on the rocks.

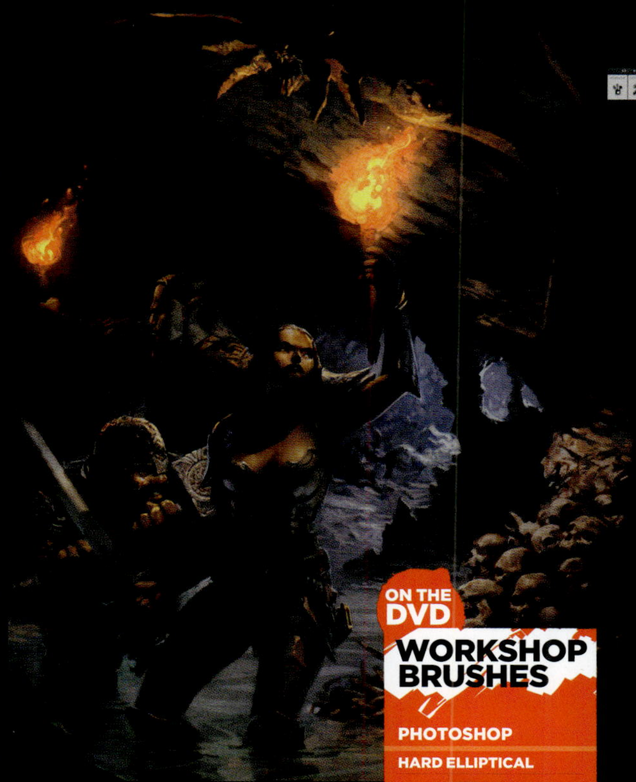

9 Tweaking the lighting

As a finishing stage, I shape and emphasise the light sources. I achieve the glow with the help of a layer set to Linear Dodge. There's light coming from the outside through the cave's entrance and into the monster's lair. It's a metaphor of good versus evil, maintained through the heroes' torches, which are ready to cast light on and defeat any malevolent entity lurking in the darkness.

10 Correcting colour

The last stage of this workshop involves using several Adjustment Layers. With these, I strengthen the contrast by controlling the intensity of the changes with the help of Layer Masks.

ON THE DVD

WORKSHOP BRUSHES

PHOTOSHOP

HARD ELLIPTICAL

HARD ROUND

PLASTIC WRAP

ROCKY

SAMPLED TIPS

These are the brushes that Svetlin used to create this scene. Find them in the Workshop folder on the DVD.

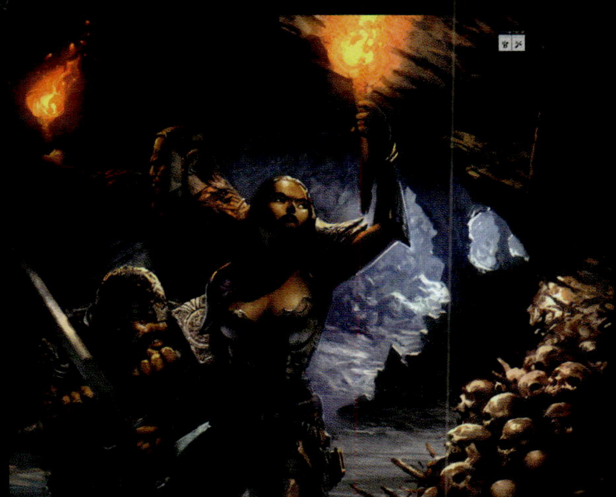

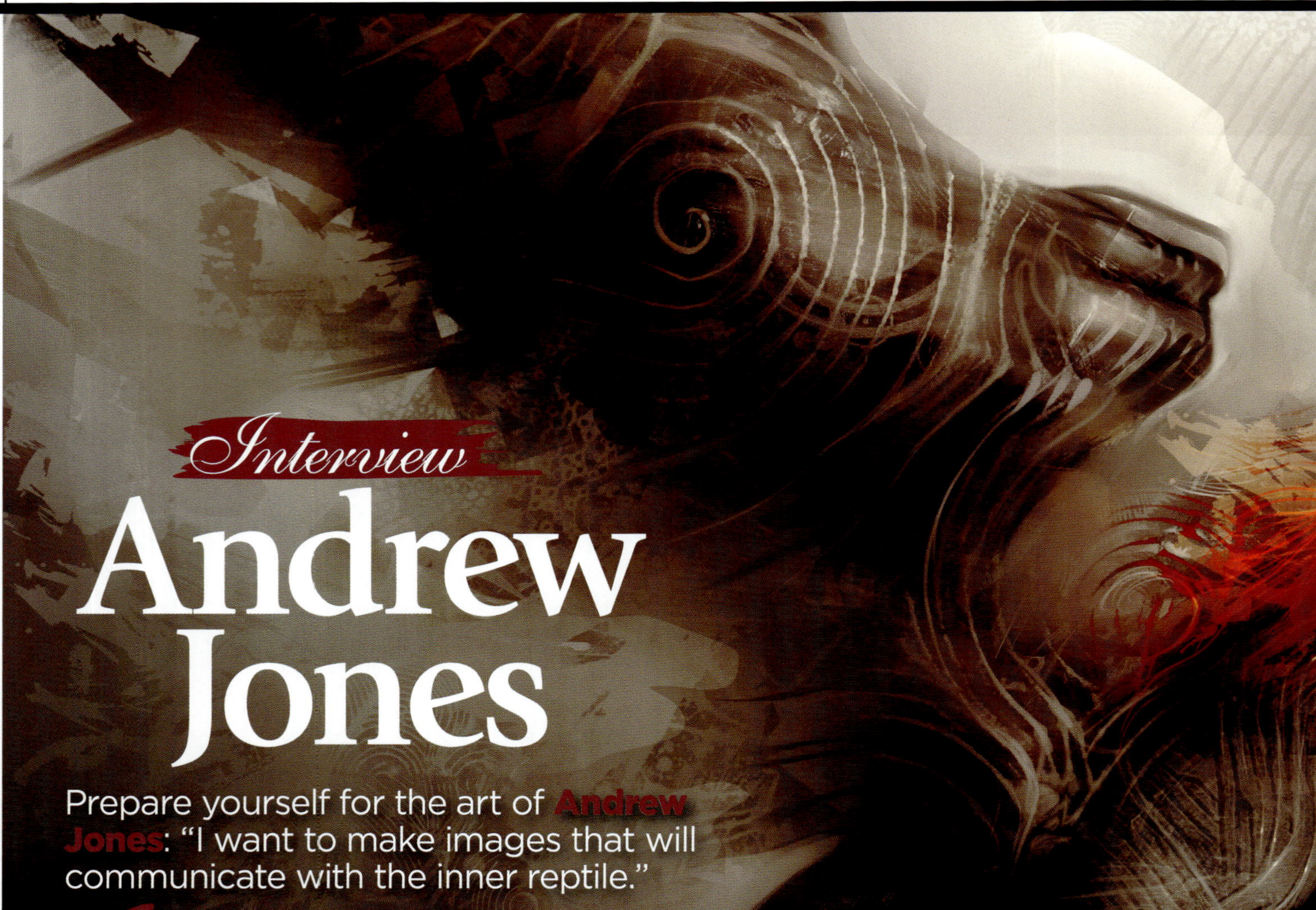

Interview

Andrew Jones

Prepare yourself for the art of Andrew Jones: "I want to make images that will communicate with the inner reptile."

As the co-founder of ConceptArt.org and Massive Black, concept artist for Metroid Prime and a former employee of ILM (Industrial Light & Magic), Andrew Jones is finely tuned to the dark emanations of the human spirit. This comes through even in the description of his hometown: "Boulder has a deeply nurturing energy," he begins, nicely enough. "However, as with all unsurpassed beauty, there is a dark side. Boulder is a vortex of souls."

You see, when white men first arrived in Boulder, Colorado, they were looking for gold. The people who lived there quickly realised they were in harm's way and that nothing good was going to come of the face-off. "They were Southern Arapaho warriors under Chief Niwot," explains Andrew. "Chief Niwot and his brave warriors were forced from the home they loved and, avoiding bloodshed, left in peace."

You can understand why Niwot cursed the valley as he left. "People see the beauty of this valley and want to stay, and their staying will be the undoing of that beauty." And Andrew has personal experience of the former: "I'm a third-generation Boulderite. It has always been my intention to return to that beautiful valley and spend my last days there," he tells us. It's a pretty morbid form of homesickness.

Artist **PROFILE**

Andrew Jones

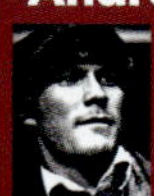

North American-based, internationally recognised conceptual and digital artist. One of the co-founders of ConceptArt.org and Massive Black. Andrew travels the world performing live digital art and teaching workshops.

www.androidjones.com

WALKABOUT

"I've searched the globe for places and communities that inspire me," says Andrew. "It took me almost a decade to finally discover a place and community that exceeded all expectations." The wandering halted, for a while at least, in the Nevada desert. Andrew's current spiritual home is the Burning Man project, an annual festival held at a temporary town in the middle of the Black Rock desert. The week-long event, which celebrates all forms of creative expression, attracts more than 35,000 people from around the world.

UNICORN OF THE APOCALYPSE
This image was created to herald the Montréal Massive Black/ConceptArt.org workshop.

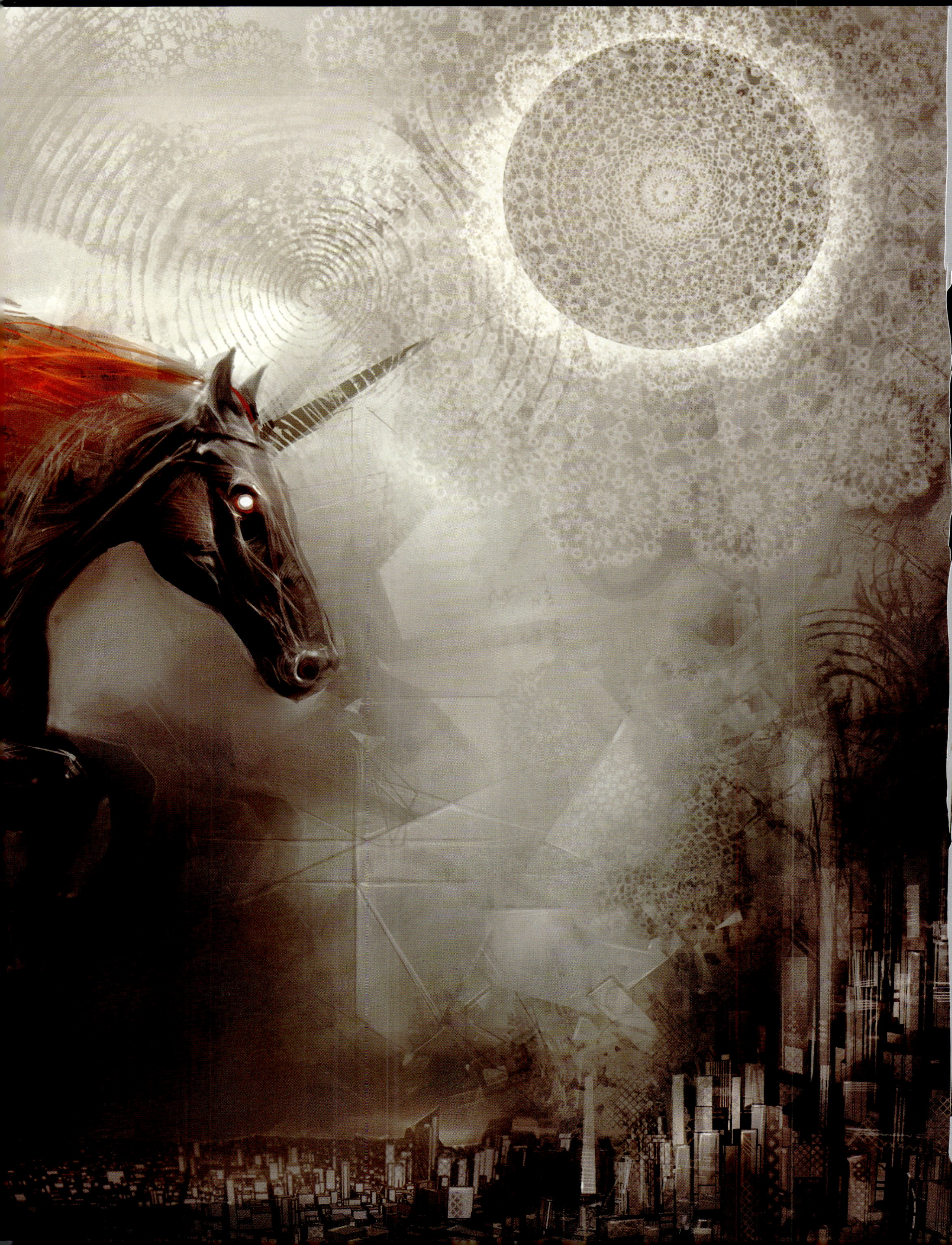

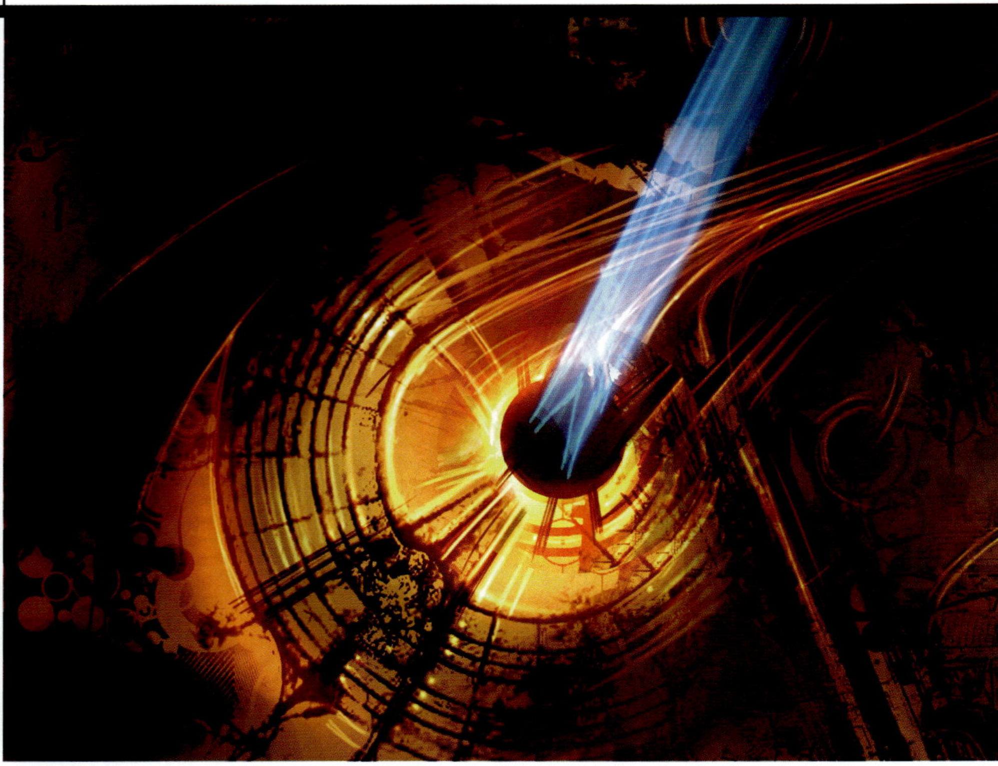

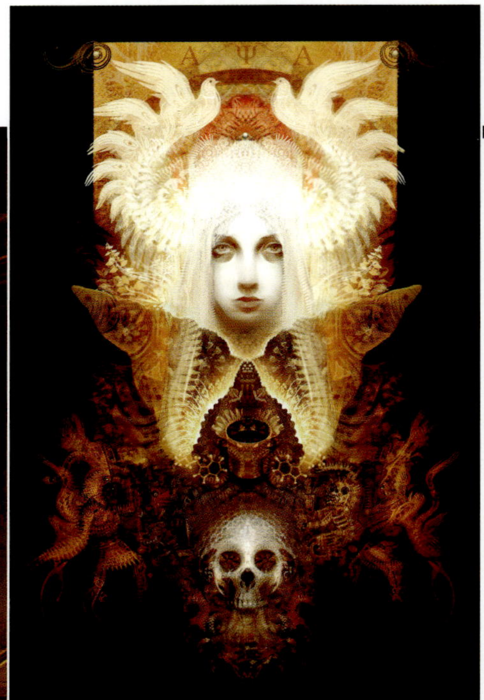

DIVINE AWAKENING
Andrew uses all sorts of meditation techniques to dig deep into his imagination, including a eye-opening visit to Peru to where he took part in esoteric tourism.

PLAYA ACTIVATED
This is how Burning Man's Black Rock city looks from Andrew's astral body.

No cash transactions are allowed and, in theory at least, no spectators – everyone is expected to take part. On the last night, they burn a giant wooden effigy.

Andrew recommends that everybody does something such as this to avoid becoming just a statistic. "Take time for yourselves, go on a vision-quest deep into the desert, talk to God and interact with the divine." And if you still can't find nuomenal transcendence, at least you had a go. "I don't claim to know what reality is but I know that it's not what most of us believe it to be."

THE DREAM MANIFESTATION GIG

"Art knew that it was going to be me, before I knew I was going to be an artist." Art, you see, is more than its name – and Andrew asks us to remember that. Art is just a three-letter word, a poor label for the thing itself. "I wish art didn't have a name, so every time we look at a painting we could see it with unjaded eyes," he says. "Words can really strip away all the inherent magic in an object."

> "Sometimes I think an unconscious part of me sabotages my life to create the drama that will fuel a new painting"

Andrew was always going to be an artist. "I was drawing and painting before I ever knew what art was," he recalls. His parents were painters, and his childhood scribbles quickly caused a stir, culminating in Andrew studying art in Florida. After that he walked the earth as a street portrait artist. He enjoyed it so much that, "If it wasn't for my student loans, we wouldn't be doing this interview and I would be covered in red chalk right about now." But that was before he got into what he calls, "the active nightmare and dream manifestation gig."

Fantasy, he says, was a natural progression for an artist looking for a challenge, "when everything else started to look really boring." But then he thinks better of his explanation: "Actually, everything in life can be fantastic." It's just a question of looking properly and that, after all, is the job of the artist.

METROID RECLAIMED

Andrew was introduced to Metroid Prime aged just 11: "I discovered that game after undergoing cataclysmic brain surgery as a child," he explains. "The world of Metroid was a safe haven for me in comparison to the real world, which I had a hard time trusting and adapting to." The recovering youngster built up a series of associations around the character. "The cold space of Norfair was something I could count on to be there for me. As a child recovering from a major trauma, little things like that make all the difference in the world."

So even though the loans had called time on his travels, a new journey was about to begin. Andrew returned from painting the tiles red in Europe to work for Nintendo.

"I seized the opportunity as the Metroid Prime concept artist. I saw it as stepping into my conceptual destiny, so to speak," he says. "I believed in the world of Metroid as a child and I gave as much as I could to make that world believable to the next generation."

EMOTIONAL CONTENT

The thing of note about Andrew's work is that in reaching towards an emotional

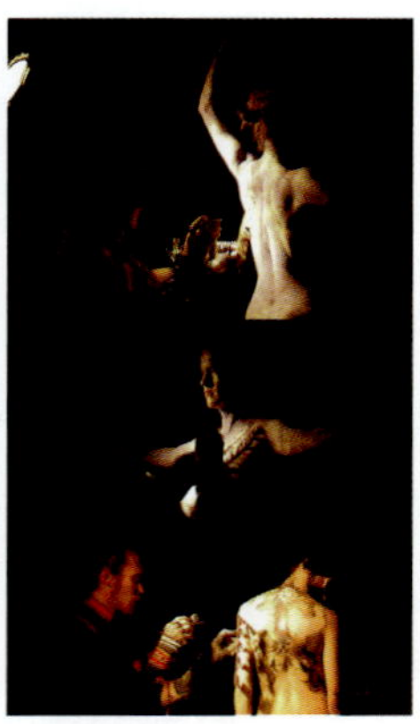

IN SERVICE
These photos were taken during the Massive Black/ConceptArt.org Montréal workshop. "I transformed the figure models into living art for the other artists to paint and draw from," explains Andrew.

Andrew Jones' ART IN FOCUS
Building images with an emotional connection

"As always when approaching a personal project," says Andrew, "I search inside myself for an emotion I want to capture; a feeling I want to cage inside of a canvas."

In the case of Lila Lost it's the feeling of countless opportunities. "Life is a vast ocean of possibilities; every step that we take in a certain direction unfolds new crossroads for us," he explains. It's this that makes us human: "To choose the right path means to choose individuality." That makes life a never-ending maze of conceptions, and in this image, the key is uncertainty. "From the very beginning, I know that I'll have to ensure the painting feels chaotic, to underline the emotion. Textures are my array that leads to chaos,".

Andrew chose to stick with earthy tones. "We as humans walk the earth. Our feet are carrying us in our struggles over the soil of the plains and deserts. So it seemed natural to stick with browns and sepias – the darker tones – as every choice we make for the future lies in a murky haze in front of us."

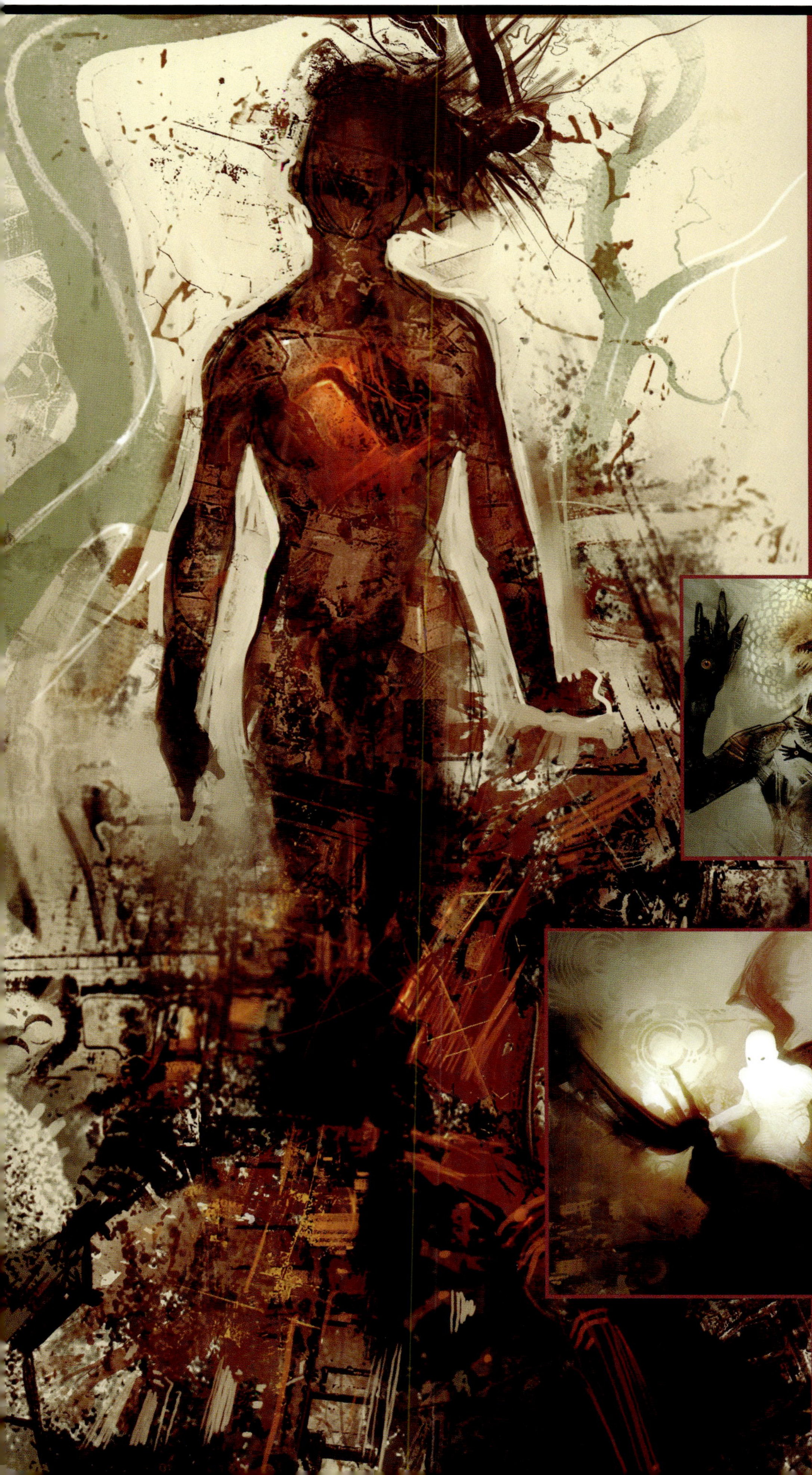

MUSIC MAKES ART
Andrew uses lyric-free, ambient music to inspire his inventive painting process.

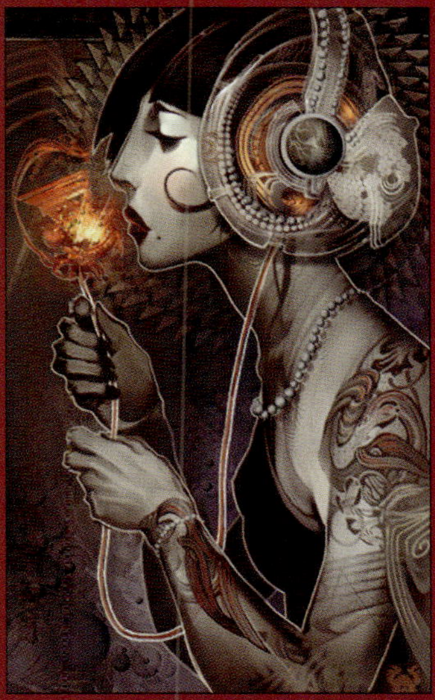

THE ARTIST
"Narkosis and Ms Goldenflame in their post-apocalyptic paradise," says Andrew.

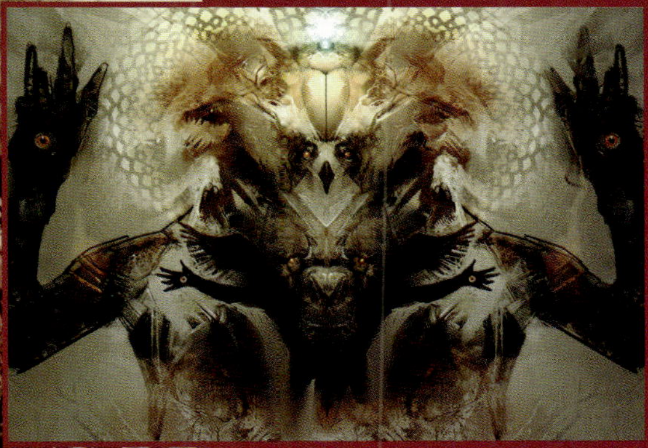

HORUS
This is a modern endomorphic vision of the Egyptian God of the morning sun.

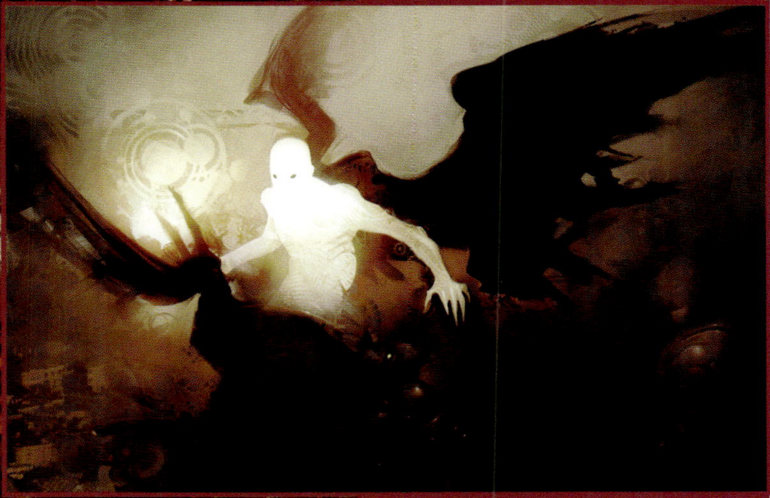

LESSER EVIL
"There is so much duality in life," says Andrew. "I wanted to make an image that captured evil in opposition to itself."

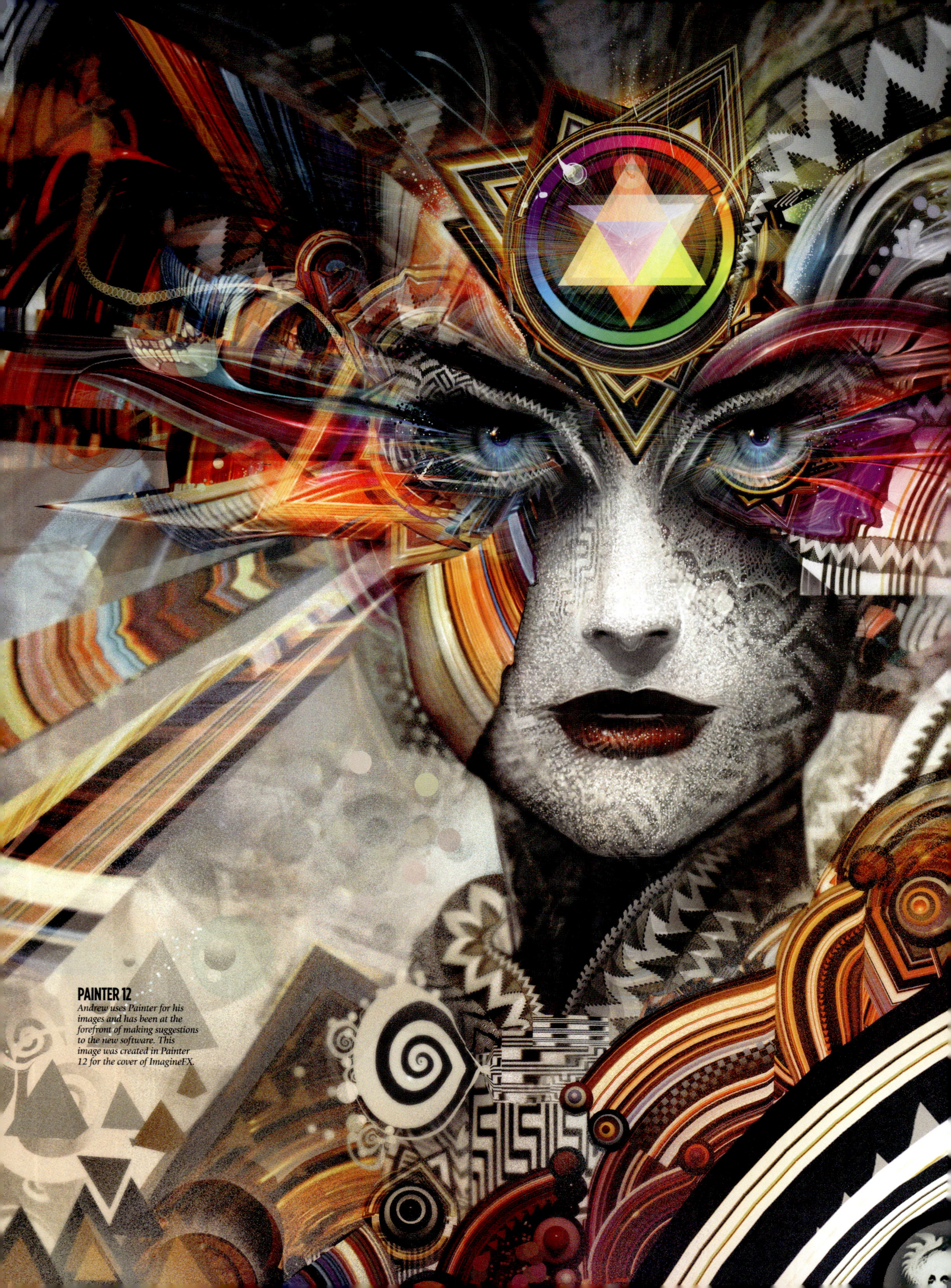

PAINTER 12

Andrew uses Painter for his images and has been at the forefront of making suggestions to the new software. This image was created in Painter 12 for the cover of ImagineFX.

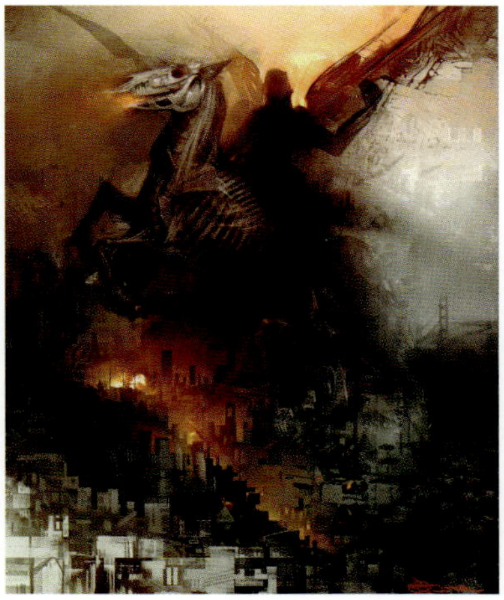

DIE SF
A vision of 2012, Andrew explains: "This piece was created during a great change in my life and points to a great change in the world that is soon to be upon us."

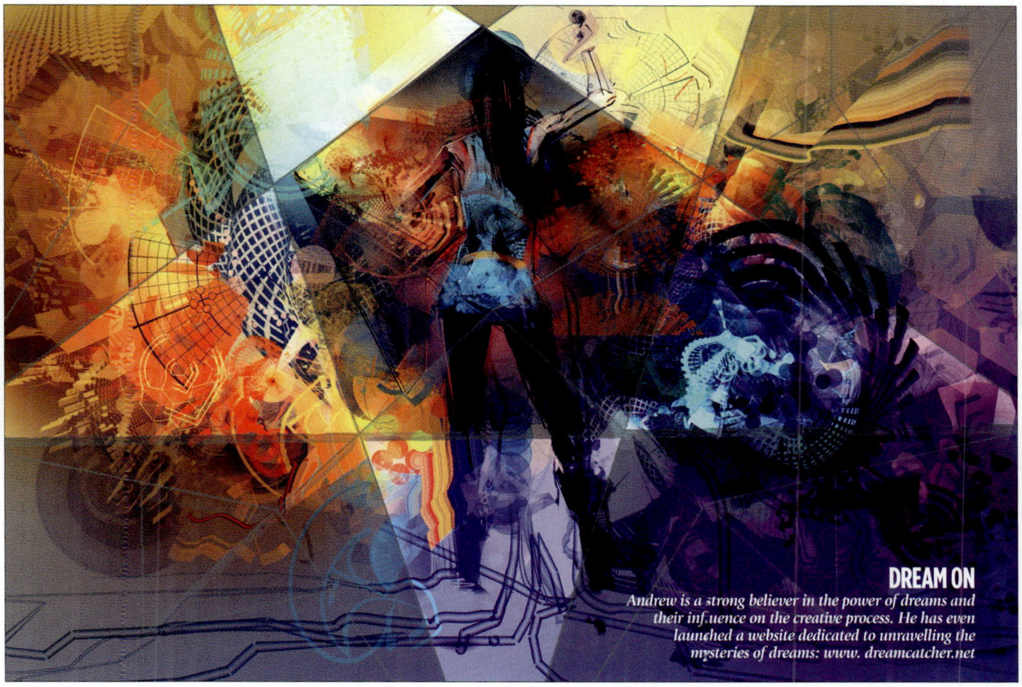

DREAM ON
Andrew is a strong believer in the power of dreams and their influence on the creative process. He has even launched a website dedicated to unravelling the mysteries of dreams: www.dreamcatcher.net

connection with the viewer, it goes beyond simple representation. "Unfortunately, bad moods make for great art," he observes. "Sometimes I wonder if there's an unconscious part of me that sabotages my life to create the drama that will fuel the next painting."

This may seem extreme, but it's about bridging the gap between creator and viewer: "The more present I can be with the emotion I'm feeling while painting, the more the viewer will recognise that emotion and share it with me," he explains. In order to do that, serious measures may be called for. "It's only when I can fully step into my shadow that I can emerge on the other side as a warrior of light."

Those planning to emulate Andrew should beware, though: "I live my life in a style that's constantly evolving, expanding and growing in abundance." That sounds benign enough but it requires dedication. "Some of the recurring themes in the overall style of my life are chaos, experimentation and pushing my boundaries – taking risks and picking myself up from failure to create something beautiful." It's not a path you can easily turn back from. So consider carefully before you begin making big changes to the way you work.

> "The more present I can be with emotion while painting, the more natural it will be for the viewer to share that emotion"

ILM TO MASSIVE BLACK

"I still have my acceptance letter mounted and framed like a deer head on the wall," Andrew reveals. He was obviously excited by the prospect of working at what is arguably the world's most prestigious animation studio: "ILM was a full-on dream vision manifestation. It was the first time I learned that you can manifest reality through thoughts."

A place of great creative significance, Andrew describes ILM as "Eye-magic-in-action." The vibe must have been incredible. "We are the creators and this is the stage, there were so many potent and powerful manifesting wizards at that place that it made my skin crawl with excitement," he recalls. And from ILM, Andrew moved to Retro Studios and Massive Black.

The artist must have freedom. "In short, Massive Black was the manifestation of not wanting to wake up to an alarm clock and never having to fill out a vacation form," he explains. Luckily, Andrew had company in his bid for freedom: "ILM was another man's dream. Massive Black was born of the vision of Jason Manley, Coro Kaufman and myself."

And that dream was accompanied by the means to achieve it. "I somehow ended up bringing, attracting and working elbow to asshole with some of the finest art warriors I could have ever asked for," he says. A studio of considerable distinction was born.

Andrew has given something back, too. In the shape of ConceptArt.org, he's helped connect a worldwide network of artists who otherwise might have continued to struggle in isolation.

"Jason Manley and I began by connecting a network of six artists together. At that time, neither of us imagined that it would exceed the tens of thousands of members and hundreds of thousands of visitors that it does today." Nevertheless, those are the figures. "It's a bit overwhelming... ConceptArt.org is a visualised dream of an overwhelming need for the artistic spirit to unite together and recognise itself."

BIG DOWN UNDER

These days Andrew is a freelancer and one of the leading digital artists in the world. He has become an evangelist for Corel Painter, the software that imitates real paints and dry media. But he uses it in a stylised, unique way to push and pull shapes, samples and fractals until beautiful faces emerge from his collage of butterfly stamp brushes and mirrored shapes.

More so, Andrew has fallen in love with projection art. He recently created the world's largest live projection installation on the walls of Sydney Opera House. In more ways than one, Andrew is even outgrowing the technology he uses.

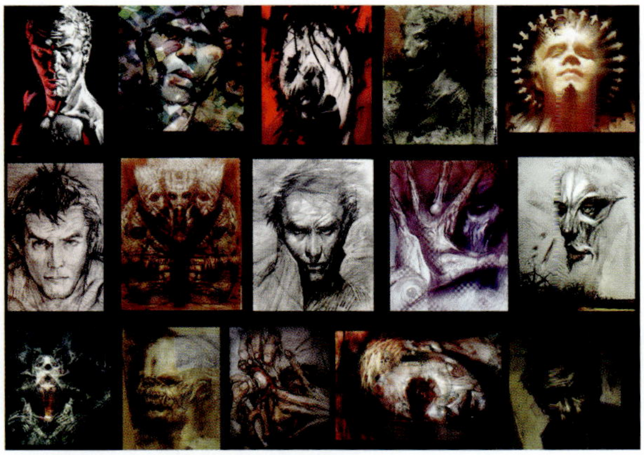

SELECTED SELF-PORTRAITS, 2002-2005
From May 2002 to Feb 2005, Andrew created 1,000 self-portraits consecutively over 1,000 days. "This is a selection of some of my favourites from the later part of the series."

Turn the page to learn to paint like Andrew Jones

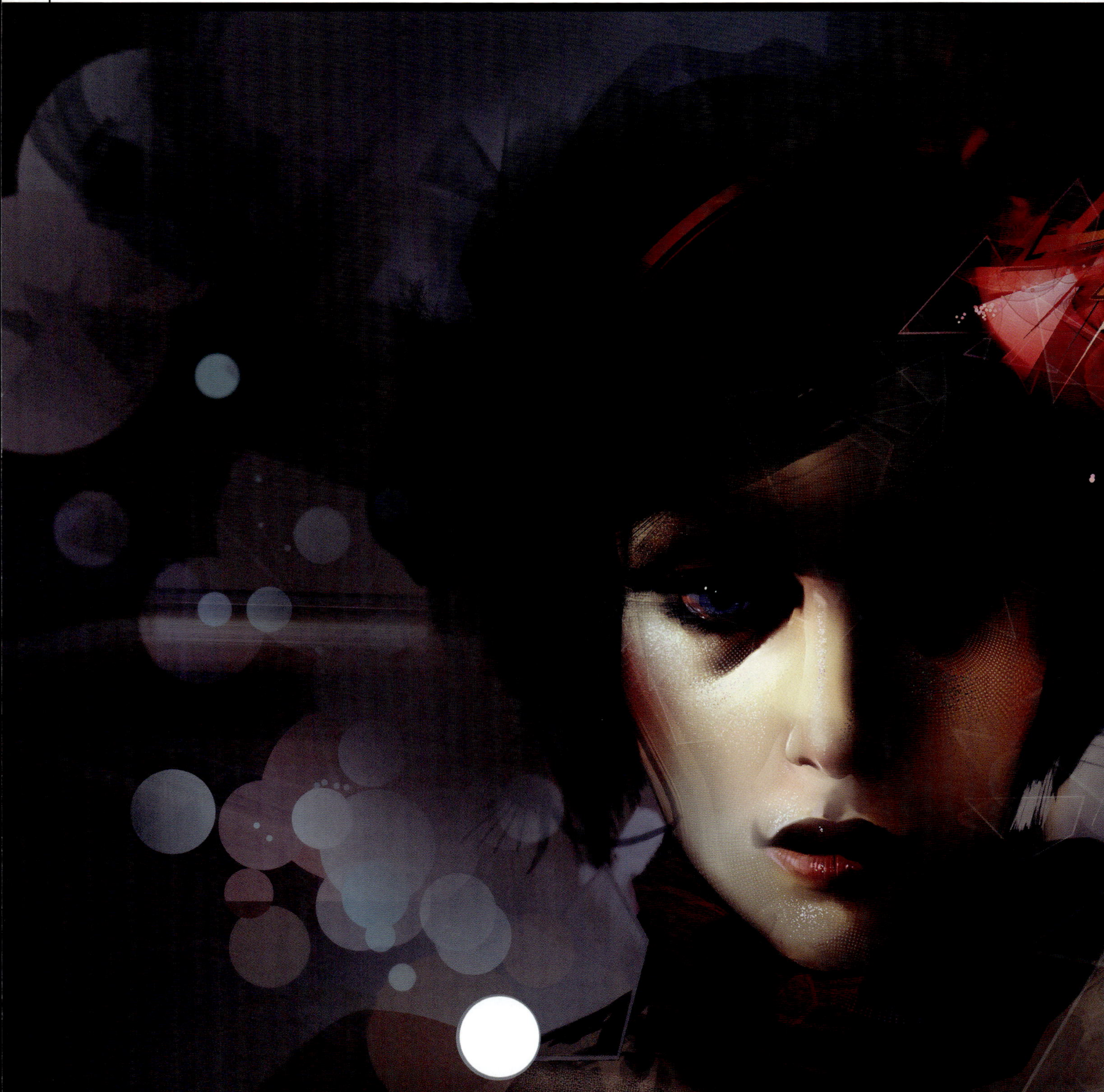

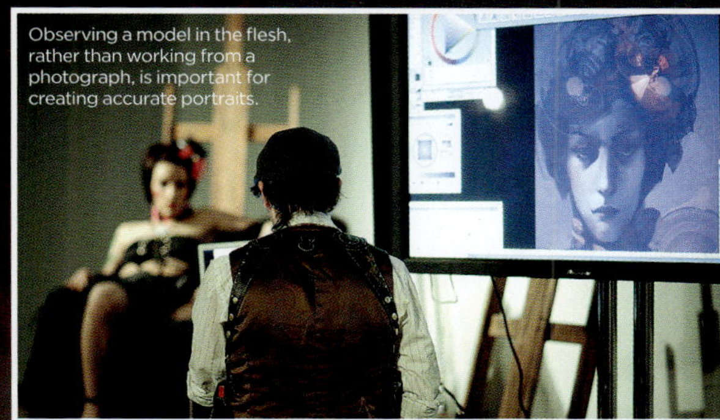

Observing a model in the flesh, rather than working from a photograph, is important for creating accurate portraits.

All photography © Phil Holland

Painter

EXPLORING THE FACE OF DIGITAL ART

Join **Andrew Jones** as he demonstrates how Corel Painter is helping to make the world a more beautiful place, one pixel at a time...

There's one simple reason why I use Corel Painter – it's the most powerful tool I've found to capture the beauty of life with the least resistance. In this tutorial I combine two of my favourite things: Painter and the timeless elegance of the female face. With their Painter Software (Painter 12 is available now), Corel has given the artist more tools and opportunity than ever before to document the natural radiance of the human form and the world inside and outside our imaginations. So, open up your beauty aperture and stare deep into the face of digital painting.

1 Finding your beauty

This demonstration was created entirely from real life observation in front of a live studio audience at the ConceptArt.org Dallas workshop. It's tempting to revert to the comfort of using a photo as reference but I can't stress enough how valuable the observation of the three-dimensional molecular reality can be. As artists we have the opportunity to communicate; there is no comparison to the amount of information you gain from observing a model in the flesh rather than a photograph. Photos can be great tools to glean insight, but I highly recommend finding a model and the space and time to create your art.

2 Set and setting

Make sure your model is comfortable and relaxed. I play music in the background, burn incense and make sure the lighting isn't in their eyes. These are all vital components to the comfort of your muse. The more relaxed they feel, the more gracefully the process will flow.

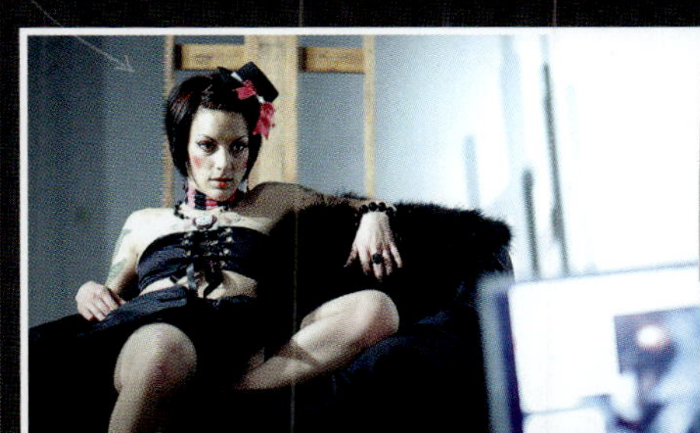

3 Fix their gaze

Decide what angle you want your model to hold. If you pick a less engaging angle, ask your model to select something to focus on. It's nice if they can look out of a window or at something interesting. Avoid having them watch TV unless you want to record that 1,000-yard stare.

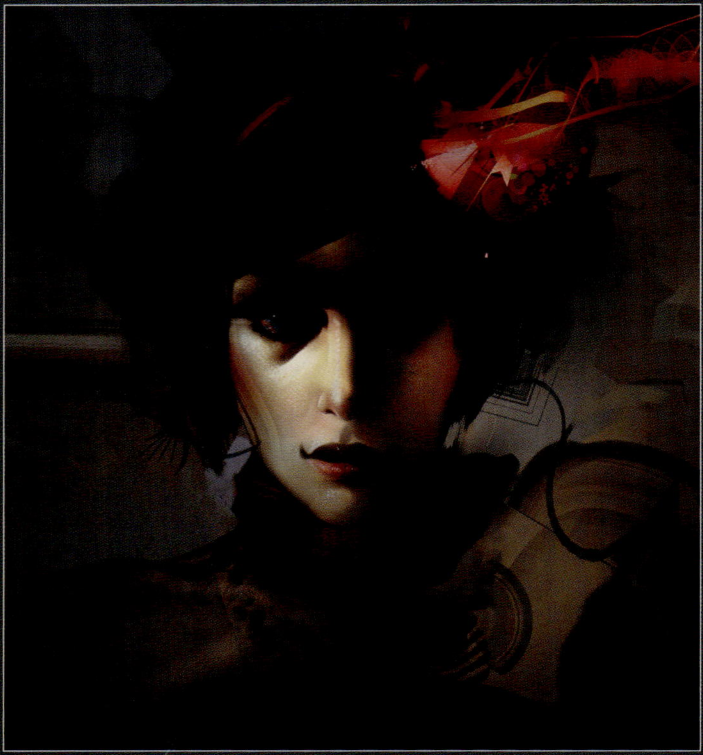

4 Define the divine

Corel has included a unique Divine Proportion aid in Painter to help composition. I begin many of my paintings with this tool, as it's a great way to break the intimidation of a fresh canvas. I don't have a set formula for using the Divine Proportion, but I just like having it there. It gives me a greater sense of control and insight into the composition, it looks cool and will impress your friends. They may think you're really good at maths, so just play along.

PRO SECRETS

Dotting your eyes

Early in the sketch, I add two dots indicating the angle of the eyes. This helps establish the gaze of the model. In this case I want her to look directly at me and the viewer. It's easy to tell if the model is looking at you by process of elimination – you know when she has your gaze. Don't stop until the painting is staring right back at you.

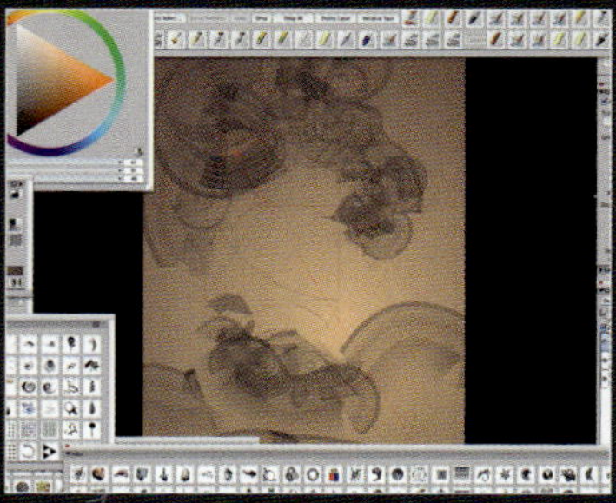

5 Throw down

As you progress into the fine nuances of portraiture, there will be many opportunities for high levels of detail and measurements. The beginning is not one of those moments. Using the Pattern Chalk tool, I select a few organic patterns and then attack the canvas with several impulsive strokes and slashes to indicate the volume of the hair and the model's clothing. There's something extremely liberating about exploring the chaos before the order. It also helps free me up and it's fun. I'll hunt and peck a bit before I find the perfect shapes, and as soon as these shapes are defined I will use them as rough reference guides to place the next series of marks.

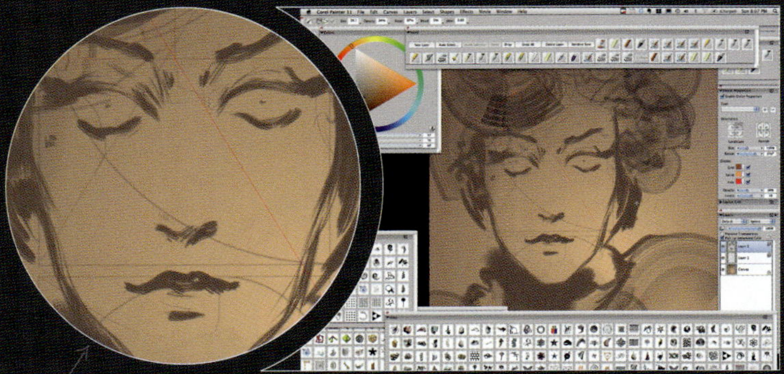

6 Nailing the sketch

Next, I'll take another favourite, the Sumi Ink brush. I like this brush for the initial sketching. It delivers a pressure sensitive irregular line, it's organic and a lot less mechanical than many digital sketching brushes. The first marks I make are the area around the eyes and the eyebrows, but the crux of this image will undoubtedly be the eyes. It's a great place to make early marks to work the rest of my measurements around. After I have the eyes roughed in, I establish the placement of the nostrils and lips and then sketch the contour outlines of the face.

7 Getting edgy

I lay in some of my initial shadows using the Digital Airbrush, because it has a very soft edge to it. I create a separate layer and, using the Airbrush, I lay in the shadow shapes. I often use the Lasso tool to get the most accurate line possible, but when using it take a deep breath, and remember – look twice, draw once! Once the selection is complete, I then paint both within and outside of my selection.

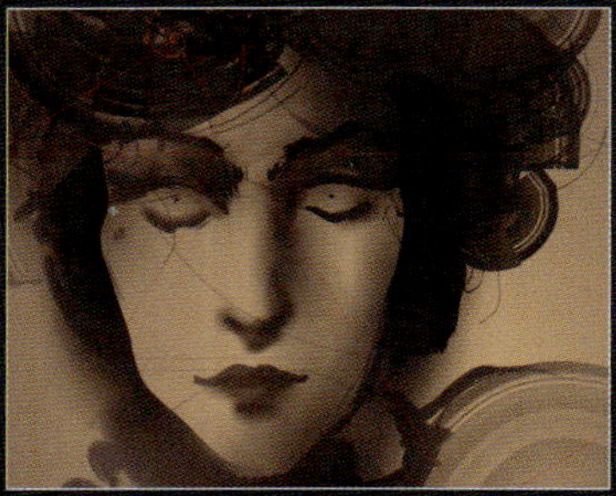

8 Soften her up

I often work back and forth between hard and soft edges. Pay very close attention to the shadow shapes – especially around the eyes. Some shadows start off with a hard edge and then transition into a soft edge. I use the Just Add Water tool to soften the edges of the shadow. When capturing a young model like this, I take a few moments to make sure that I soften off any unnecessary hard-edged lines. Too many lines and hard brush strokes will make the face appear older that it may be in real life.

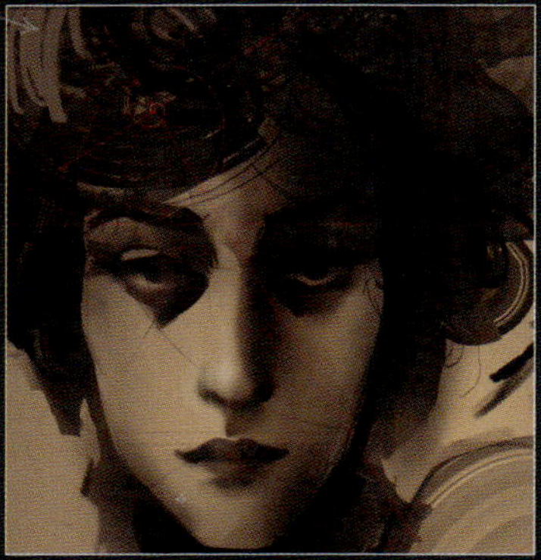

9 Let's get high

Highlights are a crucial aspect in defining the light source and rendering the form. They're also one of the most abused aspects of many portraits. Try to be sparing with them and avoid using pure white. The highlight always has a tone depending on whether the light source is cool or warm. It's a subtle distinction that makes a big difference.

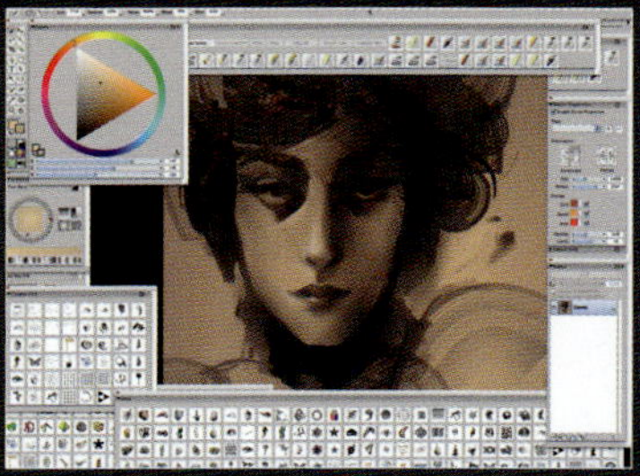

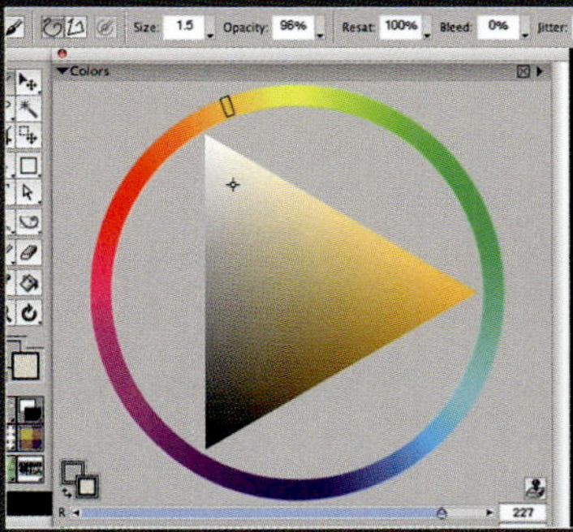

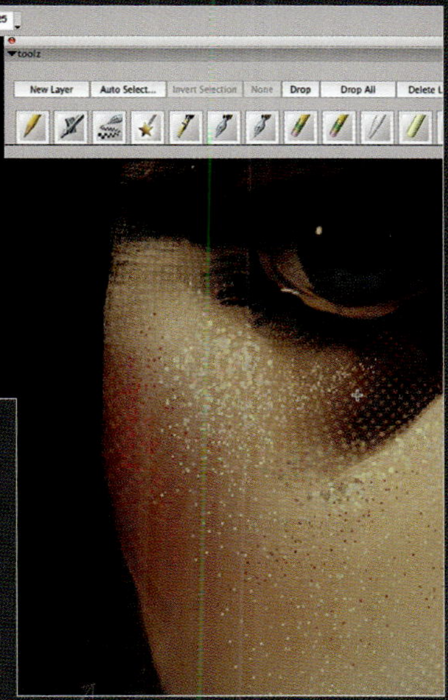

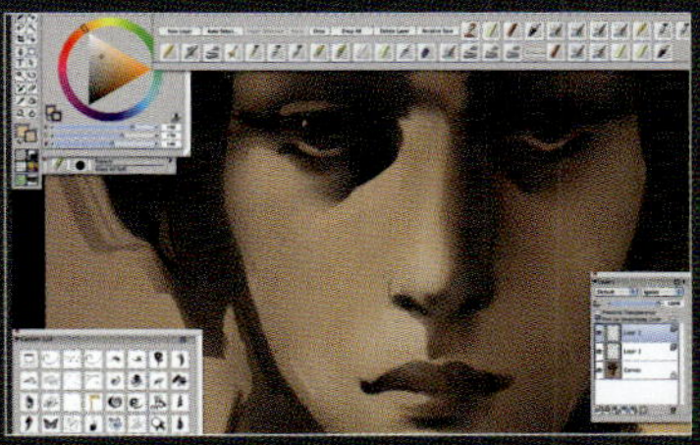

10 Let's get real

In Painter, the Real Brushes collection, which I use here, is a real asset to recreating the look and feel of traditional paints. What makes these brushes 'real' is that as you tilt the angle of the Wacom pen, it alters the thickness of the line – just like in real life with a stick of conte. It's a nice feature that works well. I select a Rough Paper texture and use the Real Conte and Real Chalk brushes to add some texture to the face.

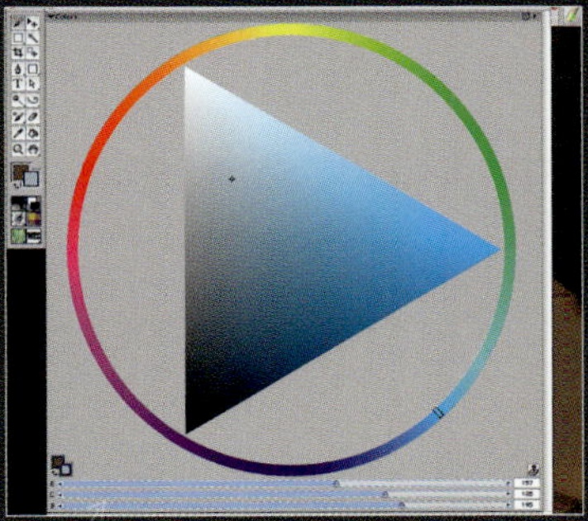

11 A world of colour

By far my favourite invention in Painter is the unique colour wheel. Corel has improved this over iterations of the software, while Painter 11 improved by enlarging the wheel and making it more accurate, Painter 12 has gone a step further with the introduction of a floating colour wheel that can be loaded on screen instantly when needed and removed automatically after a colour is selected. I can say without a doubt that this gives Painter the most sophisticated and accurate colour selection tool ever available to digital artists – and that's pretty cool. The only problem now is that I have no excuse for not selecting the right colour! I build layers of colours with the Overlay layer, adding and erasing warms and cools where needed.

12 Barbie doll syndrome

I'm adding some colour in the cheeks, but I'm confronted with how smooth and plastic it feels. The only cure is to add more texture. I choose the Leaky Pen tool, then open up Colour Variability. I set the Hue variability to four per cent, the Saturation to six per cent and the Value to eight per cent. Then, zooming in to the area around the eye, I start spackling in highlights and pores. I also use the Pattern Chalk tool to add texture using a dot matrix halftone pattern.

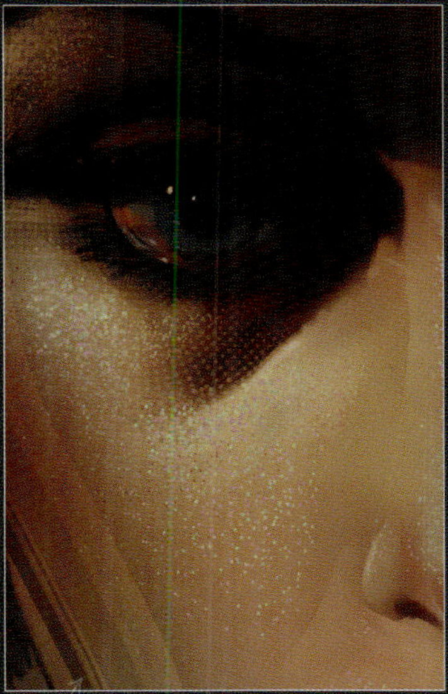

13 Look deep into my eyes

I use the Circular Lasso tool to get a perfect circle for the iris and pupil. My model has very vibrant blue eyes; because most of the tones in the painting are mainly red, I choose a cool grey for the eye colour. This gives the illusion of blue eyes without being garish. I add the spark of life highlight with the Glow brush.

PRO SECRETS

Precision Mode

I created this portrait using the new Wacom Intuos4 12x19. On this new tablet there's a function called Precision Mode. Activating this doubles the usable surface area of the tablet, giving you twice the amount of line control. I use it when drawing details around the eyes; where I need the most control.

14 Adding some flair

Now that I have a likeness of the model that I'm happy with, I add in some abstract elements to give the image more dynamic aspects. Using the Pattern Chalk tool and a number of custom abstract patterns, I place a series of geometric shapes around the hair and background of the image. I add these on a separate layer, and move and tweak them until I find just the right place. To contrast the geometric abstract shapes, I choose the Leaky Pen brush to add in some larger spots and circle shapes. I also take advantage of the Special Effects Shattered tool and use it to break up the negative space around the image. These abstract marks are to give more character to the subject's personality and make the image more interesting to the viewer.

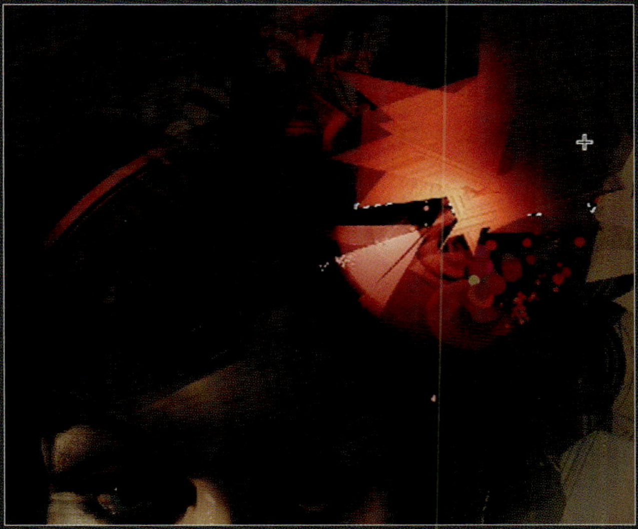

15 Finishing moves

Once all the elements are in the right places, I use Colour Correction in Image Adjustments and make slight alterations to the Brightness and Contrast of the red, blue and green spectrums. This gives me one last opportunity to get an accurate colour field. Then, I just save the image and thank the model for her time and attention.

Shortcuts

Hide everything

Tab

This will hide the palettes as much as possible and take advantage of all the screen's real estate.

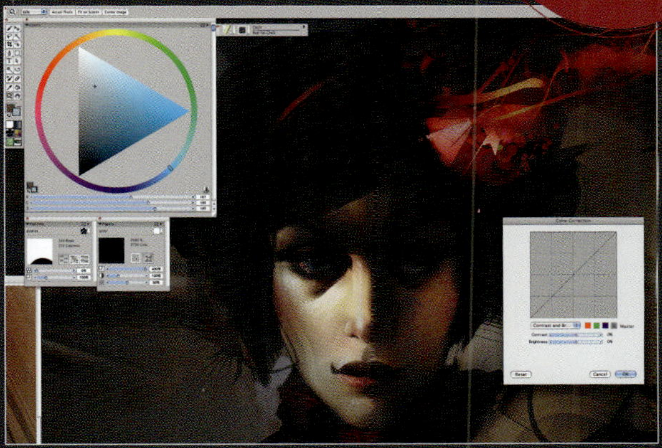

Artist PROFILE

Christian Alzmann

Illustrator and art director, Christian currently works in the film industry for Industrial Light & Magic. He's been involved with films such as The Village, and War of the Worlds. And has work printed in numerous 'behind the scenes' publications.

www.christianalzmann.com

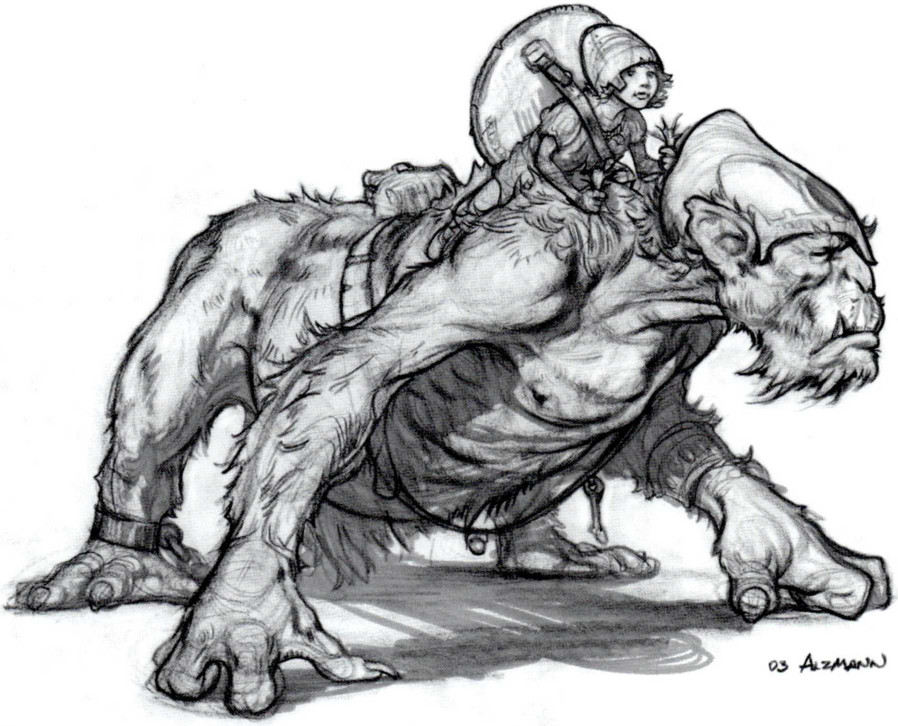

Interview

Chris Alzmann

"I enjoy making images that tell stories and ask more questions than they answer." **Christian Alzmann** and the art of creative speculation

Christian Alzmann has worked on an enviable list of movies: Pirates of the Caribbean, Star Wars: Episode II, Men in Black II… And that's just the film work; we haven't even mentioned the books and personal projects.

What makes Christian shine are his priorities. "To me," he says, "ideas are the most important thing." That's why Industrial Light & Magic (ILM) hired him right out of college and why he's art directing there now. Aspiring artists everywhere should pay attention.

CALIFORNIA DREAMING

Growing up beneath the cloudless skies of California, Christian developed a suitably sunny outlook on life: "I had the feeling that it was possible to do anything, within reason, if you worked hard at it." It didn't hurt the development of this theory that Christian's dad was a director on wholesome TV show The Waltons.

When you add to his positive disposition an early exposure to art in the form of movies such as Sinbad, Excalibur, TRON and, of course, Star Wars, you start to wonder if the world isn't just a simple mechanism after all. But life is never that straightforward. "I really wanted to be an animator at first," Christian recalls. "But when I realised how much it cost for school I sort of gave up on art for a while." It wasn't until his 23rd year that the creative pressure behind this financial dam had built up to sufficient levels where Christian made up his mind to "make a go of it".

Following in the footsteps of illustrious artists such as Ralph McQuarrie, Syd Mead and Drew Struzan, Christian enrolled at the Art Center in Pasadena. Studying illustration, Christian began to hone his craft. "Drawing human and organic forms was always very challenging," he admits. "Luckily it's also the most fun for me to draw." As a result, character design began to emerge as a strength.

LUCKY BREAK

Building a career takes considerable effort, but if you put yourself out there openings often present themselves in the form of a lucky break. In Christian's case, this was an interview with ILM. "I thought I had no chance whatsoever, I had a portfolio filled with animation artwork, backgrounds, storyboards and so on, I had nothing

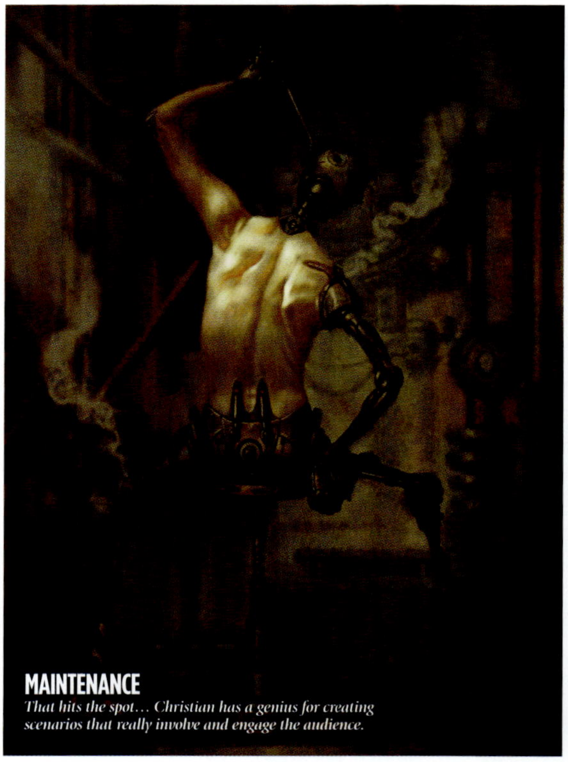

MAINTENANCE
That hits the spot… Christian has a genius for creating scenarios that really involve and engage the audience.

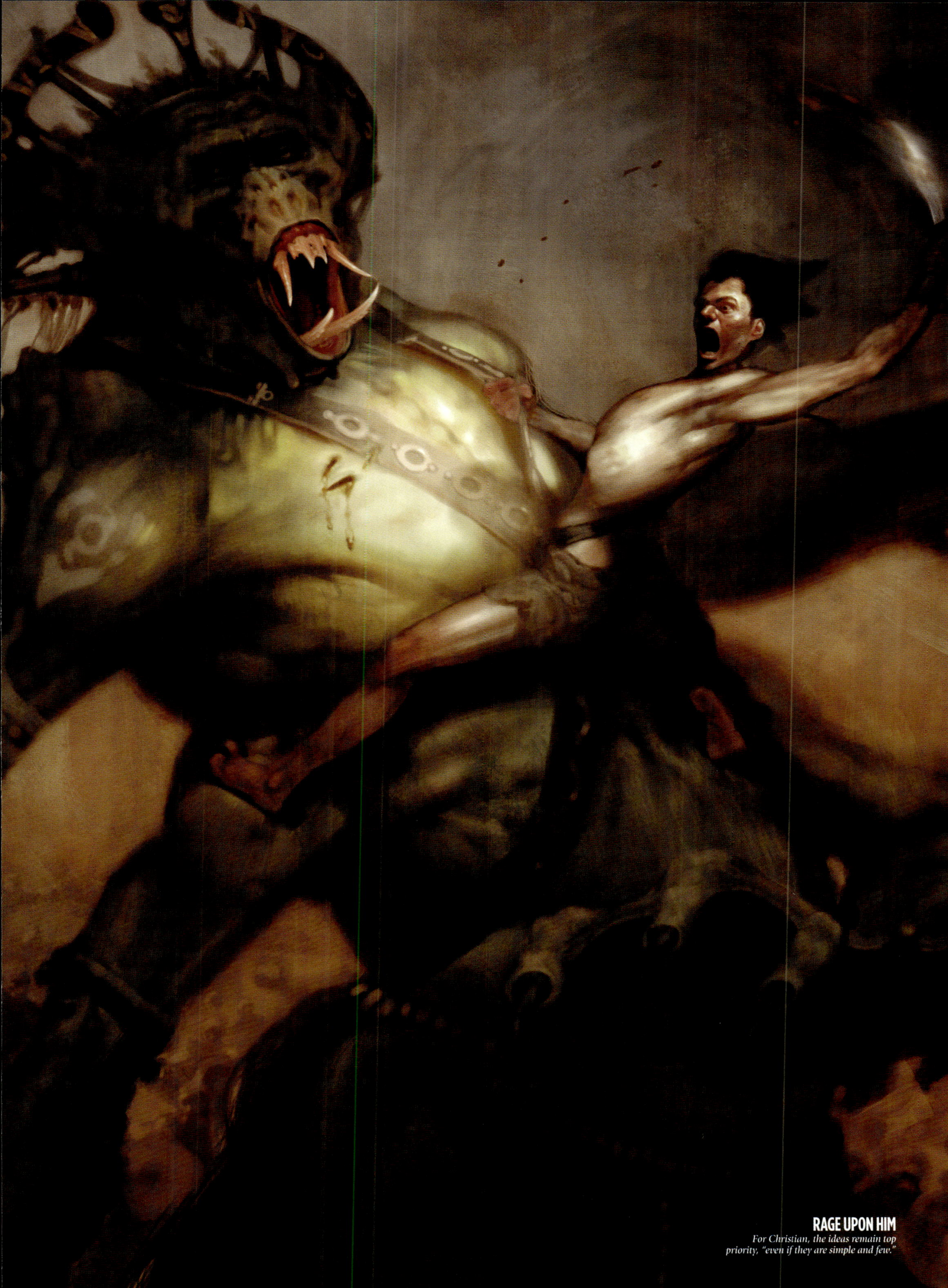

RAGE UPON HIM

For Christian, the ideas remain top priority, "even if they are simple and few."

that was particularly suitable for ILM's live action movies."

Believing he had no chance of getting a job, Christian experienced none of the usual interview nerves, which meant that everything went smoothly. "It just so happened that ILM were trying their hand at digital features, so my portfolio actually worked well," he says.

ILM signed Christian up there and then, and he was "on cloud nine."

ALL IN THE MIND

"Art school is great at building up your ego," notes Christian with a wry smile. "That ego got me through my first week at ILM." What brought him down to earth was a creative paradigm shift. "I realised that all of the paintings and drawings I was looking at there were done from the artists' imaginations," he says. The quality achieved at ILM was not a happy accident, it was the product of hard work, and lots of it.

On reflection it's obvious that this would be the approach – after all, there are no real life monsters or aliens to copy from. But at the time it was a shock to Christian who'd learnt his skills by and was used to drawing models. It forced a substantial change in his working practice. "To know something well enough to draw it from memory is to really know it," he says.

One of the reasons this skill is so critical has to do with where the world of digital effects has got to. "I think we're at the edge of being able to create anything digitally," believes Christian. "Digital characters used to be impossible to create realistically but now the industry is on the very edge of making the realistic ones a constant." If Andrew's right, and the technology is nearly there, the possibilities will begin to snowball for artists who don't need a model to work from.

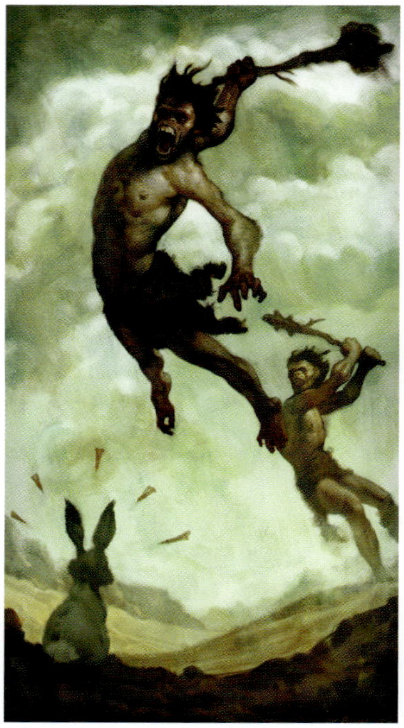

GATHERING
The leaping caveman demonstrates Christian's strong grasp of perspective, a skill that's served him well.

TELLING TALES

Today, Christian's technique is his working model. Take a book cover as an example. "I like to read the book and write down all of the items in the book that might look cool as an image," he explains. "Then I might look to combine some items in a way that gives the viewer a sense of the story." And at that point a solid composition of lights and darks can be laid down with strong shapes and values.

"Painting has always been a bit easier," notes Christian. "Shapes, values and colour made more sense to me visually than

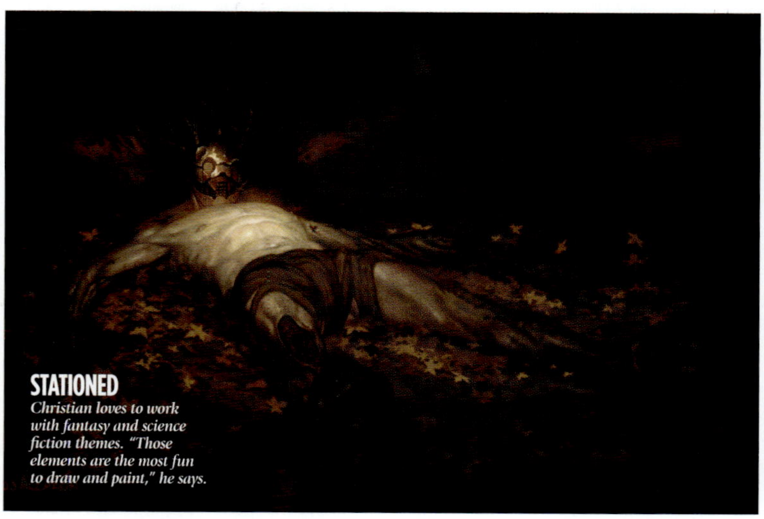

STATIONED
Christian loves to work with fantasy and science fiction themes. "Those elements are the most fun to draw and paint," he says.

THE DARKNESS

Tone and purpose in graphic compositions

Christian says he used to be surprised when people said his work was somewhat dark, but while putting the final touches to this piece entitled Listening he realised they might have a point.

"It's basically about a guy who's trying to hear or to communicate with his dead brothers," says Christian of the character with the enormous ear trumpet. It's obvious from the picture that the brothers are busy decomposing – "but he's so focused on the death of his brothers that life – the bird and the sunshine – he fails to notice."

So why is he naked? "No arty reason other than that I wanted to paint anatomy not clothing," says Christian, who quotes Norman Rockwell: "Every single object shown in a picture should contribute directly to the central theme." Wise words indeed.

Oddly, considering its weighty themes, this particular composition was worked out on sticky notes. Christian recommends this approach as they're thumbnail sized and inexpensive. And they give you a way to rapidly try out different compositions. It's eminently practical.

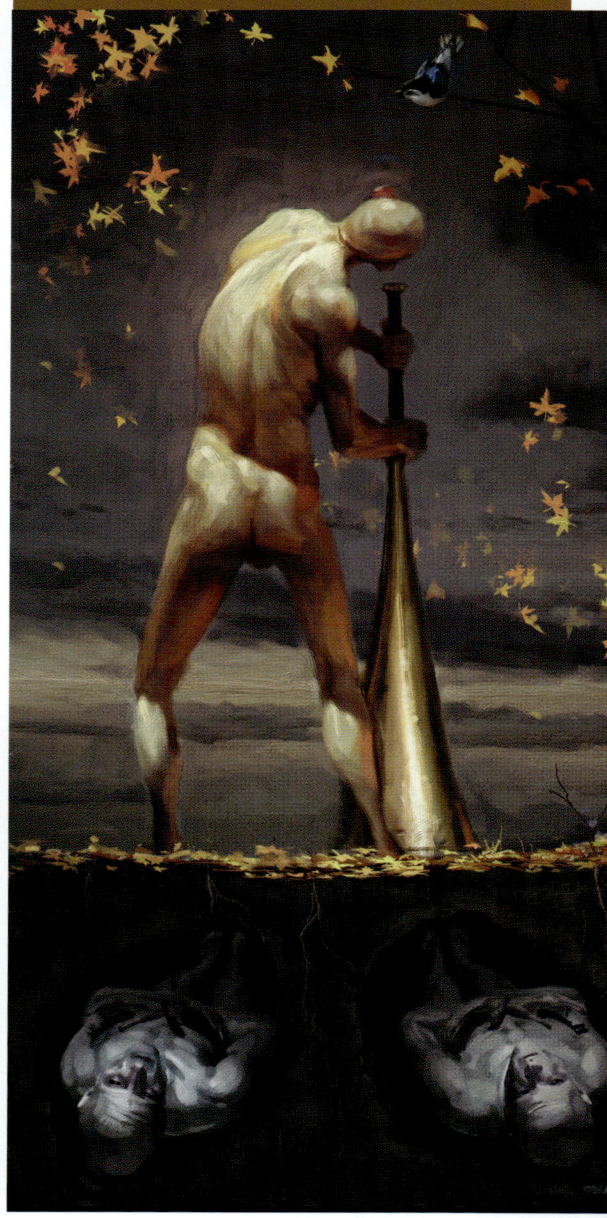

STAR WARS: EPISODE II

"Every film you're on has new things to design and new problems to solve."

Christian got the chance to fulfil a childhood dream when ILM offered him a place on the team for Star Wars: Episode II – Attack of the Clones.

Despite the obvious thrill, Christian kept his cool, observing that, "One must bury one's geekiness deep down and just approach the work professionally, at least while you are at work." Obviously, however, there are moments where this can't be maintained, "like when George puts an approval stamp on your artwork for the first time," for instance.

The job wasn't without its challenges. "I came up with architectural, colour and lighting designs for the Zam speeder chase through Coruscant," says Christian, this was tricky because he had almost no experience of designing architecture, "But you learn how to learn very quickly as a concept artist."

Fast learning is important but so is hard graft. "The great projects always make you work harder, because you never want to be the weak link of the department" says Christian. "So I did a lot of extra sketching to make sure I'd do the job well."

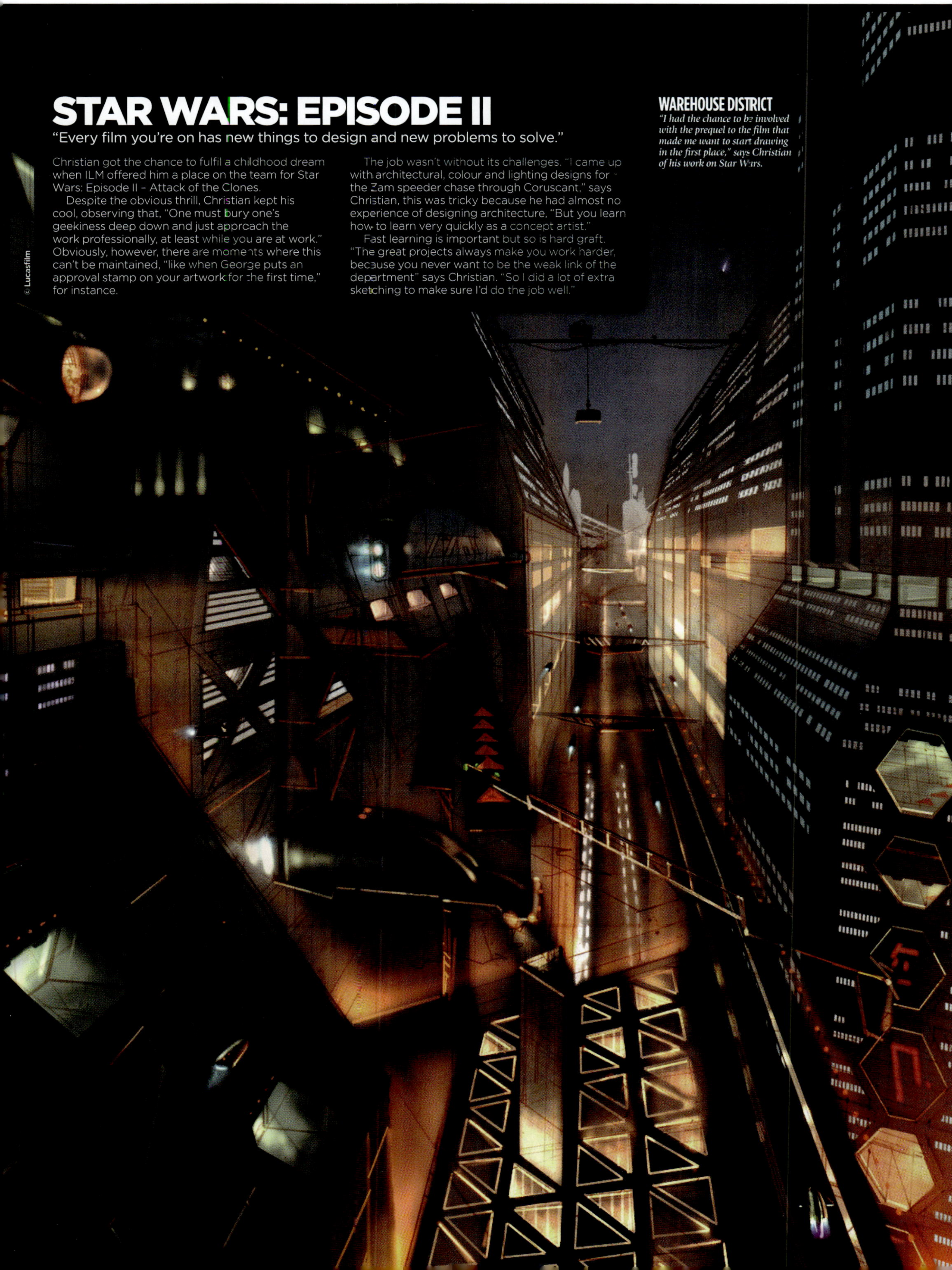

WAREHOUSE DISTRICT
"I had the chance to be involved with the prequel to the film that made me want to start drawing in the first place," says Christian of his work on Star Wars.

lines." The temptation would once have been to shy away from drawing – "early on I even looked at drawings as unfinished paintings," Christian admits. Luckily, he's since seen the error of his ways. "Now I love to look at drawings as their own finished art," he says.

That being the case, when there's a new job on the slate, Christian does drawings first to get his hand moving. Digital comes second because he "hasn't found a way to get rhythmic lines for my figures in a digital format yet." Cracking this problem has involved the purchase of a Cintiq, "so maybe that will change". Until then, it's the tried and tested route of pencils to Painter.

This sets Christian reflecting on the nature of digital production. "Creatively,

> **"Creatively, I believe that in 3D and digital animation there are places that you couldn't go, traditionally"**

I believe that in 3D and digital animation there are places that you couldn't go traditionally." 3D has an impact, even on paper (or screen). "The simplicity of the more recent programs such as SketchUp and ZBrush will have an impact on the accuracy of images," he says. "On the flipside, artwork that's so accurate to anatomy and perspective might many illustrators to stylise their imagery more."

BIGGER PICTURE

Christian's job as art director is demanding, but he loves it – just getting to be creative would be enough for him. "I have to provide any artwork that might be needed for a production," he says. "But with a good team effort you're part of something bigger, hopefully contributing to something that'll be watched generations." Under those circumstances there's an element of obligation – not to make the kids of tomorrow suffer.

Creative people act as a prism through which the world passes and emerges re-envisioned. The artist's job is to suggest an alternative universe as complex as our own, though in new and different ways. In that spirit, notes Christian; "my ideas come from everywhere."

Painter & Photoshop

A VINTAGE ILLUSTRATION CREATED WITH MODERN TOOLS

Create a traditional looking illustration using some old tools as well as a range of digital ones. **Christian Alzmann** takes you through his process for designing and painting a cover illustration.

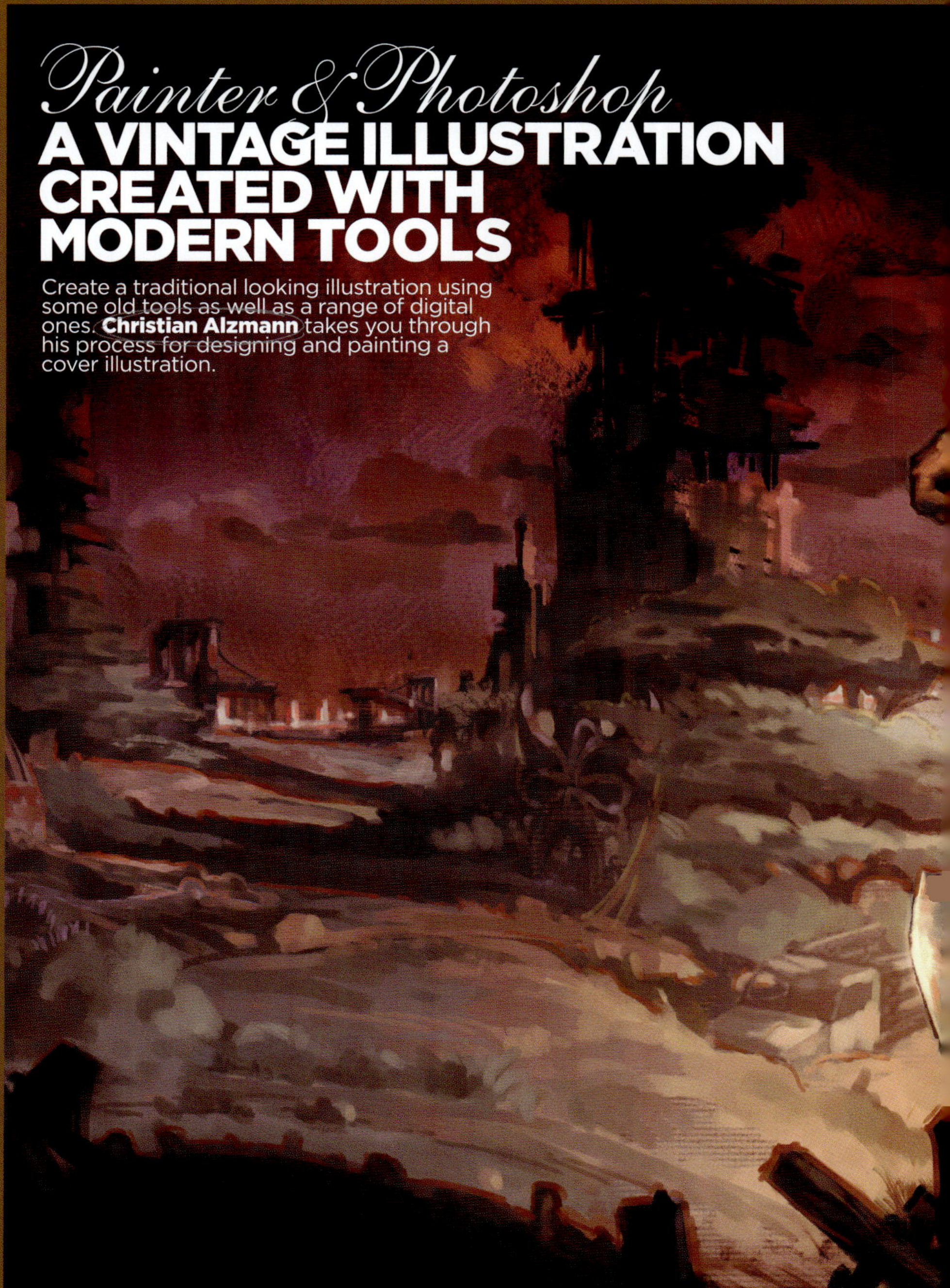

This cover painting was a Frazetta homage, and in this workshop I'll break down the process I used to create it. The steps include my thumbnail process, the study of my subjects in sketches and my use of Photoshop and Painter.

Anatomy and perspective are key to an illustration such as this, and there are many great books from which to learn these skills, but the best way to learn is to constantly draw. I recommend drawing from books and doing life studies until you're comfortable drawing from imagination. There have been times when I've not had the internet handy and was very thankful for the treasury of items I could draw from my head.

Another great learning tool is looking at photography to understand the balance of light and colour in an image. Learning to use these tools is a great advantage.

PRO SECRETS

Play with brushes

Now and then I like to take a day or so with Photoshop and Painter just to play with brushes. Photoshop has such an easy system for capturing and creating new brushes it's a shame not to master it. You can make a brush out of any 2D image, or paint an item to create the brush.

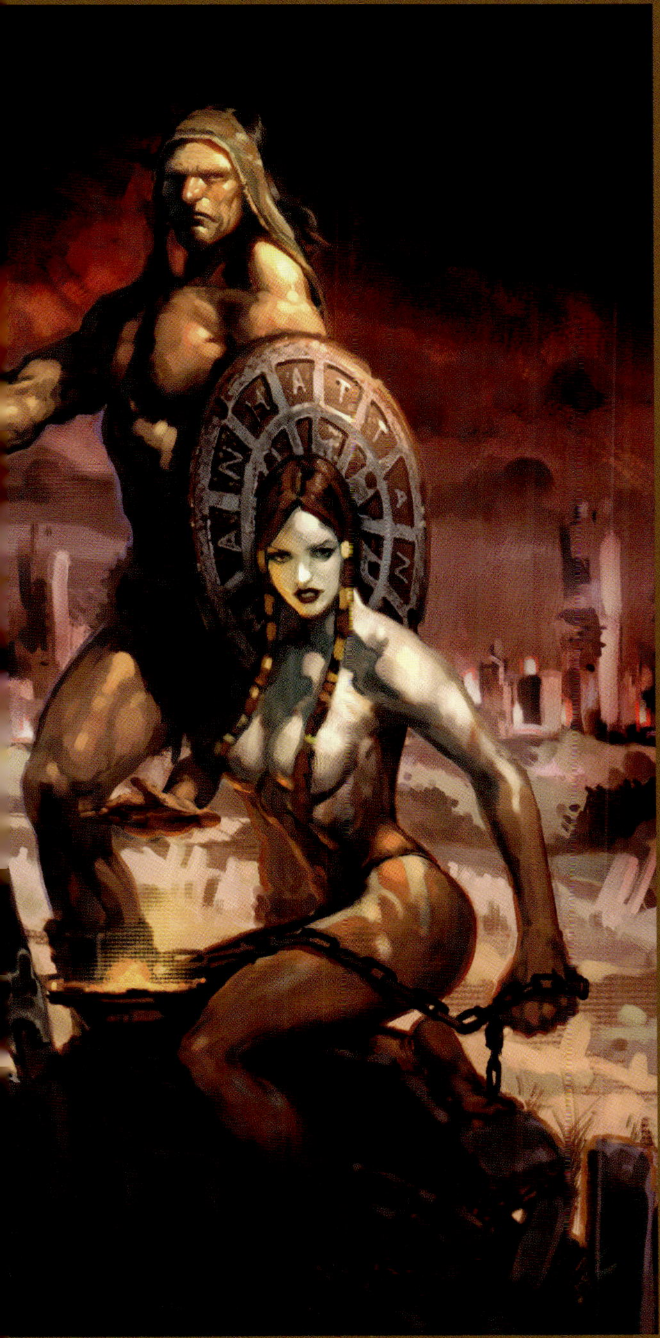

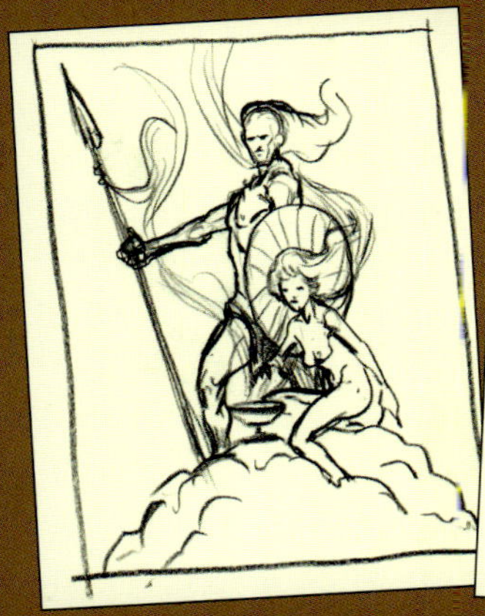

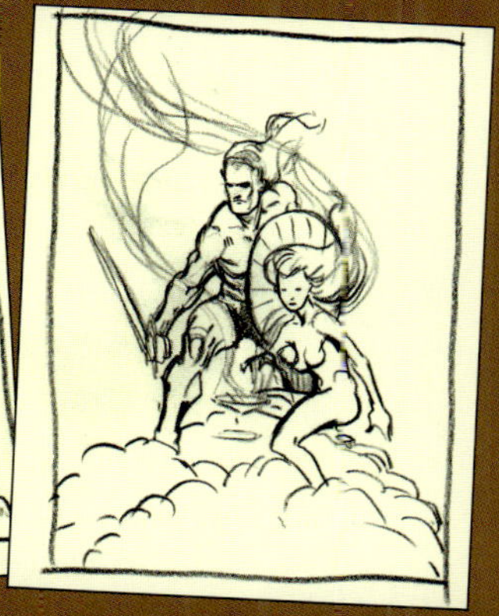

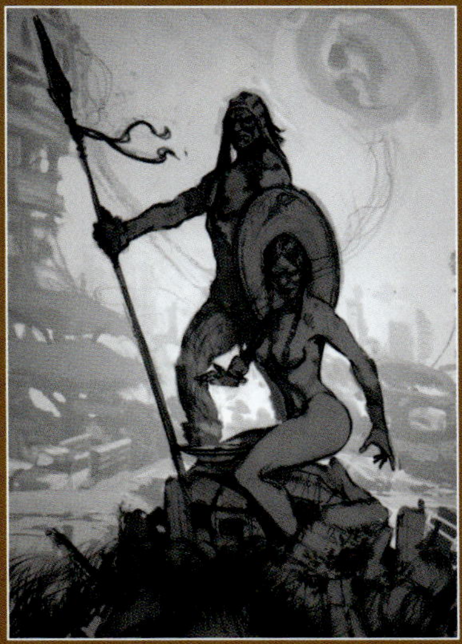

1 Thumbnails

I do a lot of thumbnails. I often use sticky notes for these throwaway drawings – if they don't work, crumple them up and move on. I consider this the most important step. Here, I'm building my composition by roughing in the shapes and sizes of all of my major elements. If it's not singing to me at this stage I won't move on. I'll often spend up to two thirds of my project time building the thumbnail. One thing to note here is that if I'm working on something that will have text on it, such as a cover for a book or magazine, the text needs to be factored into the composition.

2 Studies

Depending on the amount of time given for a project I'll study my various elements by way of sketching. If you're drawing something that you don't know intimately, make tons of little drawings from reference. I'll do sketches whenever I have a free moment. This way I'll know my subject well enough to draw them without copying reference, and by that hopefully avoid making my drawing static.

3 Drawing

I often draw figures out on paper before I go any further. Paper gives me a slightly better feel for the forms and their rhythms. I usually use a soft pencil and marker paper. Marker paper is slightly transparent so I can work the drawings up in overlays, changing, erasing and adding as I go. This keeps the process very liquid and somewhat similar to using digital layers. I then scan in the drawing of the figures and sketch in the background and rough values in Photoshop.

4 Colour study

The next thing to figure out is colour. I usually take my drawing and shrink it down as if I were painting a

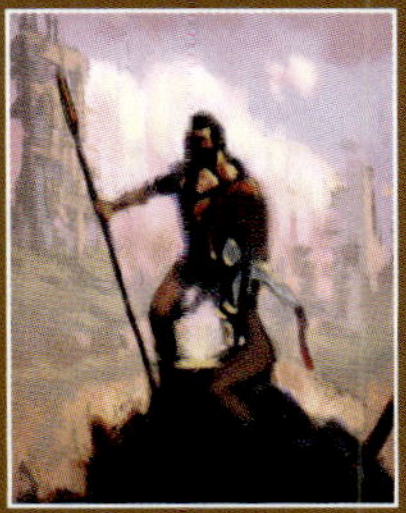

thumbnail. I paint loose and quick as it's just about rough colour here; I like to leave some of the fun of discovery for the final painting. This sketch was done in Painter using Square Chalk to paint lighter areas and Digital Watercolour to glaze in darks.

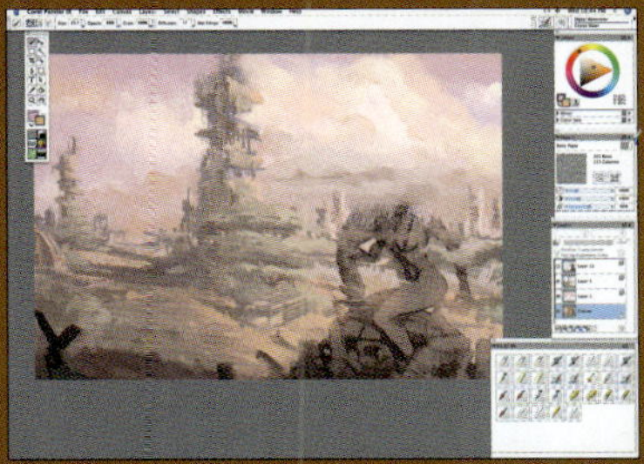

5 Paint

After toning the canvas with a Multiply layer, I start to build the painting up from back to front – the sky is the first layer, the mid-ground buildings are layer two and the heroes are on layer three.

I put 99 per cent of my brushwork down in Painter. On this piece I used Thick Wet Oils and Square Chalk on a Linen Canvas. To avoid making the painting feel stiff I build it up as a whole from dark to light. I paint in the shadows, then midtones, then the highlights. Once the brushwork's finished I bring the painting into Photoshop and do 'digital glazing' on it, where I use adjustment layers such as Levels, Colour Balance and the Photo Filter to tweak the tones. By painting in and out of these with black and white I can change areas without changing Painter brushwork. Once I have things where I want them, I add some final touches and I'm done.

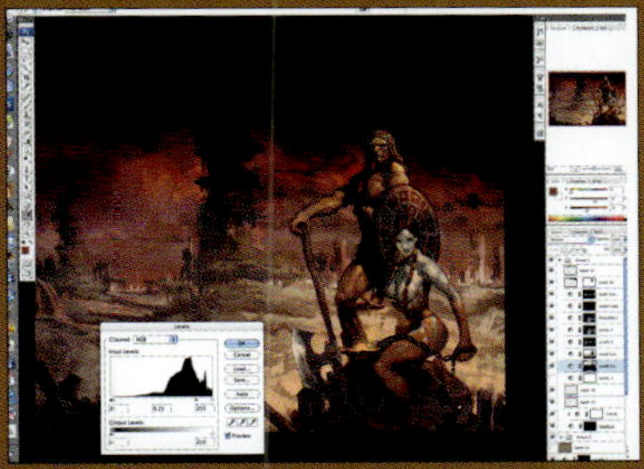

CORE SKILLS

Tips, advice and techniques from leading artists…

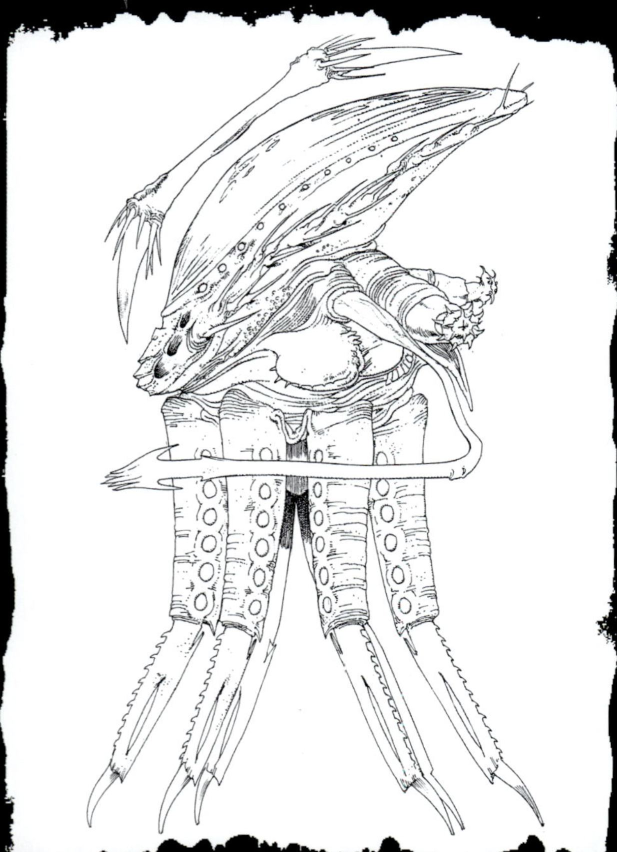

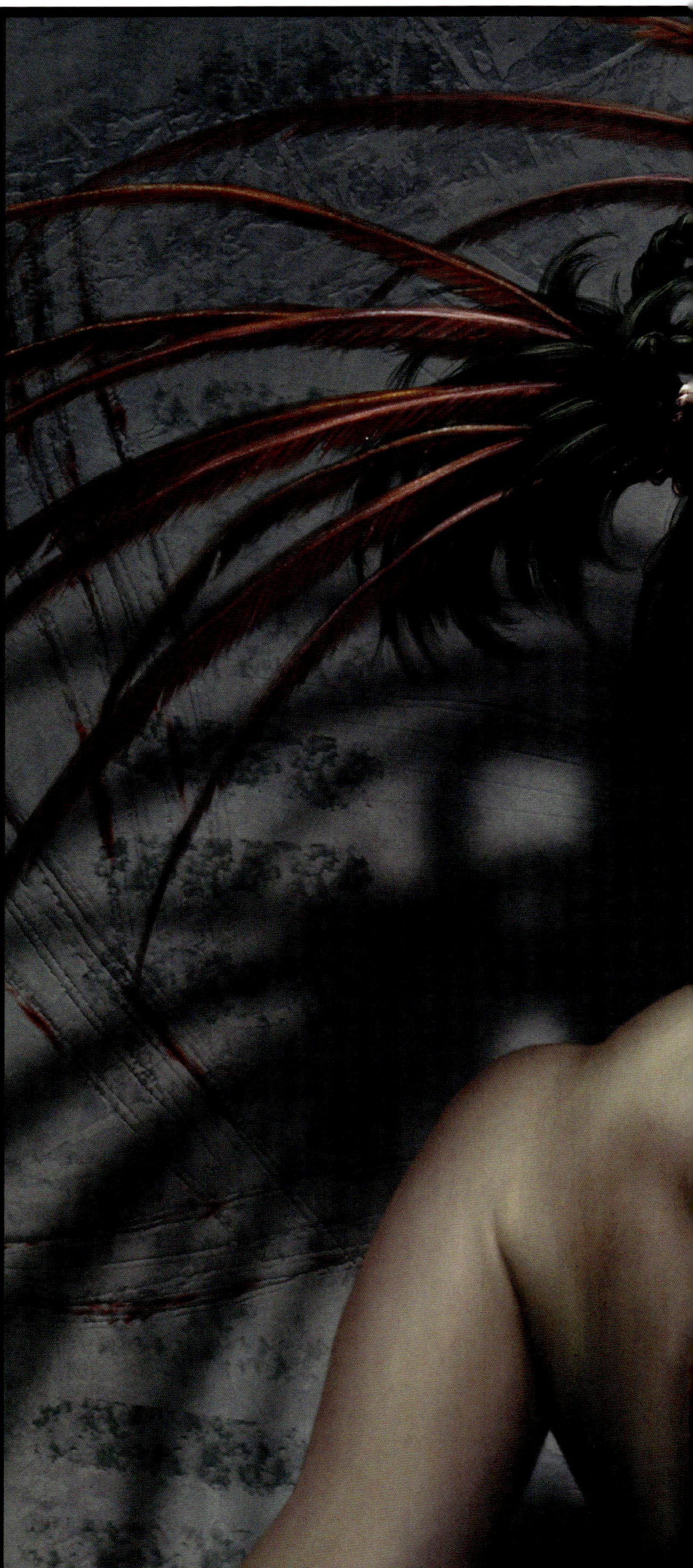

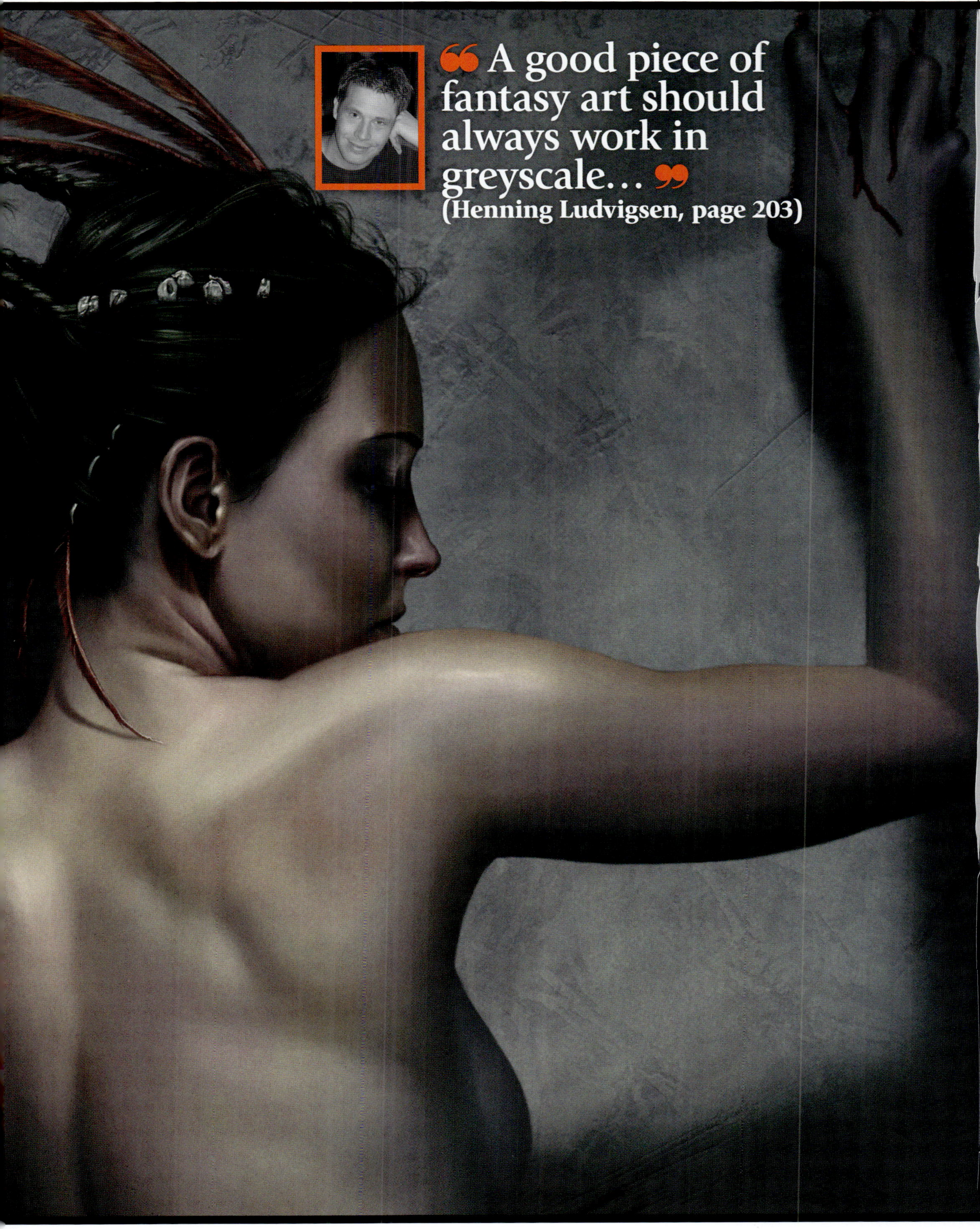

“A good piece of fantasy art should always work in greyscale…”
(Henning Ludvigsen, page 203)

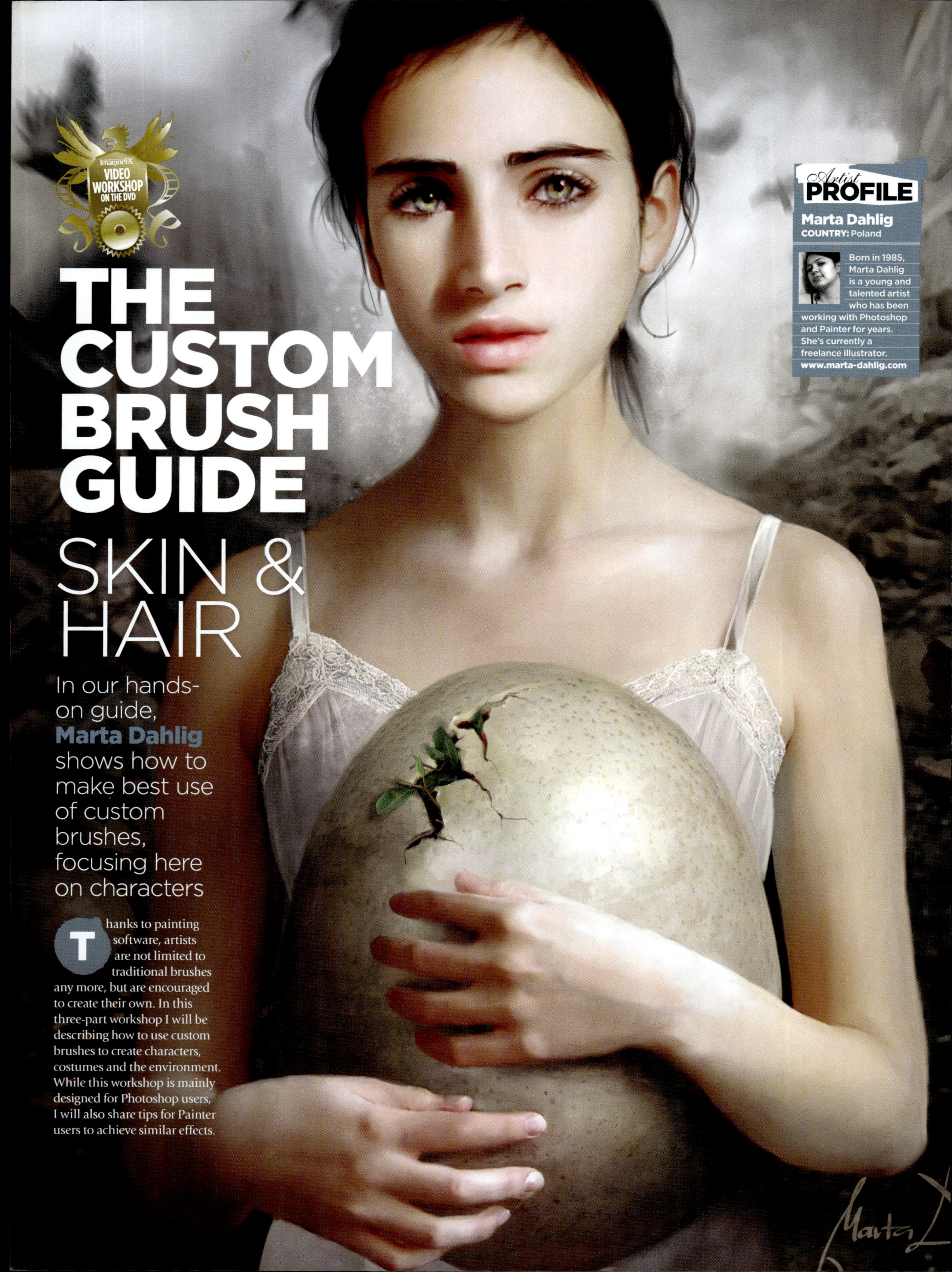

THE CUSTOM BRUSH GUIDE

SKIN & HAIR

In our hands-on guide, **Marta Dahlig** shows how to make best use of custom brushes, focusing here on characters

Artist PROFILE

Marta Dahlig
COUNTRY: Poland

Born in 1985, Marta Dahlig is a young and talented artist who has been working with Photoshop and Painter for years. She's currently a freelance illustrator.
www.marta-dahlig.com

Thanks to painting software, artists are not limited to traditional brushes any more, but are encouraged to create their own. In this three-part workshop I will be describing how to use custom brushes to create characters, costumes and the environment. While this workshop is mainly designed for Photoshop users, I will also share tips for Painter users to achieve similar effects.

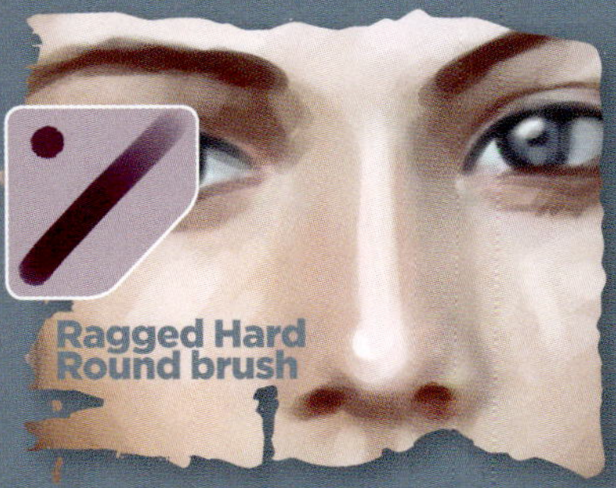

PHOTOSHOP

Opacity: 100%
Flow: 100%
Spacing: 10%
Other Dynamics:
Opacity and Flow, 0%
Smoothing: checked

PAINTER

TINTING
Basic Round
Opacity: 5-15%
Grain: 0%
Resat: 20%
Bleed:100%
Jitter: 0%

This is the first brush I use for any painting. An altered Hard Round brush with ragged edges is perfect for the first stages of colour blocking, because aside from applying colours, its edges will prevent the transitions from being too rough. The pressure sensitive opacity will enable you to create a bigger variety of skin tones.

All brushes are supplied on the DVD

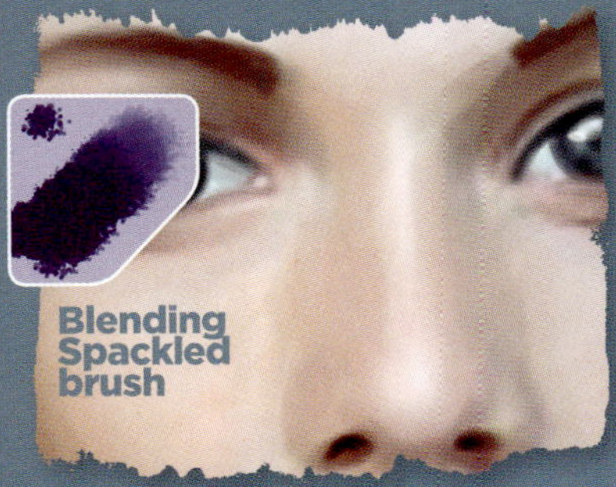

PHOTOSHOP

Opacity: 20-100%
Flow: 100%
Spacing: 6
Other Dynamics:
Opacity and Flow, 0%
Scattering: Both Axes, 109%

PAINTER

TINTING
Blender
Opacity: 15%
Grain: 0%
Resat: 0%
Bleed:100%
Jitter: 0%

BLENDERS
Just Add Water
Opacity: 15%
Grain: 0%
Bleed: 50%
Jitter: 0

A Spackled brush is the best thing to choose when you want to blend facial skin tones. Thanks to its shape and pressure-related opacity, it can blend really well and hint at skin pore texture. Smooth the transitions with this brush, while picking the colours with an Eye Dropper tool. Painter users can use the Blender brush; while it doesn't render a natural skin texture, it creates satisfying effects.

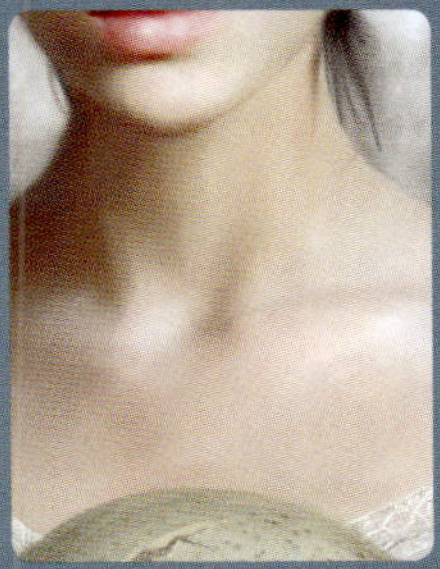

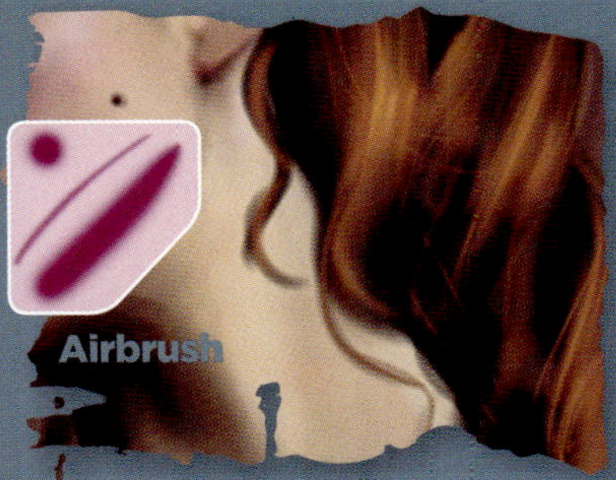

PHOTOSHOP

Opacity: 80-100%
Flow: 100%
Other Dynamics:
Opacity and Flow, 0%
Shape dynamics: (just switched on)

PAINTER

AIRBRUSH
Soft Airbrush
Opacity: 5-15%
Resat: 100%
Bleed:100%
Jitter: 0%

The Airbrush is an extremely flexible tool. It's perfect for adding in anything to your work, from painting strands of hair to adding little details, such as blushes, moles and many others. An Airbrush is also a good way to soften the edges of painted objects and those rougher transitions between certain shades, creating an illusion of beautiful fleshy softness.

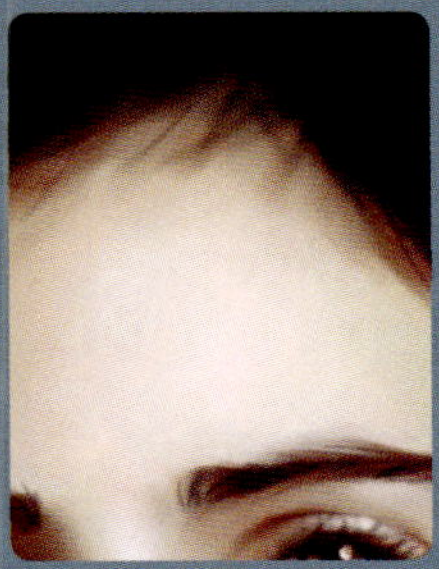

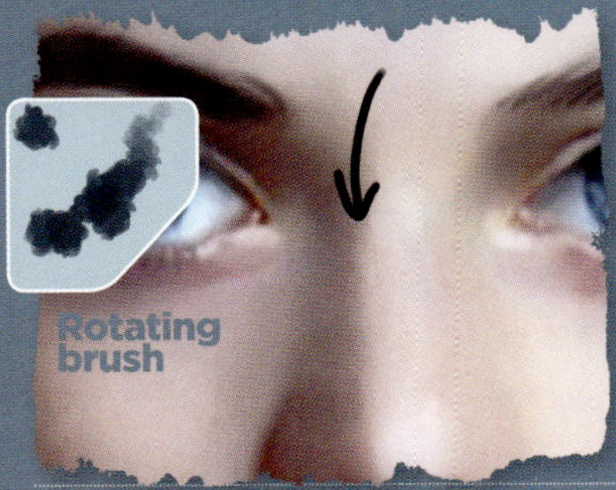

PHOTOSHOP

Opacity: 50%
Flow: 100%
Other Dynamics:
Opacity and Flow, 0%
Scattering: 100%
Shape dynamics: (just switched on)

PAINTER

AIRBRUSH
Detail Airbrush
Opacity: 2-20%
Resat: 20-70%
Bleed:100%
Jitter: 2-3

This brush is perfect for enriching the colour palette of an already painted body part, I always use it for this task. Thanks to its distinctive shape and angle variations, applying new shades naturally is extremely easy: just choose a colour and run with it over the painted skin. If you apply the colours carefully on a low opacity, you won't really require any extra smoothing. This brush also works great as a skin tone blender.

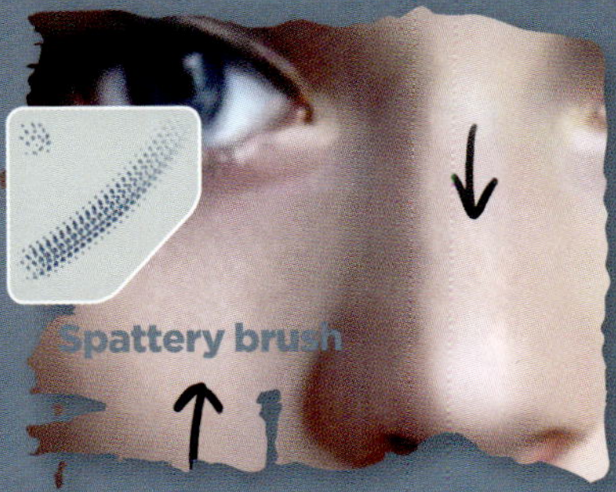

PHOTOSHOP

Opacity: 100%
Flow: 100%
Spacing: 75%
Other Dynamics:
Opacity and Flow, 0%
Smoothing: checked

PAINTER

AIRBRUSH
Tiny Spattery Airbrush
Spread: 50%
Flow: 1
Feature: 20
Opacity: 70%

The small Spackled brush is great to render skin pores with. Use it on a low opacity setting on a separate layer, so you can play with layer modes later (Soft Light usually gives the most natural effects). To enrich the 'automatic' pore effect, create another layer on top of the existing one and, with an Airbrush, randomly place some small lighter dots on top of the previous ones.

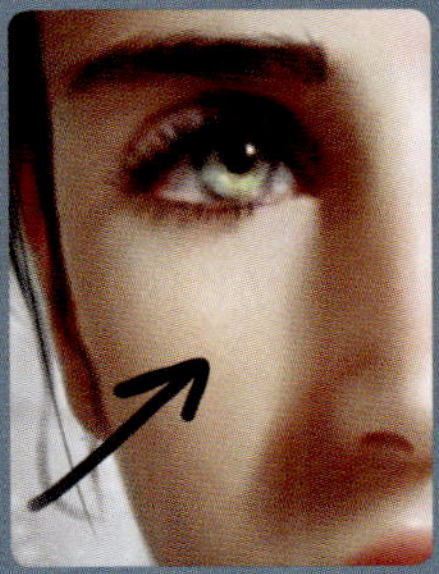

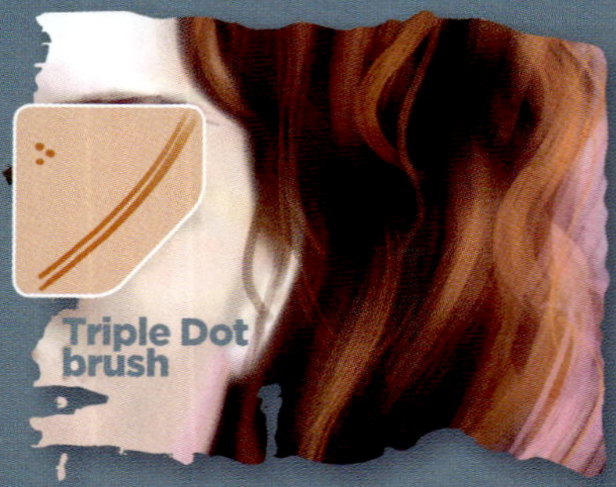

PHOTOSHOP

Opacity: 100%
Flow: 100%
Other Dynamics:
Opacity and Flow, 0%
Smoothing: checked

PAINTER

ACRYLICS
Wet Soft Acrylic
Opacity: 100%
Resat: 30%
Bleed: 100%
Jitter: 0

After having the hair basis marked with an Airbrush, it's good to start adding some texture. This simple Spackled brush is perfect for this job. Start applying the hair strands, gradually moving from bigger and darker to smaller and lighter.

In Painter, I highly recommend the Acrylic brushes – aside from a 'strandy' feel, they will automatically create a very interesting texture.

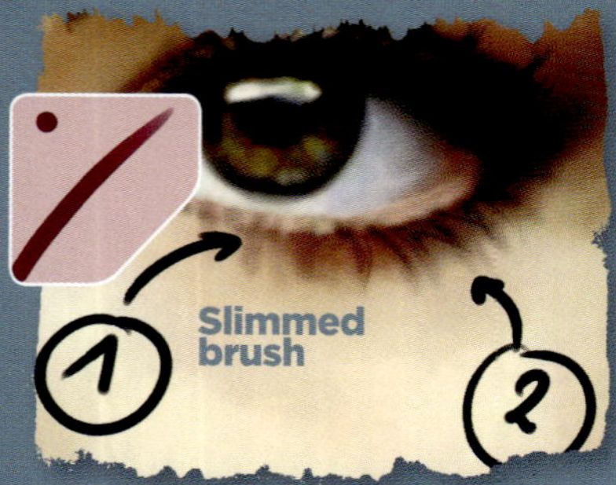

PHOTOSHOP

Opacity: 100%
Flow: 100%
Other Dynamics:
Opacity and Flow, 0%
Shape dynamics: (just switched on)
Smoothing: checked

PAINTER

PENS
Fine Point
Opacity: 10-30%
Resat: 100%
Bleed: 0%

This simple brush, thanks to its pressure adjusted size and opacity, is a natural choice for painting eyelashes. Use it on a low opacity to mark the shades under the eyelashes (1). Afterwards, size it down a bit and increase the opacity, marking the actual eyelashes (2). This brush is also a wonderful tool for hair detailing.

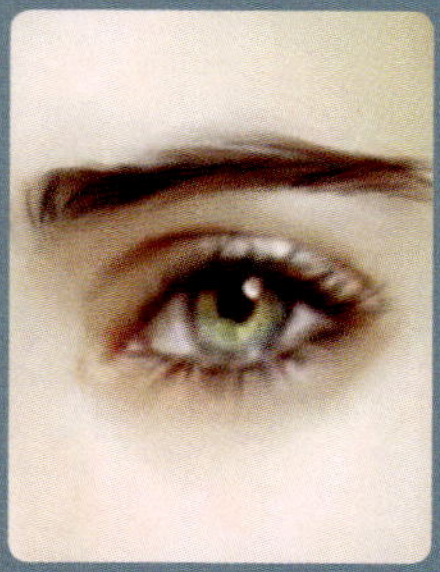

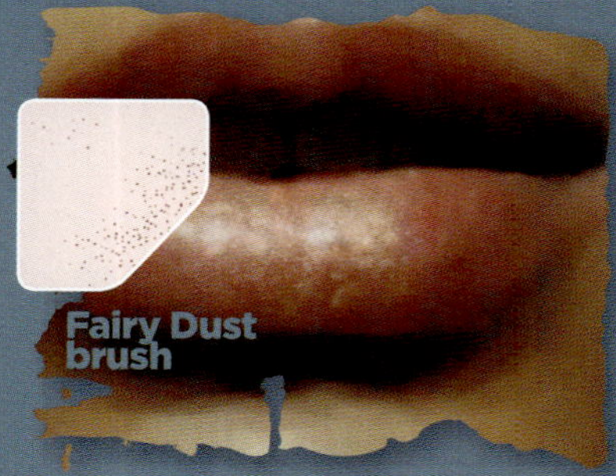

PHOTOSHOP

Opacity: 100%
Flow: 100%
Other Dynamics:
Opacity and Flow, 0%
Smoothing: checked
Scattering: Both Axes; 85%

PAINTER

AIRBRUSH
Variable Spatter
Spread: 90°
Flow: 5
Feature: 9
Opacity: 60-80%

This Spackled brush is a great special effects tool. When painting characters, you can use it to texture mouths: choose a light colour and run with the brush over the highlighted part of the lips. To achieve natural effects, switch the sizes and opacity constantly. You can also use this brush to enhance a magic spell rendition, by creating a fairy dust effect. Furthermore, you can also paint stars with it!

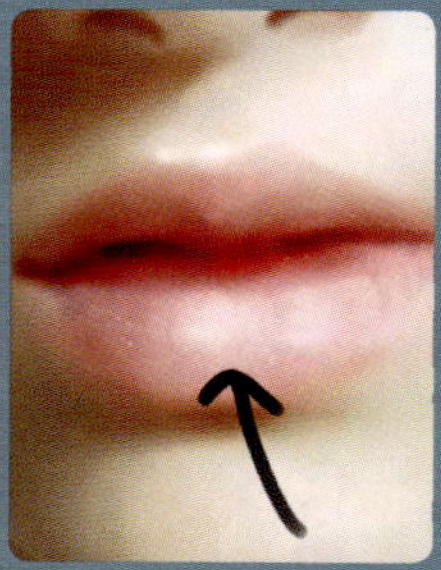

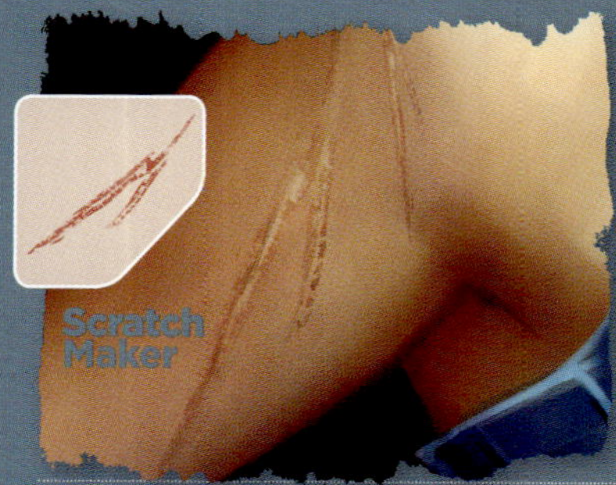

PHOTOSHOP

Opacity: 30-40%
Flow: 100%

PAINTER

Unavailable

This custom brush was made from a leaf photograph I took. It's perfect for creating scratched surfaces, but most of all for scars. Choose a neutral brown colour and use the brush over the skin (by clicking, not dragging). Then experiment with the layer modes (I recommend Overlay). Later, you might want to shrink the brush and add some lighter textures to some parts of the scar to make it look more natural.

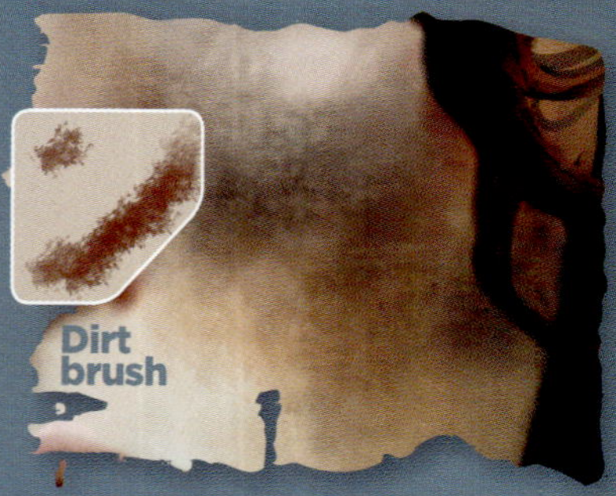

PHOTOSHOP

Opacity: 10-50%
Flow: 100%
Other Dynamics:
Opacity and Flow, 0%
Smoothing: checked
Scattering: 33%

PAINTER

Unavailable

This ragged brush is fabulous for adding dirt effects to the skin and clothing. Simply pick a darker colour and click around the surface, remembering to switch the sizes and opacity constantly. Afterwards, change the Layer mode to Multiply and add some Gaussian Blur to make your brushstrokes look natural.

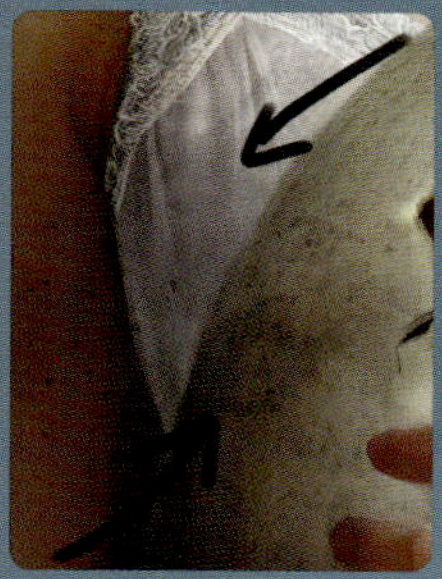

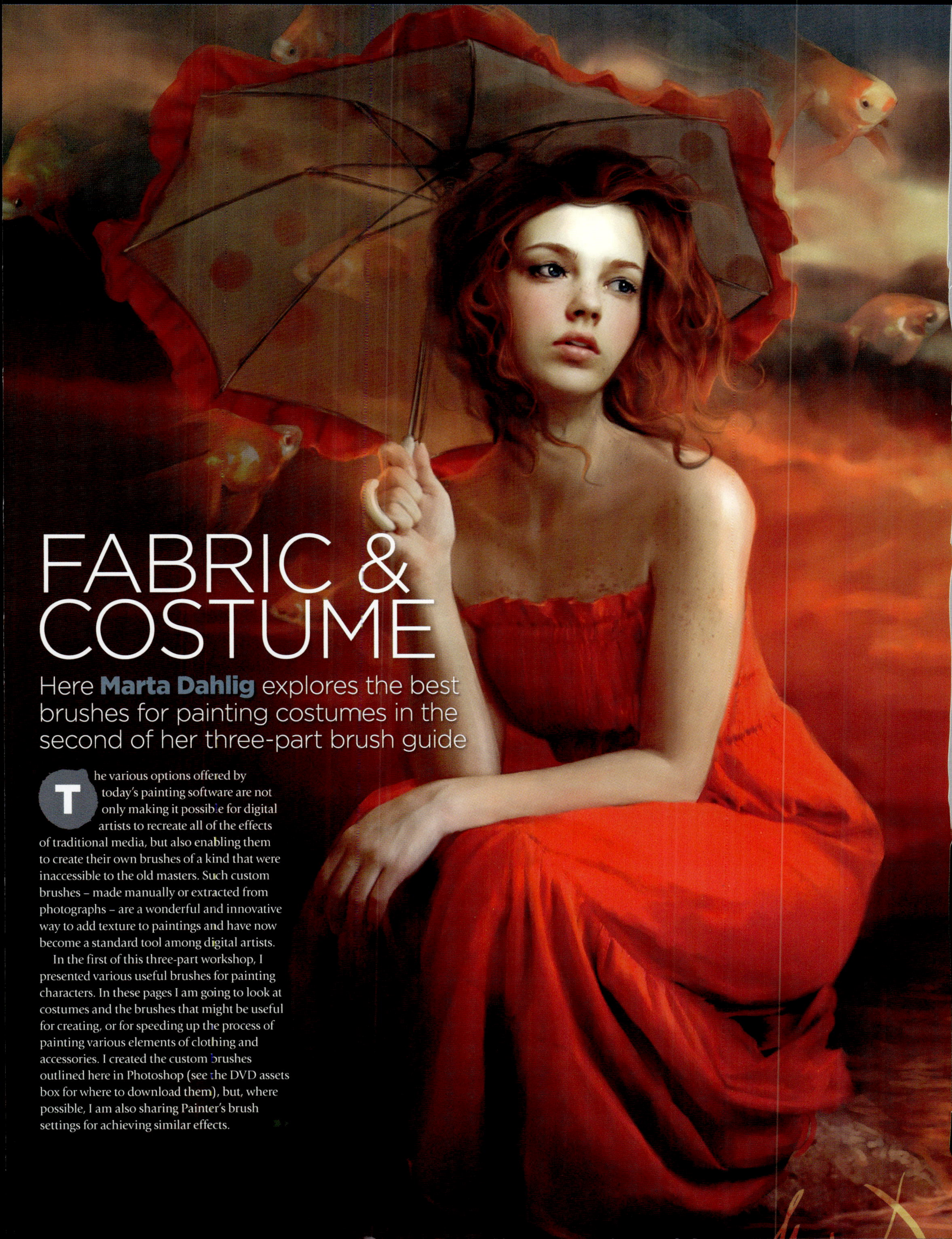

FABRIC & COSTUME

Here **Marta Dahlig** explores the best brushes for painting costumes in the second of her three-part brush guide

The various options offered by today's painting software are not only making it possible for digital artists to recreate all of the effects of traditional media, but also enabling them to create their own brushes of a kind that were inaccessible to the old masters. Such custom brushes – made manually or extracted from photographs – are a wonderful and innovative way to add texture to paintings and have now become a standard tool among digital artists.

In the first of this three-part workshop, I presented various useful brushes for painting characters. In these pages I am going to look at costumes and the brushes that might be useful for creating, or for speeding up the process of painting various elements of clothing and accessories. I created the custom brushes outlined here in Photoshop (see the DVD assets box for where to download them), but, where possible, I am also sharing Painter's brush settings for achieving similar effects.

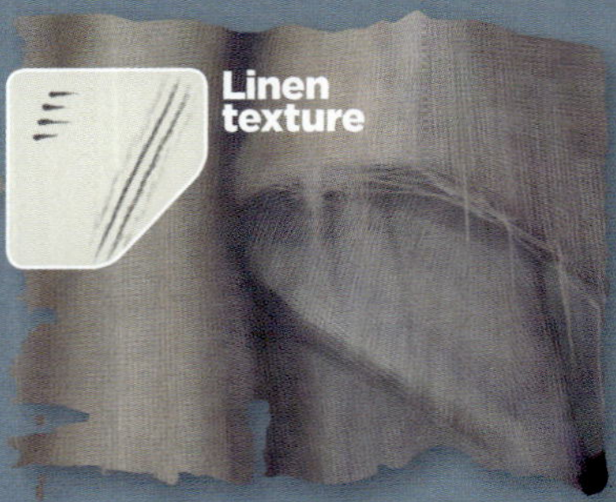

Linen texture

PHOTOSHOP

Opacity: 100%
Flow: 50%
Shape Dynamics:
Size Jitter: Off
Angle Jitter: 0%
Roundness Jitter: 73%
Minimum Roundness: 62%
Texture:
Wrinkles
Scale: 45%
Texture Each Tip: On
Mode: Multiply
Depth/Minimum Depth: 100%
Depth Jitter: Off
Dual Brush:
Diameter: 110px
Spacing: 15%
Scattering: Both axes, 0%
Count: 1
Other Dynamics:
Opacity Jitter: 0%
Flow Jitter: 0%

PAINTER

PENCILS
Sketching Pencil
Opacity: 50-100%
Grain: 18%
Bleed: 10%
Jitter: 0%

This simple Spackled brush makes texturing linen easier than ever. Just paint the desired folds and later, on a new layer, paint some vertical and horizontal brushstrokes. Remember to keep the brush size small and change the hue from time to time. To touch up, play with the Opacity and Layer modes to see if you can enhance the created effect. You might also want to use the Burn/Highlight tool in the most/least convex areas of the fabric.

DOWNLOAD MARTA'S BRUSHES FROM http://bit.ly/jcUvcl

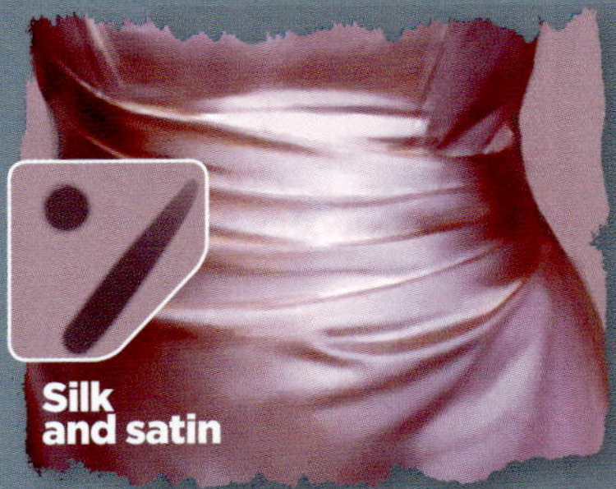

Silk and satin

PHOTOSHOP

Opacity: 20-80%
Flow: 50%
Shape Dynamics:
Size Jitter: 0%
Minimum Diameter: 10%
Other Dynamics:
Opacity Jitter: 0%

PAINTER

TINTING
Basic Round
Opacity: 10-30%
Resat: 20%
Bleed: 100%
Jitter: 0%

TINTING
Blender
Opacity: 5-10%
Grain: 0%
Resat: 70%
Bleed: 100%
Jitter: 0%

BLENDERS
Just Add Water
Opacity: 10-40%
Resat: 0%
Bleed: 50%
Jitter: 0%

This brush is a hybrid between a Ragged Edge Hard Round (described in the first part of this workshop) and an Airbrush, which makes it a fabulous blender and a texturing tool at the same time. It is especially effective when painting textiles with smooth colour transitions, such as satin or silk.

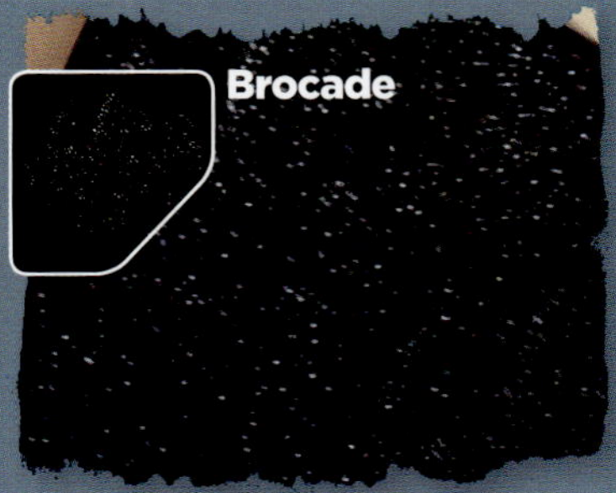

Brocade

PHOTOSHOP

Opacity: 90-100%
Flow: 50%

PAINTER

AIRBRUSHES
Tiny Spattery Airbrush
Opacity: 75%
Spread: 45%
Flow: 1
Feature: 9

I use this Spackled brush for texturing brocade fabrics. It looks plain, but used correctly it can be extremely powerful. To get the best from this brush always use it at full opacity, constantly adjusting the lightness between the applications. To push the realism of the texture, blur the specks from time to time and use the Dodge and Burn tools to accentuate singular dots to a higher extent.

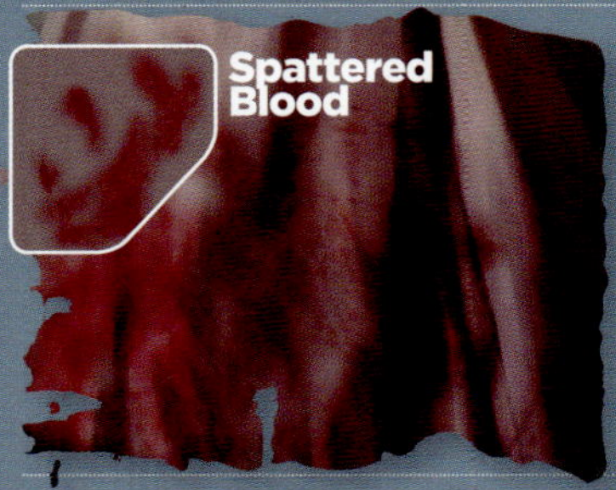

Spattered Blood

PHOTOSHOP

Opacity: 20-50%
Flow: 50%

PAINTER

Unavailable

Now here is something for your more morbid paintings! This brush was made by accident, but it proved great for creating stains on textiles, especially for a spattered blood effect. Use this as a stamp on a separate layer with Overlay mode switched on. Blur (and occasionally rotate) the colour blocks for a natural effect.

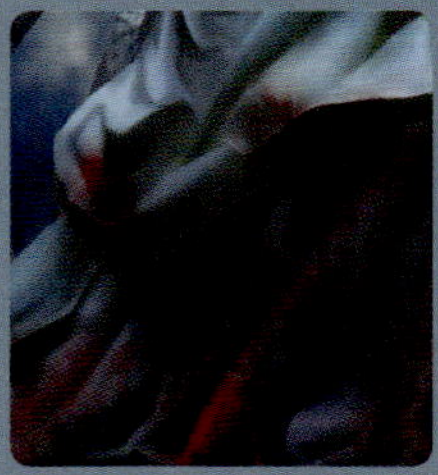

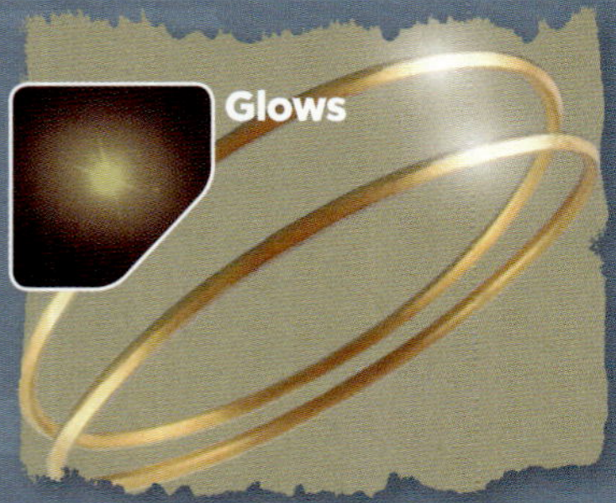

Glows

PHOTOSHOP

Opacity: 60-100%
Flow: 50%

PAINTER

TINTING
Airbrushes: Fine Tip Soft Air
Opacity: 5-10%
Resat: 100%
Bleed: 0%
Jitter: 0

This little stamp brush is extremely useful for all kinds of jobs. It can simulate all sorts of reflections and glow on metal objects, brocade and sequins, as well as act as a star or sun stamp. In addition it can be used to create the fairy dust effect.

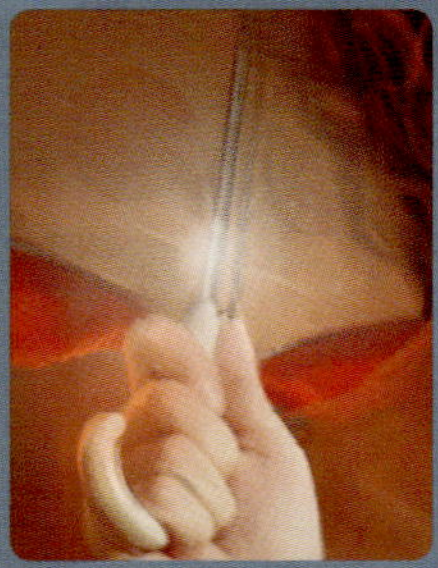

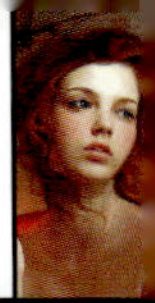

Material patterns

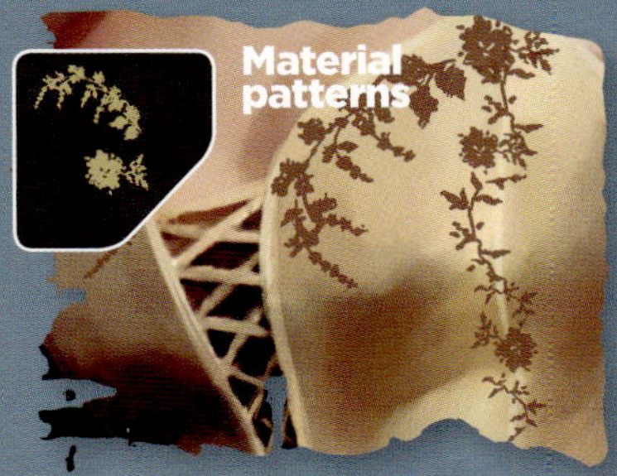

PHOTOSHOP
Opacity: 100%
Flow: 50%

PAINTER
Unavailable

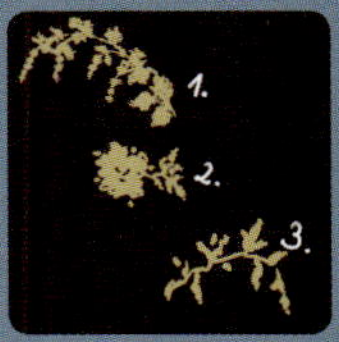

This is a set of three stamp brushes that I frequently use to create floral patterns for my characters' dresses. There are dozens of possibilities for interesting patterns, as long as you keep resizing and rotating the brushes.

By experimenting with layer modes you can create semi-transparent patterns for lace (I use Soft Light or Multiply, depending on the colour) or a nice basis to paint embroidery upon.

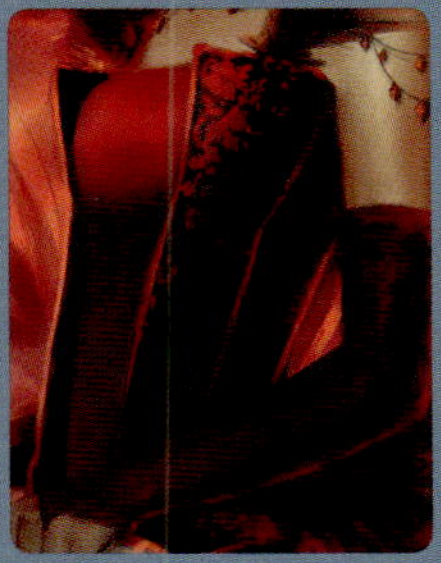

Embroidery

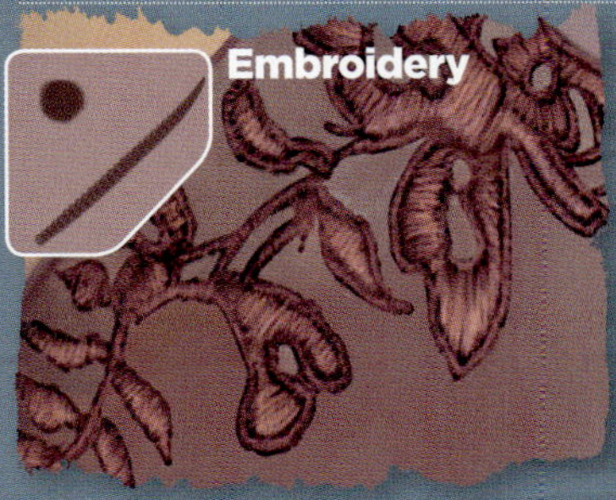

PHOTOSHOP
Opacity: 70-100%
Flow: 50%
Spacing: 50%
Shape Dynamics:
Size Jitter: 0%
Min diameter: 0%

PAINTER
PENS
Thick And Thin Pen
Opacity: 100%
Resat: 100%
Bleed: 0%

With its sparse spacing this brush looks a bit pixellated, which is a great means of achieving a realistic thread effect. Start off with a dark zigzag pattern and move to lighter colours. The more layers of thread you lay down, the thicker the embroidery will look. To underline the thickness, form your zigzags into arches instead of straight lines. Remember to keep your brush size very small at all times!

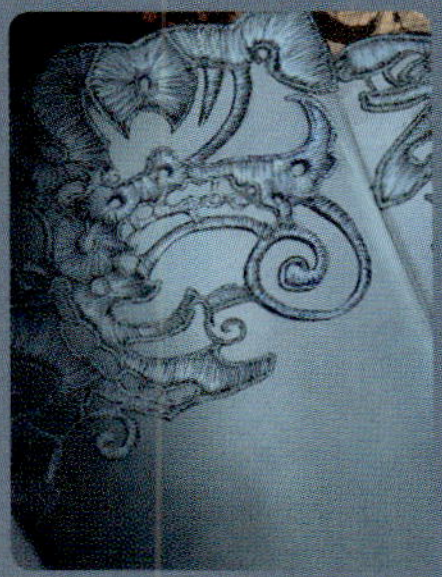

Feather boas

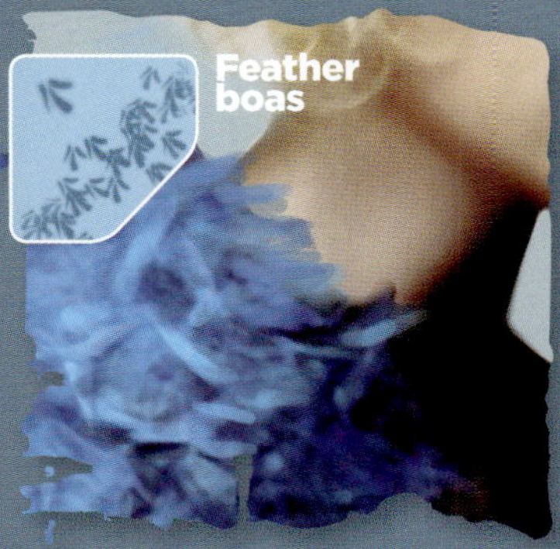

PHOTOSHOP
Opacity: 10-70%
Flow: 50%
Shape Dynamics:
Size Jitter: 0%
Minimum Diameter: 10%
Angle Jitter: 11%
Scattering:
Both axes, 294%
Count: 1
Count Jitter: 98%
Other Dynamics:
Opacity Jitter: 0%
Flow Jitter: 0%

PAINTER
Unavailable

This is a great texturing brush, which will enable you to mark out the details of a feather boa, without having to paint each individual feather separately. First, block the general shape of the object and roughly shade it, marking the highlights and shadows with an Airbrush. Afterwards, use the Feather brush on a low opacity on top of the existing shape. Switch the sizes and colour depth constantly, marking some darker and lighter areas. After you have the basic texture in place, try to underline singular feathers by giving them some extra highlights and shadows underneath. This is an easy way to create a realistic looking boa.

Fur

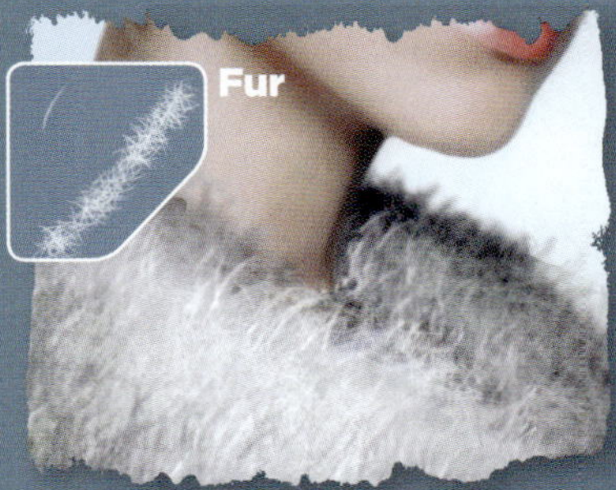

PHOTOSHOP
Opacity: 10-70%
Flow: 50%
Shape Dynamics:
Size Jitter: 0%
Minimum Diameter: 1%
Angle Jitter: 45%
Scattering:
Both axes, 109%
Count: 1
Count Jitter: 98%
Other Dynamics:
Opacity Jitter: 0%

PAINTER
F-X
Furry Brush
Opacity: 10-20%
Resat: 25%
Bleed: 0%

This is a simplified version of Painter's Furry brush. At first it is difficult to achieve satisfying results, but once mastered, it speeds up the process of painting fur. After you have the general shape marked with an airbrush tool, add fur strands on a new layer. When the first strokes are done, use the Gaussian Blur tool on it. Change the brush's hue, make another layer of strands and blur it again.

Lace

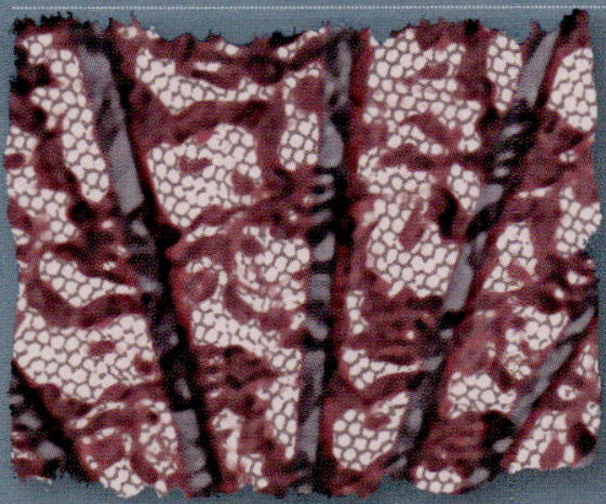

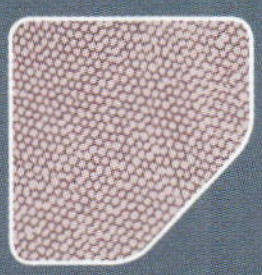

PHOTOSHOP
Opacity: 50-100%
Flow: 50%

PAINTER
Unavailable

This stamp brush is extracted from a veil photograph I took and is perfect for texturing lace in garments or objects. It's easy to use – place it on a new layer (with the Multiply mode on) over the object to texture and you're done! You might want to blur it slightly for a more realistic effect.

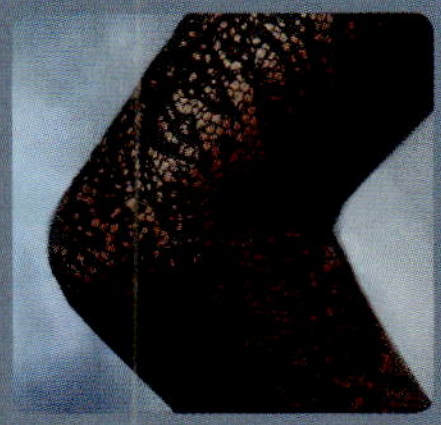

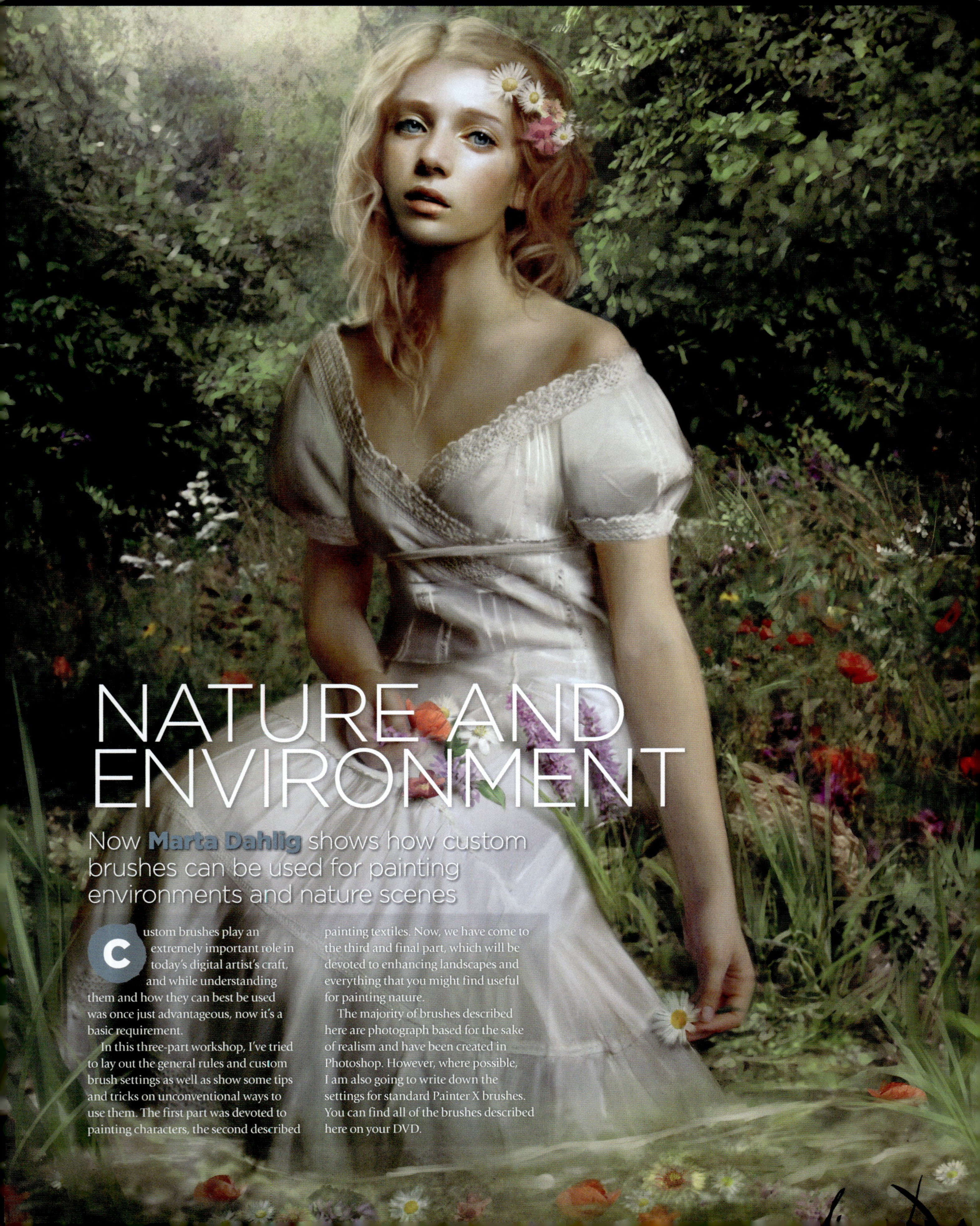

NATURE AND ENVIRONMENT

Now **Marta Dahlig** shows how custom brushes can be used for painting environments and nature scenes

Custom brushes play an extremely important role in today's digital artist's craft, and while understanding them and how they can best be used was once just advantageous, now it's a basic requirement.

In this three-part workshop, I've tried to lay out the general rules and custom brush settings as well as show some tips and tricks on unconventional ways to use them. The first part was devoted to painting characters, the second described painting textiles. Now, we have come to the third and final part, which will be devoted to enhancing landscapes and everything that you might find useful for painting nature.

The majority of brushes described here are photograph based for the sake of realism and have been created in Photoshop. However, where possible, I am also going to write down the settings for standard Painter X brushes. You can find all of the brushes described here on your DVD.

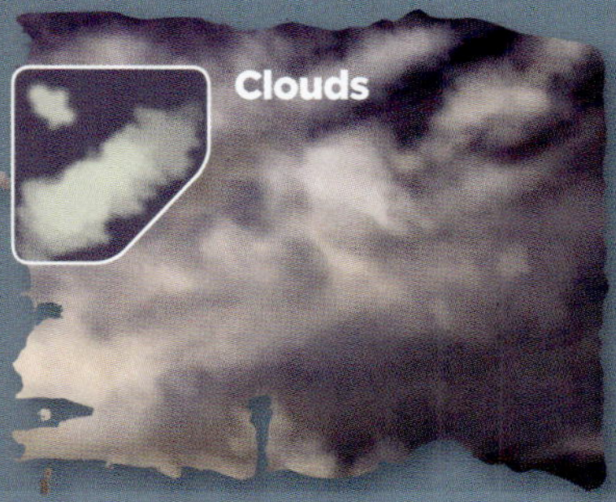

PHOTOSHOP

Opacity: 25-50%
Flow: 100%
Spacing: 3%
Shape Dynamics: Size Jitter: 20%
Minimum Diameter: 9%
Scattering: Both axes, 137%
Other Dynamics: Opacity and Flow Jitter: 0%

PAINTER

Chalk: Large Chalk
Opacity: 10-50%
Grain: 20%
Resat: 20-50%
Bleed: 0 %
Jitter: 0-1

This brush is quite a simple shape and consists of a few merged airbrush tips. It is very easy to use and highly efficient for realistic renders, so long as you remember to switch the opacity and colours constantly throughout the painting process. To use it most effectively, first off sketch out the general cloud shape with an airbrush and try the brush out on top of it on a separate layer.

All brushes are supplied free on your DVD

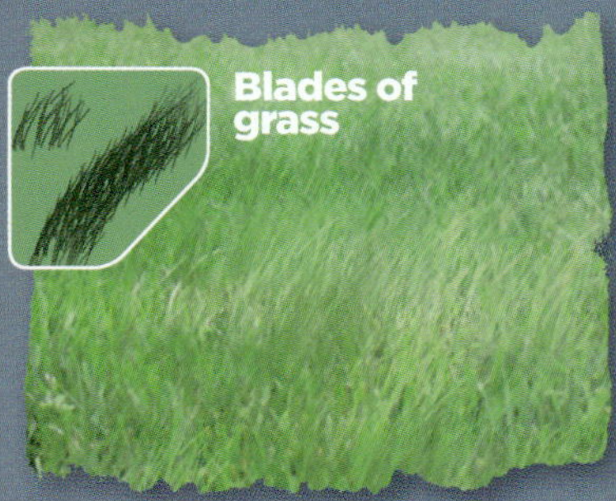

PHOTOSHOP

Opacity: 5-50%
Flow: 100%
Spacing: 25%
Other Dynamics: Opacity and flow Jitter: 0%

PAINTER

Unavailable

This brush is great for basic texturing of a grassy field. However, do not rely on it solely, as nothing can replace the hand-made touches. Once you have the basis done, pick an airbrush or hard round of a lighter colour and add some additional blades. For extra realism you can also add some loose leaves, sticks and so on. When the texture is done, duplicate that layer, flipping it horizontally and setting its layer mode to Soft Light.

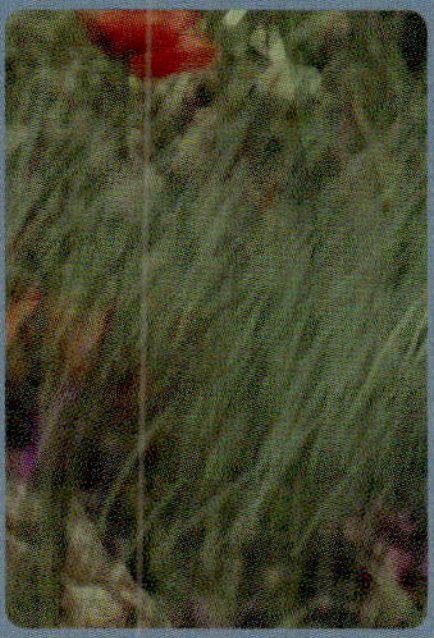

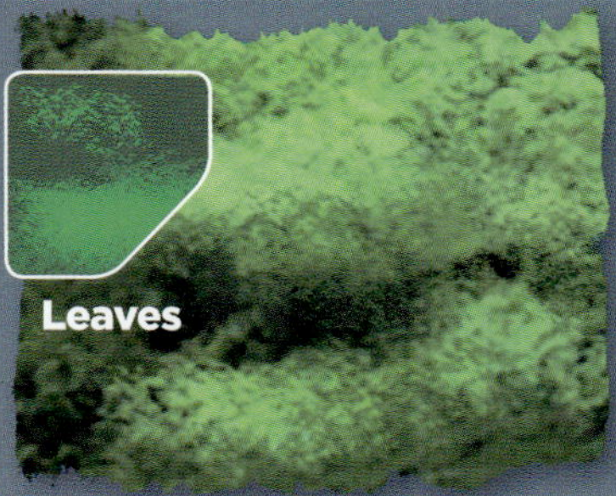

PHOTOSHOP

Opacity: 5-30%
Flow: 100%
Spacing: 25%

PAINTER

Chalk: Large Chalk
Opacity: 50%
Grain: 25%
Resat: 18%
Bleed: 0%
Jitter: 4

This photo brush is extremely useful for painting leaves in distant backgrounds. Its edges are sharp, due to the photo extraction, so be sure to blur the painted leaf blobs from time to time to avoid artificial looking results. When shading with these brushes, try to gradually move on from darkest to lightest shades. Once done, paint some individual leaves with an airbrush on top of the area.

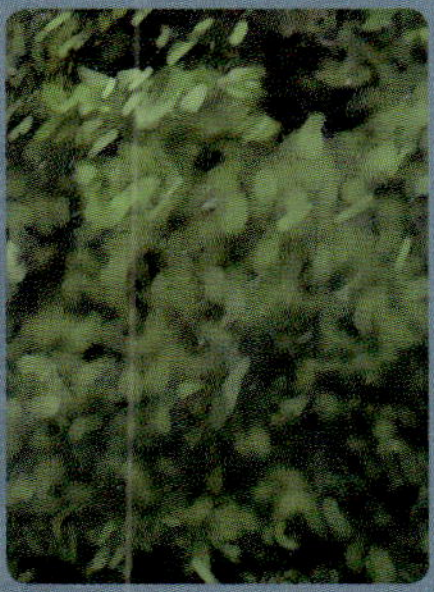

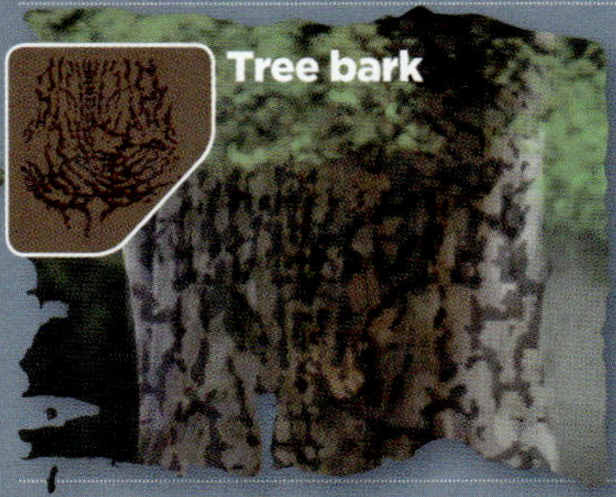

PHOTOSHOP

Opacity: 20-40%
Flow: 100%

PAINTER

Unavailable

This is another brush that I extracted from an old photo I took a while back. Using it requires a bit of patience as the stamp has to be rotated continuously, but once you're used to it, it enables you to create truly realistic effects. After you place it over an area, enhance the effect by underlining the cracked edges with a lighter stroke. This brush has a lot of functions and, aside from texturing bark, can be used for painting cracks, facial marks and scars.

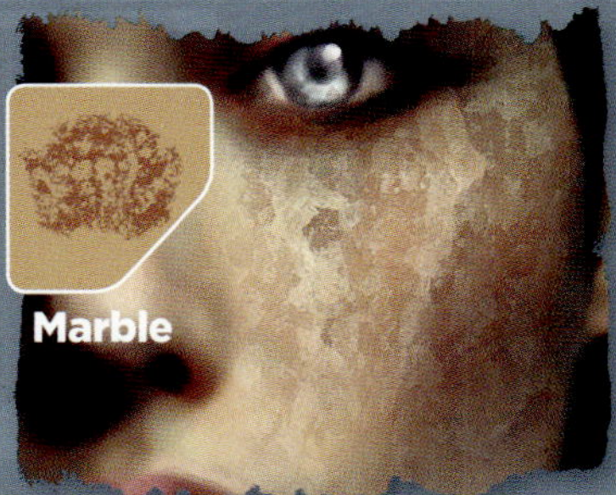

PHOTOSHOP

Opacity: 30-70%
Flow: 100%

PAINTER

Unavailable

This is a wonderful brush extracted from a marble photo, which I use excessively for a multitude of things. It can be employed for general painting and texturing, texturing of flat stone surfaces and even skin deformities. It is most efficient when used over the desired area on a separate layer with its mode switched to Overlay, Multiply or Soft Light.

Gallery
Interviews
Workshops
Core skills

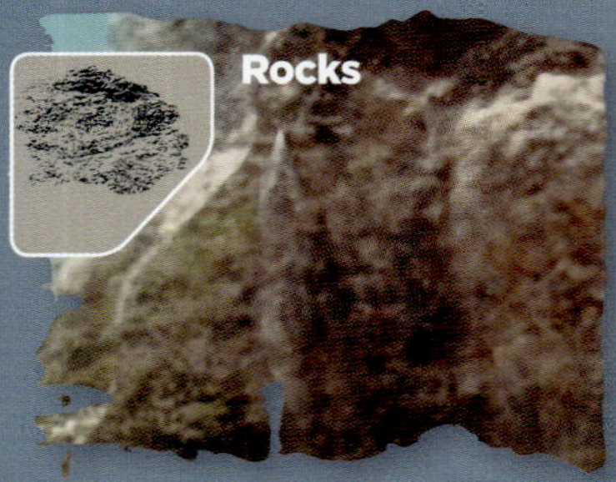

PHOTOSHOP
Opacity: 5-50%
Flow: 100%

PAINTER
Unavailable

Painting rocks is extremely hard and time consuming. This brush can't be used to create a realistic rock from beginning to end, but it is extremely useful for creating a basic texture or for hinting at the detail during speed painting. Use it as a stamp, from time to time rotating the blobs. It's definitely most effective when you blur the outcome and regularly change the hues and brightness.

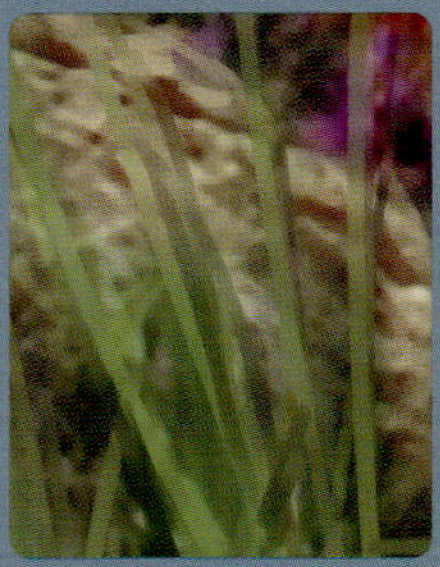

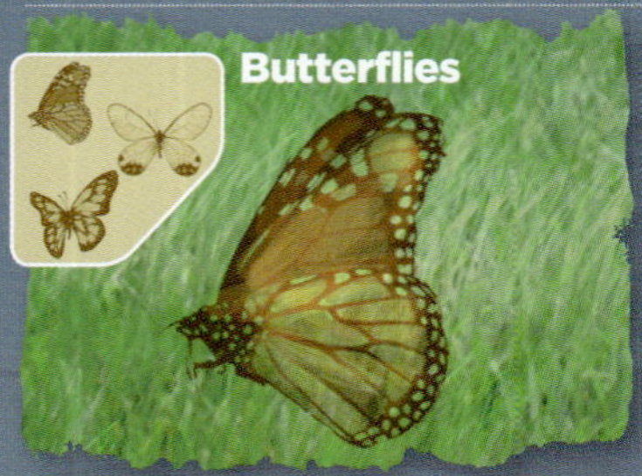

PHOTOSHOP
Opacity: 50-100%
Flow: 100%

PAINTER
Unavailable

Butterflies are very common painting elements, yet quite time consuming. So, why not make your life a little bit easier? The brushes shown here were created from photos I found on the internet. They're extremely handy if you need to add detail to your painting but are feeling a bit lazy – I always use them when painting glades, forests and such.

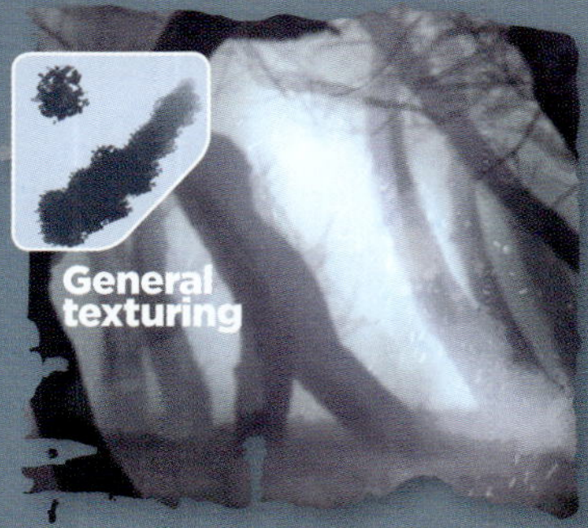

PHOTOSHOP
Opacity: 10-90%
Flow: 100%
Spacing: 5%
Shape Dynamics:
Size Jitter: 55%
Minimum Diameter: 9%
Scattering:
Both axes, 104%
Count: 5
Other Dynamics:
Opacity and Flow Jitter: 0%

PAINTER
Unavailable

I use this brush for speed painting landscapes, when I rarely switch between the brush types. This custom one is made out of some loose colour blobs – its ragged edges encourage smooth transitions between colours and so make this brush perfect for all fast jobs, as you don't need to constantly worry about colours not blending correctly. Use this brush as a typical hard round, constantly playing with the opacity and colour.

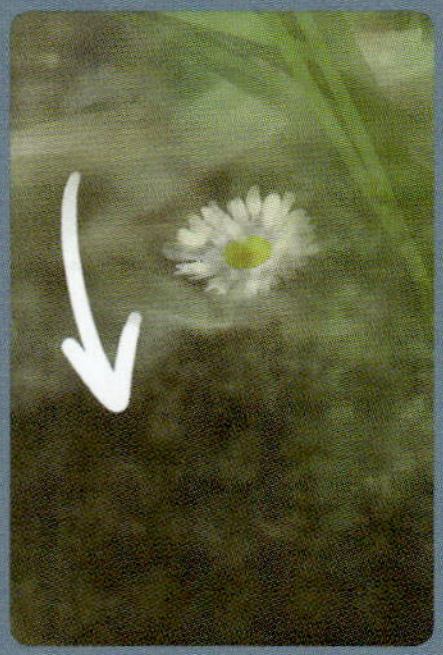

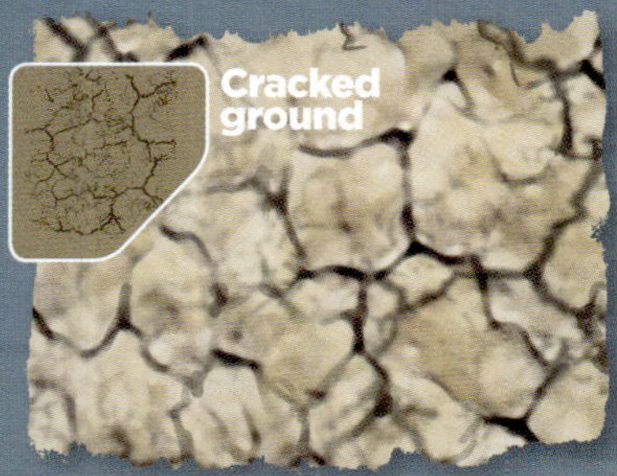

PHOTOSHOP
Opacity: 10-80%
Flow: 100%

PAINTER
Unavailable

This brush is a fast and efficient means to texture dried ground. Use it as a stamp, preferably on a multiply layer mode. It usually requires some editing and rotating, but generally greatly speeds up the painting process. Aside from its main use, it can also be handy for painting lightning.

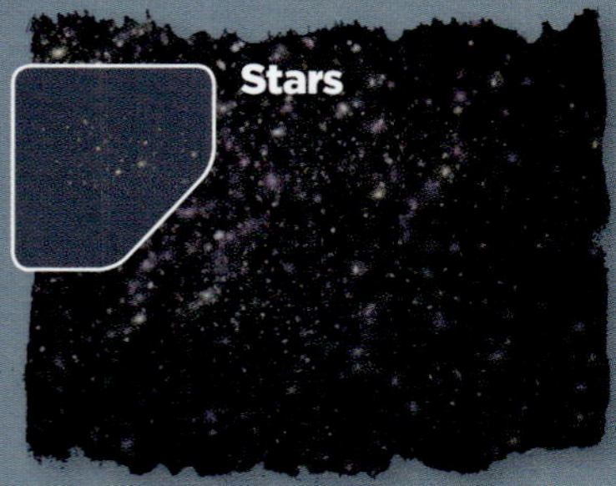

PHOTOSHOP
Opacity: 10-100%
Flow: 100%

PAINTER
AIRBRUSH
Tiny Spattery Airbrush
Opacity: 75%
Spread:
15 degrees
Flow: 2-4
Feature: 5-10

Now that is a fast way to paint a sky! Just run over the night sky with this brush, first with a larger size and higher transparency (for distant stars) gradually blurring and changing to smaller and more opaque. This brush is one of the most functional, as aside from its main purpose, it can be used to create such textures as: skin pores, brocade, smaller leaves, dust, enhanced grass and so on.

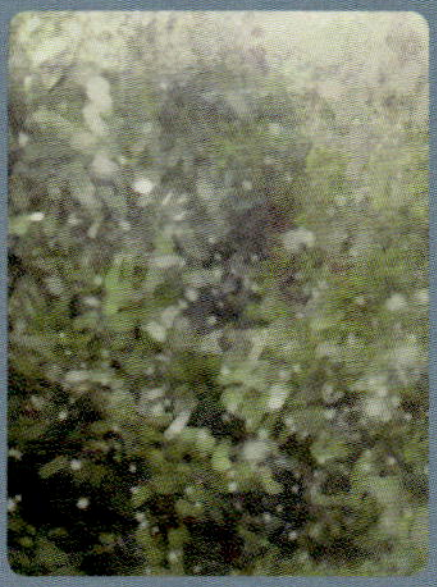

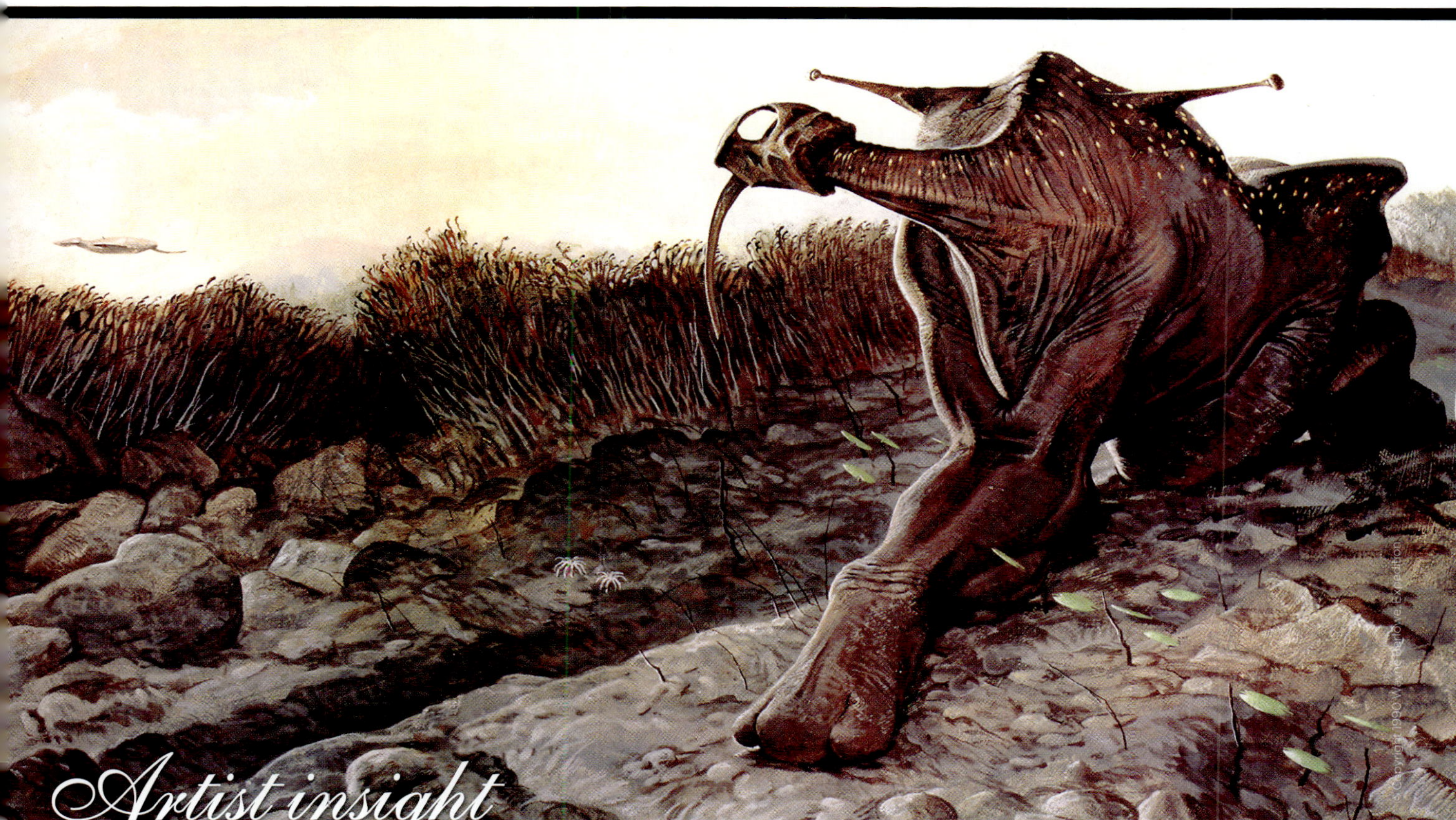

Artist insight

CREATING AND RENDERING ALIENS

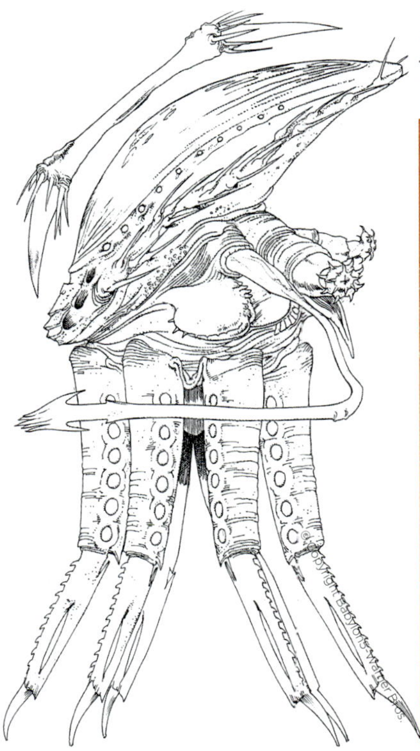

Legendary artist **Wayne D Barlowe** guides you through 25 tips on creating your own alien life-forms...

Artist **PROFILE**

Wayne D Barlowe
COUNTRY: US
CLIENTS: Discovery Channel, Activision, Time Magazine, Random House publishers

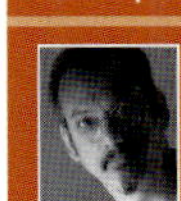

After several years in book illustration, Wayne began writing and illustrating his own books, among them Barlowe's Guide to Extraterrestrials and Brushfire. Since then he has also contributed creature designs for Hellboy, Blade 2 and Harry Potter 3 and 4. Most recently he was executive producer on Discovery Channel's Alien Planet.
www.waynebarlowe.com

In hindsight it was only natural that, as both the son of natural history illustrators and an avid SF reader, I should turn to conceiving and rendering alien life forms. And, that the logical blending of SF with the naturalist's convention of field guides should lead to Barlowe's Guide to Extraterrestrials. With that book, finished by the time I was 21, I set my course towards a life-long exploration of the extraterrestrial. Along the way I would be sidetracked by film design and artistic ventures into Hell, but my first love, aliens, was never very far from my mind.

In 1990, Expedition hit the shelves and represented the fullest realisation of where my ideas about alien fauna might take me. With over 40 paintings and numerous black and whites, it's the definitive illustration of my passion, until I approach world-building again.

Anyone who knows me knows that I am a traditionalist. While I am now delving into Photoshop, it is strictly, for the moment, due to the time constraints of film work. Otherwise, I paint in real acrylics and draw with actual pencils.

A few words on my personal philosophy regarding aliens. Aliens are not monsters in the vernacular sense. Neither are they some fabrication of our subconscious, a surrogate for our hopes and dreams embodied in the overly used, overgrown baby-forms of the Roswell "greys". They might be monstrous or child-like, true, but to my way of thinking these are Hollywood conventions that need to be countered by a more sober, scientific approach. What follow are a few provocative thoughts that might help you break the log-jam of the mundane and enable you to free your imagination from what has already been seen.

1 IT STARTS WITH A CONCEPT

If you are determined to create an alien from the extraterrestrial ground up try to have a strong theme in mind. Attempt to conceive of some umbrella concept that is compelling, some environment that is challenging to the on-looker, or some planetary phenomenon that might guide evolution in a unique direction. A passing familiarity with planetary science is a useful catalyst towards this eventual goal.

2 ORIGINALITY'S THE KEY

In a world where so many artists in film and publishing are doing **creature design**, the only true way to rise up is to be **original**. Developing a strong, unique style as well as conceiving original ideas is a sure way out of the pack. Of all these tips, perhaps, this is the most **challenging**, demanding a concerted effort on the artist's part to ignore what came before.

> **"In a world where so many artists are doing creature design, the only true way to rise up is to be original"**

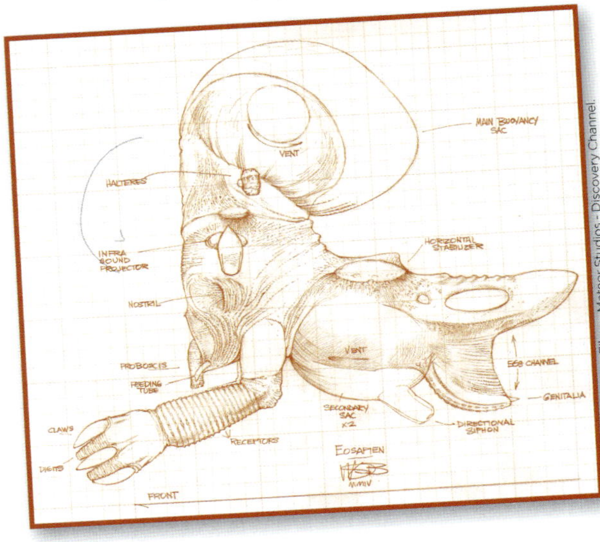

3 STRONG SHAPES ARE MEMORABLE SHAPES

I have a tendency towards cleaner, stronger forms. This is a personal approach. I like shapes with which the viewer can connect quickly and I believe they have more potency than overly baroque creations. Our animal world has a tendency towards economical solutions, an evolutionary pragmatism that appeals to me.

4 FORGET HOLLYWOOD

Perhaps the single greatest alien in film history is, you guessed it, the Alien. HR Giger's remarkable creation has inspired a generation of filmmakers and designers alike but its brilliant, viral design sensibility should not inform your work. Once something has been designed, sculpted, CG-rendered and seen on the screen it's done, finished. Enjoy it, but do not be seduced by it.

5 BUILD YOUR WORLD FIRST

Develop your world from the core outwards. Take an educated guess or contact a friendly scientist, ask some questions and see if you can create a complex world that works. Geology, gravity, climatology, are all factors that contribute to what your aliens look like.

6 FORM FOLLOWS FUNCTION

The animal kingdom on Earth solves its equations with **elegance and economy**. Complexity can be the harbinger of extinction. I would have to imagine the same holds true on other worlds. My suggestion is to go out and buy a really good reference book on **animal mechanics**. Biomechanics are fascinating in and of themselves, but when applied to conceptual alien life they can make all the difference structurally.

7 PLEASE, NO CARICATURES

Unless you are working on a Men In Black-type of project, where humour is intentional, step back and be objective. Is that spindly legged, barrel-bodied, pop-eyed creature you've just created funnier than you had intended? There are "funny" creatures on Earth but they are not the norm. And slapping huge, sharp teeth on something that is innately comical doesn't suddenly make it terrifying. If you feel there is good justification to go down this path make sure that is clear. Otherwise be careful of humour.

8 CONVINCING THE VIEWER

I'm a firm believer in the **gestalt of art**. The totality of an image is going to hit viewers and they are either going to get it right away or not. With that said, your job is to get the lighting (even if it's odd), the creature (hopefully it is odd!), its **gestures, the secondary elements and the environment**, right. It's a balancing act. If any of those elements are too broad you run the risk of losing that first moment with your audience.

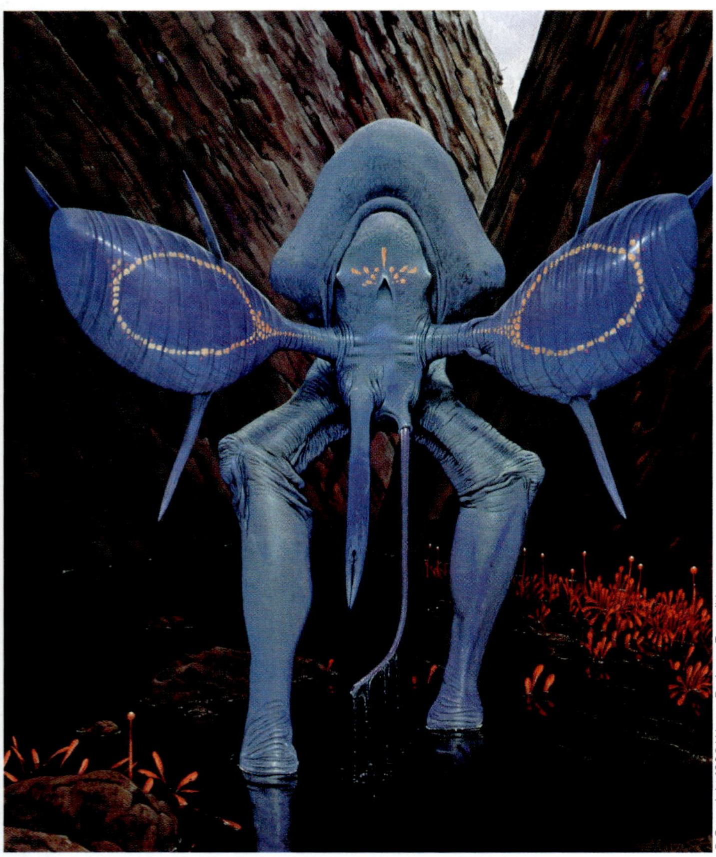

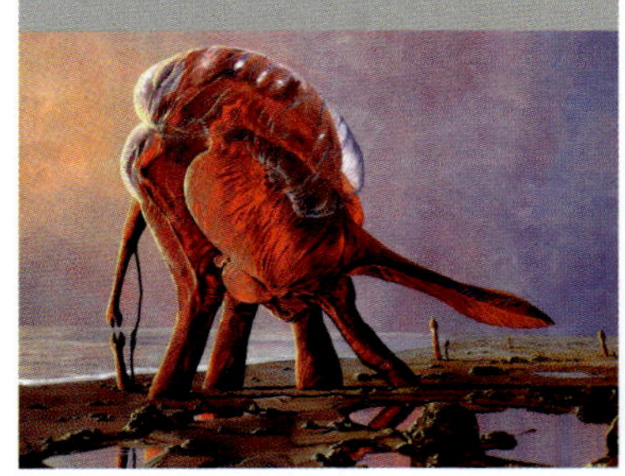

9 TEXTURES

I find textures to be **fun**. As time-consuming as it can be, I like rendering them and I have **good references** to back them up. But they are the final touch in the dressing up of any alien design. Too many inexperienced artists spend a ton of time applying great textures to less than great frameworks. It's a trap to be avoided.

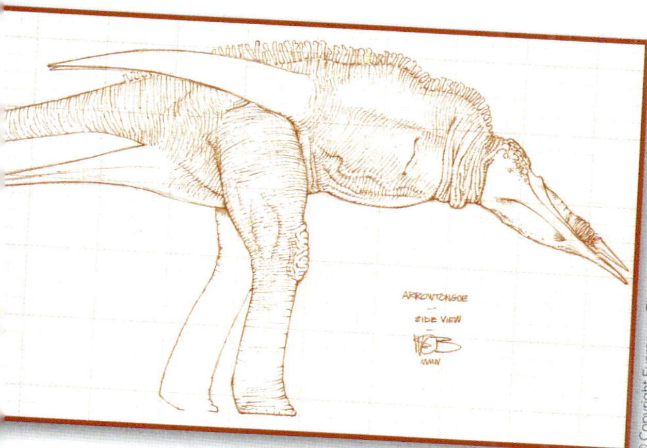

© Copyright Evergreen Films - MeteorStudios -Discovery Channel

10 THE BASIC RULES OF CREATING ART

Whatever you have learned – either in school or by looking in books, museums or galleries – applies to alien art. I, personally, tend to think of alien paintings as simply another form of wildlife art. Composition, colour theory, you name it, all go to making your work stronger and more effective. Your subject shouldn't matter; it should be rendered with the same authority that you would a conventional subject.

11 AN UNDERLYING SENSE OF INTERRELATIONSHIP

One could argue that there is so much diversity in the animal kingdom that there is no clear visual relationship between the innumerable creatures that walk or fly or swim through our world. While I believe otherwise – that many creatures do bear common traits – it may be desirable to convey an obvious sense of kinship when creating an alien ecology out of whole cloth, if for no other reason than to help your viewer feel it is an integrated planet.

12 TAKE THE SUBJECT SERIOUSLY

Call me a romanticist but I do think quite a bit about life in the universe while I'm attempting to draw it. I am certain, with the billions of worlds to pick from, that it is out there and equally certain that we would be totally amazed by its unimaginable strangeness. Creating good aliens should be, in my humble opinion, an effort to get people to think about this. See – it's not just all fun and games playing God!

> "Do I make my creatures accessible or so strange that people won't know which way is up?"

13 OUR NATURAL WORLD AS INSPIRATION

Ours is a world rich in diverse forms of flora and fauna. And equally rich are the myriad of wonderful ways these elements interact. I am always marvelling at a newly found, strange way some obscure animal traps its prey or a plant defends itself. There are many great nature films that will inspire you if you apply a large degree of objectivity as you watch.

14 MIX AND MATCH

In a word – don't! There are evolutionary reasons why insects do not have bird heads and horses don't have scales. Aliens are not mythological or **fantasy creatures** and there is no excuse for pillaging bits of terrestrial fauna to cobble together an "otherworldly" creature. Having science behind your design is essential. Physical structures may show evidence of interplanetary convergence but don't let those similarities get too close.

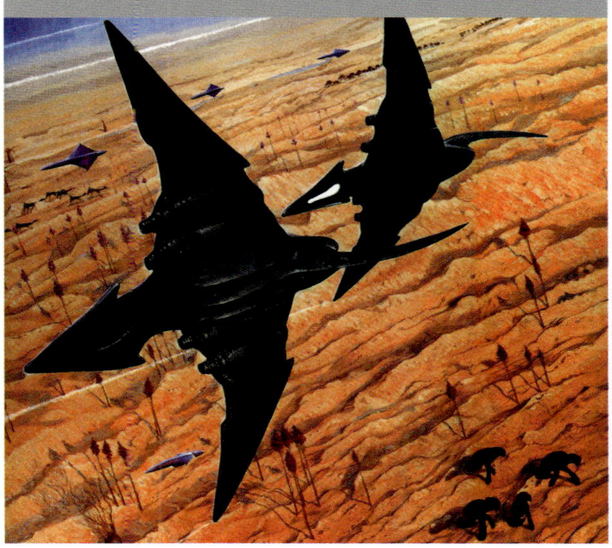

© Copyright 1990 Wayne Barlowe, Expedition.

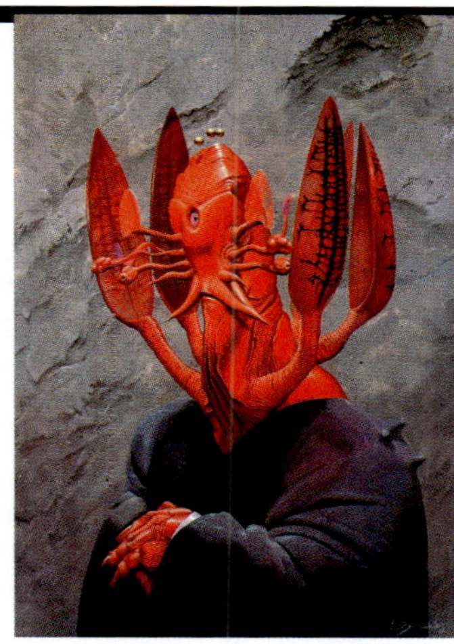

© Copyright Wayne Barlowe.

15 THE EASY WAY OUT

Odd foreheads do not an alien make. So says Yoda, anyway. Taking into account the budgetary constraints of many TV shows, it is only natural that producers would arrive at some form of inexpensive short-hand for what constitutes an **intelligent alien**. Unfortunately, not only does this create an uncomfortable sense of **Humanocentrism** but also deprives the viewer of a real feeling for the diversity that is undoubtedly out there. As an artist no such constraint is placed upon you.

16 SECONDARY ELEMENTS

Nothing better fleshes out a painting and the world it depicts than extra elements like foliage, rocks and other creatures. And this is true whether they are animal or intelligent. This is where storytelling and world-building meet. Posing a creature over another dead alien, or atop a strange tree, or fighting with another of its kind adds so much to pictorial excitement and will go far to make your world seem real.

17 ABSTRACT VERSUS CONVENTIONAL

When I wrote Expedition I wrestled with this. Do I make my creatures accessible, or so strange that people won't know which end is up? As it turned out, I **compromised**, choosing to design about three quarters of them somewhat conventionally versus the remaining oddballs. I found the latter much more **rewarding**. How bizarre one goes is a question of degrees and one you should bear in mind.

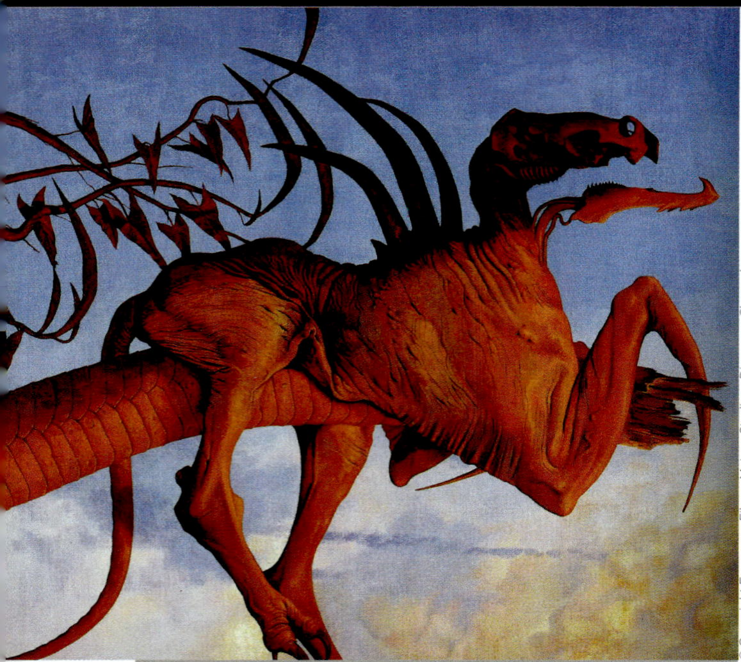

18 GESTURE

Whether your creature is intelligent or not, gesture is half the battle. So much can be **conveyed by the right gesture**. The lack of a meaningful pose, something that the viewer can connect with, is the **kiss of death**. Try to convey some behaviour through gesture; it can serve as a visual key to understanding an otherwise inaccessible alien.

19 WHAT IS ALIEN?

To my mind the term 'alien' connotes something that I may never truly be able to understand, and so should you. I have always maintained that if a human ever encountered even a benign denizen of another world it might still be a profoundly disturbing meeting; visuals, sounds, and smells may just be too overwhelming for our blinkered selves. We are too provincial in our wiring to take such strangeness casually. Make people uncomfortable with your aliens and you may be pushing the right buttons.

20 LIFE CYCLES

A simple way to give truth to your creations is to attempt to work out the details of its **conjectural life**. If you have the opportunity you can have some fun depicting creatures at varying stages in their lifecycle. But make sure to **avoid the obvious characteristics** that are prevalent on Earth. Colour and pattern, secondary sexual traits, size – all are fair game for your creativity. Strive for unpredictability.

> “Whatever you have learned in school or by looking in books, applies to alien art”

21 THE DOG'S BREAKFAST

Try to limit the grotesqueries. The hallmark of a poorly designed creature is the overwhelming aggregate of too many unfocused elements. Tentacles, pincers, scales, mouths everywhere and 50 eyes might be fun to create but a bit too much for a single creature. Simplicity can buy more from a design standpoint. Step back and see if you are leaving Alpha Centauri and entering the Land of Lovecraft.

22 THE UNEXPECTED

Our world is filled with anomalies. Tigers are beautiful but ferocious, poison dart frogs are breathtaking but lethal, vultures look horrific but rarely attack prey. What would we think of aliens so strange that they were beyond visual interpretation? Would we know what the yardstick for ferocious was on another world and how it might look? Avoid the obvious. Your job is to surprise us.

23 COLOUR AND PATTERNS

Like texture, markings are a great final touch. While you should be thinking of them throughout the design curve they should be thought of more as an accent and not a primary component of the **underlying design**. Again, there is more than enough richness in our world to inspire you but bear in mind that markings, whether they are **bioluminous or graphic**, have logical, practical reasons for existing.

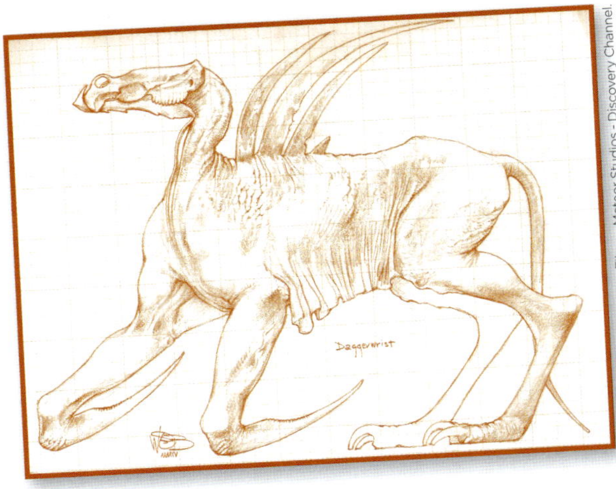

24 TRY STICKING TO ONE WORLD

There is nothing wrong with being monomaniacal. The best way to make your alien work for you is to develop it. The more layers of behaviour and environment that you can create, the more realistic it will grow. And the best way to achieve this is to keep pounding away thematically. Work out your ecology; make yourself an expert on your own planet. It's the essence of SF.

25 OTHER WORLDS, OTHER CULTURES – MISSION IMPOSSIBLE?

Designing an alien culture, its buildings and accoutrements is even more challenging, in my mind, than alien fauna. I haven't done it. Yet. We have way too many societal templates to work through such a complicated totality, and there are too many unconscious points of reference to overcome. I haven't yet been convinced by a rendered alien society. My only advice would be to ground oneself in the more distant cultures of Earth and infuse them with an incomprehensible level of abstraction. Only then might you come close!

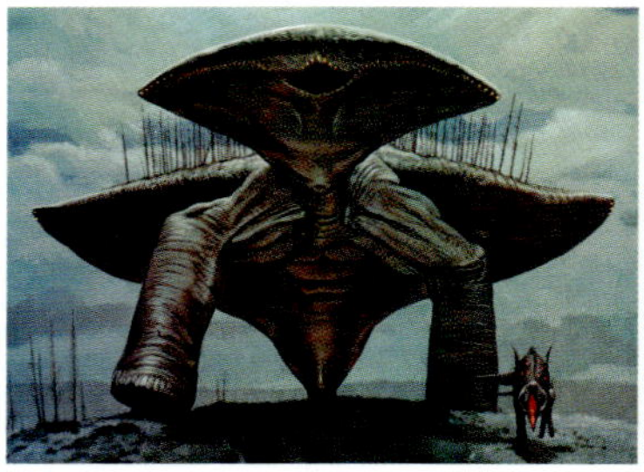

FURTHER READING

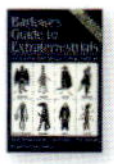

BARLOWE'S GUIDE TO EXTRATERRESTRIALS

PUBLISHER: Workman Publishing
ISBN: 0894803247

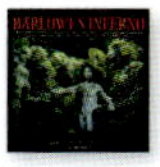

BARLOWE'S INFERNO

PUBLISHER: Morpheus International
ISBN: 1883398363

EXPEDITION

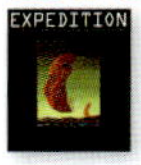

PUBLISHER: Workman Publishing
ISBN: 0894806297

Artist insight

PAINT BETTER MONSTERS

Enter the dragon's den for **Bob Eggleton's** top ten hints and tips on wings, scales and, of course, fire...

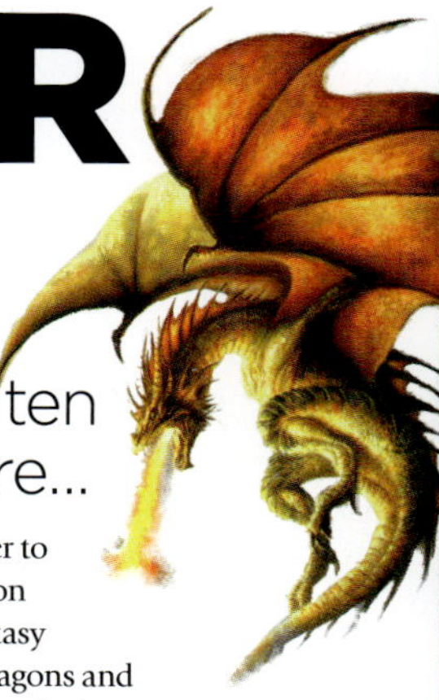

It was clear early on that Bob Eggleton was meant to be an artist. He learnt to draw when he was about four or five: "My dad sat me down and taught me perspective, and at 18 months – so Mum claims – I knew all my primary colours and could name them."

It was clear from the offset that Bob had a talent for art, and says he found SF and fantasy a perfect way to express his imagination. It's a marriage that has reaped rewards, Bob is a nine-time Hugo award-winning artist for his book covers and illustrations for Godzilla and a collection of Cthulhu tales.

Who better to offer advice on painting fantasy monsters, dragons and creatures from the imagination? Here Bob explains how idle doodles can become epic dragons and many other essential insights.

Artist **PROFILE**

Bob Eggleton

COUNTRY: US

CLIENTS: Warner Bros, Paramount Pictures, Chrysalis Books, Pyr, Overlook Press

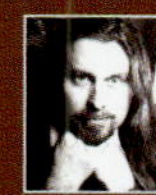

Winner of nine Hugo Awards and 12 Chesley Awards Bob Eggleton is one of fantasy art's most decorated painters. He paints book covers as well as Magic: The Gathering cards. The new asteroid 13562 was named 'bobeggleton' in his honour.

www.bobeggleton.com

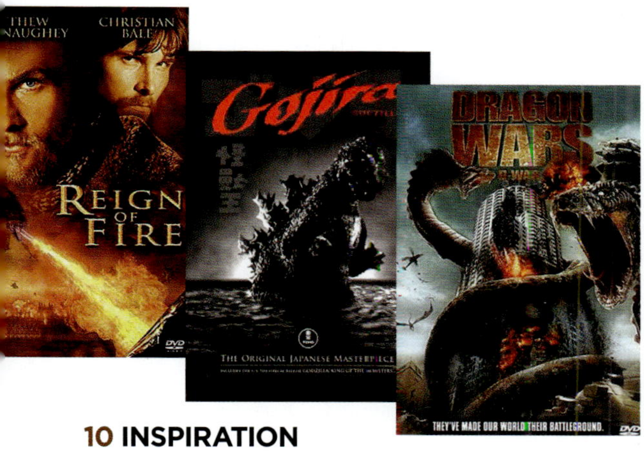

10 INSPIRATION

Let's assume you've got a total blank as to where to start. I usually get into the creative groove with movies. Some of my favourite films for this are either Reign of Fire (2002), Dragonheart (1996), Dragon Wars (2007), the original 1954 Godzilla (or really any of the sequels), or my collection of dinosaur and Ray Harryhausen work. What this does is establish a frame of mind. Often, I'll watch these as I work. This kick-starts my flow of consciousness and then the pencil starts to move.

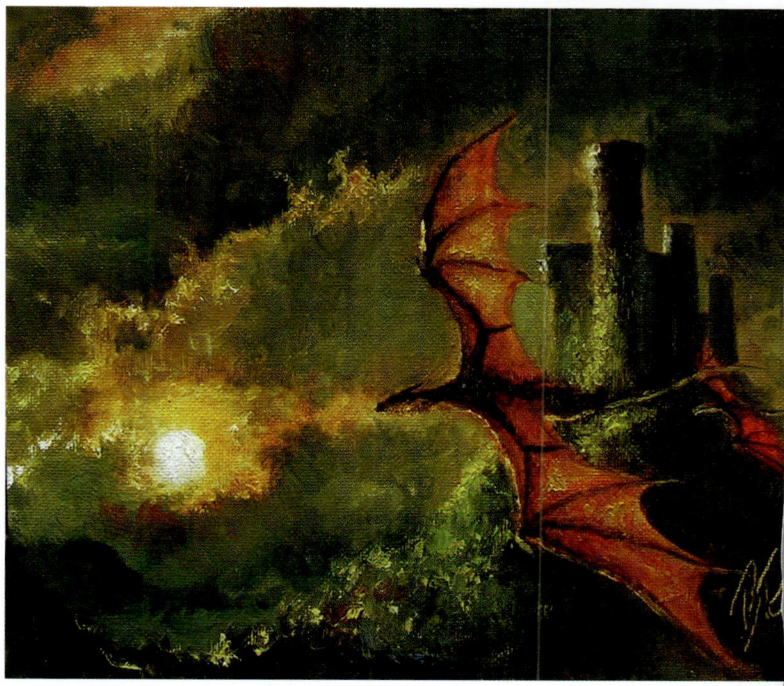

9 REFERENCE

I tend to make my creatures look as if they could really exist. One of my critics even called my dragons "too reptilian" which I thought was weird. That said, I do consult picture books and magazines that feature **reptiles, alligators, lizards** and so on, so I don't see that comment as derogatory, rather a compliment! I also study dinosaur skeletons and forms of prehistoric animals for dragon ideas.

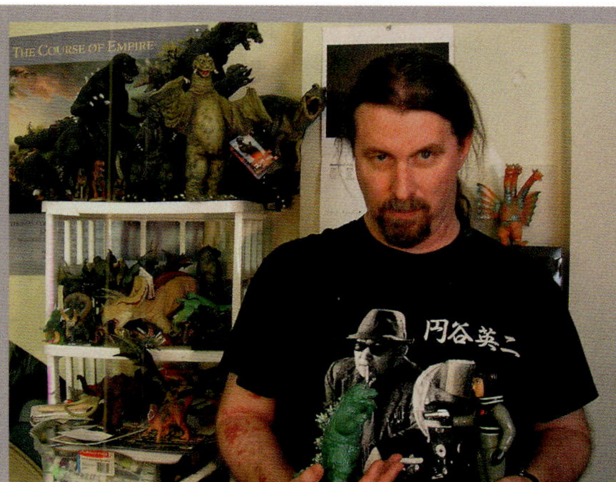

8 SETTING

If your beast – dragon, monster, or whatever – is set in an environment that's very realistic, and even prosaic, it will look even more fantastical and be the centre of attention. A good lighting effect or mood will always say something about the beast itself.

> "Study dinosaur skeletons and prehistoric animals for dragon ideas"

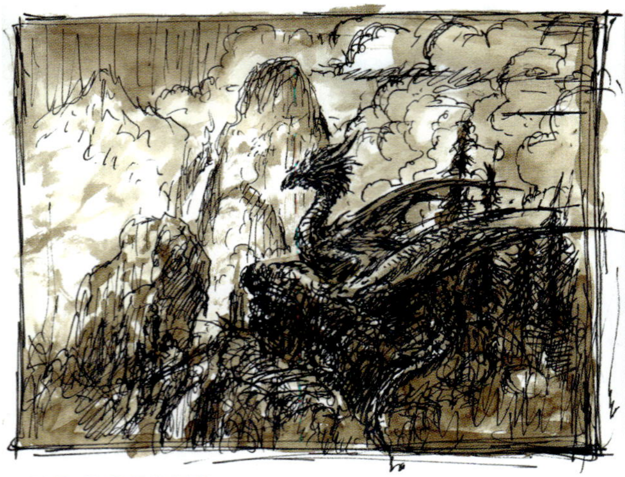

7 DOODLES

Work with a marker and just doodle shapes and ideas. Dragons should always have a **cool shape and silhouette.** I begin with the head and develop an idea until it starts to turn into something interesting. Sometimes the head will define how the rest of him looks. The same goes for any kind of monster, really. I prefer to use a good finepoint marker, or a pencil, and work in a sketchbook.

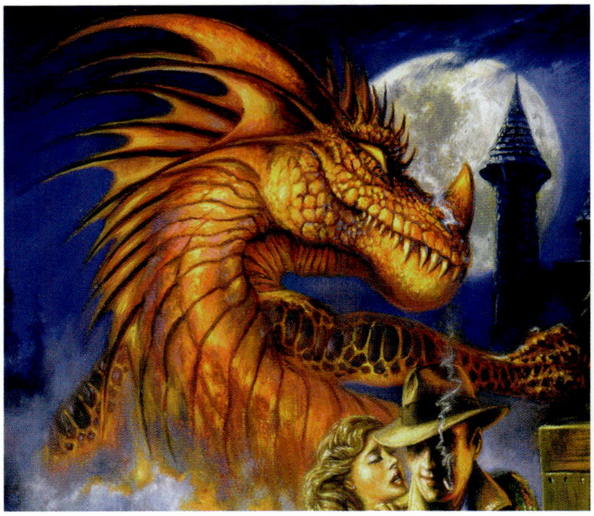

6 WINGS... OR NOT?

Should the dragon have wings? It's always a quandary for me on how to fit them into a picture. This is where "artistic licence" comes in. I've made them smaller than they might be simply because they look better that way. I recently created a great water dragon, which had water wings that were much like giant flippers.

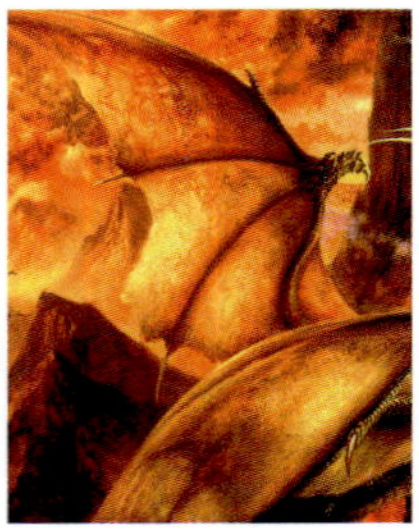

5 WINGS... INDEED

My inspiration comes from looking at pictures of bats with those unnerving, membranous wings. Putting holes, burn marks and tears in the dragon's wings gives him a bit of battle credibility. The muscles in and around the shoulders should look sort of like a double set of biceps.

4 MONSTERS VS DRAGONS

Monsters, unlike dragons, can be a complete mutation of nature. They can be **asymmetrical** and completely alien. My muse for monsters is the writing of **HP Lovecraft**. With monsters you can, in some ways, create your own anatomy. Whereas with dragons, it's kind of a given they'll have a lizard- or dinosaur-like anatomy.

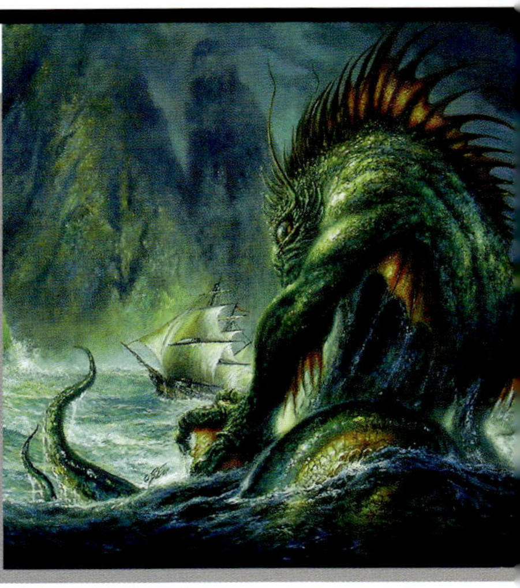

3 MOVEMENT

Despite the fact you're looking at a painting you want it to seem as though it has a life of its own, a drama that gives the illusion of something moving. I find that rendering every single scale on a dragon often just stiffens the whole thing up. The trick is to create the illusion of details. This imbues the creature with a subtle, constant motion. Too much detail can make it look unconvincing. For claws and talons note the feet of birds and reptiles.

> "The trick is to create the illusion of details"

2 FLAME ON

If your dragon is a fire-breather, one good tip is to make the fire closest to, and within his mouth, somewhat blue. This gives the appearance of a **gas blow torch** that's blue-hot as it starts and then becomes orange. It looks realistic and very hot!

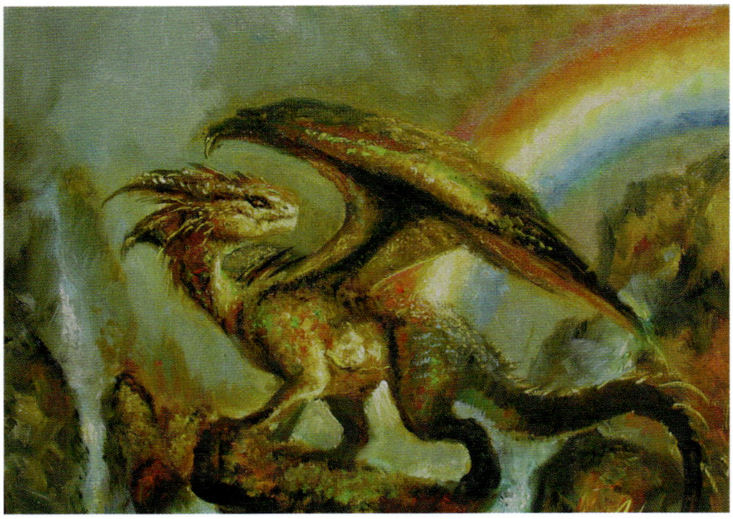

1 COLOUR ROUGHS

Do paint a small colour rough to make sure your dragon picture is working. The concept behind this painting, The Rainbow Dragon, is that this creature can absorb the **colours of the rainbow**. When you start building a 'back story' in your head, you'll start seeing more things you can build into your beast. Soon people will be dying to see more of your dragon's world.

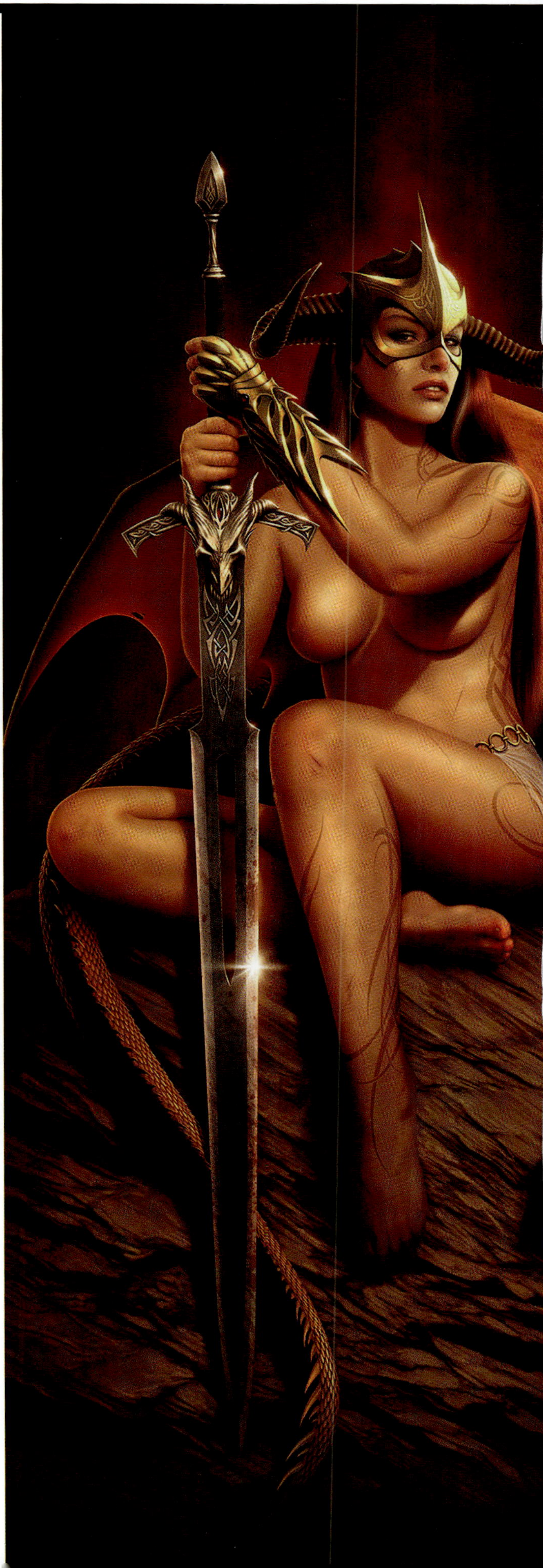

Artist insight

MATERIALS EXPLAINED

mprove your art by examining the way different materials work visually. Here **Henning Ludvigsen** offers a guide...

Artist **PROFILE**

Henning Ludvigsen
COUNTRY: Greece

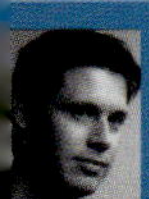

Henning is a Norwegian digital artist now living in Greece. He has more than nine years of experience in the advertising industry and over five years working as a games developer.
www.henning ludvigsen.com

DVD Assets
The files you need are on your DVD in The Henning Ludvigsen folder in Workshops.

Painting is all about tricking your viewer into believing what they're seeing. What makes us perceive that we're looking at an object made out of glass, cloth, wood, metal or even different qualities of the same material? As an artist, you have to convince your audience to accept what they're looking at. There are many ways of emulating different materials and surfaces on a flat 2D canvas, digitally or traditionally.

It's up to you to decide how deep down the rabbit hole you want to go. Do you prefer to simplify things but still achieve the look of the materials that you're aiming for? Or do you want to really understand how materials work and why the different qualities act the way they do? For example, understanding reflections can be a massive subject of study on its own. Let's get a little overview by separating the most commonly used materials into four sub-categories: matt; glossy and transparent; shiny and reflective; and organic.

FEATURED ARTISTS

Nick Deligaris
www.deligaris.com

Kulbongkot Chutaprutikorn
kay-ness.deviantart.com

Natascha Roeoesli
www.tascha.ch

Anne Stokes
www.annestokes.com

Vincent Hie
wallace.deviantart.com

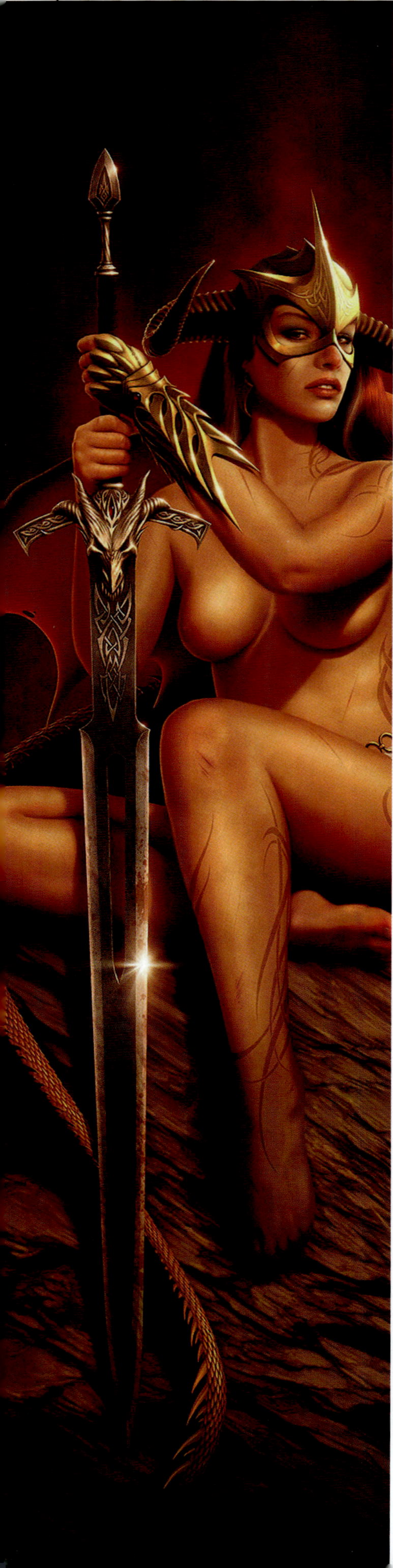

MATT MATERIALS

If you wish to create a sense of realism, it's important to understand the properties of matt materials and represent these when you put them into your work.

1 SOFT CLOTH

Think about all the different types of cloth and their qualities you have in real life and try to include these in your art. The most fundamental visual differences between various types of fabric is they way in which they fold and how they're textured. Generally, thin and soft cloth has quite small and organic folds and hardly any strong highlights; merely shadows and light. Remember that light can penetrate cloth and cause subsurface scattering, making the shadows behind the illuminated folds glow with saturated colours, as seen in some of the dark areas here....

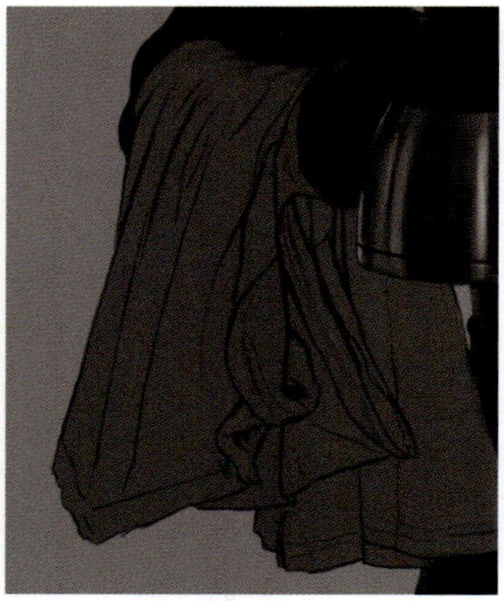

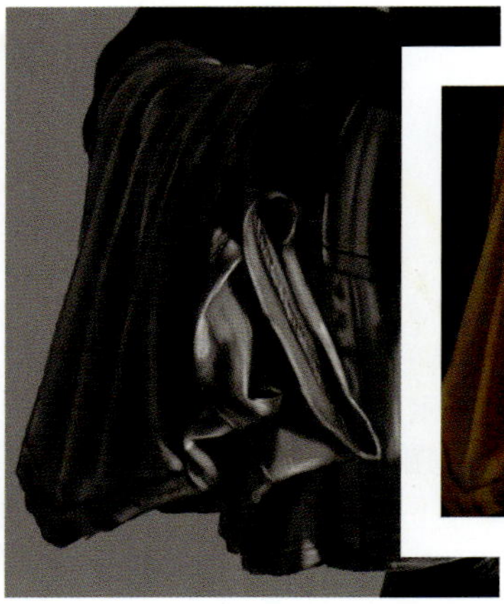

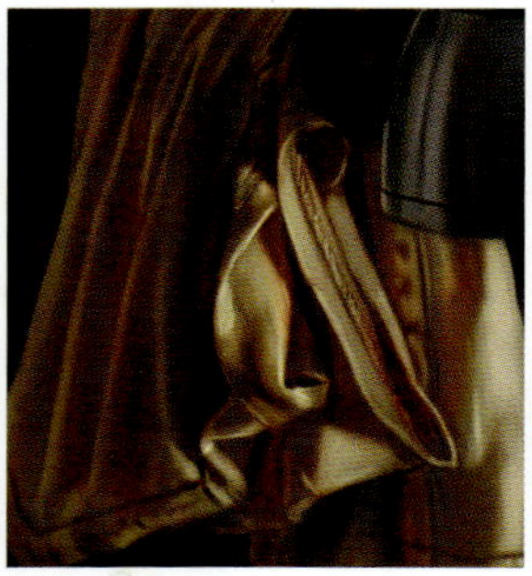

Dull highlights and subsurface scattered light is what makes soft cloth appear soft.

2 THICKER CLOTH (DENIM)

To make fabrics appear thick, the key is taking advantage of large, straight and sharp folds. Denim will not look convincing if we use the same types of folds as on soft cloth. Also, remember the final round of detailing – a dirty blue colour, with soft variations of green, grey and yellow, carefully mixed in and then vertically aligned with the texture of the fabric. I used my Speckled Hairbrush to create the lines in this example. The final yellow/brown thread trimming and the studs make it all come together and create the impression of denim. Look at references when imitating distinctive materials.

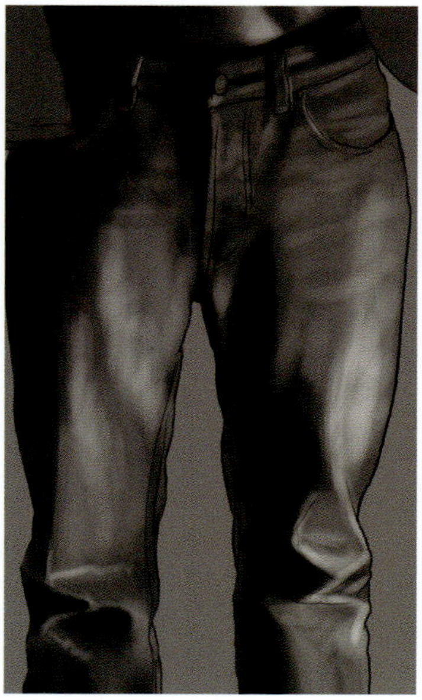

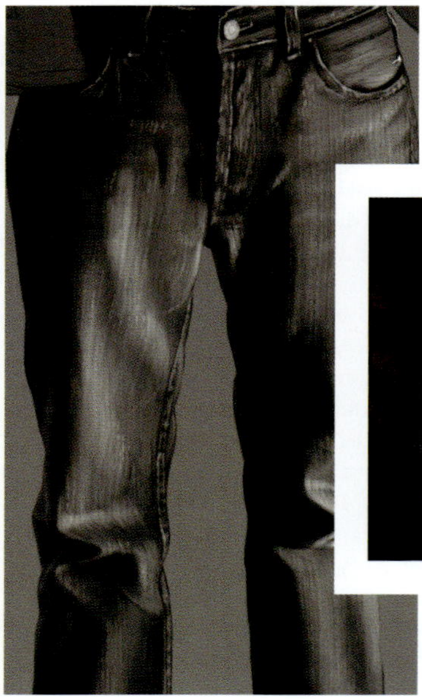

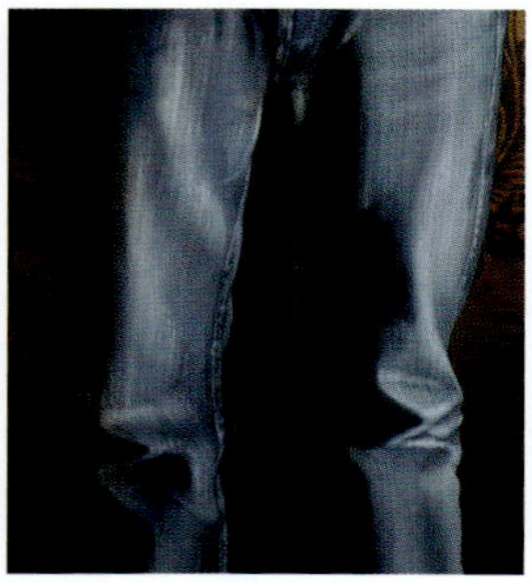

Large, straight and sharp folds make cloth appear thick. Denim has an easily recognisable texture.

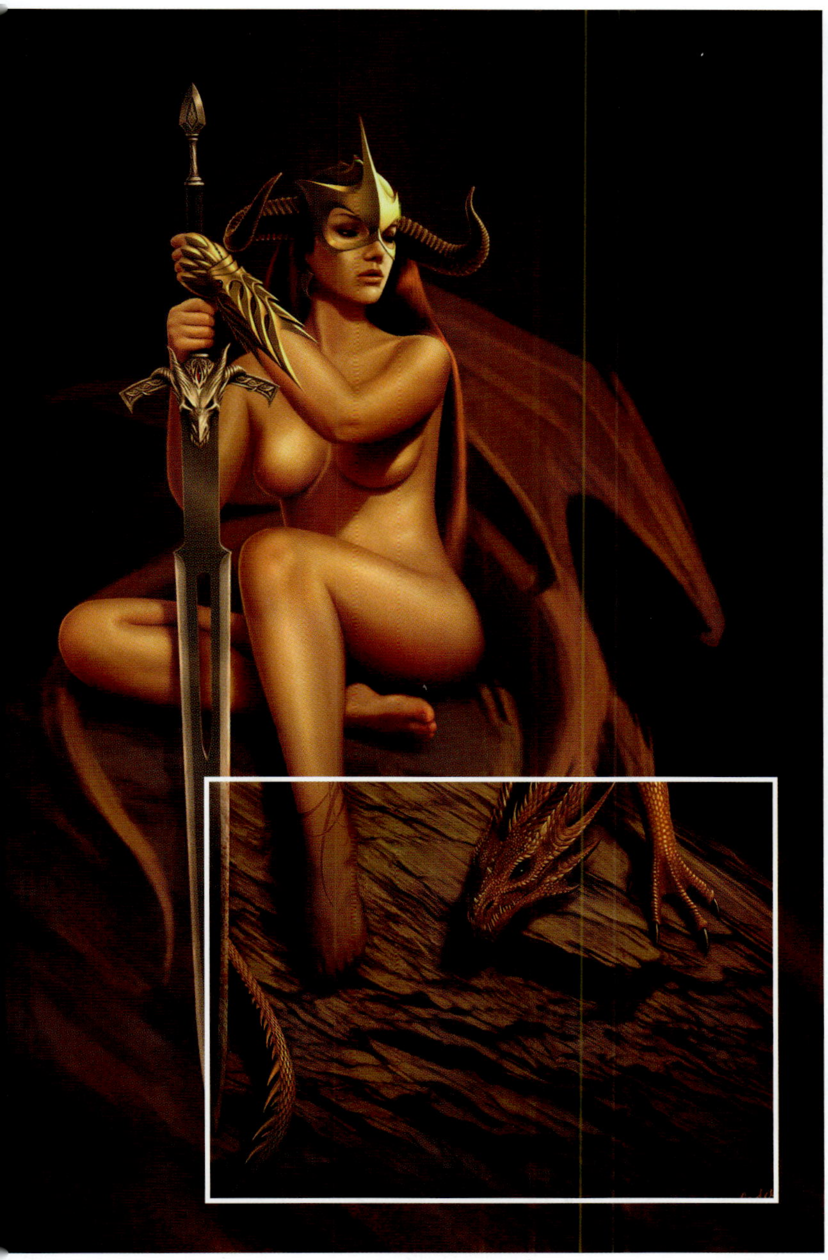

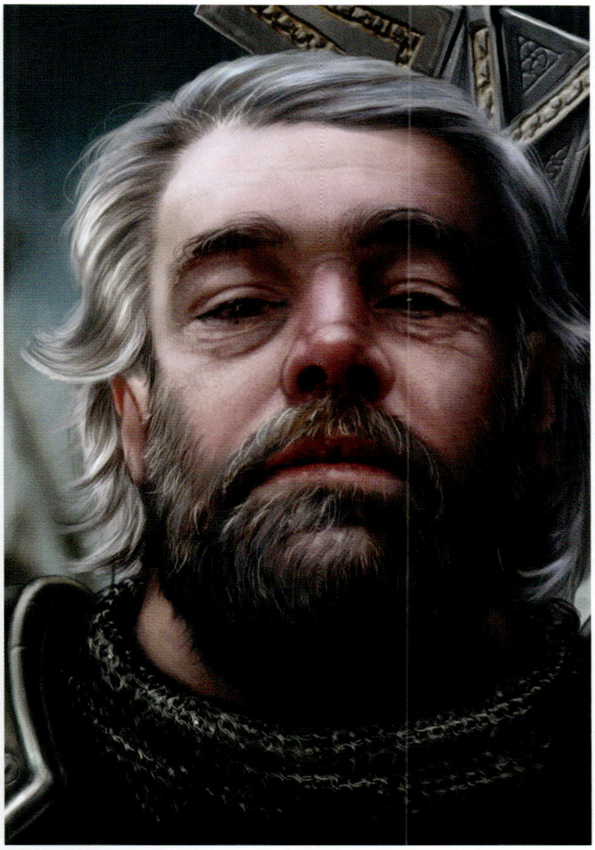

© FFG

6 SKIN

Skin is fun and consists of many colours blended together to create the final expression. Mix in **cold colours where the skin is thin** or pale (underarms, wrists, below the eyes) and use warmer values where the skin is warm or more exposed to friction or sun (nose, knuckles, knees). Even tossing in some **vague greens, greys and yellows** will make the skin look alive. Monochrome colours should be avoided if you're aiming for realistic skin tones.

3 ROCK

Rock is recreated in almost the same way as cloth, with surfaces too rough and rugged to have any major highlights. Focus on details and angles when painting rock and don't go too dark on the shadowed areas, because it's easy to make the contrast too high, which will make the rock appear noisy and artificial. Nick Deligaris has succeeded in creating a beautifully balanced rock surface in this example. Take time and hold yourself back with the contrast.

4 WOODEN PLANKS

When painting normal, untreated wooden planks, the key is to keep the highlights low. Shiny wood just ends up looking like plastic. Painting the growth rings can seem like a vast task, but this can be done quite roughly. You can even achieve it very easily with a Speckled or Dotted brush in a few seconds.

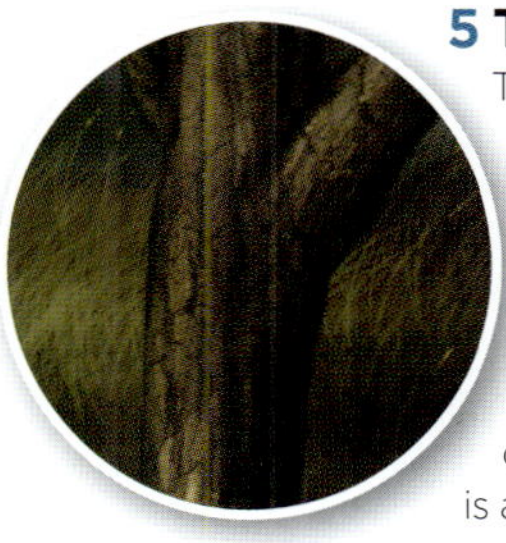

5 TREE BARK

The most important feature to keep in mind when painting tree bark is to keep the highlights low, because of the complex and rough texture of the tree trunk. It will appear realistic if you include richness in the details such as cracks and layers of bark. Tree bark is also darker than you might think.

7 RUSTY METAL

Metal works quite differently when it's rusted. As was the case with wood, keep the highlights low to make it appear accurately rough.

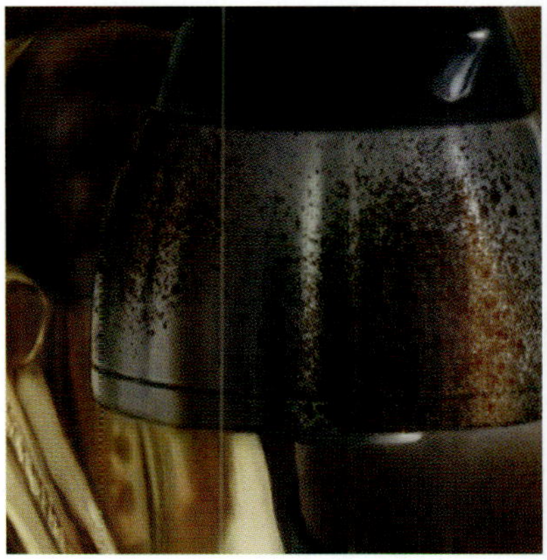

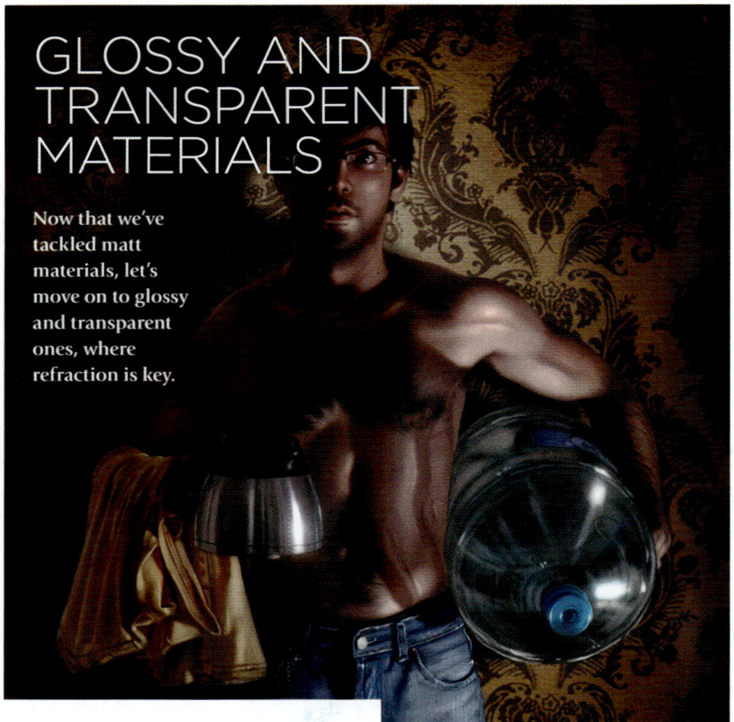

GLOSSY AND TRANSPARENT MATERIALS

Now that we've tackled matt materials, let's move on to glossy and transparent ones, where refraction is key.

1 TRANSPARENT PLASTIC AND GLASS

Transparent plastic and glass behave in a similar fashion, except that glass shows stronger refraction, distortion and highlights. For the water container in this example, the basic shape was first sketched up (figure A, right), and then a piece of the background, larger than the outline, was copied into a new layer to create refraction. This was then distorted in the areas with the most angle versus the background (B). The Liquify filter in Photoshop CS was used for this, and then cut to fit the shape of the container, to connect it with the background. The refraction layer was blended with the bottle using the Overlay layer option. To paint realistic glass or hard plastic, strong highlights and contrast are crucial (C). Try to imagine the angle from your viewpoint. The more directly you're looking towards a flat transparent surface, the more transparent and less distorted it gets. This is why looking directly down into water makes it seem clear. Because of their complexity, reflections don't have to be perfect.

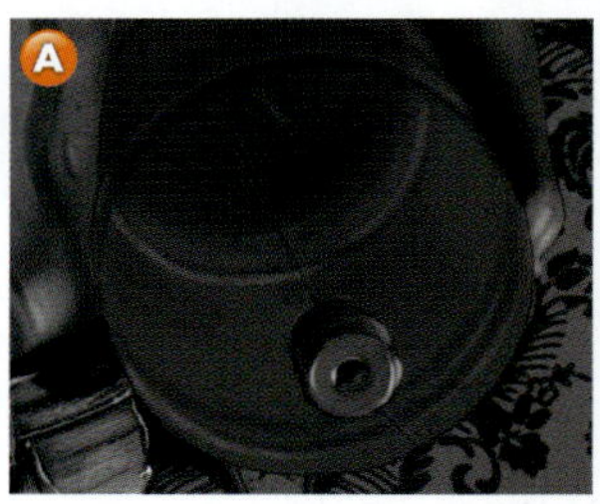

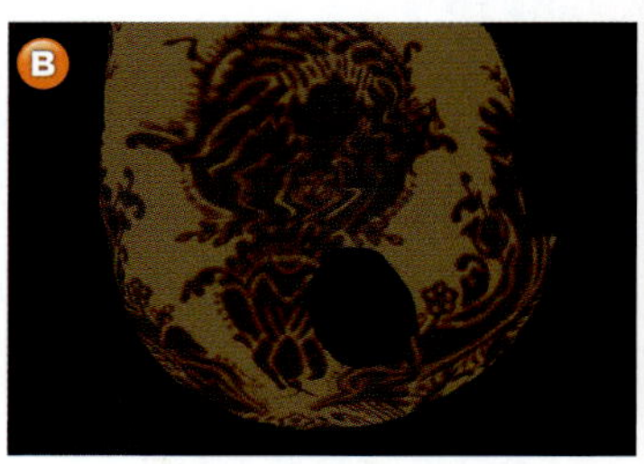

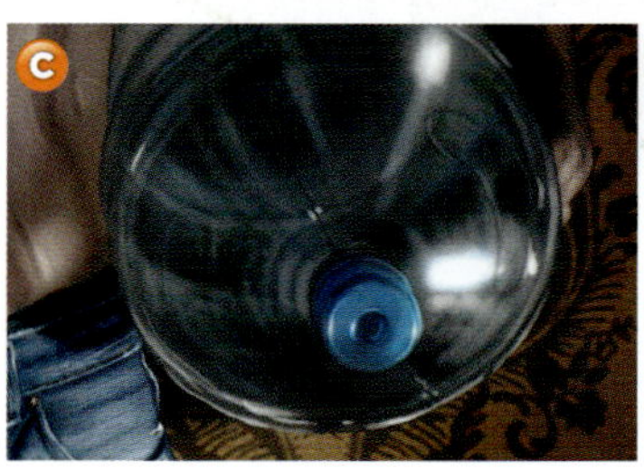

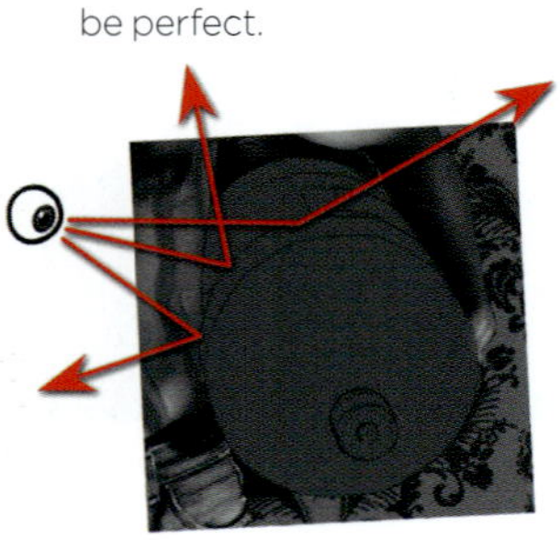

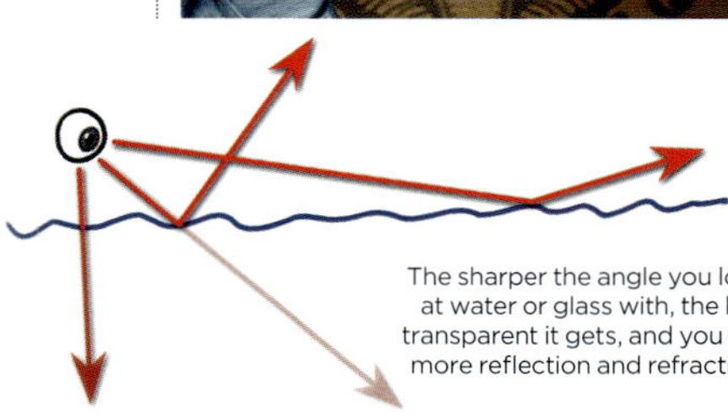

The sharper the angle you look at water or glass with, the less transparent it gets, and you get more reflection and refraction.

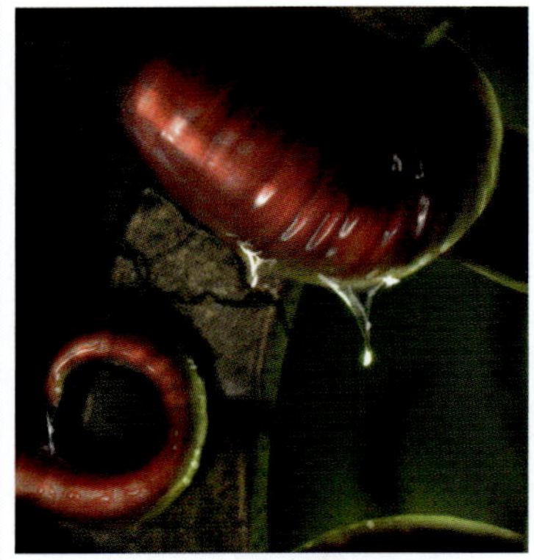

2 WET AND SLIME

Play around with some strong highlights when painting **wet or slimy things**. Plan out your shapes well, as all angles on the surfaces must correspond to the placement of the light source. Imagine you're painting glass, but focusing almost exclusively on the highlights. You can achieve similar effects using Photoshop by taking advantage of the **Plastic Wrap or Chrome filters**, and then blending these with your background layers using the different layer blending modes.

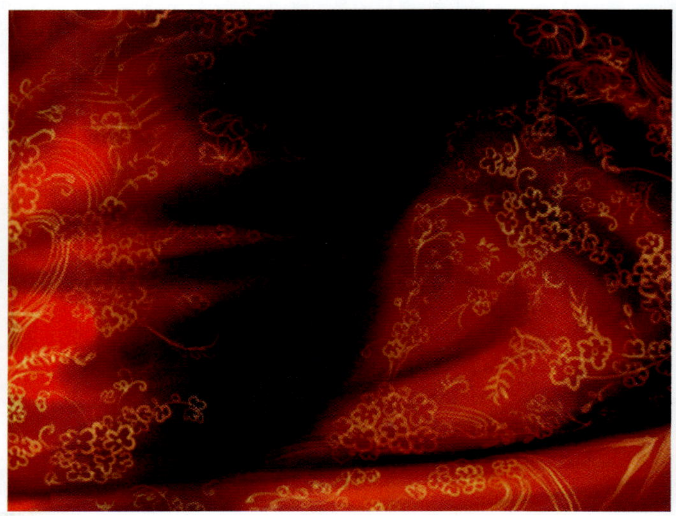

3 SILK

Silk is a beautiful material when detailed as in this example by the artist Kulbongkot Chutaprutikorn (above). To create the patterns, she used a smallish round brush in one flat colour and painted the patterns in a separate layer above the one containing the fabrics. She then went over it with a low opacity eraser, gently erasing where the folds and shadows were. To make it appear richer, she selected the Lock Transparent Pixels option on the layer with the patterns, then went over it with a brush set to Overlay, using a slightly more intense colour. At the end, Kulbongkot added another layer over the top and painted gently over the whole fabric to bring it all in together and unify the painting to give the impression of silk.

SHINY AND REFLECTIVE MATERIALS

Getting metallic objects to look right in your art is completely dependent on your understanding of how shiny and reflective materials behave.

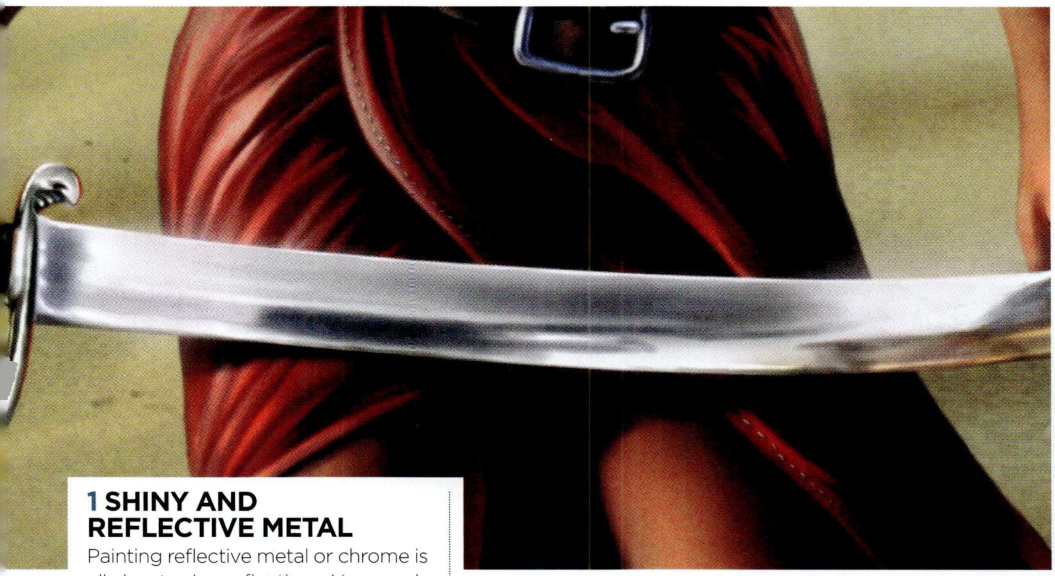

1 SHINY AND REFLECTIVE METAL

Painting reflective metal or chrome is all about using reflections. You need to know the environment your object is being placed in and make sure these two elements correspond. Otherwise the object will not seem like a part of the image. Painting reflections is a massive study and can be hard to comprehend. It helps if you use references to see howthe reflections behave. Strong highlights are, naturally, important when painting chrome. Take note of how the fingers reflect in the shiny blade in this example. It's a tiny detail, but still a vital part of the overall impression.

3 GOLD

Gold works just like painting metal, but with a strong colour overlay. Remember, gold isn't plain yellow. Try to use desaturated colours, such as greens, orange, grey and white as well.

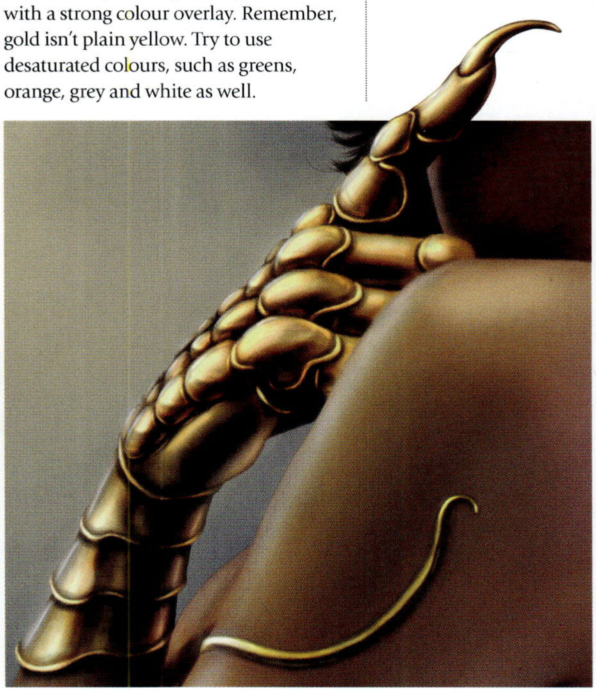

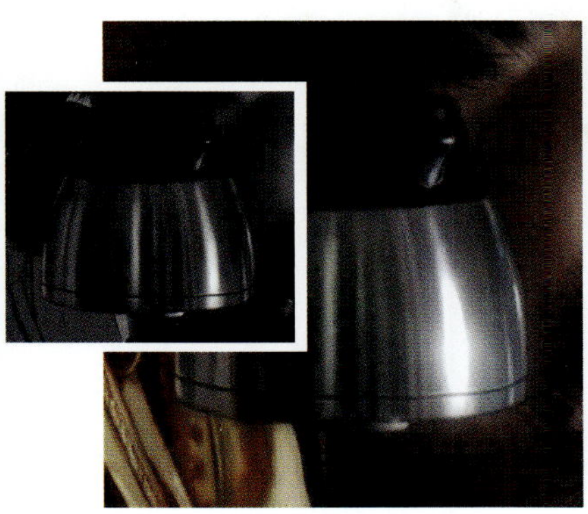

2 BRUSHED METAL

Brushed metal is easier to paint than chrome as you only need to give a hint of the reflection, using contrast and corresponding colours. For this example I used the Smudge tool, set to very low, and used my **Speckled Hairbrush** to create a vague distortion with horizontal lines along the side of the pot.

HOW TO PAINT LATEX

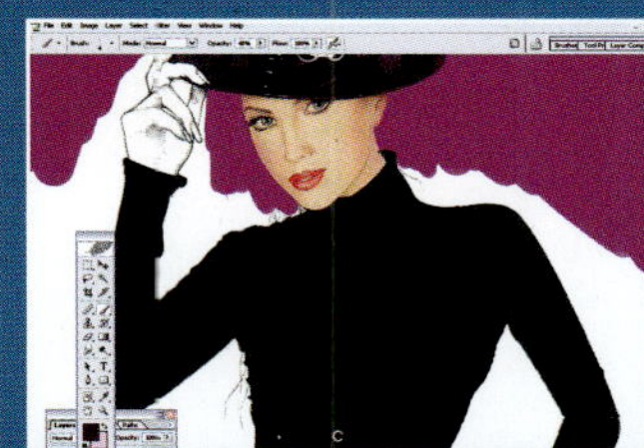

When Vincent Hie paints materials such as latex, he gets the basic shape first. Starting with a hard brush with maximum level settings, Vincent used the Lasso tool to mask out the areas as he worked on them, to be able to move the folds around in its layer to where they worked best. He then introduces some interesting lines and wrinkles, being careful that their patterns follow the wrinkles and creases in the fabric.

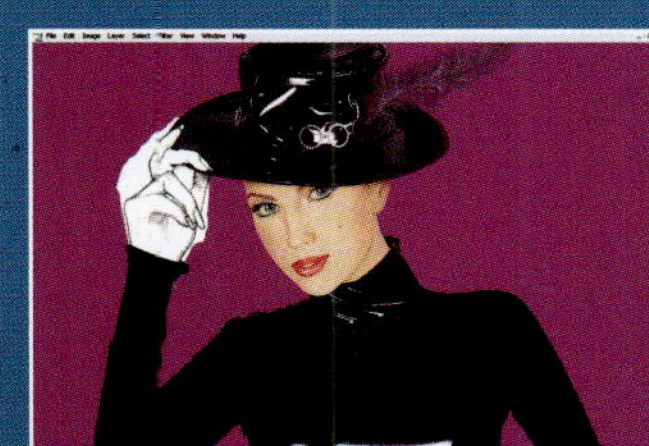

Highlights are then added in a new layer. Pure white is needed for this specific expression. A hard pencil brush is generally preferable. For bigger highlights, he makes a layer underneath and creates glow using a soft brush. Contrast is the key. Pay attention to the clean levels of colouring: almost pure black, a sharp transition to a middle yet dark value and then a leap to pure white. More middle values soften up the material.

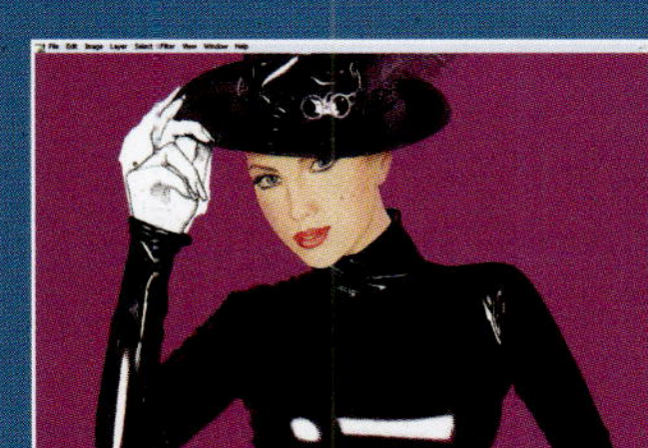

As you can see, the highlights are now long, small and vertical. The more curved the surface is, the smaller the highlighted surface becomes. Always look at references when doing this. Imagine what the shapes are like and what angle the light source is, according to them. Latex is an all-or-nothing fabric when it comes to reflecting lights. Be careful with the highlights – use them sparsely to achieve a more effective look.

ORGANIC MATERIALS

Why paint all these interesting materials brilliantly if the subjects we have around them don't look right? Painting hair, fur and scales may seem time consuming, but it's not as bad as you might think and it will drastically improve the outcome.

1 HAIR

When painting hair you shouldn't add every single strand. By simplifying it, you'll end up with a better result. These two examples, painted by Natascha Roeoesli, show how she has simplified the features of the hair. There a several important factors to remember when working on hair:

- Hair comes in layers. Start from the back and work towards the viewer.
- Hair comes in chunks that always stick together and cling on to each other. When combined with single strands, this looks realistic.
- Hair consists of many colour variations. Blonde hair isn't actually yellow, while brown hair isn't really brown. A head of hair consists of many variations as well as influences from the environment and surrounding light sources.
- As a rule of thumb, no matter how dark or bright you want the hair to be, you should always start with a darker colour as a base and then work your way up towards the brighter tones, still working in layers.

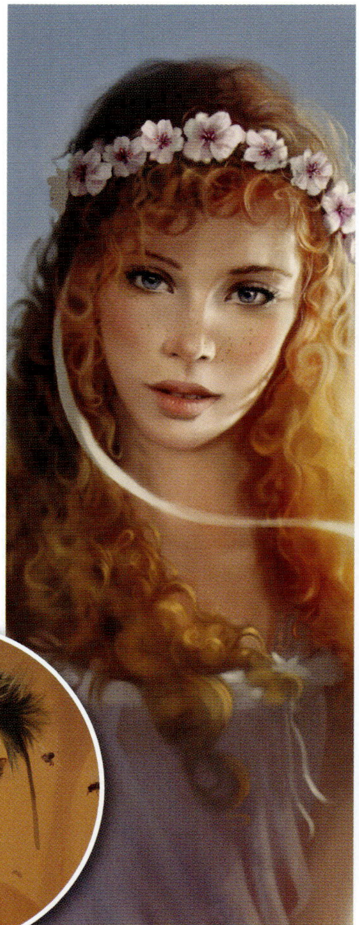

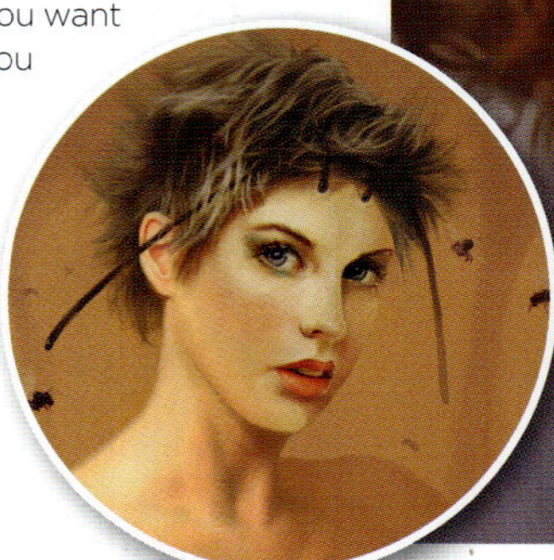

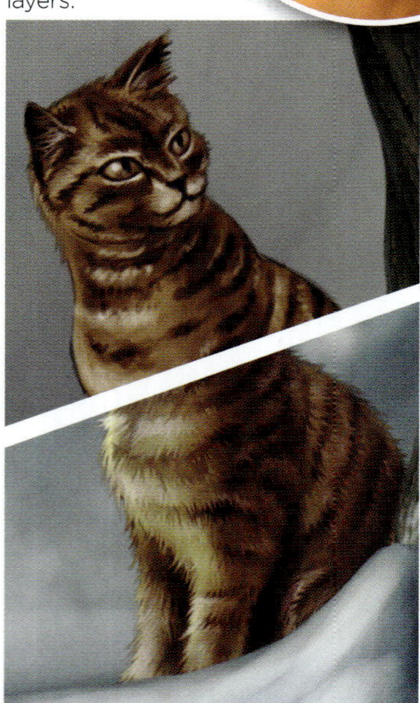

2 FUR

First, paint the creature with completely flat fur. The important thing is to include variation in tones, like the dark stripes on the cat in this example. Use a Speckled Hairbrush and the **Smudge tool** to start smudging out the fur. Work your way from the back of the creature towards the front. This way you'll get the layers in the right order and the different fur variations painted earlier will extrude, creating an interesting texture. The more variations you add the **more real** your fur will look. Finally, go over it with a sharp brush and add some lone strands.

PAINTING FUR

A handy guide to make fur painting as painless and hassle-free as is possible.

Painting fur can test your patience, but if you dedicate reasonable time to the job of detailing the fur, it can result in stunning outcomes, just like Nick Deligaris has done on this example. He began by painting a rough, non-detailed base, to decide the layout and composition of the fur and its variations.

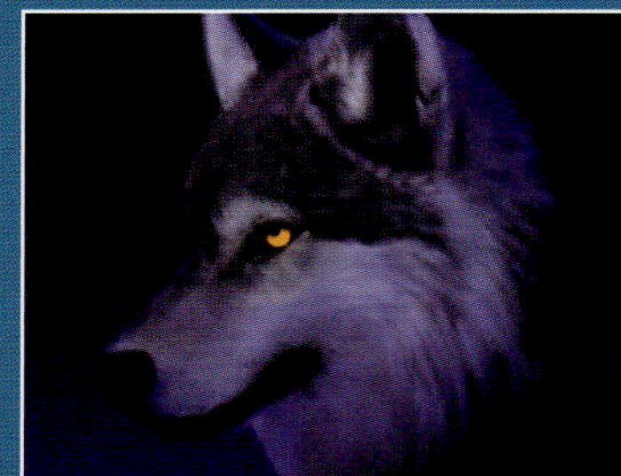

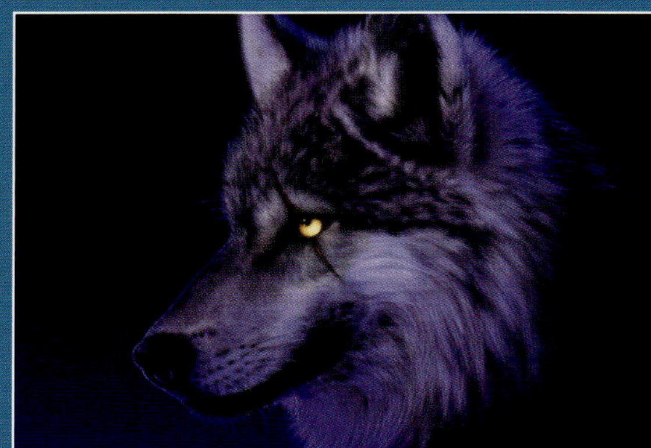

You can spend as much time as you like detailing fur. Start out using rough brushstrokes, working in patches of fur. Remember that fur is similar to hair. The strands come together in batches as they cling together and they resemble pointy spikes from a distance. Go over it again and again with thinner and thinner brushes until you've reached the level of detail you're aiming for. Nick added a beautiful rim light, as fur and hair catches light that shines from behind. Using rim lights is a good way to soften up your painting, making for a far more interesting and professional-looking final expression.

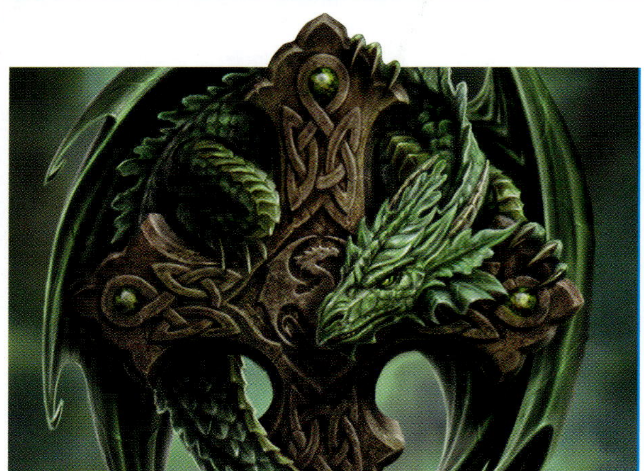

3 SCALES

Scales should be shiny. They tend to have an amazingly detailed, beautiful composition. To achieve this, invest time in putting each scale into the system before starting the detailing process, just as Anne Stokes has done on this example. Scales are almost like metal, with pretty strong highlights. For this, you can use the Dodge tool, set to Highlights, to give the fine detail.

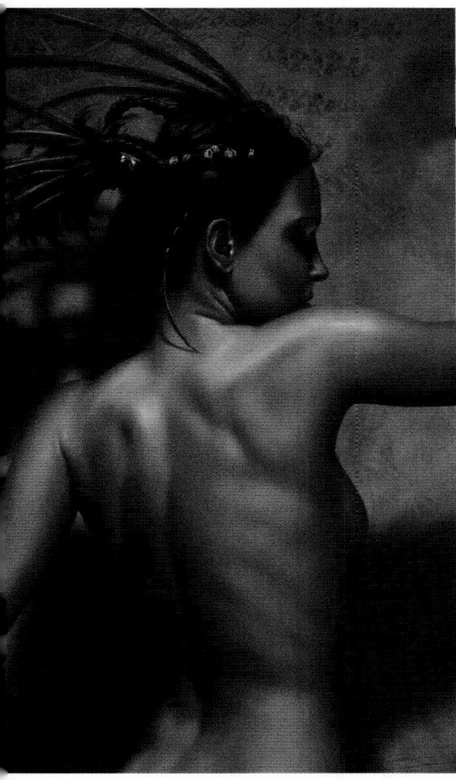

> “Apply a noise layer to your painting at the end of the creation process and you'll achieve more natural colour values”

Artist insight

20 MUST KNOW FANTASY ART TIPS

Artist PROFILE

Henning Ludvigsen

COUNTRY: Norway

CLIENTS: Fantasy Flight Games, Midway

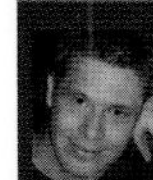

Henning is a digital artist with basic traditional art education and 12 years' experience in digital art, design and illustration. He is art director of a computer game development company and works on private commissions and projects in his spare time.

www.henningludvigsen.com

From skin tones and highlights to misty valleys and glow effects, **Henning Ludvigsen** shares his top 20 pieces of advice for creating great fantasy art every time

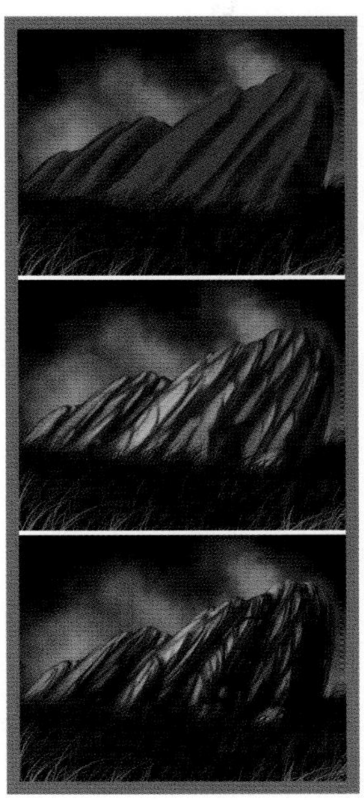

1 FANTASY SKIN

When painting skin for a fantasy piece, monochromatic tones are a good start, but even after experimenting with all the levels of colours and different skin types, you can end up with a monochromatic effect. Skin is always darker than you think, so don't take highlights too far, and use redder colours where skin is warmer.

2 THREE THINGS TO AVOID

- Unless you can hide it, avoid using filters. There's nothing less painterly than seeing a large surface covered in a custom-made Photoshop filter effect. Why not use the effect as a vague base instead and work it over from there?
- Effects such as lens flares and software-generated fire and cloud won't look natural unless they're done by hand.
- Avoid using the Smudge tool for the major parts of the painting process. Keep brush strokes clear, confident and bold.

3 LEARN TO LIMIT YOUR COLOUR PALETTE

When legendary artists such as Frank Frazetta choose their colours, they try to keep them all related. Even skin colours are mixed with colours from the surroundings. Limit your range of colours, and play more with narrower selections of the palette. That said, make sure to keep your chosen colours varied enough to not look monochromatic. You don't need all the colours in the world to make your palette lush and rich.

4 ROCKS

When painting rocks, keep the **highlights** duller than you think. Contrast is important, but you can still achieve this effect with colours that are close to each other contrast-wise. Narrow down the range of values but try to keep the lit faces more or less within the same areas of the **palette**. The same goes for the shadowed areas. A hard-edged brush is the best tool for

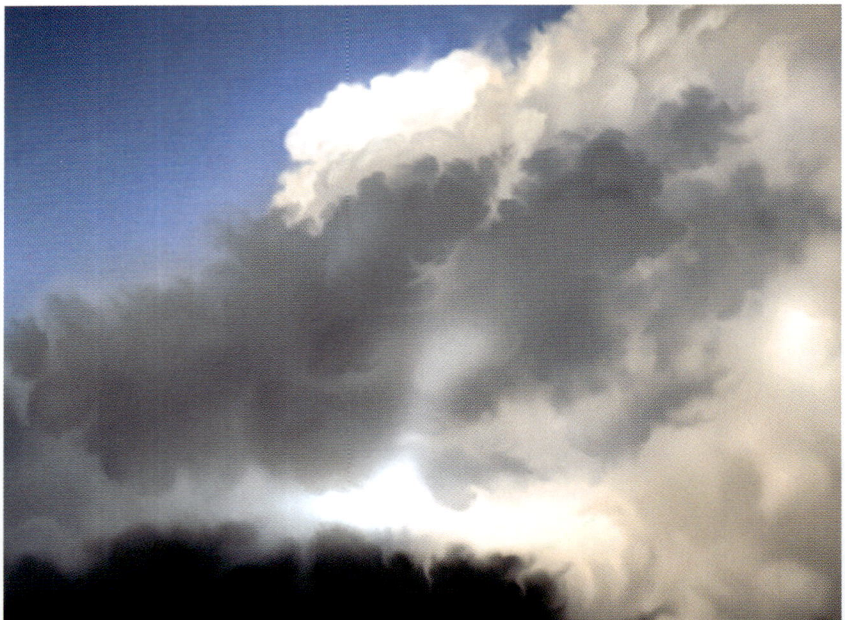

5 MOODY FANTASY SKY

Fantasy art tends to distort everyday elements. This applies to clouds too, but real references will help. Contrast is important, so be sure to have some dramatic shifts of values and colours, along with beautiful and maybe even unnatural shapes and formations.

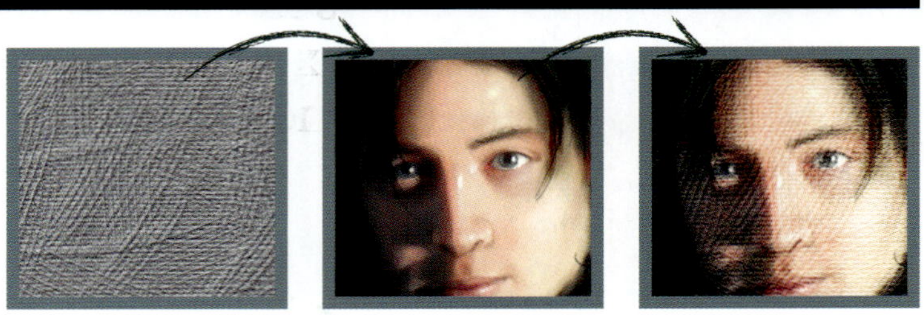

6 VISIBLE BRUSH STROKES

Get a traditionally painted effect by creating a greyscaled overlay texture that includes a vague canvas texture and brush strokes. Play around with some Palette Knife brushes and add dynamic criss-crossed brush strokes. Make sure the basic starting value for the background is close to the middle range: RGB = 128, 128, 128.

If you apply a light Emboss layer style to your brush strokes, you can get a vague 3D embossed look on the textured base. Set the Layer Blending mode to Overlay and adjust the Opacity slider until you're satisfied.

8 APPLY NOISE

Apply a noise layer to your painting at the end of the creation process to achieve more natural colour values. Make a new top layer, RGB= 128, 128, 128. Run Filter>Noise>Add Noise, set the slider at 400 per cent. Run Filter>Brush Strokes> Spatter; run the Blur filter a few times. Set Layer Blending mode to Overlay; Opacity at 3 to 10 per cent.

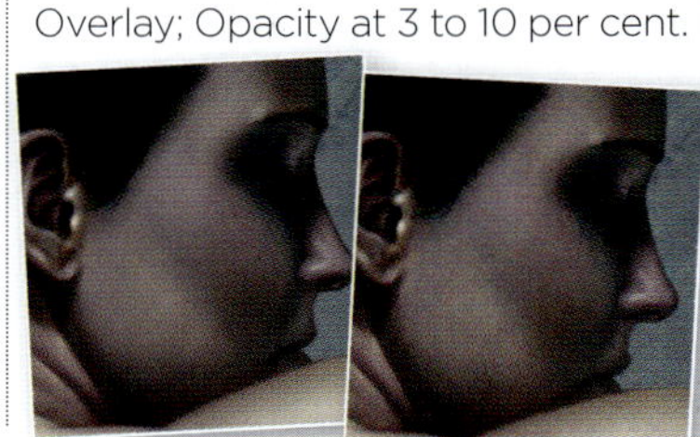

7 LAYOUT

Less is more when it comes to laying out fantasy art. Pick a **simple idea** and focus on this object in a bold and straightforward way. Heavy focus on **symmetry** can often be a good solution for a successful fantasy painting, as can making sure it balances well if you go for less symmetry and more elements.

9 SLIMY TENTACLES

Fantasy art requires monsters, and often slimy, shiny, disgusting ones. To add slime, follow these steps:

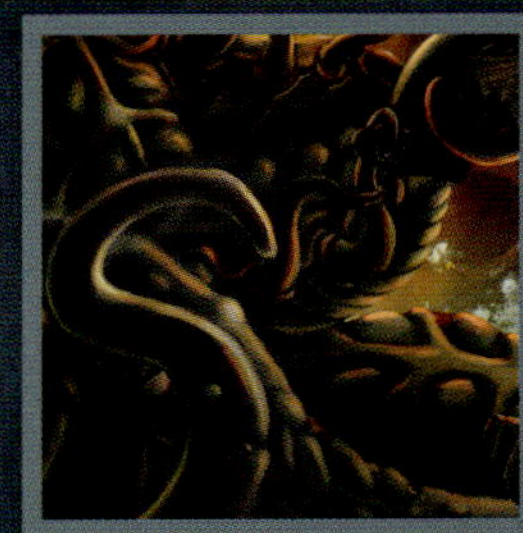

1 Copy the areas you want to make slimy into a new layer. Then make this layer greyscale.

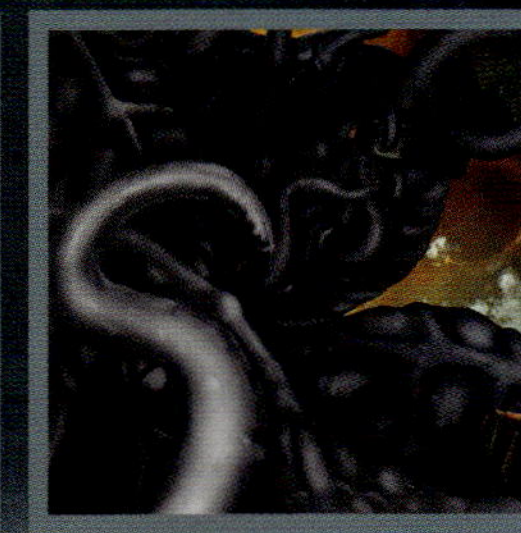

2 Smooth the layer with a soft brush. Parts pointing at you should be brighter than those pointing away.

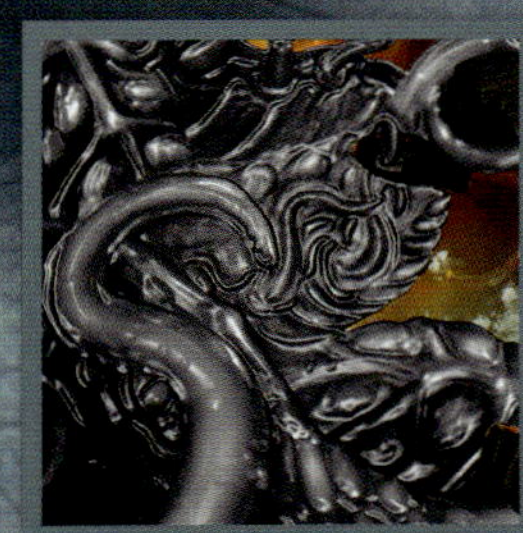

3 Run the layer through Filter> Artistic>Plastic Wrap. Keep the details to a minimum.

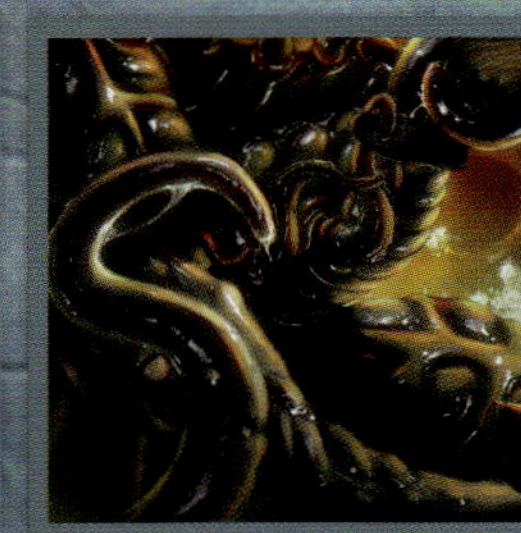

4 Set Layer Blending mode to Pin Light. Use Dodge to edit highlights in this layer, and paint strings of slime.

10 TEXTURED BRUSHES

Human imperfection is what gives art character. Custom brushes can help you emulate this imperfection. Download or make some textured brushes to give your pieces a bit of life.

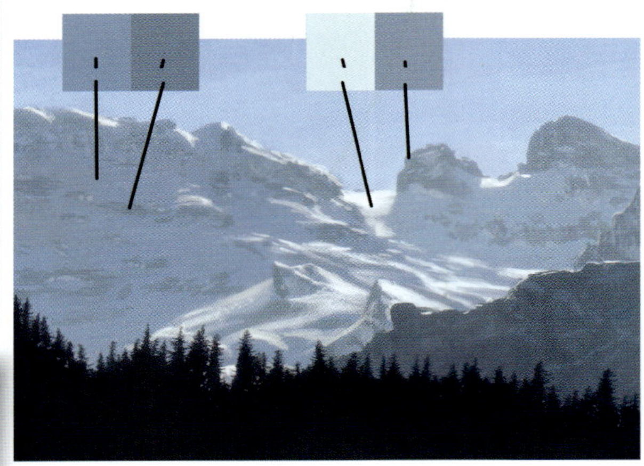

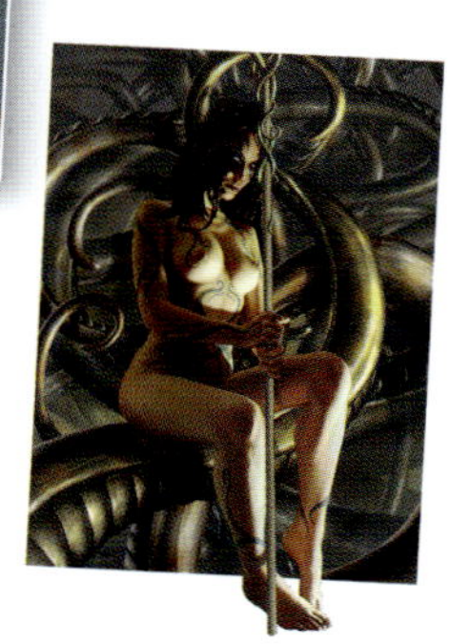

11 MOUNTAINS

Use photos as a reference when painting mountains. A good tip is to limit your range of values. Make one value each for highlighted rock and snow, and the same for shadowed versions of the two. Keeping values limited and adding detailing with a hard-edged brush will make mountains look natural.

12 MANUAL GLOW

There are plenty of ways to apply automatic glow to objects in the different painting packages; from soft brushes to layer styles. Make your artwork appear as *painted* as possible, by going for hard-edged brushes and paint it by hand. A glow doesn't have to be perfectly smooth, it will still serve its purpose and at the same time will add more of your own personality to your piece.

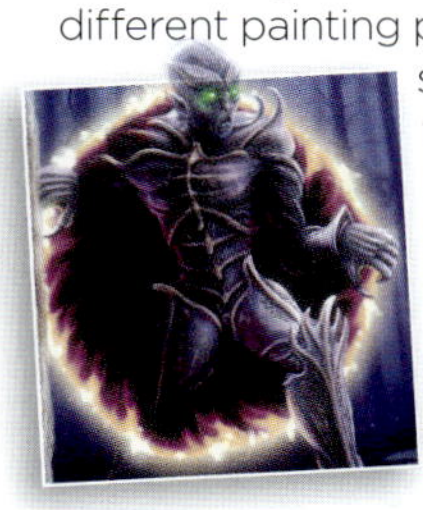

13 FANTASY GLOW

The romantic and fantasy genres are where glow effects are used most. Glows can add the extra touch – or leave you in the 80s if over-used. Add a flattened copy of your piece to a new layer on top of the others. Run Filter>Gaussian Blur, and play with the Linear Dodge blending mode and Opacity slider on the Layers palette.

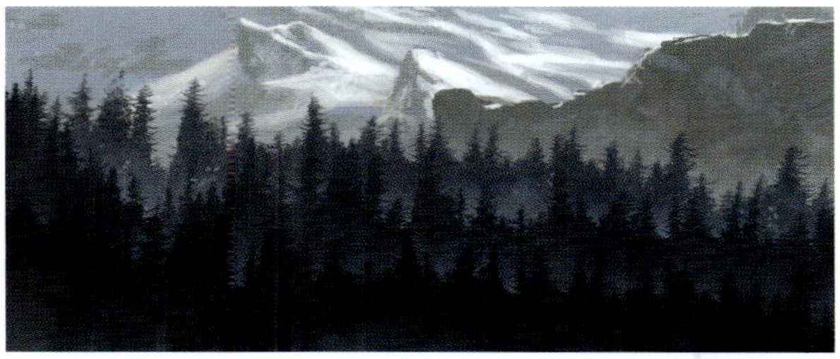

16 MIST IN THE VALLEYS

Divide the background into layers depending on distance. Applying a soft mist at the bottom, between each valley, can create an eerie feeling and add a lot of depth.

17 FORM-FIT TEXTURES

With textured layers, it can look like overlay textures are projected onto objects. To avoid this, make the noise layer cover more than you need, and use Photoshop's Liquify tool. Use the Forward Warp tool, tick the Show Backdrop box, select the base object and set Mode to Behind, then adjust the Opacity so you can see through the texture layer. Warp-change the texture layer to fit the object.

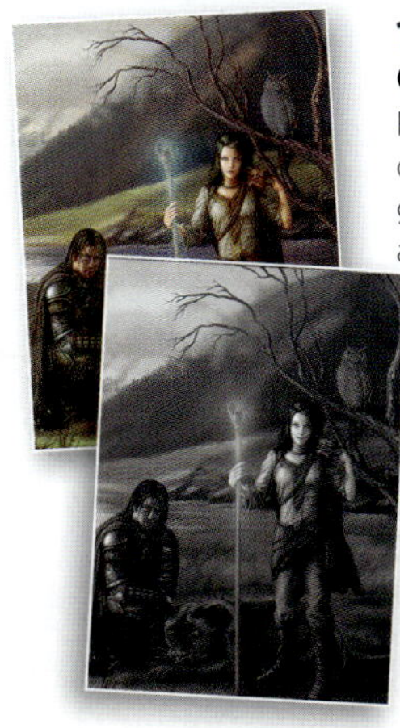

18 CHECK YOUR GREYSCALE VALUES

Fantasy art usually contains dramatic colours and contrast. A good piece of fantasy art should also work in greyscale, so check your greyscale values every now and then to get a handy overview of how your work is coming along. A quick way of checking this is by keeping a layer on top of your layer-stack with 100 per cent white colour and Blending Mode set to Colour. You can then toggle between colour and greyscale mode.

"The fantasy genre is where glow effects are used most. They can add an extra touch – or leave you in the 80s"

14 CANVAS PRINTS

Is there anything more **traditional** than a piece of art on canvas mounted in a wooden frame? Make your digital fantasy pieces come to life by printing them on **real canvas** and hanging them on the wall. The texture of the canvas makes your piece look and feel like a **traditional painting**, and it even smells similar.

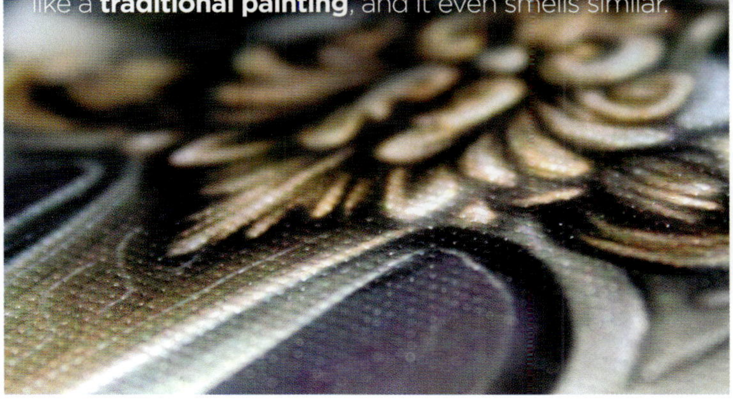

15 REFLECTIVE METAL THE EASY WAY

To create a base for metallic effects, copy the metal area into a new layer and make it greyscale. Smooth the surfaces with a soft brush and apply dark lines for etched details (bright for extruded details). Run the Chrome filter, set Blending mode to Colour Dodge, and play with the Opacity.

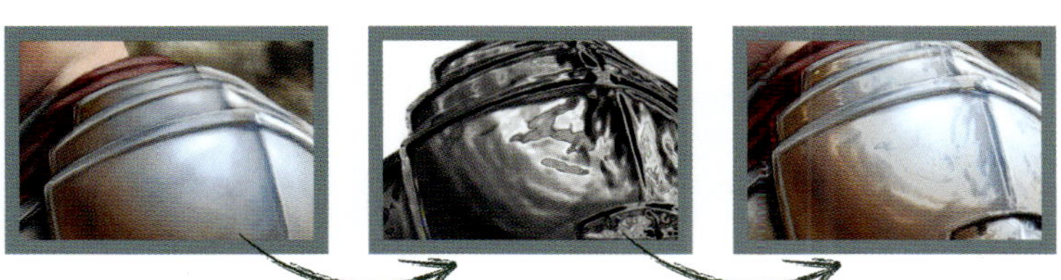

19 DISTRIBUTE YOUR DETAILS

Try to distribute detailing onto areas that are important, throughout the piece. Remember that even rough brushstrokes can appear complex if accompanied with detailed areas.

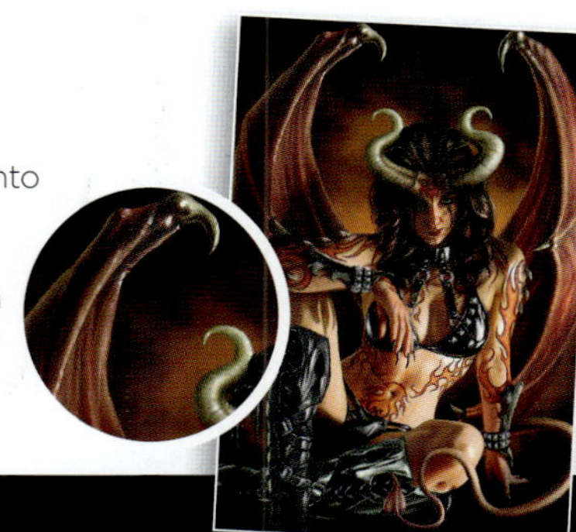

20 LIMIT YOUR HIGHLIGHTS

An important overall tip for realistic results is to avoid extreme highlights, especially on **fabric and skin** folds. Overly strong highlights on skin may cause an artificial appearance and give a comic book style to the character. Keep your **greyscale** base values under control.

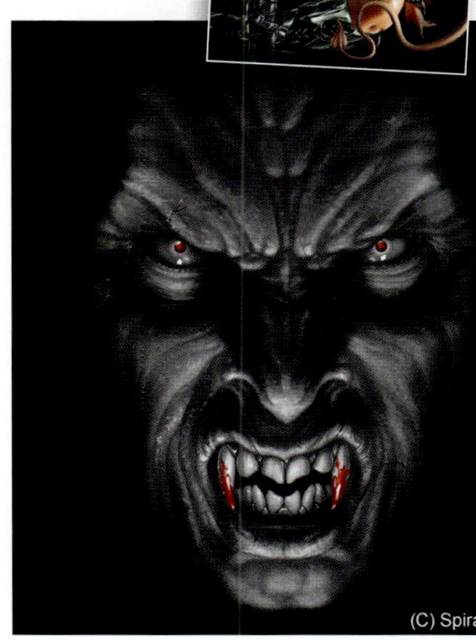

INDEX

On your disc

To support our workshops, your disc includes a wealth of resources to aid your creative process. From how-to videos to step-by-step workshop images, you'll find this disc essential.

Artist RESOURCES

Video workshops
Watch and learn from the artists, including 15 minutes of Dave Gibbon's process.

Step-by-step images
Follow the artists' steps to creating their paintings in Photoshop.

Layered PSD files
Learn how a painting is created by taking it apart piece by piece.

Artist EXTRAS

Sketches
Study the artists' rough sketches to discover their processes.

Textures
Use the same texture samples as our artists to help achieve similar results.

Custom brushes
Use the same custom brushes our artists use to recreate their digital paintings.

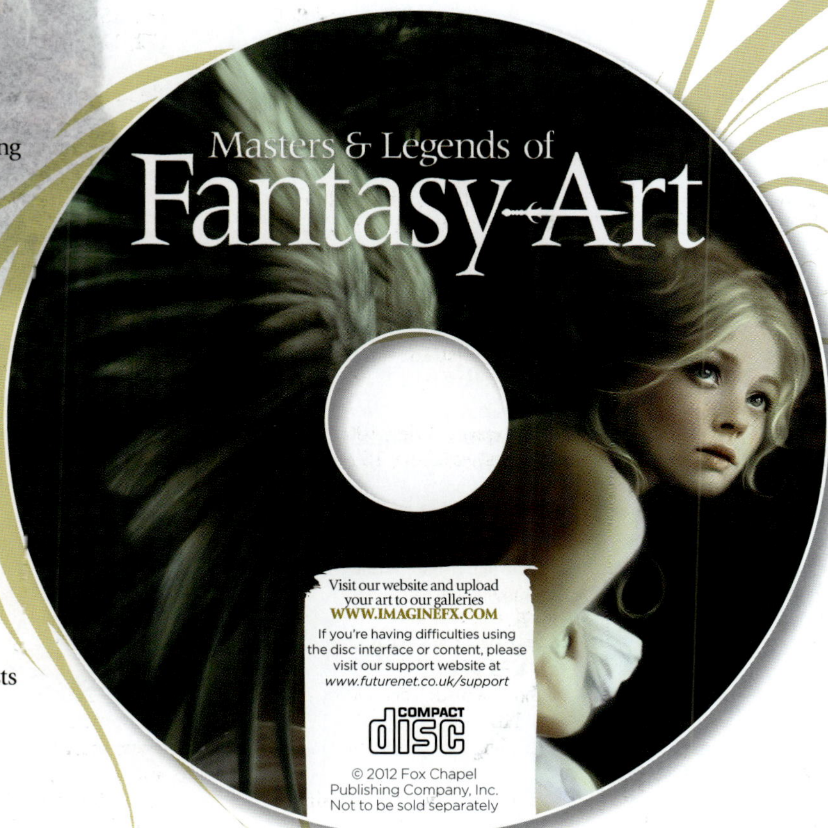

More Great Books from Fox Chapel Publishing

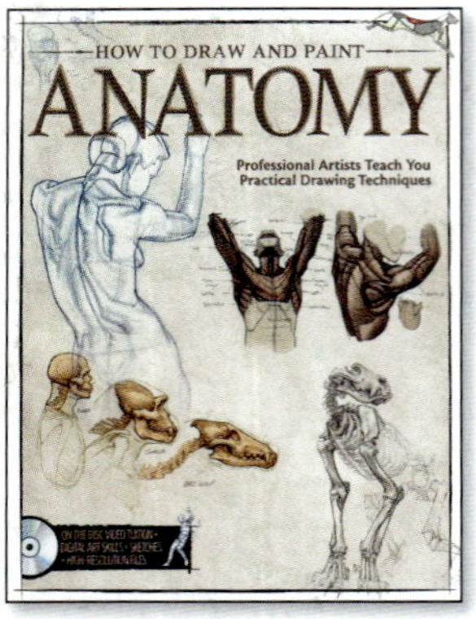

How to Draw & Paint Anatomy

Creating Life-Like Humans and Realistic Animals

By Editors of ImagineFX Magazine

Art students, professional illustrators, and amateurs alike will find inspiration and encouragement to develop their core skills and embrace innovative digital techniques. Includes CD.

ISBN: 978-1-56523-716-2
$27.95 • 112 Pages

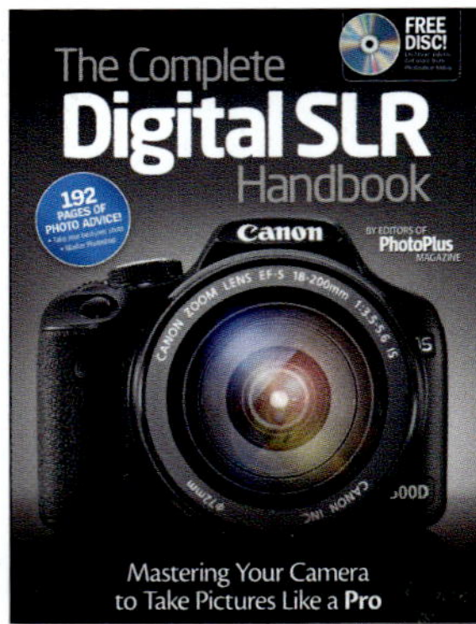

The Complete Digital SLR Handbook

Mastering Your Camera to Take Pictures Like a Pro

By Editors of PhotoPlus Magazine

Everyone wants to take great photographs, and this book shows how to make every shot a winner with expert advice on settings, sharpness, and exposure. Includes CD.

ISBN: 978-1-56523-717-9
$27.95 • 192 Pages

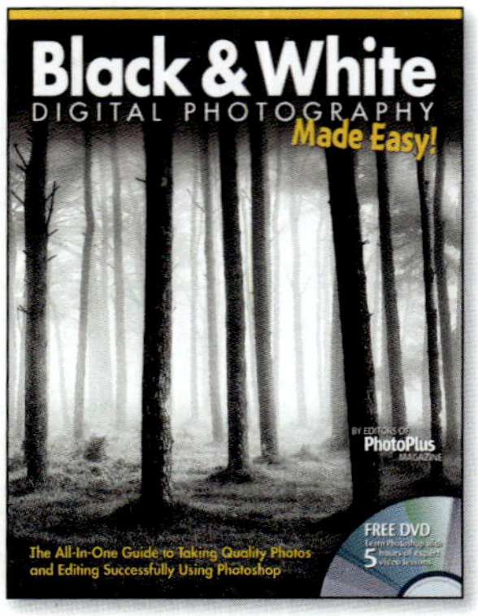

Black & White Digital Photography Made Easy

The All-In-One Guide to Taking Quality Photos and Editing Successfully Using Photoshop

By Editors of PhotoPlus Magazine

This book explores the evocative world of black and white photography and looks at exhilarating new ways to approach the mono medium. Includes DVD.

ISBN: 978-1-56523-718-6
$27.95 • 224 Pages

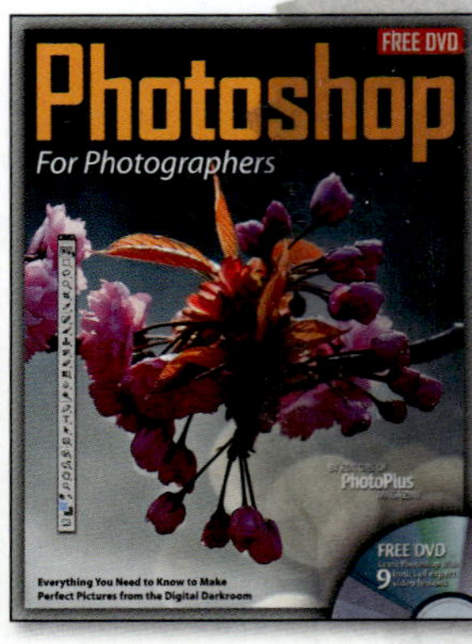

Photoshop For Photographers

Everything You Need to Know to Make Perfect Pictures from The Digital Darkroom

By Editors of PhotoPlus Magazine

This expert guide shows you how to get even better results from your digital SLR photography using Photoshop's photo-editing tools. In-depth workshops include tricks and techniques to create perfect photos. Includes DVD.

ISBN: 978-1-56523-721-6
$27.95 • 224 Pages

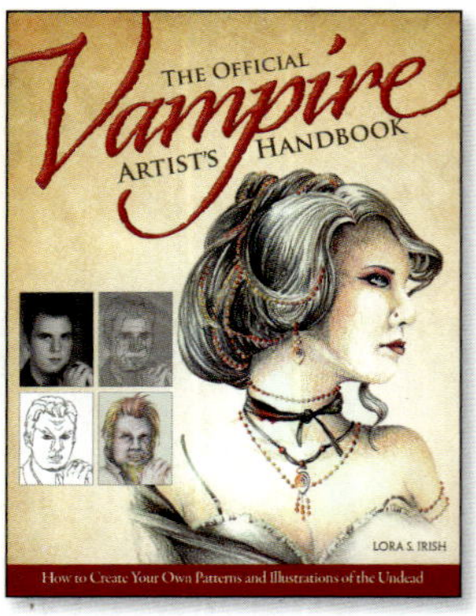

The Official Vampire Artist's Handbook

How to Create Your Own Patterns and Illustrations of the Undead

By Lora S. Irish

Learn how to draw vampire art in simple, easy steps. Instructions could be used to create patterns for various crafts and for drawing.

ISBN: 978-1-56523-678-3
$14.95 • 112 Pages

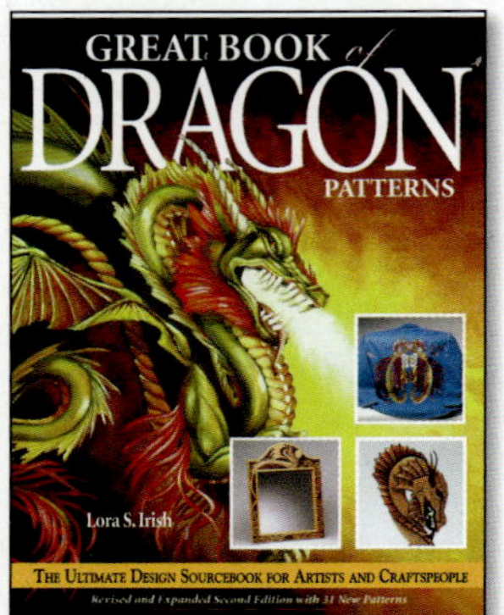

Great Book of Dragon Patterns 2nd Edition

The Ultimate Design Sourcebook for Artists and Craftspeople

By Lora S. Irish

This second edition on creating renderings of the mighty dragon includes more than 100 original patterns and a color reference chart; features dragon anatomy, historic legends, and much more.

ISBN: 978-1-56523-231-0
$22.95 • 188 Pages

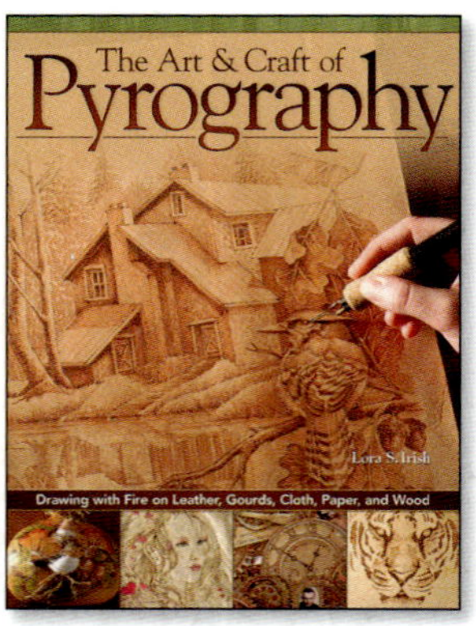

The Art & Craft of Pyrography

Drawing with Fire on Leather, Gourds, Cloth, Paper, and Wood

By Lora S. Irish

Now Lora Irish, the author of the bestselling *Great Book of Woodburning*, offers thirty-five amazingly detailed new projects that explore the craft of pyrography across the full range of inventive pyro media.

ISBN: 978-1-56523-478-9
$19.95 • 144 Pages

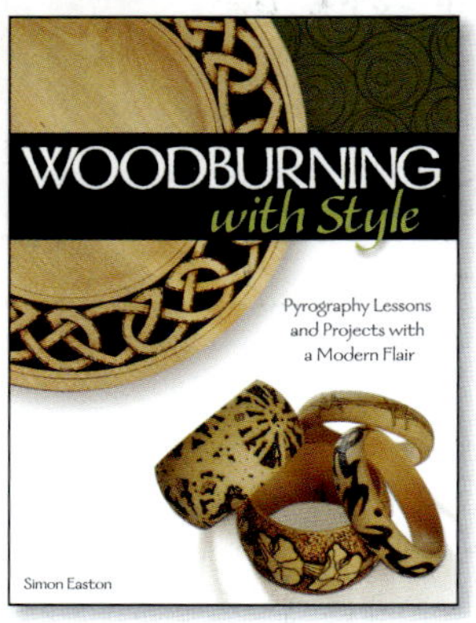

Woodburning with Style

Pyrography Lessons and Projects with a Modern Flair

By Simon Easton

This beautifully photographed, hands-on instructional guide to the art of pyrography will take you on a journey of skill-building exercises that begin at the basics and finish with stylish, gift-worthy projects.

ISBN: 978-1-56523-443-7
$24.95 • 208 Pages

Look for These Books at Your Local Bookstore or Specialty Retailer

To order direct, call **800-457-9112** or visit *www.FoxChapelPublishing.com*

By mail, please send check or money order + S&H to:

Fox Chapel Publishing, 1970 Broad Street, East Petersburg, PA 17520

# Item	US Shipping Rate
1 Item	$3.99
Each Additional	.99

Canadian & International Orders – please email info@foxchapelpublishing.com or visit our website for actual shipping costs.